From Tiberias, With Love:
A Collection of Tiberian Hasidism

אהרון בן משה ושרה

(ה' באדר א',תרפ"ד -כ"ב בתשרי, תשע"ג)

ת.נ.צ.ב.ה

From Tiberias, With Love: A Collection of Tiberian Hasidism

Volume 1: R. Menachem Mendel of Vitebsk

Edited by
Aubrey L. Glazer and Nehemiah Polen

FONS VITAE

PANUI

First published in 2019 by
Fons Vitae
49 Mockingbird Valley Drive
Louisville, KY 40207
http://www.fonsvitae.com
Email: fonsvitaeky@aol.com

Library of Congress Control Number: 2019956438
ISBN 978-1941610-817

Cover art: Elyssa N. Wortzman

To learn more about *Panui*,
write to: alongourpath@gmail.com.
Donations to support future publications can be sent to:
Panui c/o Brandstetter Law, PC
One Market, Spear Tower, 36th Floor
San Francisco, CA 94105

Printed in Canada

Table of Contents

Dedicatory Preface: In Honor of Aron Goldfarb, *o.b.m.* 7

Series Introduction: Volumes on Tiberian Hasidism
by Aubrey L. Glazer and Nehemiah Polen 13

Introduction: A Portrait of R. Menachem Mendel of Vitebsk's Spirit
by Aubrey L. Glazer 19

Reader's Guide to Volume One

The Teachings of R. Menachem Mendel of Vitebsk
by Moshe Hallamish (Bar-Ilan University). 45

Surprised by God: R. Menachem Mendel of Vitebsk's Approach to Divine Worship and Its Influence in Tiberias
by Jonathan Garb, Gershom Scholem Professor of Kabbalah (Hebrew University of Jerusalem) 71

On the Printing of Hasidic Teachings and Its Definition as "Kabbalah Made Ethos" in Light of the Doctrine of R. Menachem Mendel of Vitebsk and R. Abraham of Kalisk
by Ron Margolin (Tel Aviv University). 85

"His Spirit Speaks": Contextualizing the Vitebsker's Devotional Path within the Maggid's Circle
by Ariel Evan Mayse (Stanford University) 109

Mindfulness, Memory, Sensory Consciousness, and *Vida Contemplativa* in *Peri haAretz*
by James Jacobson-Maisels (IJS) 137

Selected Homilies of *Peri haAretz*

Translators' Introduction:
by Aubrey L. Glazer and Nehemiah Polen 153

Genesis

[1.1-1.3]. *Parashah Noach* (Genesis 6:19–11:32) 157-175

[2.1-2.3]. *Parashah Lech Lecha* (Genesis 12:1–17:27) 176-187

[3.1-3.3]. *Parashah Vayera* (Genesis 18:1–22:24) 188-198

[4.1-4.3]. *Parashah Toldot* (Genesis 23:19–28:9) 199-205

[5.1-5.3]. *Parashah Vayishlach* (Genesis 32:4–36:43) 206-213

[6.1-6.3]. *Parashah Meiqez* (Genesis 41:1–44:17) 214-224
[7.1-7.3]. *Parashah Vayigash* 1–2 (Genesis 44:18–47:27) 225-256
Exodus
[8.1-8.3]. *Parashah Bo'* (Exodus 10:1–13:16) 257-269
[9.1-9.3]. *Parashah Beshalach* (Exodus 13:17–17:16) 270-296
Leviticus
[10.1-10.3]. *Parashah Acharey Mot* (Leviticus 16:1–18:30) 293-304
[11.1-11.3]. *Parashah Behar* (Leviticus 25:1–26:2) 305-312
Numbers
[12.1-12.3]. *Parashah Shelach Lecha* (Numbers 13:1–15:41) 313-324
[13.1-13.3]. *Parashah Korach* (Numbers 16:1–18:32) 325-340
[14.1-14.3]. *Parashah Pinchas* (Numbers 25:11–30:1) 341-346
[15.1-15.3]. *Parashah Matot-Massey 1* (Numbers 30:2–36:13) 347-370
Deuteronomy
[16.1-16.3]. *Parashah VeEtchanan* (Deuteronomy 3:23–7:11) 371-376
[17.1-17.3]. *Parashah Eqev 2* (Deuteronomy 7:12–11:25) 377-382
[18.1-18.3]. *Parashah Shoftim* (Deuteronomy 16:18–21:9) 383-404
[19.1-19.3]. *Parashah Ki Teizai 1* (Deuteronomy 21:10–25:19) 405-418
[20.1-20.3]. *Parashah Ki Tavo 1* (Deuteronomy 26:1–29:8) 419-429
Glossary of Hebrew Terms 431
Hebrew Appendix . . . . 492(1)

Dedicatory Preface: In Honor of Aron Goldfarb, *o.b.m.*

In Memoriam:

Aron Goldfarb
(5th Adar I/5684–22nd of Tishrai/5773)

May his soul be nestled in the bonds of eternal life

אהרון בן משה ושרה
(ה' באדר א',תרפ"ד -כ"ב בתשרי, תשע"ג)
ת.נ.צ.ב.ה

There are times when we rejoice and utter songs of praise. There are times when we lament and offer songs of remembrance. Through it all, as Jews, *we sing* . . . Where does this strength to persevere come from?

A song of conviction—"Aron's song"!

Regardless of the situation life brings us, Judaism teaches us:

"חַיָּב אָדָם לְבָרֵךְ עַל הָרָעָה כְּשֵׁם שֶׁהוּא מְבָרֵךְ עַל הַטּוֹבָה. . ."

"One must bless God for the evil that happens just as for the good that happens."[1]

That blessing takes the form of a song in life as the song of self:

"כי לזמר צריכים שמתוך נפשו ולבו יזמר מעצמו. . ."

"For a person to sing, their integrated self—both heart and soul—must burst into song."[2]

1. *mBerakot* 9:5.

2. R. Kalonymus Kalmish Shapira, Beshalach 1942, in *Sefer Esh Ḳodesh: Amarot Ṭehorot Mi-Shenot Ha-Sho'ah She-Ne'emru Be-Shabatot Ṿe-Y. Ṭ. Be-Gẹto Ṿarsha*, ed. by Aharon Sorski (Jerusalem: Feldheim, 2007), 261; ibid., 153; idem, *Sacred Fire: Torah from the Years of Fury 1939–1942*, trans. J. Hershy Worch, Beshalach 1942 (Northvale, NJ: Jason Aronson Press, 2002), 276 [*translations emendated*].

Only once a deeper level of gratitude has been penetrated inside can a person sing to God about their pain, and indeed beyond their pain.

* * *

Aron Goldfarb, beloved husband, father, grandfather, and great-grandfather, living his eighty-eight years to their fullest as a mensch! Throughout those years, Aron's Song sounded much like the one he and children and grandchildren loved to sing around the Passover table—דַּיֵּנוּ Dayenu!

We call our prayer Dayenu!—which means "it would have sufficed" or "we would have been satisfied"—but Aron's life teaches us to consider Dayenu! as the deepest sense of gratitude. A Jew (יהוד) is defined by the capacity for gratitude (הודאה) .When a Jew is asked, "What is the opposite of nihilism? Of seeing life as 'utterly fleeing and futile,' as "הֲבֵל הֲבָלִים" as we read in Ecclesiastes 1:2?" the response is דַּיֵּנוּ Dayenu!—the ability to be thankful for what we have received, for who we are. This holds for every morning, for all generations, and surely for ours.

For each of us, every day is an act of grace, every hour a miraculous offering. *So where does such profound gratitude emanate from?* Just listening to Aron's life story makes it clear . . .

Born February 10, 1924, in Bialobrzegi, Poland, Aron was a Holocaust survivor who overcame seemingly insurmountable odds and founded a successful apparel business known as the G-III Apparel Group. The son of Moshe and Sarah Goldfarb, he was one of seven children and one of only three to survive the Holocaust.

When the Germans took Aron from his father, the last words his father said to him were "Go, my son . . . *maybe you will survive*." Those words—less "*maybe*" and more "*you will survive*"—would stay with him for the rest of his life and eventually would become the title of a book he wrote about his struggle—a book that brought tears to my eyes the first time I read it.[3]

Aron's family was sent to the Treblinka concentration camp in 1941, while Aron and his older brothers Itzhak and Abe were sent to the Pionki labor camp. Another brother, Jack, would survive the war by escaping to Russia. In 1944, Aron, his brothers, and a friend, Zisman Birman, escaped from the camp and fought for survival in the forests of Poland. While in hiding, his brother Itzhak and Zisman Birman were caught and executed. Aron and Abe would survive the war by living in a bunker they built not far from a German gunnery position near their hometown.

Armed with only their familiarity with the landscape and their courage, they would break into the German outpost not far from their hiding spot and steal food and supplies through the winter of 1944. In 1978, the brothers

---

3. Aron Goldfarb, *Maybe You Will Survive* (New York: XLibris, 2010).

returned to Poland to retrieve the remains of Itzhak and Zisman and brought them to be buried in Israel.

While in a displaced persons camp in Germany following the end of the war, Aron saw Esther Disman and immediately asked her to see *The Hunchback of Notre Dame*. Their marriage of sixty-three years was one of complete partnership in everything they did, always together, even at a restaurant, each would order something separate, finish half, and then slide their plates over to finish the other's half—a real עֵזֶר כְּנֶגְדּוֹ.

After they were married, they moved to Israel where Aron was a farmer and served in the

Israeli Army. Their son Morris was born in Israel, and the family came to the United States in 1956, where Aron, Abe, and Jack were reunited. Aron and Esther's second son Ira was born soon after. Aron used his skills learned in Poland as an apprentice to a shoemaker to start in 1956 what is today known as the G-III Apparel Group.

Like so many others who came to America as survivors and entered what was then referred to as the *shmata* business, Goldfarb started a small leather company here that grew and is still thriving as G-III—three generations of Goldfarbs working together, carrying on Aron's Song.

* * *

What is it that makes a song like Aron's so unique? The great spiritual master Rabbi Mendel of Kotzk once referred to this difference in people as follows:

> שמעתי בשם אדמו"ר הרה"ק מהר"ם זצ"ל מקאצק זי"ע שאמר על צדיק אחד שהיה בימיו שהוא צדיק אין פעלץ הפירוש: שיש אחד שעושה לעצמו בימות החורף בגדים חמים כדי שיחם לו, ויש אחד שמחמם את הבית מאד. מה חילוק בין זה לזה? שזה שעושה בגדים חמים—לו חם, אבל לאחרים אינו מועיל כלל, וזה שמחמם הבית —אזי לאחרים גם כן טוב.

> Sometimes in life you find people who are *ah* zaddik *in peltz*—"A saint in a fur coat." *What did he mean?* When it is winter and freezing cold, there are two things you can do. Build a fire, or wrap yourself in a fur coat. In both cases, the person is warm. But when you build a fire, all who gather round will also be warmed. With the fur coat, the only one who is warmed is the one who wears the coat. So it is regarding spiritual warmth—one can be a zaddik in a fur coat.[4]

That magnetism, that real fire is something that was always burning in-

4. R. Simḥah Bunem of Przysucha and Yocha Ḳadish, *Sefer Śiaḥ Śarfe Ḳodesh, He-Ḥadash: Ṿe-hu Leshon Ḥasidim, Amarot Ṭehorot*, vol. 3, no. 10, s.v. "Tzaddik" (Bnai Brak: P.M. Lev, 1988), 159a.

side Aron. Amid his humility and tolerance was a soul who was fired by unbounded compassion and caring for others. Wherever he found himself, he always could connect to people and find their inner spark—from the handyman to the shipping clerk to the waiter. He cared about everyone; you knew that when you walked between 7th and 8th Avenue and saw how every shopkeeper would greet Aron—the mayor of 37th Street! He was always lending a helping hand, lending money so that no one he met was ever in need.

Aside from these displays of courage to the world he lived in, he had a deep and abiding love for his children and grandchildren. Such a deep and abiding sense of family first! Aron's Song survives in his beloved wife of over six decades, Esther; his son Morris, daughter-in-law Arlene, and son Ira; his grandchildren Laura, Jeffrey, Scott, Samantha, and Brett; and great-grandchildren Joshua, Matthew, Amanda, Ryan, Sabrina, and Tristan.

You are the next generation to hear that story of the Exodus, just like that next generation of disciples of the sages like R. Eleazar reclining at Bnai Brak—

> כאן כמה שהיו מספרים ביציאת מצרים כל אות[ה] הלילה חשבו בענותנותם שעוד לא עשו מאומה, אבל כשראו את תלמידיהם לפניהם וראו איך הם מאירים אחר אות[ה] הלילה, וגם איך פעלו רבותיהם בסיפורם ביציאת מצרים על התלמידים, כבר פסקו.
>
> Just as the sages of the Haggadah at Passover discussed the Exodus from Egypt all night, they thought, in their humility, that they had not even begun. When they saw their disciples before them, however, they realized how their disicples' face shone after the seder night. They realized how much they had affected their disciples with their telling of the Exodus from Egypt. They knew then that they had done enough, *Dayenu*! so they could say, it sufficed, and so they stopped.[5]

Every time the Goldfarb family gather together for Passover and any moment of family time together, remember how Aron sang *Dayenu*! Remember that these kind of lessons learned from life's crucible can be taught in any moment, even playing ping pong, and you can still remain fun to be around, just like Aron modeled. Remember the resiliency, the caring, and compassion of Aron's faithful song . . . For now each of every one of us must carry Aron's Song forward.

* * *

5. R. Kalonymus Kalmish Shapira, *Esh Kodesh*, Passover 1940, 120–22; idem, *Sacred Fire: Torah from the Years of Fury 1939–1942* (Northvale, NJ: Jason Aronson Press, 2002), 68–71.

How was Aron able to sing his faithful song of Dayenu?

> אבל כשחס ושלום היסורים כל כך מתרבים עד שכל האיש נופל ונשבר. . .
> . . .לרסיסים, ולא נשאר ממנו אישיות אשר יתחזק
>
> "God forbid, one ever become so completely crushed and the mind so crumbled . . ."[6]*—lest great suffering snuff out our song!*

As a survivor, amid the horrors of the Shoah, despite it all, Aron remained a mensch of *menschen*—grateful and caring. I share these words about that faithful song that sometimes struggles to be heard, to be sung, because these words were preached by R. Kalonymous Kalman Shapira in the Warsaw Ghetto on January 31, 1942, just before the Nazis invaded and snuffed out his song. Although the Nazis tried to sever the golden chain of the famous house of zaddikim from Bialobrzegi—their song too continues from the days of the "Holy Jew" of Pashischa, until R. Chayimel (the Rebbe of Bialovzig) and his grandchildren.

Conviction matters because through it all, we do more than survive, we flourish and sing the song of life—Aron's Song! We focus on Aron's Song of conviction and love of family, love of life, which all overpower death. So by attuning your heart to hear Aron's Song that still graces all of our lives, every act of kindness and every effort to make a difference will connect you deeper to his soul.

Aron's song has survived beyond *Dayenu*! Aron's Song will continue to be sung for future generations. Out of his big heart and the soul connections he forged with each and every one of us reading this book shall Aron's Song continue to be sung. May Aron's love for life, such a sweet song of generosity and devotion continue to shine through our world!

> *עס זאל זיך זאגען שירה*
>
> "So the song should sing itself!"[7]

---

6. Ibid., Parashah Beshalach 1942, 153.
7. Ibid., Parashah Beshalach 1940, 262; ibid., 278.

Series Introduction: Volumes on Tiberian Hasidism

by Aubrey L. Glazer and Nehemia Polen

From Tiberias With Love is a journey to rediscovering the magic and mystery, the intimacy and depth of a lost moment in the history of a remarkably relevant conscious community in the Galilee that still has much to teach us. In the year 1777, a group of Eastern European Jews set sail in search of a promised land, far away from the internal and external conflicts plaguing those souls seeking the infinite within this finite world. Some who set sail identified with the burgeoning hasidic movement while others seem to have just come along for the ride.[1] Historians debate the motives that led to this minor emigration or *aliyah* to the fledgling settlement or *Yishuv* in the Land of Israel. But what is clear is that, notwithstanding the considerable socio-economic and geographic challenges, some members of this emigrating group sought to establish a center for a burgeoning hasidic *ethos* that would radiate to the Diaspora from its renewed center in the Holy Land in Ottoman Palestine. This series endeavors to re-establish an open space [*Panui*] to reflect upon the symbiotic radiance of such a hasidic *ethos*.

Our knowledge of the 1777 emigration derives from many sources, including hasidic homilies [*derashot*], prayer commentaries [*biurim*] and a large collection of letters [*igrot*]. While many scholars have studied this body of correspondence, the correlation between historio-social structures and theological records of mystical experience has not always been appreciated, and thus will be addressed in a forthcoming volume in this series.[2] This series was further inspired by a recent convening for a Tiberean Hasidism seminar, in which scholars both in the academe and the

1. David Assaf, "'The Rumor Was Spread That the Messiah Has Already Come': New Light on the Aliyah of Hasidism in the Year 1777" *Zion* (1996): 319-346.

2. See *Tiberean Hasidism,* vol. 3, ed's Glazer and Polen, (*forthcoming*). This volume will address the historio-social structures and theological records of mystical experience in regards to selections from letters of correspondence [*igrot*]. So also, Phillip Wexler, *Mystical Interactions: Sociology, Jewish Mysticism and Education* (Los Angeles: Cherub Press, 2007); Philip Wexler and Jonathan Garb, *After Spirituality: Studies in Mystical Traditions* (New York: Peter Lang, 2012).

contemporary hasidic-*haredi* world came together to critically read texts and share insights derived from both the academic field and the wisdom of spiritual practice and experience within an inter-disciplinary reading community.[3]

There already exists exemplary research and distinct methodologies which have opened the field to critically reading the hasidic social milieu as a subject of interrogation.[4] This scholarship provides a lens for reading hagiographic records in correlation with Polish and Russian archives, providing contributions that are extremely valuable and have changed the field. However, the focus of this series is to highlight the crucial theological issues affecting social formation of conscious communities in Tiberias.[5]

3. Tiberan Hasidism Seminar, *Association of Jewish Studies* (San Diego: Dec. 19-22, 2016).

4. From a methodological perspective, it is imperative to acknowledge the remarkable research on Hasidism in general, and its Tiberean iteration in particular addressing the Vitebsker's paradoxical historio-eschatological proclivities towards deep acosmicism that transcends nomos and qualia without which we would not have a scholarly roadmap. Consider some exemplars, such as Rivka Schatz-Uffenheimer, *Hasidism as Mysticism: Quietistic Elements in 18th Century Hasidic Thought,* [Hebrew] (Magnes Press: Jerusalem, 1968), pp. 30, 55-67, 88-89; Moshe Halamish, "The Teachings of R. Menahem Mendel of Vitebsk," in *Hasidism Reappraised,* ed. Ada Rapoport-Albert, pp. 268–287 (London and Portland, OR, 1996); Raya Haran, "*Shivḥe ha-Rav: Li-She'eylat aminutan shel igrot ha-ḥasidim me-Erets-Yisra'el,*" *Katedrah* 55 (1990): 22–58; Raya Haran, "*Atarah l'Yoshna—Ha'Umnam*" *Katedrah* 63 (1992): 98-102; David Assaf, "*Yesod Ha-Ma'ala*: a New Chapter in the Historiography of Hasidism in Eretz Israel," *Cathedra: for the History of Eretz Israel and Its Yishuv* (1993): 57-66; Raya Haran, "*Mah heni 'a et talmide ha-Magid la 'alot le-Erets-Yisra'el,*" *Katedrah* 76 (1995): 77–95; Naḥum Karlinski, *Historiyah sheke-neged: "Igrot ha-ḥasidim me-Erets-Yisra'el"* (Jerusalem, 1998); Yehoshu'a Mondshine, "*Aminutan shel igrot ha-Ḥasidim,*"*Katedrah* 63 (1992): 65–97, 64 (1992): 79–97; Mordecai Wilensky, *Ha-Yishuv ha-ḥasidi bi-Teveriya: 'Ad petirato shel Rabi Avraham mi-Kalisk, 570* (Jerusalem, 1988); Mendel Piekarz, *Bi-yeme Tsemiḥat Ha-Ḥasidut: Megamot Ra'ayoniyot Be-Sifre Derush U-Musar*. Yerushalayim: Mosad Byaliḳ, 1978; Gershon D. Hundert, *Toward a Biography of R. Abraham Kalisker*. Thesis, Columbus, Ohio, 1971; Yohanan Petrovsky-Shtern, "" Ḥasidei De'ar'a and Ḥasidei Dekokhvaya': Two Trends in Modern Jewish Historiography." (2008): 141-167; Zeev Gries, "From Myth to Ethos—Outlines for the History of Rabbi Abraham of Kalisk." *Uma ve-Toldoteiha (Nation and History)* 2 (1984): 117-46; Moshe Rosman, *Founder of Hasidism: A quest for the historical Ba'al Shem Tov*. Vol. 5. Univ of California Press, 1996; Immanuel Etkes, "Ba'a'l Ha-Tanya: Rabbi Shneur Zalman of Liady and the Origins of Habad Hasidism." *Jerusalem: Shazar Center [Hebrew]* (2011); Glenn Dynner, *Men of silk: The Hasidic conquest of Polish Jewish society*. Oxford University Press, 2008.

5. Here we must equally acknowledge the pioneering work of: Arthur Green, Ebn D. Leader, Ariel E. Mayse, and Or N. Rose, "Introduction," *Speaking Torah: Volume 1* (Vermont: Jewish Lights, 2013); Ada Rapaport-Albert, "Hasidism After 1772," in *Hasidism Reappraised,* ed's Weiss, J G, and Ada Rapoport-Albert (London: Vallentine Mitchell, 1996); Naftali Loewenthal, *Communicating the Infinite: The emergence of the Habad school* (Chicago: University of Chicago Press, 1990).

The hitherto binary framing of these issues, i.e., as either historical or theological, misses some deeper moments of correlation.[6]

Spiritual seekers around the globe are likely familiar with the remarkable contributions of *HaBaD* Hasidism due to their immense outreach efforts that include massive dissemination and publication.[7] What is often less understood is that *HaBaD* at its core is as a more "cognitive-based" hasidism of contemplation—and its willingness to put into practice the Ba'al Shem Tov's dedication to the mass dissemination of homilies, hagiography, and even archival-based historiography, must be applauded. Yet it is precisely for this reason that it is now so important to highlight an important lesser-heard voice —what we call *HaGaT,* or "heart-based" hasidism—that emerged around the Maggid's table.[8] The theological textures of this heart-based, anti-court, more egalitarian hasidism are made more clear when we examine those who consciously chose to leave Eastern Europe and go off to the Holy land to live in the rebuilt village of Tiberias. This series explores more deeply their choice to emigrate to such an isolated and vulnerable area of Palestine, leaving Eastern Europe far behind, in light of the many historical, sociological, theological implications. Some of the hallmarks of the Tiberean community include a focus on the ecstatic devotional prayer realized in a more horizontal relation as well as focus on mystical fellowship rather than focusing on the inherited, hierarchical office of the *tzaddik* and its vertical relation.

Throughout this series on Tiberian Hasidism, we maintain that it is not possible to truly disentangle the theological from the social-historical. [9] A fellow traveler along this pilgrimage path is R. Avraham Avish Shor, who seamlessly correlates nuances in history and mystical theology through field work and scholarship "on the ground." While his scholarship is relatively unknown within most academic circles, or even beyond the *haredi* fringes of Israel, Shor, who is editor of the Karlin-Stolin journal, *Beit Aharon v'Yisrael,*[10] exemplifies the hybrid direction of recent research.[11] While

6. For a notable exception, see Elliot Wolfson, *Open Secret: Postmessianic Messianism and the Mystical Revision of Menahem Mendel Schneerson* (New York, 2012). Compare with the challenge to the hybrid and hegemonic models of culture, see Rosman, "Forward", in Glenn Dynner, ed. *Holy Dissent: Jewish and Christian Mystics in Eastern Europe* (Detroit: Wayne State University Press, 2011) p. viii

7. Sue Fishkoff, *The Rebbe's Army: Inside the World of Chabad-Lubavitch* (New York: Schocken Books, 2005); David Eliezrie, *The Secret of Chabad: Inside the World's Most Successful Jewish Movement* (New Milford: Toby Press , 2016).

8. See Arthur Green, Ebn D. Leader, Ariel E. Mayse, and Or N. Rose, "Introduction," *Speaking Torah: Volume 1* (Vermont: Jewish Lights, 2013).

9. See above, n2.

10. Avraham Avish Shor, *Ketavim: Pirḳe Toldot Ṿe-'iyun Be-Mishnat Ḳarlin-Sṭolin*, (Mechon Beit Aharaon v'Yisrael, Modi'in Ilit, Israel: 2018), 425-430.

11. Shor's scholarship will figure more fully in *Tiberean Hasidism,* vol. 3, ed's Glazer and Polen, (*forthcoming*).

important work has been done in both historical and theological realms, Shor's more robust and integrated approach to what we are calling Tiberean Hasidism has yet to be fully appreciated.

This understudied chapter in Hasidic and *yishuv* historiography has been treated in several monographs deserving of further attention by historians.[12] These works help avoid an essentialist reduction of *Eretz Yisrael* to merely the historical moment of 1948, bringing awareness to the longer, complex historical arcs of co-habitation that preceded it. Yet after more than a decade of co-editing annotated translations, commentaries and critical reader's guides to much of this understudied period of the 1777 emigration, we continue to notice a distinct historiographic bias among both internal *haredi* and external academic scholars towards the varieties of hasidism that flourished in Eastern Europe at the expense of what we call Tiberean Hasidism. This evident preference can impede serious reflection on Tiberean Hasidism, which included such mystical luminaries as R. Menachem Mendel of Vitebsk, as well as colleagues and disciples, R. Avraham haCohen of Kalisk, and R. Tzvi Hirsch of Smorytzch—pioneering figures whose scant correspondence, homilies and emigration stories continue to challenge contemporary readers. This series serves as a re-evaluation of the white-hot spiritual intensity of these figures that continued well into the period of conventional institutionalization of hasidism in its third generation. And in the process of favorably re-assessing these mystical figures who have been mischaracterized and misunderstood, we will come to appreciate anew their complex legacies as *wade mecums* for a Hasidism for our age.

This series does not come without its challenges, especially considering that there is no group in the current hasidic-*haredi* landscape that explicitly sees itself as official inheritors of this legacy but there are those who are committed to the spiritual practices of Tiberean Hasidism. Yet our ongoing research both within the sacred literature of the *sefarim* world and in field work within living hasidic communities, including Karlin-Stolin, Slonim, or Ryzn (Ruzhyn), reflects a resurgence of interest in recovering and reclaiming some of the devotional practice, albeit fragmentary, that keep that early ecstasy of first generation hasidism afire. Further volumes in this series will be dedicated to exploring this afterlife of the Tiberean Hasidic ethos in recent communities like Karlin-Stolin, Slonim, Piacezene and Ryzn (Ruzhyn) as well as in practices of dance, music and other customs

12. M. Wilensky, *Ha-yishuv Ha-Ḥasidi Bi-Ṭeveryah: 'ad Pẹtirato Shel R. Avraham Mi-Ḳalisḳ* (1988); J. Barnai, *The Jews in Eighteenth Century Palestine: Under the Patronage of the Istanbul Committee of Officials for Palestine,* (1992); N. Karlinsky, *Hisṭoryah Sheke-Neged: Igrot Ha-Ḥasidim Me-Erets-Yiśra'el : Ha-Ṭeḳsṭ Veha-Ḳonṭeḳsṭ* (1998); as well as more recently, M. Lehmann, *Emissaries from the Holy Land: The Sephardic Diaspora and the Practice of Pan-Judaism in the Eighteenth Century* (Stanford: 2014).

that mark this unique devotional pathway.

This series seeks not only to use critical and historical lenses but also experiential lenses, drawing in experts from the hasidic-*haredi* field who are crossing devotional and academic boundaries. By engaging in critical discourse with scholars from Karlin-Stolin, *HaBaD* and other hasidic-*haredi* circles, we have discovered a treasure-trove of materials all of which, from time to time, with appropriate critical lenses, can refract light onto this nearly lost historical moment. We hope to contribute another layer to this larger project, extending its reach by means of "thicker" descriptions of the phenomenological experience of spiritual history as it unfolded and as it continues to unfold in applications for conscious community building in our own day.

Another remarkable facet of Tiberean Hasidism is the emergence of a willingness to challenge reigning assumptions about the role of the *tzaddik* in relation to the *hasid* and the imbedded experience of worship through corporeal realities.[13] There remain a web of motivations behind the hasidic emigration of 1777—notwithstanding R. Menachem Mendel's dismissive attitude to the widespread bans on a Jewish occupational mainstay like tavern-keeping—which include: opposition from mitnaggedic factions; messianic impulses; hopes of founding a center for hasidic praxis in the Holy Land; and the effects of dwelling there on spiritual practice. These latter factors of re-establishing a redemptive laboratory of hasidic praxis really distinguish, to our eyes, so much of Tiberean Hasidism. It is this shared conviction of a tight-knit mystical fellowship to transcend the evil impulse which stands in contrast to the atmosphere in R. Shneur Zalman's White Russia where his *Tanya* teaches it is only the *tzaddik* can control the temptation of the evil impulse. In Tiberias, the higher spheres of contemplative consciousness are only accessible once the emotional spheres are activated, then those higher spheres can be accessed. Those higher spheres of consciousness are revelatory.

In ascending to Sinai, Moses not receives more than Torah—he overcomes death. Receiving the Torah does not mean primarily Law, rather it really means receiving the divine kiss—this is a revelation of Love. God is kissing Moses and Moses is kissing God, and those ecstatic kisses are still palpable in this ecstatic communal bonding. These were not ordinary times in Tiberias, rather these were over-illuminated times of freedom. So when you look at *Tanya*, and even more broadly the history of the hasidic movement, especially in its earlier iteration, there was a twenty year period of ecstatic experience followed by retreat, including the power of the mitnaggedic critique. Notwithstanding the discovery and retreat, the Tiberias community is still holding in that state of earlier period of ecstatic experi-

13. Ibid., pp. 69-70.

ence still experienced as living revelation.

The case of Tiberean Hasidism may require an even more forceful gaze, since it eschewed the trend towards expansion and populism. In conclusion, this series on Tiberean Hasidism attempts to build and expand upon the scholarly research and devotional assumptions as a way of expanding the horizons of communities. Tiberean Hasidism provides a model of hasidic life that is particularly appealing to contemporary spiritual seekers for many reasons, including: its deep focus on mystical theology; devotional practice; and the ecstasy of deep friendship rather than allegiance to an institutionalized hasidism. It thus remains a rich field that is ripe for excavation, with great insight and inspiration ahead as in the unfolding of this project. The theology, devotion, and social structure offer an authentic roadmap to a future hasidism ripe for our age.

Introduction: A Portrait of R. Menachem Mendel of Vitebsk's Spirit

by Aubrey L. Glazer

Anyone who has not tasted the joyful jubilation within the fellowship of Tiberean Hasidism, may very well have never really tasted Hasidism at all. Part of the reason that so few have tasted the *joyful jubilation* of early Hasidism[1]—that spiritual renewal that swept across eighteenth-century Eastern Europe—is that one of its most prominent spiritual leaders has been all but forgotten. Before stepping into the challenges of Hasidic biographies in particular, let us take a step back to consider the the more general question of biographies that lingers: "To what end then could such a biographical portrait serve?" This challenge of the genre of biography in general, according to David Foster Wallace, is that:

> A biographer wants his story to be not only interesting but literarily valuable. In order to ensure this, the bio has to make the writer's personal life and psychic travails seem vital to his work. The idea is that we can't correctly interpret a piece of verbal art unless we know the personal and/or psychological circumstances surrounding its creation. That this is simply assumed as an axiom by many biographers is one problem; another is that the approach works a lot better on some writers than on others.[2]

In the case of the personality heading up the 1777 emigration to the Holy Land, Reb Menachem Mendel of Horodok—primarily known as Menachem Mendel of Vitebsk (1730?–New Moon 'Iyar, 1788, Tiberias)—any

1. For the foremost critical biography on the pioneer of Hasidism, see Murray J. Rosman, *Founder of Hasidism: A Quest for the Historical Ba'al Shem Tov*, Littman Library of Jewish Civilization (Berkeley, CA: University of California Press, 1996). Compare with the pioneering work of Hasidic biography, see Arthur Green, *Tormented Master: The Life and Spiritual Quest of Rabbi Nahman of Bratslav* (Woodstock, VT: Jewish Lights Pub, 1992).

2. David Foster Wallace, "Borges on the Couch," *Sunday Book Review: New York Times*, November 7, 2004.

portrait of such an outstanding Hasidic luminary would benefit from knowing the personal and psychological circumstances surrounding the creation of his spiritual art, as well as some of the historical context that spawned it. Hovering between metaphysical speculation and metaphoric contemplation, the spiritual biography undergirding the journey of Reb Menachem Mendel to the Holy Land and the life leading up to it remain shrouded in mystery, yet grounded with enough foundation points to make such a life's quest reasonably legible. When examining the traces of such a life's quest, it is imperative to keep in mind how for the mystic:

> . . . human thought, behavior and history are all the product of one big Mind, or are elements of an immense cabalistic Book that includes its own decoding. Biography-wise, then, we have a strange situation in which [the mystic's] individual personality and circumstances matter only insofar as they lead him to create artworks in which such personal facts are held to be unreal.[3]

In the case of Reb Menachem Mendel—who came to be known simply as the Vitebsker, so named after the village in which he served as rabbi—his transcendent journey led the personal facts of his life to become *hyper-real* rather than *unreal*. For example, Vitebsk—the very village portrayed years later in tones of magical realism by another of its residents, Marc Chagall—was both the physical and spiritual home to Reb Menachem Mendel and his wife, Sima. In Vitebsk, the very *real* financial struggles he endured serving there as rabbinic leader led him to the *hyper-real* realization that "wealth contradicts cleaving to the divine and so he chose poverty instead."[4] Early in his spiritual formation as a rabbi, a strong sense of uncompromising integrity emerges amid such socioeconomic challenges.

But the question that beckons this brief biographical portrait is more broadly conceived as follows: Where did such moral grandeur and spiritual audacity really begin?[5] Reb Menachem Mendel was already considered an outstanding mystical figure in his own right, within the world of Hasidic spirituality, perhaps already due in no small part to his face-to-face encounters during adolescence with the renowned disciple of the leader of Hasidism, the Maggid of Mezeritch. Along the Jewish path, meetings with remarkable mystical masters, especially in the world of Hasidic spirituality, depend on such face-to-face encounters for the transmission of the living

3. Ibid.

4. *Or haGalil*, quoted in *Toldot haRav haKadosh Peri haAretz u'Mamshikhai Darko*, vol. 1 (Jerusalem: Mechon Peri haAretz, 5771), 360.

5. I am borrowing this expression from Heschel, who sought to translate this Hasidic ethos into contemporary American Jewry, all the while deeply indebted to spiritual masters like Reb Menachem Mendel, see Abraham J. Heschel, *Moral Grandeur and Spiritual Audacity: Essays* (New York: Farrar, Straus and Giroux, 2013).

waters of Oral Torah are what bring the Written Torah to life as part of an ongoing revelation. Reb Menachem Mendel appears to have really been a wunderkind of sorts! Returning to his earliest years of spiritual formation under the auspices of the Maggid of Mezeritch, the following story of revelation is recounted:

> . . . the Maggid was studying with his students about *Parashah Yitro* [the scriptural portions dealing with revelation in Exodus] and he asked if any of the students still remembered the moment of standing at Mount Sinai [the site of Torah's revelation]. Some of them recalled, so he continued to ask them further and further, until the point that all of them were as one standing at Mount Sinai, except for one student who said he did not remember. So the Maggid returned to questioning the student in great detail and he responded that he had no recollection of this event whatsoever. The Maggid turned to his students and said: "Learn from this that his ancestor's feet never stood at Mount Sinai, and in the end, perish the thought, he is excluded from the collectivity of Israel." One of the exceptional ones who immediately remembered standing at Mount Sinai was Reb Menachem Mendel, may his merit continue to protect us and all of Israel.[6]

Aside from drawing deeply from the wellsprings of Hasidic spirituality from the revelations of the Ba'al Shem Tov as well as his own early spiritual formation under the auspices of the Maggid of Mezeritch, Reb Menachem Mendel also studied at a young age with the renowned genius R. Yosef of Pinsk along with R. Yisasschar Dov of Lubavitch.[7]

Early formation of our spiritual master includes time serving as a rabbinic leader in Lithuania and Belorussia, serving for periods in Minsk, Vitebsk, and then finally in Horodok, where he remained until his emigration to the Holy Land in 1777. By the time of the burgeoning 1777 emigration to *'Eretz Yisrael*, the Vitebsker was already seen as a prominent spiritual leader. Such renown bode well in leading and supporting the harrowing journey that included navigating the Black Sea through Istanbul to the Mediterranean Sea, until their ship docked at the port of Acco by the 5th of Elul, 1777. From a sojourn in Jerusalem, the Vitebsker went on to quickly establish a Hasidic community, briefly in Safed and then permanently in Tiberias. The deep devotional attachment of this Hasidic aliyah to the Holy Land and its imprint within the consciousness of the Hasidic

6. *Emet l'Yaakov*, 19th of Kislev, quoted *in Toldot haRav haKadosh Peri haAretz u'Mamshikhai Darko*, vol. 1 (Jerusalem: Mechon Peri haAretz, 5771), 355.

7. *Sefer haSichot*, vol. 5, 308, quoted in *Toldot haRav haKadosh Peri haAretz u'Mamshikhai Darko*, vol. 1 (Jerusalem: Mechon Peri haAretz, 5771), 360.

movement is more than merely a footnote concerning rabbinic emissaries, nicknamed *ShaDaR"im,* dedicated to collecting donations in support of the Tiberias settlement in the Holy Land. The Vitebsker's emigration to the Holy Land of *'Eretz Yisrael* was also more than merely a forfeiture of a central leadership position in the Hasidic arena of White Russia whose tsarist political infrastructure he deeply distrusted; rather, it brought the spiritual yearning for Zion home into the heart of Hasidism for successive generations. Notwithstanding strong influence in the realm of custom and melodies within Karlin-Stolin Hasidism to this day,[8] still Reb Menachem Mendel has left no explicit line of transmission or official lineage within any particular Hasidic sect. While the Vitebsker's younger students and friends became the leaders and founders of dynasties, the name and influence of Reb Menachem Mendel continues to slip away from the historiographic imagination of Hasidism. In part, this brief biographical portrait seeks to establish a rationale for the abiding influence of this great mystical master whose resonance echoes in later iterations of Hasidism to this day, including aforementioned resonances in Karlin-Stolin and Slonim, as well as in Ruzhin and Piacezene—all of such influences will be explored elsewhere.

Hasidic historiography pivots around a narrow focus for periodization. There is the pre-1772 Hasidism and then post-1772 iterations, as duly noted by Ada Rapoport-Albert, becoming more and more decentralized, likely enabling the 1777 Hasidic emigration to *'Eretz Yisrael*.[9] It is no coincidence that so many of the Maggid of Mezeritch's disciples, including colleagues who also emigrated in 1777, including esteemed rabbis Abraham of Kalisk and Shneur Zalman of Liady (who purportedly turned back to Eastern Europe somewhere along the way),[10] became devotees of the Vitebsker after 1772, which among milestones marked the death of Dov Baer, the Maggid of Mezeritch, as well as the ban of the Vilna Gaon[11]—the head of the oppositional mitnaggedic campaign against Hasidism at large.[12] When this opposition to Hasidism arose, the Vitebsker traveled to Vilna to facilitate a reconciliation with the leader of this opposition, Rabbi Eliyahu, the Vilna Gaon. As legend has it, the Gaon of Vilna refused to see the Vitebsker, slamming the door on

---

8. For the underappreciated but extensive research in this vein, see Abraham Avish Shor, "Karlin Hasidism in Its Diasporic Period—1786–1801," *Beit Ahron v'Yisrael Journal*, no. 132 (Jerusalem: Karlin-Stolin Institute, 2012*)*, 132–60.

9. Ada Rapoport-Albert, "Hasidism after 1772: Structural Continuity and Change," in *Hasidism Reappraised*, ed. Ada Rapoport-Albert (London: Littman Library of Jewish Civilization, 1997), 76–141.

10. Gershon D. Hundert, *Toward a Biography of R. Abraham Kalisker* (Master's Thesis, Ohio State University, 1971), 24n12, 27–28n25, etc.

11. Immanuel Etkes, *The Gaon of Vilna: The Man and His Image* (Berkeley: University of California Press, 2002).

12. Rapoport-Albert, "Hasidism after 1772: Structural Continuity and Change."

his face twice. Historians speculate that this may have been a key motivation for the Hasidic aliyah of 1777 spearheaded by the Vitebsker. Others scholars, like David Assaf, suggest this emigration of the Hasidic aliyah of 1777 was strongly influenced by a messianic impulse.[13] This requires further reflection, insofar as Assaf's provocative suggestion, building on Simon Dubnow's earlier intuition, is buttressed by parallel historical records in the Samaritan community of the messianic nature of this boatload of nearly 300 émigrés journeying to the Promised Land for very different reasons. It is less a question of whether there was a unique messianic impulse influencing things; rather, it is more of a question of the relative intensity of the 1777 iterative impulse, in the wake of a series of other messianic emigrations starting in earnest already in 1666. One cannot ignore the significance of 1776 as actually marking the double Jubilee anniversary of Shabbetai Zevi's failed messianic emigration to the Holy Land and the reality that Sabbateans continued to hope for the return of their messiah at this very time in history that coincided precisely with the Hasidic aliyah.[14] Historians spend less time considering the degree of messianic inclination already imbedded as part of the Vitebsker's spiritual constitution when analyzing his decision to spearhead the Hasidic emigration of 1777.

At this point, it is worth reflecting briefly on this spiritual personality. The Vitebsker's unique mystical and messianic personality is captured in a few of the following sketches transmitted by colleagues and disciples:

> Once the Maggid of Mezeritch ordered R. Levi Yitzhak of Bereditchev to blow the shofar [i.e. ram's horn]. When the Maggid called out the first blow [*of the shofar*], he saw wondrous luminosity and swooned. The Maggid of Mezeritch said: "I didn't know the capacity of [*Levi Yitzhak*]. Is not [Menachem] Mendel able to see with more [*luminosity than Levi Yitzhak*], and yet he is not nearly as intimidated?"[15]

After his passing, the Vitebsker's unique mystical and messianic personality is more deeply appreciated in terms of its abiding influence lamenting that:

> The crown of our heads has fallen, his head burnished gold, give praise to the heavens . . . as our cloud of glory has dissipated, no more glory, he revealed his glory on through the lesson of the divine ark.[16]

---

13. David Assaf, "'The Rumor Was Spread That the Messiah Has Already Come': New Light on the Aliyah of Hasidim in the Year 1777," Zion (1996): 319–46. For a critique and revision of Assaf, see R. Abraham Avish Shor, *"The Group of 'the Needy' Who Joined the Hasidic Journey of 1777"* [Hebrew] (forthcoming).

14. Assaf, "'The Rumor Was Spread That the Messiah Has Already Come,'" 340n101.

15. Yitzhak Alfassi, *Torat haHasidut: Toldot, Divrai Torah, v'Hagut shel Elef v'Shesh Me'ot 'Ishai Hasidut*, vol. ,1 (Jerusalem: Mossad haRav Kook, 2006), n487, 521a.

16. As described in a letter about the passing of the Vitebsker, as quoted in Alfassi, *Tor-*

Every spiritual venture requires courage to step out and support to sustain it. To reimagine the ever-eroding ethos of the Ba'al Shem Tov's renewal of the Jewish religion known as Hasidism, a satellite was becoming a desideratum, if not a necessity. And so this project of resettling a new center to incubate that anarchic renewal project of Hasidism in the Holy Land could not have been more apt. Nor could such a project have been possible without spiritual partnership and support. Deployment of the Vitebkser's esteemed colleague and quasi-disciple, R. Abraham haCohen of Kalisk, to join in this enterprise as a spiritual partnership and support, thus makes complete sense. Purportedly, the Gaon of Vilna refused to see the Vitebsker, given he was guilty by association—namely, in his association with the deeply intoxicated devotional lifestyle of the Kalisker, who was caught in ecstatic somersaulting in front of the Holy Ark in synagogue during prayer.[17] While their master the Maggid may have been somewhat angered by this devotion of wild abandon endangering the legitimacy of a burgeoning renewal movement as heretical, the Vitebsker remained committed and deeply connected to the integrity of his spiritual partner. Just a few years thereafter, rather than abandoning his colleague, the Vitebsker banded together in solidarity to preserve and carry forward this wild abandon away from the confines of a reifying court-based Hasidism to the terra incognita awaiting them in the Promised Land. At first the group settled in Safed, but as noted already they encountered opposition there and after three years moved to Tiberias.[18] The Vitebsker's mystical persona, bordering on the messianic, longed for the transcendence of complete immersion in the divine which was enabled through his relocation to the Land of Israel as a propitious site for such transcendent devotion.

In this regard, one can begin to appreciate the ongoing influence and pride of place that the Vitebsker's messianic impulse plays within later Israel-based Hasidism, for example:

> It is a tradition we've received from Slonim [through the author of *Yesod ha'Avodah*] who said that there are teachings in *Peri haAretz*: "if only we could practice devotion on their level of the world-that-is-coming and the messianic era of the future [now]."[19]

In returning to Zion as his renewed ancient spiritual home, the Vitebsker maintained links with his diasporic Hasidim for some time, continuing to

---

at haHasidut: Toldot, Divrai Torah, v'Hagut shel Elef v'Shesh Me'ot 'Ishai Hasidut, 521a.

17. Hundert, Toward a Biography of R. Abraham Kalisker, 32. Compare with more recently, Zvi Leshem, "Flipping into Ecstacy: Towards a Syncopal Understanding of Mystical Hasidic Somersaults," *Studia Judaica* 17.1 (33) (2014): 157-184.

18. Alfassi, *Torat haHasidut*, n487, 521a.

19. Aharon Suarsky, *Yesod ha'Ma'ale*, vol. 1 (Israel: Ziyutanim Publications, 2000), 59.

provide the most intimate spiritual guidance to them through his epistles known as *Igrot haQodesh*—what we have aptly adapted as our for this series, *From Tiberias, With Love*. Although scholarly opinion is divided, it seems that the Vitebsker did not recommend that his followers in Eastern Europe find themselves another leader: he believed that only he was capable of directing them, even from afar. The Vitebsker's move to the Land of Israel laid the foundation for a core of Hasidic settlements, supported by a structured fundraising apparatus and a network of emissaries known by the acronym *ShaDaR"im* to Europe, who delivered the leader's epistles of religious instruction and brought back letters, requests, and donations from his followers. In his last correspondence, battling the illness that would claim his life, the Vitebsker dares not shy away from describing the harsh conditions of living in a land that continues to "devour its inhabitants." The Vitebsker nonetheless maintained the conviction that his emigration to Zion was a return to a royal spiritual abode. It is fascinating to see how the anxiety of continuity of his devotional path was neither quelled nor realized through Menachem Mendel's only heir, Moshe, who married the daughter of a prominent Jerusalem Sefardic family but died young in 1799. This means that the lineage of the Vitebsker remains an open question, especially in light of a number of Hasidic leaders and their aforementioned sects claiming a strong anxiety of influence from his teachings.[20]

The Vitebsker's principal homelitical work, *Peri haAretz,* is considered to be the holy of holies in the Hasidic canon. Paradoxically, while there is no explicit lineage of Hasidism that continues the formal legacy of the Vitebsker, there remain numerous Hasidic masters that see his teaching as exemplary of their devotional path, a kind of Hasidism for the spiritual elite known as *AdMoR"im*. A case in point is to consider how Hasidic masters refer to *Peri haAretz,* the Vitebsker's principal work—

> On the table of the holy Rabbi of Ruzhin always laid the holy book *Peri haAretz*, and he said that whomever understand *Peri haAretz* [such a person] "understands how to unite upper and lower wisdom."[21]
>
> I heard from the holy Rabbi of Ruzhin, who used to say: "How did the author of *Peri haAretz* manage to include so much of the spiritual grandeur of the Master of the Universe into such a small book?"[22]

---

20. Harold Bloom, *The Anxiety of Influence: A Theory of Poetry* (New York: Oxford University Press, 1997).

21. R. Mordekhai Hayyim, *Sefer Ma'amar Mordekhai*, (Jerusalem: Yisrael Zeev Slonim publications, 2006), 62.

22. Irin Qadishin, quoted in *Toledot haRav haKadosh Peri haAretz u'Mamshikhai Darko*, vol. 1 (Jerusalem: Mechon Peri haAretz, 2011), 348.

> The holy rabbi Abraham Elimelech of Karlin said that the holy rabbi Menachem Mendel was "*the source* of Hasidism."[23]
>
> *Peri ha-Arets* was considered as the foundation stone of Hasidic methodology, even to the point where spiritual masters and saints would give *Peri ha-Arets* the nickhame of "the *RaMBa"M* and *Shulkhan Arukh* of Hasidism."[24]

Peri haAretz primarily consists of Hasidic homilies on the Pentateuch and the holy days, which appeared in print, first in 1814. This collection of homilies was redacted by the Vitebsker's close disciple, Rabbi Eleazer Zusman, son of Isaac the Cohen.[25] These teachings are unique in the Hasidic canon, as the level of the Vitebsker's innovation is second to none and reflects a one of a kind oral channeling of the Maggid of Mezeritch's teachings, then masterfully redacted by R. Zusman.[26] An abridged version called *Peri 'Etz* was then published in Zhitomir (1874). A real window into the Vitebsker's devotional life and the spiritual direction he intimately shared with his diasporic Hasidim has been published many times as *Igrot haQodesh* (1794) which includes his own epistles as well as addendums included by his colleague-disciple, Abraham of Kalisk.[27]

But it is the devotional model of arguably the greatest Hasidic sage in his generation that forgoes a secure and comfortable life, instead choosing to emigrate to *'Eretz Yisrael*, thereby having to endure great self-sacrifice. As a result, the Hasidic community in the Holy Land began to sprout and blossom. Great Hasidic leaders, like Rabbi Yisrael of Ruzhin, the grandson of the Maggid of Mezeritch, held the Vitebsker in the highest esteem, comparing Reb Menachem Mendel's emigration to the *'Eretz Yisrael* to that of the patriarch, Abraham. The emigration to *'Eretz Yisrael*, just like Abraham, opened a pathway for the Vitebsker and his progeny to enter and return to the Holy Land for generations to come.

Again we might ask: How does such moral grandeur and spiritual audacity really begin to emerge?[28] Reb Menachem Mendel of Vitebsk became rnowned as the leader of the third generation of the Hasidic movement

---

23. Peri Elemelekh, quoted in *Toledot haRav haKadosh Peri haAretz u'Mamshikhai Darko*, vol. 1, 348.

24. Suarsky, *Yesod ha'Ma'ale*, vol. 1, 59.

25. Alfassi, *Torat haHasidut*, 365a–366b.

26. *'Ohalai Ya'akov Hosiatin*, 189.

27. Raya Haran, YIVO Encyclopedia, s.v. "Menachem Mendel of Vitebsk," http://www.yivoencyclopedia.org/article.aspx/Menachem_Mendel_of_Vitebsk.

28. I am extrapolating this expression from Heschel, who sought to translate this Hasidic ethos into contemporary American Jewry, all the while deeply indebted to spiritual masters like Reb Menachem Mendel, see Abraham J. Heschel, *Moral Grandeur and Spiritual Audacity: Essays,* (New York: Farrar, Straus and Giroux, 2013).

just as it was beginning to veer away from its founding ethos.[29] Of course, the Vitebsker's leadership was contingent on its explicit connection to the lineage of the leader of the first generation—the venerated founder of Hasidism, the Ba'al Shem Tov and most importantly, to his greatest disciple was the Maggid of Mezeritch, who was accepted as mentor by the overwhelming majority of Hasidic Jewry. Recall that the third generation of Hasidism included Reb Elimelech of Lizansk and his brother Reb Zusha, who disseminated Hasidism in Poland and Galicia; and Reb Nahum of Chernobyl, who spread Hasidism in the Ukraine. Also counted among the leaders of this third-generation project of Hasidic dissemination were Reb Yitzchak of Berdichev, Reb Aaron of Karlin, and Lubavitch's founding *Alter Rebbe*, Reb Shneur Zalman of Liady. But there was clearly something unique about the spiritual grandeur of Reb Menachem Mendel of Vitebsk. The selfsame leader who spread Hasidic teachings throughout White Russia and along the border of Lithuania rose above all his colleagues gathering round the Maggid's table.[30] The Maggid of Mezeritch himself willed that, after his own son, it was Reb Menachem Mendel who would become the inheritor of his legacy to carry forward this demanding spiritual lineage known as Hasidism. This is evinced in many ways, including the fact that in all of the letters written by the disciples of the Maggid, it was always Reb Menachem Mendel whose signature appeared at the top of all signatories. The Vitebsker's spiritual stature was never in doubt.

As an exceptional student, Reb Menachem Mendel merited studying with the Maggid of Mezeritch, astounding all those who knew him with his scholarship and talent, thus making an indelible impression upon his master. Once, when the Maggid was away, preoccupied with some sacral deed, upon returning he went to open the door of young Menachem Mendel's room to find his student pacing back and forth. The Maggid noticed that his manner of walking contained an air of arrogance, as Menachem Mendel's hat was tilted to one side over his forehead. The Maggid called out to his disciple, questioning him as to how many pages of Talmud he had learned in the Maggid's absence for daily regimen. Menachem Mendel replied that he had learned five folio pages. The Maggid responded, "So what do you think—how many pages would you need to study for your hat to completely fall off your head?" Having finished speaking, the Maggid left and his young protégé understood from his master's words of the slight conceit in his behavior, so he began weeping, thus decrying: "Oh Master,

29. Alfassi, *Torat haHasidut*, 520a–521bn487.

30. See Green's lengthy introduction describing this phenomenon of transmission round the Maggid's table, Arthur Green, Ebn D. Leader, Ariel E. Mayse, and Or N. Rose, *Speaking Torah: Spiriutal Teachings from around the Maggid's Table*, vol. 1 (Vermont: Jewish Lights, 2013), 1–74.

please show me the upright path of studying the holy Torah!" The Maggid responded that he would take him to see the Ba'al Shem Tov: "For it is from our teacher, the holy BeSh"T, that we will take away what it means to truly serve the divine with devotion."

After arriving at the residence of the Ba'al Shem Tov prior to onset of Sabbath, the Maggid went in speedily to see the eminent rebbe in order to greet him, while the young protégé, Menachem Mendel, assured his master that he would return to receive Torah at the table of the holy BeSh"T during the Sabbath but beckoned the Maggid not to say anything about him. Within his small coterie of contemplatives, suddenly the BeSh"T asked for Menachem Mendel to join them during the elongated practice of contemplation for afternoon services. It was at this moment that the BeSh"T revealed many secrets with the young protégé, Menachem Mendel, which would unfold in his future lifetime. Present at this meeting were key disciples, Yaakov Yosef of Polnoyye and the Maggid, who each testified that of all present, it was only Menachem Mendel who was able to penetrate the depths of this intimate revelation. Before Menachem Mendel's emigration to the Holy Land, Yaakov Yosef of Polnoyye asked Menachem Mendel where he stood in the process of integrating this earlier, intimate revelation from the BeSh"T, to which he replied: "Already more than half of it has come to fruition"—all this, even while he was a young protégé.[31] From young precocious moments, then on to marriage, Menachem Mendel's settling into Vitebsk would not last long. A contingency of Hasidim came to visit the Maggid, seeking a way for a more proximate connection to the holy man, given that traveling from their villages to see him was too time consuming and compromised their ability to spend most of their time What? connected to their master on the levels of *Nefesh-Ruah-Neshamah* (Inner Drive-Spirit-Soul). The Maggid took one of his garments along with his sash and staff telling them: "Go to Vitebsk, there you will find a Jew by the name of Menachem Mendel. Give him these items in your hands and he will be your master. The Hasidim should do as he commands." They arrived in Vitebsk and handed over the items as instructed. Immediately the master arose and wrapped with the robe, tied the sash, and held the staff, then calling upon them in a princely voice by demanding: "Respect." The Hasidim gathered there beheld an utter transformation, albeit momentary, whereby they no longer recognized the man before them. Yet he opened the teaching and said: "Scripture states: 'From amidst your people shall you appoint a king,' but a moment ago he was just another one part of the rank and file, and then in the blink of an eye he was transformed and became the king!"[32]

31. Aharon Suarsky, *Yesod ha'Ma'ale*, vol. 1 (Israel: Ziyutanim Publications, 2000), 33–34n39.

32. Suarsky, *Yesod ha'Ma'ale*, vol. 1, 34n41.

Following the instructions of the Maggid of Mezeritch, Reb Menachem Mendel journeyed on to spread Hasidic teachings among the Jews of White Russia. Two years after being sent on his mission, Reb Menachem Mendel returned with a report to this master, the Maggid. When he arrived, Levi Yitzhak of Berditchev remarked: "Here is your most devoted disciple!" Menachem Mendel entered and the Maggid asked him for a report on his journeys. Menachem Mendel explained that there were places he was called a "gifted scholar" (*lamdan*), other places where he was called a "devoted one" (*zaddik*), and even other places where he was called a "sage" (*hakham*), "but I knew and remembered in each place who I was and the measure of my deeds." The Maggid responded, "My son, this is the correct path, to never act according to how others label you; the key is to always know your authentic value." Then the Maggid asked for an update on what he achieved with Russian Jewry. Reb Menachem responded: "I encountered Jews with torn clothes but whole hearts; so I transformed them into Jews with whole clothes but torn hearts."[33] In other words, Menachem Mendel encountered destitute Russian Jews unable to make ends meet and earn a respectable living. To his mind, their clothes being torn meant that their material concerns were rent asunder. On the other hand, their hearts were whole, insofar as they were now more deeply attuned to the soul's direction of the life in this world and the imperative to cultivate its depths. Reb Menachem Mendel succeeded in transforming them into wealthy Jews with "torn hearts"—namely, beings concerned with the necessary vulnerability and spiritual openness for cultivating a deeper contemplative life of the soul.

The contemplative life requires careful attention, especially in realizing equanimity within spiritual qualia known as *middot*. On the one hand, Reb Menachem Mendel placed heavy emphasis on the attribute of humility and meekness, repeatedly explaining that this was the most essential attribute for serving the Creator; on the other hand, though, he was adamant in adorning himself in majestic garments, suggesting a certain kind of royal sense of self. The contradictions seem striking.[34]

Once, while still a young married yeshiva student, Reb Menachem Mendel passed through the Polnoyye, the town where the renowned R. Yaakov Yosef lived. First Reb Menachem Mendel checked into an inn and took off his hat and sash, then he went out with a pipe in his mouth and a simple head covering of a yarmulke on his head. Dressed down in this manner, he went to greet R. Yaakov Yosef. To appreciate Reb Menachem

33. Ibid., 35–36n44.

34. On this contradictory royal sense of self transmitted to the Vitebsker's disciple, R. Israel Friedman of Ruzhin, see David Assaf, *The Regal Way: The Life and Times of Rabbi Israel of Ruzhin* (Stanford University Press, 2002).

Mendel's behavior, recall that R. Yaakov Yosef was one of the Ba'al Shem Tov's preeminent disciples, as well as being somewhat older than the Maggid of Mezeritch, Reb Menachem Mendel's own mentor. In addition, R. Yaakov Yosef was known to be very punctilious in his spiritual practice, and it was likely that he would become infuriated at the appearance of Reb Menachem Mendel hatless and smoking a pipe, as if he were his close friend. Yet, surprisingly, R. Yaakov Yosef received him most warmly and even escorted Reb Menachem Mendel to his own inn afterward. R. Yaakov Yosef explained Reb Menachem Mendel's behavior to his disciples by way of analogy: *There once was a king who possessed a rare pearl of unmatched value and he did not know where to hide it from thieves in his palace. Finally, the king decided to hide it in the bathroom, for no thief would think to look there. This is true concerning Reb Menachem Mendel. In truth, he is extremely humble and meek, and only in order that he not become overly proud of his humility does he adorn himself in majesty. But such deeply devotional humility should not obscure Reb Menachem Mendel's other refined qualities.*

As a diplomat, Reb Menachem Mendel was astute in assessing and navigating volatile territory. For example, following the plague that afflicted Tiberias in 1786, there was an expansion of the settlement there, primarily as a function of Reb Menachem Mendel's ability to serve as negotiator with the local Ottoman pasha, Ahmad Al-Jazeer in Acco. Given that the expansion of the Jewish settlement in Tiberias was already restricted by a previous ban set forth by Sefardic sage, R. Abulafia, prior to the arrival of the Hasidic emigration, its expansion seems extraordinary.[35] This extraordinary scenario emerged when an anonymous Russian donor from Poberzana pledged to Pasha Ahmad Al-Jazeer enough funds to cover the expansion of the Ashkenazic settlement Tiberias.

Such astuteness as a diplomat is evident elsewhere, especially in the strange incident of mass adultery in Dubno. This case drew such renown that it came to the attention of the Maggid. In order to resolve it, the Maggid specifically deployed Reb Mendel Menachem along with R. Aharon haGadol of Karlin, whom he sent as emissaries to diplomatically resolve the strange case of adultery that required both particularistic skills of Jewish law (as over 100 *gittin* or writs of divorce would need to be issued) as well as more universal skills of diplomacy (as they needed to effect a reconciliation between that Jewish community and its city official in Dubno, in the neighboring the town of Mezeritch):

> . . . once again the Maggid instructed as follows: "Reb Menachem

35. R. Abraham Avish Shor, "Olelot b'Perkai Toladah u'bMishnat Karlin-Stolin," in *Beit Aharon v'Yisrael*, vol. 31:2, no. 182 (Jerusalem: Karlin-Stolin Institute, n.d.), 186–91.

> Mendel must travel with you because he knows how to speak Polish, and also take your Sabbath white [*vestments, which Hasidim at that time were still known to wear on any holy day*]," and so they carried out these instructions. Then, on their journey, Reb Menachem Mendel said: "Behold our journey is only for the sake of arranging *gittin*, if so, why the need to speak Polish along with Sabbath vestments? It must only be because our master sees with his inner eye that the evil doers have remorse over their actions and they have become conspirators and turn coats, tale-baring to the city officials." And indeed this was the case, when these [Hasidic] emissaries arrived, the city official immediately demanded them to be brought before him, and his intention was to do them harm, while the conspirators were concealed in another room of the city official. When they arrived at the official dressed in white Sabbath finery, it pleased the official, receiving these emissaries with great dignity, and so he asked them to sit with him for a while. In the course of their conversation, the official said to them: "What do such [esteemed] rabbis have to do with what's going on here?" Reb Menachem Mendel explained: "Given that Reb Aharon is a man of God, and he saw that there are great oppositional forces, given the Jewish residents' transgressive behavior in your city who will literally lead to its demise, all the women must be given writs of divorce. Thus we have come to you, the mayor, for you must oversee their [return] to proper conduct." Once the [implications of these adulterous] deeds of these conspirators were recounted to the mayor, he demanded that these [conspirators hiding in the room next door] speak with these rabbis. Immediately Rabbi Aharon screamed at them loudly, with great anger so that they would confess all their sins before the mayor. Then the mayor ordered them to fulfill writs of divorce with great decisiveness.[36]

Diplomacy bespeaks a certain willingness to integrate, albeit at times subversively, into society so as to navigate it for the sake of an agenda. And so, most fascinating is the situation that arose while Reb Menachem Mendel was en route to *'Eretz Yisrael*, where this focus on diplomacy required him to radically challenge accepted norms in general within Jewish religious life, as well as Hasidic norms proper:

> . . . prior to emigrating to *'Eretz Yisrael*, Reb Menachem Mendel hosted a great feast for all the officials of Vitebsk. And so Reb Menachem Mendel would enter into the feasts and sit with [the

36. *Shivkhai haBesht* (Jerusalem: Mintz, 1969), 84.

> officials]. Reb Menachem Mendel suggested that his disciples assist Polish officials and their spouses in dismounting from their carriages by holding their elbows. He assured his disciples that no spiritual harm would befall them, rather that they would all be protected by an extension of his blessing . . .[37]

The image of Reb Menachem Mendel here hovers between diplomat and spiritual renegade. On the one hand, it is in his own best interest to curry favor with political officials of his day by entertaining them with the greatest dignity due to their position in secular society. By elevating these officials in the eyes of his disciples, in a sense, he is also elevating his own stature in acknowledging his equal standing to share such dignity as equally as it is being shared with him as a Jewish noble. On the other hand, by permitting his disciples to assist the wives of Polish nobility to dismount from their carriages by touching their bodies so as to enable their attendance at his farewell celebration is shocking. That sense of shock is not lost on Reb Menachem Mendel, who in the same breath assures his disciples that his blessing power as a zaddik would protect them from any untoward spiritual repercussions from this unseemly behavior. Under life-threatening circumstances, there are cases where normative rabbinic boundaries can be transgressed for the sake of saving a life. But were these such life-threatening circumstances? Hardly! This takes us back to the comment about Reb Menachem Mendel's proclivity for dressing in noble attire as befitting a "man of silk,"[38] as well as demanding his Jewish colleagues send him off with a royal farewell. To be a "man of silk" suggests that there was something else at play "beneath the folksy visage of Hasidism"[39] as it is already emerging in the time of Reb Menachem Mendel of Vitebsk. Integration through acculturation without assimilation best describes the diplomatic strategies of Reb Menachem Mendel as well as his self-fashioned sense of claim to Hasidic nobility. This latter claim is more complex than the common pattern of the Hasidic leader who becomes a court-centered zaddik that comes to define much of the third generation of disciples of the Ba'al Shem Tov, for Reb Menachem Mendel distinguishes himself from these veritable "men of silk" by abandoning the hierarchy of the Hasidic court altogether, opting for an entirely different model—emigrating to the Land of Israel to enable a more intimate fellowship community. The shift away from the hierarchical

---

37. R. Reuben Zak of Ostalia, *Liqqutim mehaRav Israel meRyzhn, z"l, Knesset Yisrael* (Warsaw, 1806), 83a–b. Compare with *Toldot haRav haKadosh Peri haAretz u'Mamshikhai Darko*, vol. 1 (Jerusalem: Mechon Peri haAretz: 5771), 417, which edits out this detail of holding onto the elbows, as later redacted in *Knesset Mordekhai* (3 Heshvan 1974).

38. Glenn Dynner, *Men of Silk: The Hasidic Conquest of Polish Jewish Society* (Oxford: Oxford University Press, 2008), 25, 72, 91, 202, 249.

39. Dynner, *Men of Silk*, 91.

model of vertical leadership in Eastern Europe towards a more horizontal coleadership model in Tiberias sheds much light on the spiritual quality of Reb Menachem Mendel. For such a majestic spiritual master to be able to share this mantle in coleadership with his most devoted disciple, R. Abraham haCohen of Kalisk, is remarkable. Such anomalous coleadership models practiced in Tiberias by these two spiritual masters, moves more deeply into an egalitarian mode of mystical friendship through the practice of *dibbuk chaverim* already within the letters of these two masters as well as in the writing of the latter's disciple, R. Tzvi Hirsch of Somyritch.

Recall that following the death of the Maggid of Mezeritch, Reb Menachem Mendel was viewed by his fellows as the most prominent among them. Already in the lifetime of the Maggid of Mezeritch was the Vitebsker acting as spiritual leader of his community, some say even as early as his bar mitzvah year.[40] When the communal leaders of Lithuania were searching for a leader, they consulted with the Maggid of Mezeritch, who promptly handed them a *Bekishe* or long silk coat, and instructed them to go and find R. Mendel, and asking him to be their leader. They journeyed to Vitebsk in search of R. Mendel, only to discover there were many men who went by this name. After they presented their case to real R. Mendel, he refused the offer. So when the emissaries offered R. Mendel the Maggid of Mezeritch's *Bekishe* or long silk coat, only then would this disciple accept the mantle of leadership, immediately agreeing to take on this role, so that all the other Mendel knew who the real R. Mendel was and showed nothing but reverence.[41]

Had he not left to live in the *'Eretz Yisrael* he may very well have attained the status of the rebbe of all Hasidic Jewry, in a manner not unlike that of the Ba'al Shem Tov in the first generation of Hasidism and the Maggid of Mezeritch in the second. Reb Menachem Mendel's standing was especially high in the eyes of the Hasidic Jews of Russia and Lithuania. In these places he was seen as master, mentor, rabbi, and leader, and all heeded his words. Even Reb Shneur Zalman of Liady, the founder of the Lubavitch trend within the Hasidic movement, took orders from Reb Menachem Mendel, aiding him in efforts to spread Hasidic thought in White Russia; and Reb Aaron of Karlin, the founder of Karlin Hasidism, helped Reb Menachem to spread teachings along the Lithuanian border. His followers reported that they had to be careful about their thoughts while in his presence, for he could sense what was in their mind. Even after his arrival in the Holy Land, he continued to be seen as their leader, and, to a large degree, Reb Shneur Zalman of Liady acted as agent of Reb Menachem by

40. *Toldot haRav haKadosh Peri haAretz u'Mamshikhai Darko*, vol. 1 (Jerusalem: Mechon Peri haAretz, 2011), 369.

41. Ibid., 369.

leading his followers. Together, Reb Shneur Zalman and Reb Aaron were responsible for gathering and sending donations from the Hasidic Jews of White Russia and Lithuania to the Hasidic community in *'Eretz Yisrael*. It is also noteworthy that the *Tzemach Tzedek*, Rabbi Menachem Mendel Schneersohn, the third Lubavitcher Rebbe, was named after him, and the seventh Lubavitcher Rebbe, also Menachem Mendel, was named after the two of them.

Given that at the time he was at his peak, many wonder what exactly caused Reb Menachem Mendel of Vitebsk to make the move to emigrate to the Holy Land. There was even some dissent about Reb Menachem Mendel's imminent emigration to the Holy Land, for example in a 1775 letter from his colleague, Abraham haMalakh, son of the Maggid, that was sent to R. Shneur Zalman of Liady. As a committed disciple and son of the Maggid of Mezeritch, R. Abraham felt it would be more worthwhile for Reb Menachem Mendel to stay and support the battle against the Mitnaggedim: "for in my opinion, it is incumbent upon this aforementioned rabbi to remain here, in order to stay interconnected in solidarity with his holy presence that should live long and protect our pathway of sacred [Hasidic] devotion."[42]

Recall that leadership of the Hasidic path did not pass on from father to son, from the Ba'al Shem Tov to R. Baruch of Mezebizc, nor from the Maggid of Mezeritch to R. Abraham haMalakh. Rather than what devolves into a familial dynastic model after the third generation, here there is still a subtle awareness on the part of a burgeoning Hasidic leadership that the capacity for spiritual inspiration and transmission is not necessarily passed on within one's biological family. Rather, the capacity for spiritual inspiration and transmission is a gift that extends through the circle of intimate fellowship. Here then is where it is important to recall that Reb Menachem Mendel was the most esteemed of the Maggid's students. This esteem was both of a spiritual and intellectual quality, enabling Reb Menachem Mendel to thus exert great influence over his disciples. That influence comes from spiritual effulgence, and so the disciples receive the transmission of their master and become lovers who are in love with their beloved master. So great was Reb Menachem Mendel's spiritual authority that we find even the leading disciples of the Maggid—fit to stand independently as great spiritual masters in their own right—submitted to the leadership and transmission of Reb Menachem Mendel.

Notwithstanding the deep love Reb Menachem Mendel aroused for this spiritual transmission, he was unique as a master who really enabled others to flourish by opening space for them too, especially within his intimate

---

42. Letter from Abraham haMalakh to R. Shneur Zalman of Liady (Thursday, 1775), Kerem Yisrael, as quoted in *Toldot haRav haKadosh Peri haAretz u'Mamshikhai Darko*, vol. 1 (Jerusalem: Mechon Peri haAretz, 5771), 413.

mystical fellowship group. Consider for example, how on the Sabbath prior to emigration, during the celebration of the *hillula'* anniversary of the Maggid's soul departing and ascending from this world on the 19th of Kislev, 1777, Reb Menachem Mendel collaborated in leading services along with his intimate fellowship. Friday night, Reb Menachem Mendel led minchah and *Kabbalat Shabbat*; R. Abraham of Kalisk led *Ma'ariv*; and Saturday morning, R. Yissachar Dov Baer of Lubavitch led *Shacharit*, R. Shneur Zalman read Torah, and R. Yisrael of Polotsk led *mussaf*, while the concluding minchah was led by Reb Menachem Mendel.[43] The existent interconnection of this holy fellowship delved deeper during these Sabbath prayers—a kind of sacred group soliloquy of sorts. During the interlude between *Kabbalat Shabbat* and *Ma'ariv*, wordless melodies of the Maggid were sung by R. Abraham and R. Yisrael which enabled Reb Menachem Mendel to enter into a state of rapture, intertwining with the soul of the departed Maggid.[44] This Sabbath *hillula'* celebration of the Maggid galvanized the import of R. Abraham of Kalisk and R. Yisrael of Polotsk joining Reb Menachem Mendel in his emigration to the Holy Land.[45] Once the date of departure was settled, Reb Menachem Mendel and R. Shneur Zalman set out to seek rapprochement with the leader of the opposition or Mitnaggedim, known as the Vilna Gaon. Reb Menachem Mendel felt a deep sense of consternation over his emigration, only insofar as it would expose the Hasidim remaining in the diaspora to the growing wrath of the Mitnaggedim. This missed moment of reconciliation remains clouded in mystery; why did the Vilna Gaon twice slam the door in the face of Reb Menachem Mendel and R. Shneur Zalman? Moreover, why did Reb Menachem Mendel not break down the door?[46] These dashed expectations of reconciliation between the warring sects of Mitnaggedim and Hasidim may have exacerbated the messianic impulse propelling the Hasidic emigration to the Holy Land. Reb Menachem Mendel, also known as *Ohev Yisrael*,[47] the "Lover of All the People Israel" may now have extended his love in becoming the "Lover of the Land of Israel."

On that same Sabbath celebration of the *hillula'* of the Maggid, when asked about the mystical meaning of the liturgy for welcoming the Sabbath of *Kabbalat Shabbat*, and the specific role of welcoming the angels with the greeting of "*Bo'acheim l'Shalom*," Reb Menachem Mendel explained that angels are referred to as messengers of shalom or peace, for their mis-

43. *Toldot haRav haKadosh Peri haAretz u'Mamshikhai Darko*, vol. 1 (Jerusalem: Mechon Peri haAretz, 5771), 392.

44. Ibid., 393.

45. Ibid., 394.

46. Ibid., 395.

47. Ibid., 400.

sion is singular—to act as emissaries carrying forward the extra-souls of the Sabbath that are endowed to every devoted human so engaged. So in this context, shalom means interconnectivity, as the exegesis on the verse "Return, return O Shulamite" (Song of Songs 7:1) teaches that she has enabled an interconnection between Me and My world. These souls enable interconnection between divinity and the world, thus making the world a vessel for divinity.[48] This final teaching in the diaspora marks a turning point in Reb Menachem Mendel's devotional teaching, for upon emigrating to *'Eretz Yisrael*, his focus shifts from interconnectivity of the divinity within the world (*hithabrut*), to interconnectivity of the divinity within the mystical fellowship circle (*dibbuk chaverim*).

And so, this decision to take an intimate group of followers to emigrate to *'Eretz Yisrael* with the intention of staying there for the rest of Reb Menachem Mendel's life may not have been as out of character as it first seemed. The aforementioned ongoing persecution at the hands of his opponents the Mitnaggedim caused Reb Menachem Mendel such hardship that he decided, in order to divorce himself from the quarreling, to move to the *'Eretz Yisrael*. And, indeed, because he succeeded in disseminating Hasidism in areas bordering on Lithuania and even enjoyed a following inside Lithuania, Reb Menachem Mendel was becoming the main target of the oppositional attacks of the Mitnaggedim. Public denouncements and excommunications were issued specifically against him, and it was due to such persecution that he was forced to leave his home in Minsk. All the same, it is difficult to accept that as a mighty personage as he would be deterred by such things—for he was succeeding and his influence was forever expanding.

It would appear that his thirst for closeness to God, and his great longing for the Holy Land—the land wherein the Divine Presence rests—shook his inner being so strongly that no worldly enjoyment could compare to living in *'Eretz Yisrael*. In addition, by settling in *'Eretz Yisrael*, Reb Menachem Mendel wished to transcend all factional discrepancy, and map out a path for mending the whole Jewish people. In emigrating to the Holy Land, Reb Menachem Mendel would be joining the ranks of modern mystical luminaries who both yearned and some of whom even realized a precursor emigration, including R. Moses Cordovero, R. Joseph Karo, and R. Isaac Luria (all of whom settled in Safed); as well as the pioneer of Hasidism, the Ba'al Shem Tov, who embarked on his emigration only to turn back from the port in Istanbul.[49]

48. Ibid., 391.

49. On the spiritual significance of this unrealized emigration and its Sufi context, see Aubrey L. Glazer, "Istanbul Mon Amour: Imaginal Journeying in Beshtian Hasidism and Turkish Sufism," in *Pillar of Prayer* (Louisville, KY: Fons Vitae, 2011), 227–45; and

In the year 5537 (ca. 1777), Reb Menachem Mendel took many of his followers amongst the three hundred who boarded the ship to set out for *'Eretz Yisrael*. The hardships involved were enormous, and one peril after another came upon the group. Even before reaching Israel one of travelers' boats sank, taking with it the lives of thirty Jews. When they arrived in Israel they settled in Safed, but the Turks and the Arabs persecuted them, so much so that eventually they were forced to leave the city and move to Tiberias. Yet they were not permitted to settle comfortably in this new setting. The difficulties of securing income were great; most of the company possessed no skill from which they could earn a living locally. As a result, Reb Menachem was forced to ask the Jews of Russia time and time again to send donations in order to support the Hasidic community in *'Eretz Yisrael*. On top of all of these difficulties, it happened that from time to time epidemics would break out, taking the lives of some of Reb Menachem's followers.

Yet, despite all of this, Reb Menachem Mendel remained adamant about staying in *'Eretz Yisrael*. It would have been easier for him to return. Many of his followers longed for him to rejoin them. But he had decided to stay and to continue to bear the heavy burden of caring for his community's livelihood. Something about this spiritual master changed on emigrating to *'Eretz Yisrael,* or so he thought.

> When Reb [*Menachem Mendel*] arrived in the Holy Land of Israel, he proclaimed that he had left behind his libidinal impulse in the diaspora, so that now he would be able to truly worship the divine in a state of holiness and purity. However, as soon as he explained that notwithstanding the deal he made to leave behind his libidinal impulse in the diaspora as he would be emigrating to the Holy Land of Israel, the inner drive did not keep to its end of the agreement. Upon arriving in the Holy Land, his libidinal impulse re-emerged, so Reb Menachem Mendel decried: "Trickster! Liar! Why have you reneged on our agreement?" The libidinal impulse responded: "That very libidinal impulse was indeed left behind in the diaspora, and I am not the same libidinal impulse that spoke to you in the diaspora—I am other—I am the libidinal impulse of the Holy Land. For here in the Holy Land, all become greater and more exalted, and so for every person who is grander than their fellow, so too their libidinal impulse!"[50]

---

more recently, see Moshe Idel, "18th Century Early Hasidism: Between Europe and Asia," in *Studia et Acta Historiae Iudaeorum Romaniae*, XII/2015 (Editura Hasefer, Iași: Editura Universității Alexandru Ioan Cuza, 2015), 49–76.

50. Mishnat Yosef haGoan R. Yitzhak Lieberman, quoted in *Toldot haRav haKadosh Peri haAretz u'Mamshikhai Darko*, vol. 1 (Jerusalem: Mechon Peri haAretz, 5771), 431.

This inner dialogue between a great spiritual master and his libidinal impulse is astonishing, insofar as it opens a window into the depths of Reb Menachem Mendel's self-awareness. Just as one can appear to be externally pious while becoming a scoundrel within the limits of the law, so too, the Vitebsker is acutely aware of the even more grandiose pitfalls awaiting him within his spiritual ascent while dwelling in the Holy Land. Just because the Vitebsker has emigrated to this spiritual center of the universe, it does not inoculate him from becoming a scoundrel within the limits of the law. The law here is not limited to rabbinic law, but extends more specifically to a comportment with all sentient beings as expressed throughout Hasidic spirituality at large. While the Vitebsker may have been partially motivated to emigrate so as to leave behind all the exacerbations of intra-Jewish conflict with the Mitnaggedim, now he was even more vulnerable to fall into the scandalous piety he was trying to escape.

There was also the very real danger of turning the Holy Land itself into a form of idolatrous worship—namely, worshipping the geographical topos disconnected from its spiritual ethos. Reb Menachem Mendel again shows great self-awareness of this challenge:

> It happened once that someone came to Reb Menachem Mendel in Tiberias and apologized in his presence, for from that moment he merited being able to have pity on the earth of the Holy Land and thus settle in it. It was not enough that this person did not feel any sort of spiritual uplift whatsoever from it, rather, this person felt that being in the diaspora, he was living on a higher spiritual plane than here [in Tiberias]. Reb Menachem Mendel answered him that he was mistaken, for the holiness of the Land certainly has influenced him. The fact that he already feels a certain sense of descent is the reason for this, for *'Eretz Yisrael* is *Eretz CaNA'AN*, from the language of "submission" [*haChNA'Aah*], and it is a great merit to be brought to place of submission and humility, and thus his soul was experiencing a descent. And so he interpreted the verse: ". . . the Land is a very, very great land." (Numbers 14:7)—namely, that the Land of Israel is uniquely capable of reaching the state of "being very, very humbled spirit" (*mAvot* 4:4). So the Kalisker responded: And from this we learn as is taught in the Mishnah (m*Keilim* 1:6): "the Land of Israel is holier than all other lands, and 'what' is Her holiness . . .[51]—namely, the condition of 'what' [*ma"h*], which is the spiritual quality of humility, that is 'Her holiness'."

And so, this deepening self-awareness emerges within the spiritual prac-

51. *Zizim u'Perakhim*, Parashah Shelach, quoted in *Toldot haRav haKadosh Peri haAretz u'Mamshikhai Darko*, vol. 1 (Jerusalem: Mechon Peri haAretz, 5771), 433–34.

tice he followed while in the Holy Land. The constant stress on this quest for humility in the service of the divine is deepened when in tune with a landscape that itself is humbled. That the spiritual grandeur of the divine only manifests in the most humble of times and spaces is aligned with the grandeur of this spiritual master who is dwelling in the most humble of spaces in the Land of Israel. It is precisely in a state of unknowing, literally asking oneself "what?" that a more humbled spirit thus emerges and is drawn into untold spiritual depths. How fitting that the entire purpose of the Hasidic spiritual pathway was already articulated with strong resonances in the Ba'al Shem Tov who taught: "The entire purpose of knowing is *unknowing*."[52]

This path of unknowing that cultivates a deeper humbled spirit, for example, is exemplified in the story that takes place in Tiberias before the Friday afternoon prayer service. At that moment, while the study hall was already filled with Jews, Reb Menachem walked to the window and stood there staring out at the water for a long time. This was the body of water known as the Sea of Galilee, also called Lake Tiberias (Hebrew *Yam Kinneret*, Arabic *Buḥayrat Ṭabarīyā*), through which the Jordan River flows. When the sun had set, he began to lead the congregation in prayer. After the conclusion of the Sabbath, Reb Menachem spoke with his students and explained to them that each Friday afternoon, all of the prayers which were offered up in the lands outside of Israel during the previous week make their way up to heaven. And the place from which they ascend is above the Sea of Galilee. Reb Menachem saw the prayers gathering above the lake, yet they were not permitted to ascend, for the Jews of the diaspora were being accused in Heaven of not sufficiently supporting the needy Jews of Israel. Only after the diaspora Jews had taken upon themselves to provide added support for their destitute brethren in the Holy Land were their prayers able to ascend.[53] It is noteworthy here how the Sea of Galilee becomes a point of contemplation within the natural landscape of the Holy Land that serves to interconnect the mystical fellowship of Tiberias with its counterpart in Eastern Europe.

Among the émigré coterie of Reb Menachem Mendel were some outstanding Torah scholars, each of whom was an important spiritual leader in their own right, though they chose to cleave to the spiritual grandeur of Reb Menachem Mendel. When the great Hasidic leader, Reb Yaakov Shimshon of Shpatibka, made pilgrimage to *'Eretz Yisrael*, he went to visit Reb Velveleh of Zebraz, a Hasid who had made his home in *'Eretz Yisrael*.

52. Ba'al Shem Tov, *Keter Shem Tov haShalem*, ed. E. Shohat (New York: Kehot Publications, 2004), 3:7–8.

53. *Toldot haRav haKadosh Peri haAretz u'Mamshikhai Darko*, vol. 1 (Jerusalem: Mechon Peri haAretz, 5771), 398.

On approaching the house of the Reb Velveleh's family, he saw, to his great astonishment, the wife of the rebbe, once a woman of means, dressed in raggedy attire and busied herself washing somebody else's clothing. Reb Shimshon could not hold back his tears. Overcome with grief, he considered turning back and not entering the house of Reb Velveleh in order to avoid having to witness the rebbe's downtrodden state. But it was too late. The wife, who had discerned Reb Yaakov Shimshon's presence, realized that he had been shocked at the sight of their poverty and called out to him saying, "Rebbe, rebbe, don't be so distressed. Come! Enter our house. We thank the Almighty for allowing us the privilege of settling *'Eretz Yisrael*, and supporting ourselves through the labor of our own hands."

Something palpable changed in the nature of spiritual insights that Reb Menachem Mendel articulated and disseminated after arriving and settling in *'Eretz Yisrael*. The aforementioned final celebratory *Shabbat hillula'* honoring the Maggid on the 19th of Kislev was indeed a tipping point towards a deeper, more interconnected spiritual path. The profundity of these spiritual pathways are evinced both in the love letters of spiritual direction as well as those homilies collected and published in *Peri haAretz*.

Given that Reb Menachem Mendel even arranged a marital match for his dearly beloved son, Moshe, who was also an outstanding scholar, to the daughter of a Sefardic family, shows that the Sefardic Jews living in Israel at that time held the Ashkenazi Reb Menachem Mendel in great esteem. Despite earlier rifts between the nascent Sefardic community and the émigré Ashkenazi community of Hasidim, through his diplomacy Reb Menachem Mendel was able to attach himself to them affectionately. In his last will, Reb Menachem Mendel advises against quarreling with the Sefardic Jews whether over issues of religious practice or any other matter, given the potential for divisiveness. His love of the Holy Land meant a love for all Jews and all sentient beings.

The tremendous challenges of settling the Holy Land while caring for the material and spiritual welfare of his followers in Israel and in the diaspora sapped the pious rebbe's strength. Ten years after his arrival in the Holy Land on Menachem-Av, 5547 (ca. 1787), he became ill. On Rosh Chodesh 'Iyar 5548 (1788), at the age of fifty-seven, Reb Menachem Mendel left this world. Disease had weakened him greatly, but his mind remained clear until his final hour as he writes:

> Regarding my prodigal son, Reb Moshe, I ask that he not be appointed to any position of authority over others, and that he distance himself from all honor and from all wantonness. He should study ethical writings on a daily basis and attach himself to people of integrity. Let him love even the lowliest of Jews and flee from

> falsehood with all of his might, even if it is for the sake of Heaven. He should not say words of Torah in my name. Let no words of praise be engraved on my headstone—just "Our teacher, Rabbi Menachem Mendel."

Regarding burial procedures Menachem Mendel instructed his disciples as follows in his will:

> I request that there should not elapse more than one hour from the moment that my soul leaves my body until the time that I am buried. They should not bury my body on boards or in a casket—just straight into the holy soil. Those responsible for carrying my body should take care to re/turn in self-reflection. And when covering my eyes with broken clay pottery as is customarily done, mention the name of the holy Rabbi Ba'al Shem Tov, and the name of our holy master, teacher, and rabbi, the Maggid of Mezeritch, of blessed memory.

Before departing this world, his disciples asked Reb Menachem Mendel whom he would like to be buried next to. Such a query may sound strange at first blush, but many people yearn to be buried near the righteous and the deeply devoted, in the hope that proximity to such spiritual merit will influence their own journey through the next world. Here we appreciate once again that the spiritual grandeur of Reb Menachem Mendel lay in his deep humility, for he was taken aback by such a question from his disciples. So Reb Menachem Mendel responded: "I would be quite happy to be buried next to any Jew—and I only hope that no Jew be ashamed of me, just as I am not ashamed of any other Jew."

The devotional posture embodied in the overall comportment, including emigrating, living, loving, and passing on within the Holy land truly lives on as a model of spiritual grandeur living within God.

25th of Sivan, 5779*
Baka, Jerusalem

**Yahrzeit* of Rabban Shimon b. Gamliel, Tanna and torch juggler for *Simchat Beth Hashoeivah* at the Second Temple in Jerusalem.

From Tiberias, With Love:
A Reader's Guide to Volume One

The Teachings of R. Menachem Mendel of Vitebsk[1]

by Moshe Hallamish
(Bar-Ilan University)

The BeSh"T seems to have spread the message of Hasidism while traveling through towns and villages and in the course of such activities as healing the sick.[2] It was only under the leadership of R. Dov Baer, "the Great Maggid" of Mezeritch, that the institution of zaddikism was properly established, with the zaddik now staying at home and a community gathering round him.[3] Among the many disciples who came together in the school of the Maggid, there may have been circles of more restricted membership which were formed by people drawn to each other by spiritual and personal affinity. Undoubtedly one of the most important personalities among them was R. Menachem Mendel b. Moses of Vitebsk.[4] It will be recalled that in the Vilna *cherem* of 8 'Iyar 5532 (1772), R. Menachem Mendel alone is mentioned as an example of a person who "had the reputation of being one of the greatest among their company, the companies of evil."[5] Equally, when the Hasidim sought to send a representative to R. Elijah, the Gaon of

---

1. This is an expanded version of a paper presented at the Tenth World Congress of Jewish Studies, which took place in Jerusalem in the summer of 1989.

2. See G. Scholem, 'Demuto hahistorit shel R. Yisrael Ba'al Shem Tov', *Molad*, 18 (1960); repr. in *Devarim bego* (Tel Aviv, 1975), 287–324; I. Tishby and J. Dan, 'Torat haHasidut vesifrutah', *Hebrew* Encyclopedia, xvii (1965), 769–821, repr. as a pamphlet by Academon, Jerusalem, and in A. Rubinstein, ed., *Perakim betorat haHasidut veToldoteihah* (Jerusalem, 1977), 250–312.

3. See Joseph Weiss, 'Reshit tsemihatah shel haderekh haHasidit', *Zion* 16 (1951): 1035, repr. in Rubinstein, ed., *Perakim betorat haHasidut*, 179–81.

4. Hasidim tell of the involvement of the BeSh"T in the birth of Menachem Mendel of Vitebsk. See *Sefer ha'otsar misipurei tsadikim* (Warsaw, 1937), tale no. 13. Hasidic legend also tells of R. Menachem Mendel's visit to the home of the BeSh"T.

5. See M. Wilensky, *Hasidim u'Mitnaggedim*, 2 vols. (Jerusalem, 1970), i. 43; see also 28, 64–65.

Vilna, to explain the doctrine of Hasidism and to prevent a further outbreak of opposition to the new movement, they turned to R. Menachem Mendel to fulfill this mission. Tactically this may have been somewhat imprudent, even if R. Menachem Mendel was accompanied by so great a Torah scholar as R. Shneur Zalman of Liady, for, as we have seen, it was R. Menachem Mendel who was the target for the attacks; nevertheless, the nomination itself shows clearly what an important position he occupied in the nascent world of Hasidism. Around him there gathered a group who were at once his close associates and his disciples, although they were people of varying stature and abilities.

R. Shneur Zalman of Liady came to the Maggid of Mezeritch as a young man of twenty-five. R. Menachem Mendel was some fifteen or twenty years his senior. There is no doubt that what brought them together was not merely their common geographical origin but their spiritual affinity.[6] It appears that R. Menachem Mendel attracted people of a particular type, and in one of his letters he refers to the great influence he had in the provinces of Volhynia, where he acquired a considerable following, although he lived in that region for only a short time.[7] For his part, he testifies in a letter written in 5541 (1781): "not a day has gone by on which I have not remembered them kindly, one and all. And through His compassion, blessed be His name, I will never forget them, *Amen*."[8] Less than four years later he was to write to his Hasidim in Belorussia (using the formal plural to refer to himself):

> Our soul longs earnestly for those who are lodged in the recesses of our heart, our [innards] yearn for them when we remember all the days we spent with them . . . the friends all over Russia who were close to our heart, who were wholehearted in their fear of Heaven, each one according to his attainments and his endeavours in serving Him, blessed be His name.[9]

While living in Tiberias, R. Menachem Mendel married into a distinguished Sefardi family.[10] We possess a letter written during the period of his

---

6. And it was not without reason that the Hasidim sent R. Shneur Zalman with R. Menachem Mendel on the mission to the Gaon of Vilna.

7. See *Likutei Amarim* (Lemberg, 1911), ii, letter 18, 25a. All references below to the letters of R. Menachem Mendel are to this collection while all references to the homilies in *Peri haAretz* (Kopys, 1814) are by name of Torah portion alone. I do not burden the reader with references to the parallel versions unless there is some special reason to do so. See note below for the various editions of R. Menachem Mendel's works.

8. *Likutei Amarim*, letter 1, 4b.

9. Ibid., letter 4, 6a.

10. "And one of the distinguished and important members of the Sefardic community, an in-law of the learned scholar in Tiberias, arranged a marriage between his daughter and R.

residence in Tiberias by R. Solomon Zalman Hakohen Vilner on 27 Shevat 5546 (1786), in which he describes R. Menachem Mendel's sermons:

> He reveals secrets and mysteries on Shabbat after Shabbat which the tongue would weary to recite and the heart to think. Even if one did not understand these things, for they are ancient . . . he displays different aspects of everything and strips them bare to their core, one layer after another, far beyond every jot and tittle—to the point of Infinity, blessed be He, as it were, and I can write no more about this, for I am not clever enough.[11]

There is also a eulogy by R. Moses Galante, one of the scholars of Damascus, written shortly after R. Menachem Mendel's death, which emphasizes, among other things, his unique qualities, his greatness, and his contemplative Kabbalistic prayer.[12] We may add here some further remarks on his character. In one of his first letters from '*Eretz Yisrael* Menachem Mendel expressed himself thus: "I, too, greatly desired to perform *yichud* and achieve unity."[13] For our purpose it is important to note that if this is not mere rhetoric, it is evidence that R. Menachem Mendel was imbued with a profound belief in the unity of God and in the need to bring about such unity in the world by raising up holy sparks and by the annulment of the *qelipot* (forces of evil) which would follow of itself. This, in turn, must find expression in the unity of mankind, in pursuit of which it was necessary to bring about the reconciliation of the Mitnaggedim to Hasidism and to establish peace with them. Indeed, in another letter he calls on people "not to scoff at those who abandon Torah." He approves (on the basis of a pronouncement by the sages) the condemnation of anything which is actually evil, but forbids it to be cursed. The reason he gives is interesting: we are all called children of God, even the sinner, and when you curse him, you are looking on yourself as distanced from him and separating yourself from the community at large. In doing so "you become a cause of decline and degradation."[14]

Moses, the charming and amiable son of the late R. Menachem Mendel may his soul rest in Eden. And he gave him a dowry of 800 'lions.'" See the section 'Nefesh Menachem: Toldot maran harav R. Menachem Mendel miVitebsk', printed at the head of *Likutei Amarim*, i. 1*1b*, 23.

11. Ibid., letter 16, 21 *b*.

12. See M. Benayahu, 'Pinkasim bikhtav-yad leHakham miDamesek', *Kiryat sefer* 35 (1960): 526. Incidentally, letter 27 in Shneur Zalman of Liady, *Igrot haQodesh* [Shklov, 1814], repr. in *Likutei Amarim: Tanya'*, bilingual ed., trans. N. Mindel, N. Mangel, Z. Posner, and J. I. Schochet (London, 1973), iv, is a letter of condolence from R. Shneur Zalman to the inhabitants of the Holy Land on the death of R. Menachem Mendel.

13. Wilensky, *Hasidim uMitnaggedim,* i. 91; and on the date of the letter, 90n1.

14. *Likutei Amarim,* letter 4, 8a.

Another characteristic of Menachem Mendel is his modesty. He frequently signs his letters "The truly humble." He also speaks a great deal about humility as opposed to self-aggrandizement.[15] However, it appears that the latter is not merely a seemly moral attribute but something that is woven into the fabric of his speculative doctrine. "The essence of the matter is the attachment [*hitqashrut*] of the humble man to the Supreme Will through humility and reverence, and from it he arrives at contemplation and study through [the application of] intellect and wisdom, to introduce these into every *mitzvah* with which he occupies himself."[16] The explanation is, apparently, that only through humility and self-annulment is it possible to attach oneself to the Godhead.

To conclude this brief description, a further interesting point may be observed. In a letter to his Hasidim written exactly a year before his death, R. Menachem Mendel testifies to his telepathic, or telecommunicative, ability:

> My dear ones, my friends, my brethren . . . have you not known, have you not heard, has not the saying of our Sages been told you from the beginning (see Isaiah 40:21). More than the calf desires to suck, the cow desires to give suck, and all my desire and the yearning of my love towards each one of you is many thousands of times greater than yours towards me, and each one is engraved on the tablet of my heart, as a sign on my hand, and as a memorial between my eyes, directed always towards the Lord, as if their likeness stands before me so that I may recognize their appearance while their hearts, their nature and quality and the sum total of all their concerns stand revealed. And let not any newcomer entertain the thought that perhaps I am unaware of matters concerning them, the manner in which they conduct their religious life and their [spiritual] wisdom, the path which they tread and the deeds which they perform. For how should a thing be known which I have never seen, how can I explain this wonder. Behold, they know not, neither do they understand, they walk in darkness (Psalm 82:5), but it is God's truth that nothing concerning them is hidden from my eyes. I know every one of them from beginning to end. And I am not a prophet or a seer,[17] but it is in accordance with Torah of truth

---

15. E.g., ibid., letters 3, 6*a* and 4, *7b–8a.*

16. *Peri 'Etz* [Zhitomir, 1874] (Cracow, 1937), end of Parashah Noah. The humility of R. Menachem Mendel is also attested by R. Jacob Joseph of Polonnoye, according to the tale by M. L. Rodkinson, *Adat Tsadikim* [Lemberg, 1864], 16*b* (not paginated in the original), repr. in G. Nigal, ed., *Sipurei Michael Levi Rodkinson* (Jerusalem, 1988), 46–47.

17. This expression, modeled on Scripture (cf. Amos 7:14), also occurs in another letter. See David Zevi Hillman, ed., *Igrot ha'al haTanya' uvenei doro* (Jerusalem, 1953), 26.

> and the design of the Lord that I should know all the people He has created [*anshei ma'asehu*]—possibly a pun, referring also to the quality of *anshei ma'aseh*—men of righteous deeds—which characterizes those who had been converted to the "fear of Heaven" by R. Menachem Mendel, since I have been favoured from the outset with the knowledge of the beginning of their fear of Heaven, knowledge derived from those long known to me in this respect. In this way I can tell the end of any matter in all its details precisely as it will present itself to the eye, and I will not err in my vision, with the help of the Lord . . .
>
> You are my children just as if I had borne you; since you were initiated in the fear of Heaven by me, you will remain close to me. I shall never forget the times when you visited me, for through them you have given me life,[18] even into hoary-headed old age neither height nor breadth, neither horse nor chariot shall separate us from each other.[19]

This remarkable personal description shows that even while he was in *'Eretz Yisrael*, new Hasidim joined his congregation in Belorussia, which is a fact of some significance.

The two colleagues mentioned, R. Shneur Zalman and R. Abraham of Kalisk, however close they were to R. Menachem Mendel, were different from each other. They both had strong personalities. For example, a man such as R. Abraham of Kalisk, who followed the controversial practice of *kolyen sich,* that is, turning somersaults in the street, and ignoring everyone who jeered at him, would certainly do so not merely out of a particular belief or a certain view of the world; the act itself demands an extraordinary temperament to stand up to such a situation. In my opinion, R. Abraham aspired more to centralist authority. Even the concept of *dibbuk chaverim,* the cleaving together of friends,[20] seems to me to be connected with, and indeed to issue from, this aspiration to be able to stand at the head of a closed and close-knit group, directing it along a single path. R. Shneur Zalman, too, was a man of forceful personality, but he allowed every individual room to develop his own personality; his charisma was such that he could still unite

18. After Psalm 119:93.

19. *Likutei Amarim*, letter 18, 24b–25a ff.

20. See J. G. Weiss, "R. Abraham Kalisker's Concept of Communion with G-d and Men," *Journal of Jewish Studies* 6 (1955): 87–89, reprinted in idem, *Studies in Eastern European Jewish Mysticism* (Oxford, 1985), 155–69. And similarly Ze'ev Gries, 'Mimitos le'etos: Kavim lidmuto shel R. Abraham miKalisk', in the anthology *Umah veToldoteihah*, 2 vols. (Jerusalem, 1984), 2:117–46. The psychological point discussed here briefly may explain the dual personality of R. Abraham of Kalisk, on which Gries commented, 'Mimitos le'etos', 126.

them under his leadership.

Undoubtedly, during the time they spent together at the court of the Maggid, R. Menachem Mendel and R. Shneur Zalman would have discussed and clarified many issues. The close connection between them can be detected in expressions, turns of phrase, and terminology, although these were sometimes used to convey differing concepts.[21] As for their *Weltanschauung*, there were shared viewpoints as well as points of dispute. In

21. E. Steinman, *Be'er haHasidut,* 10 vols. (Tel Aviv, 1951–62), 2:39, goes too far when he declares that "We find whole paragraphs almost word for word the same in the *Tanya'* and in *Peri haAretz."* I regret to say that I have found no such paragraphs, but there are expressions, and subjects, which correspond closely. See, e.g., '*hetokpam ugevuratam'* ("by their power and might") in *Peri haAretz* on Parashah Ki Tavo, and frequently in the *Tanya', 'helek eloha mima'al mamashi* ("an actual part of God on high") in Parashah Vayeshev, and Shneur Zalman of Liady, *Tanya',* ch. 2; for the evaluation of the body as flesh and not as the essence of man's being, see *Likutei Amarim,* letter 4, 6*b* and *Tanya',* ch. 29, etc.—although the idea is very widespread in the literature of Kabbalah; for the expression from *Tiquney haZohar* that fear and love are pinions on which to raise up thought, see *Peri haAretz* on Parashah Matot and Parashah Massey, and *Tanya',* ch. 41; for the explanation of the Tetragrammaton *(shem Havayah)* as *mehaveh hakol,* "bringing everything into being," transforming everything from *ayin* to *yesh*, see *Peri haAretz* on Parashah Korach and *Tanya',* Sha'ar hayichud veha'emunah', ch. 4, as well as other Kabbalistic works such as those of the Shelah and Remak [R. Moses Cordovero]; for the notion that "All apparent evils are from Him, blessed be He, [and] in truth they are kindnesses," see *Peri haAretz* on Parashah Vayera and *Igrot haQodesh,* s. 11, as well as the homilies of the Maggid of Mezeritch; for the negative assessment of Torah study otherwise than for its own sake, in the sense of "for one's own benefit," see *Likutei Amarim,* letter 3, 5*b,* and *Tanya',* ch. 39 and *passim,* but also in various other Hasidic works. On the other hand, R. Menachem Mendel's use of certain other expressions is quite distinctive, such as the epithets "He who fills all worlds" and "He who encircles all worlds," which refer to divine immanence (as in the *Ra'aya Me'heimna).* Compare *Likutei Amarim,* letter 9, 15a, with R. Shneur Zalman, who, following the Ari, draws an essential distinction: R. Menachem Mendel emphasizes the greatness of the Creator precisely on the evidence of the constant and natural guidance of the world (see *Peri haAretz,* on Parashah Bo'), whereas for R. Shneur Zalman the miracle is revealed only by concealment (R. Shneur Zalman of Liady, *Seder tefilot mikol hashanah im perush hamilot* [Zhitomir, 1863] (Brooklyn, NY, 1965), 44b); in R. Menachem Mendel's view (and that of the school of the Maggid) it is *Keter* which stands at the head of the *sefirot,* whereas for R. Shneur Zalman it is *Chokhmah*; for R. Menachem Mendel, *Da'at* is not an attribute in its own right (see *Peri haAretz* on Parashah Matot-Massey and similarly *Peri 'Etz* on Parashah Matot), but for R. Shneur Zalman, *Da'at* is the third *sefirah (passim*). On the subject of Keter and *Da'at*, see also M. Hallamish, *"Mishnato ha'iyunit shel Rabbi Shne'ur Zalman miLiady: Mekorotav bakabalah veyahaso lereshit haHasidut"* (PhD thesis, Hebrew University of Jerusalem, 1976), 84, 217; and cf. below, nn. 22, 52, 57,105, 106. Finally, it is worth mentioning that in several cases R. Menachem Mendel himself uses Kabbalistic terms but gives them a new connotation: e.g., *Shekinah* is a name applied to the divine manifestation which is below *Chokhmah*; "zaddik" can be "He who has nothing of his own," which is generally a name for *Malkut*, but for R. Menachem Mendel it is important to refer to the zaddik in this way in order to point out that it is his function to destroy corporeality and reduce it to nothing so as to raise everything up to its root (see *Peri haAretz* on Parashah Lech Lecha).

general, R. Menachem Mendel was nearer in his ideas to his teacher the Maggid, whereas R. Shneur Zalman was influenced more by the world of Kabbalah. A number of basic issues in R. Menachem Mendel's doctrine become clear through a comparison with that of R. Shneur Zalman.[22]

The world was created through the free and "simple" (not complex) will of the *'Ein Sof.* This implies also the principle of man's free will. Since

---

22. For the purpose of compiling an account of the doctrine of R. Menachem Mendel the following sources are available: *Peri haAretz* (Kopys, 1814; Mogilev, 1818; n.p., n.d., but clearly later than 1818; Zhitomir, 1849; n.p. [Konigsberg], 1857, Lemberg, 1862; Zhitomir, 1867; Warsaw, 1879, and Jerusalem, 1965 and subsequently). *Peri 'Etz* (Zhitomir, 1874; Cracow, 1937). *'Etz peri* (Safed, n.d. [the approbation is dated 1873, in fact a reversal of the title of *Peri 'Etz,* apparently a copy from a corrupt MS] Zhitomir, 1874; Lvov, 1880). Important material is contained in letters from *'Eret Yisrael.* Some of them are printed at the end of *Peri haAretz* (except for the edition of unidentified date and place and those of Mogilev and Lemberg). Further letters were printed in *Likutei Amarim* (see n. 6 above). Some were reprinted by Israel Halpern, *Ha'aliyot harishonot shel haHasidim le'Erets Yisrael* (Tel Aviv, 1947); Hillman, *Igrot Ba'al haTanya');* Jacob Barnai, *Igrot Hasidim meErets Yisrael* (Jerusalem, 1980). These books also note additional bibliographical sources.

Other discourses on doctrinal matters appear in *Likutei Amarim,* i, and also in *Igrot haQodesh,* at the beginning of which there are several such passages. This has been reprinted many times (perhaps because of its brevity): 1799, 1800, 1810, 1840, etc. See also the "testament" printed at the head of *Likutei Amarim,* ii; and *Mikhtavim Qedoshim mehaBesht vetalmidav,* ed. J. Margulies and A. H. Bierbrauer (Czernowitz, 1921), 15–16.

It must be borne in mind, however, that, according to the testimony of the publisher on the title page, even *Peri haAretz,* which is regarded as R. Menachem Mendel's principal work, was printed from material discovered by R. Eleazer Susman of Tiberias and arranged in the order of the sabbath sermons. The publisher adds that at the beginning, material has been added from the writings of R. Abraham "the Angel," comprising Parashah Bereshit as far as the *kavanah* ("intention") of the *mikveh,* where it is stated: "Here end the holy words of the aforesaid, our master and teacher Rabbi Abraham, which we found" (3b). However, in the body of the text there is no indication of where R. Abraham's remarks begin. That problem can be solved by consulting Abraham b. Alexander Katz of Kalisk, *Chesed le-Abraham* [Czernowitz, 1851], (Jerusalem, 1954), where, indeed, all the sermons appear, from the beginning of Genesis onward. But the intention of the *mikveh* is not there. The whole question of the attribution of Hasidic discourses to various sages, sometimes correctly and sometimes not, needs more rigorous examination than it has yet received, and it is doubtful whether we shall get to the bottom of the matter. By way of example in the present context, I would point out that the preface to *Chesed le-Abraham* appears not to have been printed in full, since MS New Haven 72 has a continuation. In any event, I have used all the material as published in *Peri haAretz,* including the beginning, since it accords with the doctrines of R. Menachem Mendel as they appear in the rest of the book.

It should be pointed out further that some of the homilies are incomplete. See, e.g., *Peri haAretz,* on Parashah Vayeze at the end.

A further problem is the language used at the beginning of Parashah Vayeshev: "the rabbi began [*patah harav*] . . . and the rabbi explained by another matter." What is the reason for this choice of words? If the reference was to R. Menachem Mendel, it is interesting to note the application to him of the title "rabbi."

hitpashetut (egression) cannot be infinite, there is a second stage in which *zimzum* (contraction) occurs, and this is followed by a further series of *zimzumim,* the purpose of which is to obscure the divine light. If this were not so, nothing could exist but the *'Ein Sof.* Thus R. Menachem Mendel follows in the footsteps of the Maggid in his account of the doctrine of *zimzum,* whereas R. Shneur Zalman is more firmly grounded in the traditional world of Kabbalah, and subjects such as *zimzum*, whether taken literally or merely figuratively, as well as other theological questions, are considered by him with meticulous attention. Thus, for the Maggid and R. Menachem Mendel *zimzum* is not a primary act which took place within the *'Ein Sof*; it is not a first stage as in Lurianic Kabbalah, but occurs in the *sefirah Chokhmah*, after the "egression," and it means the concealment of the *ayin* in order to render possible the revelation of the material world. Hence the saying that *olam*, the world, is derived from *he'alem*, to be hidden.[23] It is interesting that R. Shneur Zalman too explains *zimzum* in this way.[24]

Every descent of light to a lower stage increases the number of *zimzumim*, but the main point is that there is here a revelation of the divine from within the *ayin*—the *sefirah Keter* (crown), which makes immanence possible.[25] For this reason, the *Shekinah*, too, is explained not necessarily as the tenth *sefirah* but literally: the Godhead residing (*shokhenet*) in the world. In this connection the verses "the whole earth is full of His glory" (Isaiah 6:3) and "You preserve [or "give life to"] them all" (Nehemiah 9:6) are frequently quoted. This immanence is sometimes also called *galut Shekinah*, the Exile of the divine presence,[26] without any reference to the Kabbalistic meaning of sins and the war against evil: the concealment of the Godhead for the purpose of its revelation in the world is itself exile. That is a given situation of the very nature of immanence itself. Consequently the concept of *le'okama shekhinta me'afra* (to raise up the divine presence from the earth), which is referred to in R. Menachem Mendel's letters, for example, in connection with the giving of charity to the poor of *'Eretz Yisrael*, is explained as *haf-shatat halevushim*—stripping off the outer coverings: "to strip off all the ways of corporeality, which is 'earth,' and to raise them

23. I have been told several times by Chabad Hasidim that this flash of linguistic inspiration originated with R. Shneur Zalman. It should be pointed out, however, that it is quoted in Aaron of Opatow, *Keter shem tov*, 2 vols. (Zholkva [Zolkiew], 1794–95), name of the BeSh"T. It is also mentioned in *Peri haAretz* on Parashah Mishpatim; and in the same period in R. Nahum of Chernobyl's *Me'or Einayim* ('Yismakh Lev'), at the head of Tractate *Beitzah*; and frequently in R. Shneur Zalman's writings.

24. See Hallamish, "*Mishnato ha'iyunit*," 95–104.

25. It is apparently for this reason that R. Menachem Mendel writes, in *Peri haAretz* at the start of Parashah Bereshit, of the *emanation* of the worlds and the creation of *yesh ayin*.

26. *Peri haAretz,* "Sabbath falling during Passover" (after Parashah Vayikra); *Likutei Amarim,* letter 4, 6*h,* etc.

up to the place of the [divine] Will,"[27] such as devoting the money of the corporeal world to the holy purpose of charity for those in need, those who are broken vessels. And thus the giver, too, "is raised up together with it to the *'Ein Sof*," although it is important that his intention should be to do the will of God and have no thought of "reward and personal advantage."[28] Man's duty is to discover the divinity concealed in those very things which are furthest removed from the source, to see the true light in everything, to elevate the divine vitality to its origin and root, to nullify and become null. "And man's function above all is to bring forth the precious from the vile (Jeremiah 15:19) . . . in whatever he turns to he will succeed and in all his ways he will know what it is that the Lord caused to happen to him and why, and who created these things—the Lord, of course, who brings all things into existence and endows them with life, who surrounds them and fills them," and so on.[29] When man, contemplating God, sees Him in the state of greatest *z̲imz̲um* and concealment, that is itself the greatest revelation of the *Shekinah*. For this reason, anyone who does not see that the perpetuation of the natural order is due to divine providence and thinks that it occurs by chance is nothing but a fool. The true service of Heaven consists in recognizing also "the nature and habitual state and continuous management of everything, and in truth it is I, even I, *'Ein Sof* blessed be He, but this, however, is in concealment." Man must match the "returning" to the "running" (*shov* and *razo*—see Ezekiel 1:14), both of which serve to veil the celestial "creatures"—the standard Kabbalistic symbol of divine vitality and energy.[30] In other words, the function of the animal body and soul is to serve the rational, contemplative soul, and if a man follows his animal soul, that is to say if his vision remains limited by the horizons of the material world, he is "an animal in human form."[31] However, "man was created for no other reason than to raise everything up from a lower to a higher level, and to subordinate the outward to the inner reality by discovering His divinity, blessed be He, in everything, there being no place where He is not."[32]

A person who has attained this condition is, indeed, already in a state of *devequt,* and therefore it is only a man of irreproachable character, a zaddik, who can fulfill this function.[33] In this context we find the expression "*devequt* to the *Shekinah*," again without any connection with the *Shekinah* as female but in the sense of the divine immanence which pervades and fills

27. *Likutei Amarim*, letter 4, 6b–7a.
28. Ibid., 7a.
29. *Peri haAretz,* Parashah Korach.
30. Ibid., Parashah Bo'.
31. Ibid., Parashah Behar.
32. Ibid., Parashah Vayigash.
33. Ibid., Parashah Bereshit, etc.

all worlds. This sort of *devequt*, it is true, represents a stage which is low in the process of the ascent to *devequt* in the highest sense, but in the process of stripping off the outer coverings it is possible to become absorbed into the *'Ein Sof*. It should be noted that, in these descriptions, the chain of the *sefirot* is not mentioned, as if its sole purpose were to serve as the contraction (*zimzum*) of the light of the *'Ein Sof* descending from *ayin* to *yesh*. However, on the way upward again, the climb is really rapid.

Devequt is not a state of spontaneous illumination but is attained stage by stage. First comes fear. R. Abraham of Kalisk placed the utmost emphasis on the fear of punishment; he wrote in the name of his master R. Menachem Mendel:

> The beginning of worship every day is one of the aspects of the fear of punishment. And this [*fear*] is very necessary. That is where you begin, and once you see that you have attained the utmost fear of punishment, you ascend from that to fear of God's eminence [*romemut*] and to true love. And anyone who discards the fear of punishment will inevitably fall into the pit of destruction.[34]

However, this fear denotes distance, a condition which is opposed to *devequt*. Therefore, a higher stage is constituted by the fear of God's eminence, or the fear of shame before the One who is the absolute master and ruler of the very essence and root of all worlds. It is true that even in this state a certain distance remains, but there is nevertheless a greater affinity and the gap is narrowed. The next stage is a fear which is above all the varieties of love and beyond all the attributes, "and that is when you clothe yourself in the *Shekinah* and apply yourself wholly to serving as a chariot for Him, blessed be He . . . for they [who act thus] annul themselves and are absorbed into the channels of divine flow, and in that case fear is perfect *devequt*, for one becomes a part of the *'Ein Sof*."[35] That is to say, self-annulment and, correspondingly, clothing oneself in the *Shekinah* or inclusion in the *'Ein Sof* is perfect *devequt*.[36]

Coupled with the references to fear, references to faith frequently occur. "Let him first accept the yoke of the kingdom of Heaven, which is fear and faith, as is well known. And then let him accept the yoke of the commandments and the yoke of Torah," and this "will teach him attachment to the Lord (*hitqashrut*) and love of Him and cleaving to His attributes,"

34. *Likutei Amarim*, letter 38, 42a.

35. *Peri haAretz*, Parashah Eqev.

36. I would not conclude from this sentence, in the context in which it appears, that we have here an actual reference to *unio mystica*, as was alleged by Moshe Idel, *Kabbalah: New Perspectives* (New Haven, CT, 1988), 308. (Incidentally, there is an error in the page reference there because of incorrect pagination. "24b" should read "32b.*")* However, other sources will be quoted below, which clearly refer to the experience of *unio mystica*.

while at the same time overcoming the evil inclination, "which would not be the case if he did not give first place to fear and faith in the Lord and Torah . . . All Torah and the commandments would be of no avail, and he would remain as grossly material a person as ever."[37] R. Menachem Mendel returns repeatedly to the concept of faith. He sees the absence of faith as the cause of the Exile.[38] Faith is what leads to *devequt*, through the development of the personal attributes. In this arrangement, the intellect has no place, and this is no accident. "Certainly all one's [intellectual] attainments are quite without value and devoid of any *devequt* whatsoever. Let him live in his faith, to cleave to Him, blessed be He . . . for this faith emanates *from none other than Him Himself blessed be He*."[39] Here the intellect is set in opposition to faith, for two reasons which are really one and the same: (a) the direct source of faith is the divinity, while the intellect is human—an argument which is of fundamental importance to the mystics; (b) therefore active faith has positive consequences, whereas the exercise of the intellect does not lead to religious achievements. Even the patriarch Abraham "did not rely on his intellectual grasp" and overcame his doubts only through the power of faith.[40] And if that was true of Abraham, how much more must it apply to ordinary men. "When a person falls, Heaven forbid, into opposition to Him, blessed be He, on rational grounds, what mainly helps him and enables him to ascend is simple faith, without any reasons or reasoning at all, for it [faith] can rend mountains and break rocks into pieces (1 Kings 19:11). If he is of stone, he is softened by the power of faith, and without it there is no cure or remedy for him; he cannot gain strength by the exercise of reason or intellect."[41] The fact that the intellect is a human faculty carries with it its own limitation. The intellect sees multiplicity and restriction where faith points to wholeness and inner unity.[42] It needs to be added that multiplicity is a characteristic feature of the *sitra achra*, the forces of evil. That is how we should interpret the statement: "The greatest knowledge of all is not to know." That is to say, "Whatever one succeeds in comprehending of the Divinity is itself a limitation . . . except only by faith, which is infinitely higher than the intellect can reach."[43] The best example for R. Menachem Mendel is the contrast between Noah and Abraham. The faith of the righteous Noah was not founded on any process of reason: he overcame

---

37. *Peri haAretz,* Parashah Devarim. With regard to fear and faith, cf. also the letter of R. Abraham of Kalisk written in 1797, *Likutei Amarim,* letter 38, 41a.

38. *Peri haAretz,* Parashah Vayigash.

39. Ibid., Parashah Lech Lecha, at the end. For the evaluation of the intellect, see more below.

40. *Likutei Amarim*, letter 6,11b. Cf. *Peri haAretz,* Parashah Vayera.

41. *Likutei Amarim,* letter 11a. Cf. *Peri haAretz,* Parashah Vayera, at the beginning.

42. *Likutei Amarim,* letter 18, 24a (written in 1787).

43. Ibid. Cf. also the letter of R. Abraham of Kalisk, ibid., letter 38, 41a.

troublesome questions through his perfect faith in the Creator.[44] Abraham, on the other hand, recognized his Creator when he was three years old, according to the exegesis; that is, he had a highly developed intellectual consciousness, and in the end, in spite of this, he realized the limitations of the intellect in the endeavor to reach the *'Ein Sof*. And then he returned to faith—"And he believed in the Lord" (Genesis 15:6). Emphasis is therefore laid on the verse "And the righteous shall live by his faith" (Habakuk 2:4). At any rate it appears that R. Menachem Mendel did not totally deny the achievements of the intellect, on the grounds that Abraham himself made use of it, but he points out its limitations.[45] He explicitly states: "The essence of the service of Heaven and of attachment (*hitqashrut*) to Him, blessed be He, is to attain the true *devequt* which is reached *after* all that the intellect can succeed in understanding." However, in what he goes on to say there are indications that he rejects the intellect and holds it in open contempt: "After all his intellectual and speculative endeavours to grasp *devequt*, let him believe with true faith, because of his own humility, that he must regard himself as dust and ashes, and then certainly all his intellectual attainments will be seen to be worthless."[46]

The great importance that R. Menachem Mendel attached to faith can be seen in the astounding example (admittedly linked to the interpretation of scriptural verses) which he adduced in order to explain in concrete terms the difference between a person who fulfills Torah and the commandments spontaneously and one who fulfills them after faith is implanted in him. Torah not preceded by fear and faith is valueless, like consorting with a prostitute in order to satisfy a momentary appetite, in contrast to regular marital intercourse.[47] In other words, faith has a kind of settling and stabilizing power.

It should be pointed out that for R. Shneur Zalman, in contrast to R. Menachem Mendel, faith is a *fundamental* attribute presumed to exist in all Jews as a matter of course, since belief is inherent in them, and at *this* level faith exists without any special cause. But by passing through and beyond a stage of profound rational speculation, one reaches the highest stage of faith and *devequt*.[48]

Devequt appears on various levels in R. Menachem Mendel's writings.

44. According to R. Menachem Mendel, this is why the reasons for the commandments were not explained in Torah, for "what is important above all is to cleave to what is beyond one's understanding" *(Peri haAretz* Parashah Tezaveh). Cf. also Rivkah Schatz-Uffenheimer, *HaHasidut keMistikah* (Jerusalem, 1968), 57.

45. Cf. Tishby and Dan, "Hasidut," 812.

46. *Peri haAretz,* Parashah Lech Lecha.

47. Ibid., Parashah Matot-Massey 2.

48. See Hallamish, "Mishnato ha'iyunit," 200–208, where the point is treated more extensively.

Its importance can be judged from one sentence: "That from occupying oneself with Torah and the commandments one arrives at perfect *devequt.* For Torah is a spice (*tavlin*)[!]"[49] A spice or condiment can indeed impart flavour, but the essential is *devequt.*

R. Menachem Mendel frequently couples faith with *devequt,* just as, indeed, there similarly occurs in one place in *Maggid Devarav leYa'akov* the explicit statement that "faith is *devequt.*"[50] In other words, *devequt* is faith without the application of reason. Man cannot attain any element of divinity, but he can perceive the unity and interconnection of everything with the immanence of God in our world. By the very fact that he recognizes and believes in the constant presence of God, he achieves *devequt.* "But *devequt* in Him [cleaving to Him] is by faith alone, unaccompanied by any reasons of love, affection or desire."[51] In one place he quotes the rabbinic saying "Let man always first offer (*yesader*) praise to God and then pray" (b*Berachot* 32a), and he explains that it is not a question of the arrangement (*seder*) of times based on a hierarchic concern to show due honor—that is, first to adopt a proper attitude to the Holy One, blessed be He, and then to ask for the fulfillment of one's needs—but first to meditate on the immanent totality of the Divinity, and this would of itself lead him to prayer, which is to say, to *devequt.*[52] Man reaches *devequt* through the world, through corporality. In this sense, "the great delight" is that "he was distant and has drawn near."[53] And that is the meaning of the terse statement: "It is the *Shekinah* that is called prayer, which consists in truly cleaving to (*devequt be-*) the Supreme Will through faith without any reason."[54] That is to say, prayer seeks the Divine Presence because man's contemplation is directed toward the manifestations of the Divinity in the world, without any need for rational processes of thought: it is enough to have faith in this axiom, which, of itself, leads to "*truly* cleaving to the Supreme Will." Other passages, too, demonstrate that no distinction is drawn between "a man's business and his speech, his [observance of the] commandments, his [study of] Torah and his prayer."[55]

There are, however, passages emphasizing that *devequt* is attained through "holiness which is not the observance of the commandments or the

---

49. *Peri haAretz,* Parashah Devarim, at the end.

50. See I. Tishby, *Mishnat haZohar*, 2 vols. (Jerusalem, 1971); trans. as *The Wisdom of the Zohar*, 3 vols. (Oxford, 1989), 3:1015n446.

51. *Peri haAretz,* Parashah Lech Lecha.

52. Ibid., Parashah Bo'. For a similar idea cf. *Keter shem tov* [Korets, 1797] 12*b*.

53. Ibid., Parashah Korach, where, incidentally, this path to *devequt* is called *ahavah mesuteret*—concealed love. The term is interpreted variously in the literature, e.g., by the Shelah, R. Shneur Zalman, and others.

54. *Peri haAretz,* Parashah Lech Lecha.

55. Ibid., "Sabbath falling during Passover," at the end.

study of Torah or prayer."[56] It seems that the intention here is to stress that this attainment is possible only through religious action and not through contact with corporeal and material things. Similarly in another passage: "*Mitzvah* means *tzavta*—togetherness—which is true *devequt* even in the lowest and most earthly of the low, a pleasant savour to the Lord who spoke and whose will was done. And that is the greatest joy before Him, blessed be He, and there are no bounds to the joy of the worldly ones [through observance of the commandments], exceeding that of all the spiritual beings."[57]

A higher level of *devequt* finds expression in his statement that entry into the religious world demands the absolute abandonment of everything that went before, since attachment to any particular thing of itself demands severance from the past. In other words, one must abandon the material world in order to be able to realize *devequt.* For since Torah and the fulfillment of the commandments "are, in a literal sense, Divinity," and since "man is literally part of God on high," it follows that "when a man immerses himself and all his thoughts in them with all his heart and soul and might, with desire and longing and *devequt,* and, as stated, this path exists, empathically, only *when a man enters with his whole self* into some holy matter, some *mitzvah* or Torah and prayer, with such complete *devequt* that he divests himself of his previous attachment to material things and no longer notices them at all . . . he now clothes himself in a holy spirit. And when he clothes himself in the words (*teivot*) of Torah and prayer, the scriptural verse (Genesis 7:1) applies to him: 'Go into the ark (*teivah*), you and all your family,' for he enters into it with his whole self . . ."[58] "The annulment of the remnants of his previous feelings constitutes complete unity with Him, blessed be He . . . he enters into communion with Him, blessed be He, with nothing intervening between them"—"and experiences something of the taste of the world to come."[59] Without doubt he thus attains a superlatively high degree of spiritual elevation.

56. *Peri haAretz,* Parashah Vayeshev, Sabbath preceding Hanukkah.

57. Ibid., Parashah Re'eh. See also Ibid., Parashah Yitro; *Peri 'Etz,* Parashah Beshalach. This idea serves R. Menachem Mendel to explain why the pious look forward to the resurrection of the dead, for they desire to be in their bodies "out of the greatness of the joy of bodily service of the Creator, blessed be His name" (ibid., on Parashah Re'eh). A similar view was expressed by R. Shneur Zalman of Liady in *Likutei Torah* [Zhitomir, 1848] (Brooklyn, NY, 1984) on Parashah Behar, 42. And the same reason is advanced to explain why a repentant sinner is greater than a zaddik, for he has already used his physical attributes for material purposes, and he now elevates them by his service of Heaven (*Peri haAretz,* Parashah Ki Tezai).

58. This exegesis of the verse is apparently that of the Maggid. Cf. the opening of *Likutim Yekarim* [Lemberg, 1792], ed. Abraham Isaac Kahan (Jerusalem, 1974); *Tsava'at haRibash* [n.p. (Ostrog?), 1793; Zolkiew, 1795], ed. J. I. Schochet (Brooklyn, NY, 1975), 8.

59. See n. 55 above. On *devequt* which demands the abandonment of everything corporeal, including family ties, cf. *Tanya',* ch. 49, 137.

It may sometimes occur that a man reaches a stage of ecstasy, and this precisely when he is turning from his past in penitence: that is to say, when he considers his sins and grieves ("out of his great bitterness") that he has allowed the vitality of holiness to enter into the *qelipot,* the husk of evil, he reaches a state in which his bitterness is so great that "a fire not fanned [by man] (Job 20:26) takes hold of him, to which he cannot respond in any words but only by an inarticulate groan . . . and he simply cries out to the Lord, and God answers him by a voice (Exodus 19:19), for thereby the letters are raised above evil."[60] What is described here is a condition so exalted as to be beyond the possibility of utterance in words, and which can be expressed only in an ecstatic mystical experience. Another matter connected with this is the *simhah shel mitzvah* (joy of fulfilling a religious precept), to which R. Menachem Mendel returns.[61]

Devequt at its highest level is sometimes formulated in very strong terms. For example, "The path of *devequt* consists in the annihilation of self, which is perfect unity [in a bond] of love which is as strong as death (Song of Songs 8:6) and which makes parting difficult."[62] Or "to bind them and unify them with Him so that they become one in perfect *devequt.*"[63] And spelled out in detail: "The meaning of *devequt* is that there should be nothing intervening, then it is possible to achieve *devequt.* Like the comparison drawn by the Ba'al Shem Tov, that it is impossible to solder two pieces of silver together unless one scrapes down to the actual silver at the point where the joint is to be made; then it holds well . . . It is necessary to scrape one's personality so that no tarnish remains on it, nor any separating covering, but only the essential personality; then *devequt* becomes possible."[64] It would seem unnecessary to add to formulations expressed in such clear terms, but it is further stated that the basis of *devequt* is that "since man is an actual part of God on high, he should be able to join himself in perfect unity to Him, blessed be He, without any intervening barrier or separating curtain."[65] This same starting point, of the return of the branch to its root, of the cleaving of the part to the perfect whole, also appears in another homily, and entitles us to conclude that there is nothing casual in this entire approach:

> for when he concerns himself with the root of their [the worlds']

60. *Peri haAretz,* Parashah VaEtchanan. Incidentally, the expression "to cry out to the Lord" used by R. Menachem Mendel is apparently not lightly chosen. Cf. M. Hallamish, *Nativ laTanya'* (Tel Aviv, 1987), 250n22.
61. *Peri haAretz,* on Parashah Ki Tezai, Parashah Ki Tavo, etc.
62. Ibid., on Shabbat Nahamu.
63. *Peri haAretz,* Parashah Noach.
64. *Peri haAretz,* Parashah Ki Tissa.
65. Ibid., Parashah Vayeshev, Sabbath preceding Hanukkah.

> creation and touches it, all the branches are moved by the root, and when man is included in them because he resembles an angel [!] . . . and then he delivers his soul to be united with the *Shekinah (moser nafsho baShekinah),* then he climbs upward *through* the worlds and *together with* all the worlds, ever upward by means of the *mitzvot* . . . until his soul succeeds in divesting itself of concrete attributes, namely love, fear, etc., in order that he should cleave to their root and touch it directly, without any intervening barrier.

This mystical and ecstatic description of "cleaving to their root directly without any intervening barrier" is referred to further on as "a marvelous and impenetrable secret, which cannot be revealed because it is disclosed to none but oneself."[66] There is no doubt that in these descriptions R. Menachem Mendel rose to an extremely high mystical level for which it is not easy to find parallels. A similar statement, however, is made by R. Shneur Zalman:

> And it is in the nature of a merging of the Jewish people *into the Source that hewed them out*, with a unification so perfect that they are regarded as actually one body, etc. For example, when one joins two different things together with glue, the advantage of glueing them together is that they become so closely united as to be regarded as a single body . . . and it is as if he were actually glued to the Lord, etc., and through the strength of this adhesion he could never be separated . . . *and although he concerns himself with business affairs all day long* and is in close proximity to the influence of the "external" [evil] forces of the desire for alien [material] things, this will not in the least break his unity with the Lord, because he has been united to Him through prayer and joined with Him in a union so close as to be inseparable forever etc. And that is what is meant by "And to Him you shall cleave" (Deuteronomy 13: 5), i.e. *in true devequt* so as to become literally one.[67]

Particularly in the remarkable latter description, the word *devequt* is given its simplest meaning, derived from *davak,* to stick. But the power of the description is obvious in both cases, and it seems to me that herein lies the secret of the close bond between these two outstanding men. In any event, we have here clear evidence to counter Gershom Scholem's assumption that the concept of *unio mystica* does not exist in Jewish thought.

We need, however, to set the matter in proper perspective. The late

66. *Peri 'Etz,* Parashah Ki Tezai.

67. Preface to the prayer book, *s.v.* "aharei hashem," 26. And see similar remarks in Shneur Zalman of Liady, *Ma'amrei Admor haZaken 5562* [1801–2] 2 vols. (Brooklyn, NY, 1964–81), 58.

Professor Rivkah Schatz-Uffenheimer defined R. Menachem Mendel's doctrine as consisting "*entirely* [*the emphasis is mine—M.H.*] of extreme spiritualism while deliberately preaching the daily fulfilment of the commandments."[68] In my opinion, the matter needs to be seen in a somewhat different light, or at least certain additional points need to be mentioned in order to complete the picture.

Two contrasting strata may be distinguished in R. Menachem Mendel's doctrine. The first is that of simple faith, without any reason or logical explanation (i.e., without any *sevara*). The justification for this is that in an intellectual argument it is always possible to advance a counterargument,[69] and no clear-cut decision can be reached. This is also made clear in another passage in which R. Menachem Mendel puts forward the principle of *zeh le'umat zeh,* the existence of opposites, which is a central principle of Creation. Man therefore encounters things which are "upside down."[70] The mind confines man within the limits of his intellectual grasp, that is to say, still in this world, where dualism and lack of clarity are part of the normal order. But if a man rises beyond the world to the realm of the *'Ein Sof,* he discovers there that in the Source everything is one, without any alteration or substitution, and that that is the true creative principle which endows everything with life. This insight can be attained only by means of faith, which is firmly anchored in the true reality of things and which alone can define them. It goes without saying that to achieve this a man must be active in his religious life. The fulfillment of practical *mitzvot* is a vital stage. Moreover, it generates social uniformity.

Contrasting with the stratum of simple faith there is the spiritual level. This is not a matter for simple folk, but a personal path appropriate solely for the elect, a path that cannot even be explained to others. However, this contrast is the very soul of Hasidism, a movement within which simple folk and people of exalted spirit are closely associated. The factor common to all of them is their final goal; where they differ is in the means of attaining that goal, and the means, of itself, confers a certain distinctive quality on the goal.

The contrast referred to may be observed in another area: the difference between the fear of punishment and the fear of God's majesty. In a homily on Torah portion Balak (Numbers 22–25), R. Menachem Mendel lets slip almost casually the observation that the fear of punishment is universal, necessary even to "the great and the zaddikim." On the other hand, the fear of God's majesty is personal, "and therefore it is impossible for any man

68. Schatz-Uffenheimer, *HaHasidut keMistikah,* 64.

69. *Likutei Amarim*, letter 6, 11a.

70. *Peri haAretz,* Parashah Lech Lecha. There is no need to interpret this word as meaning "paradoxical," as Schatz-Uffenheimer does, see *HaHasidut keMistikah,* 58.

to attune his deeds and thoughts and ways to the ways of some zaddik in order to be like him, because sometimes the ethical norms and conduct of that zaddik will be of no use to him. And even for one man it is impossible to be the same in his own eyes and [*unchanging in*] his ways and ethical standards day by day; everything depends on the time."[71]

To return to our main topic: in a letter written in 1784, R. Menachem Mendel says:

> As soon as he rises in the morning, a man ought to be ready to serve his Creator, and to give first place to the soul. For it is the soul that is the principal thing and not the material being, which perishes and is lost. And to be in as spiritual a state as possible, that is the great principle, and therefore one should not act or calculate one's actions with a view to the world to come. For whatever he achieves in this world while he is still in his body is corporeal. And even if he takes care, in his endeavour to attain the world to come, to refrain from any kind of worldly action, by whatever means he attains his goal it will still be corporeal, since he has attained it while still inhabiting his body.[72]

That, then, is the fundamental aim: "to give first place to the soul," to aspire to spiritualization through renunciation of the thoughts and possessions of this world.[73] And if a person follows this path, he perceives no distinction between "the affairs of this world and the performance of the commandments," for:

> such is the way of all *devequt* and union with God's holiness, blessed be He and His *Shekinah*, in the affairs of this world or the performance of the commandments and Torah; it is to cleave [to Him] in perfect *devequt* and to continue to clothe oneself in that same holy vitality that resides in one's business affairs, one's speech, one's fulfillment of the commandments, one's study of Torah, and one's prayer. It is that which cleanses the bodily organs and all material substance, releasing them from the power of evil (*qelipot*). For when he admits the Lord, blessed be He, into himself, there all the doers of evil are scattered (Psalm 92:10).[74]

When one reaches "the root of the whole Torah and the commandments, which is . . . simple unity and *'Ein Sof*, when he stands there, the wings of all the commandments and statutes droop limply, and all are nullified,

71. Cf. also *Peri haAretz,* Parashah Matot-Massey.
72. *Likutei Amarim,* letter 4, 6b.
73. Cf. Schatz-Uffenheimer, *HaHasidut keMistikah*, 33, 42, and elsewhere.
74. *Peri haAretz*, Sabbath falling during Passover, at the end.

for that condition is the dissolution of the evil inclination."[75] True, Adam required only one commandment—*devequt*—and Abraham only love, but "because of the inadequacy of the human mind everyone [else] needs . . . all the commandments of Torah and the fences round it, which are combinations of principles of conduct and counsels for cleaving to the Creator, blessed be He."[76] Even one who is spiritual on the most exalted level fulfills *mitzvot,* but he does so naturally, as a matter which has no heteronomous significance but springs autonomously from the depths of his heart.[77]

The clearest description of this spiritual state occurs in a homily in which R. Menachem Mendel mentions:

> the ancients who did not know whether it was night or day or how many days it was since they had entered into that state of wisdom which consisted in casting off everything corporeal . . . The man who applies himself and his vitality entirely and solely to speculative wisdom and contemplation of the greatness of the Creator, may His name be blessed, and leaves behind all corporeality and all the various worlds and attributes until he has ascended to the greatness of intensive contemplation of divine wisdom with all his strength and vitality and with his whole self . . . such a man is called *a godly man* . . . to sum up, that he himself should be as if he did not exist, abandoning both his body and his soul, in some manner to be blotted out of this world and the world to come for the sake of the sanctification of His name, blessed be He, and in any event that he should not be drawn by his desires in any direction save only towards Him, blessed be His name, through the intensity of his contemplation of the greatness of the Creator . . . *for what does it matter to him how or what he is and in what manner he exists, or whether he was never created or whether he was created and perished* . . . for his individuality has already been altogether annihilated through his contemplation of the greatness of the Creator, blessed be His name. And all his desire and his longing are only that His name, blessed be He, should be magnified and sanctified and that His divinity should be revealed. Now *certainly a wise man such as this will be detached from everything,* for he has no desire for anything, "and the Lord alone will be exalted on that day" (Isaiah 2:11).[78]

So hyperbolic a description ranks R. Menachem Mendel with the quietists.

---

75. Ibid., Parashah Toldot.
76. *Likutei Amarim,* letter 18, 24b.
77. *Peri haAretz,* Parashah Toldot.
78. *Peri haAretz,* Parashah Qedoshim [*italics mine*].

There is, however, another side to the coin. Certainly, it would be a noble thing for a man to start his day with worship of the Creator, to persevere in his worship to the point of perfect *devequt,* and to strive to attain such lofty pinnacles. But life is complex, and man is put to a severe test every day in contending with material and corporeal things. Moreover, R. Menachem Mendel says explicitly that it is impossible to practice complete abstinence from everything corporeal, since Scripture says "and live by them" (Leviticus 18:5). But the reason he goes on to give is much more "convincing": we are not commanded to be angels! "If indeed one were, of a certainty, pure and holy—one would be like the ministering angels. Nevertheless, Torah was *not* given to the ministering angels."[79] That, he says, is why the practical commandments were given, for "matter can be purified by nothing but [the fulfillment of] *practical* commandments."[80] That, too, was the purpose of the practical instructions concerning "worship through corporeality," the battle against "straying thoughts" (*mahshavot zarot*), and so on. "In sum," says R. Menachem Mendel, "without contemplation and the attainment of *devequt,* the fulfillment of commandments [is itself corporeal, and conversely, without the commandments] which are a corporeal matter, contemplation and the attainment of *devequt* do not bring a man into communion with the Creator."[81] In this way, it appears, the emphasis on spirituality is softened. It is not clear whether the remarks are addressed to all who seek to share this experience, to inform them that no one is entitled to forego corporeal matters and religious worship,[82] or whether the intention is to distinguish between different types of people: there are some who can ascend by purely spiritual endeavor, while others must always couple spirituality with practical endeavor, in order to ascend.

This leads to a consideration of the opposite aspect, that of the material world. Professor Schatz-Uffenheimer was indeed right in saying that R. Menachem Mendel showed "no enthusiasm for worship through corporality,"[83] but nevertheless he did express himself explicitly in its favor. Two points of view must be distinguished. The first concentrates attention on the central cosmic principle that the Divinity lies concealed in everything. Therefore, when a person *chances to encounter* some object of love, he should not love its material aspect but should realize that it is "its inner vitality" that inspires him with love for the material substance and "therefore he should cleave in his love to the inner vitality in that thing."[84] That, then, is the way

79. *Peri haAretz,* Parashah Re'eh.

80. Ibid., on Parashah Naso.

81. *Peri haAretz,* Parashah Noach, at the end.

82. And see the treatment *in extenso* in Schatz-Uffenheimer, *HaHasidut keMistikah,* ch. 5.

83. Ibid., 61.

84. *Igrot haQodesh*, 1b, *s.v.* vezehu bekholderakheikha da'ehu. And cf. *Likutei Amarim*, letter 9, 15a.

to bring the divine element to the surface, as explained above. But there is another point of view which places not the Divinity but man at the center. For example, R. Menachem Mendel speaks of physical pleasure "which is to serve a bodily requirement and fulfill a commandment." And then the Holy One, blessed be He, pays regard to the intention of the doer, and therefore the blessing pronounced by the doer is not "on the corporeal act" but on the fulfillment of the commandment, "which is in the nature of 'In all your ways acknowledge Him' (Proverbs 3:6)."[85] The very link with "In all your ways" shows that it is possible to strip *every action* of its corporeal covering and to intend by it or by means of it the performance of a spiritual act "which is in the nature of 'In all your ways acknowledge Him' so as to act in all corporeal matters with *devequt* and attachment to the *Shekinah*."[86] As a corollary of this approach, "if a man regards himself during his meal as consuming food given to him from the house of the King, the Holy One, blessed be He, and he eats and drinks and beholds God, drawing near to Him by means of the meal . . . the vitality he acquires in eating is increased, and this vitality itself has reached the level of 'this is the law for man' (1 Samuel 7:19), and by everything that he does subsequently for the sake of Heaven, the vitality, too, is exalted."[87] Moreover, it is possible that he will come to acquire the supernatural power of control over matter, and then he will even be able to bring about supernatural changes in the physical world.[88]

It is true that this approach is accompanied by the risk that a man may become immersed in material things and externalities and will not rise to become exalted. Fundamentally, to be sure, "our teaching [*toratenu*] is one of truth and faithfulness, that man is certainly forbidden to expose himself to temptation, to immerse himself in straying thoughts in order to raise them up, Heaven forbid, for who knows if he will be as strong as a lion and rise up or whether he will descend ever lower and not be equal to the test."[89] And from the injunction against immersing oneself in straying thoughts, it follows all the more clearly that "it is not the intention, nor is man commanded, Heaven forbid, to transgress—may that be far from us—in order to arouse his ardor";[90] unless, that is, "he unintentionally finds himself confronted by the test, when certainly it is sent by the Lord to test him, and he must exert all his strength and devotion to prevail over it."[91] That is to say,

85. *Peri haAretz,* Parashah Re'eh.

86. Ibid., Sabbath falling during Passover.

87. Ibid., Parashah Vayigash, second sermon.

88. *Likutei Amarim,* letter 9, 15a.

89. See n. 30 above; and also Tishby and Dan, "Hasidut," 787.

90. *Peri haAretz,* Parashah Ki Tissa.

91. In principle, this is also the approach expounded in *Tsava'at haRibash,* where we read: "If he has *suddenly* looked on a beautiful woman," and not that one should deliberately

he is not to content himself with rejecting the straying thought, but must elevate it—unless it is to be feared that he will be unable to direct his mind to performing the action for the sake of its merit but will act for his own benefit, for then it would be better "not to use it [the extraneous thought, the *qelipot*] at all."[92] But "when a man genuinely draws near to God in his innermost heart . . . [and] straying thoughts or attributes are awakened in him, since their desire is to be raised up, for behold, there is a place prepared beside them [an echo of Exodus 33:21—"behold, there is a place beside Me"], to raise them up through repentance so that he becomes ready to serve in the Sanctuary,"[93] then undoubtedly the obligation is imposed on him to bring them to repentance.

This point of view is also evident in another place, where R. Menachem Mendel "resolves" an alleged contradiction between two scriptural verses. Psalm 33:18 says: "Behold, the eye of the Lord is on them that fear him," "eye" being in the singular, whereas Psalm 34:16 says: "the eyes of the Lord are on the righteous." Consequently R. Menachem Mendel distinguishes between the God-fearing man and the zaddik. The God-fearing man is afraid of war against the evil inclination, and therefore rejects the evil inclination outright. He serves the Lord only with his good inclination, and hence "eye" is written in the singular. By contrast, the zaddik brings both inclinations, the good and the evil, into equal partnership and "binds together all the worlds, from the lesser spiritual levels (*katnut*) to the greater (*gadlut*) and to simple unity . . . and he does not reject *katnut*." It is the latter person, of course, who is the better of the two (for which reason "eyes" is written in the plural).[94] This viewpoint is similar to that expressed by R. Shneur Zalman in chapters 27–28 of the *Tanya'*: the average man must reject temptation, and is advised against doing otherwise, because a man who wallows in the dust with what is vile becomes vile himself. But the zaddik is at the level of converting evil to good; he is allowed, or even obliged, to concern himself also with deviant thoughts, and thereby to elevate them too (though these are the thoughts of others, since the zaddik himself, *ipso facto,* no longer entertains evil thoughts, according to the view of R. Shneur Zalman).

R. Menachem Mendel's doctrine of the zaddik contains some of the distinctive ingredients of Hasidism. For example, from a personal point of view, "sometimes a certain descent from the level of their thoughts is

seek out such temptation. The text goes on to explain that one should immediately begin to think of the source of her beauty and see the divine vitality, etc., similarly to the sentiments we shall find expressed in the immediately following passage. See *Tsava'at HaRibash,* 23; Dov Baer of Mezeritch, *Or torah* (Jerusalem, 1968), on "Tehilim," 105b.

92. *Peri haAretz,* Parashah Bo'.

93. *Peri haAretz,* Parashah Bo'.

94. *Peri haAretz,* Parashah Vayeshev, at the end.

brought about in the zaddikim, but the truth is that this descent is only for the sake of further ascent." This topic appears in Hasidism in various contexts, but in the present context the matter is not elaborated. And from the social point of view R. Menachem Mendel establishes an important point: the zaddik, who is also called *ha'adam hakasher,* the man of unblemished character, is the socio-religious center, like the Temple. "To sum up, in the case of each and every zaddik, everything that he encounters must pass through his thoughts until it reaches the place of his spiritual elevation. And even if a person claiming to be a Hasid says that he has already annulled all his feelings and desires, a fool does not realize that if he has not got them in one respect he has them in others."[95]

Sometimes the figure of the zaddik appears cosmic in scale, "binding together all the worlds from *katnut* to *gadlut,*"[96] or "a zaddik . . . binds together all the worlds from the supreme root to the lowest depths, and through them [the zaddikim] all the worlds are conducted."[97] But the most striking statement made about the zaddik is that it is within his power to bring about changes in the processes of nature and perform miracles and wonders. It is true that we also find similar remarks in R. Joseph Gikatilla's *Sha'arei Orah*, but there the reference is to "proper prayer," by means of which treasuries on high are opened up, "and nothing can stand before him."[98] It appears, therefore, that the passage refers solely to prayer. The subject of the "change" (*hishtanut*) effected by the zaddik sometimes appears in *Maggid Devarav leYa'akov,* too.[99] But in R. Menachem Mendel's writings the idea is repeated in striking fashion. It is the zaddik who leads all things to the Source, and at the starting point it is possible to begin a new order of life. This even takes place "of itself, without any additional preparation."[100]

95. Ibid., *Parashah Matot-Massey.*

96. Cf. Dov Baer of Mezeritch, *Maggid Devarav leYa'akov,* ed. R. Schatz-Uffenheimer (Jerusalem, 1976)41 ,.

97. *Peri haAretz,* Parashah Eqev, at the end. Cf. *Maggid devarav le Ya'akov,* 275: "The intellect of the zaddik encompasses the entire universe."

98. To quote him more fully: "Proper prayer which gathers strength and ascends from *sefirah* to *sefirah* until it reaches the Will, which adheres to the *sefirah Keter* . . . and when the prayer reaches the place of the Will, all the gates above and below are opened before him and there is none there to hinder or obstruct his petition, for he is in the world of compassion *[rachamim],* And then all his needs and requests will be fulfilled, and nothing can stand in his way, for he draws [power] from the place of the Will, and can perform new signs and wonders as if the world were only then being created" (Joseph Gikatilla, *Sha'arei Orah* (Warsaw, 1883), Sha'ar no. 9, 95a). And see also Ephraim Gottlieb, *Mehkarim haSifrut haKahatah* (Tel Aviv, 1976), 36.

99. See, e.g., *Maggid Devarav leYa'akov,* 220: "that the zaddik can effect a change whenever he wishes." Similarly ibid., 23: "If the zaddik attaches himself to the primordial Will, he will be able to draw changes] from there [if] he wishes to perform a miracle."

100. See *Peri haAretz,* Parashah Vayigash, *s.v. kelala demilta.*

So great is the power of the zaddik that he is called "*ba'alah dematronit,* husband (or master) of the 'matron'—*Shekinah* or *Malkhut*—for he is master of the conduct of all the worlds" of which she is in charge, according to the Kabbalistic scheme, and it is within his power "to effect any change, miracles and wonders."[101] He gives more light to the world than the sun at noon, and he is called the *memale makom,*[102] the deputy—literally one who fills the place—of the *'Ein Sof.* What is meant by this designation is a person who makes it possible for God—who is *mekomo shel olam,* the place of the world, according to the exegesis (and is also known as *Hamakom,* "the Place")—literally to fill all the earth with His glory (as in Isaiah 6:3). A man who comes to recognize this is called *hakham*, wise—not, however, in the intellectual sense, but in the sense that he is identified with the *sefirah Chokhmah*, which derives from *ayin-Keter*, from which the spread of immanence begins.[103]

The position of the zaddik in his *devequt* is not one of absolute self-annulment but, on the contrary, one of positive emulation of the Holy One, blessed be He, in that he becomes a source of the flow of divine bounty to all the worlds, and even to the *qelipot,* the forces of evil, for Scripture says, "and You give life to them all" (Nehemiah 9: 6; the versions translate "You preserve them all"). For all the righteous deeds of the zaddikim, their chief desire is to cleave to the Lord, for the characteristic of the zaddik is *hitqashrut,* attachment to Him.[104]

R. Shneur Zalman's image of the zaddik is very different. He sees the zaddik's activity as essentially introspective—the conversion of the evil within him to holiness—whereas R. Menachem Mendel sees the zaddik's activity as directed toward the world. Even so, R. Shneur Zalman also speaks of the zaddik as elevating stray thoughts that are not his own but those of the members of his congregation, which is somewhat akin to R. Menachem Mendel's view that it is the duty of the zaddik to raise up his followers. The resemblance extends to a further point which it is surprising to encounter in R. Menachem Mendel. It is surprising, in the light of what has been said above, that when R. Menachem Mendel was asked by one of his disciples to bless him with a child, he answered sharply:

> I am overcome with shame, for am I in the place of God? (Genesis 30:2) The word of God was indeed in the hand of the Ba'al Shem

---

101. Ibid., Parashah Eqev. Generally, in Kabbalah, *matronita* is a name for the *sefirah Shekinah*, and her husband is, of course, *Tiferet*. But R. Menachem Mendel is faithful to his doctrine: the *Shekinah* for him denotes the divine immanence in the world. It follows that the husband of the *Shekinah* is he who has the power to introduce and determine changes in the order of the world.

102. *Peri haAretz,* Parashah Bo' (twice).

103. *Peri haAretz,* Parashah Qedoshim.

104. *Peri haAretz,* Parashah VaEtchanan.

> [Tov] and what he decreed would come to pass. He was unique, and among the ancients there arose none like him, and after he has returned to the dust who will arise? Although some of the great men among the zaddikim of our generation are talkers and make such announcements as they do, I do not regard myself thus.[105]

It may be that his remarks reflect opposition to the "practical zaddikism" which existed in his time,[106] and the fact that unworthy men represented themselves as wonder-workers. His objection would then have been on practical grounds, although in principle his attitude to this question was extremely positive, as I have argued. R. Shneur Zalman, too, was opposed to "practical zaddikism" and did not allow his Hasidim to speak to him in private except on subjects connected with guidance on divine worship.[107]

R. Menachem Mendel's description of evil reveals a distinctly monistic viewpoint. Evil springs from the divine source, and stress is repeatedly laid on the verses "and You give life to them all" (Nehemiah 9:6) and "His kingdom rules over all" (Psalm 103:19).[108] But evil exists only in the sense that there should be something to nullify or elevate. R. Menachem Mendel also uses the parable of the harlot, that is to say, the evil inclination was sent into the world in order that man should not submit to its temptations.[109] He sometimes makes use of the philosophical rule that "nature abhors a vacuum"—there is no empty space in the world—to teach that there will always be either impurity or holiness.[110]

Where holiness is absent, evil will automatically have a hold. We therefore do not have to make any great effort in order for evil to exist. By contrast, man needs devotion and self-sacrifice in order to draw down holiness on himself.[111] According to the order of events as seen by R. Menachem Mendel, evil does not take hold until it is necessary to fight against it. It is true that he once makes allegorical use of the olive, pointing out that its skin must be broken in order for oil to be extracted from it. But in general, or by the very fact of seeing the divine root of all things, it follows *automatically* that "all the doers of iniquity are scattered"[112] (Psalm 92: 2).[113] R.

105. *Likutei Amarim,* letter 7, 13a.

106. Cf. a similar appreciation with regard to R. Shneur Zalman in Hallamish, "Mishnato ha'iyunit," 362–63.

107. See M. Hallamish, "Yahasei tsadik ve'edah bemishnat RaSha"Z," *Hevrah vehistoriah* (Jerusalem, 1980), 79–92.

108. E.g., *Peri haAretz,* Parashah Matot-Massey.

109. *Likutei Amarim,* letter 4, 7a.

110. *Peri haAretz,* "Sabbath falling during Passover"; and Parashah Acharey Mot.

111. Ibid., Parashah VaEtchanan.

112. Ibid., Parashah Noach, at the end.

113. See, e.g., ibid., "Sabbath falling during Passover, at the end"; Parashah Naso; Parashah Ki *Tezai*, etc.

Shneur Zalman, on the other hand, maintains that evil does not exist in the metaphysical sense, but that on the cosmic and human plane evil is engaged in a mighty struggle against good. The whole of R. Shneur Zalman's basic typology of humanity—the zaddik, the wicked, and the average man—is set in the context of the power of evil and the need to subdue it.

The motives for R. Menachem Mendel's immigration to *'Eretz Yisrael* at the head of a congregation of Hasidim—an immigration regarded by scholars as important and successful—have recently become the subject of scholarly debate. The main opinions are that the immigration was motivated by disappointment at the failure of the mission to the Vilna Gaon or by messianic beliefs. Let us therefore observe that in the extant homilies and letters of R. Menachem Mendel there is relatively little speculative material connected with the subject of redemption or with that of *'Eretz Yisrael*. There may be some who will take R. Menachem Mendel's relative silence on these questions as a possible pointer towards his messianic orientation, but, in my opinion, the evidence is far from compelling.[114]

---

114. On these issues in the writings of R. Menachem Mendel of Vitebsk and R. Shneur Zalman of Liady, see my "Hasidism and the Land of Israel—Two Models," in *The Land of Israel in Modern Jewish Thought*, ed. Aviezer Ravitzky (Jerusalem: Yad Ben Zvi, 1998), 225-55.

Surprised by God: R. Menachem Mendel of Vitebsk's Approach to Divine Worship and Its Influence in Tiberias

by Jonathan Garb
Gershom Scholem Professor of Kabbalah
(Hebrew University of Jerusalem)

Introduction

While the remarkable spread of Hasidism in the late eighteenth and early nineteenth centuries is mostly a European story, the movement (just like the opposing school of the Vilna Gaon), spread to Palestine (the Land of Israel in the eyes of these immigrants), especially the Galilee. While the successive generations of Hasidic writing in Tiberias render broad generalizations hazardous, one can nonetheless point at a clear starting point and thus anchor the writings of R. Menachem Mendel of Vitebsk. R. Menachem Mendel was regarded as the heir of his teacher, R. Dov Baer of Mezeritch, at least within the branch operating in his original area of activity—Northeastern Europe.[1] Following his emigration to Palestine in 1777 and especially after his death in 1788, a fierce controversy over the succession erupted, the main antagonists being R. Shneur Zalman of Liady, founder of the Chabad dynasty, and R. Abraham haCohen of Kalisk, who operated in Tiberias.

As Nehemia Polen has also argued in a forthcoming volume in this series, and as A. Avish Shorr has recently shown in a series of groundbreaking articles, this was far from a mere political dispute. Rather, it went to the foundations of the correct path in divine worship. Here I shall attempt to re-examine the basic approach of R. Menachem Mendel to these ques-

1. On the relative closeness of R. Menachem Mendel's views to those of the Maggid, see the article by Moshe Hallamish in this volume, pp. 43-68 (and compare to my concluding comments).

tions and then inquire as to its possible reception in a selection of texts culled from later generations of Tiberian Hasidism. My focus here shall be primarily textual. Thus, I shall largely rest content with Shorr's meticulous historical narrative, while noting a recent response on the part of the leading Chabad in-house historian.[2] Furthermore, I shall not enter into a sustained dialogue with existing research on R. Menachem Mendel of Vitebsk and related topics, which until the present volume was relatively sparse (especially compared to the numerous studies of Chabad or even the thorough volume recently devoted to the Chernobyl dynasty, itself but one of numerous branches of the Maggid's following).[3]

Peri haAretz[4]

Our first text is located within a discussion of speech: "The more a person accustoms his speech to note and understand that it does not come from him, but rather the good comes from God and it is He who is talking, then he creates new heavens and new earth."[5] At first blush, this is a passive (or "quietistic," as R. Shatz-Uffenheimer had it), approach.[6] Creativity is enabled by the recognition that one is a medium for speech, originating from the divine, rather than being its source. However, a bit further into the homily, R. Menachem Mendel continues in a far more radical vein:

> . . . but such speech is abstracted from the *middot* [emotional traits,

2. See Shalom Duber Levin, "Rabeinu ha-Zaqen ve-Admorei Karlin," in Ha-Rav, ed. Nahum Gruenwald, Machon Ha-Rav 2015, 659–84.

3. Besides the studies cited below, the other articles in this volume (and the further studies cited wherein), one can mention the writings of Raya Haran, esp. "What Motivated Hassidic Jews to Emigrate to Eretz Israel in the Late Eighteenth Century?" *Cathedra 76* (1995): 77–95 [Hebrew] and the different (and in my view more accurate) approach of David Assaf, "'The Rumor was Spread that the Messiah has Already Come': New Light on the Aluyah of Hasidim in the Year 1777," Zion 61 (1996): 319–46 [Hebrew]. The Chernobyl volume is: Gadi Sagiv, Dynasty: The Chernobyl Hasidic Dynasty and its Place in the History of Hasidism (Jerusalem: Merkaz Zalman Shazar), 2014.

4. As this is not a philological study, I am utilizing a recent convenient edition rather than entering the history of print. Likewise, diachronical issues in the history of the texts shall not be addressed here.

5. Compare to Zohar 1: 4b.

6. Rivkah Shatz-Uffenheimer, Hasidism as Mysticism: Quietistic Elements in Eighteenth-Century Hasidic Thought, trans. J. Chipman (Princeton and Jerusalem: Princeton University Press and Magnes Press, 1993), 78, 115–19, 158 (and see also Jonathan Garb, *Shamanic Trance in Modern Kabbalah* (Chicago: University of Chicago Press, 2011), 105–8). For a good example of a passive model in *Peri haAretz*, Parashah Shoftim (Jerusalem: Mechon Peri haAretz, 2011), 498. Ideational themes in R. Menachem Mendel's epistles (printed in a separate volume in this edition and the subject of some controversy among scholars), are briefly addressed in Moshe Hallamish's articles on the Land of Israel (see below) and in this volume, and further genre-sensitive research is called for.

> but also alluding to divine attributes],[7] whilst speech that emits from a *middah*, is already enclothed in a *middah* and the *middah* is connected to all material things, for all the lower debased creations are through the *middot*.
>
> And also as each *middah* has a habit, so it is impossible for the divine speech to be clean and clear, for habit causes forgetfulness, and even the subtle words of *musar* [self-refinement] and wonderful intellects [*sekhalim*] and sounds of sounds[8] following on habit do not awaken, for habit is the cause of forgetting the active power[9] and its wonders, after one has already seen or heard or known a few times.

I understand this distinction as follows: Speech that is mediated by one's emotional virtues is prone to habituation, occluding the constant creative power of the emergence of speech from God. Even if habit is cultivated and refined, it nonetheless remains trapped within this limitation. This point immediately becomes more evident:

> Unless speech is without any clothing of a *middah*, but only faith in the words of the living God . . . speech which is not occasioned by *middot* is a flowing fountain,[10] for it is connected to the Infinite and flows from it, and all mouths weary of speaking its words . . . unlike speech which is enclothed in a *middah*, according to the extent of the *middah*, it operates in the limbs [of the body], for the *middah* accustoms the limbs to speak in its tongue. . . . And thus Moses of blessed memory, who was abstracted from all the *middot* in his speech, was known as "heavy of mouth" (Exodus 4:10) . . . and actually every person who speaks words of Torah in this fashion is like him.[11]

In other words, speech transcending habit and emotional dispositions can tap in to the infinite flow, and this is a constantly available option. The ethos here is one of bypassing both supernal structures and their human counterparts (in the Kabbalistic tradition of isomorphism between the divine and the human), in favor of direct, spontaneous access to the infinite.[12]

---

7. *Peri haAretz*, 164–65.

8. Possibly alluding to loud prayer, still customary amongst his followers, the Karlin Hasidism.

9. I.e., "Koah ha-po'el ba-nif'al," or the notion of the divine power constantly renewing and animating reality, as developed by the Maggid.

10. See *mAvot* 2, 8; 6, 1. On faith in R. Menachem Mendel's thought, see the article by Moshe Hallamish in this volume, pp. 43-68.

11. *Peri haAretz*, Parashah Vayera, 498, 161–66.

12. Cf. Ariel Evan Mayse's article in this volume pp. 107-134, which accords the *mid-*

This suggested reading, part of a wider history of *middot* (as both divine and human attributes or even emotions) in Jewish mysticism, is borne out by numerous locutions, of which I shall cite only samples (with further supporting texts footnoted).[13]

In his first homily on pericope Vayeshev, R. Menachem Mendel writes of the need to be totally absorbed in prayer or study or performing a commandment, until one is divested of erstwhile connections to material matters, until one no longer feels them. This trancelike state is that of "complete union" with God.[14] "However, in order to be in complete union with Him, blessed be He, one needs to totally go out of the *middot*, which are clothing . . . and ascend above the *middot*, through the letters which are the *tzeirufim* [combination of the *middot*] themselves."[15] This sentence, in the author's usual terse manner, is making three points: First, the need to transcend the *middot*, as we have already seen, yet here in pursuit of total unity. Secondly, as we have seen, this is accomplished through language.[16] Thirdly, R. Menachem Mendel taps in to the rich Hasidic and Kabbalistic discourse on combinations of letters, and argues that through recombining the letters one can recombine the *middot* and thus transcend their present form.[17]

Before continuing with our present text, I wish to pause to consider a parallel view in *Or haMeir*, by R. Zeev Wolf of Zhitomir, a senior student of the Maggid: After discussing the pleasure that God receives from "the numerous renewed combinations of the zaddikim [righteous in every generation]," he moves to address the erotic pleasure "as in the first hour"[18] that each individual can receive in countering "aging" of one's worship. The technique is as follows: Rather than praying habitually, "as arranged in the prayer book," one needs to "imagine that he does not see before him any combination of letters and words but rather now . . . he has to assemble

---

dot a much more positive role in R. Menachem Mendel's thought, while acknowledging the imperative to transcend them. Compare also to his treatment of language, emphasizing silence or "a wordless cry" as forms of transcendence of speech, while my own analysis focuses on spontaneous speech.

13. See also Parashah Lech Lecha, 498; Parashah VaEtchanan, translations no. 2.2, 15 in this volume, as well as Parashah Chayye Sarah, 60, 63, on freedom from the *middot*, Parashah Shelach Lecha, 361, on transcending the *middot*.

14. *Peri haAretz*, 94–95. Such passages are part of the massive evidence in favor of the existence of the model of *unio mystica* in Jewish mysticism.

15. Ibid., 96.

16. See also ibid., the first homily Parashah Vayigash, 137–38 (also on *zimzum*-contraction, as discussed shortly below).

17. On letter combination in Hasidism and its sources, see Moshe Idel, *Hasidism: Between Ecstasy and Magic* (Albany, NY: SUNY Press, 1995), 56–60 (adducing also our text), 276n55.

18. See the erotic context of this quote in *bEruvin* 54b; *bYomah* 29a. See a further sharp erotic image shortly after the portion of the text quoted here.

the letters according to his apprehension of Him, blessed be He, through his enclothing, and render them combinations of letters in praises . . . that is to make combinations of words out of the heap of letters that wait for the arrival of the speech of the zaddik."[19]

Again, the method of recombination counters habituation, though in a theurgical (giving pleasure to God) rather than an unitative mode, and while emphasizing (unlike our text) the special role of the zaddik.[20] Returning to our text, one should note that R. Menachem Mendel describes the combination of letters of the constantly transforming divine thought into *middot* (here in the sense of the divine attributes) as *zimzum* (contraction). Prayer begins with *middot* (here human emotions such as the aspiration for kindness and mercy), and then should reverse the process of contraction by ascending past understanding (through adhering to letters emerging from the heart), into constantly fluctuating thought, eventually reaching the *'Ein Sof* (Infinite) or "simple unity." This is what grants prayer its efficacy, for this infinite potential enables the worshipper to rearrange reality and "perform all change."[21] This, concludes R. Menachem Mendel, is the entire purpose of human existence and that of the world: "to uplift the contraction to the simple."[22]

A final text is found in a *midrash*-like reading of Psalm 118:24—"This is the day which the Lord has made; we will rejoice and be glad in it"—

---

19. Zeev Wolf of Zhitomir, *Or ha-Meir*, vol. 1, *Song of Songs* (Jerusalem, 2013), 291–92. As Moshe Idel, *Absorbing Perfections: Kabbalah and Interpretation* (New Haven, CT: Yale University Press, 2002), 386, notes, this book "betrays a fascination with the method of combination of Torah letters, which is unparalleled in Hasidism from the point of view of the recurrence of this concept." For an earlier parallel for the expression "heap of letters," see Gershom G. Scholem, *On the Kabbalah and Its Symbolism*, trans. R. Manheim (New York: Schocken, 1974), 74–75. Moshe Hallamish and Ariel Evan Mayse, in their articles in this volume, have addressed R. Menachem Mendel's unique view of the zaddik. See also on the zaddikim as transcending the *middot* in the homily for Shabbat Teshuva, 565–66.

20. Giving pleasure to God is briefly addressed in *Peri haAretz*, Parashah Qorah, 367. See at length in Moshe Idel, "Ta'anug: Erotic Delights from Kabbalah to Hasidism," in *Hidden Intercourse: Eros and Sexuality in the History of Western Esotericism*, ed. Wouter Hannegraaf and Jeffrey J. Kripal (New York: Fordham University Press, 2010), 111–51, which gives especial attention to R. Zeev Wolf of Zhitmoir.

21. *Peri haAretz*, 97–99. For constant change as the human condition, see the second homily on Parashah Vayeshev, 107–9. This text is discussed from different angles in Elliot Wolfson, *Giving Beyond the Gift: Apophasis and Overcoming Theomania* (New York, 2014), 321n178; Jonathan Garb, *Modern Kabbalah as an Autonomous Domain of Research* (Los Angeles: Cherub Press, 2016), 52–53. On constant change and "the point of the heart" (to be discussed below), see the first homily on Parashah Ki Tavo, 538–42, where pleasure is also a major theme. On change as constant return to the source of the *middot*, see Parashah Bechuqotay, 335–36. On *zimzum* (contraction) in the thought of R. Menachem Mendel, see the articles by Moshe Hallamish, Ariel Mayse, and Ron Margolin in this volume.

22. Ibid., 101.

found in pericope Qorah:

> Whatever illumination comes to a person is called day, from whatever *middah* it happens to be, for it is an illumination from God. Can one by joyful of the "day," that is to say in the illumination in the measured *middah*? Rather one should be joyful of "it" (*Bo'*), to be joyful in God, that is to understand that the illumination is the essence of God. . . . So when the King suddenly comes to dwell with him, he has to leave all of his house and utensils and if he abandons all of his house and utensils to the King, then automatically (*meimele*) he becomes as naught.[23]

In this creative misreading, "it" refers to God rather than to the day, thus turning the verse into a dialectic leading to the transcendence of the *middot* in favor of being surprised by joy, surprised by God into total self-abandonment.[24]

The locutions analyzed here reveal not only the radical and unique nature of R. Menachem Mendel's thought, requiring a Zen-like spontaneous presence to the call of the moment, but also assist in assessing its disputed heritage. As claimed already by and recently at greater length by Shorr, the approach of R. Abraham of Kalisk is far closer to the views emerging from these texts by R. Menachem Mendel than that of R. Shneur Zalman of Liady.[25] One could follow this mystical lineage, as it were throughout the history of the Karlin dynasty that was allied with R. Abraham,[26] yet here I shall focus on two lesser-known Tiberian sources from the twentieth century and then work backwards, as it were, in assessing the continuity of

23. Ibid., 383. The term *meimele*, repeated in this book, denotes a passive model.

24. On "true self-abandonemnt (*hefqerut amiti*)," see Parashah Bo', 172.

25. See A. Avish Shorr's article in a forthcoming volume, especially on the infinity of faith as opposed to the limitations of the forms of knowledge propounded by R. Shneur Zalman and on the need to limit one's speech in matters of divine worship, and rather to spend long periods of time internalizing one dibbur or utterance. Shorr correctly adduces *Peri haAretz*, Parashah Naso (337–41 in the edition used here and compare to 343) as support for R. Abraham of Kalisk's view, as well as Noah (24–27 in the edition used here). Cf. the more hesitant (as it is based on less textual research) approach of Shatz-Uffenheimer, *Hasidism as Mysticism*, 258–61, 286, and the different path taken by Ariel Evan Mayse in his article in this volume, noting both commonalities between R. Menachem Mendel and R. Shneur Zalman (in turn differentiating both from the Maggid) and striking differences. See also See Zeev Gries's article in this volume on the commonalities between the approach of R. Abraham of Kalisk and that of the Maggid.

26. On Karlin as continuing the approach of R. Abraham of Kalisk (as opposed to that of R. Shneur Zalman of Liady), see A. Avish Shorr, "Qarlin be-tqufat ha-galut 4," *Qovetz Beit Aharon ve-Yisrael* 171 (2014): 137–45. Shorr correctly identifies this approach with an emphasis (to be greatly developed in later branches of Hasidic writing), on "the point of the heart" (and see below soon on the opening of the heart). See also Ron Margolin's article in this volume.

Tiberian Hasidism. My focus shall be on the question of adherence to or divergence from, R. Menachem Mendel's approach as presented here.

Inner Work

The first of these sources is *'Avodat Pnim* (Inner Work), by R. Aharon Yosef Luria (1894–1969), written in 1931–35. These writings were part of a creative wave occasioned by the visit of the Slonimer (Branovitcher) rebbe, R. Abraham Weinberg the second (the *Beit Abraham*), in 1929. Although not all of the manuscript has been published, this is considered a classic of Slonim writing to this day, and like any collection including epistles, is highly revealing as to more practical exchanges on divine worship, as opposed to theoretical formulations.[27]

Although it is hard to find any teachings that even approximate the radical approach of R. Menachem Mendel of Vitebsk, one can point at a strong rejection of spiritual schedule in favor of a spontaneous response to the challenges of the moment in a letter "to a young man":

> As for your request to write you a schedule, this is not the way of our holy teachers, may their merit protect us. As they taught us, that one who wishes to enter the worship of God is like a warrior who enlists in the army in order to combat the enemy, which is the evil impulse that renews itself every day [as in *bSukkah* 52 a–b]. And it changes from time to time in different matters, and in this not every person is the same, and the person himself is not the same from day to day. And he also changes depending on location . . . and how is an uniform schedule for each day relevant [*shayach*], as one needs to combat the matter which is relevant for that hour or place.[28]

This formulation is joined by a critique of *middot*-based worship, as in the following passage (also demonstrating an awareness of the contemporary theory of the unconscious):

> You can find a person whose entire worship and study is founded

27. I shall not address existing writing on Slonim, which is far from extensive (it shall be discussed at length in Noga Bing's forthcoming doctoral dissertation, which like my present discussion and her Master's Thesis, written under my supervision), focuses on the twentieth century and on contemporary developments. For English-language discussions, see Shaul Maggid, "In Search of a Critical Voice in the Jewish Diaspora: Homelessness and Home in Edward Said and Shalom Noah Barzofsky's *Netivot Shalom*," *Jewish Social Studies* 12 (2006): 193–227; idem, "The Holocaust as Inverted Miracle: Shalom Noah Barzofsky of Slonim on the Power and Divine Nature of Radical Evil," in *Spiritual Authority: Wrestling with Cultural Power in Jewish Thought*, ed. Haim Kreisel and Boaz Huss (Beer Sheva: Ben Gurion University Press, 2010), 33–62.

28. Aharon Yosef Luria, *'Avodat Pnim* (Jerusalem: Bahran Press, 2004), 139 (and see also 6, 8). Compare to 118 for an image of "first aid," and 78, 82, 96 for further military images.

> on haughtiness, for the nature of man . . . is to wish to be a great person, and not necessarily to be regarded by others as such, but he himself desires and yearns to be a great person, and sometimes he directs himself toward lowliness after hearing from zaddikim and great ones that their greatness was in the *middah* of lowliness, and so on for the other *middot*, that he is excited by them and desires them and all because he wants to be great. And even if this is not conscious, in any case this thought creeps into his heart. And a slight sign and aspect of this is if he, God forbid, fails in his worship in some sin and becomes sad and depressed and downcast, and all because it is not suitable for him that he too should experience this.[29]

The relative rarity of vestiges of R. Menachem Mendel's teachings in *'Avodat Pnim* raises doubt as to long-term continuities between Tiberian Hasidism at its inception and in its later forms. Furthermore, it is worth observing the manner in which Luria describes his chain of transmission in a gathering held in 1945:

> Which one of us does not still remember the festivals and Sabbaths when our rebbe R. Abraham [Weinberg] was with us in the Holy Land eleven years ago . . . his holy Torah was like a key that opens the doors of the closed and blocked heart. . . . And this key he received from his ancestors, and our teachers the Kobriner [R. Moshe, leader of Slonim Hasidism after 1833] and the Lechovitzer [R. Mordekhai, student of R. Menachem Mendel of Vitebsk's follower R. Shlomo of Karlin], until the Ba'al Shem Tov, that drew down this aspect from heaven and transmitted it to his holy disciples, so as to say words of Torah in such a manner that one word will open the heart of the man of Israel . . .
>
> And the key was delivered in inheritance until the Lechovitzer, and the Kobriner received it from the Lechovitzer . . . for the way of the Ba'al Shem Tov was delivered from teacher to student like the aspect (*behina*) of the reception of Torah at Sinai . . .[30] and the hint is that when our rebbe R. Abraham passed away, this key was delivered to his son, the rebbe R. Shlomo David Yehosu'a [1914–43], and since the outbreak of the [second world] war, for several years we have no news [from him] and our hearts are closed and blocked

29. Ibid., 20 (and see 123).

30. See there on five "renewals in the world": creation, Abraham (not coincidentally the name of his teacher), the reception of Torah at Sinai, the writing of the Oral Torah in the Talmuds, Midrash, Zohar and the code of Law (itself a Galileen composition) and the Ba'al Shem Tov, as the opener of the hearts.

> and we don't have anyone to open our hearts . . . thus we have joined together today. . . . Perhaps we can make an inclusive [*kolel*] key, through each one being included with the other as one heart with friendly love.[31]

Besides the very focus on historiosophy (albeit in a Hasidic vein), alien to the present-focused thought of R. Menachem Mendel, he himself (as well as R. Abraham of Kalisk and even R. Dov Baer of Mezeritch) is strikingly absent in this fascinating narrative.[32] What one can learn from this text is that Luria's alliance is to a European tradition up to his own rebbe, although we are also speaking of early figures, such as R. Mordekhai of Lechovitz, loyal to R. Menachem Mendel of Vitbesk's approach. In other words, also due to a constant flow of epistles (published by Jacob Barnai), Tiberian Hasidism's point of reference was always its region of origin rather than its present setting, as Zionist historiography would have it (though see my brief note below on the place of the Land of Israel). Together with my previous point, this observation should lead to caution as to a bounded construct of "Tiberian Hasidism."

Beit Genazay

This sense of discontinuity is reinforced by a second, somewhat later source: the large (and partly unpublished corpus) *Beit Genazay*, by R. Aharon Yosef's nephew, R. Raphael Moshe Luria (1937–2009). I see his yet un-researched writing as the most important product of the Slonim dynasty in the twentieth century, as we are speaking of a figure with strong ties to the Kabbalistic elite, as a leader of the *Sha'ar haShamayim* Yeshiva.[33] Predictably, Luria's writing is replete with a rich assortment of Kabbalistic sources, not only the obvious (the writings of R. Yitzhak Luria and of R. Shalom Shar'abi), but also a corpus not always viewed favorably in the Hasidic world—the historiosophical writings of the Vilna Gaon, arch-opponent of Hasidism, and those of R. Moshe Hayyim Luzzatto and his close associate R. Moshe David Vallee.[34] Luria's transition towards granting the Land of Israel a central, at times almost erotic, role in his teaching and its

31. *'Avodat Pnim*, 181–83. Compare to 80 on three branches of Hasidism: Poland, Lithuania, and Volohin, with two Lithuanian sub-branches: Chabad and Lechovitz, followed by Kobrin and Slonim. On the blocked heart, see 20. I shall not go into the question of friendly love here, as it has enjoyed some attention in writing on Tiberian Hasidism (most notably Zeev Gries's article in the forthcoming second volume in this series).

32. See the critique of modernity and technology ibid., 92.

33. On the role of this yeshiva as a "hub" in contemporary Kabblah, see Jonathan Garb, *Yearnings of the Soul: Psychological Thought in Modern Kabbalah* (Chicago: University of Chicago Press, 2015), 15, 120–21.

34. On the conflicted Hasidic reception of Luzzatto, see Jonathan Garb, *Kabbalist in the Heart of the Storm* (Tel Aviv: Tel Aviv University Press, 2014), 322–25 [Hebrew].

antinomian implications, as well as the general question of the place of the Land of Israel in Tiberian Hasidism, deserve a separate study.[35] Here I wish to focus on vestiges of R. Menachem Mendel's approach. However, before doing so, one must note that even more than in *'Avodat Pnim*, the very resort to technical Kabbalistic terminology and quotes from the Jewish mystical library, contrasts strongly with the relative absence of these textual phenomena, especially Lurianic and post-Lurianic sources, in the writing of R. Menachem Mendel (not to mention the ideological rejection of dwelling on Kabbalistic matters in the writings of R. Abraham of Kalisk).[36] This absence is even more evident when one compares the place of Kabbalah to the role of this literature and language in the writings of R. Shneur Zalman and even those of R. Dov Baer of Mezeritch.[37] As far as I have seen, there is very little here that is reminiscent of *Peri haAretz*, besides a general stress on experiences of radical dependence and other passive states.[38]

Thus, rather close to our own time, a leading figure from a central branch of Tiberian Hasidism, who was actually born in Tiberias, shows very little loyalty to the teachings of the founding figure of Tiberian Hasidism. There are several possible explanations for this striking discontinuous development, and here I shall point at but one of them.

ONE TURNING POINT

Not surprisingly for one whose inner world was transformed by encountering R. Abraham the second, R. Aharon Yosef Luria is openly influenced by the works of R. Abraham Weinberg the first (1804–83), who was active in supporting the settlement in Tiberias (and wrote repeatedly of the merit of the Holy Land and of Tiberias in particular). When asked to describe the way of Slonim Hasidim, Luria responded: "The book *Yesod ha'Avodah* is open in front of us." If one consults the un-researched writings of this figure, and especially this work (which helpfully contains numerous letters),

35. On the Land of Israel in the thought of R. Menachem Mendel, see Moshe Hallamish, "Hasidism and the Land of Israel—Two Models," in *The Land of Israel in Modern Jewish Thought,* ed. Aviezer Ravitzky (Jerusalem: Yad Ben Zvi, 1998), 225–55. The historiosophical tendency, the connection to Luzzatto, and the antinomian stress on the Land of Israel (and other matters not addressed here) all bring Luria close to the circle of R. Kook and indeed he reportedly supported the Kook circle's opposition to the 2005 disengagement from the Gaza Strip.

36. See A. Avish Shorr's article in a forthcoming volume in this series. See, however, *Peri haAretz*, first homily on Vayigash, 141. One should note here the frequency of references to the Zohar in *Peri haAretz*. While this is not uncommon in early Hasidic writing, it should by no means be taken for granted.

37. His uncle R. Aharon Yosef also cites the writings of R. Yitzhak Luria as evidence for his claims (*'Avodat Pnim*, 81).

38. See Rapahel Moshe Luria, *Azai: Ori Ve-Yish'i*, 2nd ed. (Jerusalem, 2003), 150, 233; idem, *'Eretz Yisrael Ma'amarim*, vol. 2 (Jerusalem, 2011), 648.

one can locate a precise point of swerve away from R. Menachem Mendel's teachings and those of R. Abraham of Kalisk. On the one hand, both of these figures (alongside with the Maggid of Mezeritch and R. Mordekhai of Lechovitz) are repeatedly and admiringly quoted by Weinberg, who suitably emphasizes themes such as faith, constant self-renewal, friendly love, the point of the heart, self-abandonment, and *ayin* (nothingness). And yet for him this was part of a wider modern panorama, including seventeenth-century figures such as the works of the Italian Lurianic writer R. Menachem 'Azariya of Fano, R. Isaiah Horowitz's *Sheney Luhot haBerit,* and the works of R. Yehudah Loewe (Maharal) of Prague (for whom he has fulsome praise). The latter corpus may have influenced the historiosophical discourse found here, as well as in his *Chesed le-Abraham*, which betrays the influence of the Luzzatto circle (as well as extensively quoting the Lurianic corpus).[39] As a result, themes of divine will and power, relatively rare in the writings of R. Menachem Mendel, are highly prominent here. To these one should add his original contributions, including striking sexual imagery, extensive psycho-physical discussions of the four elements and the purification of the senses, and also quotes from other Hasidic streams (such as Ruzhin).[40]

However, the most striking swerve away from the thought of R. Menachem Mendel lies in his treatment of the *middot*, occupying a very large place in his works.[41] First, as opposed to the somewhat anomian (R. Menachem Mendel) or at times almost antinomian (R. Abraham of Kalsik, as interpreted by Gries) approach of his predecessors, Weinberg firmly asserts a nomian stance.[42] The *middot* as God's clothing can be bypassed (as R. Menachem Mendel claimed), but only by means of Torah, as a direct and continuous connection.[43] Otherwise, *devequt*, or adherence to God (famously one of the most central values for all of Hasidism), "can only descend to the person through the illumination of the enclothment of the *middot* through *zimzum* [contraction]." Weinberg then expands this idea by detailing the

---

39. See, e.g., Abraham Weinberg, *Chesed le-Abraham: 'Asara M'aamarot*, 1974 reprint of the Yozefov 1886 edition, 11a, 17a, 21a. In this context one should note the extensive discussions of time itself in this work, as well as Weinberg's interest in current political and military events (see *Yesod ha'Avodah*, vol. 2 [Warsaw, 1892], 9b). In turn, this may reflect the prominence of the theme of inner warfare in his writing.

40. See, e.g., *Yesod ha'Avodah*, vol. 2, 17a, on becoming like a virgin.

41. See, e.g., *Chesed le-Abraham*, 8a; *Yesod ha'Avodah*, vol. 1 (Warsaw, 1892), 135A.

42. See Zeev Gries's article in a forthcoming volume in this series.

43. Idem, *Yesod ha'Avodah*, vol. 1, 46a. The nomian salience of Weinberg's writing is reinforced by his frequent recourse to the Lurianic system of *kavvanot*, or intentions of the commandments and prayers. Inter alia, such textual findings should give pause with regard to claims as to the annulment of these practices in Hasidism.

correspondence between human emotions and divine attributes.[44] One should add that in some aspects, as in the stress on angelology, Weinberg's writing is closer to that of R. Shneur Zalman than to his own school.

R. Weinberg's writing, in style, sources. and themes, thus demonstrates a significant departure from the deliberate simplicity of R. Menachem Mendel's approach (in which Kabbalistic sources are not referenced in detail, intricate cosmologies are avoided, and the *sefirotic* system itself (alongside with its customary Hasidic translation into *middot*) often bypassed in favor of direct access to the infinite. Rather, it reflects the transformation of Slonim into a scholastic (and thus profoundly Lithuanian) form of Hasidism as described by Alan Nadler.[45] If his writings still extant in manuscript are ever published, this will hopefully further clarify the nature of this transition.

Conclusion

Just as we have noted the complexity of continuity of R. Menachem Mendel's own teachings, the marked divergence between his own approach and that adopted in Europe by the Chabad school demonstrates the remarkable diversity of opinion amongst the disciples of the Maggid of Mezeritch, R. Dov Baer Friedman. These varieties in turn point to the complexity of the Maggid's own thinking, reflecting his effort to merge various stages in his own thought with various strands of the teachings of his teacher, the BeSh"T, and earlier Kabbalistic views, especially Lurianic vocabulary.[46]

---

44. Ibid., vol. 2, 20A. One should note that Weinberg at times resorts to color imagery to describe aspects of the psyche. This is relatively rare in Hasidic writing and thus contributes to the sense of the uniqueness of his thought and hence the need for further study of it. On *devequt* in the thought of R. Menachem Mendel, see the article by Moshe Hallamish in this volume.

45. Alan Nadler, "The Synthesis of Hasidic Pietism with Lithuanian Torah Scholarship in Slonimer Hasidut," in *Yeshivot and Battei Midrash*, ed. Immanuel Etkes (Jerusalem: Merkaz Shazar, 2006), 395–415 [Hebrew]; see also the expanded English translation of this article in a forthcoming volume in this series. As evident here, my discussion of the place of Kabbalah in Slonim literature differs substantively from that of Nadler.

46. See A. Avish Shorr's article in this volume, and especially his plausible hypothesis that the approach of R. Shneur Zalman continues that of the Maggid's son, R. Abraham haMalakh ("the angel"). I believe that comparing the teachings of "the angel" and R. Menachem Mendel on the same periscopes will bear out this suggestion. The scholarly literature on the Maggid is not large, yet is rapidly growing. For two notable recent studies, see Ariel Evan Mayse, "Beyond the Letters: The Question of Language in the Teachings of Rabbi Dov Baer of Mezeritch," (PhD dissertation, Harvard University, 2015); Menachem Lorberbaum, "'Attain the attribute of 'Ayin': The Mystical Religiosity of Maggid Devarav Le-Ya'akov," *Kabbalah* 31 (2014): 169–235. Two indispensable requisites for further study are a comprehensive philological examination of the writings and teachings attributed to him (joined by a diachronical exploration of the evolution of his thought), and then a thorough mapping of the differences between his approach and that of the other disciples of the BeSh"T. Part of this massive undertaking is due to be included in Eli Mosenson's forthcoming dissertation.

Certainly, this constant proliferation of stances toward the very foundations of divine worship both confounds facile generalizations as to the "Hasidic" way and challenges constructs such as "Tiberian Hasidism." These findings reinforce the need to more rigorously adopt the methods of intellectual history in the study of Hasidism. However, the unique and radical nature of the main approach presented here that understandably did not last long in its original form also points at the necessity of including an increasingly rich and varied selection of Hasidic writing in the library of world mysticism.

On the Printing of Hasidic Teachings and Its Definition as "Kabbalah Made Ethos" in Light of the Doctrine of R. Menachem Mendel of Vitebsk and R. Abraham of Kalisk

by Ron Margolin
(Tel Aviv University)

In 1961, Gershom Scholem set forth in *Commentary* his objections to Martin Buber's interpretation of Hasidism.[1] Scholem raised two main arguments, one, that the spiritual message that Buber introduced into the world of Hasidism originated in Buber's own philosophy, and the other opposed Buber's focus on the Hasidic legends, or legendary literature, and his disregard of what Scholem called the Hasidic theoretical–homiletical literature. Buber responded to Scholem's critique in a short article that appeared in the following issue of *Commentary*.[2] In the beginning of his response, Buber distinguished between two different ways of transmitting the spirit of a religious doctrine to a generation that had lost direct access to the faith of its forefathers. One way was the theoretical scientific approach championed famously by Scholem and others. The other way, which was characteristic of Buber's own approach, is not satisfied with merely indicating new knowledge; it rather must "convey the reality of the way of life that was once informed by these teachings, the life of faith that was lived by exemplary individuals and by the communities they founded and led."[3] In such matters Buber was a student of Wilhelm Dilthey and Georg Simmel. He assumed throughout his scholarly literary activity that not only did his way not contradict academic methodology, to the contrary—it enrichened

1. Gershom Scholem, "Martin Buber's Hasidism: A Critique," *Commentary* 32, no. 4 (1961): 305–16.

2. Martin Buber, "Interpreting Hasidism," *Commentary* 36, no. 3 (1963): 218–25.

3. Buber, "Interpreting Hasidism," 218.

it with a vital perspective that was hidden from most other scholars. Buber responded in short to the concise and focused attacks by Scholem and Rivkah Schatz-Uffenheimer on his interpretation of Hasidism during his last years; therefore, many were convinced of the correctness of the attacks by Scholem, who ended his article with the words, "we shall, I am afraid, have to start all over again."[4]

Scholem divided the Hasidic literature into two types. The first comprised, until the beginning of the twentieth century, more than a thousand theoretical and homiletical works, mainly expositions and sermons, biblical commentaries, booklets on prayer, and other aspects of religious life, most of which did not break new theoretical ground, with the exception of the books of Chabad.[5] The second type was a rich literature concerned with legends, biographies, and tales of the wonders of the zaddikim, along with collections of memorable sayings that were published especially after 1860, from which Buber fashioned the world of the Hasidic masters that he includes in his *Tales of the Hasidim*.[6] This division was especially undermined after Mendel Piekarz's book on the *Beginning of Hasidism*, in which he argued that the *drush* (homiletical) literature of nascent Hasidism should not be viewed as a systematic theoretical literature.[7]

> The transition from the *drush* and *musar* [ethical teachings and homilies] books to the writings of R. Jacob Joseph of Polonnoye,

---

4. Scholem, "Martin Buber's Hasidism," 316. Shortly before he died, Buber responded to the trenchant criticism by Rivkah Schatz-Uffenheimer that she first presented in her article in *Molad* 149 (1960): 596–609. For the English version of the critique, see Rivkah Schatz-Uffenheimer, "Man's Relation to God and World in Buber's Rendering of the Hasidic Teaching," in *The Philosophy of Martin Buber*, ed. Paul Arthur Schilpp and Maurice Friedman (La Salle, IL: Open Court, 1967), 403–34. Buber's response to this article appears in the same collection, 731–34. For a comprehensive discussion of the Hasidic attitude to the life of this world, which is actually a new examination of the disagreement between Schatz-Uffenheimer and Scholem, on the one hand, and Buber, on the other, see Ron Margolin, *Human Temple* (Jerusalem: Magnes, 2005), 145–287 [Hebrew].

5. Scholem maintains that most of the contents of this literature were formulated until 1815, and even if new ideas were added to it afterward, most of the books published after this date are repetitions and variations of the fundamental motifs that were developed in the earlier books (Scholem, "Martin Buber's Hasidism," 308).

6. This division corresponds with what Buber wrote in his introduction to *Tales of the Hasidim*, in which he distinguished between the Hasidic theoretical literature and the popular books that constitute Hasidic legend. "In addition to these, there are several teachings and sermons which are given because of their profound significance. But not a single passage hails from the extensive theoretical writings of Hasidism; all are taken from the popular literature, where they supplement what is told of the lives of the zaddikim" (Martin Buber, *Tales of the Hasidim* [New York: Schocken, 1991], xxii).

7. Mendel Piekarz, *Beginning of Hasidism: Ideological Trends in Derush and Musar Literature* (Jerusalem: Bialik Institute, 1998) [Hebrew].

> the first author of Hasidism, of premier quality and importance, is like the exodus from an arid desert to a settled land . . . Although his words are anchored in a whole and distinct worldview, a second look reveals totally contradictory conceptions and ideas within them, and the reader will struggle in vain to discern the marks of intellective development by means of a historical philological examination . . . Central ideas recur in different formulations, at times at length, and at other times, fragmentary and implied; at times things are attributed, and at other times the very same things are not attributed . . . It seems they were printed based on various handwritten notes and copies, and were not touched by the hand of an editor.[8]

This argument is of importance for the disagreement between Scholem and Buber since Piekarz rejects the presentation of the ramified Hasidic *drush* literature as theoretical literature that is the continuation of theoretical Kabbalistic works such as *Pardes Rimonim* by R. Moses Cordovero, or the description of Lurianic Kabbalah in R. Hayyim Vital's *'Etz Chayyim*. On the one hand, Piekarz opposed Scholem's terminology of "Hasidic theoretical literature," while, on the other, he intensified Scholem's famous position that Hasidic literature contains nothing new. Although Scholem accepted Buber's early twentieth-century definition that Hasidism is "Kabbalah made ethos,"[9] in practice he rejected the meaning that Buber gave to the concept of "ethos," arguing that we cannot accept Buber's notion that "Hasidism in the first instance is not a category of teaching but one of life."[10] Buber's decision to base this argument mainly on the Hasidic legendary literature correctly aroused scholarly opposition, but this does not negate the depth of Buber's understanding that in Hasidim Kabbalah was made ethos. Zeev Gries opened this discussion in his article "From Mythos to Ethos."[11] In the current article I wish to continue this inquiry. Following Buber's view, the Hasidic *drush* literature is primarily intended to teach of the spiritual way of life that was fashioned by the circle of the Ba'al Shem Tov and the circle of the students of the Maggid of Mezeritch. The speedy development of the Hasidic zaddikim as the leadership of the

8. Piekarz, *Beginning of Hasidism*, 15–16.

9. This phrase appeared for the first time in Buber's introduction to his German collection of the tales of R. Nahman that was first published in Frankfurt in 1906. See Gershom G. Scholem, "Hasidism: The Last Phase," in *Major Trends in Jewish Mysticism* (New York: Schocken, 1969), 342.

10. Scholem, "Martin Buber's Hasidism," 308.

11. Zeev Gries, "From Mythos to Ethos: An Outline of the Image of R. Abraham of Kalisk," in *Nation and History: Studies in the History of the Jewish People. Based on Papers Delivered at the Eighth World Congress of Jewish Studies, Jerusalem 1981*, vol. 2: *The Modern Period*, ed. Shmuel Ettinger (Jerusalem: Zalman Shazar Center, 1984), 117–46 [Hebrew], included in a forthcoming volume in this series..

masses by some of the Maggid's disciples, already in the third generation of Hasidism,[12] obviously justified the claim made by Scholem and others that Hasidism is a mass movement with populist characteristics. I, however, find the attribution of the populist element to the transformation of the Kabbalah to ethos to be flawed. On the one hand, this reflects disregard for the force and depth of the social forces and ideas that motivated the Hasidic leadership, while attesting, on the other hand, to a lack of comprehension of the profound and elitist nature of several of the outstanding books that were included in what scholars call the medieval *drush* and *musar* literature, and especially those belonging to the Hasidic literature.[13] In my opinion, the importance of the study of the *musar* and *drush* literature lies in its showing that what Buber called Hasidism's religious–spiritual ethos clearly had its roots in the interiorization orientation of the philosophical and Kabbalistic ethical-teachings literature.[14]

The argument that Hasidism is Kabbalah made ethos has been universally accepted by scholarly research, but the question of the nature of this ethos remains unanswered. We will discuss the question of the nature of the *drush* literature in nascent Hasidism, through an examination of the letters of R. Abraham of Kalisk (1741–1810) that were sent to his Hasidim in Russia and the teaching on Torah portion of *Acharey Mot* in the book *Peri haAretz* by R. Menachem Mendel of Vitebsk (ca. 1730–88). We should take into account Buber's assertion that historical theoretical knowledge of Hasidism cannot ignore the spiritual character of the life of individuals, and that of the Hasidic testimony.

A Study of the Letters of R. Abraham of Kalisk

The letters by R. Abraham of Kalisk to his Hasidim in Russia vividly attest to the thinking current in the court of the Maggid of Mezeritch on the question of the reason for writing and printing of homiletical books of the Hasidic masters.[15] After the Maggid's death, R. Menachem Mendel of Vitebsk

12. On this process among the disciples of the Maggid, see Ada Rapoport-Albert, "The Hasidic Movement after 1772—Structural Continuity and Change," in *Hasidism Reappraised*, ed. Ada Rapoport-Albert (London: Littman Library, 1996), 76–140; Arthur Green, *The Heart of the Matter: Studies in Jewish Mysticism and Theology* (Philadelphia: Jewish Publication Society, 2015), 119–66.

13. See Patrick Benjamin Koch, "Human Self-Perfection: A Re-assessment of Kabbalistic Musar-Literature of Sixteenth Century Safed" (PhD diss., Hebrew University of Jerusalem, 2011).

14. See Piekarz, *Beginning of Hasidism*, 7.

15. On R. Abraham of Kalisk, see Joseph Weiss, "R. Abraham Kalisker's Concept of Communion with God and Men," in *Studies in Eastern European Mysticism* (Oxford: Littman Library, 1985), 155–69; Gries, "From Mythos to Ethos"; Ra`aya Haran, "The Doctrine of R. Abraham of Kalisk," *Tarbiz* 66 (1997): 517–41 [Hebrew].

was considered to be his leading disciple in Russia,[16] and we therefore should carefully consider the critique by R. Abraham of Kalisk, who was his student and successor in leading the small Hasidic court that the two founded in Tiberias after their immigration to the Land of Israel in 1772, and remained the leader of their loyalist Hasidim in Russia.[17] This testimony is most telling in the criticism that was directed to R. Shneur Zalman of Liady (1745–1812) that was included in a personal letter to the latter immediately following the publication of the *Tanya'* in 1797.[18] R. Abraham of Kalisk's criticism corroborates Buber's claim of the secondary importance of the Hasidic *drush* books, at least in the beginning of Hasidism.

Two letters by R. Abraham of Kalisk to his Hasidim in Russia from 1793 and 1794, six years after R. Menachem Mendel's death, and three to four years before the printing of the *Tanya'*, patently oppose the printing of Hasidic teachings in books:

> Last year I responded at length [in the spirit of] "he who loves him disciplines him early"[19] regarding the written Torah . . . as the dictum of the Rabbis in the Palestinian Talmud, "If the words of Torah seem old, etc."[20] For, with God's help, may He be blessed, you have with you, the beloved rabbi, the holy one of the Lord, our teacher and rabbi Shneur Zalman, may his light shine, your eyes see your teacher, "You water the mountains from Your lofts, the earth is sated from the fruit of Your work" (Psalm 104:13),

16. On R. Menachem Mendel and his book *Peri haAretz*, see Moshe Hallamish, "The Teachings of R. Menachem Mendel of Vitebsk," in this volume, pp. 43-68..

17. On immigration to the Land of Israel, see Raya Haran, "What Motivated Hassidic Jews to Emigrate to Eretz Israel in the Late Eighteenth Century?" *Cathedra* 76 (1995): 77–95 [Hebrew]; Moshe Hallamish, "Hasidism and the Land of Israel—Two Models," in *The Land of Israel in Modern Jewish Thought*, ed. Aviezer Ravitsky (Jerusalem: Yad Izhak Ben-Zvi, 1998), 225–55 [Hebrew].

18. I accept the argument by Gries that the teachings of R. Menachem Mendel of Vitebsk and his successor R. Abraham of Kalisk are more reflective of the spirit of nascent Hasidism than are those of R. Shneur Zalman and his successors. This claim is supported by Moshe Hallamish's observation that R. Menachem Mendel was generally closer to the Maggid than was R. Shneur Zalman, who was more faithful to the original Kabbalistic meaning of concepts such as *z̲imz̲um* (withdrawal), *katnut* (smallness), and *gadlut* (greatness). See Hallamish, "Teachings of R. Menachem Mendel," in this volume. On the disagreement between R. Abraham of Kalisk and R. Shneur Zalman, see Raya Haran, "R. Abraham of Kalisk and R. Shneur Zalman of Ladi—A Friendship Cut Off," in *Rivkah Shatz-Uffenheimer Memorial Volume*, vol. 2, ed. Rachel Elior and Joseph Dan (*Jerusalem Studies in Jewish Thought* 12; Jerusalem, n. p., 1996), 399–428 [Hebrew].

19. Following Proverbs 13:24.

20. "'Do not despise your mother when she is old' (Proverbs 23:22)—R. Yose ben Bun said, If the words of Torah seem old when you say them, do not despise them. What is the reason? 'Do not despise your mother when she is old'" (jBerakot, 9:5, 68a).

> and pearls come forth from his mouth. This is especially so since the world is full of new and old [holy] books on most lofty matters, and so they scream all the day, "Ho, all who are thirsty, come [for water]" (Isaiah 55:1). All of this is because the light of Torah has become very antiquated in their eyes. [And] now, the duty of the hearts, the secrets of Torah, of which only the main points are revealed to the wise one who understands from his own mind, to delve in it and delve again all the time, have poured out their heart before Him, may He be blessed, "they are renewed every morning, ample is Your grace" (Lamentations 3:23). If they have not reached this level, then the clouds are His concealment. "What advantage is there to the owner thereof, saving the beholding of them with his eyes?" (Ecclesiastes 5:10). When a person's mind ages, the power of his faith and fear [of God] diminishes. The Torah so cries out, "These words, etc., shall be on your heart" (Deuteronomy 6:6)—that every day they should be as if they were new in a person's inner eyes. This is the main thing of the complete acceptance of the kingdom of Heaven, to constantly renew every day the old, as if it were given today. Let everyone know in his soul the first hour that he approaches the service of the Creator with a fire [i.e., in his heart] on account of the new light in which his inner eyes are illuminated with the light of truth, thus they will be renewed every day.[21]

In this letter R. Abraham of Kalisk criticized the novel practice in the life of the Hasidim, namely, the printing of new religious books.[22] At this juncture, it is not evident that he blames his friend R. Shneur Zalman for this innovation; he might even hint here that the closeness of the Hasidim to R. Shneur Zalman could substitute for these books. We might think that this is a call for elitist esotericism, in opposition to exposing the secrets of Hasidic doctrine to the public. His reliance, however, on the dictum from the end of j*Berakot* and the emphasis on the acceptance of the kingship of Heaven links the printing of the books with spiritual aging. That is, R. Abraham of Kalisk viewed the printing of Hasidic teachings as a mark of institutionalization, which he calls "aging." He deems this institutionalization, because he critiques transforming the daily routine of the Hasidim into religious activity by rote, without fervor and vigor. Consequently, for him, learning

21. Letter of R. Abraham of Kalisk from 1793 to the Hasidim and "Those of Standing in the Country of Russia," in *Hasidic Letters from Eretz-Israel: From the Second Part of the Eighteenth Century and the First Part of the Nineteenth Century*, ed. Ya'acov Barnai (Jerusalem: Yad Izhak Ben Zvi, 1980), Letter 59, 226–27 [Hebrew].

22. The first Hasidic book to be printed was *Toldot Ya'akov Yosef* (Koretz, 1780); *Maggid Devarav leYa'akov* was first printed in Koretz in 1781.

Hasidic teachings from these books is a sort of substitute, an escape from the loss of personal passion in religious activity. Daily spiritual renewal is the ideal that he presents in contrast to spiritual aging. Enthusiasm that is constantly renewed is like the taste of receiving Torah for the very first time. R. Abraham of Kalisk's letter indicates that the way to spiritual renewal depends solely on man's heart—his inner self. It cannot be attained by any scholarly erudition, whatever its content. This message becomes even clearer in a letter that was sent a year later:

> I wrote this only so that the generation that seeks Him [i.e., his disciples who remained in Russia] will know all that they bear, [you] do not need [additional] Torah [i.e., notions]. "He whose wisdom [surpasses his deeds"] (*mAvot* 3:17), as the saying, "where [*me-ayin*] can wisdom be found" (Job 28:12) [according to the Maggid, this verse teaches that wisdom comes from *ayin*—the divine nothingness]—a sort of revelation. A person must look within himself: to bring his heart back to Him—to know the Lord in all His ways; and if there is no understanding, from whence knowledge, nor will they have wisdom [based on the fundamental *Chokhmah-Bina-Da'at* triad of the Hasidism founded by R. Shneur Zalman]. Plead, please, to the Lord with the prayer, give us comprehension, and I, too, raise my hands to the Lord, to plead for them. For many distinguished books [in which] the reasons of Torah and fear [of God] are revealed—as the taste of the manna that became all the tastes in the world, both all those that you know and heard, and here, too, new teachings are delivered, by their king at their head, this is the honored, the renowned, the divine rabbi, my brother, our teacher, Shneur Zalman, may he live long, his words are always with you.
>
> This is certainly from God: not to write down any Torah teaching, not even a single letter, lest they multiply, and they are very many. By the Lord's life, I stood before the honored *Admor* [our lord, teacher, and rabbi], may the memory of the righteous be for a blessing, and each teaching of his remained with me for a long time. Then as now, it is as if it were said now. But I wrote all this to teach you the way in which the righteous walk, that it may be good for them.[23]

The sentence "if there is no understanding, from whence knowledge" apparently alludes to the acronym *Chab"ad* (*Chokhmah* [wisdom]—*Bi-*

23. This letter was not included in the collection edited by Barnai. It appears, e.g., in *Peri haAretz* (Zhitomer, 1867), 90; see also the Hamesorah edition (Jerusalem, 1989), Letter 34, 215–16.

nah [comprehension, understanding]—*Da'at* [knowledge]) chosen by R. Shneur Zalman, which is a paraphrase of the dictum in *mAvot* 3:17: "If there is no understanding, there is no knowledge; if there is no knowledge, there is no understanding," and of the dictum in j*Berakot* 39b, 5:2: "If there is no knowledge, where is prayer? And, here, if there is no knowledge, where is *Havdalah*?" R. Abraham of Kalisk argues that "understanding" is not intellective wisdom, but the understanding of the heart, from the wording "to bring his heart back to Him." Inundating thought with intellective wisdom, even if its content is the Hasidic teachings of his close friend R. Shneur Zalman, is liable to serve as a substitute for the inner awakening that he calls the "awakening of the heart." R. Abraham of Kalisk joins the teaching of their common teacher the Maggid of Mezeritch of "where [*me-ayin*] can wisdom be found"[24] together with the withdrawal and lessening of the cognitive aspect that is expressed in theoretical knowledge. The printing of Hasidic teachings and their study from books is a flight from the difficult challenge of daily inner renewal, and its substitution by the intellectual interest in spirituality. This diverts the service of the Lord from the mystical experiential way of the Maggid to that of intellective study, which was not the way of their teacher. R. Abraham of Kalisk explains to the readers of his letter that the way of the Maggid and of R. Menachem Mendel was different.[25] Their teachings were concise but profound, and in general, aroused their listeners to long-lasting inner religious fervor.[26]

---

24. Dov Baer of Mezeritch, *Maggid Devarav leYa'akov*, ed. Rivkah Shatz-Uffenheimer (Jerusalem: Magnes, 1990), *Torot* 1, 6, 46, 56, 60, 100, 154.

25. Netanel Lederberg maintains that the appellation *Admor* in this letter refers to the Maggid of Mezeritch, and not to R. Menachem Mendel of Vitebsk. See Netanel Lederberg, *The Gateway to Infinity: Rabbi Dov Baer, the Maggid Meisharim of Mezirich* (Jerusalem: Rubin Mass, 2011), 37 [Hebrew].

26. Further to the letter from 1794, R. Abraham of Kalisk directed additional criticism against R. Shneur Zalman, while comparing his Hasidic path with that of their teachers: "and the honored rabbi, the beloved . . . he is asked as a person asks, etc. (see 2 Samuel 16:23) about every matter, minor or major! Explanations are not sought of the king regarding the prophets or dreams—this is not the way of Jacob to trouble [the religious authority] in trifling matters. Our old rabbis did not do so, not even concerning the needs of the public . . . Even in the time of our teacher, may the memory of the righteous be for a blessing, I did not see that they acted in this manner, that people entered and left without the beadle's [intervention]. And if they nevertheless entered for some great matter, they did so before the beginning of the prayers, and they nevertheless took care as to how and what to say, so as not to burden him. And all the tales that are related when [the Hasidim] gathered together to tell the tale—it just seems to them that this was a constant occurrence. But I know and can testify that this was not so, but only infrequently, once a year or during *Shemittah* [= the Sabbatical year, i.e., only once in seven years!], and this was not a daily occurrence" (letter from 1794, in *Peri haAretz*, ed. Zhitomer, 90–91; Hamesorah edition, 211).

This contains scathing criticism of the populist leadership of zaddikim that began to spread among the early Hasidic masters in the time when R. Menachem Mendel and R.

This critique is most intense in a third letter that R. Abraham of Kalisk wrote to R. Shneur Zalman in 1797, the year in which the *Tanya'* (also known as the Book of Intermediates) was published. Here his fundamental critique of the printing of Hasidic teachings is joined by specific criticism of R. Shneur Zalman's theoretical doctrine:

> My beloved brother . . . now the mountain is high, the distance between us is great, and I have come to write things . . . additionally, I carefully [read] the entire letter that was sent to me from there. It is evident from your letter that it went ten levels backward, and I myself was not pleased with the light of the sun that his eminence of the holy Torah brought forth. That is, to enclothe the words of the holy rabbi of Mezeritch, which are the very words of the holy rabbi, the Ba'al Shem Tov, within the holy words of R. Isaac Luria, of blessed memory. Additionally, everything goes to one place, the words of Torah separately, and the words of the wise [an allusion to R. Shneur Zalman] separately, and especially because of the danger that, due to our numerous sins, despite his trenchant words, the generation is not fit for them. Accordingly, choose unadorned language, through which the ways of fearing and loving [God] will be revealed and understood. . . . [W]e saw the Book of Intermediates [= the *Tanya'*] that his honor printed. I did not find it of especial avail to save souls, for it [= the *Tanya'*] is overburdened with thoughts, as if learning by rote. The fruits of this erudition are as the ancient difficulty [of Torah without its spirit]. But for

Abraham of Kalisk left for the Land of Israel, and to which R. Shneur Zalman was party. Such conduct was not accepted in the Maggid's circle, and it apparently began in the first years after his death. This practice that began to characterize the Hasidic leadership, and was expressed in the giving of advice and directives on material matters, was anathema to R. Abraham of Kalisk, who saw it as a deviation from the elitist spiritual path of the members of the Maggid's circle. We may conclude from this that turning Kabbalah into ethos, in terms of shifting attention from theoretical Kabbalistic doctrines to a means for personal religious revitalization, preceded, both in principle and historically, the process of popularization that characterized Hasidism as a mass movement. On the transition to leadership of the masses among the Maggid's disciples, see Rapoport-Albert, "Hasidic Movement after 1772"; Green, *Heart of the Matter*. This passage from the letter by R. Abraham of Kalisk contradicts Green's assertion about R. Menachem Mendel and R. Abraham of Kalisk, that "once in Tiberias, they had to give up on their original intent of spreading Hasidism far and wide" (150). Green seems to have confused the desire of the two to establish an elitist Hasidic community in Belorussia with the later actions taken by R. Shneur Zalman and R. Levi Isaac of Berditchev that were directed to broader audiences. I would also draw a substantive distinction between R. Shneur Zalman's leadership of his community and the public activity of R. Levi Isaac, who acted in Berditchev within the context of his position as rabbi of the community, and not as a zaddik in the spirit of the courts established, for example, by R. Elimelech of Lyzhansk and his disciples.

> those who receive [Torah properly] a single spark suffices, to be divided into several reasons. For this is the way of Torah; and an excess of oil in the lamp is, Heaven forfend, the cause of its being extinguished; man's inclination overcomes him, "day to day makes utterance" (Psalm 19:3), [saying:] see this new thing, with wisdom, discernment, and knowledge [i.e., an allusion to *Chokhmah*, *Binah*, and *Da'at*] [but] it lacks a heart, and thus [the reader] will not understand, as Elijah, of blessed memory said, "Wisdom is the heart," and through wisdom, the heart [that is, and not the intellect] understands. I call to you: "What good is money in the hand of a fool to purchase wisdom, when he has no mind?" (Proverbs 17:16). This was the practice of our masters, to take exceeding care regarding their words, to speak to the majority of the Hasidim only in the way of *musar* and to bring them into the covenant of belief in the sages. Torah talk is little but good, much is contained in little, and blessing is in that speaking of the hidden light, which will shine for him.[27]

For R. Abraham of Kalisk, R. Shneur Zalman's theoretical way is a regression, since it clothes the teachings of the Ba'al Shem Tov and the Maggid in clearly Lurianic garb. Excessive study of books of Kabbalistic thought, and likewise, the *Tanya'*, is like an excess of oil that extinguishes the lamp of inner fervor. Chabad's path is rationalist, and does not contain the understanding of the heart. The hidden light that Hasidism seeks to ignite in its followers is not the product of deep and extensive study of Kabbalistic teachings, but of short and measured Torah teachings that penetrate the heart to arouse continuous inner renewal in the life of the Hasid. With the exception of the writing tradition of the rabbis of Chabad, the great majority of the Hasidic masters remained faithful to the idea that speaking Torah is meant to invigorate man to serve the Lord with all his inner being. The attempt to present R. Abraham of Kalisk's stance, in the name of his teacher, as marginal because he opposed the printing of Hasidic books per se is not tenable, in light of his disagreement with R. Shneur Zalman's singular Hasidic path, which was, and remains, exceptional in the Hasidic world.[28] These letters prove Buber's arguments on the question of brevity. This is so, despite the weakening of this emphasis on conciseness in the years that passed since the Maggid's death due to the printing of Hasidic books in which these short teachings were collected in lengthy discussions on Torah portion. A very large part of the teachings printed in these works retained

27. Barnai, *Hasidic Letters*, 238–40.

28. R. Jacob Joseph's book is composed of homilies that are longer and more tortuous than usual. This is not surprising, in light of the fact that he served as a rabbi, but did not lead a Hasidic community of the type led by the Maggid's disciples.

features faithful to those to which R. Abraham of Kalisk subscribed. These are short teachings with the primary task of arousing the Hasidim.

The Exposition of Torah Portion of Acharey Mot in the Book *Peri haAretz*[29]

Since R. Abraham of Kalisk drew a fundamental distinction between the way of the Maggid and R. Menachem Mendel and the theoretical method of R. Shneur Zalman, I wish to examine a typical homiletical exposition from R. Menachem Mendel's *Peri haAretz* that discusses some of the ideas that R. Abraham of Kalisk mentions in his letters. From many aspects, a comparison of this homily with those characteristic of many books of early Hasidism plainly shows that R. Menachem Mendel's thought and writing are much closer to the writings of the early Hasidic masters, unlike that of R. Shneur Zalman. R. Menachem Mendel's exposition on Torah portion of *Acharey Mot* exemplifies the nature of the ethos that was fashioned in the school of the Maggid, as it was taught by R. Menachem Mendel. The book *Peri haAretz*, first published in 1814, contains the expositions of R. Menachem Mendel, who had died in 1788. This thin volume includes an important spiritual ideational precis that originated in the court of the Maggid, and in the expositions of R. Menachem Mendel, who, according to Hasidic tradition, met the Ba'al Shem Tov in his youth, by merit of his father, who was close to the founder of Hasidism. Although the homily was published as a single unit, I divided it into paragraphs in the following ideational analysis.

1. Opening

> It was asked[30] [about] the dictum "Pray for the welfare of the ruling power [since but for the fear of it, people would swallow each other alive"] (m*Avot* 3:2). The rabbi began with the verse "After the death of the two sons of Aaron [who died] when they drew too close to the presence of the Lord" (Leviticus 16:1). Rashi, of blessed memory, compared this to a physician, etc. ["What does this Scripture teach? R. Eleazar ben Azariah explained this by means of a parable: This is comparable to a sick person who was visited by a physician, who told him, 'Do not eat cold foods and do not sleep in a damp place.' Another came and told him: 'Do not eat cold foods and do not sleep in a damp place, lest you die as did so-and-so.'"] This [the latter] motivated him more than the former.

29. Following the version in *Peri haAretz*, Hamesorah edition, 76–78; I also made use of the edition published by the Peri haAretz Institute (Beitar Eilit, 2004) (emphasis added).

30. The opening wording "it was asked" (*nishal*) indicates this was not written directly by R. Menachem Mendel, but rather was committed to writing by one of his disciples.

The homily's beginning with a question on the dictum from m*Avot* seemingly teaches that this is an interpretive homily on mishnah Avot typical of the popular ethical-teachings literature on this tractate. We expressly learn from the continuation, however, that the querier casts doubt on the spiritual value of the fear of punishment that the mishnah in *Avot* extols. Referring to Rashi's interpretation of the reason for Torah's repetition of the death of Aaron's sons enables R. Menachem Mendel to declare his intent to discuss the reason for fear of punishment, as compared to the fear of sin. The first physician tells the sick person what is forbidden, while the second adds a warning, to intimidate his patient regarding the perils entailed in not following the medical instructions. The double mention of the death of Aaron's sons is therefore meant as a warning with a didactic purpose, as is typical in homiletical chastisements. The following analysis, however, will show that the importance of the homily, beyond its justification of the reason for fearing punishment, lies in revealing the new religious contents that apparently had led R. Menachem Mendel's audience to doubt the need for fear of punishment.

2. A Second Example of the Principle of Chastisement

> He explained this in the manner of the teaching of Akaviya ben Mahalale'el: "Consider three things and you will not fall into the hands of sin. Know whence you came, etc." (m*Avot* 3:1). He repeated and explicated: "Whence you came—from a putrid drop, etc." The world asks about the duplication of his words, and their answer is that what he says first is to **remind man** that he is a guest in this world, since it is customary when you first see a guest to ask him, after greeting him, where he came from, where he is going, and what are his affairs and his needs. Then he explained that it is insufficient that he is a guest, rather, all his affairs are repulsive and repulse, from when he first arrives to his return to dust. In the meantime, he put his head between great mountains [i.e., between a rock and a hard place], and will have to give an accounting to the King of kings, the Holy One, blessed be He.

The teaching ascribed to Akaviya ben Mahalale'el, which was meant to serve as a deterrent against the performance of sins, includes a duplication that here too is understood as following the above interpretation by Rashi, as a rhetorical means to intensify warning and reproach. The first warning, which parallels the directive of the first physician, is the simple mention of the transitory nature of human life: in light of the fact of his death, a person is as a guest in this world. The second warning that is analogous to the addition in what the second physician says, is meant, according to R.

Menachem Mendel, to recall the repulsiveness of life in this world and the total nullity of death, that is, to intensify the explicit intimidation that appears in the continuation of this teaching: "and where you are going—to a place of dust, worm, and maggot; and before Whom you will have to give account and reckoning, before the King of kings, the Holy One, blessed be He." This second opening, too, is characteristic of the medieval ethical-teachings literature that mentions the day of death to deter and intimidate.[31] The shift from a typical exposition of reproach to a Hasidic homily that expresses the spiritual world of the Maggid and his disciples occurs in the following passages.

3. Where One Thinks, There One Is

> But **the moral** may be understood from the repetition of his words and their order that "from whose belly came forth" (Job 38:29) [referring to God] and a garment is precious to its wearer (b*Shabbat* 10b; another veiled reference to God), for here, regarding Akaviya ben Mahalale'el, the Rabbis, of blessed memory, said: "The Temple Court was never shut against the face of any man in Israel so wise and sin-fearing as Akaviya ben Mahalale'el" [m*'Eduyot* 5:6]. The matter of fear of sin is **the fear of sin itself more than the punishment** that comes to him, as is explained several times: punishments are a remedy for the soul and cleanse it of the evil of the sin. Certainly, one must fear and be frightened of the blow itself more than from the remedy. Additionally, this is understood by every person, "a living one should take it to heart" (Ecclesiastes 7:2): since the essence of man is inwardness and his life-force, and the body is flesh and blood and his garb, apparently after the life-force departs, the body is a carcass (see *Peri haAretz*, Parashah Te*z*aveh), and from this principle you hear that **wherever a man thinks and cogitates, to which he puts his soul, his eye, and his heart, there he is, and it is named after him**. For if a person thinks of a transgression, he himself is the husk [*qelipot*] and the spirit of impurity that vivifies it and rests on it, as the Rabbis, of blessed memory, said: "a person does not commit a transgression unless a spirit of folly enters into him" (b*Sotah* 3a). As soon as sanctity and fear of Heaven departs from him, the spirit of impurity rests on him; as is known, there is nothing empty in the world. If one is not called pure, he will be called impure, impure, from the *mezikin*

31. See Avriel Bar-Levav, "Story, Ritual and Metaphor: Contemplating the Day of Death as a Spiritual Exercise and the Internal War in Jewish Ethical Literature," in *Peace and War in Jewish Culture*, ed. Avriel Bar-Levav (Jerusalem: Zalman Shazar Center, Center for the Study of Jewish Culture, Haifa University, 2006), 145–63 [Hebrew].

> [harmful forces] and the plagues of humans (see Zohar 3:51b, and *Peri haAretz*, the teaching for a Sabbath within Pesach). For no body or matter can exist without form that shapes and vivifies it, and the transgression was infused with vitality only in order to test men, the righteous. The worlds that were created, were created for the righteous. And what is the life-force of the transgression? The possibility of performing it and the pleasure derived from it. **Consequently, when man commits it [i.e., a transgression] he is the transgression itself, or by his thought there, he is the life-force of the transgression** and the plague itself of the plagues of men, that was transformed from the holy to the profane, from the pure to the impure.

R. Menachem Mendel maintains that Akaviya ben Mahalale'el's uniqueness does not lie in his famous reproach regarding the day of death, but rather in his depiction in Tractate *Eduyot* as a sage and fearing sin. For R. Menachem Mendel, this is testimony from the sources of the superiority of fear of sin over fear of punishment, that is compared to a remedy that is meant to prevent the sin by means of deterrence, and therefore is secondary to the act of the sin itself, which is the heart of the problem.[32] R. Menachem Mendel bases his explanation of the nature of sin on the dictum that became a fundamental principle in nascent Hasidism: "Where man thinks, there he is." The early Hasidic masters were troubled, more than anything, by the question of how to prevent man's detachment from the divine inwardness, from the spiritual element within him, in the wake of his immersion in mundane worldly affairs. This inwardness is evident in the life-force that maintains the body, and which is a spark of the divine above—the divine in man. The pleasure derived from transgressing, that is, from immersion in the material, whether in deed or in thought, was perceived by the Hasidic masters as lowering the divine vitality to a lower level. Lowering the original, pure spirituality to within the material world turns the holy into the secular. Instead of connecting through the body by means of the thought to the godly that sustains it, it is a "carcass." We see here the combination of (a) the worldview that tends to dualism which penetrated to the very heart of medieval Jewish thought with (b) the aspiration of Hasidic thought to overcome the dichotomy expressed in the desire to weaken the body to the greatest extent possible. In Hasidism, the principle of epistemological interiorization that, I argue, has its beginnings in the Maimonidean doctrine of Providence, became an unshakable—and unprecedented—foundation in the life of the Hasid.[33] R. Menachem Mendel uses this principle in the

32. R. Menachem Mendel thereby confirms the reason for the question.

33. See Ron Margolin, *Inner Religion: The Phenomenology of Inner Religious Life and Its Manifestation in Jewish Sources (from the Bible to Hasidic Texts)* (Jerusalem: Bar-

context of fear of sin. Fitting fear is not of punishment, but of the sin itself, of the consequent spiritual evil. In the spirit of the rabbinic dictum: "the reward of a commandment is a commandment, and the reward of a transgression is a transgression" (m*Avot* 4:2), he argues that the act of the transgression turns man himself into the transgression. His essence and life-force are seemingly painted in the colors of the transgression, for he is there. Instead of external reward and punishment, we have a typical interiorizing conception. At this point, the exposition already contains a new element. The remedy is one of thought and consciousness, by thinking of the life-force that sustains the body, as well, the Hasid can free himself from the sin of immersion in the material that detaches him from the spiritual and godly.

4. "Where Can Wisdom Be Found": The Conception of *Zimzum* and Creation in the School of the Maggid

> The truth of the matter of the creation of the husks and impurity: their root is mainly from the beginning of Creation, **from the necessity of *zimzum* and the departure of the spread of the holiness of *'Ein Sof***, and from the *zimzum* something new is created. Similarly, it is the way of any renewal to sprout, like the sprouting of a plant from the kernel and the creation of a chick from the egg. For the renewal of the transformation from the original form to the new one cannot begin until the first form will be totally lost, and the kernel must mainly consist of the beginning of the complete annihilation and loss—so, too, for the egg. Afterwards, the remnant of the primal matter is capable of change, acquiring the new form in the creation of the chick and the sprouting. When something lacks both forms, this is called *ayin*, which is the matter of *zimzum*, which is "where can wisdom be found" (Job 28:12).
>
> Like the order of creation, **in which no new revelation is possible without the return to the initial** *ayin*, as is explained elsewhere (*Peri haAretz*, Parashah Vayigash 1), is man's ability to undergo change and miracles, by reaching humility, [self-]dissolution, and *ayin*, which is wisdom.

As is asserted in the above letter by R. Abraham of Kalisk, the notion of "where can wisdom be found" (which appears a number of times in the homilies of the Maggid) was a fundamental principle in the world of the early Hasidic masters. The Ba'al Shem Tov gave an existential interpretation to the verse "I turn my eyes to the mountains; from where [*me-ayin*] will my help come?" (Psalm 121:1): "anytime when I see some [divine] withdrawal, Heaven forfend, then *me-ayin* will my help come—by my see-

Ilan University Press and Shalom Hartman Institute, 2011), 402–13 [Hebrew].

ing and understanding this, by my heart breaking and becoming *ayin*."[34] The Maggid's doctrine presumably emphasizes the idea of Creation ex nihilo [*yesh me-ayin*], but the concept of *zimzum* is not perceived here in its Lurianic sense, namely, as the formation of the *halal ha-panui* (the void), but as a metaphor for the twofold depiction of all existence, as in the Ba'al Shem Tov's parable of the partitions.[35] Paradoxically, wisdom, the source of the orderly and comprehensible reality, dwells in *ayin*; consequently, there is no void. Rather, "the whole world is filled with His glory." In the original Hasidic doctrine, wisdom is understanding the importance of the principle of humility, self-dissolution, and *ayin* and its realization in life. For the Maggid as well, the discussion of Creation and *zimzum* is not meant to provide a theoretical explanation for the formation of the worlds; it rather facilitates a positive existential way of facing the mental and universal reality. From this aspect, the Maggid's doctrine of "where can wisdom be found," as explained by R. Menachem Mendel, is the best example of Buber's assertion that Hasidism is "Kabbalah made ethos"—by the metaphorical use of Kabbalistic concepts, theoretical Kabbalah becomes a spiritual way of life. "Wisdom" here is not rationality in the usual sense of the word; it rather teaches of the imperceivable and incomprehensible factor that enables ex nihilo procreation and creation. This is a synthesis of the primal conception of ex nihilo, primal Creation that includes the kernel and chick parable and the idea of *zimzum* in its Lurianic sense in order to create a new and revolutionary meaning. This is why R. Abraham of Kalisk was taken aback by reading the *Tanya'*. He thought that R. Shneur Zalman had restored the theoretical Kabbalistic meaning and context to these fundamental Hasidic concepts. The idea of "where can wisdom be found" is a spiritual existentialist argument, and not a conceptual one. It can be called mystical-experiential, but certainly not mystical-theoretical.

Understanding "where can wisdom be found" as a religious directive reflects the Hasidic theological revolution that demolished the conclusions of the various types of Kabbalistic theosophy and called for direct communication with the divine, infinite, and imperceivable *ayin*, the *'Ein Sof*. The worship of God in nascent Hasidism was focused on *'Ein Sof* as the divine nothingness, thereby transferring the emphasis from simple devotion.

5. The Concept of *Zimzum* in Corporeality and the Sin of the Withdrawal of Sanctity

"The fiery ever-turning sword" (Genesis 3:24), God forfend, and turning from holy to profane and from pure to impure, a destruc-

34. See Moses Hayyim Ephraim of Sudylkow, *Degel Mahaneh Efrayim* (Jerusalem, 1963), *Shabbat Teshuvah*, 267.

35. See Margolin, *Inner Religion*, 414–17.

> tive husk and human ills is the way of man, for sanctity and fear of Heaven departed from him after the limitation of sanctity and its spread. [*Man*] changed into a destructive spirit of impurity and a husk, and his body became a body for the husks. He becomes a demon with a body which is harder and more material than other demons and spiritual husks. This is the fear of sin: [*the fear*] **lest he change and become the sin itself, which is a harsher blow than the punishment, which is the remedy**.

Following the application of the principle of "where man thinks, there he is" (which I call the principle of epistemological interiorization), R. Menachem Mendel asserts that fear of sin is actually a person's fear that his essence will change—from the divine spiritual essence that dwells in him by means of his life-force to a material physical essence, with all his vitality concentrated in his corporeality—which, in actuality, is the state of *z̲imz̲um*. The proper fear is not that of punishment, but of the sin of man's immersion in physicality. This would seem to reveal acute dualism that pertains to the depth of the disagreement between Scholem and Buber with which we opened this article. Since, however, the key to change is thought—the manner in which man relates to physical pleasure—it does not require the negation of physicality. When pleasure is entirely physical, man descends to the husks, but when he is capable of elevating the pleasure to its divine root and ascribe it to its divine source, the danger of descent is replaced by spiritual ascent and dwelling in sanctity. The first Hasidic masters had not completely freed themselves of the culture of mortifications and weakening the body that had been held by many Kabbalists, but they shifted the focus from physical action or inaction to the inner consciousness.[36] This passage reveals the revolutionary conception of sin held by R. Menachem Mendel and his teacher the Maggid. Sin is not action that is contrary to the will of God, as it was commonly seen in rabbinic thought (or in the present-day world of Torah scholarship). Sin is immersion in evil, in what is not divine. This idea complements the alternative view of commandment that R. Menachem Mendel sets forth in his homily on Parashah Noah, in which his definition of commandment (*mitzvah*) is derived from *tzavta* (literally, association)—connection with the divine.

36. For Buber, this is attained by means of the I-Thou relationship, and not by the instrumental I-It relationship. Obviously, this is interpretation, and the Hasidim themselves did not talk in the language of dialogic philosophy. Notwithstanding this, the change in their attitude to the vitality in pleasure as a means for bringing the divine into the life of man and the encounter with it is at the heart of the Hasidic thought typical of the school of the *Maggid* of Mezeritch.

6. Creation Ex Nihilo [Me-ayin] as Rebirth and Its Opposite, Creation Me-Ein

> This fear of sin devolves from wisdom, one who is wise, who negates himself and becomes *ayin*, facing the holy life-force to become a new creation every day, as it is said, "You are My son, I have fathered you this day" (Psalm 2:7). Consequently, he fears the sin itself, since he knows that after the negation and departure of the first form he changes, and he therefore fears. This is what the Rabbis, of blessed memory, said about Akaviya ben Mahalale'el, that he was of the level of wisdom and fear of sin, since one is drawn from the other. These are his words, which he reiterated, for first comes the simple interpretation, and afterwards, the explanation, that one comes from a putrid drop, which is after loss and annihilation—the negation of the drop's power to become a creature, as is known. And where he goes—this is the second *ayin*, to change from a pure creature to an unclean one and a husk, which is "worm and maggot." The difference between the negation of the first *ayin* and the second is that **what changes from holiness to husk is not called *ayin*, with [*the letter*] *yod*, but *En*, without the *yod***, which is the holy half-shekel. Rather, he introduces the sparks of the vitality of the [*letter*] aleph [*representing God—**Elohim***] by its expansion to the final nun [*with the numerical value of fifty, representing impurity itself, after having traversed the forty-nine "gates of impurity"*] to what remains [*i.e., beyond the pure*] and the husk.

R. Menachem Mendel's innovativeness is evident in his exegesis of the dictum by Akaviya ben Mahalale'el, "Know whence you came—from a putrid drop." Impregnation from a drop of semen is a metaphor for creation ex nihilo. In the above medieval conception, the sprouting of a seed, like the conception of the fetus, come from the rotting that the medieval thinkers viewed as immersion in *ayin*. This notion is linked here to the idea of continual rebirth as a metaphor for spiritual renewal that is symbolized in the verse (Psalm 2:7): "You are My son, I have fathered you this day." This constant rebirth always leads to one of two contradictory directions. The first is birth to sanctity from within *ayin*, and the other, birth within impurity, which is signified here by the word *en–ayin* without the intervening letter *yod*. In contrast to the Sabbatean notion of "a commandment performed through a transgression" that required the descent to impurity toward the goal of redemption, the Hasidic masters were extremely fearful of the descent to the husks, which they regarded as the very heart of sin. The principle of "where can wisdom be found" presumes the descent to *ayin*, but this is attained by the negation of the ego, and not by a plunge into total physicality and physical pleasure, that were perceived as impurity. States of descent are facts of life, because life is *ra<u>z</u>o vashov* ("dashing to and fro"; the phrase comes from Ezekiel 1:14), as is frequently stressed by R. Jacob Joseph of Polonnoye, in the name of the Ba'al Shem Tov.[37] The purpose, however, of this natural descent is the possibility of rebirth and the renewal it entails.

The emphasis placed on rebirth after every stay within *ayin* is decisive proof that this is not a quietist doctrine that strives for withdrawal into *ayin* for total annihilation of the self. The *ayin* is entered for rebirth, a new creation that is made possible by this entry. This is not a doctrine that negates life: it rather affirms life by connecting it with *ayin*.

7. Justification of the Fear of Sin as a Stage to Spiritual Fear or as a Compromise with Human Weakness

> It is said, "and you will not fall into the hands of sin," because "hands" are called love and fear. Now, there is fear, and there is fear of punishment, which are punishments and death, as the Rabbis, of blessed memory, said, that "there is no death without sin" (b*Shabbat* 55a). This fear is called outer fear, that is felt by all in the world, even among the non-Jewish nations, as it is said, "Those among Pharaoh's courtiers who feared the Lord's word" (Exodus 9:20), which is the fear of punishment, which is the fear of harm to oneself. **But the main element of fear**, of the Principal and Root of all the worlds [i.e., the Holy One, blessed be He; *Zohar Chadash* I:11b] is **called "His sovereign rule is over all"** (Psalm 103:19). For all the fears branch off from it, these are of punishments, tribulations, and death, that purge the filth [and] pollution of souls, for it is the remedy, the balm, and dressing for souls from every wound and every ailment.
>
> For the person who is good in the eyes of God, the fear of the *chi<u>z</u>onim* [i.e., all that is bad] will not seem bad and bitter to him, as the Rabbis, of blessed memory, said, "'And God found it very good' (Genesis 1:31)—this refers to death." As this is explained in the Zohar [II:149b], many times man returns [i.e., in repentance] to his Maker because of this fear, therefore it is very good. And even for the greatest of the righteous, not all times are the same: at times, one can attain true fear only by beginning with outer fear, to imagine in his mind. Since all the fears are from a single source, from it [i.e., the outer fear] he rises upward and senses the pleasantness of fear and fervor for Him, may He be blessed. Accordingly, the righteous thank and bless Him, may He be blessed, for all that He created of the punishments and tribulations. Whoever has not seen lights [i.e., the di-

37. See Margolin, *Human Temple*, 216–18.

> vine lights] in his lifetime, who knows only outer fear and fear of the loss of his body, the application of tribulations and death seems bad to him. **In truth, however, this is called "the welfare [*shelomah*] of the government [*literally, kingship*]"** [m*Avot* 3:2], because He "imposes peace [*shalom*] in His heights" (Job 25:2), **to return to Him**, as was mentioned, and also, "It shall be well [*shalom*], well with the far" (Isaiah 57:19). It [i.e., the fear of all that is evil] imparts life and balm, as was mentioned. Consequently, at any rate, **it is fitting for a person to never remove this fear from his sight, for if he merits, he will distinguish between the true kingship and it [= fear]**, and if not, Heaven forfend, he should keep away from evil and do what is good out of fear.

In this passage R. Menachem Mendel returns to the beginning of the homily and the question of the reason, for the pious who truly fear sin, for the existence of the fear of punishment that is represented in the concept of "fear of the ruling power." His answer, which is based on the rabbinic principle of "out of [performance of a commandment] not for its own sake comes [the intent] for its own sake" (b*Sanhedrin* 105b), also contains a very realistic argument concerning individuals who desire the spiritual service of the Lord, whom he calls "righteous." They, too, are not always successful in meeting the high spiritual demands that they set for themselves, and there are times when they, too, need the simple fear of death that awaits every man, whether as punishment or as spiritual catalyst. R. Menachem Mendel clearly preferred positive worship, out of the desire to adhere to God, as concern for the "welfare of the ruling power," to negative worship that is motivated by fear of tribulations and that is worship based on "fear of the ruling power." For him supreme fear is that of the loss of connection with the kingship of God, but fear of sin, too, is of importance and possesses value. This expresses the traditionalist element characteristic of R. Menachem Mendel and of many of the early Hasidic masters. Along with his innovativeness and obvious inclination for the interiorization of religious life, he opposed the tendency of his disciples to negate the rationale for more external aspects of religious life, such as fear of punishment. This was grounded in a sober assessment of the weakness of the spirit—including his and those of his fellow Hasidic masters. This awareness of the force of the physical in every individual's life is lucidly formulated in the following passage.

8. The Resolution of the Difficulty: The Essence of the Homily as Referring to the Soul

> This is the meaning of "Pray for the welfare of the ruling power," namely, **to adhere to this fear**, in any case, "since but for the fear

> of it, people would swallow each other [*literally, his fellow/friend*] alive," for **the soul is called friend**, as it is said, "your friend and your father's friend" (Proverbs 27:10), **and while still alive the husks would swallow him up**, as we said above—so that he will not become a husk and harmful like it, by being drawn after it [= the husk]. For the difference between the intellective soul and the animative soul is that the animative soul is the vital soul, that causes to grow, nourishes, and desires—all these were created for the needs of the body, which is the form and life-force of the body. This is what is said, "a beast's [*breath = spirit*] does sink down" (Ecclesiastes 3:21). By the body's elevation, all these are elevated, which is not so regarding the intellective soul, which was not created for the body. To the contrary, the body and all the animal souls were created for the intellective soul, to act through them and draw them, for them to ascend with it. Consequently, as soon as a person draws his intellective soul after bodily pleasures, then it becomes an animal soul; he is a beast, and the animal soul swallows up the life-force within them. **All the contractions [*strictness of punishments*] and lovingkindnesses come into being by the first *ẕimẕum*, for creation is possible only by contraction.** Likewise, every contraction, strictness of punishment, and death of the body and the soul—all is lovingkindness and good, for if not for fear, people would swallow each other alive, as was mentioned; and by this one draws near to the Lord.

R. Menachem Mendel concisely sets forth the distinction between the animal and intellective souls that became a fundamental element of the doctrine of his disciple and friend R. Shneur Zalman, by the former's interpretation of the phrase "people would swallow each other alive." The greatest spiritual danger facing the devout Hasid is the swallowing of his vitality, which is divine in nature, by the outer reality (*in Kabbalistic terminology, the* qelipot—*"husk"*). R. Menachem Mendel bases this on the exegesis in *Exodus Rabbah* that calls the soul "friend."[38] He combines the Kabbalistic concept of *qelipot*, the exegesis, and the phrase from Tractate *Avot* to produce a lively and instructive description of earthly life that, as it were, swallows man's soul and causes it to forget the divine source of its life-force, which is now drawn into the earthly reality. This existential state is necessary, since the entire world is a product of the initial divine contraction and has its source in *ayin*. The goal, therefore, is not to flee from the world, but to elevate it, to turn the low into the sublime. Accordingly, the justification of the fear of punishment is more than a mere compromise with weakness; it rather is a

38. "'Your friend' (Proverbs 27:10) is the Holy One, blessed be He" (*Exodus Rabbah* 27:1).

sort of bridge, one that provides an opening to the fear of sin, that is higher than it. The path to drawing close to the Lord begins with the lowly fear of punishment (which is, mainly, the fear of death and tribulations), that leads man to the positive fear of the sin of immersion in the husks and the loss of perfection—namely, the connection with the godly. This, then, is the meaning of the dictum: "Pray for the welfare of the ruling power since but for the fear of it, people would swallow each other alive."

9. Summation: Coming Full Circle and Connecting the Dictum in Avot with the Verse from Acharey Mot

> This is the meaning of "After the death of the two [*sheney*] sons of Aaron"—for every changed [*shinuy*] deaths—this is "the sons of Aaron," which is lovingkindness (*Zohar Chadash* 1:266b) "when they drew too close to the presence of the Lord"; and this is the interpretation of Rashi, the parable of the physician, etc., for whatever motivates another person not to die as did so-and-so is for the best and [for one's] welfare. The "welfare of the ruling power"—this is the unification of the Holy One, blessed be He, and His Divine Presence, as is known.
>
> This is the meaning of what the Rabbis, of blessed memory, said (*Zohar Chadash* 2:158b), that Torah exists only by means of the one who kills himself in the tent [of Torah], **who recalls all the deaths to himself, and imagines them in himself, to strengthen fear and Torah**.
>
> It is known that the observance of Torah is called *Nezach* and *Hod*, "the sons of Aaron who died when they drew too close to the presence of the Lord" (*Tiqunei Zohar*, *Tiqun* 70), as is the interpretation of the verse (Exodus 1:16): "look at the birth-stool [literally, stones]"—the Rabbis, of blessed memory, said (b*Sotah* 11b) that the thighs become as cold as stones, which is their death so that the newborn will live. The interpretation: "And the Lord spoke to Moses" (Leviticus 16:1)—this is the intellect; "after the death of the two sons of Aaron" meaning after he killed himself in the tent, as above; "when they drew too close to the presence of the Lord"—which is the Written Torah, as is known.

The fear of punishment that leads to the higher level of fear of sin, too, effects the unification of the Holy One, blessed be He, and the Divine Presence to which the wording "the welfare of the ruling power" alludes. This unification was understood in nascent Hasidism as the unification of the Israelite [*represented by the term "Divine Presence"*] and God, the aspect of *'Ein Sof*, thereby differing from the original meaning of this unification in the Kabbalistic literature.[39] Contradictory understandings of the episode of Nadab and Abihu are present from the Talmudic literature to the Zohar.[40] The ending of the homily shows that R. Menachem Mendel's stance is closer to the positive interpretation that is based on the Zoharic tradition. The death of Aaron's sons was a warning to a good purpose, and not a bad one. They "killed" themselves in the tent of Torah, that is, they knew to die in order to be born anew, to be reborn to draw closer to the Lord, and not to fall to a total nothingness. The death depicted here is a spiritual death that is necessary for spiritual renewal. "After the death of the two sons of Aaron" alludes to the change that occurs at the moment of contraction, and their change was for the purpose of attaining closeness to the Lord. The exegesis of the stones in b*Sotah* 11b teaches that in order for the infant to be born, the thighs must become as cold and hard as stones. That is, cold, which is death in minor degree, is beneficial for life. In the spirit of what is written in *Avot de-Rabbi Nathan*: "Is it your wish not to die? Die, so that you will not need to die. Is it your wish to live? Do not live, so that you may live."[41] R. Menachem Mendel interprets the death of Aaron's sons as alluding to the need for remembering the day of death, and the annihilation of the "I" that derives pleasure from physicality, for the sake of rebirth from the divine source of this pleasure.

Summation

When Gershom Scholem sought to define the ideational innovation in Hasidism, he made use of the books by R. Shneur Zalman of Liady and his successors, although he was well aware of their rejection by his peers, the disciples of the Maggid. Scholem maintained that Hasidism created a mystical psychology in which the concepts of theosophic Kabbalah became perceptible states in man's psyche. Following on the phrase coined by Buber, "Kabbalah made ethos," Scholem spoke of practical Kabbalah at its foremost, in terms of focusing on the individual's relation to his God.[42] This article enabled much greater precision on this issue, both because R. Abraham of Kalisk's substantive distinction between concentration on the individual's relation to his God and the popularization instituted by some of the Maggid's disciples emphasizes that they are not to be bound together, as Scholem did, and because the definition of this focus as mysticism hinders a full understanding of the phenomenon. Presenting nascent Hasidism, theoretically, as

39. Margolin, *Human Temple*, 234–41.

40. See Ruth Kaniel Kara-Ivanov, "Consumed by Love: The Death of Nadav and Avihu as a Ritual of Erotic Mystical Union," in *Itamar Gruenwald Festschrift*, ed. Gideon Bohak, Ron Margolin, and Ishay Rosen-Zvi, *Teuda* 26 (2014): 585–653 [Hebrew].

41. *Aboth de Rabbbi Nathan*, Version B, ed. Salomon Schechter (London, 1887), chap. 32, 36; translated as *The Fathers according to Rabbi Nathan*, trans. Antony J. Saldarini (Leiden: Brill, 1975), 193.

42. Scholem, "Hasidism: The Last Phase," 341–42.

a transition between theosophy to psychology prevents us from seeing the profound change in the conception of the religious mission of the exceptional individual, and the significant change in the purpose of Torah study, in the broad sense of the term that included philosophy and Kabbalah, in addition to the Written and Oral Law. This turn was initially alluded to in the book *Chovot haLeb̲ab̲ot*, appears in the ethical-teachings and homiletical works by several late medieval authors such as R. Elijah de Vidas (author of *Reshit Chokhmah*) and R. Isaiah Horowitz (author of *Sheney Luhot haB̲erit*), and reached its peak in nascent Hasidism. All these shared their changed attitude to theoretical study (rabbinic, philosophical, and Kabbalistic). The conception that study itself was the very heart of the religious ethos was replaced by one in which study was one of a diverse range of means to the end of the interiorization of religious life, in the broad sense of the term, and not only in the narrow ethical sense ascribed it by some scholars. Interiorization and not mysticism was emphasized, because the experiential mystical element that Moshe Idel calls the ecstatic is only one of many components. Its centrality and importance in the inner spiritual world of different individuals, as indicated by their writings, varied from one to the other.

The Maggid and his disciples were faced by the question of how to escape the spiritual death entailed in immersion within the husks. Such a fate resulted from absorption in the outer material world because it presumably was bound up with detachment from the divine life-force. How is one to experience and sense the connection with the divine source of vitality, without which life is impossible, although most of the time, due to the concerns of physical existence, the basic experience of life is that of contraction, that is evident in God's distance from the world? The spiritual problem faced by the Maggid of Mezeritch, R. Menachem Mendel, and their fellow Hasidic masters concentrated on a fundamentally existential question, while the mystical dimension was one of the ways in which they met this challenge.

It apparently was the Kabbalist Dov Baer of Mezeritch's meeting with the Ba'al Shem Tov that was responsible for such a radical change in the former's way of thinking. It caused him to shift the focal point of his life from discursive Kabbalistic life as the aim of religious life accompanied by the ascetic lifestyle of the Kabbalists to bridging the gap between the godly and the material, to the never-ending search for the paths to inner communion with God. The Maggid's way of teaching Torah was one of these paths. This is what Buber meant when he wrote in the introduction to *Tales of the Hasidim*: "for with him [= *the zaddik*] speech is an essential part of action."[43]

43. Buber, *Tales of the Hasidim*, xxi.

"His Spirit Speaks": Contextualizing the Vitebsker's Devotional Path within the Maggid's Circle

by Ariel Evan Mayse
(Stanford University)

> One who wishes to taste the words of [the Maggid's] teachings should look his disciples' books, for his spirit speaks in them and his word is on their tongue (cf. 2 Samuel 23:2). But were someone to ask me, "I would have liked to understand the Maggid's greatness and grasp his exalted level from his own interpretations of Torah—where might I find them?" I would reply, "The [sermons] of R. Mendel Vitebsker *are* those of the Maggid."[1]

RABBI MENACHEM MENDEL OF VITEBSK was a crucial figure in the history of early Hasidism. His creative and illuminating teachings, collected and published as *Peri haAretz* (1814) some years after his death, bespeak a unique mode of devotional theology. The sermons of the Vitebsker, as we shall call him, synthesize the conceptual worlds and vocabularies of Safed and Zoharic Kabbalah and elements of medieval Jewish philosophy,[2] interpreting them through the Hasidic ideas as imbibed from his teachers.[3] His

1. R. Ya'akov of Husyatin, *Ohalei Ya'akov* (Jerusalem: 2006), 86–88.

2. Identifying these earlier sources of influence and the Vitebsker's creative deployment thereof would make for a very interesting and important future study. For one interesting example, see *Peri haAretz*, vol. 1 (Beitar Illit: 2014), Parashah Lech Lecha, 60, where the Vitebsker interprets a passage from Maimonides in light of Kabbalah while admitting that the author could not have meant it in that way. All citations in the present article refer to this edition.

3. The Vitebsker refers to teachings from the BeSh"T in a few places; see, inter alia, *Peri haAretz*, vol. 2, Parshah Pinchas, 203. He rarely cites direct traditions from the Maggid, a puzzling fact mirroring the way that R. Dov Baer's sermons do not often quote teachings from his own master the BeSh"T. The Vitebsker does, however, cite a passage from *Lik-*

homilies underscore the themes of self-transcendence, contemplative and ecstatic prayer, spiritual poverty and absolute humility, and the transformative power of devotional community. Above all, however, the Vitebsker's sermons describe the worshipper's quest to unite with God, thus achieving release from the finite vessels of humanity and stepping into the infinite expanse of the ineffable Divine. His theology is hardly systematic, for it is neither cohesive nor coherent and it is pitted with many unresolved tensions. But the picture that emerges from these homilies is one of a remarkably intense Jewish mystic that suffered no mediocrity.

The Vitebsker's sermons also afford a unique perspective on the school of his teacher R. Dov Baer Friedman (d. 1772), better known as the famed Maggid or "Preacher" of Mezeritch.[4] The Vitebsker came to Mezeritch at some point in the 1760s and seems to have been among the elder members of the Maggid's circle. The Vietbsker also served as a teacher to his younger colleagues R. Abraham of Kalisk and R. Shneur Zalman of Liady, both of whom had journeyed to Mezeritch from White Russia as well. The impact of the Vitebsker's thought on these two figures was quite significant.[5]

The Vitebsker led his own community in White Russia after the Maggid's death, and he continued to do so after moving to the land of Israel together with Rabbi Abraham of Kalisk in 1777 and a small number of followers. The Vitebsker attempted to maintain control of his Hasidim through a series of letters, offering them spiritual guidance and assuring them of his sustained attention even from afar.[6] In the Holy Land, this band of Hasidim and fellow-travelers founded an enigmatic devotional fellowship. Charting the teachings of the Vitebsker and his place in the contours of this mystical community, which endured for some years after his death, are the subject of the present volume.

The Vitebsker's homilies reveal the sustained influence of the Maggid of Mezeritch, although he rarely refers to R. Dov Baer explicitly. In fact, the Vitebsker's sermons were so similar in thrust and style o those of the

---

kutei Amarim (Korets: 1781), a work that he could have seen either in its printed form or as a manuscript. See *Peri haAretz*, vol. 2, Parashah Korach, 174–75, likely based *Maggid Devarav leYa'akov*, no. 123, ed. Rivkah Schatz-Uffenheimer (Jerusalem: Magnes Press, 1976), 209. But similar images appear in *Peri haAretz*, vol. 2, *Acharey Mot*, 45–46, without any reference to the teachings of the Maggid. Cf. *Maggid Devarav leYa'akov*, ed. Schatz-Uffenheimer, no. 60, 91.

4. See Ariel Evan Mayse, "Beyond the Letters: The Question of Language in the Teachings of Rabbi Dov Baer of Mezeritch," (PhD diss., Harvard University, 2015).

5. For a more personal reflection on this bond, see the letter printed in *Likkutei Amarim-Tanya'* (Brooklyn: Kehot Publication Society, 1998), iggeret ha-kodesh, ch. 27, 145b–147b.

6. Future research comparing the epistles to his printed sermons is needed to demonstrate the extent to which these letters may reveal a different accent of the Vitebsker's theology.

Maggid that their works were confused with one another by later printers.[7] But the Vitebsker was no mere carbon copy of his master. His teachings are original, innovative, and often quite inscrutable. Thus situated as a creative disciple of the Maggid and the teacher of R. Shneur Zalman of Liady and R. Abraham of Kalisk, the Vitebsker offers a critical view into the formative debates that characterized the emergent Hasidic ethos as Hasidism transformed from small groups of elites into a mass movement.

Moshe Hallamish has suggested that the sermons of the Vitebsker were quite close to those of the Maggid, whereas the homilies and theology of his colleague and disciple R. Shneur Zalman reveal a very different sort of Kabbalistic inflection.[8] I will argue, however, that this framing requires some nuance. On some important issues, the teachings of the Vitebsker and R. Shneur Zalman are much closer to one another than either are to the sermons of the Maggid of Mezritsh. R. Shneur Zalman's theology does differ significantly from the Vitebsker's teachings. It may do so, however, not because of R. Shneur Zalman's inclination toward the intricacies of Kabbalah, but because he held a unique vision for the mode of leadership and the strict social hierarchy that came to define his Hasidic community. In this matter his approach, I believe, represents a clear departure from *both* the Vitebsker and the Maggid. Finally, I hope to demonstrate that R. Shneur Zalman actively tempered elements of the Vitebsker's teachings, restraining devotional postures that he found to be too extreme in the realms of theology, spiritual service, or the social sphere.

I shall illustrate these alternative models of influence and affinity by highlighting a few issues in the teachings of the Vitebsker. We will examine them with an eye to his place vis-à-vis the Maggid and the Mezritsh circle, and the works of R. Shneur Zalman of Liady in particular.[9] This

7. See *Likkutei Amarim* (Lemberg: 1911), reprinted with the correct attribution as *Sefer Likkutei Amarim* (Jerusalem: Shuvi Nafshi, 2009). Among the introductory materials included in the 1911 printing is a "bill of sale" (*shetar mekhirah*) that establishes the origin of the manuscript in Safed, where R. Menachem Mendel's teachings had apparently written down by one of his close students. If this manuscript was indeed purchased in Safed, it may represent a bundle of the Maggid's teachings taken by the Vitebsker when he moved to Israel; see Zeev Gries, *The Book in Early Hasidism: Genres, Authors, Scribes, Managing Editors and Its Review by Their Contemporaries and Scholars* (Tel Aviv: Ha-Kibbuts ha-Me'uhad, 1992), 111–12n11, 118n83 [Hebrew]; and Mayse, "Beyond the Letters," 69–70. Similar confusion exists between the Vitebsker's homilies and the sermons of Rabbi Abraham "the Angel," the Maggid's son (d. 1776), to whom several of the initial sermons in *Peri haAretz* are also attributed.

8. See the article by Hallamish reprinted in the present collection.

9. My remarks here focus on devotional issues of worship and service rather than points of cosmology or metaphysics, such as the nature of *zimzum*, the mythic account of God forming the world through Torah, or the nature and ideational core of the Scripture given through Revelation. Additional research is needed to take up these complementary questions.

angle will provide a new set of data points for the study of dispirit spiritual streams and theological currents among the key figures in the Maggid's school whose teachings shaped the course of Hasidism.[10]

Devequt and the Commandments

The quest for *devequt* is the devotional heart of Vitebsker's mystical path. This emphasis surely does not make him unique, but R. Menahem Mendel's fiery, impassioned descriptions of this ecstatic state reveal his theological creativity and intensity. In the works of some early Hasidic figures, the term *devequt* may refer to a heightened sense of God's presence in the physical realm, an expansive awareness of the Divine in all moments, or even an intensified acceptence of the "fear of heaven" (*yirat shamayim*).[11] But the Vitebsker consistently portrays *devequt* as nothing less than absolute and unmitigated unity with God.[12] He calls the worshipper to cultivate a burning desire for God when performing the commandments, withdrawing from all external stimuli and focusing the entirety of his being into contemplation of the Divine:

> When you enter with all of yourself into some holy deed, be it a commandment, [*studying*] Torah, or prayer, with total attachment (*devequt gamur*), so that your initial connection to the physical is stripped away and you feel nothing at all—this is called "removing the defiled garments and wearing robes" (Zechariah 3:4). You are now enclothed in the spirit of holiness (*be-ru'ah kedushah*).
>
> Become cloaked in the words (*teivot*) of Torah and prayer, fulfilling [*the verse*]: "go into the ark (*teivah*), you and all of your house" (Genesis 7:1). Devote the totality of your being into nullify-

---

10. In this way my work dovetails with the recent studies of Arthur Green, "Around the Maggid's Table: Tsaddik, Leadership and Popularization in the Circle of Dov Baer of Miedzyrzec," *Zion* 78 (2013): 73–106 [Hebrew]. See also Tsippi Kauffman, *In All Your Ways Know Him: The Concept of God and Avodah be-Gashmiyut in the Early Stages of Hasidism* (Ramat-Gan: Bar-Ilan University Press, 2009) [Hebrew]; and idem, "Typology of the Tsaddik in the Teachings of R. Abraham the Angel," *Kabbalah* 33 (2015): 239–72 [Hebrew].

11. Mendel Piekarz, *Between Ideology and Reality: Humility, Ayin, Self-Negation and Devekut in the Hasidic Thought* (Jerusalem: Bialik Institute, 1994), 154 [Hebrew]; Gershom Scholem, "*Devekut*, or Communion with God," in *The Messianic Idea in Judaism and Other Essays on Jewish Spirituality* (New York: Schocken, 1995), 203–227; Rivkah Schatz-Uffenheimer, *Hasidism as Mysticism: Quietistic Element in Eighteenth-Century Hasidic Thought*, trans. Jonathan Chipman (Princeton and Jerusalem: Princeton University Press, 1993), esp. 21–79.

12. Rather than distinguishing between *gadlut* and *katnut* ("expansive" or "diminished" consciousness), the Vitebsker is more interested in distinguishing *devequt ha-amiti* from the lower stages of devotional attunement; for example, see *Peri haAretz*, vol. 1, Vayakhel-Pekkudei/Parah , 408–9.

> ing your previous senses (*hargashotav ha-rishonim*). This is called absolute unity (*achdut gamur*) with the blessed One.[13]

This beautiful passage builds on the famous Hasidic teaching instructing the worshipper to enter fully and completely into a word of prayer (*teivah*).[14] This focused commitment to the aural resonance of the liturgy envelops the seeker in the sacred ark (also *teivah*) of his spoken words of prayer. The Vitebsker is claiming that in worship one must become so wrapped up in performing a sacred deed—including, but not limited to, holy forms of language—that he becomes divested from the world. Communion with God, not an encounter but the process of merging into the Divine, requires the worshipper to sever any connection with the material or phenomenal realm.

Two elements of this text bear further comment. First, the Vitebsker suggests that *devequt* involves a kind of spiritual death in which the senses melt away.[15] This is true even of the very first stages of the ladder of ascent that leads to ineffable rapture. Reimagining certain Jewish rituals and liturgical units (such as *tachanun* and the accompanying confession) as spiritualized death has long been a feature of Kabbalah.[16] However, the Vitebsker strikingly extends this to all *mitzvot*, foregrounding spiritual death as a definitional element and necessary prerequisite for *devequt* in all sacred deeds. The worshipper must be transformed into a sanctified vessel for divine energy by severing all connection to the material world. This entails experiencing the physical sensations of physical death, thus shattering attachment to the body and even the perceived self, then becoming reborn anew in God.[17]

---

13. *Peri haAretz*, vol. 1, Parashah Vayeshev, 144–45. Reflecting the devotional tenor of these homilies, I have translated them from third person into second person. See Arthur Green, "On Translating Hasidic Homilies," *Prooftexts* 3 (1983): 63–72.

14. This teaching is attributed variously to the Ba'al Shem Tov and the Maggid. See the translations in Arthur Green and Barry W. Holtz, *Your Word is Fire: The Hasidic Masters on Contemplative Prayer*, second revised edition, with Ariel Evan Mayse (Nashville: Jewish Lights Publishing, 2017), 41–42.

15. See his remarks in *Peri haAretz*, vol. 2, Parashah Korach, 66–81.

16. Michael Fishbane, *The Kiss of God: Spiritual and Mystical Death in Judaism* (Seattle: University of Washington Press, 1994); Elliot R. Wolfson, "Weeping, Death, and Spiritual Ascent in Sixteenth-Century Jewish Mysticism," in *Death, Ecstasy, and Other Worldly Journeys*, ed. John J. Collins and Michael Fishbane (Albany: State University of New York Press, 1995), 209–47; idem, *Alef, Mem, Tau: Kabbalistic Musings on Time, Truth, and Death* (Berkeley and Los Angeles: University of California Press, 2006), 156–74; Isaiah Tishby, "Prayer and Devotion in the Zohar," in *Essential Papers on Kabbalah*, ed. Lawrence Fine (New York: New York University Press, 1995), 341–99.

17. See the Vitebsker's surprising usage of Psalm 2:7 ("You are My son; this day I give birth to you") in *Peri haAretz*, vol. 2, aharei mot, 48. See also Arthur Green and Ariel Evan Mayse, "'The Great Call of the Hour': Hillel Zeitlin's Yiddish Writings on Yavneh," In Geveb (March 2016), accessed April 13, 2016.

The second point is the Vitebsker's stress on the commandments as crucial tools for attaining the ecstatic state of *devequt*. The Vitebsker does not advocate, as some scholars have suggested, spiritualizing the commandments because such deeds are fundamentally incompatible with in favor of inner service.[18] In the continuation of the sermon quoted earlier, we read:

> The garments of the commandments, which surround and enclose you, for you are within them, unite you to God without any interruptions, as it says, "You have spread your wings on your servant" (Ruth 3:9). It is this garment that unites [you with God], since Torah and the commandments are truly divinity (*Elohut mamash*), as is known. You unite with the blessed One by entering into them, tasting something of the world to come.[19]

The *mitzvot* and nomian structures are themselves are the spiritual link between the human being and God. *Devequt* is possible in part because there is an element of the Divine that dwells within the human form, but the span between the sacred realm and finite world may only be truly breached through studying Torah and performing *mitzvot*. These sacred deeds transform the worshipper and refine as the cosmos by allowing the divinity within to shine forth.[20]

But the unitive power of the commandments is by no means automatic. Rote worship, says the Vitebsker, has no power. To perform the commandments without *devequt* is essentially meaningless, for "all Torah and *mitzvot* are of no avail to a person if, God forbid, they are done without *devequt*."[21] Indeed, the Vitebsker's teachings include fierce polemics against non-devotional study and religious practice.[22] He even argues that without self-transcendence and awe, the commandment actually becomes the most idolatrous of deeds when so performed. It corporealizes the Divine without leading to uplift or illumination, thus dragging God's vitality further into the debauched material realm.[23]

18. See Rivkah Schatz Uffenheimer, *Hasidism as Mysticism: Quietistic Elements in Eighteenth Century Hasidic Thought*, trans. Jonathan Chipman (Princeton and Jerusalem: Princeton University Press and Magnes Press, 1993), esp. 113–19; and the rebuttal by Jerome Gellman, "The Figure of Abraham in Hasidic Literature," *The Harvard Theological Review* 91, no. 3 (1998): 291–92. Here we should recall the important study of Naftali Loewenthal, "The Apotheosis of Action in Early Chabad," Daat 18 (1987): v–xix. See more broadly, Daniel C. Matt, "The Mystic and the *Mitzvot*," Jewish Spirituality from the Bible through the Middle Ages, ed. Arthur Green (New York: Crossroad, 1986), 367–404.

19. *Peri haAretz*, vol. 1, Parashah Vayeshev, 145.

20. See ibid., vol. 2, Pesach/*Sefirat haOmer*, 25–26; and ibid., vol. 2, Parashah Naso, 119, interpreting Psalm 92:10.

21. Ibid., vol. 1, Parashah Ki Tissa, 391.

22. Ibid., vol. 2, Parashah Devarim/Shabbat Chazon, 255–58.

23. Ibid., vol. 1, Parashah Noach, 32–33.

All sacred actions must be accompanied by inner desire and longing for God, for this intent alone distinguishes between divine service and idol worship. This element of his religious ethos conforms with the spiritualist reading suggested by Rivkah Schatz-Uffenheimer, but the Vitebsker takes pain to assert that contemplation on its own is not enough.[24] The *mitzvot qua* physical deeds are essential for escaping—and transforming—the intractable corruption of the corporeal world, since "the physical only becomes purified through the performance of the commandments."[25] Cultivating knowledge and even sacred wisdom is sufficient. The Vitebsker argues that absorbing the correct intellectual tenets or theological postulates will not necessarily bring the worshipper to ethical or moral perfection. In true Hasidic fashion, he notes that even scholars may become scoundrels. Only fulfilling the precepts of Torah by means of physical deeds frees the worshipper free from ulterior motivations and self-interest. He illustrates this point with a beautiful image: just as the heat of a forge burns away the impurity of metal, so do the fires of *devequt*—as expressed in sacred deeds—cleanse the worshipper of any self-interest.[26]

The teachings of the Vitebsker, as do those of R. Shneur Zalman of Liady, underscore the necessity of sacred deeds to a far greater degree than the sermons of the Maggid. The latter uniformly embraced sacred language as a vehicle of *devequt*, but his attitude toward physical actions of all types was rather complicated. While the Vitebsker and R. Shneur Zalman may have been responding to their teacher's ambivalence toward physical deeds, they did so in very different ways. R. Shneur Zalman consistently emphasizes the power of the commandments to bring the light of the transcendent and infinite Divine (*'Ein Sof*) into the physical world.[27] He suggests that this power, though augmented by intention, remains even if the *mitzvot* are performed without the fiery devotion demanded by the Vitebsker. If my reading is correct, R. Shneur Zalman's insistence on the independent efficacy of the commandments and their ability to invest *this* world with the light of *'Ein Sof* can be read as a departure from and even a polemic against the path of the Vitebsker. He may even have been responding to the sentiment behind some of the Vitebsker's trenchant condemnations of non-devotional study and prayer. This criticism, conceivably aimed at the Mitnaggedim, was also anathema to R. Shneur Zalman's path.

Some elements of Vitebsker's take on *devequt* and the role of the *mitzvot* differ from that of his teacher. The erotic dimensions of the Vitebsker's

24. See also ibid., vol. 1, Parashah Vayeshev, 142–43.

25. Ibid., vol. 2, Parashah Naso, 115.

26. Ibid., vol. 2, Parashah Devarim/Shabbat Chazon, 252.

27. *Likkutei Amarim-Tanya', Sefer shel Beinonim*, ch. 23, fol. 28a; ibid, ch. 49, fol. 70a; ibid, ch. 41, fol. 56a–58a; ibid, ch. 38-39, 51a–54a; and cf. *Kuntres Acharon*, ch. 1, fol. 153b.

devequt as loving communion with God fostered by intense yearning, are quite in keeping with much of Kabbalah and early Hasidism.[28] But this amorous turn is unlike the tenor of the Maggid's sermons, in whose works the metaphor of God and Israel as lovers is nearly absent. Such musings are more characteristic of his other disciples, including R. Shneur Zalman of Liady. Moreover, the Vitebsker's extreme descriptions of mystical ecstasy are not characteristic of the Maggid's teachings.[29] Although terms like *devequt* and even *achdut* appear in the Maggid's sermons, the notion of becoming fully incorporated into the divine expanse (and especially *hitkolelut* and its various verb and noun forms) is significantly more prominent in the sermons of R. Shneur Zalman.[30] And the Vitebsker's meditations on mystical extinction and spiritual death are a departure from the teachings from the Maggid and different than those of R. Shneur Zalman; for the latter, the journey into the divine nothing (*ayin*) from which all change and transformation proceeds is described not as death but as a journey into the beneficent beyond.[31]

The Vitebsker emphasizes the necessary power of performing the *mitzvot*, but he explores the question of whether service of God can exist outside of their boundaries.[32] The idea that the patriarchs fulfilled the commandments in spiritual form, either through simple meditation or by means of ordinary deeds infused with sacred attention, is a common Hasidic trope adopted from classical rabbinic sources. It appears in the Vitebsker's teachings as well, but in several passages he combines it with a rather distinct notion that the *mitzvot* are a method of attaining a spiritual consciousness (and experience). This definition extends far beyond the typical notion of

28. On the broader dimensions of erotic love and gender imagery in Jewish mysticism, see the differing evaluations: Moshe Idel, *Kabbalah and Eros* (New Haven, CT: Yale University Press, 2005), esp. 53–178; Elliot R. Wolfson, *Circle in the Square: Studies in the Use of Gender in Kabbalistic Symbolism* (Albany: State University of New York Press, 1995), 1–78; Yehuda Liebes, "Zohar and Eros," *Alpayim* 9 (1994): 67–119 [Hebrew]; Arthur Green, "Intradivine Romance: The Song of Songs in the *Zohar*," in *Scrolls of Love: Ruth and the Song of Songs*, ed. Peter S. Hawkins and Lesleigh Cushing Stahlberg (New York: Fordham University Press, 2006), 214–27; and Melila Hellner-Eshed, *A River Flows From Eden: The Language of Mystical Experience in the Zohar*, trans. Nathan Wolski (Stanford: Stanford University Press, 2009), 190–203. See also Peter Eli Gordon, "The Erotics of Negative Theology: Maimonides on Apprehension," *Jewish Studies Quarterly* 2, no. 1 (1995): 1–38.

29. Cf. Mayse, "Beyond the Letters," 367–69.

30. See Leah Orent, "Mystical Union in the Writings of the Hasidic Master, R. Shneur Zalman of Liady," *Studies in Spiriutality* 18 (2008): 61–93.

31. See *Maggid Devarav leYa'akov*, ed. Schatz-Uffenheimer, no. 177, 275–76.

32. See Arthur Green, *Devotion and Commandment: The Faith of Abraham in the Hasidic Imagination* (Pittsburgh: Hebrew Union College Press and University of Pittsburgh Press, 2015), 16–24.

cut-and-dry precepts or obligations, even going beyond many kabbalistic attempts to attribute meaning to the various commandments:

> When you journey from strength to strength, ascending higher and higher, you may come to the root of Torah and the *mitzvot*. This is "I am YHVH your God" (Exodus 20:2)—the undifferentiated unity of the infinite One (*ha-achdut pashut ve-ein sof*). When you stand there, the wings of all the *mitzvot* and statutes are let down (*terapeinah*).[33] You have nullified the Evil Inclination, standing above and before (*le-ma'alah ve-kodem*) the beginning of Creation.[34]

When one ascends to the greatest heights of mystical contemplation, says the Vitebsker, one truly moves beyond the confines of the *mitzvot*. In this place of utter and pure unity is reached, the menaing of such nomian formulations melts away. In the moments of absolute rapture, then, the worshipper can step into the realm before Creation and in achieving this go to a place where the *mitzvot* become irrelevant. Thus, the Vitebsker's unique take on the commandments emerges in his description of their ultimate goal (*telos*): they deliver the mystic into the pre-Creation—pre-Revelation—realm of divine oneness in which even the precepts of Torah melt away.[35]

I believe that this text should not be misconstrued as suggesting an antinomian stance vis-à-vis the commandments, for the *mitzvot* are essential

33. Referring to Ezekiel 1:24: "And when they went, I heard the noise of their wings like the noise of great waters, like the voice of the Almighty, a noise of tumult like the noise of a host; when they stood, they let down their wings." In rabbinic literature it is often negatively associated with laxity in performing the law; see b*Bekhorot* 5b.

34. *Peri haAretz*, vol. 1, Parashah Toldot, 101.

35. It is thus noteworthy that the Vitebsker invokes the notion that God is in need of human deeds in order to uplift the fallen *Shekinah*; see vol. 2, Parashah Korach, 158–60. Cf. *Maggid Devarav leYa'akov*, ed. Schatz-Uffenheimer, no. 118, 192. R. Shneur Zalman, by contrast, uses the phrase *tsorekh gevo'ah* (lit. "supernal need") in reference to the worshipper directing his thought an action toward God alone; see, for example, *Likkutei Amarim-Tanya'*, ch. 10. Cf. *Torah Or* (Brooklyn: Kehot, 2001), Parashah Terumah, fol. 80a, where he claims that while God is sustained by Israel through the commandments which illuminate the *sefirot*, but he insists that this fact does not reflect a divine need per se. This notion of God's need for the commandments, often found in Hasidic sources, is rooted in Ramban's comments to Exodus 29:46. See Elliot R. Wolfson, "Mystical Rationalization of the Commandments in *Sefer ha-Rimmon*," *Hebrew Union College Annual* 59 (1988): 223–35; Morris M. Faierstein, "God's Need for the Commandments in Medieval Kabbalah," in *Jewish Customs of Kabbalistic Origin: Their History and Practice* (Boston: Academic Studies Press, 2013), 97–114; and Arthur Green, "God's Need for Man: A Unitive Approach to the Writings of Abraham Joshua Heschel," *Modern Judaism* 35, no. 3 (2015): 247–61. For Rabbi Shneur Zalman's deployment of the term *tsorekh gevo'ah* in classical rabbinic literature, see b*Menahot* 64a.

for bringing the worshipper to this heightened stage of consciousness.[36] It is thus the nomian performance of ritual obligations that leads the seeker into the supra-legal realm of devotion and religious ecstasy.[37] But teachings such as this offer fascinating picture of religious practice as leading the mystic toward a divine vantage point that reveals the commandments to be nothing more than a way of suppressing humankind's basest carnal instincts and rising beyond the physical. It is not surprising, then, that the Vitebsker elsewhere describes the *mitzvot* as a post-Edenic necessity. Everything became more grossly corporeal and physical after Adam and Eve were banished from Garden, and thus sacred deeds became necessary in order to bridge the human and divine realms.[38] The Vitebsker also notes that the *mitzvot* are *toldot* (i.e., the offspring or a derivative class) of the true essence of divine service.[39] The commandments are a means of attaining the pre-Creation moment, allowing the worshipper to reclaim the experience of Sinai and thus relive the self-effacement that characterized the theophany.[40] This ascent, or, more precisely, the inward journey, into the unity beyond the commandments and beyond the *sefirot* is a constant theme in the Vitebsker's teachings.

Service through the Phsyical

The Vitebsker's sermons have a striking ascetic thrust. In this way his teachings mirror those of the Maggid and may have informed the sermons of R. Shneur Zalman, but the Vitebsker stakes out a more extreme position

36. For an anomian reading of the certain of the Vitesbker's teachings, see Shaul Maggid, *Hasidism Incarnate: Hasidism, Christianity, and the Construction of Modern Judaism* (Stanford: Stanford University Press, 2015), 51–80. It should be noted, however, that the Vitebsker suggests that *devequt* and connection to God leads to a supererogatory performance of the commandments, especially of those in the interpersonal dimension. For recent reconsiderations of Hasidic sources arguing for a more integrated reading of the relationship between halachah and spirituality, see Ariel Evan Mayse, "The Ever-Changing Path: Visions of Legal Diversity in Hasidic Literature," *Conversations* 23 (2015): 84–115; and Maoz Kahana and Ariel Evan Mayse, "Three Models of Hasidic Halakhah: Reappraising the Interface of Spirit and Law," *AJS Review* 41.2 (2017): 375–408.

37. This attitude seems to support the argument that Kabbalists often sough to push beyond the inherent duality of a legal or moral system, reaching toward a realm in which nomian dichotomies fall away; see Elliot R. Wolfson, *Venturing Beyond: Law & Morality in Kabbalistic Mysticism* (Oxford: Oxford University Press, 2006), esp. 186–285.

38. *Peri haAretz*, vol. 1, Parashah Vayezey, 114–15.

39. Ibid., vol. 1, Parashah Noach, 43. Here the Vitebsker seems to be cleverly reinterpreting the rabbinic division of certain legal precepts into primary (*avot*) and secondary (*toldot*) categories; see m*Shabbat* 7:2 and m*Bava Kamma* 1:1; and cf. the extensive commentary in this edition of *Peri haAretz* correlating *toldot* to generativity See the extensive commentary to Parashah Noach in this volume correlating *toldot* to generativity.

40. Ibid., vol. 2, Parashah Behar, 89–98.

than either of them.[41] The Vitebsker's resounding denial of the material realm, and of physical pleasure in particular, is unequivocal. He refers to the world as saturated with divinity, in keeping with the teachings of Hasidism, but the Vitebsker portrays humankind as terminally poised to become ensnared in the material and increasing the *qelipot* that obscure this sacred energy.[42] Humanity seems to have little chance of becoming freed from the material, for the physical is precarious as the sword of Damocles looming over all spiritual aspirations.[43] An individual who is engrossed in this world corrupts the sacred vitality of his *middot*,[44] and following earthly desires makes him subject to his "animal soul" (*nefesh habehemit*). One subjected to the whims of these carnal appetites is nothing more than a beast in human form.[45] Underscoring that *devequt* requires eradicating all attachment to this world, the Vitebsker invokes the image attributed to the Ba'al Shem Tov: the bond between two pieces of metal can only be forged if the surfaces are totally effaced.[46] The ego, and, more fundamentally, any strand of connection to the physical, represents an intractable barrier between the worshipper and God.[47] Only through constantly striving to transcend the confines of one's physical body can the uprush of *devequt* be attained.

This aspect of the Vitebsker's thought is complicated by the fact that he does not appear to be advocating monastic withdrawal from the world. Rather, he emphasizes that the worshipper must interpret everything that happens to him (and around him) as a divinely-ordained message. This requires one to be focused quite intensely on the happenings of the world as well as the individual people in his community, albeit without any attachment to the sense or physical pleasures.[48] Given this spiritual ideal, it comes as no surprise that the Vitebsker gave up all material comfort in undertaking the journey to Israel, where he and his community lived a life of fervent devotion amid abject poverty. Indeed, in one passage he remarks that the Land of Israel, like Torah and the World to Come, is

41. On this point his sermons differ from the world-affirming posture voiced by Rabbi Menachem Nahum of Chernobyl, and are even more extreme than the approach of R. Ze'ev Wolf of Zhitomir, who was skeptical but ultimately embraced the imperative to serve God through eating and drinking. See also Kauffman, *In All Your Ways*, passim.

42. *Peri haAretz*, vol. 2, Parashah Naso, 17–19.

43. Ibid., vol. 1, Parashah Vayezey, 110–11.

44. Ibid., vol. 2, Parashah Shelach, 139–45.

45. Ibid., vol. 2, Parashah Behar, 91. See also ibid, vol. 2, Parashah Acharey Mot, 53, where the *nefesh habehemi* is contrasted with the *nefesh hasikhli*. Of course, this repercussive term has a central place in R. Shneur Zalman's theology of the *beinoni*.

46. Ibid., vol. 1, Parashah Ki Tissa, 389–90.

47. For this reason physical suffering can be positive, since it breaks one's attachments to the material realm and purifies the soul; see ibid., vol. 1, Parashah Vayigash, 210–11; ibid, vol. 2, Parashah Shelach, 139–45.

48. Ibid., vol. 1, Parashah Vayeẕey, 114–15.

beyond the *middot* and therefore cannot be attained through any element of physicality.[49]

The abject grotesqueness of the physical world and his unabiding fear of even the commandments devolving into corporealizations of God did not lead the Vitebsker to eschew the idea of serving the Divine by means of ordinary deeds. This path of "knowing God in all one's ways" is called a lower form of divine Wisdom (*Chokhmah tat'a*), a type of service of modeled by the patriarchs as well as in the famous exegesis of Enoch the Shoemaker.[50] Through ordinary deeds, he suggests, one may cleave to *Shekinah* and, through engaging with divine Wisdom even in this diminished form, eventually come to realize that the sacred divine vitality amid the physical is sustained by an endless reservoir of unknowable—and indeed ineffable—transcendent Wisdom.

As in all realms of service, including the commandments, the worshipper must connect the two realms and thus unify the blessed Holy One and *Shekinah*. Yet the same deed—for example, eating and drinking—can have spiritual benefit or negative consequences entirely depending on intention.[51] There is no such thing as an empty, meaningless act—all deeds are either totally holy or absolutely impure. There can be no middle ground, for even seemingly discretionary actions are either truly sacred or truly profane.[52]

The Vitebsker's distrust of the material often appears in the context of his disdain of divine anthropomorphism.[53] This issue seems not to have troubled the Ba'al Shem Tov or the Maggid, but rarely in *Peri haAretz* do we find the parables of the parent and child that characterize the sermons of these earlier Hasidic figures.[54] In one case where he does invoke the tender image of father and son, the Vitebsker eviscerates the metaphor of any trace of humanity: An earthly parent receives joy or pleasure for watching

49. Ibid., vol. 2, Parashah Shelach, 150. On the *middot*, see below.

50. Ibid., vol. 2, Pesach/Sefirat haOmer, 20–22. On Enoch the Shoemaker in Hasidism and Kabbalah, see Moshe Idel, "Enoch was a Sandal-Maker," *Kabbalah* 5 (2000): 265–86 [Hebrew]; and idem, *The Angelic World: Apotheosis and Theophany* (Tel Aviv: Yediot Aharonot, 2008), ch. 4 [Hebrew].

51. *Peri haAretz*, vol. 2, Parashah Vayikrah/*Shabbat haChodesh*, 7–13; ibid., Parashah Shelach, 147–48.

52. Ibid., vol. 2, Pesach/Sefirat haOmer, 19.

53. See ibid., vol. 2, Parashah Vayyiqra/*Shabbat haChodesh*, 7–13.

54. This too seems to have been an element shared by the Vitebsker and R. Shneur Zalman that distinguishes them from their teacher the Maggid; see *Likkutei Amarim-Tanya'*, sha'ar ha-yichud ve-ha-emunah, ch. 10, fol. 87a–b. See also Avinoam J. Stillman, "Transcendent God, Immanent Kabbalah: Polemics and Psychology in the Hasidic Teachings of R. Avraham haMalakh," *Be-Ron Yahad: Studies in Jewish Law and Theology in Honor of Nehemia Polen*, ed. Ariel Evan Mayse and Arthur Green (Boston: Academic Studies Press, forthcoming).

his child, but such terms have absolutely no meaning when applied God.[55] The Vitebsker's profound abstraction of the Divine complicates our previous description of God's need for human action, for he claims that the Divine can only give and *cannot* ever receive. This is not the answer that one generally finds in the Maggid's school, where descriptions abound of how a vulnerable God in need of human service are grounded in the loving divine act of self-limitation (*ẕimẕum*).[56] The Vitebsker even claims that the famous Talmudic maxim of the cow longing for her calves to suckle, frequently deployed in Hasidic as a metaphor for God's desire for Israel's service, would impugn divine perfection if applied to God.[57] In painting a theological portrait that is largely consistent with the abstract deity of the philosophers as well as dynamic, living God of the Kabbalisits, the Vitebsker shows that his primary devotional focus rests upon the ineffable and infinite expanse toward which *Keter*—the most elusive and transcendent of the *sefirot*—can only gesture.

The Zaddik

The Vitebsker's teachings on the concept of the zaddik follow the Kabbalistic descriptions of pious, sanctified individuals that are bound to the spiritual vitality of the cosmos and whose words and deeds shake the heavens.[58] Rarely in the Vitebsker's sermons is there any suggestion that the zaddik functions as a communal leader.[59] His zaddik is a dynamic figure

55. Ibid., vol. 1, Parashah Lech Lecha, 58–59.

56. See, for example, the striking but not atypical image of a feminine (i.e., receptive) God in the source translated in Arthur Green, *Speaking Torah: Spiritual Teachings from around the Maggid's Table*, with Ebn Leader, Ariel Evan Mayse, and Or Rose (Woodstock, VT: Jewish Lights, 2013), vol. 2, 150–51.

57. Such teachings stand in tension with homilies in which the Vitebsker asserts that the cosmos exists to fulfill a divine need. See *Peri haAretz*, vol. 2, Korach, 155–160. He describes the love between God and man that is possible because of the way the cosmos occludes divine unity as *ahavah mesuteret*, or that emerges from hiddenness. This, says the Vitebsker, may be compared to the love between man and wife, versus the constant but less passionate love between two relatives. We should note that R. Shneur Zalman uses the term *ahavah mesuteret* in a very different context, as the hidden love imbued within all Jews that needs only to be awakened through performing the commandments. See *Likkutei Amarim-Tanya, sefer shel beinonim*, ch. 18, 23b, and see ibid., ch. 31, 40a-b. Cf. ibid., ch. 19, 24a–b.

58. See *Peri haAretz*, vol. 2, Parashah Eqev, 307–9.

59. Drawing on the image of Moses erecting the Tabernacle, in one homily the Vitebsker refers to the leader as having caused *Shekinah* (associated with the Tabernacle, or mishkan) within each and every Israelite. Read as a veiled reference to the zaddik, he may be suggesting that the role of the spiritual leader is to transform those around him and connected to him. This point, however, goes unsaid. *Peri haAretz*, vol. 1, Parashah Vayaqhel-Pequdey, 413–17. On this issue there may be indeed a significant difference between the image projected in the Vitebsker letters and the homiletical sermons, perhaps reflecting their intended audiences. If the sermons do indeed represent homilies delivered in Israel to a small group

who is always in motion and constantly seeking God. Aspiring to overcome his shortfalls, the Vitebsker's zaddik is imperfect and thus progressively reaching toward higher levels of divine service.[60] Even what he calls a *zaddik gamur* (a "completely righteous individual") is continuously striving to achieve greater uplift by abandoning self-interest and emptying himself of all connection to the physical realm. The zaddik has set himself on a quest, described by the Vitebsker in terms both inspirational and aspirational, but has not necessarily arrived at the final stages of perfection.[61] For this reason the zaddik is always afraid, lest some sin distance him from the Divine.[62] In fact, the zaddik interprets the events of the world as revealing his defects and thus demonstrating how he might return to God's intimate embrace.[63] This attention, however, is something that the zaddik shares with *every* individual. The Vitebsker emphasizes that all people must be alert to the ever-changing spiritual "call of the hour,"[64] suggesting that the zaddik is essentially the fulfilled potential of all people.[65]

The Vitebsker's zaddik is quite different from the figure of the ideal leader as it came to be understood in late eighteenth-century Hasidic teachings.[66] The following sermon from R. Abraham Hayyim of Zlotschev is

---

of elite disciples (i.e. zaddikim-in-training) it makes sense that he spends more time on the inner work and divine service of the zaddik rather than his place vis-à-vis other worshippers. In the letters addressed to his followers, however, it seems reasonable that he would be more interested in demonstrating the great power and spiritual efficacy of the zaddik and his unique place in the spiritual community.

60. *Peri haAretz*, vol. 2, Parashah Acharey Mot, 51.

61. Ibid., vol. 2, Parashah Shelach, 149–50.

62. Ibid., vol. 1, Parashah Vayishlach, 128–30.

63. Vol. 1, Parashah Vaye̲zey, 118–20. This is the Vitebsker's reading of the key phrase *zaddik yesod olam* ("The zaddik is the foundation of the world," Proverbs 10:25): not only that the zaddik is the fulcrum or "axis mundi" of the cosmos, but also that the zaddik senses the foundational interconnectivity of the world and the events therein as demonstrating his own insufficiencies. See below.

64. Ibid., 116–17.

65. For example, see ibid., vol. 1, Parashah Vayaqhel-Pequdey, 409.

66. In addition to the studies cited above, see Arthur Green, "The Zaddiq as *Axis Mundi* in Later Judaism," *Journal of the American Academy of Religion* 45 (1977): 327–47; idem, "Typologies of Leadership and the Hasidic Zaddiq," in *Jewish Spirituality II: From the Sixteenth-Century Revival to the Present*, ed. Arthur Green (New York: Crossroad, 1987), 127–56; Ada Rapoport-Albert, "God and the Zaddik as the Two Focal Points of Hasidic Worship," *History of Religions* 18, no. 4 (1979): 296–325; Louis Jacobs, "The Doctrine of the Zaddik in Elimelech of Lizansk," in *Their Heads in Heaven: Unfamiliar Aspects of Hasidism* (London: Vallentine Mitchell, 2005), 73–89, and Rivkah Schatz-Uffenheimer, "On the Essence of the Zaddik in Hasidism," *Molad* 144–45 (1960): 365–68 [Hebrew]; Haviva Pedaya, "On the Development of the Social-Religious-Economic Model of Hasidism: The Pidyon, the Havurah, and the Pilgrimage," in *Zaddik and Devotees: Historical and Sociological Aspects of Hasidism*, ed. David Assaf (Jerusalem: The Zalman Shazar Center for

typical of a common interpretation of the zaddik that appears, mutatis mutandis, in the sermons of many other thinkers in the Maggid's circle in various forms:

> The leaders of Israel, those who guide and teach the people God's ways and Torah, receive even more from those they teach. ["I learned much from my teachers, more from my compatriots,] but from my students most of all."[67] In the outflow of mind and awareness that comes from God, they receive more so that they can pass the flow on to others. Proof of this is found in the fact that all the years that Israel were in the wilderness because of the sin of the spies, divine speech stayed away from Moses [because he was not prophesying to Israel].
>
> This is: "And you, command (*tezaveh*) the Children of Israel" (Exodus 27:20). The word may be derived from *tzavta* (or "togetherness"). Join yourself to the Children of Israel, to teach them and lead them. "They will bring you pure olive oil" (Ibid.): it is they who will cause that pure flow of wisdom and Torah to come on you.[68]

The message of this homily is resounding and clear: the sacred teacher is obligated to share instruction and give to those around him. In doing so, however, the master becomes the receiver of an even greater measure of inspiration. Rather than diminish his own attachment to God, the leader's connection to the people and his willingness to engage with them actually increases his own wisdom.

In his own sermon on this verse, the Vitebsker invokes much of the same symbolic language but extracts quite the opposite meaning from the original verse.[69] The zaddik, manifest in the figure of Moses, is commanded by God to connect himself not to his disciples but to the words of his own speech (represented by the Children of Israel, who collectively embody the divine Word). This contemplative moment brings together the scattered letters of the zaddik's speech and allows him to see how the disparate sounds are linked to one another by a hidden, flowing reservoir of divine wisdom. The zaddik's inward journey through the letters and their viscous and ever-flowing sacred energy (the oil of the biblical verse) leads him deeper into his own mind and heart, thus coming to the seat of consciousness and eventually to the Divine. This exclusively introspective mystical trajectory is, of course, precisely the

---

Jewish History, 2001), 343–97 [Hebrew].

67. b*Ta'anit* 7a.

68. Translated in Green, *Speaking Torah*, vol. 1, 223–24.

69. *Peri haAretz*, vol. 1, Parashah Tezaveh, 381–83.

inverse of the communally oriented model adduced above.[70]

This issue of the zaddik may have been one of the great gulfs between R. Shneur Zalman and the Vitebsker. The latter interprets the Talmudic passage outlining different types of zaddikim,[71] a notion that becomes the foundation of *Tanya*'s strict socio-spiritual hierarchy, as referring to imperfect individuals whose faith must be strengthened and increased through divinely ordained afflictions.[72] But difference in their attitudes on this subject cannot have emerged because of R. Shneur Zalman's attraction to Kabbalah. It seems, rather, that R. Shneur Zalman was interested in developing a totally new doctrine of leadership by the time he rose to power in the 1790s.[73] Furthermore, Rabbi Shneur Zalman's invention of the *beinoni* ("the intermediate individual"), a unique move in the conceptual world of early Hasidism, may well have been his way of tempering the extreme demands of the Vitebsker, for whom the path to spiritual development is binary: true zaddik or total *rasha*. This identity is not foreordained by birth, as it is for R. Shneur Zalman, but is forged anew in every moment as the worshipper either answers or refuses God's sacred call. Those who do not submit to the divine beckoning are justified as wicked, but those spiritually-attuned individuals who incline their ear and embark on the quest are described as zaddikim in full.

The Emotional Realm—The *Middot*

The work of refining and uplifting the *middot* is critical—and even prima-

---

70. Cf. *Or Torah* (Brooklyn: Kehot, 2011), Parashah Tezaveh, no. 102–3, 142–44, for a pair of teachings attributed to the Maggid inhabit the middle ground between those of R. Abraham Hayyim and the Vitebsker. See also Haviva Pedaya, "The Ba'al Shem Tov, R. Jacob Joseph of Polonnoye, and the Maggid of Mezeritch: Outlines for a Religious Typology," Daat 45 (2000): 25–73 [Hebrew]; idem, "Two Types of Ecstatic Experience in Hasidism," Daat 55 (2005): 73–108 [Hebrew]; and Mayse, "Beyond the Letters," 227–45, 460–71.

71. See b*Berakhot* 7a, and cf. *Likkutei Amarim-Tanya'*, ch. 1.

72. *Peri haAretz*, vol. 1, Parashah Vayera, 72–73.

73. See Nehemia Polen, "Charismatic Leader, Charismatic Book: Rabbi Shneur Zalman's *Tanya'* and His Leadership," in *Rabbinic and Lay Communal Authority,* ed. Suzanne Last Stone (New York: Yeshiva University Press, 2006), 53–64, who argues that the publication of *Tanya'* was in part R. Shneur Zalman's attempt to concretize his vision of a rigid socio-spiritual hierarchy. For a different perspective, see Naftali Loewental, *Communicating the Infinite: The Emergence of the Chabad School* (Chicago: University of Chicago Press, 1990), where the author focuses on the literary works and oral teachings of early Chabad as an attempt to develop a linguistic discourse capable of transmitting the deepest spiritual matters. See also Ariel Evan Mayse, "The Sacred Writ of Hasidism: The *Tanya* and the Spiritual Vision of R. Shneur Zalman of Liady," *Books of the People: Revisiting Classic Works of Jewish Thought*, ed. Stuart Halpern (New York: Maggid and Yeshiva University Press, 2017), 109–56.

ry—for the Vitebsker.[74] "The essence of divine service," he says, "is connection to the blessed One through each and every *middah*."[75] The notion that God may be worshipped with every emotion and all parts of the self is a fundament of Hasidism. Everything has a holy source and must therefore be "returned" to its divine origin. For example, lust for something physical should be transformed into desire for God.[76] One who does not use the *middot* for a divine purpose allows a spirit of impurity to settle down upon him. As it is with physical deeds, for the Vitebsker there is no middle path when it comes to the *middot*: exile or redemption, or building or destroying the Temple, may be accomplished at any moment.[77] Of course, God does not withdraw the sacred vitality from the *middot* if they are used to a less sublime end. And, although one must not test himself by conjuring up strange thoughts, if they do emerge he must seize the day and correct the fundamental problem by tracing the desire back to its divine root and transforming it there.[78]

This inner work has implications for the cosmos as well. The human being is a microcosm of the Divine, with his *middot* corresponding to those of God.[79] Therefore, arousing the human *middot* inspires a similar movement in God's attributes, and human beings raising up their misguided thoughts and repairing their *middot* repairs an element of the fractured cosmos. To refrain from doing so would be to leave some aspect of holy vitality amongst the *qelipot* ("husks"). The material world, the domain of the *middot*, has trapped the divine presence and the worshipper must draw forth the latent sacred energy.[80] He then becomes cloaked in the mantle of this life-force, attaining *devequt* but also liberating the divine vitality and shattering the material grasp of the *qelipot*.

The work of the *middot* is fraught with danger, however, for one who becomes invested in the physical world is cut off from his divine source—

74. The *middot* are the seven emotional and ethical character traits or human attributes, which, together with the three intellectual faculties, embody the divine superstructure (the sefirot) within man. See Arthur Green, *A Guide to the Zohar* (Stanford: Stanford University Press, 2004), 28–59.

75. *Peri haAretz*, vol. 1, Parashah Chayye Sarah, 87. Cf. ibid., vol. 2, Parashah VaEtchanan/*Shabbat Nachamu*, 265–80. See also ibid., vol. 1, Parashah Bereshit, 3–5, for a kindred notion found in a teaching also attributed to R. Abraham haMalakh ("the Angel"), the son of the Maggid of Mezeritch, and the parallel quote in R. Abraham's name in *Me'or Eynayyim* (Jerusalem: 2012), vol. 1, Parashah Beshalach, 170.

76. For a remarkable teaching from the Vitebsker on how, and under which circumstances, one might be called on to uplift this type of lust, see Green, *Speaking Torah*, vol. 1, 153–55.

77. *Peri haAretz*, vol. 1, Parashah Chayye Sarah, 85–92.

78. Ibid., vol. 2, Parashah Nizabim, 442–49.

79. Ibid., vol. 2, Parashah Behar, 89–98.

80. Ibid., vol. 2, Pesach/Sefirat haOmer, 22–26.

a greater punishment than this could scarcely be imagined. This path is a constant struggle, for the Evil Inclination comes to a person hidden within one *middah* after another in an attempt to catch him unaware.[81] To raise the *middot* by correctly returning them to their godly sources requires constant focus. The ever-flowing cosmos and the changing emotional states of each individual mean that task cannot be the same for any two moments, people, or situations.[82] Yet he who successfully cleaves to the Divine with all of his *middot* becomes empowered. The worshipper is linked to the entirety of Being like a part of single organic body, and streams of sacred energy course unencumbered through his or her *middot*.[83]

The Vitebsker poses a fascinating question very much of the moment to one interested in attaining union with the Divine: Given the inherent danger involved in working with the *middot*, why should one not seek to bypass them and ascend immediately for the ineffable divine realm? Why not defer the gritty work of the emotions in favor of abstract or contemplative intellection? This unknowable region, which he calls the *eino musag*, is surely the heart of religious experience and the locus of *devequt*.[84] The Vitebsker suggests that such immediate uplift is both impossible and undesirable. Just as the sanctity of Shabbat is predicated on the work of the six days of the week, purifying the *middot* must happen slowly. It is an extended process akin to assembling the Tabernacle, thus composed of many small acts of construction that together add up to something great.[85] Therefore, one cannot arrive at the *eino musag* without the entry point established through the work of the *middot*. In this context, he mentions the rabbinic tradition of the pious ones (Hasidim) who had no time to perform their labor—referring to the work of their *middot*—because they are too engrossed in contempla-

81. Ibid., vol. 1, Parashah Vayeshev, 161–71. Here, as elsewhere, the Vitebsker asserts that divine service that is constantly changing brings the greatest pleasure to the worshipper as well as to God.

82. Ibid., vol. 1., Parashah Chayye Sarah, 85–88.

83. Ibid., vol. 2, Shabbat Nachamu, 289–91.

84. See vol. 1, Parashah Vayaqhel-Pequdey, 416–17. This phrase of *eino musag* (also a key term in the teachings of R. Abraham haMalakh) may have been his translation of the notions of *kadmut* or *kadimat haSekhel* found in the Maggid's sermons. Gershom Scholem, "The Unconscious and the Concept *Kadmut ha-Sekhel* in Hasidic Literature," in *The Latest Phase: Essays on Hasidism*, ed. David Assaf and Esther Liebes (Jerusalem: Magnes Press, 2008), 268–76 [Hebrew]; Ahron Marcus, *Hartmanns inductive Philosophie im Chassidismus* (Vienna: 1888); Siegmund Hurwitz, "Psychological Aspects in Early Hasidic Literature," trans. Hildegard Nagel, in *Timeless Documents* of the *Soul* (Evanston: Northwestern University Press, 1968), 149–240; Mayse, "Beyond the Letters," 228–37.

85. Arthur Green, "Sabbath as Temple: Some Thoughts on Space and Time in Judaism," in *Go and Study: Essays and Studies in Honor of Alfred Jospe*, ed. Raphael Jospe and Samuel Z. Fishman (Washington, DC: B'nai B'rith Hillel Foundations, 1980), 287–305.

tion.[86] The Vitebsker, however, cites this ostensibly pious model of rapture as a negative precedent.

But the Vitebsker complements this line of inquiry by raising the inverse point as well. If the world is saturated with holiness, representing the presence of God, why should one expend himself to transcend the *middot*? And why are the commandments the primary instruments for rising above the *middot*, since all things—and theoretically, all deeds—include Divinity?[87] His answer to the latter point is that emotional expressions of love and awe that are not rooted in *devequt* are essentially false. This includes religious experiences that are less intense than spiritual death (and hence are imagined) as well as uplift achieved outside the framework of halachah. The *middot* are crucial to attaining divine wisdom, for they shelter the unbounded and infinite realm by giving it both boundary and expression. They are the true gateways to infinity.[88] So although it should not be misunderstood as the end goal of the mystical journey, transforming the *middot* is the essential groundwork for the next stages of higher religious consciousness. Yet the ultimate point, says the Vitebsker, is for the worshipper to infuse the *musag* with new vitality.[89] The divestment from self and physicality, though intense and absolute, is always impermanent.

R. Shneur Zalman offers a contrasting vision of perfectly aligned *middot* as restricted to the messianic future. This state cannot be attained by most people, and surely remains impossible for the *beinoni*.[90] And yet for the Vitebsker, as for the Maggid, directing the *middot* toward God is both possible and necessary in the present moment. Furthermore, R. Shneur Zalman's spiritual teachings emphasize time and time again that it is the intellectual faculties that must rule over and constrain the *middot*. While R. Shneur Zalman's cerebral form of contemplation should not be mistaken for dry or stultified intellection, the emphasis is always on the power of the mind to harness the *middot*.[91] For the Vitebsker, even knowledge of Torah is broadcast through the *middot*, and therefore wisdom takes on a positive or a negative instantiation based on the refinement of the person in whom it is embodied.[92] Thus refining the *middot* is essential. And for the Vitebsker, the journey has the opposite trajectory: awe, submission and unwavering humility enable the worshipper to transform his *middot*, thereby illuminating them with the light of God. Only then can the worshipper travel on, delving deeper into the mind and eventually into the Unknowable, and

86. b*Berakhot* 32b.
87. *Peri haAretz*, vol. 2, Parashah Korach, 169–70.
88. Ibid., vol. 2, Parashah Ki Tavo, 428–30.
89. Ibid., vol. 2, Pesach/Sefirat haOmer, 21–22.
90. See *Likkutei Amarim-Tanya'*, *Sefer Shel Beinonim*, ch. 37, 36b.
91. Ibid., ch. 42, fol. 59a–b.
92. *Peri haAretz*, vol. 2, Parashah Naso, 118.

eventually returning to the *middot* and recharging them with an even greater measure of sacred energy.

'Emunah

Scholars have long since moved beyond Joseph Weiss's dichotomy of "Hasidism of mysticism" and "Hasidism of faith," but the shell of this essentialist typology still informs many readings of the Vitebsker's sermon and his description of "faith" or *'emunah*.[93] The concept is a critical theme in the Vitebsker's sermons, but his understanding of the concept must not be misunderstood as unsophisticated and unreflective belief, often derisively described as "blind faith."[94] The contemplative path outlined in his sermons—absolute focus on every deed, strict asceticism, attention to every human emotion and element of the self, and the desire for nothing less than absolute of unity with God—belies such oversimplifications. Nor is the Vitebsker's *'emunah* a type of mystical belief predicated on a palpable and (nearly) unbridgeable rift between man and God, a common formulation in the modern world and not uncommon among later Hasidic writers.[95] Indeed, his sermons invoke the term *'emunah* in reference to the human being's capability to unite with God as a single and total unity, with no barrier standing between the worshipper and the Divine.[96]

'Emunah is crucial because it brings the worshipper to a state of ecstatic knowing (*gnosis*) that cannot be achieved through any degree of intellectual exploration or contemplation on its own.[97] The Vitebsker's goal is to attain *Keter*, the *sefirah* associated with divine will and an element of

93. See Joseph G. Weiss, "Hasidism of Mysticism and Hasidism of Faith," *Studies in Braslav Hasidism* (Jerusalem: Bialik Institute, 1974), 87–95 [Hebrew]; translated as "Mystical Hasidism and the Hasidism of Faith: A Typological Analysis," in *God's Voice from the Void: Old and New Studies in Bratslav Hasidism*, ed. Shaul Magid (Albany: State University of New York, 2002), 277–85. Among the others who have challenged this binary, see Zvi Mark, *Mysticism and Madness in the Work of R. Nahman of Bratslav* (Tel Aviv: Am Oved, 2003) [Hebrew].

94. One might do well to contrast the teachings of the Vitebsker with those of Rabbi Aharon of Karlin on this subject.

95. Such is often the definition of mystical belief, reflecting the origins of "mysticism" as a category in the modern study of religion. See Michel de Certeau, *The Mystic Fable, volume one: The Sixteenth and Seventeenth Centuries* (Chicago: University of Chicago Press, 1992); Leigh Eric Schmidt, "The Making of Modern 'Mysticism,'" *Journal of the American Academy of Religion* 71, no. 2 (2003): 273–302. See also Shalom Noah Barzofsky, *Sefer Netivot Shalom: Meshubav Netivot Da'at be-Inyanei Torah va-Hasidut, Sha'arei Avodat Hashem ve-Tohorat ha-Middot*, vol. 1 (Jerusalem: 1982-89), 41–49, in which the author makes use of the Vitebsker's teachings to explore the meaning of *'emunah* in the contemporary religious world.

96. *Peri haAretz*, vol. 1, Parashah Vayeshev, 142–46.

97. Ibid., vol. 1, Parashah Lech Lecha, 60–61.

the Godhead that is so abstract and boundless that it cannot be construed by means of rational thought. The worshipper cannot, says the Vitebsker, ever hope to grasp this aspect of the infinite Divine by means of the limited tools of reason. *Devequt* requires that the worshipper relinquish rational methods of inquiry, which in a sense hinder the deeper stages of the mystic quest; only *'emunah* lifts him beyond the realm of the *middot*.[98] *'Emunah* is the key to the devotional life, for only it—and not merely intellection—generates the awe necessary for complete self-effacement.[99] Trust in divine omnipotence and omnipresence leads to spiritual poverty and unqualified humility, which produces an awe that then gives rise to the worshipper's burning, all-consuming love for and attachment to God.[100]

But true unity with God is attained after even this erotic experience of desire for God.[101] This is a point that the Vitebsker repeats in many different ways throughout the sermons in this book—the state we might rightly describe as "ecstasy" (in the sense of *ekstasis*) is located beyond all intellect, feeling, and even beyond all *ta'anug* (pleasure).[102] This last point is one that the Maggid's students debated: Should one experience *ta'anug* in the service of God?[103] R. Dov Baer himself refers to *devequt* as an experience of *olam ha-ta'anug* (the "world" or "realm of pleasure").[104] But the Vitebsker claims that even spiritual pleasure risks becoming just another form of temporal distraction, like even love and awe, to be transcended via *'emunah* leading to total *devequt*.

This emphasis on the power of *'emunah* might lead us to expect him to extoll Noah, the silent and trusting biblical figure, as a paragon of trust or faith in God without any investigation or protest. But the Vitebsker surprises on this point, vaunting the spiritual example of Abraham, who, according to rabbinic tradition began his search for God through rational inquiry and

98. Ibid., vol. 1, Meiqez, 175–87. Here he refers to this realm as chokhmah instead of Keter, mirroring a terminological inconsistency present in the Maggid's teachings as well. Mayse, "Beyond the Letters," 284–87.

99. See *Peri haAretz*, vol. 1, Parashah Ki Tissa, 389–92. It is worth noting the affinity between the Vitebsker's account of extinction into the Divine and the famous Sufi metaphor in which self-effacement is likened to polishing a mirror: the illuminating and animating light of divinity can only begin to shine through the soul as the sediments of ego and self-awareness are cleared away. See Michael A. Sells, *Mystical Languages of Unsaying* (Chicago: University of Chicago Press, 1994), 63–89.

100. *Peri haAretz*, vol. 2, Shabbat Nachamu, 289–91.

101. Ibid., vol. 1, Parashah Lech Lecha, 61–62.

102. Ibid., vol. 1, Parashah Vayaqhel-Pequdey, 408–9.

103. This topic was addressed in Arthur Green, "Around the Maggid's Table: Issues in the Devotional Life," delivered at *The Maggid's Court: 1760–1772*, a conference at Johns Hopkins University (April 2015, unpublished).

104. *Maggid Devarav leYa'akov*, ed. Schatz-Uffenheimer, no. 170, 267–68.

only then came to the rung of "'*emunah* alone."[105] Although only *'emunah* can bring the worshipper to rapture in all of its fullness, physical deeds, the work of the *middot*, and intellection are necessary preparations:

> This matter depends upon *'emunah* . . . in truth, no understanding can comprehend or grasp true *devequt*. No intellect, and all the more so sensation or pleasure [can attain it] . . . True *devequt*, which is beyond feeling and cannot be sensed through any understanding or sight, "for no man shall see Me and live" (Exodus 33:20), can only come about through *'emunah* without any sensation whatsoever. This dissolution of existence cannot be fully grasped even by oneself, and all the more so [it cannot] be communicated or made intelligible to others . . .
>
> Yet it is truly impossible to arrive at *'emunah* and *devequt* of this sort until one has exhausted all possibilities of understanding, such as awe, love, and cleaving to things that can be comprehended. This is preparation, a throne for the unknowable that comes afterward. This is the essential thing.[106]

The search for God through the faculties of sense and reason is both valuable and necessary. The worshipper must expend himself in this rational quest, together with performing the commandments, for these failed efforts come together as the foundation on which ecstatic experiences are built. The highest rung of *devequt* is more powerful than can be conveyed or even encountered through language, just as it is beyond all intellectual reasoning. This notion of the incommunicability of *devequt* will concern us shortly.

The Vitebsker maintains that one must have absolute trust, and indeed a deep *'emunah*, in the capacity of the commandments and Torah to transform the worshipper.[107] This power may not be immediately apparent, but when performed with *devequt* the *mitzvot* draws together God and man. This is the Vitebsker's interpretation of the repercussive verse "the righteous one lives through *'emunah*" [*zaddik be-emuntato yihiyeh* (Habakuk 2:4)]. The true life of the seeker comes through *'emunah* that his deeds connect him to the infinite divine power coursing through cosmos. Through *'emunah*, expressed through actions, the worshipper comes to bind his *middot* to the supernal realms and illuminates them together with the rest of the material realm. This infusion of vitality underscores that the Vitebsker's quest

105. *Peri haAretz*, vol. 1, Parashah Lech Lecha, 57. In this sense the Vitebsker occasionally employs different versions of phrase "the ultimate goal of knowledge is unknowing" (*takhlit ha-yediah she-eino yodea*), inherited from medieval Jewish philosophy and cited in a crucial teaching from the BeSh"T in the frontispiece of *Ben Porat Yosef* (Korets: 1781). See *Peri haAretz*, vol. 1, Parashah Beshalach, 302; and *Behinat Olam* 13:1.

106. *Peri haAretz*, vol. 1, Parashah Vayaqhel-Pequdey, 408–12.

107. Ibid., vol. 2, Parashah Devarim/Shabbat Chazon, 254–56.

into the heart of *'emunah* is not focused on escape *per se*, but is a journey toward transcendence (of self and world) that leads to ecstatic and transformative rapture.[108] *Emunah* is the unique key to opening the heart and the mind to a new level of religious experience, a spiritual death that turns the worshipper into a channel for sacred energy. Blending *Eros* and *Thanatos*, the Vitebsker's *'emunah* appears to be an amplified version of the spiritual dimension of Zoharic *raza de-meheimnuta* ("mystery of faith"), an experiential state in which the scholar or worshipper steps into a profound awareness or consciousness of the unified Godhead.[109]

The Vitebsker refers to prayer as the ideal moment for *devequt*, suggesting that worship has a devotional property that even study does not have.[110] It is a-rational, grounded in *'emunah* rather than intellection, and thus offers a mode of cleaving to the God that dwells utterly beyond reason. Like many other early Hasidic thinkers, the Vitebsker seeks to transcend obvious understandings of petitionary prayer, taking an even more radical stance than some. *Devequt*, he suggests, will open a channel through which the spiritual wounds of the self and the cosmos are healed.[111] The Vitebsker's emphasis lies not in praying on behalf of *Shekinah*, a common Hasidic approach to the quandary of petitionary prayer, but in the exclusive focus on *devequt* which then spills over into the world and effluence of blessing.

This cluster of ideas suggests that we may do well to interpret R. Shneur Zalman's emphasis on the primacy of the intellect as an alternative to the Vitebsker's conception of *'emunah* and the crucial work of the *middot*. *Emunah* and ecstatic *devequt*, argues R. Shneur Zalman, are not the primary means of attaining of *Keter*. God's will is expressed through Torah and more specifically through the intricate matrices of *halachot*, and it is precisely through study that the gap between human and divine may be bridged. Not so in the teachings of the Vitebsker, for whom *Keter* is an experiential realm (albeit one beyond the senses) accessed through divine service and *'emunah*. Sacred study is another manner of achieving *devequt*, but it holds nothing unique and may indeed encumber the worshipper's ascent beyond the intellect. The Maggid of Mezeritch was a deeply contemplative, highly introspective mystical thinker, and he was intensely concerned with the inner workings of the human mind. But he did not prioritize the intellect like R. Shneur Zalman of Liady, and we should note that the Maggid also

108. Ibid., vol. 1, Parashah Chayye Sarah, 90–92.

109. Hellner-Eshed, *A River Flows From Eden*, 172. See also Liebes, "Zohar and Eros," 67–119.

110. *Peri haAretz*, vol. 1, Parashah Lech Lecha, 53–55. But cf. ibid., vol. 2, Parashah Devarim/Shabbat Chazon, 253–54, for some very positive remarks on study. Even here, however, he says that efficacious mystical study requires intention, *'emunah*, and burning desire for God.

111. See also ibid., vol. 2, Parashah Naso, 119–23.

refers to *'emunah* as a tool for drawing spiritual vitality through the *middot.* In some teachings, the Maggid even goes so far as to suggest that *'emunah* as a mode for inspiring the flow of divine energy can accomplish something more than studying Torah and observing its precepts.[112]

But the fact that prayer is the nearly exclusive focal point of his devotional system distinguishes the Vitebsker from both his teacher Maggid and R. Shneur Zalman of Liady, who emphasized the centrality of Torah study as a sacred activity. This is even more the case for R. Shneur Zalman, whose hyper-intellectual approach to the spirit is well known. Perhaps this emphasis reflects the fact that the Hasidim in Tiberias were not building a yeshiva or a Hasidic court in the sense of what it would come to mean in Podolia or White Russia. They were establishing a devotional center and semi-monastic communal locus in which members could devote themselves solely to *avodat ha-kodesh*—a hub for divine service.

LANGUAGE

Exploring the role of language in the spiritual life, our final project, will provide us with one more lens through which to view the Vitebsker's theological creativity.[113] He inherited the Maggid's understanding of thought as governed by language and letters, as well as his description of human speech as a manifestation of the divine Word (*Shekinah*).[114] For the Vitebsker, as for his teacher, sacred energy dwells within all of human words as well as our thoughts.[115] Therefore the letters and words of our speech,

112. *Maggid Devarav leYa'akov*, ed. Schatz-Uffenheimer, no. 145, 245–46.

113. This issue is, of course, one of the core subjects in the study of Jewish thought. For a few of most relevant works, see Gershom Scholem, "The Name of God and the Linguistic Theory of the Kabbala," *Diogenes* 79 (1972): 59–80; and the continuation in *Diogenes* 80 (1972): 164–94; Joseph Dan, "The Name of God, the Name of the Rose, and the Concept of Language in Jewish Mysticism," *Medieval Encounters* 2, no. 3 (1996): 228–48; Moshe Idel, "Reification of Language in Jewish Mysticism," in *Mysticism and Language*, ed. Steven T. Katz (New York: Oxford University Press, 1992), 42–79; idem, "Modes of Cleaving to the Letters in the Teachings of Israel Ba'al Shem Tov: A Sample Analysis," *Jewish History* 27, no. 2–4 (2013): 299–317; idem, *Absorbing Perfections: Kabbalah and Interpretation* (New Haven, CT: Yale University Press, 2002); Elliot R. Wolfson, *Language, Eros, Being: Kabbalistic Hermeneutics and Poetic Imagination* (New York: Fordham University Press, 2005), passim; Rachel Elior, *The Mystical Origins of Hasidism*, trans. Shalom Carmy (Oxford: Littman Library of Jewish Civilization, 2006), 41–58; Ron Wacks, "The Yichud in Speech in Hasidism," *Daat* 57–59 (2006): 143–63 [Hebrew]; Steven T. Katz, "Mystical Speech and Mystical Meaning," *Mysticism and Language*, ed. Steven T. Katz (New York: Oxford University Press, 1992), 3–41; Mayse, "Beyond the Letters."

114. *Peri haAretz*, vol. 2, Parashah Matot-Massey, 234–46.

115. See ibid., vol. 2, Pesach/Sefirat haOmer, 17. The Vitebsker even describes human thought as "supernal speech" (*dibbur elyon*), a sublime revelation of God's energy within the one's mind; see ibid., vol. 2, Parashah Matot-Massey, 237.

which are the same linguistic tools through which the cosmos was created, are vessels into which divinity must be drawn.[116] The worshipper must pay attention to his thoughts and speech, which, like the *middot*, must be devoted solely to God. Thus, the individual comes to unify all aspects of the self in reaching for the Divine. And the worshipper must constantly remember that God speaks through him; only thus do his words have creative power. One who does not pay attention to his inner world, and all the more so to his inner words, cannot devote them to God. In that case, human speech only serves to further rend the link between the divine and material realms.[117]

However, for the Vitebsker the task of restoring the *middot* to God also means ascending beyond language, a climb that he describes in radical and unapologetic terms. He variously refers to this ascent as moving into the realm "above speech" (*le-ma'alah min ha-dibbur*) or "above the letters" (*le-ma'alah min ha-otiyyot*).[118] For the Vitebsker, and unlike for the Maggid and R. Shneur Zalman, this process involves striving beyond the contemplative depths of the mind which are governed by the structures of language and entering the ineffable realm of godly silence.[119] Others in the Maggid's circle seem to have been drawn in this direction. These other Hasidic thinkers generally affirmed the importance of remaining primarily within the realm of language, for words play a necessary role in the leader's devotional life and serve as vehicle of communication to his students. But the Vitebsker was not nearly as restrained or circumspect. He emphasizes that a wordless cry allows one to transcend the *middot*, creating a bridge between the mystic's heart and the infinite expanse of God.[120] Though he does not say so explicitly, but perhaps the Vitebsker would extend this power to song as well. Indeed, contemplative silence allows one to connect to the ineffable Divine, ushering in a form of ecstasy that transpires beyond words.[121]

'Emunah allows the worshipper to attain this state, which the Vitebsker describes in glowing and illuminated terms:

> The fear of YHVH that gives life (Proverbs 19:23) is the *devequt* that is higher than all loves and all *middot*. It is thus: you become garbed in *Shekinah*, aligning yourself to become a throne for the One in all that you receive from Him, and all of the subtle pos-

116. Ibid., vol. 2, Parashah Shelach, 139–40.

117. Ibid., vol. 1, Parashah Vayera, 249–55.

118. Ibid., vol. 1, Parashah Tezaveh, 390.

119. Among the other figures in the Maggid's circle, R. Ze'ev Wolf of Zhitomir seems to have been drawn in this direction. See, inter alia, *Or ha-Me'ir* (Jerusalem; 2000), Parashah Vayezey, 49; translated in Green, *Speaking Torah*, vol. 1, 125–26. See also *Or ha-Me'ir*, vol. 1, Parashah Zav, 212–13.

120. *Peri haAretz*, vol. 2, Parashah Shelach, 140.

121. Ibid., vol. 1, Parashah Meiqez, 184; and ibid., Parashah Vayaqhel-Pequdey, 408–9.

> sible understandings. These are the origin of the letters of thought (*otiyyot ha-mehushavim*),[122] which constantly lose their form and become invested in another [i.e., thoughts are fluid and ever-changing] . . . As you gaze into the root of the origin of your understanding that come from the blessed One, you are astounded. God is infusing you and you are receiving; it is the way of all those who receive to be astonished. This leads to their extinction (*bittulam*), for they lose their own identity and becoming incorporated into the One who gives. This awe is complete *devequt*, for you are incorporated into the infinite One (*'Ein Sof*), above all the *middot* . . . If you attain this fear of heaven, becoming included in the One and losing your self and your own [individual] life-force, remaining above the letters of thought, you can effect any change, such as miracles and wonders, for all the worlds are in your hands. You have become incorporated into the One . . .[123]

The worshipper cloaks himself in the immense power of the divine Presence, becoming a throne for the divine. He gazes into the source of the letters, entering the deepest recesses of the mind and transcending even conscious thought. Thus, one is astounded by the silently overwhelming rush of divine vitality from the ultimate Source of all Life, an outpouring that is silent as well as overwhelming. Attaining unity with God means rising above the letters, the most primal and inchoate form of language.[124] There one is fully incorporated into the Divine, reaching total self-dissolution. The worshipper attains the Sinai moment, a time of absolute clarity in which the boundaries between human language and divine words melt away. It is the pre-Creation moment, attaining a beneficent pool of silence that is above all fear, all love, and far beyond the *middot*. As the zaddik attains this Sinai moment of total freedom, stepping into an internal theophany above the letters and beyond the *middot*, a return to the world and drawing forth of new energy is absolutely crucial.[125]

In longing to enter the divine ineffable, the Vitebsker was much closer to the Maggid than R. Shneur Zalman of Liady. But there is a curious historical fact here that is also of interest. The Maggid, perhaps because of temperament and in part because of a distrust of writing, did not transcribe his own teachings.[126] The Vitebsker, however, attempted to lead his Hasidic

122. Cf. the Maggid's teachings on *otiyyot ha-mahshavah*; see Mayse, "Beyond the Letters," 204, 222–27.

123. *Peri haAretz*, vol. 2, Parashah Eqev, 304–6.

124. *Peri haAretz*, vol. 1, Parashah Tezaveh, 381–83.

125. Ibid., vol. 2, Parashah VaEtchanan/Shabbat Nachamu, 275–80.

126. There is, however, a very early tradition claiming that the Maggid asked one of his disciples to write down his teachings; see Mayse, "Beyond the Letters," 47–49.

community in White Russia through letters of spiritual instruction and religious encouragement. This is something that Rabbi Shneur Zalman seems to have learned from him, but taken in a different way: the power of the written word. The Vitebsker wrote a number of significant letters, many of which include theological teachings or spiritual guidance for the reader, but he did not transcribe his own sermons. R. Shneur Zalman, however, embraced the medium of written language to such an extent that he authored *Tanya'*, a shining classic of early Hasidic literature and a work that is renowned for its clarity of vision and striking ideas. For the Vitebsker, reinfusing the world with vitality was key, but he never relinquished the call of ascending above into the beckons of contemplative silence. It is surely no surprise that he never founded a court, preferring to nurture a tight-knit group of mystical disciples.

Conclusions

Rabbi Menachem Mendel of Vitebsk was a fierce and uncompromising mystical thinker. He developed ideas already found in the teachings of the Maggid, often by amplifying their intensity and centrality, but he also extended them into a new realm of ascetic piety and ecstatic spirituality. Yet R. Shneur Zalman, a fellow disciple of the Maggid and later the Vitebsker's student, took the Maggid's intellectual legacy in a different direction.

Instead of reducing the rift between their theological projects to an assumption that R. Shneur Zalman was more immersed in the world of Kabbalah and that the Vitebsker was closer to his teacher, I believe that in some cases R. Shneur Zalman was alert to the radical spiritualism of R. Menachem Mendel of Vitebsk and sought to reign in it. Thus when R. Abraham of Kalisk accused R. Shneur Zalman of charting a new course different than the Maggid, claiming that the latter was developing a novel form of leadership as well as a new sort of theological language and devotional posture, it seems that Rabbi Abraham was keenly attuned to the fundamental differences between R. Shneur Zalman and the Vitebsker. Both of these Hasidic thinkers should be considered creative interpreters of the Maggid's legacy, but carefully reading the sources of their divergent intellectual projects reveals the extent to which both R. Shneur Zalman and the Vitebsker carried forward and transformed the spiritual legacy of Mezeritch.

Mindfulness, Memory, Sensory Consciousness, and *Vida Contemplativa* in *Peri haAretz*

by James Jacobson-Maisels
(IJS)

R. Menachem Mendel of Vitebsk, in his work *Peri haAretz*, touches upon many classic themes of early Hasidism. These include such important subjects as non-duality, faith, the release of desire, panentheism, the danger and divinity of corporeality, and others. In addition, he introduces a theme little discussed in the study of Hasidism, that of "mindfulness." By this I mean nondiscursive, direct, nonjudgmental, perceptual-like awareness, akin to the use of term in Western Anglophone Buddhist-inspired practice and its broader cultural adoption in contemporary English. While there is no one exclusive technical term in the Vitebsker's writing that refers to this type of awareness, the term *lehistakel*, to look or gaze, in its various forms, is particularly associated with this type of consciousness. Indeed, in *Peri haAretz*, every use of *lehistakel* which is not a quotation, as far as I can discern, refers to an operation of consciousness rather than an actual operation of the senses.[1] In addition, we will see him utilize other terms which together help us

1. See, for instance, the use of *lehistakel* in the following parshiyot of *Peri haAretz*: Noach, Vayera, Vayeshev: Sabbath before Hanukkah, Mishpatim, Qedoshim, Behar, Matot-Massey, Eqev, Re'eh, Shoftim, and Vayelech. Interestingly, this is precisely the word used to describe mindfulness practice in the texts of R. Kalonymus Kalmish Shapira, The Piaseczner Rebbe. See, for instance, *Bnei Maḥshava Tovah, Seder Emtzaei VeYesod HaHevra*, §6, 17–18 and §10, 25–26, Jerusalem: Va'ad Ḥaside Piaseczno (Committee of Piasczno Hasidim), 5749 (1989). R. Shapira is particularly significant as he provides the most developed concrete description of mindfulness in Jewish sources. See his unparalleled, to my knowledge, description of mindfulness as a concrete practice both in the "Technique of Quieting," *Derekh HaMelekh* (Jerusalem: Va'ad Ḥaside Piaseczno [Committee of Piasczno Hasidim], 5755 [1995]), 451–52 and *Hakhsharat HaAvrekhim*. See also *Hakhsharat HaAvrekhim, Mevo HaShearim* (L'Ḥovat HaAvrekhim), *Tzav VeZeruz* (Jerusalem: Va'ad Ḥaside Piaseczno [Committee of Piasczno Hasidim], 5761 [2001]), 9:4. The Vitebsker here is a possible source of this terminology.

form a picture of a certain type of consciousness and relationship to experience which is akin to and best captured by the contemporary term "mindfulness." What we will note about these terms is their use of sensory metaphors to describe this consciousness (such as *lehistakel*, as we have mentioned) and explicitly mental terms (such as *lizkor*, bringing to mind).[2] In this article, I aim to evoke the basic meaning and task of mindfulness in the Vitebsker's writings and its key aspects and functions through a close reading of a select series of teachings from *Peri haAretz*. As we read each of these texts in turn, a picture of a certain type and texture of consciousness, which we can most felicitously label as mindfulness, will emerge. In this way, this article represents both a textual analysis but also a kind of constructive praxology which organizes and orients us towards a certain practice of consciousness in Hasidic texts that offers itself to the contemporary reader.

1. Behar

We will begin with a teaching from Parashah Behar in which the Vitebsker lays out many of the key elements of mindfulness and its function in his thought.

> Let us ask concerning the teaching "Whoever appraises [*haSham*] his ways in this life becomes privileged to see [*roeh*] the salvation of the Holy One, blessed be He, for it is said: "[and to him] who orders [*ve-sam*] his way I will show the salvation of God" (Psalm 50:23)" [see b*Moed Katan* 5a].
>
> [The Vitebsker] opened with the words of Rashi [on the opening of our parashah]: "What is the connection between *Shemittah* (the sabbatical year) and Mt. Sinai? Just as with *Shemittah*, its general principles and its finer details were all stated from Sinai, likewise, [all of them were stated—their general principles together with their finer details—from Sinai]." . . .
>
> In this way every action of a person, his ways and thoughts in this world, that occur every season, hour and moment are like "an arrow that flies by day" (Psalm 91:5) "commanding . . . His lovingkindness" (Psalm 42:9). Or [so too is the case concerning] every *middah* [disposition, quality, *sefirah*] which is aroused on him. The arousal of his *middot* are paralleled by the arousal of the upper worlds as it says, "Abraham aroused lovingkindness in the world" [based on Zohar I:87b, III:262b] whom the verse called "Abraham my lover" (Isaiah 41:8). So too is the case with all the zaddikim and their *middot*. And when a bad *middah* or alien thought passes through him

2. Compare this, for instance, to the primary technical terms R. Shapira uses to refer to mindfulness *maḥshavah* (thought) and *lehistakel*. Here too there is a focus on the perceptual (see) and cognitive (think, remember) as terms to refer to "mindfulness."

> he gazes on it [inquiring] "what is this?" and "what caused this?" and he is ashamed before God until the thing is annihilated and ascends through the holy life-force which "dwells in them within their uncleanness" (Leviticus 16:16) and God's statement through which God created that thing which is its good life-force hidden within. Through gazing at this she cleaves to God through that very life-force. And through her ascent, the thing which came to her in thought or in her *middot* ascends as well as do all the upper worlds. . . .
>
> And this is "Whomever appraises [*haSham*] his ways in this life becomes privileged to see [the salvation of the Holy One, blessed be He]" and so to with every *middah* which is aroused on him until he receives the merit of them all. So too Noah and Abraham received the merit of them all. The general principle is that the end of everything includes everything that preceded it, for it is the purpose of them all, and everything is like nothing, annulled and annihilated, before it and pulled after it. And this is the matter of shemittah. For the six years are included in the seventh and annulled before it. Therefore all purchases are annulled and go free (see Exodus 21:2). And everything is from Sinai which is annihilation and nothingness (*ayin*). For Sinai is humility and nothingness . . . which is the end of wisdom, which is nothingness and gazing. And from the seventh we learn about all the *mitzvot* which are raised through the last act (*sof hama'aseh*) from Sinai which is annihilation and nothingness . . .[3]

Our teaching begins with a Talmudic passage which plays on the word orders or places [*ve-sam*] in the verse Psalm 50:23 and reads it as "appraises" [*haSham*], a word spelled almost the same way but with a *shin* rather than a *sin*. It also indicates, in both the biblical verse and Talmudic commentary, that one who does this putting or appraisal, is gifted with sight, both "see" in the Talmudic passage and "show" in the verse, coming from the same root of "to see" (ראה). That is, we begin with this connection between looking, seeing, and reflection, appraisal, placing one's attention, and ordering one's way in the world.

Then we are brought Rashi's classic question on our parashah,which asks why *Shemittah* in particular is brought in connection with the revelation at Sinai, as Parashah Behar opens:

> YHVH spoke to Moses on Mount Sinai: Speak to the Israelite people and say to them: When you enter the land that I assign to you, the land shall observe a Sabbath of YHVH. Six years you may sow your field and six years you may prune your vineyard and gather in

3. *Peri haAretz*, Parashah Behar. Jerusalem: HaMesorah, 5747 (1986–87).

> the yield. But in the seventh year the land shall have a Sabbath of complete rest, a Sabbath of YHVH: you shall not sow your field or prune your vineyard (Leviticus 25:1–4).

Rashi's answer is that it comes to teach a general principle that just as all the general principles and finer details of *Shemittah* were given at Sinai, so too in reference to "all of them," that is all of the *mitzvot*. However, the Vitebsker will read this "all of them" hyper-literally as referring to everything, all created things, that all of them come from Torah, the divine word.

The Vitebsker then describes, through multiple images and quotations, how our actions, dispositions, and thoughts arouse parallel energies in the upper worlds. Thus, our actions or thoughts (of lovingkindness in this case) are arrows we shoot forth that command and bring God's lovingkindness to the world. That is, our actions, dispositions, and thoughts are never isolated occurrences but always have wider implications and reverberations in the cosmos. This itself is an important and challenging Kabbalistic concept which claims that even our thoughts are never just ours, and that every thought, feeling, and action has the potential to cause harm or healing for ourselves and the world.

Mindfulness now is introduced, picking up on themes of sight and placing attention in the opening paragraph to answer the question of what one is to do when a harmful thought, disposition, or action arises in one's experience. One is instructed to gaze upon it (*mistakel*),[4] investigate it, recognize its harmful nature and its holy root or life-force, and thus allow that which has arisen to be annihilated and to ascend back to its holy source. The first step, however, is mindfulness par excellence. It is seeing the thought itself and having a direct perceptual-like experience of the thought rather than thinking about it or analyzing it, though that will come. Rather, it is simply, in the Vitebsker's sense-based language, seeing it. This gazing, this mindfulness, accomplishes this because the gazer, in truly seeing the action, feeling, disposition, or thought, connects to its holy life-force and thus cleaves to God, ascending herself and pulling the action, feeling, disposition, or thought along with her. That is, mindfulness, truly looking, allows the practitioner to see the nature of what she is looking at, rather than just its surface appearance, and the nature of whatever she gazes at is always ultimately the divine. By gazing at, seeing, and recognizing the divinity of that which she interacts with, she liberates that thing, connecting it to its divine source and freeing it, through annihilation from the impurity in which it has been trapped. This connection between mindfulness and annihilation, both as a way to release the impure and evil and as a way for that which is seen to disintegrate into its divine

4. See above, n1.

sources is another crucial task of mindfulness here.[5]

This is the meaning of our opening Talmudic passage. One who appraises his ways, that is, gazes upon and investigates what arises within him, is privileged to see the Divine, because he sees the essence of whatever he is looking at. In particular, the passage goes on to explain, whatever he is looking at is the end result of a whole series of processes, and in seeing the thing before him truly, he also sees and raises and liberates (annihilates) all the processes that went into its creation. This is the esoteric meaning of the *Shemittah*, the seventh year, which includes the six years before it (and also, implied, the esoteric meaning of *Shabbat*, the last act [*sof hama'aseh*], as we are told in *Lecha Dodi*,[6] which includes the six days before it). That is why, on this reading, slaves, people who are purchased, go free in the seventh year and their purchase is annulled (as is true for land in the Jubilee year, seven cycles of seven years).

The connection to Sinai, answering Rashi's question, is that coming from Sinai means that everything is ultimately rooted in divine nothingness or emptiness and humility, which is wisdom and gazing/mindfulness. What is fascinating here, for our purpose, is the equivalence of Sinai, humility, nothingness, wisdom and gazing/mindfulness. The equation or connection between humility and nothingness in Hasidic thought is hardly new. Similarly, the connection of wisdom and nothingness is a standard trope based on Job 28:12. What is unusual is that, however, all of these aspects being described as revelation and that in turn are described as gazing, the direct perception of reality. Yet if we consider how mindfulness functions as the ability to see the underlying nature of things and release the false impurity which has been overlaid on that phenomenon, for the Vitebsker here, we can understand the connection.

What the Vitebsker seems to be claiming is that the ultimate nature of everything we experience is emptiness, is the divine nothingness out of which they emerge. That is why when we look at them closely, when we are mindful, we can see their inherent nature, their inherent nothingness or divinity, and therefore allow them to pass and allow ourselves to no longer be attached to them but rather to cleave to their inherent nature and source which is the radical openness or divinity which underlies them. Mindfulness is seeing the emptiness of all things, their lack of any separate existence, and in doing so it is Sinai/revelation. This mindful way of seeing reveals

5. This again parallels the Piaseczner's view of mindfulness as annihilating the false or impure and revealing the divine. See the discussion in my dissertation, "The Self and Self-Transformation in the Thought and Practice of R. Kalonymus Kalmish Shapira" (University of Chicago, 2014), 495–98.

6. The liturgical poem, composed by Shelomo HaLev Alkabetz (sixteenth century), that forms the climax of the Friday/Sabbath evening Kabbalat *Shabbat* service.

the genuine nature of that thing. When the practitioner sees that truly in any particular instance, it allows him to see that it is also true of everything included in that thing. When he sees the nothingness of bread, which means both that it is underneath just a divine gift and that it is just an ongoing process, not a thing in itself, not a self-sustaining and separate entity, but rather a just part, a wave, emerging momentarily from the nothingness which is the source of everything, we see also that everything that made it up: the sun, water, soil, winnowing, grinding, etc. are all empty as well, all simply processes of divine nothingness—not things unto themselves.

Mindfulness or gazing is then what allows the practitioner to see the true nature of things as they are—which is their divine nature for the Vitebsker and which is also their nothingness—and allows the release of that which is false, anything, such as impurity or evil, which is contrary to its divine nature. Mindfulness, truly gazing at that which arises in our experience, has a dual and connected power according to the Vitebsker, allowing us to see nothingness and divinity and to let go of harmful *middot*, thoughts, feelings, and actions. This dual power of allowing the practitioner to see truth and release falsehood is the basic capacity of mindfulness in the Vitebsker's thought, as we will now see in a series of other teachings.

2. Vayeshev

We can see a parallel function of mindfulness and gazing in the Vitebsker's teaching on Parashah Vayeshev in *Peri haAretz*. The teaching begins by discussing Potiphar's wife's garments, which she uses to entice Joseph, and that serves as a jumping off point to discuss the garments of God. The teaching describes the impermanent and constantly changing nature of reality where the underlying divine life-force constantly assumes new forms, new garments, which is the beauty, diversity, and wonder of creation:

> For this is the nature of the human, he undergoes change every occasion and every moment, as it is written, "You examine him every moment" (Job 7:18). This is the flowing of his life-force, as is known, which is the matter of "stripping off a form and donning a form" . . . The changing of a person in his spiritual practice for God is also called garments, "The clothing he wears in the morning, he does not wear in the evening." . . . The matter of all the garments . . . is the matter of beautification (*hitpa'arut*), as is known . . . From the day God created Adam unto the last generation of humans there is not a single person equivalent to his fellow, nor is there any hour or moment which is equivalent to its fellow in the operation of all of the worlds from the highest heights to the lowest depths. There never was and never will be, from the six days of

> creation until the end [of the world], two moments that are the same or two people that are the same,[7]

The teaching then ultimately concludes thus:

> When a person is enclothed in the evil inclination, in whatever specific garment, love or fear, when he stops and investigates from where this growth draws life, lo it is God who shines within it and is enclothed within it to beautify (*lefaer*) its Creator through the name of His glorious kingdom ruling over all (b*Yoma* 35b and Psalm 103:19), even in this *qelipot* (the shells of separation/evil), due to [God's] compassion. In having looked (*hibit*) at the stone from which he has been hewn "all workers of iniquity are scattered" (Psalm 92:10) as it says "as wax melts before fire, so the wicked shall perish before God" (Psalm 68:3) and the evil inclination shall be annihilated from him. . . . When Joseph entered to fulfill his needs [lie with Potiphar's wife] because of the beauty of the corporeal clothing she donned morning and evening, he looked (*hibit*) at his quarrying place in the window of his mind and comprehension, as it says "Gazing (*mashgiach*) through the window" (Song of Songs 2:9), and saw the image of his father who is the splendor [*Tiferet*] of Israel, as mentioned above. He therefore stopped himself [from lying with her]. Therefore, he certainly "makes culpable the wicked" who do not investigate and see "the glory of God has shone on" them (Isaiah 60:1), light will shine "for the upright" (Psalm 112:4).[8]

In this text, these garments, are understood as nothing less than the multiple diverse manifestations of God, whether in holiness or "evil" [*qelipot*]. These garments, as explained earlier in the teaching, are understood to be the fact of diversity, the wondrous and blessed uniqueness of every moment and creature. Hence, the previous paragraph of the teaching tells us, one blesses, as the Talmud commands: "If one sees beautiful creatures and beautiful trees, he says: Blessed it is that thus it is in His world" (b*Berakot* 58b). R. Menachem Mendel, living in an Eastern Europe and Israel filled with persecution at the hands of non-Jews, points out that this applies even to one he and his listeners may consider the "enemy," Potiphar's wife. Even the beauty of the oppressor must be praised as part of the diverse beauteous splendor [*Tiferet*] of the world and that person must be seen as one of the garments of God. When one is able to do this "all workers of iniquity are scattered" (Psalm 92:10), a stock phrase employed by the BeSh"T to indi-

7. *Peri haAretz*, Parashah Vayeshev.
8. *Peri haAretz*, Vayeshev.

cate that, when certain shifts of consciousness are achieved, all suffering and all "evil" vanish.[9]

Returning to an earlier question posed in the teaching, this final paragraph explains how Joseph makes culpable the sinners [b*Yoma* 35b] because Jacob symbolized by the sphere of *Tiferet* that is compassion/change/diversity/unification does not appear to him by chance but rather because he made the effort to "gaze through the window," to bring his mindfulness to bear and to see through the momentary manifestation of form to the divine underneath. Taking gazing or looking again as movements of consciousness which are akin to "seeing" rather than "thinking about," his directly seeing the object allows him to be aware of the divine manifested in the appearance of his father Jacob that is lurking underneath. And making that effort to investigate and see is possible for anyone. This is why, as the verse more fully reads, "light shines for the upright in the darkness" (Psalm 112:4) for they make the effort to see the light that is always already present, even in the darkness, while the wicked do not see that "the glory of God has *shone* on" them (Isaiah 60:1), notwithstanding that it always already has.

That is, mindfulness, consciousness, a capacity available to us all and again described using terms for sight (looking, gazing) allows Joseph to the see the divine source underneath the changing forms of the world (the garments). It allows him to connect directly with divinity while releasing the evil and ultimately false shells which are the passing forms of the divine nothingness at this moment. Moreover, it allows him to directly see the impermanent and constantly changing nature of reality. As above, it is this direct seeing of that which arises and the uncovering of its divine essence that allows this process to take place.

3. VAYKIRA-ZACHOR

These same themes are seen in a teaching on Parashah Zachor found in *Peri haAretz* in Parashah Te<u>z</u>aveh. Here we will again see mindfulness as a type of sensory consciousness connected to sight and the connection of mindfulness to both revelation and nothingness. However, we will also see a new type of imagery which describes mindfulness as a kind of remembrance or bringing to mind and its opposite as forgetfulness, an imagery that is also used elsewhere in the Vitebsker's writings to describe this form of consciousness.[10] The teaching proceeds:

Remember (*zachor*) what Amalek did to you [on your way, in your

9. See, for instance, the BeSh"T, brought in R. Jacob Joseph of Polonne, *Ben Porat Yosef*, Brooklyn, 5755, 339–40. See the discussion of this text in Immanuel Etkes, *The BeSh"T: Magician, Mystic, and Leader* (Waltham, MA: Brandeis University Press, 2004), 135.

10. See *Peri haAretz* on Meiqez, and see the equation of these two terms, *histaklut* (gazing) and *zikaron* (bringing to mind) in Parashah Shoftim.

exodus from Egypt]" (Deuteronomy 25:17). The literal interpreters ask how it is possible to command a memory as a person cannot control whether she forgets. Their words concern the corporealized human who has already damaged his inner-powers and dispositions (*middot*) through his grasp of corporeality which is the *qelipot* (evil shells), the place of forgetfulness. This is not the case [for another kind of person concerning which] Torah says, for "God created humans aligned" [based on Ecclesiastes 7:29][11] to receive Torah and grasp "its ways, ways of pleasantness" (Proverbs 3:17), to know God in all God's ways. And Torah is itself remembrance/mindfulness (*zekhira*), which is the commandment of bringing to mind [*zikaron*] standing at the revelation at Mt. Sinai (Deuteronomy 4:10). God created the world through Torah (Zohar I:5a) and it is the tool of God's craft (Genesis Rabba 1:1). Certainly the power of the person who brings something to mind (*haZokher*) who was created through it [Torah] is the commandment of these remembrances (*zekhirot*) mentioned above [remembering Amalek and Mt. Sinai]. How could forgetfulness be possible, as the verse says "Shall He who implants the ear not hear, He who forms the eye not see?" (Psalm 94:9), if not in the case of someone who has already damaged his dispositions and inner-powers in opposition to Torah, God forbid. But the difficulty raised by the literal interpreters still stands. For insofar as Torah is eternal and practiced in every generation and by every person and "[the words of Torah] are healing for his whole flesh" (Proverbs 4:22) and they are a spice for the evil inclination (b*Kedushin* 30b), [we must understand] how this commandment still applies to the one that has damaged [his inner-powers and dispositions]. . . .

Following the general assumption that in every *yesh* (being, somethingness, form, conditioned) "God made this in contrast to that" (Ecclesiastes 7:14), [we must ask] who is the maker? Lo it is his *ayin* (nothingness, formlessness, emptiness, unconditioned) which gives life to his *yesh*. Therefore, the essence and root of the matter is to be saved from the evil inclination which operates in his *yesh* by bringing himself to *ayin*. There "all workers of iniquity will be scattered" (Psalm 92:10). As it says, "as wax melts before

11. Ecclesiastes 7:29 literally reads that "God made humans *yashar* (plain, straight, in contrast to the confusions of intellect), but they have engaged in too much reasoning." Here the Vitebsker takes the meaning of *yashar* as straight or aligned and uses it, as it is often used, to describe the moral and mental character of a person who is direct, straight, aligned and so not damaged by "corporeality" but able to directly, straightly, receive the divine message.

> fire, so the wicked shall perish before God" (Psalm 68:3) which is the *'Ein Sof* (infinite) which gives life to it. . . .
>
> This is the meaning of "Remember (*zachor*) what Amalek did to you [on your way, in your exodus from Egypt]" (Deuteronomy 25:17) which is the evil inclination in all of her matters and actions. One should arrive at the *middah* (quality, disposition) of mindfulness/memory (*zachor*) to be saved from it (the evil inclination). This is what the Sages said, "one whose fear of sin is primary to his wisdom [his wisdom endures]" (m*Avot* 3:9). This is fear/awe which is infinite for lo this awe comes from '*Ein Sof* (the infinite).[12]

The Vitebsker begins with a classical question on the command to remember Amalek: How can we be commanded to remember? How can we be *commanded* (rather than encouraged) to pay attention, recall, bring to mind, or be mindful when, as we all know, forgetfulness or mindlessness is not entirely under our control? The question applies, he tells us, to those who are corporealized. This does not mean those who are in bodies. Every human is in a body. Rather the term corporeal in this context refers to the dualistic, the limited, and the patterned.[13] That is, the claim is that this problem of forgetfulness and hence the command to remember applies to those of us (which is all of us) that are in some way caught in the illusion of separation, of dualism, of being trapped in preexistent patterns, of believing in limitation and habituation (*yesh*).[14]

In contrast is the "Torah individual" who is "aligned" in mind, heart and action because he is not lost in the intellect [dualistic, patterned, form-based] as made clear from the full verse "God made humans aligned, but they have engaged in too much reasoning" (Ecclesiastes 7:29).[15] Here we see mindfulness contrasted with intellectual thought and analysis. This person is aligned with Torah, which is the blueprint and tool of creation and remembrance or mindfulness (*zekhira*) itself and so is naturally mindful. Indeed, this is the nature of all beings. For "certainly the power of the one who brings to mind (*haZokher*) who was created through it [Torah] is the commandment of these remembrances (*zekhirot*) mentioned above

---

12. *Peri haAretz*, Tezaveh.

13. See my discussion in *The Self and Self-Transformation in the Thought and Practice of Rabbi Kalonymus Kalmish Shapira* (PhD diss., University of Chicago, 2014), 178–82.

14. For the connection between forgetfulness and habituation and the way mindfulness overcomes them both, see also *Peri haAretz*, Parashah Vayera.

15. Again, Ecclesiastes 7:29 literally reads that "God made humans *yashar* (plain, straight, in contrast to the confusions of intellect), but they have engaged in too much reasoning." Here the Vitebsker takes the meaning of *yashar* as straight or aligned and uses it, as it is often used, to describe the moral and mental character of a person who is direct, straight, aligned, and so not damaged by "corporeality/duality" but able to directly, straightly, receive the divine message.

[remembering Amalek and Mt. Sinai]."

That is, Torah is mindfulness, which is the tool and blueprint of creation, which is therefore the nature of every being that was created through Torah, which is again revelation, which is "the power of the one who brings to mind" (i.e., that which enables the person to be mindful), which is the commandment to be mindful, to remember, which here is then simply the affirmation and claiming of one's nature. This must be so for "how could forgetfulness be possible, as the verse says 'Shall He who implants the ear not hear, He who forms the eye not see?' (Psalm 94:9)." That is, the divine source is that which pays attention, the origin of the eye and the ear, and so too, in its nature, is that which has come forth from that Source. Note once more the way in which this remembrance or mindfulness is again represented by sensory images, the bringing to mind clearly not being only a remembering of that which has passed but a paying attention to what the eye can see and the ear can hear in the present moment. Only one who has somehow violated his nature [Torah] can forget or be mindless. To be mindless is to be out of touch with who we are, to lose touch with our divine source. The question then is how one commands those who have lost touch with who they are to come back into touch with who they are. How does one make the mindless mindful? How does one help people recall their nature?

This is done, our next paragraph explains, by bringing yourself to *ayin*, to a place of formlessness and openness in which one is no longer trapped in one's patterned and habitual ways of being [*yesh*]. Again, mindfulness is here the ally of nothingness, here the open and non-habitual nature of nothingness making mindfulness possible. This is the natural "contrast" to *yesh*, as indicated by the Ecclesiastes verse, and that which in fact animates and gives life to all *yesh*. *Ayin* is the emptiness out of which all form arises. When one enters this state of mindfulness/annihilation, change happens automatically. Psychic enemies and distorted inner states, here represented by the "workers of iniquity" and "the wicked," scatter and melt before the fire of the infinite awareness.

This then is the meaning of the commandment to remember Amalek. It is to purposefully bring oneself back to mindfulness, back to the unconditioned, *ayin*, infinite and non-habitual when one realizes that one has become lost in Amalek/the evil inclination, *yesh*, the conditioned and the habitual. One cannot control if one forgets. One cannot even control if one remembers. But one can consciously train oneself and, when aware, bring oneself to a state of paying attention and non-dualistic awareness. Mindfulness here, which is again revelation, nothingness and sensory perception (hearing as well as sight), is what it means to remember. It is to remember both who one is and the underlying divine nature of reality.

4. Conclusion

Mindfulness, in my reading as presented in *Peri haAretz*, is then a quality and capacity which while distinct in its nature, fulfills many of the core goals of Hasidic spirituality. Mindfulness is described in *Peri haAretz* as a fundamentally natural capacity, one aligned with our true nature—Torah itself. In this way, it is a type of memory, or recall, a recalling of the nature of what is and the true nature of the practitioner who utilizes it. It is not a remembering of the past but rather a bringing to mind, in a direct way, of the truth of how things are for the Vitebsker. In addition, it is portrayed as a kind of direct sensory consciousness akin to sight or hearing, which allows the practitioner to once again see things just as they are. It is, in both these senses, a type of consciousness radically different from intellectual analytical reasoning. It is rather the direct experience, sensing or recalling of the truth of what is before the practitioner.

This capacity serves many of the key goals of Hasidic spirituality. Perhaps most centrally, it is this direct seeing or calling to mind of the truth that allows the practitioner to see the divine nature of reality whether described as the Divinity beneath the changing forms, *ayin*, or Torah. In this way mindfulness is associated with revelation in the Vitebsker's thought, for it is what enables the divine to be revealed to the Hasid who utilizes it.

Connected to these capacities, mindfulness is a crucial instrument of change. By allowing the practitioner to see the root and essential emptiness of everything which arises, it enables the healing and annihilation (which are one and the same) of harmful thoughts, dispositions, or actions by connecting them to their divine source and allowing the Hasid to see their genuine nature. Similarly, mindfulness undoes the habitual, particularly harmful habitual patterns, by allowing the dropping away of the structure of habit. That is, mindfulness is here again a kind of annihilation, connected to its contrast with *middot* or the self. It provides an awareness that is no longer filtered through the specifics of some particular quality or the ego of the practitioner but one which is clear and clean and allows the seeing of the divinity, the nothingness, which underlies all.[16] The mindful practitioner recognizes the changing forms of the world, which include her own habits and peculiarities, and believes and attaches to none of them, rather recognizing the divine nothingness out of which all of these patterns emerge and to which they will return. In these ways, mindfulness is a powerful tool for

16. See, for instance, in addition to the discussion above, "Every *middah* has a habit [connected to it] and thus God's words cannot be clean and clear for the habit causes forgetfulness," from *Peri haAretz*, Parashah Vayera. Here the particular quality, *middah*, limits, sullies and causes forgetfulness, the antithesis of mindfulness. Mindfulness goes beyond the particularity of any one quality or personality to provide the clear and clean speech and awareness, which is the nature of genuine remembrance for the Vitebsker.

embodying the deep goals of Hasidic spirituality for the Vitebsker and for realizing, in a direct nonintellectual way, the Hasidic cry that there is "none other," that all is God.

Selected Homilies of *Peri haAretz*

Translators' Introduction:

by Aubrey L. Glazer, and Nehemia Polen

Translation is the art of interpretation. As Walter Benjamin astutely noted in his masterful 1923 essay, "The Task of the Translator":

> Therefore it is not the highest praise of a translation, particularly in the age of its origin, to say that it reads as if it had originally been written in that language. Rather, the significance of fidelity as ensured by literalness is that the work reflects the great longing for linguistic complementation. A real translation is transparent; it does not cover the original, does not black its light, but allows the pure language, as though reinforced by its own medium to shine on the original all the more fully. This may be achieved, above all, by a literal rendering of the syntax, which proves words rather than sentences to be the primary element of the translator. For if the sentence is the wall before the language of the original, literalness is the arcade.[1]

We have taken to heart Benjamin's suggestion to be "transparent" while "longing for linguistic completion" in these translations. This requires both a withdrawal and expansion, as Benjamin lusciously invokes the Kabbalistic doctrine of *shevirat ha'keilim*, the breaking of the vessels as a process of gathering up of the scattered sparks of light to usher in Messianic time:

> In the same way a translation, instead of resembling the meaning of the original, must lovingly and in detail incorporate the original's mode of signification, thus making both the original and the translation recognizable as fragments of a greater language, just as fragments are part of a vessel.[2]

These fragments of a greater language bring the reader to then expect the

1. Walter Benjamin, "The Task of the Translator" (1923), trans. Harry Zohn (1968), in *The Translation Studies Reader*, ed. Lawrence Venuti (London: Routledge, 2000), 21.
2. Ibid.

unexpected, and to realize that "fidelity and freedom in translation" are not conflicting tendencies but a creative tension throughout. So, I urge the reader to consult with the footnotes as well as the glossary for the more literal renderings amid the range of meanings. The body of the translated text, however, will endeavor to be not only transparent but also allow "the pure language . . . to shine on the original more fully." In so doing, the intention is to present these timeless texts of spiritual direction to contemporary readers from both particular and universalist backgrounds, to touch both philosopher and the devoted one, to provoke the metaphysician and the mystic. The assumption is that mystics, regardless of their traditions, have an understanding as expressed through their religious culture. Nevertheless, there remains a universal ground of experience. All mystics then are looking back at the ground of experience, which is available to any seeker who has knowledge of it and seeks to look in that direction. There is then the universal ground of being that converges with a particular tradition that mediates it and expresses it in ways that are meaningful to that tradition, but it is always grounded in a *gnosis* that is universal.

Notwithstanding this approach, the language of the homilies herein translated is terse and often highly esoteric. Despite this terse style common to the esoteric tradition, there are three recurring terms in the Vitebsker's homilies and letters: *hitqashrut*, *devequt*, and *'emunah*. The Vitebsker's teachings need to be framed within the context of "mystical fellowship" (*dibbuk chaverim*), the forty-six usages of "connectivity" (*hitKaSHRut*, *mitKaSHeR*, *le'hitKaSHeR*), the forty-one usages of "cleaving" (*DeVeKut*, *DaVuK*, *le'hitDaBeV*, *mit'DaBeK*) as well as nine usages of "integration" (*kallelut*). The thirty-nine usages of *'emunah* have proven most challenging to render in English, but depending on the context we have approximated *'emunah* as denoting a spiritual support system, spiritual practice, training, or simply conviction. It must be duly acknowledged that while the act of translation can be a solitary act, this has been a group project, so that these translations are not only the fruit of dedicated *hevruta* between Aubrey and Nehemiah over many years, but also part of further *hevruta* studying shared with David Greenstein and Miles Krassen. Aubrey is grateful to all his study partners for their commitment, erudition and patience along the path. Any errors remain his own.

The quality of unknown and beckoning that undergirds the core of *'emunah*, opening the aspirant to the unknown and inexhaustible is lost in translating *'emunah* merely as "faith" or "belief." As one contemporary thinker suggests, we are speaking here "of intimations that border on convictions and lead to belief systems." When speaking of faith or belief, too often these approximations substitute "ongoing originary intimations."[3] So

3. Michael Eigen, *Kabbalah and Psychoanalysis* (Karnac Publications: London, 2012), 43.

each of these key terms prove important in formulating and influencing the nature of mystical experience within the context of intimate fellowship in Tiberias.

Whereas most Hasidic courts that began to arise generations after the BeSh"T were focused on limiting the intimate exposure between zaddik and Hasid, here the opposite is true and fellowship takes on a more central role, both in text and its translation process as noted above. This deep concern with interpersonal connection allows for the transpersonal mystical experience to take shape.

A master of masters, there is something to the Ruzhiner rebbe's comment about the *Peri haAretz* as a book that never left his desk, saying: "Whomever understands this book, is someone who understands how to interconnect wisdom beyond to below."[4]

The posthumous printing history *Peri haAretz* ranges from the 1814 Kapost edition, to the 1874 Zhitomir edition, concluding with the 1911 Lvov edition. More recently Mechon Peri haAretz has republished two new annotated editions in 2011 and 2017, all of which have been consulted, the latter being the most helpful in deciphering the spiritual landscape beyond the words on the page. Acknowledgment of gratitude is due to Elizabeth-Noa Andrews who patiently and punctiliously reviewed the complete manuscript of translations with Aubrey and in her own unique way managed to brilliantly midwife and massage a more readable text before you that retains its nuance.

4. R. Mordekhai Hayyim of Slonim, *Ma'mar Mordechai*, vol. 2, no. 18 (Yisrael Ze'ev Slonim: Jerusalem, 2007), 62.

Genesis

[1.1]. *Parashah Noach* (Genesis 6:19–11:32)

INTRODUCTION TO HOMILY:

The contemplative life is complicated in its search for simplicity. What the seeker yearns to experience through spiritual practice in intentional community presents both great potential and challenge. Does the contemplative practice of quieting the busy mind allow for a merging into the calm of nothingness, breeding deeper bonding? Or does the contemplative practice of emptying the mind altogether allow for a merging into a more fully present self-actualizing in relation to others? The present homily endeavors to investigate this line of inquiry through a thirteenth-century Castilian Jewish mystical text known as the Zohar as applied to spiritual practice centuries later in eighteenth-century Tiberias. Even at this remove, questions like this could easily be asked of other spiritual practices dedicated to cultivating the contemplative life. For example, in Sufism one might consider the journey that leads from cultivating self-effacing quietism of "Fana" to the manifest self-actualization of Baka.[1] *Or consider the practice of "zazen" in the Mahayana Buddhist tradition, in which one seeks the focused, quiet-mind, emptied state of "Shunyata" on the path leading to liberation of the self through "Satori."*[2] *Consider too the Christian practice of kenosis or "self-emptying" that leads to the merging of self within the divine pleroma. In many spiritual traditions, often it is the master who cultivates the calm mind. But what happens when such a spiritual elder begins to speak and share this experience with others? Is a new constitution of "self" (re)generated amidst the sharing and devotional service in a contemplative community? Is there a language of devotion that could be said to derive from an innate knowledge that constitutes the "initial state" of the language faculty. The primary linguistic data of one's experiences of language during childhood, according to linguists like Noam Chomsky, gives rise to a new*

1. Neil Douglas-Klotz, "The Key in the Dark: Self and Soul Transformation in the Sufi Tradition," *Modern Psychology and Ancient Wisdom: Psychological Healing Practices from the World's Religious Traditions* (2003): 149–72.

2. A more fruitful parallel to the robust Zoharic cosmology, for example, would be to the Tantric school of Kūkai (ca. 774–835 AD; aka Kōbō Daishi), founder of Japan's Shingon Sect of Esoteric Buddhism, which is more akin to Kabbalah than Mahayana Buddhist practice of *Zazen*.

body of linguistic knowledge, namely, knowledge of a specific language (like Hebrew or English). This "attained" state of the language faculty constitutes one's "linguistic competence" because it includes knowledge of the grammar of one's language. It is this knowledge that is needed in order to speak and understand a language, but it remains insufficient for this ability. Extrapolating from Chomsky's linguistic insights into the Hasidic milieu, one could say that much additional knowledge is brought to bear in "linguistic performance," that is, in the actual grammar of devotionality. It raises the question as to whether knowledge of devotional language is an inborn human language faculty, and if so, then how did such inborn knowledge evolve into a more robust grammar of devotionality? This underlies the current homily's reading of the Deluge. While both human and animal prototypes are brought onto the ark for the sake of preserving and then regenerating each species, there remain differences. While humans are distinct from animals, given their linguistic capacities, it is instructive to turn to the natural world to understand generativity and what some linguists like K. Sterelny call "cumulative downstream niche construction." This occurs when a generation of animals modifies an environment already modified by earlier generations, for example, a mountain thornbill's nest embodies "downstream niche construction," seeing that its offspring are affected by the thornbill's efforts. The construction of the nest, however, is not cumulative, given that the nest is built anew each year. By contrast, a rabbit warren extends and generates over several generations, which then serves as an instance of cumulative construction, namely, that successive generations of offspring inherit an ever-more-complex niche and their other behaviors are accordingly attuned. Such "niche construction" is not limited to the physical world, for animals also make changes to their social and epistemic worlds as well. For example, chimpanzees mark a social niche by living in groups, while dogs mark their territory, eliminating any need for remembering where the boundaries of their territory are, thus changing their epistemic niche. As niche constructors "with a vengeance," humans however embody multiple, cumulative modifications that are made to their physical, social, and epistemic environments, including the grammar of devotion. Such cumulative modifications allow for a "ratchet effect," that is, a cycle of improvement being made that then becomes standard for the group, which then serves as the foundation for further innovation.

Turning back to eighteenth-century Tiberias, the grammar of devotion for the Vitebsker's teaching posits that sacral deeds devoid of contemplation remains illusory and dualistic. However, the Vitebsker teaches that contemplation alone is not enough: sacral deeds that are embodied do not fully realize the divine-human interconnectivity. Judaism yearns for a contemplative life that is firmly grounded in this world while not of it. Strad-

dling this tension between living in community and being at one with the divine marks the mystical path in much of Kabbalah and Hasidism. This homily offers a unique window into the grammar of devotion as it generates its "ratchet effect" from Noah and his generativity, namely, a cycle of spiritual elevation of devotion being enacted which then becomes standard for the group dedicated to the intimate and austere contemplative life of eighteenth-century Tiberias.

[1.2]. *Parashah Noach* (Genesis 6:19–11:32)

HOMILY:

"These are the generations of Noah. Noah was a deeply devoted one; he was blameless in his generation . . ."[3] And this is expounded upon by R. Shlomo Yitzhaki as follows: "To teach you that the core value of the deeply devoted is embodied in good deeds."[4] [*This claim requires further explanation as to why sacral deeds are the "generations," that is, why such acts are generativity and progeny? Good deeds are a supple movement of the heart of generosity to give pleasure to others. This then allows the embodied deed to rise higher into something more eternal. Furthermore, why is it that, to the deeply devoted, sacral deeds, and good deeds are the core of generativity? And, why, for the deeply devoted does the matter of their "generations"—as generativity and progeny—become the sacral deeds themselves? Awe allows seeing beyond the self, to the other, and the vitality imbued in the fruit of intercourse, through the child, the insight, reaching prior to creation, then returning back in to the world of generosity and new creation. In order to recapture the infinite benevolence that is encapsulated with the initial vision for creation, then new creative energy can be channeled down and extended through new modalities of expression within the material world. When the sacral deed has en-spirited cognition, then the act itself is divine; otherwise the act remains in the corporeal state.*]

The matter is as our blessed Sages expounded the verse, **"Happy is the one who has not followed the counsel of the wicked, or taken the path of sinners . . ."**[5]

"Happy is the one"—this is Noah.

"Who has not followed the counsel of the wicked"—this is the generation of the Flood.

"Or taken the path of sinners"—this is the generation of the Tower of Babel.[6] [*This now requires a deep excursus into the nature of sacral*

---

3. Genesis 6:9.
4. R. Shlomo Yitzhaki ad loc Genesis 6:9.
5. Psalm 1:1.
6. *Genesis Rabbah* 26:1.

deeds, their purpose as well as the way they are practiced, and then the homily will return to its original question.]

The root of the matter [*from which the spiritual practice of sacral deeds and their order*] is that there is a type of *Yirah* (terror) [*moving to Awe and leading to Transparency of Self*] of a sacral deed, when one contemplates the reality that enacting it is itself divinity. [*The sacral act itself serves as an enshrouding of the divine totality embodied through the Indwelling Presence that is Shekinah. The object of the sacral deed is a crystallization of the divine, which elicits terror in touching divinity in this way. Yet paradoxically, one's humility causes the physical action to become a genuine and secure channel in allowing physicality into the spiritual realm.*] So when one enters into enacting a sacral deed wholly embodied with all its accoutrements [*because the spirit knows the divine cannot be fully embodied*], one gets anxious. One's spirit actually becomes agitated by the prospect of corporealizing the divine. Alas, were the divine corporealized, *perish the thought*! [*One should be agitated and troubled if the only focus of the sacral deed is a thickening of the spirit, by extension tainting it. It is this murkiness that emerges in dragging divinity into the realm of physical appetites. Within Kabbalah there is an interconnection of the spheres from Yesod to Malkut, referring to the channel of energy through all the levels, which serves as an interior connection to feel the animating of the divinity within every sacral deed and within an interconnectivity of all levels.*]

[*On enacting a sacral deed wholly embodied*] numerous agitations may emerge; nonetheless, one's conviction of the divine is strengthened. The sacral deed is itself the interconnection between embodied act and divinity. Namely, from the *Ratzon 'Elyon* (Original Will) "is the One that spoke and whose Will is realized,"[7] flowing all the way through the chain of being to

7. Rashi *ad loc* b*Zebahim* 46b; Rashi ad loc Leviticus 1:9. The divine pleasure happens when the divine will is being fulfilled, rather than simply being a pleasure that is corporealized with the eating of sacrifices. This tension is found already in the Tannatic debate on sacrifices between R. Ishmael and R. Akivah. The former position argues that the purpose of sacrifices was to wean the Israelites from idolatry, whereas the latter position argues that the sacrifices and their aroma were commanded to satisfy the divine will. See Abraham J. Heschel, *Heavenly Torah: As Refracted through the Generations*, trans. Gordon Tucker and Leonard Levin (New York: Continuum, 2005), 82–88. The Vitebsker's homelitical turn here is to refocus on the deeper spiritual meaning of fulfilling the Original Will. The Hasidic perspective is building upon the mystical stance of R. Akivah that sacrifices are offered not merely fulfilling a duty; rather, this is an expression of the divine will as it emerges from the primordial state of creation. Whereas the school of R. Ishmael transforms "aroma" (*reiah*) into a more transcendent "spirituality" (*ruhani*) so that the literal becomes concretized within the spiritual, by contrast, the school of R. Akivah is willing to remain more literal in identifying the true divine need as the aroma alone, thus opening a door to greater divine immanence. Therefore, it is an eruption of the primordial will into the physical realm. By taking something physical, animating it with spirit, then the aspirant allows the garb of

the lowliest forms, thus [*we gain*] understanding of how the *Shekinah* is enshrouded in that sacral deed. [*This becomes an opportunity to slip into the garb of the Shekinah as manifest in this physical sequence of movements and to feel how it moves up the levels, ultimately to the emergence of divinity in the creative process.*]

This enshrouding of the *Shekinah*, interface of the divine realm with the human phenomenal realm, connects all embodiment through one's limbs performing the sacral deed, *hitqashrut* (interconnecting through unfolding of emotional states), [*including*] one's *Da'at* (nexus point between emotional states and cognition) and *Binah* (discernment) all the way to the *Chokhmah* (root of their origin), reaching to the *'Ein Sof* (infinite without end). [*All the spiritual dispositions here refer to the six spheres from Chesed (compassion) through to Malkhuth (grounding), encompassing all sentient beings. Intuition (Da'at) remains the innermost electromagnetic energy that unifies all the spheres of spiritual dispositions, and its point of origin is nestled in the womb of Binah (discernment). She towers above these five other spheres, so that all sentient beings are interconnected through the other spiritual dispositions below Binah (discernment), including the innermost force field of divine dynamism of Da'at (nexus), thus in a sense, the lower dispositions return to their origin in Binah (discernment). This is not the negation or erasure of the physical; rather, it is the absorption of the physical back to its source in a higher spiritual state restoring it to its original nobility. In that integration, it does not lose its physicality, rather it has been re-energized and elevated, seen for its higher original aspect.*]

This is [*the meaning behind the verse*]: **"for sacral deeds are a lamp [serving as a vessel for the light of Torah of *HaBa"D*]."**[8] [*With Torah of the higher spheres, the earthenware vessel holding the oil, and cradling this light, then itself becomes the enshrouding of the divine light. Torah enables one to see the sublime status of the lamp itself*]. For the sacral deed is the lamp which is illumined by way of the light [*of transformed consciousness*] embedded in the teaching itself, given that *Chokhmah* and *Binah* (discernment) are known as "Torah light" [*namely, contemplative potential within every seeker*]. This is the esoteric meaning of the aforementioned verse, namely, that by way of contemplating *Chokhmah* (primordial point) and *Binah* (discernment) the sacral deed is imbued and then transformed [*to manifest*] that ethereal, transcendent light [*within the manifest world*].

But without this [*contemplation of Chokhmah (primordial point) and Binah (discernment) that imbues the sacral deed*] there is only duality and

---

the *Shekinah* to interface with the physical world and touch Her primordial source in the emergence of this eruptive moment when the infinite first expresses itself in the created condition.

8. Proverbs 6:23.

delusion [*so that the lamp is not manifesting true luminosity*]. So the interconnection [*of the human being and all corporeality to*] the divine totality, is through [*the sacral deed that interconnection takes place with the divine totality enshrouded in the corporeal realm*].

The sacral deed of a *miTZVah* is so called because of basis in the language of bonding and togetherness, *l'TZaVot* [*from TZaVtah, which means interconnection in Aramaic*], implying such interconnectivity and the unification of disparate elements into one organic whole.[9] [*This is an interconnectivity at the core and purpose of each and every sacral deed, namely, the interconnection of all sentient beings with the divine totality.*]

However [*this divine interconnectivity through the sacral deed*] is by way of the *Haskeil* (enspirited cognition)[10] and *Binah* (discernment) that [*the practitioner*] brings to each sacral deed [*to illumine it and so make it divine. Thus, it is the intellect and discernment of the practitioner that illuminates the sacral deed, and they*] are a function of the terror and trembling that takes hold lest one betray the divine by corporealizing it. [*This is the transparency born of a kind of "performance anxiety" by corporealizing the sacral deed through discipline and sharpness of focus to the point of not lapsing into excess or a missed opportunity, whereby*] this terror then nourishes one's steadfast conviction integrated through *'emunah.* [*It is by way of the intellect and discernment that the sacral deed is divine. It is fraught with the awareness of the delicate balance and necessary mindfulness of uplifting the physical to the spiritual without sinking the spiritual into the throes of coarse materiality and while remaining mindful of opening to such higher horizons. It takes effort to be constantly reminding oneself of aiming for this higher horizon*].

[*The process begins in awareness and clarity as to why the aspirant is engaged in the sacral deed through the path of the intellect and discernment so as to strengthen the inner conviction, so that*] one is then able to draw forth [*from this bolstered inner conviction*] of *Ahavah* (love) and *Simha* (joy) [*within the divine totality. This relates to the spheres of divine consciousness such that joy is an elevated expression of lower level terror, while love is an elevated expression of lower level enspirited cognition*]. All of this transpires on the level of spiritual disposition and integration [*in merging with the divine. Merging through spiritual dispositions and spheres is a further deepening beyond intellect and discernment*].

[*And the drawing forth of these spiritual dispositions of the love and*

9. b*Berakot* 6b.

10. This is a different modality which is the aspect of intellect that can grasp spirit; on *haskeil*, see "You gave also Your good spirit to instruct them, and withheld not Your manna from their mouth, and gave them water for their thirst" (Nehemiah 9:20), but the reading here is the gift of "en-spirited cognition."

joy in the divine totality, happens by way of] contemplation of the divine grandeur and supreme love to be a channel for this splendor from the Original Will [*until it reaches the corporeal immanence of the sacral deed itself. This is a pathway of ascent to the divine desire to share, to give, to bring the light into emergence*].

[*This splendor that shines forth and flows through its channels is the divine interconnectivity that is being drawn from the Original Will of the Limitless until it reaches the corporeal matter of the sacral deed itself*], enabling the enshrouding of the *Shekinah* into [*material*] manifestation. [*This is Her purpose, namely,*] to bind and unite [*the realm of manifestation*] with the [*divine totality*], thus making [*the divine reality present within the manifest realm*] in unity and complete merging. [*The challenge is to be mindful of conducting this cosmic symphony into physical form through general cognition and awareness. This requires a deep discipline of the interiority fused with a stillness and precision in the exteriority, with an abiding awareness of how difficult it is to remain precise while experiencing so much pleasure.*]

[*Thus, the contemplation of the divine grandeur and supreme love draws forth through the spiritual dispositions of love and joy merging the divine totality with the human aspirant. For it is the very contemplation of these supreme threads of love that channel the splendor of the Limitless and Original Will in order to connect the manifest and unite it in complete absorption.*]

However, all of this [*regarding the channeling of splendor through the spiritual dispositions of love and joy*] cannot begin its transformative process [*on the practitioner*] until the aforementioned *Yirah* (anxiety) and *Pahad* (awe) [*elicit an opening within the transparency of sacral deeds, which lies at the root of Awe. This opening leads to bolstering of inner conviction and from that foundation, a deeper contemplation is then possible*]. All the spiritual dispositions [*of love and joy,*] along with any accompanying joy that one elicits voluntarily cannot be genuine if they [*namely, the spiritual dispositions*] are not formulated within the mind. [*Such cognitive formulation is not effective unless it is*] preceded by [that shudder of] terror leading to awe, which then strengthens one's inner convictions. Joy can be self-generated [*and perhaps is therefore suspect*], and not necessarily genuine or real; rather, it is merely a fantastical projection. [*Such a determination may not be justified insofar as when this joy is actually emerging from a deep place*]. True spiritual joy must be preceded by the power of the tremendum. [*Without awe, one lapses into imaginative projection and possibly self-indulgence.*] A profound sensibility of inner conviction uniting all being is then strengthened, so that what then emerges with *Ahavah* (love) and *Simcha* (joy) that genuine—that is, the Holy Spirit. [*Inspiration of the Holy Spirit refers to the merging through love and joy. Proper awe leads to joy in the sacral deed. By allowing the infusion of the divine spirit to intake within one's self, thereby transforming one, emerging as the true love of attachment to the divine. This true joy is a realization that one is being animated by a new vital divine spirit. This is all to say that the love and joy are not self-generated, trying to agitate one's being; rather, one is aligning one's true self to be the vessel that is infused by vital divine spirit, which will surely animate one's being in joy and in a profound feeling of participatory emotion and love.*]

This is in line with what is reiterated many times in the Zohar[11] and Talmud:[12] awe must precede [*the process of merging with the divine totality, by allowing for an emptying of one's ego with love*], for without this preceding *Yirah* (awe) [*that is, when merging with love and all other dispositions are not authentic*], everything is delusional and vexed spirit rather than divine inspiration.

[*Continuing on this theme of generativity, there is a shift to the situation of the woman whose ovum inseminates first and "births" a male, which is here interpreted as generativity of the deeply devoted ones and their good deeds, which began the present homily.*] And as our blessed Sages teach: **"A woman who inseminates . . ."**[13] [*is interpreted as follows*]:[14]

"Insemination"—refers to the matter of [*both spiritual dispositions of*] *Yirah* (awe) and *Ahavah* (love). For it is known that during the moment of insemination, one can be overcome by both the most sublime levels of *Yirah* (awe) and *Ahavah* (love), with orgasmic shuddering [*mindful not to lapse into self-indulgence*], as explained in the Zohar,[15] **"and from physical act of sexual arousal shall I see the divine arousal."**[16]

"Woman"—this refers to the sacral deed, which is the *Shekinah* [*as explained above that the sacral deed is the enshrouding of the Shekinah, engendered as the divine feminine*].

[*After expounding on the matter of insemination interpreted as love and awe, as well as the feminine engendering of the sacral deed, the homily shifts to explain the verse and its rabbinic interpretation.*] This is the meaning of the verse: **"When a woman inseminates and births a male,"** [*that is*] if the awe overtakes a person from the sacral deed as it is embodied, then [*this embodiment flows all the way*] until it reaches to the spiritual dispositions like love and joy in the divine totality.

11. Zohar I:7b.
12. b*Shabbat* 31b.
13. Leviticus 12:1.
14. b*Berakot* 60a.
15. Zohar III:43a.
16. Job 19:26.

[*Inner convictions are bolstered*] through what was spoken by the One [*ordaining the embodied sacral deed*] and the Original Will was realized [*to continue drawing forth the divine interconnection from this source to the embodied sacral deed*].

Given that [*the Original Will*] is the world of re/membering, it then includes the memory of life, blessing, and flow of all effulgence into the universe. For it is through the Original Will that the world was created and creation is renewed [*through the Will*] constantly each day. From this effulgence flows forth the generativity of the sacral deed [*which is divine interconnectivity flowing from the Original Will. If sexual practice is on this level, it leads to divine generativity*]. When it gives birth [*within each sacral deed*], what emerges is something completely unique, unlike any other moment.

Since the Original Will preceded creation, it is through the Original Will [*that creation*] was instantiated [*thus it is through the generativity of the sacral deed emerging from this Will preceding creation that something completely unique can come into being and regenerate. Through this mindfulness in sexual practice, one is allowed to rise beyond the level of creation, returning all the way to the Original Will. For example, early Hasidic tales confirm this approach to spiritualizing sexual practice, so that in the hour that that the Maggid of Mezeritch begot his son, a pure spirit from the angelic sphere entered his wife's womb, and from there the angelic sphere was born for a brief space into the human realm. Teaching and expunging memory are assigned to two different angels, so that a concentration on the sacred during intercourse precludes the latter angel from expunging memory of natal Torah*].[17]

This is the guiding principle: "To teach you that the core value of the deeply devoted is embodied in good deeds"[18] [*that are generated spiritually from the Original Will. This comment of Rashi is attempting to disentangle a limited biological genealogy into the generative impact of good deeds upon the world and their legacy*]. From there [*namely, this place of spiritual generativity*] returns to an embodied generativity [*on an entirely different register*].

It is no coincidence that the first act of all sacral deeds is procreation [*for it is in the power of such generativity that the Original Will is drawn forth to flow into embodiment. Given that this generative act is foundational to the order of creation, if one is able to find purchase from an inward posture, then one is above the order of creation. That is what the new*

17. See Nehemia Polen, "Rebbetzins, Wonder-Children, and the Dynastic Principle in Hasidism," in *The Shtetl: New Evaluations*, ed. S. T. Katz (New York: New York University Press, 2007), 63.

18. R. Shlomo Yitzhaki ad loc Genesis 6:9.

generativity means, because one is replicating the first verse of generativity in Genesis 1:1 rather than in Genesis 1:24. From this position anterior to creation, then the child born of this generative act is from an entirely new order of creation and is imbued with a completely new vitality].

So once the deeply devoted are engaged with this sacral deed [*of procreation known physiologically now extended with the more inclusive body of generative acts*] through the aforementioned path [*of making the sacral deed transparent through awe that then bolsters one's inner conviction*], then [*this sacral deed*] ascends [*all the way to the Original Will that*] transcends the order of creation. The spirituality adds perpetuity to the physical. So **"you shall live by them"**[19] so that divine vitality expresses itself from this endless chain of generativity.[20] [*Beyond the biological baseline of every sexual act, additionally, there is the thread of divine vitality cascading through all of creation. This unique feature of the sacral sexual act is what enables the self to exist beyond the natural order.*]

[*This vitality is drawn to the generativity that becomes manifest from the Original Will and is*] separate [*from the spiritual vitality generated*] by the sacral deed itself. [*Namely,*] what is realized [*in the sacral deed of procreation is also the spiritual vitality that resides in every sacral deed. Yet this spiritual vitality of the sacral deed is not identical with whatever is generated and birthed into manifestation. The spiritual vitality of the sacral deed emerges*] also through this process of generativity.

And aside from [*the spiritual vitality of the sacral deed*], it becomes manifest forever and endures—[*so that the practitioner is*] living within [*these acts*] from multiverse to multiverse [*unlike the generativity of corporeal matters that are born and degenerate, without any sustaining power. This is why spiritual generativity of the sacral deed of procreation is not ancillary to the embodied creation that results from it; rather, it is significant to its very identity*].

So this matter [*regarding the transparency generated through the awe of the sacral deed and its generativity, from which the practitioner can ascend to the primordial, Original Will*] only comes about through humility and a subdued spirit. When the spiritual practitioner reflects and contemplates their subdued spirit and insignificance, such a person is anxious at the mere thought of embodying a sacral deed.

---

19. "You shall therefore keep My statutes, and My ordinances, which if one does, he shall live by them: I am YHVH" (Leviticus 18:5).

20. Divinity becomes human, not in any one particular person or body, but in the unending chain of generativity; see Charles Mopsik, "Union and Unity in the Kabbalah: The Proclamation of the Divine Unity and the Male/Female Couple," in *Sex of the Soul: The Vicissitudes of Sexual Difference in Kabbalah* (Los Angeles, Cherub Press, 2005), 128–49; ibid., "The Body of Engenderment in the Hebrew Bible, the Rabbinic Tradition and the Kabbalah," in *Zone: Fragments for the History of the Body*, vol. 3 (New York, 1989), 53, 57.

This is to be distinguished from the one whose false piety[21] becomes a tumultuous spectacle in performance of the divine sacral deeds [*lacking the deeper interconnective disposition of humility and a subdued spirit*], with one's ego swelling into inauthentic heights, projecting spiritual greatness fed by smug self-satisfaction. All of the spiritual dispositions and joy that then emerge for the practitioner are merely the fantasy of one's egocentric projection [*insofar it nurtures one's pride in achievement*]. All such sacral deeds are corporeal, lacking any vitality within, so all ensuing sacral deeds are manifest and embodied, without any bit of vitality within them [*that is, they lack the Shekinah enshrouded and are devoid of any human merging with the divine*].

This is what is meant by the verse [*regarding Noah as the second Adam given the permission to eat meat*]: **"And the fear of you and the dread of you shall be on every creature of the earth"**[22] and its placement after the sacral deed of procreation [*as stated in the previous verses: "And God blessed Noah and his sons, and said unto them: 'Be fruitful and multiply, and replenish the earth'."*] For as one engages in the sacral deed of procreation as a spiritual practice, then such awe propels this ascent into transparency, ascending beyond the natural order to the Original Will and drawing down the Primordial Vitality antecedent to creation [*as alluded to in "every creature (HaYaT) of the earth," which is the vitality (HeYuT) from which the earth itself was created. Any person who is able to engender a child in awe or even engendering awe and trembling before the immensities within daily life, will have a purchase of creation and will enjoy the reverence of the created condition by having preceded it*].

From [*the primordial Original Will*] is the vitality drawn into whatever is becoming manifest so that others will also feel this overwhelming sense of awe. [*Thus*] one's anxiety is over the awe [*that generates transparency*] over all sentient beings. So too, regarding [*the deeply devoted one*] in transcending creation then the awe [*that generates transparency*] permeates one's perception of all sentient beings. As the verse states: **"in-**

21. "False piety" derives from a reflexive verb, *mitHasid*, alluding to smug spiritual self-satisfaction that one is a pious person expressed openly. A common critique of the first generation of Hasidism was this very loud, tumultuous ecstatic spiritual practice. Suggestions by scholars like Pierkaz that this type of Hasidism is suffused with the ethical content and practice of musar, but it is much more sublime than suggested, insofar as genuinely reaching the state of *devequt* only out of true humility through genuine surrender, see Mendel Piekarz, *The Beginning of Hasidism: Ideological Trends in Derush and Musar Literature* (Bialik Institute, 1978).

22. "And the fear of you and the dread of you shall be on every creature of the earth, [and on every fowl of the air, and on all wherewith the ground teems, and on all the fishes of the sea: into your hand are they delivered]" (Genesis 9:2).

cline the [rule] of the many."[23]

"[T]he many" is represented here by the deeply devoted one [*emerging from this awe within the primordial Original Will serving as axis mundi*]. In this way [*that the deeply devoted one enacts the sacral deed of procreation as a spiritual practice, such a person ascends with this awe to transcend creation, so too with*] the vitality of the fruit [*of every sacral deed*].

It is due to the vitality within whatever is generated and its primordial awe transcends all sentient beings, emerging from the primordial Original Will. This is what [*is being expressed in this verse by the usage of these terms*]: And **"And the fear of you and the dread of you,"**[24] which is interpreted by R. Shlomo Yitzhaki as whatever does not precede awe and the extension of vitality of the birthing [*namely, the vitality generated from awe that transcends creation*], see further there.

This is to be distinguished from awe disconnected with its primordial root [*within the sacral deed*], and the drawing forth of vitality into that which is generated [*from its source in the primordial Original Will*]. How then would one be [*in this aforementioned state of*] **"one's vitality and awe imbuing all the creatures of the earth"[?]**

[*The homily shifts now into a more existential direction, by returning to the rabbinic quandary of whether it would leave human beings better off and at greater ease (b'noah in Hebrew) if they were never created. But since the human was created, one must search within and contemplate one's deeds. All this is a prelude to interpreting the verse in question about Noah and his genealogy, which we now recall opened the present homily.*]

This is the meaning behind the teaching of the blessed Sages: "Better off if the human being was not created, but now that the human being has been created . . ."[25] And the rabbinic super-commentary *Tosafot* problematized the assumption behind this teaching: "Come, let's bolster our ancestors for the good, for without them we would never have come into existence,"[26] which means that humanity is better off for having been created [*which contradicts the earlier rabbinic assumption*].

So from this response [*of the Tosafot, one can then adduce that it is better that*] the deeply devoted ones [*were created*], while the wicked [*are better off without having been created*]. Yet even upon being created, there

---

23. Literally, "You shall not follow a multitude to do evil; neither shall you bear witness in a cause to turn aside after a multitude to pervert justice" (Exodus 23:2); "incline"—this is the language of inclination towards awe; "the many"—this refers to the deeply devoted one whose awe overtakes all sentient beings.

24. "And the fear of you and the dread of you shall be on every creature of the earth, and on every fowl of the air, and on all wherewith the ground teems, and on all the fishes of the sea: into your hand are they delivered" (Genesis 9:2).

25. b*Eruvin* 13b.

26. *Tosafot ad loc* b*Eruvin* 13b.

is no good that comes from all the human being's toil under the sun [*the very place of one's creation*], unless one is able to transcend [*the toil*] beyond the sun, reaching a primordial state preceding creation [*which is the Original Will, coming to such a realization once one engages in spiritual practice of sacral deeds*].

Such a person might reach this [*primordial state of transcendence*] by self-reflection on past actions, to really take stalk, to then recognize one's ultimate insignificance. [*Being in this state of humility and subdued spirit opens one to the fully awesome quality of sacral deeds, and the anxiety over embodying anything so divine*], thus one shudders in enacting a divine sacral deed. [*After this anxiety over enacting any sacral deed then*] one will be more self-reflective with each ensuing sacral deed. This entanglement [*of anxiety and awe that now emerges within every sacral deed*] bolsters one's inner convictions [*that the practitioner's purpose is to make sacral deeds divine*].

This [*process of self-reflection and entanglement then*] leads one to emerge with an attitude of "divine inspiration" [*of merging through love*] and joy—[*which is the merging with the divinity of the sacral deed. Once this divine inspiration of merging within the divinity of the sacral deed begins,*] then one realizes the primordial Original Will—which is that [state] "of not being created."

This is what is intended by the rabbinic statement "it is better off if the human being was not created"—[*namely, it is better off*] to reach that point [*of uncreated nothingness, which is the primordial Original Will*].

"And now that the human is created," one will reach that state of "being uncreated"—[*which is the primordial Original Will*] through the aforementioned process of self-reflection and entanglement.

It is no longer that difficult [*regarding the opening rabbinic dictum that it would be better off not having been created*] to [*come to the Tosafot's position*] that "we should come and acknowledge the good of our ancestors" that has brought us into existence. This is what the *Tosafot* are addressing "in the deeply devoted ones"—[*namely, implanted within the spiritual practice of those engaged in deep self-reflection and entanglement, leading to awe that interconnects one to the primordial, Original Will*].

So this is the meaning of [*the opening verse*]: **"These are the generations of Noah,"** namely, [*the generations of better off for the human being*] to not have been created, [*which are generativities emerging from the place of the primordial Original Will*].

This is the esoteric meaning [*of the verse*]: **"Noah was pristine [*as*] a deeply devoted one within his generation"**—which are his good deeds [*namely, the sacral deeds which bring the practitioner to the Original Will*].

"In his generation"—that is the place of the Original Will, which is [*the source and root of all*] the ensuing generations;

Or another way of interpreting **"In his generation"**—that is, the sacral deed of procreation [*which is solely concerned with continuity and generativity, and in this very sacral deed*] Noah was "deeply devoted in a pristine way" as well [*as with other sacral deeds*]. He realized the manifestation of this sacral deed [*of procreation*] to its primordial point.

Along this path [*of procreation which is solely concerned with continuity and generativity through this very sacral deed*], one could say that every sacral deed has embedded within its own kind of generativities. So the verse continues: **"And Noah begot three sons, Shem, Ham, and Japheth."**[27] From this aforementioned spiritual practice of the sacral deed of procreation, was he able to manifest three physical progeny [*which drew forth the primordial Original Will*]. So too can one interpret their three names.

"Ham"—[*the younger*] is the corporeal manifestation of the sacral deed [*as it becomes enshrouded and embodied*]. As the smallest [*in terms of corporeality*], it follows the explanation of R. Shlomo Yitzhaki in the middle of the genealogical order [*regarding his comment on Genesis 9:24, suggesting that Ham was the most "unworthy and despicable" in his materiality*]. And since Ham is a name denoting corporeality [*of the sacral deed*], he becomes overwhelmed by the spiritual energy within the material [*and whether it was even possible to manifest the awesome quality of the divine through any sacral deed*].

Then one reaches **"Shem"**—who symbolizes the *Shekinah* [*which draws forth enshrouding of the sacral deed*]. As Scripture states: **"And David got him a name [*Shem*]"**[28] [*which symbolizes the Shekinah*].

And from the *Shekinah* [*which is the awe of divine interconnectivity within the sacral deed*] one arrives at **"Japheth,"** who is the eldest [*the antithesis of the reductive quality of manifestation*] which is love. [*Namely, merging with the divine is the spiritual reality of the sacral deed.*]

As Scripture states [*when read hyper-literally*]: **"Elohim was beautiful to Japheth"**[29] [*for the root of YaPHet is beauty or YoPHi, which is the spiritual disposition of love*]. For love is the spiritual disposition and joy [*that one realizes on being overtaken with the awe of the sacral deed, bolstering one's inner conviction of the supreme love*] as the spiritual practice.

This explains why verse continues: **"And Noah the husbandman began, and planted a vineyard,"**[30] which is interpreted to mean that Noah

27. Genesis 6:10.

28. "And David got him a name when he returned from smiting the Arameans in the Valley of Salt, even eighteen thousand men" (2 Samuel 8:13).

29. Literally, "God enlarge Japheth, and he shall dwell in the tents of Shem; and let Canaan be their servant" (Genesis 9:27).

30. Genesis 9:20.

entered the mundane, according to R. Shlomo Yitzhaki's comment. In becoming **"a man of the earth,"** he was manifest corporeally.

"And planted a vineyard"—that is, the sacral deed itself, as Scripture states: **"but mine own vineyard have I not kept"**[31] [*namely, that as a one becomes more embodied and grounded upon the earth, then it is necessary to be implanted in spiritual practice*] which is embodied.

The verse continues**: "And Ham saw [*the corporeal facet of the sacral deed which is*] the nakedness of his father"**[32]—that is, [*Ham judges the divine, seeing the sacred in a contemptible context which is an utter*] neglect of his Heavenly Father in becoming trapped in so coarse a manifestation.

"[A]nd told his two brothers without"[33]—whereby **"told"** is the language of drawing forth [*the divine reality and the enshrouding of the Shekinah in the sacral deed, so that it would not devolve into coarseness of manifestation*].

"[S]tream . . . drew forth"[34]—[*whereby **"drew forth"** is equivalent to **"told,"** which is from the language of the river that **"issues"** and comes forth. The reasoning of **"and he told"** as **"spoken word"** is because it rectifies the corruption of materializing the sacral deed by drawing into it the spiritual vitality of the divine*] for the spoken work is what orchestrates all spirituality that arises. [*That is, all arousal and spiritual comportment is drawn through the spoken word*], and the materialization as well [*is aroused and orchestrated in this manner*], as is known.

And so this is why it is called a **"spoken word"**—from the language of comportment. This is also the case with the [*Aramaic*] translation of the verse—**"and human became a living soul"**[35]—rendered as "spirit speaking" [*that is, translating "living" as "speaking" which is the "spoken word"*], for the spoken word is the vitality [*namely, spiritual comportment. Now the homily focuses on the three levels of every sacral deed, from the physical to its becoming nestled into categories, and from there to love and beauty*].

"And Shem and Japheth took a garment"[36]—which is the aforemen-

31. "Look not on me, that I am swarthy, that the sun has tanned me; my mother's sons were incensed against me, they made me keeper of the vineyards; but mine own vineyard have I not kept" (Song of Songs 1:6).

32. "And Ham, the father of Canaan, saw the nakedness of his father, and told his two brethren without" (Genesis 9:22).

33. Genesis 9:22.

34. "A fiery stream issued and came forth from before him; thousand thousands ministered unto him, and ten thousand times ten thousand stood before him; the judgment was set, and the books were opened" (Daniel 7:10).

35. "Then the YHVH God formed human of the dust of the ground, and breathed into its nostrils the breath of life; and human became a living soul" (Genesis 2:7).

36. "And Shem and Japheth took a garment, and laid it on both their shoulders, and

tioned enshrouding [*of the Shekinah in the sacral deed, which allows the seeker to elevate corporeality as a gift rather than something despicable*].

"[A]nd their faces were backward"[37]—which is [*the humility of*] subdued spirit and awe [*drawn through the sacral deed becoming transparent*] and turned away in fear of approaching him [*that is, lest they materialize the sacral deed, and afterward the awe of the sacral deed draws forth the enshrouding of the Shekinah within it so as not become fully materialized*].

In this way **"and they saw not their father's nakedness"**[38]—[*namely, they engaged in spiritual practice of the divine sacral deed that would not materialize it*].

[*To conclude, this homily now reiterates the spiritual practice of sacral deeds, which interconnects the practitioner with the Original Will*]. The general principle: one's lower connection to the Original Will [*by way of spiritual practice of the sacral deed is initially*] through a subdued spirit, anxiety, and the awe that generates transparency. Through this does one come to contemplation, speculation, and wisdom, which one will then integrate into every sacral deed engaged in, as mentioned above. But without [*such*] actively applied contemplation and discernment the sacral deed remains just corporeal. And so too, the inverse, namely, a disembodied spirituality of the sacral deed, neither actively applied contemplation nor discernment serves to effectively connect one to the blessed Creator. [*One only gains that transcendence when the devotion of mindfulness is grounded in physical practice.*]

The prooftext here is King Solomon, of whom it is said: **"He was the wisest of all men."**[39] [*He was more integrated than any other human through contemplation, intellectual speculation, and wisdom.*] But because he tried to be wise without [*following*] the sacral deed which warned the king **"not to multiply horses and women"**[40]—saying, "I will multiply and not go astray"[41]—he faltered notwithstanding [*his wisdom*]. [*Solomon tried to separate his contemplation from being actively applied to his embodied deeds, and without something to hold onto, the spiritual insight then gets lost.*]

This is the meaning of our blessed Sages' statement [*with which we began*][42] **"Happy is the one"**—this is Noah [*the one who transcends the generation of the flood who are constantly tossed by the waves of the intel-*

---

went backward, and covered the nakedness of their father; and their faces were backward, and they saw not their father's nakedness" (Genesis 9:23).

37. Genesis 9:23.
38. Genesis 9:23.
39. 1 Kings 5:11.
40. Deuteronomy 17:16-17.
41. b*Sanhedrin* 21b.
42. *Genesis Rabbah* 26:1.

lect that ceaselessly break against the mind of the intellect; on the other hand, this is one who transcends standing in one place like the generation of Babel, stuck in a physical existence without any devotional practice].

"Who has not followed the counsel of the wicked"—this is the generation of the flood [*that only follows the counsel of the intellect; this is insufficient. If one only follows pure intellect in disembodied contemplation, then one succumbs to becoming flooded with mind over heart*].

The meaning of [*the generation of the flood*] refers to use of the intellect divorced from the spiritual practice of sacral deeds. For one can become flooded with excessive awareness [*and overwhelmed by the incessant and relentless flow of ideas*], as the verse says: **"YHVH sat at the flood and YHVH will sit as king forever,"**[43] as referred to in the Zohar.[44] [*For the Vitebsker, there is a negativity to the Waters of Quarrel that undergird this flood, so it is only through divine intervention that any quieting of this mind overwhelmed by divisive ideas will quell the flood. Intellectuals are in love with ideas, but sooner or later the idea will fall out of fashion. The Vitebsker is putting forth the problematic of the spiritual life quite starkly—namely, that being "flooded by idea"' is problematic (i.e., waters of strife) but so is standing in one place (i.e., waters of peace). The physicality becomes bonded with deeper integrity with all levels of the being, up to the level beyond mere Intellect, resting in Intuitive Apperception. This then enables one to be both fluid and grounded. This integration is what allows one to be supple and fluid while still retaining continuity.*][45]

43. Psalm 29:10; b*Zevahim* 116a.

44. Zohar I:64b trans. Matt, Pritzker edition, 377: "The secret is: 'YHVH sat at the flood' (Psalm 29:10). What does sat mean? If the verse were not written, we could not say it. He sat by, alone, not accompanying Judgment. Here is written: sat, and there is written: 'Along . . . sit' (Leviticus 13:46)—all alone." See Matt, 377n257: "YHVH, symbolizing Compassion, sat alone, uninvolved in the Flood, while Judgment, symbolized by the name Elohim, wrought the catastrophe." The Vitebsker is using this passage in Zohar to contrast different types of contemplation. For any mere mortal sitting alone in such a singular form of contemplation, as in the case of God sitting alone in contemplation, such contemplation would cause the mind to be flooded. Noah was not engaged in pure contemplation and therefore was not swept away. Rather, Noah's form of contemplation exemplifies this subtle fusion that allows for the ethereal to be grounded in an embodied way, thus preserving the insight of contemplation through its application to the physical world.

45. Zohar I: 65b, trans. Matt, Pritzker edition, 386–87: "'And I, I am about to bring the Flood, waters on the earth' (Genesis 6:17). Rabbi Yehudah opened, 'These are the Waters of Quarrel, where the Children of Israel quarreled with YHVH, and through which He was hallowed' (Numbers 20:13). Didn't 'the Children of Israel quarrel with YHVH' anywhere else? What's different here, that the verse should state: 'These are the Waters of Quarrel,' and not others? But these were really 'Waters of Quarrel,' potently empowering the masters of judgement. For there are sweet waters and bitter waters, clear waters and turbid waters, waters of peace and waters of strife. So 'these are the Waters of Quarrel, where the Children of Israel quarreled with YHVH,' attracting to themselves the one they must not, through

"Or taken the path of sinners"—this is the generation of the tower of Babel" who had [*only*] external awe [*only allowing them to work on the exteriority of the sacral while remaining devoid of the contemplative interiority otherwise practiced. This is a fear and anxiety of lapsing into complacency*].

As Scripture states: "**[*And they said, 'Come, let us build us a city, and a tower with its top in the sky, to make a name for ourselves*;] lest we shall be scattered [*all over the world*].**"[46] [*The builders were anxious because they were afraid that they would disperse spiritually. This fear of dispersion by the generation of the Tower of Babel is an instance of exterior, lower Yirah. However, the potential for an integrated approach to spiritual practice is nascent here. Indeed, as in any mitzvah, only a fraction of it as a sacral act is made corporeal: as spiritual seekers we are permitted to, and even must, begin by "getting a toehold" in the material world. Once the seeker "gets a toehold" s/he begins the process of fusing the spiritual core with embodied practice. Then, s/he is spiritually readied to access the inner divine reality of the Shekinah enshrouded in the sacral deed.*] May God implant within every mind a keen heart, an aware heart, a knowing heart, insight, and divine knowledge integrated in [*the inner landmarks of the mind-heart state of*] Zion [*the inner compasses that guide us in this fusion of the spiritual with the embodied to the divine within homeward so this supple fluidity can move forward with continuity and integrity. The practice is integrated with the highest level of contemplation. This integration guards one against over-intellectualism or religious-behavioralism by ensuring that the ethereal insights from contemplation remain grounded in an embodied form of devotion*], *Amen.*

[1.3]. *Parashah Noach* (Genesis 6:19–11:32)

QUESTIONS FOR REFLECTION:

1. How do you ensure that your contemplation is never devoid of sacral deeds embodied?

2. When is it most challenging to be fully aware of this divine–human interconnectivity through the spiritual practice of sacral deeds?

3. How do love and joy serve as helpful guides preceding awe to avoid delusion? Does your spiritual practice more effectively draw on other spiritual dispositions to achieve a similar non-duality?

---

whom they became defiled, as is written, 'through which he was tabooed.'"

46. Genesis 11:4.

4. Once your steadfast conviction is bolstered, how do you react to the expansiveness of supreme love then being contemplated? How does this contemplation maintain any sense of grounding amid the merging experience?

[2.1]. *Parashah Lech Lecha* (Genesis 12:1–17:27)

INTRODUCTION TO HOMILY:

Truly immersive experiences of human consciousness within the divine emerge by way of an expansive spiritual support system—namely, 'emunah, as articulated in Genesis 15:6. Typically translated as "faith," 'emunah lies at the heart of this devotional literature of Tiberian Hasidism, to elucidate that 'emunah is anything but simplistic, passive, blind acceptance of dogmatic assertions. To really appreciate 'emunah, it is important throughout this homily to reflect upon 'emunah as a continuum with many levels of spiritual development. One thus needs to appreciate that there are two systems of esoteric gnosis: Keter (No-thing)-Chokhmah (Wisdom)-Binah (Discernment) versus Chokhmah (Wisdom)-Binah (Discernment)-Da'at (Intuition). Da'at is the lower reflection of Keter. The Vitebsker seems to be integrating the Kabbalistic system of Keter-Chokhmah -Binah into his experience of 'emunah, which begins lower and then ascends higher beyond. 'Emunah is thus a way of being grounded while soaring to the highest level. This is another aspect of its being anything but simplistic, "blind faith." Chokhmah-Binah-Da'at teaches the truth of divine immanence and a limited contemplation of this truth of permeating divinity, but does not really invite experience. This is precisely what the Vitebsker will be attempting to invite here through 'emunah. It is through 'emunah then that the spiritual being as subject has the capacity to operate supra-rationally. The supra-rational realm of consciousness is not irrational but builds upon the faculties of cognition, which feature thinking as a process of discernment, understanding, and categorization of the infinite. The expansive 'emunah, or spiritual support system, being sought here is one that extends beyond thinking as a process of discernment, understanding, and categorization. True 'emunah transcends mundane experiences of ephemeral pleasure and bliss, opening to a deeper, limitless joy that paradoxically lies at the heart of circumcision, which is articulated for the first time in Genesis 17:10. The rationale behind circumcision as the "diminishment of pre-sentient desire" is what opens the subject to feelings of infinite bliss that emerge through the ultimate interconnectivity, which is the circuitry of an expansive spiritual support system being reframed here as 'emunah. The spiritual alignment with the divine totality advocated here is not based on the entanglement of personal experience or ephemeral spiritual pleasures; rather, there is an austere turning to detachment from the world to reach the place of infinite bliss. Recall that being passionately in the world is possible within the panentheism of the pioneering hasidism of the Ba'al Shem Tov, while the acosmicism of his disciple the Maggid leads to seeing the world as illusory, having reached the Chokhmah level as the detachment of bittul (dissolution), thus demanding a deeper modality of ascetic contemplation. The challenge here could not be starker—if one truly yearns for alignment with the divine perspective, it requires a devastating degree of detachment, to live beyond the world of natural human spiritual pleasure, dissolving deeper into the limitless spiritual pleasure of the divine.

The "I am" level of consciousness is the point which recognizes the impossibility of separating the self from phenomenal experience, but it does not yet recognize where the "I am" comes from—for it is an indefinable experience of existence. Thus the "I am not" is a prior, higher level of consciousness. But considering this level of bittul (dissolution)—such a devastating degree of detachment—as the ultimate is confusing a deep state of consciousness as the final state of consciousness. However, if the seeker knows how to carry the inquiry further, then one might realize the level of Keter (No-thingness), which is an integration of above and below—the state where consciousness recognizes there is no difference between darkness and light. Rather, what is real hovers there in the dark and there in the light. Thus, to merge into this state of consciousness does not require detachment from phenomenal experience. Devotional life requires an integral balance of the "I am" and the "I am not" as opposite sides of the same coin—the contemplation of the spheres of Chokhmah and Binah. This allows for the self-negation of bittul (dissolution) that exposes the transparency of a deeper underlying reality, and the engagement of serving the ultimate reality (yegiah) as a form of agency of the transcendent without any contradiction.

[2.2]. *Parashah Lech Lecha* (Genesis 12:1–17:27)

HOMILY:

Our blessed Sages explore the question of why circumcision [*according to its scriptural foundation*] is inscribed on the genitalia.[47] As Scripture states: **"every male among you shall be circumcised"**[48]—on the very site of masculinity [*as the engendered site of remembering*].[49] The matter is explicated in the verse: **"And because [Abram] put his trust in YHVH, so Abram achieves self-realization [so all of his spiritual achievements flow freely] with no compelling cause."**[50] In turn, this verse is then un-

47. b*Shabbat* 108a.

48. "Such shall be the covenant between Me and you and your offspring to follow which you shall keep: [every male among you shall be circumcised]" (Genesis 17:10).

49. Compare with the polemical shift in Christian theology that supersedes circumcision, replacing it with faith, for example, in Paul's Letter to the Galatians 5:6: "For in Christ Jesus neither circumcision nor uncircumcision avails anything, but faith working through love."

50. "And because [Abram] put his trust in YHVH, so the One reckoned it to his merit"

derstood anew when linked with what our blessed Sages teach that "one should always first recount the Holy One's praise, and only then engage in petitionary prayer"[51]—for the *Shekinah* is also called "Prayer" [*by virtue of receiving without causing anything of Her own.*[52] *The Shekinah is considered to be "Prayer" as the symbol of spiritual support known* as *'emunah, so*] it is only possible to take place through the merging of *devequt*[53] into the Original Will [*known as the sphere of Keter*] by way of a *'emunah* trusting in what lies beyond[54] without any incentive[55] [*using the intellect to transcend the intellect, beyond all discernment and apperception. This is only possible after building on the rational side of cognition, but it is only after exercising the heights and limits of cognition that the mystical experience is possible. The fact that Original Will of Keter (Crown) is above Chokhmah (Primordial Point) and Binah (Discernment) means it is an emergent and developmental property from the heights of the intellect, resting entirely on the foundation of the intellect itself. The ladder cannot be thrown away once the insight is reached; rather, the ladder remains a foundational path that is continually nurturing the aspirant from what comes before. The profundity of the intellect is the realization that the intellect can only take one so far. Nothing could be further from the misperception and mistranslation of this as "blind faith." This is what is meant above by "ordering of praise before engaging in prayer," which tends to be intellectual and cognitive, yet "Prayer" is itself the Shekinah—namely, expansive spiritual support of 'emunah, without any discernment and apperception*].[56]

(Genesis 15:6). See R. Joseph Gikatillia, *Shaarai Orah, Second Gate, Ninth Sphere:* "Zaddik gives, Tzedek receives, where the secret act of giving, conjoining and interlocking is called Tzedakah."

51. "R. Simlai expounded: One should always first recount [literally "order"] the praise of the Holy One, and then pray in a petitionary manner." See b*Berakot* 32a, b*Avodah Zarah* 7b. On the embodied choreography of salutation of praise preceding the petition in rabbinic liturgy follows the etiquette of approaching the sovereign power, see more recently Uri Erlich, *The Non-verbal Language of Jewish Prayer [Kol . . . Tefila]* (Jerusalem: Magnes Pres, 1999).

52. Zohar I:24a.

53. *Devequt* is a pure and simple reaching out and surrendering without any ground of being which thus requires *'emunah*. The spectrum of mystical experience being described ranges from sympathetic alignment to total absorption.

54. *'Emunah* is more than merely "belief"; rather, it is the "conviction" at the ground of being and thus enables a deeper connectivity between self and Other, between pray-er and the source of blessing. If the Vitebsker only meant "blind faith," he would not be sublimely invoking the Supernal Will.

55. One uses the intellect to transcend that intellectual apprehension, surrendering it to the higher level that is yet to be apprehended in ongoing process. This approach of the Vitebsker finds full expression in later Hasidism; see R. Yehudah Aryeh Leib of Ger, *Sefat Emet*, Parashah b'Hukotai [1872] (Jerusalem, 5757), 202a–b.

56. The unconditionality is Tzedakah whereby there is a conjoining between *Zaddik/Yesod* and *Tzedek/Malkhut* has no rationalization and is simply the incessant yearning to be

The nuances at play [*in the "ordering of praise before engaging in prayer"*] become more evident through the following verse: **"All streams flow into the sea, Yet the sea is never full; / To the place [from] which they flow / The streams flow back again."**[57] The Indwelling Presence of the *Shekinah* [*is the "sea" which*] **"has nothing of Her own"**[58] [*without any discernment and apperception*]—except that which she receives from other spheres of divine consciousness [*namely, the "Streams"*]. The one attempting to pray has to then set in place praises in order to turn on the flow of these spiritual qualities from above [*which are the six lower emotionally based spheres of Chesed (Compassion)-Gevurah (Rigor)-Tiferet (Splendor)-Neẕach (Endurance)-Hod-(Humility) Yesod (Foundation)*] down into *Shekinah.*[59] These [*lower six emotional*] spheres are at once a description of the divine [*engaged by "ordering of praise before engaging in prayer"*], as well as that very overflow of the divine. There is only one way to merge Her with the blessed Holy One; it is simply impossible except by way of "Prayer" through spiritual transparency [*which is expansive spiritual support without any apprehension and apperception, as it is only this path that opens up the possibility of the merging experience. As Scripture describes it in the verse*]: **"in this way does . . . one enter into the holy."**[60] Merging with the Holy One is possible through *Tefillah* (surrender) [*with Shekinah, serving as the pathway to enter into a sacred state merging with the divine*] which is also an overflow through transparency.[61] The *Shekinah* **"has nothing of Her own"**[62] [*which is the groundedness that allows one to surrender. Reaching this higher level provokes a deeper level of Tefillah,*

connected. *'Emunah* is about interconnecting one's allegiance to a loving relationship that leads to trust, which then leads to deeper connection. See the opening sections of *Genesis Rabbah* about *'emunah* where this post-verbal relationship is depicted as a kind of spiritual art or craft. More importantly, the subtext here is the polemics of Paul's *Letter to the Galatians* 2:1-14, where the covenantal relationship inscribed through circumcision in the flesh is superceded by "faith" inscribed in the heart.

57. Ecclesiastes 1:7.

58. Zohar II:218b.

59. The ordering of prayer is an emptying out of language through praise, so that the pray-er is ready to receive just like the *Shekinah*. The associative cluster of *Shekinah* [Neighboring Presence]-Tefillah [Prayer]-Yirat haRomemut [Awe] requires that the first step of ordering praises by the pray-er. This process that makes the divine possible the process through ritual is known as theurgy as defined by Mopsik, see Charles Mopsik, *Les grands textes de la cabale: Les rites qui font Dieu* (Paris: Verdier, 1993).

60. Literally, "Thus only shall Aaron enter the Shrine: with a bull of the herd for a sin offering and a ram for a burnt offering" (Leviticus 16:3).

61. Through *yirah*, which is translated here not literally as "fear" or "awe," but the spiritual embodiment of awe, which is "transparency"—also etymologically related to the seeing/being seen within *yirah*.

62. Zohar II:218b.

enabling further surrender. This is a recursive loop at ever higher levels. The paradox of spiritual advancement is that each level of advancement requires surrender, rather than grasping, which is already a fall. One hopes to ascend higher and higher, surrendering that higher level, if one is to pray as a form of surrender. The expansive spiritual support has no apprehension and apperception of its own, thus will the human being seek Her], then one must set in place praises in order to turn on the flow of these qualities. [*The ordering of these lower six spiritual spheres carries forward energies into a state of "Prayer," symbolized as the Shekinah*]. This [*ordering of the lower spheres is what*] then enables the *Shekinah* to remark: **"Take heed of this wonderful child I bring before You."**[63] [*The Kabbalistic mapping renders the spheres into the following familial groups: "father," "mother," "son," "daughter," "child," or "son" refers to the lower six spheres in relationship to the Shekinah, as these children bring Her as expansive spiritual support of 'emunah and "Prayer," for which the human being seeks to merge with the divine.*]

[*Notwithstanding the understanding and comprehension of "giving order to praise of the One," which arouses and brings it toward 'emunah and tefillah, behold*] when [*in prayer*] one reaches a merging state of *devequt* [*which is 'emunah beyond understanding and comprehension*], then a deeper apperception becomes possible by way of a trusting *'emunah*. For one has yet to apperceive [*the divine, and still*] there is no sensorial perception.[64] Once in this state of *devequt*, the aspirant realizes that all preparatory prayer has not even grasped the Holy One whatsoever until entering [*a consciousness of*] the *Shekinah*. The glory [*of the Holy One*] is felt in this [*deeper*] merging of *devequt* by way of *'emunah* alone that comes after cognitive and philosophical apperceptions [*which precede prayer, when one is "giving order to praise of the One"*]. All apperceptions are incapable of truly grasping the Holy One [*thus using the intellect to transcend it*] which is actually [*an extension of the*] Limitless. [*So that all cognitive and philosophical apperceptions which precede prayer, when one is "giving order to praise of the One"*] only serve to strengthen *'emunah* [*but are not*

63. Zohar III:3a, compare with the paraphrase in *Ketem Paz* (a forthcoming volume in this series) of Zohar II:217a, which evokes a tone in the dialogue of the *Shekinah*'s as akin to a proud mother who derives pleasure from her children in front of the angels.

64. All prayer is preparation, yet this preparation to pray through prayer is necessary for the true merging of *devequt*. Of the four characteristics common to William James's definition of the "mystical experience" (i.e., Ineffability [difficult to articulate in language]; Noetic Quality [presenting themselves as states of knowledge]; Transiency [unable to be sustained long term]; Passivity [unable to control their coming and going]), the state of consciousness being described here is akin to Passivity, whereby "the mystic feels as if his own will were in abeyance, and indeed sometimes as if he were grasped and held by a superior power," see Robert S. Elwood, *Mysticism and Religion* (Seven Bridges Press: New York, 1999), 33.

true depth apperceptions of the divine. The pray-er shines in a higher level of praise through greater wonder, inculcating a deeper state of devequt, continuing in this endless cyclical process. Shekinah is the groundedness that allows the pray-er to transcend and elevate].

[*Just as "giving order to praise of the One" strengthens one's 'emunah, so too*] the strengthening of one's trusting *'emunah* expands and shines as the aspirant engages in "giving order to praise of the One endlessly" [*from its original state*]. The more one "giving order to praise of the One" exults in the wondrous ways that transcend self and knowing, the more the aspirant can merge through *devequt* with transcendent "Prayer" [*as Shekinah*], beyond any causation. [*From "giving order to praise of the One, and then entering into prayer" comes a state of a more expansive 'emunah. So one is able to ascend from one degree to the next, beginning from cognitive comprehension and ascending to a more expansive state of 'emunah, which is a truer merging in devequt with the divine.*] **"But the earth [as *Shekinah* in Her expansive state of *'emunah*] remains the same forever"**[65]—namely, beyond apperception of the Holy One, the purpose of *'emunah* is getting the aspirant to reveal the concealment of the *Shekinah.* [*In each degree of ascent, there is an expansion through "giving order to praise of the One," then a spanning emerges from there to the "earth" which is the state of*] pristine *'emunah* beyond cognitive understanding of the divine, **"because [Abram] put his trust in YHVH."**[66] As discussed above, this is continuous. [*The higher advancement of spirit that is fueled by 'emunah and devequt must then promote a more sweeping surrender through this spiraling virtuous loop. Surrendering the pride of accomplishment is being called for.*]

"Those tributaries [of spiritual qualities which are precisely those components of 'giving order to praise' through cognitive comprehension] all run to the Sea [of the *Shekinah*, expanding Her pristine spiritual support of *'emunah* beyond comprehension and perception to the

65. "One generation goes, another comes, / But the earth remains the same forever" (Ecclesiastes 1:4). Needing to bring the experience of prayer "back down to earth," the Vitebsker draws on this verse from Ecclesiastes. While "the earth" is a common symbol of the *Shekinah*, it also can be translated as "the land," which may refer to the heightened presence of the *Shekinah* in the Land of Israel. Notwithstanding the Exile of the *Shekinah* since the destruction of the Jerusalem Temples, the Vitebsker understood one key function of his 1777 emigration was to "reveal what is concealed" of Her presence within the Land of Israel as a way of deepening prayer experiences for their community in Tiberias as well as on behalf of diaspora communities.

66. "And because [Abram] put his trust in YHVH, so the One reckoned it to his merit" (Genesis 15:6). See R. Joseph Gikatillia, *Shaarai Orah, Second Gate, Ninth Sphere*: "Zaddik gives, *Tzedek* receives, where the secret act of giving, conjoining and interlocking is called *Tzedakah*."

next degree of ascent] but the Sea is never full"[67] [*namely, that this cyclical process is never ending on the path to the Limitless, so that whatever is grasped intellectually is transcended and surrendered*], as discussed above.

Now take note of the distinction in the exegesis between Noah and Abraham.[68] Noah is likened to the King's beloved, who sits back in the dark and waits for the King to come to turn the light on for him, whereas Abraham is likened to the King's lover, who comes forward to serve the King by illuminating the [*palace*]. The King says to the lover: "Instead of shining a light in darkness, come and shine a light in a luminous place." So, the language of [*the exegesis on these scriptural verses*] could not be more clear when it states: **"Go forth [*into the luminous place*]**."[69]

The matter can be understood as follows: given his capacity for expansive, supra-rational *'emunah*, Noah was a saint [*without any philosophical apperceptions or contingencies*]. This is why the Holy One illumined the way for Noah. But it was altogether different in the case of Abraham [*who arrived at his relationship with the divine through philosophical apperceptions and contemplation*]. By way of [*philosophical apperceptions leading to his own*] contemplation, at age three Abraham already knew of his Creator,[70] so that he matured spiritually and grew in intuitive capacity, discernment, and cognition. Still after all this [*philosophical apperception, deepening his cognitive capacities for intuition, discernment, and intelligence*], Abraham remained unblemished in all of his deeds, thus utterly embodying [*that rare combination of pristine and profound*] *'emunah*. [*'Emunah then is most meaningful when it builds upon cognitive insight from intuition, discernment, and intelligence, the very opposite of "blind faith."*]

As Scripture teaches [*regarding the divine call to Abraham*]: **"Walk with Me [before there is even any formally revealed law],"**[71] which is [*an anomian way of being*] transcending [*the implied duality of*] spiritual attributes [*of an expansive state of 'emunah. The lower seven spiritual attributes are themselves the product of a preliminary cognitive apperception that requires a constant cycle of apperceiving and surrendering that apperception to a deeper and more expansive state of 'emunah. The bonding here emerges from a succession of cognitive grasp and surrender, which is an endless cycle linking to the limitless divine consciousness through its spherical unfolding from the non-manifest to the manifest*].

"And be pristine"[72] afterward—for transcendental apperception is lim-

67. Ecclesiastes 1:7.

68. *Genesis Rabbah* 30:11.

69. Genesis 12:1.

70. b*Nedarim* 32a.

71. Literally, "When Abram was ninety-nine years old, YHVH appeared to Abram and said to him, 'I am *El Shaddai*.' Walk in My ways and be blameless" (Genesis 17:1).

72. Genesis 17:1.

itless, whereby interconnectivity and true merging of *devequt* to the blessed Holy One happens through the steadfast conviction of *'emunah* alone.

[*This issue of interconnectivity which emerges through 'emunah rather than through cognitive apperception is also operative in the process of creation, which can be seen in the exegetical imagination. Consider this*] parable to explain how the interconnective tissue of the worlds is evident within *'emunah*. In the terrestrial world, there is that precognitive moment of child while still connected to their parent. It is precisely in this state that precedes cognitive recognition by the child that gives the parent such immense pleasure.

This was the intention of the blessed Holy One **"to create the world in the beginning."** Just as the child experiences pleasure that is manifest in a precognitive recognition of the parent, which brings such immense joy to the parent, so too with Israel [*the One who sees divinity*], known as *Reishit* [*that primal point of beginning*], endowed with the precognitive pleasure of knowing how to glorify the Creator and then call out "Our Father, Our King."[73] What greater delight could the blessed Holy One hope for? As our blessed Sages teach: "More than the calf wants to suck, the cow wants to suckle."[74] In this core of interconnectivity, where the worlds are pouring forth from one to the next, there is a greater desire of the upper showering that below it with goodness. And in its showering goodness, the upper receives greater pleasure than that below it in its receiving this overflow of goodness. [*One of the reasons that motivates our spiritual growth and one of the delights that propels spiritual development from level to level, is precisely the increasing levels of pleasure in knowing that we can continue to hold on to and develop. As much pleasure as I receive as a child, it only increases with further development and an even richer bond. That joyous experience of the emerging horizons promises deeper receiving and transmitting from continuing elevating multiverses of consciousness.*]

But the parable has limitations. The fact that the creation of the cosmos happened through such interconnectivity suggests it was programmed into the world from creation; yet the blessed Holy One is the cause of all causes, thus infinite and beyond all causality. While nature was created to give necessary order and rhythm to the world, by contrast, the blessed Holy One is not compelled by any form of contingency whatsoever; rather, it is all dependent on this divine desire. [*Unlike the human nature of delighting, the divine created that nature and therefore is not subject to the contingency of that delight. The highest levels of divine consciousness are pointing toward to the realm of pure will, thus ultimately there is no analysis that could capture it. The only way to bind with this will is to align with the limitless*

73. *Pesikta Zutarta*, Genesis 1:1.

74. b*Pesachim* 112a.

nature of Keter. Cognition is necessary as a building block to the limitless.]

If so, this interconnectivity of the divine to shower goodness on the world does not compel the nature or essence of the blessed Holy One to flow forth. [*The only way to bond with the divine is to launch from the cognitive, propelling one beyond it to the place of divine will. This is an ethereal and sophisticated transcendence of the intellect.*] Rather, this interconnectivity is only the pristine desire, as is taught: **"When the first inkling of desire was aroused [to create the world]"**[75]—the will to create a primordial interconnection, sustains the world, showers goodness, and causes pleasure, while remaining beyond contingencies. There is no way to grasp [*whether cognitive, philosophical, theological*] this interconnection.

It is known that one rationale for the command of circumcision, according to Maimonides, is "to diminish pre-sentient desire."[76] And this prosaic

---

75. See R. Hayyim Vital, *'Etz Chayyim*, Sha'ar haKelalim, chapter 1: "When the first inkling of desire was aroused in the Holy One to create the world in order to improve conditions for sentient beings to come to know the grandeur of this One, and to merit becoming a chariot to ascend and merge with the Holy One, then one point emanated forth which included within it all ten (which are the ten spheres of the Bounded Stripes which were contained in one vessel) all of which were invisible."

76. Compare with Philo of Alexandria's fourfold rationale for circumcision: (1) protection against the "severe and incurable malady of the prepuce called anthrax or carbuncle"; (2) the promotion of the cleanliness of the whole body as befits the consecrated order; (3) the prophetic analogy of the circumcised member to the heart; and (4) the promotion of fertility. Moreover, for Philo, circumcision "spiritualizes" the Jewish male by decreasing pride and pleasure, hence enhancing the spiritual persona of the Israelite male (*De Circumcisione*, 11:210). Compare with Maimonides, *Guide for the Perplexed* III:49. Circumcision, for Maimonides, simultaneously quiets pre-sentient desire and perfects moral defects. The "diminution" of the phallus is not a "correction" of a congenital problem but a "diminishment of the pleasure principle" through the painful surgical process. This process alters masculine sensibilities to become more attuned with the moral life prescribed by Judaism for the Jew. This correlation of asceticism and Abraham informs Maimonides' rationale for circumcision in *Mishne Torah, Hilchot Milah* 3:8, 9. Finally, the distinction in translation here between "pre-sentient" and "sentient desire" is that the former applies to instinct and involuntary needs known as the pleasure principle or libido, while the latter applies to conscious and voluntary needs. While applying this contemporary distinction between "pre-sentient" and "sentient desire" helps to illuminate the issue at hand, it may have been lacking in Maimonides's paradigm of medicine that relied so heavily on Galen. Maimonides was familiar with his older contemporary al-Ghiifiqi and the Arabic translations of Greek medical writings. That being said, Maimonides was highly regarded as a physician among the Muslims, evident from historians Ibn al-Qifti (c. 1248) and Ibn Abi Usaybi'a (c. 1270) as well as of the physician 'Abd-al-Latilf of Baghdad, who visited Maimonides when he was in Cairo in 1201. Attesting to Maimonides's holistic approach to healing the body and soul, a song of praise which was written by a grateful patient, Sa'id 'al-Mulk, has been preserved—an integration sought and carried forward by the Vitebsker—by Ibn Abi Usaybi'a: "Galen's art heals only the body / But Abu-Amran's [Maimonides's] the body and the soul. / His knowledge made him the physician of the century. / He could heal with his wisdom

rationalization of the command was more profound than he knew—an esoteric truth of great depth.[77] The [*diminishment of*] desire [*by circumcision*] which Maimonides addressed is not merely the pre-sentient desire; rather, it is a desire for interconnectivity. The cutting of the foreskin is related to first fruits, **"like an early fig / Before the fruit harvest"**[78]—namely, every first arrival is true delight because this incipient moment is connected to what follows. Such an incipience points to its [*fecund*] futurity which is the real pleasure of the worlds.[79]

However, the main purpose of devotional interconnection to the divine is to reach the point of true merging beyond mere perceptions to realize transcendental apperception. One transcends all concepts of nature, delight, and immanence to make this interconnection to the Creator of everything. True *devequt* then happens through *'emunah* alone, beyond any possible contingencies inherent to natural love, delight, and desire [*which serve as a building block for supernatural bliss*].

This deeper truth [*implied in Maimonides's teaching*] points to "diminishment of pre-sentient desire" for the sake of interconnection. This command of circumcision is inscribed on the body [*to create life*], bringing forth souls into the world—the ultimate connectivity—yet the very locus of this power needs to be cut back as a reminder that the ultimate goal is not to be generative but to be steadfast through the spiritual support system of *'emunah*. Cultivating transcendental apperception is the point here—to emulate the Limitless One in becoming truly infinite [*beyond contingencies*].

This *devequt* and ultimate interconnectivity serves to conjoin the pristine will that is devoid of causality or rationale. The difference between the Limitless One and any force of influence in nature is that the latter is fulfilled in realizing itself as an influence. But the Master of the Universe does not ultimately take pleasure in the realization of this pleasure; rather, the Limitless One is pure influence without the need to receive anything.

This then explains why [*the blessed Sages teach*]: **"every male among you shall be circumcised"**[80]—on the very site of masculinity—pure in-

---

the sickness of ignorance." See Benjamin Lee Gordon, *Medieval and Renaissance Medicine* (Philosophical Library: New York, 1959), 235.

77. For this affirmation of phallic desire through its negation in circumcision, see: Elliot R Wolfson, *Language, Eros, Being: Kabbalistic Hermeneutics and Poetic Imagination* (Fordham University Press: New York, 2004), 11-141, esp. 119, 135, 141.

78. Literally, "The wilted flowers— / On the heads of beings bloated with rich food— / That are his glorious beauty. / They shall be like an early fig / Before the fruit harvest; Whoever sees it devours it / While it is still in his hand." (Isaiah 28:4).

79. For further reflections on desire and time in the kabbalistic tradition, see Elliot R. Wolfson, *Alef, Mem, Tau: Kabbalistic Musings on Time, Truth, and Death* (University of California Press: Berkeley, 2006).

80. "Such shall be the covenant between Me and you and your offspring to follow

fluence without the need to receive anything. By diminishing pre-sentient desire and the influence of the pleasure principle, the supra-rational sign of the *Y"oD,* as *Chokhmah* (Primordial Point) [*is thus the truly circumcised inscription*]. As Scripture teaches: **"Wisdom is found within No-thing"**[81]—this is the No-thingness, and circumcision is the inscription of truth and *'emunah.*

Now we can appreciate the opening verse [*concerning Abraham that*]: **"The *'emunah* is purely unwarranted"**[82]—namely, this *'emunah* transcends all philosophical proofs and contemplations, for they do not constitute true understanding. Such *'emunah* is beyond causation. This is what allows Abraham to experience the shift from perception to apperception, as Scripture states: **"I am but dust and ashes"**[83]—namely, a connection to *Chokhmah* (Primordial Point), which is humility and nothingness, as Scripture states: **"Wisdom is found in No-thing."**[84]

In the apperception of *'emunah* there is no ego involved. All self-directed contemplations, cognitions, proofs, and even *devequt* need to ultimately be shed. Such shedding of the self leads to a state whereby one sees the self as **"dust and ashes"**[85] such that anything which precedes is necessary preparation, but never fully sufficient. [*With this realization in mind, one can then*] open to true *devequt.*

Thus, this is a specific type of *'emunah*—a merging of *devequt* with the Holy One. This is why Scripture recalls this spiritual development through the chronology of the narrative itself. **"And besides, [*'emunah*] is in truth my sister, my father's daughter though not my mother's; and [*'emunah*] became my wife."**[86] The latter *'emunah* is pre-conditional and preconsequential, where its flow functions as the blessed Sages teach: "More than the calf wants [*to suckle, the cow wants to give milk*]."[87]

Thus, in this kind of *'emunah,* the ordering of Scripture is meant to teach a process of spiritual evolution toward true *devequt.*[88] The degrees

---

which you shall keep: [every male among you shall be circumcised]" (Genesis 17:10).

81. Literally, "But where can wisdom be found; / Where is the source of understanding?" (Job 28:12).

82. Genesis 15:6.

83. Genesis 18:27.

84. Job 28:12.

85. Genesis 18:27.

86. Literally, "And besides, she is in truth my sister, my father's daughter though not my mother's; and she became my wife" (Genesis 20:12).

87. b*Pesachim* 112a.

88. That evolution of spiritual consciousness is about to be summed through the three key verses that encapsulate the journey: (1) Apperception that all philosophic proofs and contemplations are nullified in relation to the Holy One; (2) Apperception of the lowliness of No-Thing and Emptiness; (3) Apperception of *'emunah* through the masculine level of consciousness.

of *devequt* are thus ordered as follows: (1) it begins with a preliminary *devequt* **"that has no incentive";**[89] (2) then realizing [*the need to shed the self to the stage of*] **"I am but dust and ashes";**[90] (3) finally realizing [*that final stage of dissolution into devequt whereby*] **"[*'emunah*] is in truth my sister, my father's daughter."**[91]

[2.3]. *Parashah Lech Lecha* (Genesis 12:1–17:27)

QUESTIONS FOR REFLECTION:

1. How does thinking about and/or sending, and even feeling the divine affect your prayers?

2. Does your spiritual support system of *'emunah* depend on sense perception or emotions? What happens when you move beyond sense and emotions within a given spiritual experience?

89. Literally, "And because [Abram] put his trust in YHVH, so the One reckoned it to his merit" (Genesis 15:6).

90. Genesis 18:27.

91. "And besides, she is in truth my sister, my father's daughter though not my mother's; and she became my wife" (Genesis 20:12).

[3.1]. *Parashah Vayera* (Genesis 18:1–22:24)

INTRODUCTION TO HOMILY:

Religions can often be problematic insofar as the spiritual journey is concerned. To a certain extent, religions can preserve authentic source material, but too often that authentic material becomes sealed off from its originary sources of spiritual inspiration and realization. Part of that inclination to preserve the originary spiritual inspiration by sealing it off leads to a reification of the spiritual into the boundedness of religion. With religion, there comes its singular way of thinking or orthodoxies, which leads often to dogmatic statements about "faith." Too often genuine seekers of the spirit are forced to flee from the path because of dogmatic demands surrounding "faith." If as the hasidic take on Judaism purports that indeed there is no such thing as "blind faith," then there is a real need for reappraisal of 'emunah as a continuum. To take responsibility for the heavenly yoke, then today's spiritual seekers need to continue to discover new forms of evolutionary spiritual consciousness that are authentic to the expansiveness of 'emunah. Can new wine be put into old bottles? As a perennial truth rather than any kind of orthodoxy, a pristine 'emunah can accommodate continual evolution and updating. With any kind of philosophical apperception, formulated as a dogma or intellectual position as this homily explores, there is always an opposition to it. To realize a state of 'emunah that is beyond the ken of opposition, is thus incontrovertible. To get through suffering, one needs 'emunah, so that with such 'emunah, suffering serves as an aid to shift consciousness deeper into a state of 'emunah. While the afflictions experienced in life raise doubts, it is 'emunah that then allows one to leap over the mind's habit of creating doubts. To be an authentic spiritual person, one has to be able to leap over the mind, so that the very nature of the mind can serve as an aid rather than as a source of confusion and despair. In order to be sustainable and have the integrity of shleimut, there is a need to implace the ideal spiritual goals as levels to be attained gradually through some kind of extended spiritual process. Once again, the Vitebsker will be expressing the yegiah aspect of this teaching—the aspect is devotional, which requires effort toward transformation. In the Vitebsker's case, the focus tends to be on personal transformation and is not yet cognizant of the all-inclusive, planetary condition. The responsibility for achieving the highest objective on earth requires universal cooperation of all sentient beings. It cannot be fully realized by a singular tradition, path, or culture; rather, it involves the recognition of the deepest level that all sentient beings are derived from the same source and ultimately aspire to the optimal way of living on the earth redemptively. Redemption is a liberation from our own shortsightedness grounded in egocentrism and ethnocentrism.

[3.2]. *Parashah Vayera* (Genesis 18:1–22:24)

HOMILY:

The exegesis of R. Yitzhak Nafkha[92] opens with the scriptural verse: **"Make for Me an altar of earth and sacrifice upon it."**[93] A person makes a sacrifice of burnt offerings and well-being offerings upon it so that **"in every place where I cause My name to be mentioned I will come to you and bless you."**[94] How much more so when Abraham sacrificed himself,[95] [*whereby Scripture*] thus [*proclaims*]: **"And the Holy One appeared."**[96] [*What is the meaning of the exegesis in suggesting that Abraham sacrificed himself, and why does the divine then appear to him?*]

Let us review the issues in this preliminary reading. First, why is the trial of the [*rabbinic reading of the*] binding named after Abraham and not after [*scriptural rendering of the*] Isaac who surrendered himself to the Holy One? As R. Shlomo Yitzhaki teaches [*regarding the binding of Isaac in Genesis 22 which opens in the following way*]: **"Sometime after these words."**[97] These are the words spoken by Ishmael [*bragging over his own circumcision late in life at thirteen years old rather than succumbing to the rite earlier on in life as a baby on the eighth day*] to which Isaac responded with a readiness to surrender himself completely [*namely, offering his very life*].[98] Secondly, why [*is Abraham's*] trial through the furnace in Ur of Chaldeas not mentioned in Scripture?[99]

---

92. *Midrash Tanchuma*, Parashah Vayera 1.

93. "Make for Me an altar of earth and sacrifice on it your burnt offerings and your sacrifices of well-being, your sheep and your oxen; in every place where I cause My name to be mentioned I will come to you and bless you" (Exodus 20:21).

94. "Make for Me an altar of earth and sacrifice on it your burnt offerings and your sacrifices of well-being, your sheep and your oxen; in every place where I cause My name to be mentioned I will come to you and bless you" (Exodus 20:21).

95. The nature of the sacrifice here is ambiguous. The Vitebsker could be suggesting that in offering Isaac, his son, Abraham was sacrificing himself as a father. More likely, however, the Vitebsker is referring to the rabbinic tradition which outlines the ten trials which Abraham withstood, the tenth being the binding and the first being this trial by fire in Ur of the Chaldeas; see m*Avot* 5:3.

96. Genesis 18:1.

97. Literally, "Some time afterward, God put Abraham to the test" (Genesis 22:1).

98. Rashi ad loc Genesis 22:1—"Others say [that it means] 'after the words of Ishmael' who boasted to his brother Isaac that he had already been circumcised at thirteen years of age without resisting. Isaac replied to him: 'You think to intimidate me by [*mentioning the loss of*] one limb of the body!?! If the Holy Blessed One were to tell me: "Sacrifice yourself before me" I would not hesitate even a moment.' (*Genesis Rabbah* 55; b*Sanhedrin* 89b)."

99. See above n. 44, m*Avot* 5:3.

The matter is known: "The greater the person, the greater their inner impulse."[100] And [the Sages also] taught: "This inner impulse is constantly attempting to derail a person from their path, so were God not there to assist, that person would be overwhelmed—as Scripture states: '**The wicked watches for the righteous, / seeking to put him to death; YHVH will not abandon . . .**'[101] etc."[102]

Notice how [*this notion of oppositional forces that catalyze challenges*] is read by the author of *Akeidat Yitzhak*, R. Yitzhak of Arama through this verse:[103] **"I will make a fitting help-mate *against* him"**[104] [*which implies contradiction of two mutually exclusive terms. What the Akeidat Yitzhak goes on to then teach here is how*] the dynamic tension within every dialectic can actually be helpful.[105] [*What follows are three scenarios where oppositional force can be helpful*]. (1) Without oppositional forces [*of the errant impulse that one experiences in all divine service*], as Scripture states: **"The one no less than the other was God's doing,"**[106] so free will would then be abolished, with neither reward nor consequence. [*That evil choices exist means there is a necessary oppositional force to the good, which then allows for conditions of embracing the goodness of that choice once made.*] (2) Moreover, as we discuss elsewhere,[107] without oppositional forces there would be a complete dissolution of bliss [*and its perception, for constant bliss is not true bliss. There is a real need for oppositional force, which lends bliss and its perception the reality of constant renewal*].[108] (3) A person could not bare the pleasure of illumination unless it occurred in a condi-

100. Literally, "The greater one person is from another, so too is that person's inner impulse greater" (b*Sukkah* 52a).

101. "The wicked watches for the righteous, / seeking to put him to death; YHVH will not abandon him to his power; / He will not let him be condemned in judgment" (Psalm 37:32-33).

102. b*Sukkah* 52a–b.

103. According to R. Yitzhak of Arama (1420–94), *Akeidat Yitzhak*, vol. 1: Genesis, Eighth Gate (n.p. Israel: 1974), 86b–88b, (esp. 87a which uses the term "dialectical opposition" or hitnagedut).

104. Literally, "[YHVH God said, 'It is not good for man to be alone]; I will make a fitting help-mate for him" (Genesis 2: 18).

105. Living in a world of opposition, this dialectical tension is not antagonistic but actually ends being complementary. Much like the "loyal opposition" in government, challenging the status quo for the sake of the greater good beyond individual desires is what allows for good governance and vibrant communities.

106. "So in a time of good fortune enjoy the good fortune; and in a time of misfortune, reflect: The one no less than the other was God's doing; consequently, a person may find no fault with God" (Ecclesiastes 7:14).

107. See *Peri haAretz*, Parashah Bechuqotay, whereon enjoyment is part of a dialectical system, following on its absence.

108. See below, *Peri haAretz*, no. 9: Parashah Korach.

tion of oscillation, and such **"dashing to and fro"**[109] is by its nature dialectical [*which nullifies the apperception so that it would not remain constant*].

[*After completing the reflections upon the teaching of the Akeidat Yitzhak, this homily continues to explicate two outstanding issues in the aforementioned rabbinic dictums: (1) The greater the person, the greater their inner impulse; (2) This inner impulse is constantly attempting to derail a person from their path, so were God not there to assist, that person would be overwhelmed. The concluding point here being that every spiritual apperception requires an equal and opposite force, and now additionally, in accordance with the magnitude of the apperception, there is equal opposition, as will now be further explained*]. This is the operative principle regarding spiritual apperception and devotion—its grandeur depends on its oppositional force. For example, dissolution of ego requires a greater magnitude of oppositional force, especially in thinking of an external reality [*that separates one from non-duality flowing from such a dissolution*]. Each according to their capacity—a minor realization requires minor opposition, and major realization requires major opposition. This oppositional force should serve as assistance to realizing [*non-dual consciousness*]. Lest one fall away from the magnetism of an oppositional pull as it becomes more intensified, one should draw on this simple, powerful *'emunah.*

The more one grows in spiritual apperception and devotion, the more oppositional energy emerges as a counterbalance. When opposition befalls you, then fortify yourself as intensely as possible by holding onto this simple, powerful *'emunah.* [*'Emunah is what allows you to re-set the pendulum, seeing that you stand outside the continuum.*] *'Emunah* is the act of grasping onto the Holy One outside that reality system of opposition. Complete support is possible through such *'emunah.* [*If your relation to the absolute is based on intellectual argument or dogma alone, it is vulnerable, for it can always be undermined by a better argument. 'Emunah is an ability to realize that what you believe in is not contingent upon the way you explain it; rather, you have a direct and clear relationship with that which cannot be apperceived. The mind is not the absolute arbiter of the spiritual relationship, for the purpose of knowing is unknowing. This is not "blind faith"; rather, it is a knowing that is not-knowing, enlightened agnosis, which is key for 'emunah.*]

[*Since 'emunah is simplex and not complex, there is nothing that can oppose it,*] for whenever one's mind is operating through intellectual constructions, at some point, it will collapse. It is necessary to go back to the simple, powerful *'emunah* of a knowing that is not-knowing, an enlightened agnosis, so sublime. [*The power of this 'emunah is in its form of*

109. "Dashing to and fro [among] the creatures was something that looked like flares" (Ezekiel 1:14).

gnosis, which is the unknowability of what you are knowing, never producing an intellectual apprehension, whereby the "purpose of knowing is unknowing."[110] *It is pure wonder and radical amazement.*] This is the greatest "help" that there is, for nothing can defeat it, so that one's daily connection with the divine can withstand the fall of any paradigm or construct, thus never falling into depression.

This allows for a new understanding of theodicy—namely, why does a righteous person suffer?[111] **"And YHVH tests the mind"**[112] so that there are times when the oppositional force in spiritual apperception and devotion is necessary for healing. [*Divine consciousness is of oppositional forces within the human mind that cannot access such 'emunah.*] Such healing precedes the wound and thus brings about a simple, powerful *'emunah*. Or the Holy One intervenes to mitigate the negative pull and to weaken its force, through afflictions or poverty—this is the grounding of divine awe leading to the dissolution of lust and heretical faith. [*The affliction one experiences has the effect of weakening or canceling the oppositional forces inside the mind.*]

In truth, it is known: transgressions are more bitter and painful than falling away from the Holy One [*in that one becomes distanced from the Holy One when one's spiritual support systems become neglected*]. Such transgressions [*of distancing*] have no atoning quality, whereas afflictions and death do have the capacity for atonement. While afflictions might appear to be degenerative [*on the exterior*], whenever a righteous person is suffering this allows one to grow [*on the interior*]. The negative corresponding energy created through greater spiritual apperception and devotion allows one to grow in otherwise unexpected ways. And from here "a righteous person suffers"—surely one could fall into this abyss of oppositional force, never being able to escape were it not for the ostensible affliction and poverty that mitigates complete submersion. [*A righteous person suffering is not really experiencing something negative; rather, the afflictions actually restrain and eliminate the oppositional forces, namely, whatever would contradict that person's devotional service. If it is the case that the afflictions themselves weaken the evil impulse, then such afflictions are constructive, sparing this person from the conflict that arises from oppositional forces. The moral universe operates with oppositional forces as representative of the Other Side from the Limitless until the individual is awakened.*]

Regarding [*the opposite case of*] "A righteous person flourishes"—

---

110. Compare with Ba'al Shem Tov, *Keter Shem Tov Hashalem*, ed. E. Shohat (New York: Kehot Publications, 2004), 3:7–8.

111. b*Berakot* 7a.

112. "For silver—the crucible; / For gold—the furnace; / And YHVH tests the mind" (Proverbs 17:3).

whatever one has accomplished in terms of spiritual apprehension and devotion through their opposition requires no further afflictions. [*Such a person has the capacity to withstand the oppositional forces without having to weaken the evil impulse and has no need to be motivated by suffering.*] Without afflictions, such a person can withstand suffering; meanwhile, "no one is objective enough regarding another person"[113] to truly judge their situation [*especially in regard to degrees of afflictions and perseverance through a given situation*]. But when it comes to the Holy One, there is no issue with objectivity: **"the One who forms us together and understands."**[114] Since each person has a unique path to follow with a different impulse, judging others will tend to be biased based on his/her own subjectivity, but if his/her consciousness includes the field itself, then there would be awareness of the individual itself. Such a mind would know what is needed for each person to advance and fulfill themselves.

Thus [*in regards to theodicy*], the blessed Sages teach about it through the grandeur of R. Eleazar ben Pedat's afflictions. When he questioned these afflictions, the response was simple—"Even if the entire world would be recreated, there is no guarantee of things being different."[115] In terms of R. Eleazar ben Pedat's own mind and soul, his encounter with the dialectical process of existence leads him to [*the*] question [*of*] whether these afflictions could possibly have been avoided in alternate worlds or whether indeed it was impossible to have grown in perspective [*with his 'emunah*] without such afflictions of poverty. [*R. Eleazar ben Pedat's afflictions are necessary, for without them he might not be strong enough to withstand the oppositional force pushing back against his level of spiritual apperception and divine service. There is something oppositional that exists within every spiritual apperception, except when it comes to 'emunah, which experiences no oppositional forces.*]

[*Now the meaning of the trial of the binding of Isaac that opened this homily is explained.*] And so it is with the real trial of this binding, according to the exegesis[116] captured by R. Shlomo Yitzhaki, as the moment when

113. b*Baba Batra* 75a.

114. Psalm 33:15, which suggests that the Holy One has this intimate knowledge and can thus prescribe the proper treatment.

115. b*Ta'anit* 25a, recounts how R. Eleazar ben Pedat was in straits and attempted to break through, first through bloodletting, fasting, and then took garlic only to faint into a stupor. The Sages came to visit him and by now Pedat was crying and laughing while a flame was coming out of his nose. When asked what happened, Pedat explained that he was sitting with the Holy One. I asked, "What is going on here? How much longer will I suffer?" So the Holy One responded: "My son, Eleazar, what would you prefer? That I recreate the world? Maybe then your fortune would change and you would be assured of living in a more prosperous situation!?!"

116. *Genesis Rabbah* 56:12.

Abraham had to be self-reflective about his actions and spiritual values. "So as R. Aba taught: Abraham said: 'I shall share with You all my inner struggles that have arisen since yesterday, when You said to me: **"for it is through Isaac that offspring shall be continued for you"**[117] and then You seemed to go back on Your word and said: **"Take your son [. . . and offer him]"**[118] and now You are saying to me: **"Do not raise your hand against the boy"**[119]—so how can You authentically be the Eternal Creator if there is constant change happening to the divine will?' At that moment, Abraham should have already been disturbed, as his ruminations could have constituted the basis of heresy, *perish the thought*, that the absolute is unstable."

Quandaries such as these arise—like theodicy which contradicts the moral assurances of Torah [*as constructed by the rabbinic imagination*] or any other forsaken belief about "divine retribution measure for measure." This corresponds to the desire for the apperception of divine wisdom and the yearning for union of *devequt* with the Holy One. These questions only become more intense as you approach the Holy One. For as we learn in Rashi: **"Now the serpent was more subtle than all the wild beasts"**[120]—according to the height of his subtlety was the depth of his fall.[121]

Whereas regarding Abraham, in the trial of the binding, he did not fall into the side of the oppositional force [*both psychologically and cosmically*]. Rather, he withstood [*the oppositional forces in his mind by being shrewd*] and by fortifying his simple and deep *'emunah*. How a person understands the way things work from below to above is not the way the absolute truly functions from above to below.[122] Doubt only emerges in the

---

117. But God said to Abraham, 'Do not be distressed over the boy or your slave; whatever Sarah tells you, do as she says, for it is through Isaac that offspring shall be continued for you'" (Genesis 21:12).

118. "And God said, 'Take your son, your favored one, Isaac, whom you love, and go to the land of Moriah, and offer him there as a burnt offering on one of the heights that I will point out to you'" (Genesis 22:2).

119. "And [the angel] said: 'Do not raise your hand against the boy, or do anything to him. For now I know that you revere God, since you have not withheld your son, your favored one, from Me'" (Genesis 22:12).

120. "Now the serpent was more subtle than all the wild beasts that YHVH God had made. [The serpent] said to the woman, 'Did God really say: You shall not eat of any tree of the garden?'" (Genesis 3:1).

121. Rashi ad loc Genesis 3:1. "'Now the serpent was more subtle than all the wild beasts'—What connection is there between the following narrative and the statement just made? The latter should have been followed by: 'and He [YHVH God] made for Adam and his wife garments of skin and clothed them' (3:21), but Scripture informs you with what plan the serpent assailed them: he saw hem naked and unashamed and he coveted [Eve] (*Genesis Rabbah* 18)."

So the nemesis of the greatest animal was precisely its shrewd character.

122. He is ready to relinquish his drive to analyze and understand compared with the

world of oppositional forces.

From whatever perspective one has from below to above, oppositional forces appear to be evil. But even the oppositional forces that appear from above to below are actually from a different source, in truth all emanating are from one source—the Holy One. The inability to understand this oneness is a human limitation from below to above: **"For this is not a trifling thing for you."**[123] There is no faculty of apperception that can even process the divine word: **"Those who call evil good / And good evil,"**[124] whereby the divine commands something good, the human mind cannot discern whether it is meant for good or for evil and vice versa, and ultimately even being unable to discern the pristine divine will. It is in this space of relinquishing the natural drive to analyze and know matters with apparent certainty that Abraham could connect to this simple and deep *'emunah*. The trial for Abraham was to no longer solely depend on his faculty of perception and philosophical analysis.

The general principle underlying all trials has to do with *'emunah,* as Scripture teaches: **"that [God] might test you by hardships to learn what was in your hearts."**[125] So all the trials that Abraham *o.b.m.* had to undergo then passed through this path, for example, in the case of the famine, when God said **"Go forth"**[126]—so that following such a famine it appears as though there is a fluctuation in divine will, as R. Shlomo Yitzhaki discusses regarding all such cases [*of trial. The trial then is a trial of 'emunah and not that the absolute is unstable. All the spiritual guidance one receives is really a trial, for even it cannot be completely accurate, always being mediated by things you are unaware of*].[127]

But the trial [*here for Abraham in regard to*] surrendering one's soul to the divine is an act beyond knowledge [*which is a trial for Isaac but was not the case for the 'emunah within Abraham's mind*]. This requires an attuning to the Creator as the force that created the world through divine fiat and commanded this person to surrender his soul and sacrifice himself for

possibility of options that come through analysis; see Ramban ad loc Genesis 3:6.

123. "For this is not a trifling thing for you: it is your very life; through it you shall long endure on the land that you are to possess on crossing the Jordan" (Deuteronomy 32:47).

124. "Ah, / Those who call evil good / And good evil; Who present darkness as light / And light as darkness; Who present bitter as sweet / And sweet as bitter!" (Isaiah 5:20).

125. "Remember the long way that YHVH your God has made you travel in the wilderness these past forty years, that He might test you by hardships to learn what was in your hearts: whether you would keep His commandments or not" (Deuteronomy 8:2).

126. "YHVH said to Abram: 'Go forth from your native land and from your father's house to the land that I will show you'"(Genesis 12:1).

127. See Rashi ad loc Genesis 12:10. "A famine in the land"—in that land only to test him [through a trial] whether he would take exception to God's commands in that He had bidden him to go to the land of Canaan and now forced him to leave it (*Pirkai d'Rabbi Eleazer* 26).

the sake of the divine. When one does not have this a priori knowledge to truly understand the command—how could this be considered a real trial? The problem is when the command itself appears [*to the human mind to be*] contradictory [*to the divine will*], which was not the case regarding our holy ancestors [*whose minds were merged in attunement with the divine mind thus avoiding cognitive dissonance*].

Therein arise the universal problems [*of the philosophers*]: Even with omniscience [*that enables knowledge of all things before they occur*]—regarding one being commanded by the Holy One with certainty of this command to surrender their life [*even someone who may not be as spiritually elevated as Abraham*]—this does not constitute a real trial [*for any Jew would perform this command of sanctifying the divine name*]. This is why these aforementioned trials are not necessarily mentioned in Scripture.

As the teaching of our blessed Sages suggests,[128] Torah should really have begun [with the verse]: **"This month shall mark for you"**[129]—yet Torah begins [*with the verse*]: **"He revealed to His people His powerful works."**[130] [*Although the opening stories in Genesis may appear to be contradictory,*] they are meant to teach every generation and every person who contemplates what is written about the interaction of *Chokhmah* (primordial point) within everyday life—to purify the impure, to extract good from evil, so that all judgments are really [*at their core*] energies of compassion, and **"Everything goes to the same place,"**[131] given that the root of everything resides within the pristine Will of the One, within pristine and empowered *'emunah*.

Through [*this process of contemplative discernment*] the severity of judgment within compassion is sweetened, for this pristine and powerful *'emunah* plummets to the abyss [*of primordial Wisdom*], wherein all these apparently contradictory qualities are intertwined into unified consciousness. After embracing this pristine and powerful *'emunah*, there remains no oppositional force or contradiction, just as the Holy One responds to Abraham in the narrative.[132] And just as R. Shlomo Yitzhaki points out on that verse: from the source of blessings everything is blessed—namely, by the coherence of this pristine and powerful *'emunah*, allowing for such bless-

128. *Yalkut Shimoni* 187a.

129. "This month shall mark for you the beginning of the months; it shall be the first of the months of the year for you" (Exodus 12:2).

130. "He revealed to His people His powerful works, / in giving them the heritage of nations" (Psalm 111:6).

131. "Everything goes to the same place; everything came from dust and both return to dust" (Ecclesiastes 3:20).

132. "And [the angel] said: 'Do not raise your hand against the boy, or do anything to him. For now I know that you fear God, since you have not withheld your son, your favored one, from me'" (Genesis 22:12).

ing to simply flow through all the worlds of consciousness right down to the smallest creature in the sea.

And this is the [*meaning of the*] opening teaching of R. Nifkha: **"in every place where I cause My name to be mentioned"**[133]—as is known, **"My name"** is both feminine and [*refers to*] the *Shekinah*—while **"I cause to be mentioned"**[134] is masculine. This means that in every place where [*these oppositional forces are*] unified, bringing together compassion and judgment—**"I will come to you and bless you"**[135] in this way—blessing flows so the embodied world is blessed.[136] So when [*the exegesis*] mentions that "Abraham sacrificed himself"[137]—this indicates how much more of a trial of *'emunah* this is, like undergoing the worst, most painful sacrifice [*of intense psychological suffering and inner conflict*], as opposed to merely being called to sanctify the divine name by surrendering one's life. This is why Scripture reads, **"YHVH appeared to him"**[138]—by slightly revealing the divine pathway of knowing [*that is unknowing. In sum, this homily presents a journey into 'emunah through three levels, (1) what begins with oppositional forces then requires 'emunah to overcome opposition, (2) it then becomes blessed, (3) so then that emerging blessed apperception stands beyond 'emunah, only slightly, changing one's perspective on the stability of the absolute*].

[3.3]. *Parashah Vayera* (Genesis 18:1–22:24)

QUESTIONS FOR REFLECTION:

1. How do you react to oppositional forces in your life? Are you like Abraham in being more submissive in your responsiveness? Are you like Sarah in being more reactive in your opposition?

2. Have you ever experienced oppositional force as something constructive rather than destructive? Why is it so difficult to respond instead of reacting to such oppositional forces in life?

---

133. "Make for Me an altar of earth and sacrifice on it your burnt offerings and your sacrifices of well-being, your sheep and your oxen; in every place where I cause My name to be mentioned I will come to you and bless you" (Exodus 20:21).

134. "Make for Me an altar of earth and sacrifice on it your burnt offerings and your sacrifices of well-being, your sheep and your oxen; in every place where I cause My name to be mentioned I will come to you and bless you" (Exodus 20:21).

135. "Make for Me an altar of earth and sacrifice on it your burnt offerings and your sacrifices of well-being, your sheep and your oxen; in every place where I cause My name to be mentioned I will come to you and bless you" (Exodus 20:21).

136. Zohar III:271a.

137. *Midrash Tanchuma*, Parashah Vayera, Chapter 2.

138. "YHVH appeared to him by the Terebinths of Mamre; he was sitting at the entrance of the tent as the day grew hot" (Genesis 18:1).

3. What would be necessary in your spiritual support system of *'emunah* to allow for encounters with oppositional forces and evil to be sweetened into something that could somehow be for the good? What does it mean for your spiritual support system of *'emunah* to be a sui generis force of blessing in your life? When was the last time you felt this source of blessing and why?

[4.1]. *Parashah Toldot* (Genesis 23:19–28:9)

INTRODUCTION TO HOMILY:

The particular is rooted in the cosmic. The particular forms of sacred texts and traditions that as Jews and seeker venerate, like the form of Torah, are not necessarily capable of fully expressing the cosmic dimension that they point to. The Torah of the Future will still be subject to the same limiting principle, but it will contain particulars that were not present in previous paradigms. These particulars necessarily manifest in a different paradigm wherein the information available concerning the nature of life on the planet and the cosmos has radically changed. There are innumerable levels of understanding, attuned to the capacities of particular minds. Since the particular minds are distinguishable in terms of the nature and quality of information they can process, there will thus be different paradigms of meaningfulness that model the Ultimate through Torah's capacity to function as a primordial myth. One of the most important insights that is now occurring as a result of the information available concerning human experience on the planet is the interconnection that everything shares. The recognition of everything that we think is external to ourselves is actually present in the same unifying field of existence that includes us as well—such that inter-being exists without any single center. Every locality may seem to be its own essential center, even though in reality the center can be anywhere, anytime. Torah as an ever-flowing, evolving tradition cannot claim to be self-existent or privileged within the paradigm of planetary consciousness. Torah is one of many streams of wisdom that serve as primordial myth for various cultures encompassing the entire earth. So, for example, in many of these streams of wisdom, pointers are available that enable one to acquire the awareness of the undifferentiated oneness, in Hasidism called 'Akhdut haPashut (which is analogous to what Vedanta calls "Paramashiva"), in contradistinction to a source of multiplicity, in Hasidism called "z̲imz̲um" (which is analogous to what Vedanta calls the power of "Shakti"). Analogy here means that each of these particular modalities are functionally parallel within their cosmological systems, without implying that there are exactly the same. The process that results in phenomenality brings with it the possibility of self-awareness, which is otherwise impossible until there is something that can enable the pre-existent to witness and recognize its own reflection. The meta-programming process enables the limited self-identity to gradually realize that its real nature is inseparable from the single, underlying reality of everything. This arises when the desire for self-knowledge becomes important to a person as explored in this homily.

[4.2]. *PARASHAH TOLDOT* (GENESIS 23:19–28:9)

HOMILY:

"This is the story of Isaac, son of Abraham,"[139] as explained by R. Shlomo ben Yitzhaki, *o.b.m.*: this story is referring to Jacob and Esau in the [*preceding*] scriptural reading.[140] The issue at hand in need of explication then follows the path of how Hillel responded to the heathen seeking to convert by being taught all of Judaism on one foot. [*Hillel*] accepted him [*as a student*] and thus agreed to teach him: "What is contemptible to you, do not do to others."[141] R. Shlomo ben Yitzhaki, *o.b.m.*, then explains that this refers to the [*positive*] commandment, **"Love your fellow as yourself."**[142] [*Regarding this same story of Hillel and the convert,*] the comment by R. Shmuel Eleazer haLevi Ideles[143] raises a quandary: Why make this core statement in the negative rather than in the positive? Even in the Aramaic translation of Leviticus 19:18, it is nonetheless framed in the language of a negative command. Yet [*here in the Talmudic passage about Hillel and the convert this core concept of Judaism*] is framed negatively through a negative command: "Whatever is despicable to yourself, do not do to someone else."[144]

But the matter is as discussed by the blessed Sages: "The world was created through ten divine speech utterances,"[145] which map onto the ten commands, also mentioned by the blessed Sages: "[*God*] looked at Torah and created the world."[146] [*Notice how Torah and Creation of the world are one matter, thus the ten speech utterances of Creation are linked here to the ten utterances of command revealed at Sinai.*] With regard to the Creation of the world [*there are two roots: the first root—the undifferentiated oneness of the Creator which is the root of all beings; the second root—the restraint which is the root of Creation's renewal since*] from its incipience the Creator was undifferentiated oneness and so was the Name. This undifferentiated oneness is boundless beyond any apprehension, apperception—the very nature of being limitless [*such that the reality and root of all beings emerges from the true reality of the Necessary Existent*]. At that turning point when the impulse for complexity within the undifferentiated oneness to create [*the delimited, contracted world of boundaries, then*] as

139. Genesis 25:19.

140. Compare with Nahmanides's Commentary on Genesis 10 where it is read as "the offspring" rather than the "story."

141. b*Shabbat* 31a.

142. "You shall not take vengeance or bear a grudge against your countrymen. Love your fellow as yourself" (Leviticus 19:18).

143. R. Shmuel Eleazer haLevi Ideles (1555–1631), also known as *MaHaR"SHA*.

144. *MaHaR"SHA* ad loc b*Shabbat* 31a.

145. m*Avot* 5:1.

146. *Genesis Rabbah* 1:2.

is known, there was necessarily a filtering [*of the limitless divine presence*] to make space for the creation.[147]

Behold [*the two roots of the world's creation, which are undifferentiated oneness and filtering, also serve as the roots of Torah, such that*] all positive commands are in the category of speech spoken from [*the beginning of the commandments known simply as*] **"I am [YHVH your God]"**[148]—that flow from the primordial state of undifferentiated oneness. [*All the positive commands are really branches of this flow from the primordial, undifferentiated oneness of that "I."*] By contrast, negative commands [*of Torah*] emerge from the place of filtering as limitation and are thus in the category of [*the second of the ten commandments*]: **"You shall have no other [gods]."**[149] All the supernal roots, branches, general and particular manifestations of divine energy come into fruition below through the commands [*which are all branches from the root of limitation and filtering, implicit in the manifest act of Creation*]. All these roots and branches, both universal and particular [*of the undifferentiated oneness that is delimited*], emerging from its supernal source, are embedded in the very constitution of the sacred Torah, along with all of its commands, statutes and teachings [*as already discussed regarding positive commands, which are rooted in the undifferentiated oneness of the utterance "I," while the negative commands are rooted in the delimiting utterance of "You shall have no other." Divine service also needs delimitation and constraint, for example, in the case of enthusiasm and ecstasy. All the shaping of our way of being is from the filtering. These forms of divinely empowered doing are rooted in the divine creative power of manifestation known as "I"-Anokhi as both cosmic and individual existence. The particular is rooted in the cosmic. The fruits that emerge from this terrestrial communication from the supernal roots and branches is what is known as the holy Torah.*]

Our blessed Sages teach [*regarding the verse*]: **"inasmuch as Abraham obeyed Me and kept My charge: My commandments, My laws, and My teachings."**[150] How could Abraham have intuited what the Sages would later interpret that Torah commands, right down to the details of observing of *'Eruvai tavshilin*?[151] If you respond, that [*Abraham*] was able to intuit [*by himself all of*] these details by contemplation, then what about the statutes without rationale that cannot be deduced by reason alone, as with

147. R. Hayyim Vital, *'Etz Chayyim* 1:2.

148. "I YHVH am your God who brought you out of the land of Egypt, the house of bondage" (Exodus 20:2).

149. "You shall have no other gods besides Me" (Exodus 20:3).

150. See b*Yomah* 28b and its usage of Genesis 26:5.

151. *'Eruvai tavshilin* refers to a "shared cooked dish" that is used as part of a legal fiction to permit cooking on the holiday for a purpose beyond the day's usage, namely for a Sabbath immediately following.

the case of the Red Heifer and other such statutes?

Yet according to our teaching [*as described above, that Torah and all of its legislations and commands have roots in the supernal realm*] it becomes clear why the blessed Sages then teach: "[*God*] told Moses: 'To you, shall I reveal all the reasoning of the Red Heifer [*so that for you, with this revelation it is no longer a statute*], while to others it shall appear as a statute [*given the lack of revelation. It appears then*] for every statute [*in Torah that*] there is an underlying reason and supernal root in the order of creation. For creation was enacted through Torah [*and every detail embedded within it having an analogous root in the order of creation itself*]. Not every mind has the capacity [*to fully understand and apperceive these supernal roots*], thus for others [*who lack such spiritual capacities, the Red Heifer, for example, is merely*] a statute.'"[152] But Torah does not speak to the spiritual elite alone, like Moses and Abraham, *o.b.m.*, whose elevated souls can see how every command derives from the supernal root. With this kind of spiritual elevation, no statute stands as anything more than a command, given the connection between their cognition, apperception, genealogy of all commands and their supernal rootedness.

This seems impossible: for the statutes to become commands!?! Then the commands must change too whereby they are nullified and no longer relevant [*to such an elevated soul*]. For example: the prohibitions of "**You shall not murder. / You shall not commit adultery. / You shall not steal**"[153] are not appropriate for the spiritual elite, seeing how much they have shattered any impulses for such transgression to the point where they no longer have any use for their physical character traits. Rather, such souls dedicate every impulse to the Holy One, seeing that anything self-serving feels disgusting. Such a soul does not need to be told to refrain from desecrating itself, for [*desecration*] is not integral to its sense of self. There is a natural repulsion to transgression whereby prohibitions become meaningless in the sense of needing constraints commanded by a higher authority [*when such a refined soul is already so attuned.*]

Along these lines, King David, *o.b.m.*, says: **"and my heart is empty within me."**[154] For such a cultivated spiritual person, the commands do not function as commands, so the statutes then appear as commands. This is what the Sages, *o.b.m.*, meant by claiming that in the messianic era, that there will be no more commands, **"For the land shall be filled with devo-**

152. *Numbers Rabbah* 19:4.

153. "You shall not murder. / You shall not commit adultery. / You shall not steal. / You shall not bear false witness against your neighbor" (Exodus 20:13).

154. Literally, "For I am poor and needy, / and my heart is empty within me" (Psalm 109:22).

tion to YHVH."[155] So for [*the spiritual elite*] there shall be a different Torah, one that flows naturally, whereby statutes become commands, [*and everything becomes a simple, complete unity with undifferentiated oneness*].

The force of commands weaken, becoming completely no-thing, seeing as there is no longer a libidinal impulse [*rather, all that exists in the soul is transparent, supernal bliss*]. This spiritual ascent reaches the point preceding the advent of the libidinal impulse, preceding the filtering of the pristine impulse to create wherein such dualistic libido does not exist—until it reaches the point of the command **"I YHVH am your God"**[156]—the simple undifferentiated oneness of the Limitless Primal Reality. All the force of commandedness fades away insofar as all commands and statutes are concerned, residing in the primordial state of unimpeded Limitlessness. Commands are the overcoming of impediments, so being unimpeded obviates the relevance of commands.

In terms of apperceiving commands, the practice begins with **"shunning evil"** and then **"doing good,"**[157] for in the beginning **"a wild ass is born a man,"**[158] whereby one starts at the lowest of all levels. At that point, the continuum moves from a creaturely nature toward a divine nature, taking the mundane reality and continually sanctifying it and elevating it to reach the state of **"I YHVH am your God."**[159]

This then applies to the case of the heathen yearning to convert to Judaism while standing on one principle—that is, the foundational axiom, to truly learn this path. Indeed, Hillel could have taught the heathen the principle that everything is **"I YHVH am your God,"**[160] but this capacity within was not yet fully cultivated. Rather, he started with the negative rendering according to his capacity, **"You shall have no other,"**[161] for spiritual cultivation begins at a lower level, which is why Hillel said, "the rest is commentary, go study,"[162] which is the root of **"Love your fellow as yourself,"**[163] and the negative rendering of this axiom is "what is contemptible to you do not do to others"[164]—which is the paradigm of **"I YHVH am**

155. "In all of My sacred mount / Nothing evil or vile shall be done; / For the land shall be filled with devotion to YHVH / As the water covers the sea." (Isaiah 11:9).

156. "I YHVH am your God who brought you out of the land of Egypt, the house of bondage" (Exodus 20:2).

157. "Shun evil and do good, / seek amity and pursue it" (Psalm 34:15).

158. "A hollow man will get understanding, / When a wild ass is born a man" (Job 11:12).

159. Exodus 20:2.

160. Exodus 20:2.

161. "You shall have no other gods besides Me" (Exodus 20:3).

162. b*Shabbat* 31a.

163. "You shall not take vengeance or bear a grudge against your countrymen. Love your fellow as yourself" (Leviticus 19:18).

164. b*Shabbat* 31a.

your God"[165] and **"You shall have no other."**[166]

This then is the [*true esoteric*] meaning of the opening verse: **"This is the story of Isaac, son of Abraham,"** which is the order of creation. **"Isaac"** is the [*spiritual force within the dialectic of*] filtering and rigor, **"son of Abraham"** is the [*spiritual force within the dialectic of*] the flow of compassion and undifferentiated oneness, and from the [*collision of these*] two [*oppositional*] forces did the entire world came into being. This is the meaning behind R. Shlomo ben Yitzhaki's interpretation of **"This is the story"**[167]—referring to the difference between Jacob and Esau in this scriptural reading [*and the developmental process that differentiates them*].[168] [*Given that*] Esau is completely formed at birth,[169] accordingly the teaching of the Zohar[170] [*that builds on this through*] the verse: **"When an ox or a sheep or a goat is born."**[171] Immediately on the day of its birth it is called an ox because its features are fully formed on birth, which is not the case with a human being.

But in truth all of a person's physical properties are formed at birth, as Scripture states—**"sin couches at the door"**[172] and **"an old but foolish king"**[173]—thus at birth he was called **"Esau"** and afterward **"Jacob was grasping onto the heel of Esau."** The meaning of **"his hand"** [*YaDo*] is the grasping for uncultivated wisdom [*Y"oD*].[174] From that point of uncultivated wisdom, there is the transcendence of the terrestrial towards *Chokhmah*—Primordial Point—the [*ultimate*] command of **"I am,"**[175] which is undifferentiated oneness, and this is well understood by the mystic.

---

165. Exodus 20:2.

166. Exodus 20:3.

167. Genesis 25:19.

168. Rashi ad loc Genesis 25:25. "And they called his name Esau"—every one called him thus because he was made and fully developed with hair as a lad several years old.

169. See above, Rashi ad loc Genesis 25:25.

170. Zohar III:91b.

171. "When an ox or a sheep or a goat is born, it shall stay seven days with its mother, and from the eighth day on it shall be acceptable as an offering by fire to YHVH" (Leviticus 22:27).

172. "Surely, if you do right, / There is uplift. / But if you do not do right / Sin couches at the door; / Its urge is toward you, / Yet you can be its master" (Genesis 4:7).

173. "Better a poor but wise youth than an old but foolish king who no longer has the sense to heed warnings" (Ecclesiastes 4:13).

174. *Tiquney Zohar*, Tiqqun no. 40: 80b.

175. "I YHVH am your God who brought you out of the land of Egypt, the house of bondage" (Exodus 20:2).

[4.3]. *Parashah Toldot* (Genesis 23:19–28:9)

QUESTIONS FOR REFLECTION:

1. Why is it such a challenge to reallocate the focus of your life to the point of making egocentric needs repulsive?

2. Have you ever encountered a moral dilemma for which the road to goodness was inductive or intuitive? Do you rely more on induction, intuition, or commands to live the good life?

3. In striving to live the good life, do you find it more worthwhile to first clean your spiritual house and then do good in the world? Or do you find it more worthwhile to attempt to first do good in the world and then use that goodness to inspire internal change? What can you learn from ordering the spiritual practice according to the former rather than the latter?

[5.1]. *Parashah Vayishlach* (Genesis 32:4–36:43)

INTRODUCTION TO HOMILY:

Being human creates a sense of separation, in that a person experiences the self as an independent actor within the context of time-space-circumstance. This condition suggests an independent will, in contrast to one that is completely guided by providential oversight. This condition of vulnerability is explored in this homily as it brings with it a state of 'Yirah,' implying a deep, existential concern as to how one will be able to fulfill the divine need. Divine protection is never absolute. Through self-reflection, one can be relieved of much illusion and self-deception. The great problem is that a human assumes that because thinking is occurring in the mind that one is awake, but this is not necessarily the case. There is a tension between divine protection and human fallibility. The deeply devoted one is aware that just deserts and consequences of their fallibility will override the divine protection. An individual, even though self-crafted, is under a certain protection while that individual is still part of the totality that might lead to deployment elsewhere. But the promise of divine protection is conditional on the perfected action of the recipients. This homily illustrates the nature of Yirah as represented by two exemplars, Moses and Jacob. Two qualities that are illustrated through these exemplars that are essential here are: (1) 'bakhur,' the ability to make a virtue of necessity in seeing even the most painful events as potentially beneficial to one's spiritual development and (2) 'Yirah,' the sense of self-doubt based on a clear understanding of one's nature and limitations.

[5.2]. *Parashah Vayishlach* (Genesis 32:4–36:43)

HOMILY:

In the exegesis, R. Pinchas says in the name of R. Reuben: we find amongst the most refined of the patriarchs and the most choice of the prophets that these are the ones who are frightened and full of fear. For example, Scripture states [*regarding the Patriarch Jacob*]: **"Jacob was greatly frightened,"**[176] and it is also written **"For YH has chosen Jacob for Himself."**[177] [*And regarding*] Moses the prophet, *o.b.m.*, Scripture states: **"had not Moses His chosen one,"**[178] and it is also written regarding the battle of Sichon and 'Og

176. "Jacob was greatly frightened; in his anxiety, he divided the people with him, and the flocks and herds and camels, into two camps" (Genesis 32:8).

177. "For YH has chosen Jacob for Himself, / Israel, as His treasured possession" (Psalm 135:4).

178. "He would have destroyed them / had not Moses His chosen one / confronted Him in the breach / to avert His destructive wrath" (Psalm 106:23).

"Do not fear him [*tirah*]"[179]—which means that he had become frightened [*mityareh*]. [*The exegesis points to the need for further elucidation here, namely, how is it that yirah is connected with being most refined?*]

Behold, this exegesis settles the contradictions and eliminates the quandaries that appear to emerge. [*Namely, there is shock and surprise surrounding theodicy that emerges surrounding a devoted person who suffers, which seems to contradict Torah's assurance that a devotional life is rewarded, rather than punished.*] For example, Scripture makes assurances against a devoted person suffering from evil, to the point where God even vouchsafes this from happening:[180] **"Remember, I am with you: I will protect you wherever you go."**[181] And so it is with God's assurances for Moses,[182] but in the end all the guarantees in the world for divine protection cannot assuage such a lingering fear that perhaps a sin would cancel any such guarantee.[183] [*In this context, Jacob's fear emerges not only from the terror of Esau and Laban, as explained by Rashi's comment, but also a deeper existential fear that God would abandon him despite the promise, for perhaps he had sinned in the meantime and this would cause the annulment of the promise.*]

This is no longer fear of another, rather it is the [*within oneself*] fear of sinning. There is no reason that these characters should have fear, except perhaps if they had sinned their fear was a function of worrying over losing their merit for individual providence and protection. The real sin is a sense of self-satisfaction that would distance one from devotional service to the divine and that distancing is what cancels the providence. Once you have that fear of separation from the divine, it is at that point that one is now open to the whole spectrum of lower human emotions including primal fear for survival. From this explanation, one should not be constantly in fear of sinning, rather fear the sense of self-assuredness that damages sincerity of intent in being in proximity with the divine—that is precisely what alienates a person from the divine. The higher level of fear is that the divine assurance of providence may be ruptured, so that now the lower fears gush through the gates of consciousness. [*Such an assurance could potentially*

179. "But YHVH said to Moses: 'Do not fear him, for I give him and all his people and his land into your hand. You shall do to him as you did to Sichon of the Amorites who dwelt in Heshbon'" (Numbers 21:34).

180. b*Berakot* 7a.

181. "Remember, I am with you: I will protect you wherever you go and will bring you back to this land. / I will not leave you until I have done what I have promised you" (Genesis 28:15).

182. Exodus 3:12 and elsewhere.

183. Rashi ad loc Genesis 28:15, 32:10. "'I am with You'—God promised [Jacob] this because he was in terror of Esau and Laban." Compare with b*Berakot* 4a, b*Sanhedrin* 98b, b*Shabbat* 32a.

make one reckless precisely because one is protected by providence. But what comes with this sense of being protected is the fear that it is not protection from everything as a function of human limitation. The fear of being separated is a function of losing one's intimacy with the divine and disconnecting from the merging consciousness of devequt.]

[*The human incapacity to maintain the intimacy is what is at stake here.*] Here is the issue: on the one hand, the Zohar explains this verse—**"Jacob sent messengers ahead to his brother Esau"**[184]—as referring to the great shrewdness [*as a function of fear*] that Jacob had in sending emissaries to assuage Esau; while, on the other hand, rather than just minding his own business and keeping on his path, the exegesis suggests Jacob failed as a function of fear by sending emissaries and **"A passerby . . . who seizes a dog by its ears."**[185]

But the core of the matter at hand is really this: **"the decrees of YHVH are enduring / making one aware just how much wisdom is folly."**[186] [*By virtue of self-reflection on the mechanical nature of one's persona, then one becomes relieved of much illusion and is much less self-deceived. The greatest problem is that the human subject thinks it is thinking, but this is not the case.*] The core of devotional study and spiritual practice is all about this intention: to teach us our own lack of worth and foolishness, further linked to our materiality. Being formed from the earth—the more illusory and insubstantial a person perceives oneself to be, the more such knowledge draws that person to the Limitless. The more one sees the vanity of oneself, the more attraction the Limitless has, so then every desire and yearning should move us to cleave in *devequt* to the blessed Holy One.

In truly understanding that one cannot ultimately understand this, there emerges a certain distance from the Holy One. Thus, all of one's purpose is to actively shake up the self through devotional study and spiritual practice so that the spiritual counsels comes from divine knowing: **"Lest, seeing with its eyes . . . It also grasps with its mind"**[187] through spiritual practice of **"good counsels"** as expressed in the aforementioned Zohar.[188] [*First, these good counsels make a wise person think they are a fool. Secondly, these good counsels make wise a person with wisdom*

184. "Jacob sent messengers ahead to his brother Esau in the land of Seir, the country of Edom" (Genesis 32:4).

185. "A passerby who gets embroiled in someone else's quarrel / Is like one who seizes a dog by its ears" (Proverbs 26:17).

186. "The teaching of YHVH is perfect, / renewing life; / the decrees of YHVH are enduring / making the simple wise" (Psalm 19:8).

187. "Dull that people's mind, / Stop its ears, / And seal its eyes— / Lest, seeing with its eyes / And hearing with its ears, / It also grasps with its mind, / And returns and saves itself" (Isaiah 6:10).

188. Zohar II:96b.

think of oneself as a fool.]

In truth, this is what happens with spiritual practice: all engagement in spiritual practice itself endows the practitioner with vitality **"YHVH grants wisdom; / Knowledge and discernment are by His decree"**[189] to understand and to learn that **"all who practice it gain sound understanding."**[190] This is the meaning of the verse: **"the decrees of YHVH are enduring / making the simple wise"**[191]—specifically, the word **"simpleminded"**[192] acknowledges that the person who is foolish is made wise enough to find the spiritual practice. Such a spiritual practice through commandments allows for an evolution from being inherently unworthy **"And the knowledgeable will be radiant like the bright expanse of the sky"**[193] to know the divine mind.

This is the underlying meaning of the verse **"the decrees [*'edut*] of YHVH are enduring"**[194]—**"the decrees" [*'EDuT*]** can be then collocated as divine **"knowing" [*DE'oT*]**, for the commands allow for a sacred linkage [*between human self and divine self*]. This is not the case when a person is self-assured in their wisdom, because then the commands do not **"make one wise."** [*For how could the commands make any difference when the ego obstructs a way to serve as a sacred linkage?*] For the commands only serve as good counsel making wise those who are **"simpleminded"** in their own eyes and seeking wisdom. But one who is wise and righteous in their own eyes and lacking nothing—such a person does not seek for their devotional learning and spiritual practice to shed light on individual shortcomings. Rather, such an egocentric person will continue following the light of their own path. In so doing, what illumines one's path and what kind of counsel is then given through the command? If one does not seek the counsel [*of this light that catalyzes self-reflection*], then what use is the command itself? Advice then is only worthwhile for those seeking it [*so enacting a command should be an invitation to seek counsel so as to shed light on one's own spiritual comportment and evolution*].

[*The homily now returns to the opening quandary of the deeply devoted one's concern over losing the intimate connection with the divine. Either*

189. "For YHVH grants wisdom; / Knowledge and discernment are by His decree" (Proverbs 2:6).

190. "The beginning of wisdom is the fear of YHVH; / all who practice it gain sound understanding" (Psalm 111:10).

191. "The teaching of YHVH is perfect, / renewing life; / the decrees of YHVH are enduring / making the simple wise" (Psalm 19:8).

192. "Simpleminded" does not quite capture the negative connotation of being lowly and debased in terms of squandering our human potential.

193. "And the knowledgeable will be radiant like the bright expanse of the sky, and those who lead the many to righteousness will be the stars forever and ever" (Daniel 12:3).

194. Psalm 19:8.

a person is self-aware enough to see his/her own lack and is in need of higher guidance and open to Torah embodied in the persona of Jacob, or a one has a false sense of greatness, preventing him/her from become wise and open to sacred linkage, embodied in the persona of Esau in opposition to seeking intimacy with the divine.] For the issue is really encapsulated in this episode about Jacob and Esau in the following way: Esau is the egotist in opposition—the force that stands against **"an eagerness for the divine intimacy,"**[195] for it is perceived as a threat to his own egotism, as Scripture states: **"her son of higher [*but ultimately false*] stature, Esau."**[196] And later on, when his grandeur is felled [*when the blessing is switched*]—instead of acceding, Esau is full of ire and seeks revenge from his brother, Jacob. [*The impulse first leads to inflated ego, followed by unwise actions, so it then takes vengeance by exacting a price on the self for falling prey to such inflation.*]

This is what Jacob says to Esau: **"Thus shall you say, 'To my lord Esau, . . . I stayed with Laban and remained until now,"**[197] according to R. Shlomo ben Yitzhaki's interpretation, "and I fulfilled the six hundred and thirteen commands."[198] What this really means is that Jacob remained devoted to his spiritual practice while he **"stayed with Laban"**—that is, he dwelt with the libidinal impulse of Laban for all those years without succumbing to egocentrism and false arrogance. **"I have acquired cattle, asses, sheep and male and female slaves"**[199]—these are the ephemera of the material world that every human contends with—"so I remained within the creaturely realm, keeping myself transient and in a lowly station, all the while I was keeping the commandments."[200]

To be like **"Jacob, the transparent one encamped in the unifying source of all that exists"**[201] means being angelic, great, and unblemished. This is why Jacob always needed to work on himself, to be sure to constantly see himself as transient and lowly. Jacob never falls into the false assumption that he has not overcome that inflated sense of overconfidence

195. "To be sure, they seek me daily, / Eager to learn My ways. / Like a nation that does what is right, / That has not abandoned the laws of its God, / They ask me for the right way, / They are eager for the nearness of God" (Isaiah 58:2).

196. Literally, "Rebekah then took the best clothes of her older son Esau, which were there in the house, and had her younger son Jacob put them on" (Genesis 27:15).

197. "[A]nd instructed them as follows, 'Thus shall you say, "To my lord Esau, thus says your servant Jacob: I stayed with Laban and remained until now'." (Genesis 32:5).

198. Rashi ad loc Genesis 32:4.

199. "I have acquired cattle, asses, sheep and male and female slaves; and I send this message to my lord in the hope of gaining your favor" (Genesis 32:6).

200. R. Shlomo ben Yitzhaki on Genesis 32:5.

201. Literally, "When the boys grew up, Esau became a skillful hunter, a man of the outdoors; but Jacob was a mild man who stayed in camp" (Genesis 25:27).

and impulse for invulnerability by constantly denying any realization of that **"transparent"** state. When Jacob sent Esau a mixed message—all the learning and devotion he completed with the awareness that still **"I have been living with Laban"**[202]—he was trying to remain vigilant and self-conscious of this impulse for invulnerability.

This then assuages the commentators' perplexity: Jacob sent Esau contradictory messages—on the one hand, surrendering himself through humility; yet on the other hand, there is a sense of spiritual grandeur: **"I have been living with Laban,"** for according to this both spiritual qualities are one. [*Jacob kept up his spiritual practice of sacral deeds through grandeur that in no way affects his humility. The reason for keeping up the practice of sacral deeds appears to be tied intimately to living with surrender rather than living with inflated arrogance. It is necessary as long as one is susceptible to the impulse of inflated arrogance, but what lies beyond that?*]

For it is known—Jacob is the most refined patriarch, while Moses is the most refined prophet, so that the "most refined" [*BakHiR*] really refers to the intermediate, that force which balances opposing forces so that one side takes the other side and it is the "most refined" as the connector [*me-HaBeR*], combining and unifying everything into a complete unity.

For in truth, **"there is no evil that emanates from the divine totality,"**[203] so that all imagined evils or any traits that can be measured all flow to a good telos or end, except that the human mind cannot understand this—so **"exiled, for want of knowledge."**[204] [*Exilic consciousness is an inability to both think expansively and transcend beyond it as well to know that everything is leaning toward the good.*] *Da'at* is the synergy that flows through all the spiritual qualities, allowing the system to work and unifying the whole system together [*toward the good*]. What joins them together is *Chokhmah* (Primordial Point) through blessing in disguise residing in everything [*namely, there is a more temporal context to Wisdom of Chokhmah, which means there is a providential movement toward the good, a kind of gnosis beyond what the mind is able to think*].

Thus, the early *Tana'aim* had this knowledge [*that there is a providential movement toward the good regardless of what is happening*] to make this kind of unified way of knowing [*Da'at*], like Nahum Ish Gamzu,[205] who apperceived that it is all connected back to the unity. [*In all of the trials suffered by Nahum Ish Gamzu, he remained in a vigilant connection*

202. The insight here is conveyed in the translation of the verse no longer simply as past "I lived with Laban," but as past continuous: "I have been living with Laban."

203. "Out of the mouth of the Most High proceeds not evil and good?" (Lamentations 3:38).

204. Literally, "Therefore My people are exiled, for want of knowledge; and their honorable men are famished, and their multitude are parched with thirst" (Isaiah 5:13).

205. b*Ta'anit* 21a, where the name Nahum Ish Gamzu is explained in the context of his own sufferings and mishaps to mean "the man for whom this is also for the good!"

of knowing that there is a providential movement toward the good because there is a process and purpose at work, even amid any apparent experiences of suffering. It is also possible that if one experiences something negative and harmful, then after seeing that negativity for what it is, the suffering becomes a cause for deeper awakening rather than for madness; the suffering is transformed and deepens one's aspirations.] This was also the case with R. Akivah, who appeared to be suffering but was dwelling in the blessing in disguise.[206] For this kind of knowing ties it all together into unified goodness in the face of any chaotic phenomena—this way of seeing actually transforms the curse into something positive, and such knowing, that the totality is a singular field, with nothing standing outside of it, this is the sweetening of judgment of what is otherwise unpleasant [*on the way to goodness, all serving as an instrument of awakening*].

Thus Jacob and Moses are thus called "most refined," alluding to the unifying knowledge of the "connective agent" (*Da'at*) [*in encountering both sides of Judgment and Compassion*], consequently remaining in a state of constant *Yirah*. [*To be connective agents, there is a need for such a fulcrum point between Judgment and Compassion, so that Yirah is the experience of unpleasantness that is sweetened. When something limited occurs to such a person, instead of separating that unpleasantness as evil, it is sweetened by not allowing it to be separate and holding fast to the knowing that there is a providential movement toward the good because there is a process and purpose at work.*]

[*Now the homily comes to explicate the contradiction between the rabbinic and zoharic exegesis that juxtapose Jacob's confronting or fleeing Esau.*] In truth, if life were just a series of compassionate experiences, there would be nothing to be afraid of, then one would travel along life's path with an assured sense of security, as the exegesis teaches on the verse **"Jacob sent."**[207] Jacob did not enjoy the bliss of ignorance; rather, as one of the "most refined patriarchs," he holds on to and integrates both extremes of life's experience [*namely, the compassion and the rigor bound through the mediating sphere of Tiferet-Splendor*]. There is a great wisdom in that **"Jacob sent angels to Esau,"**[208] as explained in the Zohar,[209] for being able to remain cautious with regards to Esau, and yet Jacob was able to integrate the external anxiety and fear to elevate it into [*a higher state of fear regarding the potential forfeiting of the providence due to his own inadequacy, which is*] the internal knowing that everything is part of a process moving

206. b*Berakot* 60b.

207. "Jacob sent messengers ahead to his brother Esau in the land of Seir, the country of Edom" (Genesis 32:4).

208. Genesis 32:4.

209. Zohar I:166a.

toward the good. Namely, by elevating this fear, it is possible to remain vigilant, never letting go of one's own inadequacy with the looming possibility of sin. [*If Jacob would not have feared, he would not have sent messengers along with any preliminary gifts to Esau. The distinction being made here is that Jacob and Moses each had to be able to integrate the unpleasant into the wholeness of their existence by sweetening it. It is through this knowing that there is a providential movement toward the good because there is a process and purpose at work.*]

And so too, Moses serves as a refined connector of both sides of knowledge, being in that place of fear, but this fear emerged from a deeper awareness [*of transforming severe situations into a blessing in disguise*] all the while not becoming seduced by impulse of invulnerability; it was the mysterium tremendum that impinged directly on Moses's connection with the divine [*regarding the battle of Sichon and 'Og "Do not fear him"*[210]], so may divinity grant us the merit to be among the wholly fearful—*Amen.*

[5.3]. *Parashah Vayishlach* (Genesis 32:4–36:43)

QUESTIONS FOR REFLECTION:

1. Has there been a moment in your life when *'emunah* and knowledge have overturned even the external and incidental in your life toward the good? If so, describe; if not, describe.

2. In what ways do you engage in self-deception? How does Torah help to break through this spiritual quagmire? While complete self-deception is understandably a threat to society and self, is it healthy in moderation?

3. Why would the coarsening of your heart cause a separation between yourself and the divine?

210. "But YHVH said to Moses: 'Do not fear him, for I give him and all his people and his land into your hand. You shall do to him as you did to Sichon of the Amorites who dwelt in Heshbon'" (Numbers 21:34).

[6.1]. *Parashah Meiqez* (Genesis 41:1–44:17)

INTRODUCTION TO HOMILY:

Trusting in the grander scheme of existence provides one with the support of what is called 'emunah. The homily parses out different stages of 'emunah. The first stage of 'emunah is situating a higher power within nature. It leads to a basic conviction that there is a concealed higher power, which connects the world as experienced through the senses and connected to an egocentric mind. That egocentric mind can either be with or without 'emunah. However if one can be persuaded that there is a higher power, then that entrance level 'emunah emerges. In order to develop and be productive, one needs to recognize and pursue that second stage of 'emunah on a deeper interior level, namely, a recognition of a higher power within the depths of one's own consciousness—known as Chokhmah. The third stage of 'emunah builds on the first stages; one then is able to draw the higher stage into the lower levels through sacral deeds. The capacity to draw positive energy into the realm of sensory experience from the inner locus of the higher power transforms the realm of experience known as nature. To connect above and below, the two stages of 'emunah are then integrated through this alchemical practice of lighting the Hanukkah lamp. Joseph as the archetype of master consciousness transforms himself from the level of forgetting through nature to the level of remembering. There are two levels of transformation operative here: (1) the awakened state of remembering abides in the higher spheres of Chokhmah (in the realm of the formless of Intelligibles) and Binah (in realm of conceptual Intelligibles); whereas (2) the forgetful state is associated with the seven lower spheres, from Chesed (Compassion) to Malkut (Grounding), which constitute nature. By elevating consciousness to the source of blessing, then everything from there is blessed. There is a distinction between the outside of forgetting and the inside of remembering, both in the realm of the phenomenal, but here the homily is pointing to the site where disclosure can occur and the awareness of the divine can be recognized. The process of moving through stages of 'emunah is empowering, but the power one needs is then drawn from Chokhmah to extend blessing into the lower spheres of the externality of the world of sensory experience.

[6.2]. *Parashah Meiqez* (Genesis 41:1–44:17)

HOMILY:

"R. bar Hama bar Manyumah said that Rav: If a Hanukkah lamp is placed above twenty cubits [*from the ground*] it is ritually unfit, like a *Sukkah* and a crossbeam over [*the entrance of*] an alley [*which are also ritually unfit placed above twenty cubits from the ground*]."[211] [*It is then necessary to explain why a Hanukkah lamp is ritually unfit when placed above twenty cubits from the ground.*] So the issue [*is explicated through the following*] understanding of the scriptural verse: **"It was after two years when Pharaoh dreams"**[212] as it relates to the eighth level of reliance [*which one will benefit by trusting in a spiritual system*] called *'emunah*, as discussed in the book by our teacher, Rabbi Bahya.[213] It is this recognition of the unlimited nature of particular providence in cultivating a humility and lowliness that allows for such reliance, [*whereby*] **"one relies on the pristine Rock and its workings"** for everything is being seen with an awareness of master consciousness [*that is holistic and pristine*] that encompasses everything. As Scripture states: **"Who was it that gave Jacob over to despoilment . . ."** [*whereby despoilment refers to the humble and lowly level from which one becomes able to trust in a deeper reliance in the divine totality, the pristine Rock and its workings, which explains why the verse concludes with the assurance*] **". . . Surely YHVH."**[214] Even if your mind is not able to figure out what is good about the given situation [*for it is the nature of being small-minded that causes the human being to continually focus on the fragmentary and thus lack in everything*], still there remains justice in the system of providence [*when one shifts from being small-minded to a more expansive, holistic, integral perspective of the divine totality*]. Since the human intellect is too limited to perceive causality in a positive way in comparison to the mind of the divine totality, the perspective of the human mind must be dropped. *'Emunah* in the divine totality is the hidden good [*which is only possible to experience from the perspective of the humbled mind open to the greater good, even beyond conception and understanding*]. For Scripture states: **"Wisdom is found beyond the level of conception and conceptualization,"**[215] so that it is beyond the capacity of any embodied being to simply grasp it. There is nothing outside of this providential perspective of the expansive mind in its turning to experience how all particulars rely on the divine totality. [*What emerges now are two degrees of 'emunah: the first degree, focusing on the divine totality overseeing all of existence through particular providence; the second degree, focusing on the truth of the divine works and its evolution toward the greater good.*] In

211. b*Shabbat* 22a.

212. Genesis 41:1.

213. Rabbeinu Bahya, *Commentary to Torah*, Parashah Meiqez, 257a–b.

214. "Who was it gave Jacob over to despoilment / And to Israel plunderers? / Surely YHVH against whom they sinned / In whose ways they would not walk / And whose Teaching they would not obey" (Isaiah 42:21).

215. Literally, "But where can wisdom be found; / Where is the source of understanding?" (Job 28:12).

accessing the expansive mind full of reliance [*in these two degrees of 'emunah*], then the cause of one's alienation from the divine is resituated and elevated in the context of *Chokhmah* (Primordial Point). This then is the spiritual quality of master consciousness wherein everything in all worlds is interconnected [*to the ultimate human purpose with the hidden good*] in *Chokhmah* (Primordial Point). This is the esoteric meaning of the scriptural verse: **"Now Joseph is the master consciousness . . . distributing and nourishing everything,"**[216] namely, for the elevated spiritual being who has realized master consciousness of *Chokhmah* (Primordial Point), then blessings flow through such a person, **"distributing and nourishing everything."**[217]

[*This issue of interconnection between the lowly level of the humbled human mind with the supernal level of wisdom*] has a direct application to prayer [*whereby divine consciousness is always overseeing and in so doing, is looking downward, entrusting that everything is attuned to this directionality*] so too should one's heart should be uplifted and one's eyes downcast.[218] The divine eyes are lowered to look upon the lowest of the low, so as not to miss anything, while the human is lowering its gaze in appreciation for this complete reliance on providence. If the one praying cultivates *'emunah* in this gaze from above looking over every particular providence, then such a person is aware of the eye seeing everything, reaching the point where one becomes part of this providential web. Depending on the clarity of one's understanding of the providence, so is it reflected in the condition of providence one experiences. If one cultivates awareness in individual providence, then one is cared for individually even to bruising a finger.[219] [*This particular providence extends to the slightest movement: the least thing that happens is all part of this providential web but if one withdraws entrustment in such attunement to the providential web, then one's experience becomes subject to causality, namely, the lower nature.*] Unawareness then is that state whereby one is in denial of this spiritual reality [*kofer*]. Thus, [*there is an etymological basis for*] understanding prayer as binding [*namely, binding one's lower and higher natures*], whereby one's eyes should be lowered in their gaze into the more expansive providential realm. If the person in prayer is truly in a state of non-dual awareness, then there is only One looking down, which is the providence itself. The immediate consequence of non-dual consciousness that is providence leads to the

216. Literally: "Now Joseph was the vizier of the land; it was he who dispenses rations to all people of the land. And Joseph's brothers came and bowed low to him, with their faces to the ground" (Genesis 42:6).

217. Genesis 42:6.

218. b*Yebamot* 105b.

219. "One does not bruise a finger below, unless it was decreed so from above" (b*Hullin* 7b).

elevation of the heart above the mind to a realm higher than the seven lower spheres of consciousness.[220] The human mind is limited in its capacity to perceive the good, while providence exceeds what such small-mindedness can truly understand. It is crucial to realize this: the further one is in a condition of lowliness and humility, the more one has any capacity for reliance upon providence. Under circumstances where something is irritating, s/he finds himself/herself disconnected from this providential web, so then s/he falls into a situation where [*s/he would expect*] the providential web to remain concealed. Being caught up in one's lower nature is the cause for disrupting this providential web, yet in the context of this absence one is able to discern the presence of divine totality [*of Chokhmah (Primordial Point)*]—precisely in that very absence: **"Surely [there is] YHVH."**[221] This is what is meant by Joseph exemplifying master consciousness [*symbolized as the sphere of Yesod (Binding) that binds all causation to the sphere of Chokhmah (Primordial Point)*], precisely when he is thrown into the pit, immersed in the very depths of the husks [*which is the lowliest of realms wherein one is not able to conceive of anything good. Yet it is from this lowly place of descents that it is possible to discover a binding that interconnects with Chokhmah (Primordial Point), which is the hidden good one is unable to perceive*]. As long as Joseph [*does not bind in interconnection with of Chokhmah (Primordial Point) that is above the lower nature and rather*] trusts in the **Cup Bearer** [*namely, causality*], hoping to be remembered by him, yet [he is at risk as *the Cup Bearer*] is precisely the one **"who forgot him."**[222] Experiencing matters by the condition of the lower nature is one of forgetting, whereas the source of remembrance is higher than this lower nature [*of causality*]. Since Joseph entrusts the Cup Bearer to liberate him from the dungeon, relying on the conditions of the lower nature [*and thereby trapped by its small-minded limitations*], it is for that very reason he was forgotten and subject to forgetfulness. [*The clearer and deeper one's remembrance, the more one's expansive mind is connected to the providential web of of Chokhmah (Primordial Point).*]

And if indeed Joseph [*did not abandon his trust in the divine totality, rather by trusting the Cup Bearer to liberate him from the dungeon through the lower nature, he thus*] was in a condition of master consciousness [*as the sphere of Yesod (Connector) that binds all causation to the sphere of*

220. That is, to a higher level or sphere of consciousness known as *Primordial Wisdom* (*Chokhmah*), which is above the lower seven spheres of Grounding (*Malkhut*) to Compassion (*Chesed*). Each of the seven days of creation represents a sphere from which the world was created, which then comes to encompass the entire nature of reality.

221. "Who was it gave Jacob over to despoilment / And to Israel plunderers? / Surely YHVH against whom they sinned / In whose ways they would not walk / And whose Teaching they would not obey" (Isaiah 42:21).

222. Genesis 40:23.

of Chokhmah (Primordial Point)], **"for there was [nature as the] interpreter between them."**[223] Joseph wanted to connect the lower nature with what is beyond it.[224] Maintaining the condition of the lower nature does not involve any miraculous change in the natural order. When something changes, it only takes place in the higher realm of all possibilities, beyond nature—which is the level of pure divinity. Joseph wanted to change nature in order to transform the lower nature itself, so as to elevate it above the level of forgetfulness to the consciousness of remembrance. Thus, Joseph was causing this condition of forgetfulness to maintain the lower level.

[*The matter of redemption which eventually comes to Joseph through a seemingly miraculous change in the natural order happens through his binding of causation through the sphere of Yesod (Binding) to the sphere of Chokhmah (Primordial Point) where the hidden good abides. This now allows for the explication of its depiction in the scriptural verse.*] **"It was after two years when Pharaoh dreams,"** which is really upon the completion of two degrees of transformation [*in the natural order*], along the lines of zoharic reading "years" [*shanah*] as "change" [*shinuy, wherein this change is the dissolution of the natural reality in its ascent beyond the lower nature*].

"Pharaoh dreams"—[*the word*] **"PhaRaoH"** [*here is derived from the language of PeRiyaH, flowering and revelation*], namely a revelation which is the lower nature [*namely, coarser and thus conceivable*]; whereas **"dreams"** refers to the World of Concealment [*for the dream takes place at night when one is sleeping, in a state of concealment and covering, which is the degree of the lower nature. This lower nature is covered and concealed, thus it cannot be conceived. The matter at hand in the verse "Pharaoh dreams" is an attempt to interconnect the coarse, concealed, lower nature of Pharaoh and elevate it to the World of Concealment or the dream, which is above the lower nature*].

This is the meaning of the verse **"It was after,"**[225] which is also [*to be understood in the aforementioned esoteric manner as a liberation from the lower nature*] explained in the Zohar as [*from the lowliest level*] where **"darkness ends"**[226] [*that is precisely*] the place where one becomes aware of the *Chokhmah* (Primordial Point) in that very lowly place of absence [*which is a way of already overcoming the darkness*]. And so **"It was**

223. "[For they did not know that Joseph understood them], for there was [nature as the] interpreter between them" (Genesis 42:23).

224. The interpreter binds the realm above and below, bringing them together, so that the above is also understood to be below. This is the function of the *Zaddik yesod olam*, that is, Master Consciousness as the foundation of the world serving as interpreter.

225. Genesis 41:1.

226. Job 28:3.

after"[227]—due to the end and concealed lower degree [*which cannot understand nor conceive of the good within it, so there is a need for an interconnection with the hidden, Chokhmah (Primordial Point) above the lower nature*], so then when he apperceives **"Surely [there is] divinity here"**[228] [*and only the divine totality knows of the good therein*], **"for the wise one knows the interpretation of the matter"** [*namely, Chokhmah (Primordial Point) which knows the interpretation of all that is concealed in the lowliest level over which reigns darkness*]. For it is only within the divine totality whose workings are wondrous that the good remains hidden. [*Namely, the good hidden in the darkness of the lowliest, concealed level remains a great wonder for the divine alone.*]

This is then the place wherein [*Joseph*] interconnects to *Chokhmah* (Primordial Point), which is above the lower nature, by reaching to the place where darkness ends two degrees above while still remaining tethered to the lower nature. These two levels areabove the lower seven spheres, namely *Chokhmah* (Primordial Point) and *Binah* (Discernment), which fell into the lower realm. [*Recall that Binah (Discernment) is above the lower nature, and in turn that Chokhmah (Primordial Point) is above Binah (Discernment), ultimately above the lower nature by two degrees.*] And then these are **"the ears and cows all swallowed up by the seven solid and full ears and cows"**[229] [*which are the seven lower spheres*] **"but when they did not know how bad things really were"**[230] [*which is the descent into the lower nature embodying the absence of the divine reality. Joseph was able to connect the lowermost with what is beyond the lower nature. Since he elevated everything from the lowermost nature, forgetfulness was also elevated, here symbolized by the Cup Bearer, only then to be remembered and brought him up to Pharaoh*]. Everything was transformed through the consciousness of the source of blessing [*in Chokhmah (Primordial Point) and the hidden good*], uniting the lower seven elements of nature with the upper realm [*thus causing a revealing of this providential web even from this darkness*]. And this is [*what Joseph said:*] **"God has revealed to Pharaoh what He is about to do,"**[231] so at that point, what was hidden became revealed. [*The coarser level of Pharaoh that is perceptible and thus revealed is the lower nature, which then becomes blessed through the source*

227. Genesis 41:1.

228. "Who was it gave Jacob over to despoilment / And to Israel plunderers? / Surely YHVH against whom they sinned / In whose ways they would not walk / And whose Teaching they would not obey" (Isaiah 42:21).

229. Job 28:3.

230. Literally, "but when they had consumed them, one could not tell that they had consumed them, for they looked just as bad as before" (Genesis 41:21).

231. "It is just as I have told Pharaoh: God has revealed to Pharaoh what He is about to do" (Genesis 41:28).

of blessings.]

[*From here the homily shifts to explain how one is to discern whether one is interconnected within Chokhmah (Primordial Point) in the higher nature or whether one is in the grasp of the lower nature and garbed in the coarser, material body.*] The general principle here is that so long as a person is suffering from the condition of descent in a given situation seeking to be liberated, such a person is held in check, lost in the lower nature, and is thus unable to connect to *Chokhmah* (Primordial Point). By contrast, if one can attune to the providential web present in a situation of descent from divine presence, then regardless of what is experienced, there is no suffering and complaining. It is impossible for the mind to comprehend the purpose of suffering, so then it is best to connect to the higher realm of *Chokhmah* (Primordial Point). Rather than remaining in an embodied state of consciousness wherein one suffers over why something is not right, leaving that mind-state is possible by becoming bound to *Chokhmah* (Primordial Point). As one accepts the afflictions of suffering with true love [*whereby one is not out of sorts in suffering and does not seek relief, given that one is bound to the concealed good within it*] then one apperceives that **"Surely [there is] divinity here"**[232]—[*precisely in these afflictions*] there is good concealed therein. When it is impossible for one to apperceive the greater good [*the divine totality*], then it is preferable to be bound to *Chokhmah* (Primordial Point) [*which is the hidden good that is imperceptible*]. For, behold, when one is not out of sorts by suffering, then one has transcended embodiment [*which is the principal reality of the perceptible lower nature*], and interconnected to *Chokhmah* (Primordial Point) [*which is the hidden good above the lower nature*].

"Silence is the remedy of afflictions."[233] For "silence" is then [*like a tourniquet holding one, enabling one to be*] bound to the awareness of *Chokhmah* (Primordial Point) [*which is deeply interconnected within the divine. Being interconnected in this way to Chokhmah (Primordial Point), one receives from this very source of blessings an emanation with the cure providing healing*]. This is aligned with the meaning of **"A fence to wisdom is silence,"**[234] which speaks to [*an awareness of the power of silence in suffering that binds one to Chokhmah (Primordial Point). Through such an interconnected awareness in the moment of suffering, one realizes that*] "this [*suffering*] is also for the good,"[235] which then allows one to accept

232. "Who was it gave Jacob over to despoilment / And to Israel plunderers? / Surely YHVH against whom they sinned / In whose ways they would not walk / And whose Teaching they would not obey" (Isaiah 42: 21).

233. b*Berakot* 62a.

234. m*Avot* 3:13.

235. b*Ta'anit* 21a.

afflictions with love [*that interconnects to the hidden good. This is the very opposite of complaining over suffering*].

[*This understanding of interconnected awareness allows now for a deeper explication of the opening rabbinic statement regarding the inappropriateness of the Hanukkah lamp placed above twenty cubits from the ground. Such positioning invalidates it from serving to fulfill the obligation of seeing its true illumination for the season. The unsaid shift here from Hanukkah to Chokhmah (Primordial Point) is the shared motif of illumination through the symbol of oil. During Hanukkah, when the cognitive functions are despoiled,*] behold wisdom is called **"oil,"** as in the verse which describes **"your head never lack anointing oil"**[236] [*which is the Chokhmah (Primordial Point) on the head called oil*]. This is the issue of Hanukkah [*based on the miracle of the oil, which is Wisdom*]. When the mind that is coarse and secular, lacking awareness of the totality of the presence [*akin to the Greek mind*], entering into the subjectivity of the soul [*that is the inner Temple*], it leads to suffering when everything is so blurred. Amid the blurring of the mind-stream [*when one no longer sees any more of the divine presence in the world*], there still remains one tiny container of sealed oil [*that is the pristine capacity to trust in the providential web evolving toward the greater good*] in the seal of the High Priest [*which kept his mind-state from becoming contaminated*]. The priestly seal [*which was inscribed on this vessel of oil was*] truth and trust [*namely, the capacity to trust that the seal will guard against the contamination of the husks that interrupt the mind from apperceiving the divine totality*]. This [*oil is the Wisdom of providence evolving towards the greater good albeit*] an imperceptible good which the mind cannot fully grasp. [*This is the seal which encloses and prevents ways of thinking from ruling the mind and contaminating it.*] For [*this providential web of divine totality interconnecting every sentient being in its evolution towards the good*] is that imperceptible good [*from the perspective of the human being, although the one can still bind the self toward its apperception only through the trusting path of 'emunah rather than only through intellectual perception*].

[*The true miracle of Hanukkah then is that the cruse of oil, which is the depth of trusting in 'emunah that remains imperceptible actually stopped for eight days, which are the intellectual perceptions of the lower nature.*] For this [*oil of illumination*] is only enough for one day, which is the quality of Wisdom [*namely, imperceptible Chokhmah (Primordial Point), and the other intelligibles below it were governed by contaminated thinking, distracted from the divine totality*], but all the other eight lower intelligibles are blessed through it [*being blessed by Wisdom and so they are purified*

236. Literally, "Let your clothes always be freshly washed, and your head never lack ointment" (Ecclesiastes 9:8).

from the contaminated thinking, distracted from the divine totality].

[*And so given that the miracle of Hanukkah really is the blessing drawn from Chokhmah (Primordial Point) to the lower eight intelligibles, thus*] lighting then proceeds from this light of Wisdom, from which the rest of the levels are blessed for the entire eight days. Therefore the blessed Sages teach why the level of the *Chanukiah* cannot be poised higher than twenty cubits, which is the level of *Keter* (Crown) [*a nexus of unknowing between above and below, with the capacity for receptivity of prophecy beyond our limitations*]. The gaze from twenty cubits and below is the gaze from the level of *Chokhmah* (Primordial Point) that sees everything below *Keter* (Crown), and this is precisely what allows for an apperception of this providential web. Above this level of twenty is where the eyes cannot see, for the level of *Keter* (Crown) [*where even the trusting eye of 'emunah has no capacity to oversee and draw down blessing to the lower intelligibles, thus*] it cannot light the *Chanukiah* [*given it has no content*]. Rather from the consciousness of Wisdom [*where the trusting eye of 'emunah oversees the providential web evolving toward the good*], thus enables seeing with a good perspective, and only then is one able to light the *Chanukiah*. [*If the purpose of the sacral deed is to draw down blessings to the lower intelligibles, then it is ritually unfit to light the Chanukiah above twenty cubits, the level of Keter.*]

Behold the blessed Sages are divided as to whether lighting begins with one candle and is augmented each day [*as the School of Hillel opines*] or to whether lighting begins with eight candles and is then reduced each day [*as the School of Shammai opines*]. What abides is that both opinions are the word of the living God. For in truth **"everything have you created according to Wisdom"**[237] such that all the lights are already contained within Wisdom [*but the rectification of the sphere of Hod (Splendor) is below and not above, therefore it is necessary to reveal incrementally what is hidden*]. The power of the actual is always already included in the potential such that all beings' potential is an extension of the divine [*Wisdom*].

And so too with the [*structure of the levels*] below [*Wisdom*], each higher level must include [*and build upon*] the level that preceded it. For if this was not [*structured*] so [*namely, that the lower level is already encompassed in the higher level*], then from where would the existence [*of what was lower*] then emerge if the power of the actual was not indeed always already included in the potential? [*All eight levels of illumination in potential are then included in the first actual light. Following this structure would then require a reorientation of the order of lighting the eight candles of the Chanukiah.*]

237. Psalm 104:22.

The truth is that on the first night [*namely, the first stage of actual illumination*] one should really light all eight candles [*encapsulating all of the eight potential degrees*], given that all [*eight degrees of illumination*] are included in [*the first supernal degree*]. And so it should then follow afterward on the second day [*which is the second stage of actual illumination that one really ought to light*] seven [*candles*], given that all [*seven potential degrees of illumination*] are included in [*the second supernal degree*]. But as human beings, we are unable to apperceive [*all these stages*] of this integral form [*in its supernal positioning*], except through extension and revelation [*which is a process of releasing these integral forms and extending them into a revealed form that is stepped down, thus capable of being apperceived by the human mind*].

[*Given that all our apperception of these degrees is only perceptible through extension and revelation of integral forms*], it follows that the lighting of one candle each day is a process of extension. [*This allows for the contemplation of each new day of lighting as a process of extension and revelation. By contrast, the order of light proffered by the School of Shammai is the contemplation of a messianic consciousness, given that the light of the divine in its totality is already present, without any need for extension or revelation.*] This incremental process of augmentation [*following the School of Hillel*] allows for concealment to abide, which then allows for an incremental revelation. This process of extension is what then augments our apperception. [*This explains the reasoning behind the sacral deed of lighting the Chanukiah which is contingent on human perception, namely, the way in which the miracle is publicized.*] So the devotional work is to publicize the miracle. [*It is precisely in this process of seeking of a fuller revelation of messianic consciousness that extension and revelation of this light takes place, allowing the gnosis to actually flow and extend beyond the boundaries of its actuality, realizing its integral potential already inscribed within it.*]

[6.3]. *Parashah Meiqez* (Genesis 41:1–44:17)

QUESTIONS FOR REFLECTION:

1. How do I experience the sacral deed of lighting the Chanukiah? How does it allow me to open my awareness to the limitations of my spiritual apperception when limited solely to my mind?

2. Is my experience of illumination heightened in a public space or in a private space—why?

3. If it is through this process of seeking of a fuller revelation of messianic consciousness that extension and revelation of the light

takes place, then how do I allow space in my regular week for such seeking to emerge?

4. Is my potential sense of seeking already actually flowing and extending beyond the very boundaries of my mind that tends to obstruct this flow through rationalization and cynicism?

[7.1]. *Parashah Vayigash* 1–2 (Genesis 44:18–47:27)

INTRODUCTION TO HOMILY:

This homily parses spiritual reality as the spinning wheel of objects versus the inner consciousness that is aware of them. The appearances of the objective world are constantly changing regarding these combination of letters. There is something perceiving them separate from those objects. But the energy of perception is intrinsically connected to what appears. The sacred language expresses the view that comes from the inner source of perception, symbolized by the trunk of the Tree-That-Is-All. None of those things which appear are sui generis; rather, those appearances are dependent upon the source of perception, represented by the sap of the Tree. The energy that extends from the source of perception and enlivens all objects that appear is called the sacred language of Torah, as opposed to its limbs, which are the objects that appear, symbolized by the Zodiac wheel and its permutations. Those letters have their source within the innermost center of the wheel. The world of appearances is constantly changing. In Kabbalah, it is called the World of Exchanges or 'Olam haTemurot. It is dependent upon an inner source, the source that perceives it. The process of appearance or creation depends upon energy coming from the creative source, represented by the letters of the sacred language. The closer an appearance is to its creative source, the less limited it is in terms of separateness and the more it partakes of an eternal quality and therefore the less it is subject to change. Letters are the delimiting powers of creation from the source. Letters have the capacity to condense the divine light. The mind is creating the world of experience by picking out certain elements as concepts, so that one can recognize the world within a certain constitution. The world of perception is thus meditated by the sphere of Da'at, which in this homily is understood as the mind's capacity to form concepts through combining letters of the sacred language. This sacred language is the material of creation, expressing itself as names. The name is a particular kind of light that constitutes the object that appears through the power of that name. This is what the world consists of—for everything that exists is named. A person does not truly live up to their name unless one's comportment aligns with the potential of the powers that constitute one's name. Everything other than the human inherently corresponds to its name, whereas the human being must perfect their actions to realize the inner meaning of their name. To fulfill one's purpose, one must relate to the objects of their experience as constituted by the sacred letters that are the basis for their existence. Satisfaction then comes from what is the case, namely, the sacred energy within each letter. What the mind thinks is not dependent upon the sacred energy of these letters. If one is not seeing everything as the embodiment of sacred letters that names it, then one is either attracted or repelled by it based on some subjective view, which is not factual from a spiritual perspective. Rather, by relating to everything through the letters of its sacred language, then one is making use of its deep interiority and root, which is ultimately satisfying. A spiritual perception based upon a metaphysical assumption that in order to have clarity one needs to disconnect one's self from the sense of solidity of the existence of everything being perceived. If a person lives by the metaphysical reality represented by the letters, then one is participating in a transformative spiritual experience. This supports the divine intent to reveal itself through the creative process; but if one does not, then it impedes it, leading to greater degrees of concealment. This process is the effort of the divine to disclose itself within nature.

[7.2]. *Parashah Vayigash* 1–2 (Genesis 44:18–47: 27)

HOMILY:

"Behold, you can see for yourselves, and my brother Benjamin for himself, that it is indeed I speaking to you"[238]—namely, that according to Rashi's explanation, Joseph showed his circumcised membrum to his brothers to prove to them that he was circumcised just like them; **"I am the one speaking to you"**—in Hebrew.[239] [*Covenantal loyalty, even though it may appear concealed, is most effectively revealed as expressed through circumcision as well as the Hebrew language.*] But on this point R. Eleazar Mizrakhi [*in his super-commentary, called Gur Aryeh on Rashi*] raises an objection that Joseph made an oath to Pharaoh not to speak in Hebrew [*lest it embarrass him by exclusion due to his ignorance of the language of Canaan not Egypt*] as indicated in Tractate *Sotah*.[240] The *MaHaRsH"A* [*in his Talmudic glosses to this same narrative*] then raises concern over the apparent quandary: Joseph was indeed talking Hebrew to his brothers [*which would then exclude and embarrass Pharaoh, thus violating the terms of their oath*].[241]

But I think there is another [*way of understanding the original challenge posed by R. Eleazar Mizrakhi that Joseph made an oath to Pharaoh not to speak in Hebrew lest he embarrass him by exclusion due to his ignorance of the language*], namely, to explain this situation without going into ethnographic distinctions of language [*and by extension, the ritual of circumcision to prove their connection*]. Recall it is known that the Exodus

238. Genesis 45:12.

239. Rashi ad loc b*Sotah* 36b.

240. b*Sotah* 36b.

241. *MaHaRsH"A ad loc* b*Sotah* 36b.

from Egypt was due to the four markers of identity for evolving from spiritual exile: "preserving one's names; preserving one's language; preserving righteous conduct; [*as well as refraining from gossip*]."[242]

[*The homily now needs to define holiness and how it obtains in language, namely, Hebrew. To convey this esoteric teaching, the homily assumes familiarity with two key symbols in Jewish mysticism. The homily will now freely associate both distinct symbols that on the surface share similarities. Each symbol, however, is steeped in some of the earliest layers of Jewish mysticism. The first symbol is the Wheel of the Zodiac, extrapolated from the Sefer Yetzirah, while the second symbol is the Cosmic Tree-That-Is-All, extrapolated from Sefer HaBahir*].[243] In order to understand this issue [*regarding the ontological status of the sacred within the Hebrew language*], we need to delve into [*esoteric teaching in Sefer Yetzirah regarding all that is ephemeral being dependent upon*] the 231 gates. [*Each one of the letters has qualia and quantity from the Limitless light so that when two letters are collocated and conjoined, they form one gate. As each of the twenty-two letters of the Hebrew Aleph Bet are paired with each other forming gates, the sum total of 22 letters x 10.5 remaining unpaired partners = 231 gates.*] The perennial qualia at the center of the wheel are imbued with the **"divine portion within children of Jacob"**[244] to then serve as the axis point upon which everything revolves [*given that this divine portion was not created from the aforementioned 231 gates*]. Even the heavenly throngs [*including archangels of other nations*] as well as all sentient beings, regardless of their elevated status, are as branches when viewed from the World of Distorted Mirrors[245] [*at a distance from the sacred center*]. While the roots of all other seventy languages emerge from branches of the Cosmic Tree,[246] the trunk is composed of the Hebrew

---

242. *Leviticus Rabbah* 32:5.

243. The most recent scholarly consensus on the dating of these two key Jewish mystical texts (which is always evolving) dates *Sefer Yetzirah* to the late Gaonic period, while *Sefer HaBahir* to the early medieval period in Provence. The present concern of the homilist is with the devotional power of the symbol rather than with its dating per se, although the more ancient the symbol, the more authenticity it tends to garner in exoteric and esoteric circles alike.

244. Deuteronomy 32:9.

245. "World of Distorted Mirrors" is an approximate translation of the Kabbalistic concept of *'Olam haTemurot*. While in mishnaic terms, *Temurah* denotes a kind of substitution or replacement wherein the human being can be substituted by an animal sacrifice, its extrapolation in to the Kabbalistic tradition suggests however, that the replica of a given spiritual reality reproduces, at best, the distorted reflection of a flawed mirror. Just like an ape resembles a human being, much of what appears in such an external comparison of mirroring may show much in common between the exterior qualia but that parallel dissolves on reflection of the interior qualia.

246. "Cosmic tree" is an approximate translation of *'Ilan*. The homily does not go into

language and Israel. These branches ultimately culminate in exterior forces [*in the tree analogy, more bark than sap*], so that all other nations and languages do not necessarily have intrinsic access to the [*unique divine vitality or sap of this mapping of the world as a cosmic*] tree. While all existents depends upon this center of the wheel for existence, many remain [*unwilling and*] unable to connect to the center of the divine permanence that energizes the wheel [*from a place of devotional interiority rather than from the exteriority manifest in language, as is the case with the 231 aforementioned gates that structure external communication through Hebrew. The homily is suggesting that amidst the dichotomy of interiority and exteriority the only authentic, immediate connection with the divine totality takes place from a place of devotional interiority rather than through the mediated vehicle of any language, so that even the holy tongue of Hebrew has its limitations*].

There is a boundary point marking the sacred from the profane. This is why Torah is not [*primarily or necessarily*] concerned with connections to foreign languages or ethnos [*because there is a deeper interiority that energizes the sacred center*]. This focus upon the interior vitality that animates the center point of the wheel is the [*ontic spiritual reality that is ontologized into a*] reason for delimiting boundaries of the sacred from exterior forces of dissipative energies within language and ethnos.

This is [*a way to understand the otherwise shocking rabbinic teaching as to*] why "a gentile who studies Torah is condemned to death."[247] It is [*this sacred center that originates in the prophetic thinking which delimits the sacred from the profane as evinced in the scriptural teaching that*] **"Israel is YHVH's hallowed portion, the firstfruits of increase; all that devour him shall be held guilty."**[248] [*Just as it would be ritually*

---

great detail about this *'Ilan*, but from its usage here, it is most likely the *'Ilan d'kol Hai*, the Tree-That-Is-All, which makes a veiled appearance early on in Ancient Israel; see Ziony Zevit, *The Religions of Ancient Israel: A Synthesis of Parallactic Approaches* (Continuum, New York, 2001), 559a; Moshe Weinfeld, "Feminine Features in the Imagery of God in Israel: The Sacred Marriage and the Sacred Tree," *Vetus Testamentum* XLVI, no. 4: 515–29. What concerns our homily directly, however, is more likely the *'Ilan d'kol Hai,* the Tree-That-Is-All, with its first sustained appearance in early medieval Jewish mystical literature of Provence. On this usage of the *'Ilan d'kol Hai*, the *Tree-That-Is-All*, see *The Book Bahir: An Edition Based on the Earliest Manuscripts, Sources and Studies in the Literature of Jewish Mysticism*, ed. Daniel Abrams (California: Cherub Press, 1994), no. 14, 125. For a most comprehensive and astute analysis on the origin of the "Tree-That-Is-All" and its implications for Jewish mysticism in relation to its more theosophic iteration as the "Tree of Life" [*'Etz Chayyim*], see Elliot R. Wolfson, "The Tree That Is All: Jewish-Christian Roots of a Kabbalistic Symbol in *Sefer ha-Bahir*," in *Along the Path: Studies in Kabbalistic Myth, Symbolism, and Hermeneutics* (New York: SUNY Press, 1995,) 63–88, esp. 70–88.

247. b*Sanhedrin* 59a.

248. "Israel is YHVH's hallowed portion, the firstfruits of increase; all that devour him shall be held guilty, evil shall come on them, says YHVH" (Jeremiah 2:3).

inappropriate] for "a stranger to eat sacred sacrifices" [*which assumes prerequisite ritual preparation*] whereby such a person, ab initio, is forbidden [*to cross this boundary and*] consume [*such spiritual produce relegated to an appropriately prepared Israelite, one who struggles with the divine*], so it is also related to [*the ritual readiness required to offer*] *Terumah* and *Challah* [*which are forbidden without such ritual preparation, and, more importantly, Terumah and Challah are considered first offerings. By virtue of their symbolic value as firsts, these offerings are only appropriately offered by priests who are in a state of ritual readiness for such devotion*]. It is known that the "beginning" of this zodiac wheel is the central point of the sacred from which the center emerges [*radiating outward concentrically to the profane; thus, all beginnings are aligned with the most intensely sacred, given that everything emerges from this sacred center*]. Thus, Torah [*as one expression of this sacred center*] is relevant to Israel [*namely, those that struggle with the divine and are thus open to receive this gnosis. These series of concentric circles of holiness accord with the terms, Torah, God and Israel, which are all concerned with beginnings and are really one given their relationship to the sacred center*]. As the dictum states: "Torah, God and Israel are really one reality"[249] [*for Torah and Israel emerge from the sacred center while the divine sustains all sentient beings, which is actually the essence of this sacred center*].

[*The homily has thus far explicated an integral vision of the reality of the sacred, which is a divine portion. Now the homily turns to an extended explication of the holy language of Hebrew*]. Behold, Rashi comments on the verse: **"This one shall be called Woman, / For from man was she taken."** "Hence we may learn that the language used to create the world was the Holy Tongue [*Hebrew*]."[250] This interpretation works well [*as proffered by Rashi*]. The rabbinic teaching is interpreted [*as well is proffered by Rashi*]: **"In the Beginning created Elohim."**[251] At first ["*In the Beginning*"] it arose in the divine mind to create the world through the attribute of strict Justice, but afterward allied Mercy [*YHVH*] with Justice [*Elohim*].

249. Zohar III:1a.

250. "The Adam said: 'This one at last / is bone of my bones / And flesh of my flesh. / This one shall be called Woman, / For from man was she taken" (Genesis 2:23). See Rashi ad loc. "'This one shall be called Woman, / For from man was she taken'—Here we have a kind of play on words [*the words 'ish and 'ishah sounding similar*]: hence we may learn that the language used at the time of the Creation was the Holy Tongue [*Hebrew*]."

251. "In the Beginning created Elohim" (Genesis 1:1). Rashi ad loc. "'God [*as Judge*] created'—it does not state 'YHVH created' because at first God intended to create [*the world*] to be placed under the attribute [*and rule*] of strict justice, but God realized that the world could not thus endure and therefore gave precedence to Divine Mercy allying it with Divine Justice. It is to this that what is written in Genesis 2:4 alludes—'In the day that YHVH God made heaven and earth.'"

[*To explicate the matter further,*] the issue [*at hand*] is known that in the beginning of Creation, the Infinite had to undergo self-circumscription, thus allowing space for the Finite. Restraint is the root of *Din* (Judgment), for the more that something is limited, the denser and more distinct it is than that which preceded it. The vessels are more ephemeral, while the spirit is more abiding, unchanging, and thus the proximity of the spirit to the Infinite. The whole concept of ephemerality and destruction is associated with the dissipating energy of exteriority, evil, and judgment. [*Ephemerality and destruction are an expression of Din (Judgment), for that which is delimited is embodied in an ephemeral vessel. This explains why*] the very terms delimitation and restraint are the root of *Din* (Judgment) and thus considered a manifestation of mortality and deterioration.

Behold the epitome of restraint is represented linguistically by the letters [*being the lowest spiritual level according to a Kabbalistic mapping of T"ANTA (trope, vowels, letters), which serves as the embodiment of the infinite within the finite, as Scripture states:*] **"from my embodiment I shall envision the divine."**[252] When engaged in contemplating the restless thoughts moving in the mind-stream, this quality of the mind in its constant motion is like the **"creatures fluttering to and fro."**[253] Everything in motion takes the form of letters. Such motion is conceptual, for it is impossible to discern any concepts in the mind without recognizing thoughts. But if thoughts are conceptual and formed through letters, then it is precisely letters that enable one to grasp a given thought and conceive it. Otherwise, it remains undifferentiated. One cannot even speak of a concept or thought until there is some reduction of the abstraction to the linguistic realm. The energy of thought itself is constantly taking on conceptual forms. The restraint that gives rise to the letters, once purified, then permutates with *Chokhmah* (Primordial Point), then it is conceptualized in the combination of different letters. Within restraint, the content of the mind takes the form of letters, after which comes a comprehension of the letters, called *Binah* (Discernment). [*So the letters themselves are a form of restrained limitless light that extends from the realm of thinking that can then be conceptualized and apperceived once restrained. The process of the limitless light becoming manifest is now described as it moves through the realm of thinking into apperception by way of the spheres of divine consciousness known as sefirot. Expansive light originates in the sphere of Keter (Crown), the most supernal of all the spheres. From there light flows into the sphere of Chokhmah (Primordial Point) where restrained light is embodied in letters.*] This process of understanding [*as a restraining of the limitless light*

252. Job 19:26.

253. "And the living creatures ran and returned as the appearance of a flash of lightning" (Ezekiel 1:14).

of gnosis originally abstracted] is what leads to a more intimate kind of knowing the meaning of the concept, which is *Da'at* (Bridging Connector) [*energy that is a continually moving stream that connects thought along so it can be ramified in different forms. Until this point, the sphere of Da'at is now revealed even though it remains primarily concealed. Da'at as the sphere of knowing is precisely the essence of that which is known and delimited into thought itself. From here the sphere of Binah is then able to form a comprehension. At the beginning of the limitless light manifesting before it is restrained, thought is expansive without a capacity to be apperceived, so Da'at remains concealed. Following the restraint of limitless light, only then can Da'at emerge from a concealed to a more revealed state*]. It is this sphere of *Da'at* which actively mediates in its being composed of both the formalizing energy of *Chokhmah* (Primordial Point) and the understanding of *Binah* (Discernment). [*Da'at as the delimited light that emerges into thought is then apperceived by the sphere of Binah. The contours of its delimitation come from the sphere of Chokhmah (Primordial Point) as well as from the contours of comprehension within the sphere of Binah, given that all of human knowing encircles and is bound up in the spiritual qualia known as middot.*] It is only after this intimate knowing of *Da'at* that a movement from concealment to revealment is possible, whereby these spiritual qualia are aroused and thus able to emerge. These spiritual qualia operate as *Ahavah* (Love) and *Yirah* (Awe) [*and it is through these qualia that Da'at is able to emerge in the midst of the human experience of life*]. The greater revealment of *Da'at* happens through its mediating position, thus becoming more manifest through its next iteration in *Tiferet* (Splendor). The capacity of *Tiferet* (Splendor) is to mediate between *Ahavah* (Love) and *Yirah* (Awe) [*while Da'at meditates between the spheres of Chokhmah (Primordial Point) and Binah (Discernment)*]. And similarly this [*process of making manifest the limitless light emerging now restrained*] takes place throughout all the spiritual qualia. [*The spiritual qualia being alluded to here further along the realm of manifestation are Neẕach (Perpetuity), Hod (Humility), and Yesod (Bonding), wherein the latter sphere serves again in the meditator between the former two spheres. Once again, at this level, there is even more revealment of emerging light from Da'at in this meditated iteration through Yesod (Bonding).*]

What then really characterizes the primary role of *Da'at* is its mediating capacity to integrate two oppositional spheres into one [*place for more revealment of its manifesting light. Given this mediating role between the spheres of Chokhmah-Primordial Point and Binah-Discernment*] thus the sphere of *Da'at* is called *Lashon haQodesh* (Holy Tongue). [*In serving in its mediating capacity, Da'at is thus*] as meditator between the sphere of *Chokhmah* (Primordial Point) also known as *Qodesh*, while *Binah* (Discernment) is referred to as the *Lashon* (Tongue/Language). [*Regarding this image of mediation, consider the image of*] the scale with one balance and two cups, oscillating from one side to the other, balanced by the beam of the weights through the tongue of the scale's vertebrae [*which mirrors the capacity for human reflection by meditating oppositional cups through the tongue's scale*]. In Yiddish, this beam of the scales is called *lashon*, as it contemplates the balance, causing the beam to shift from one side to the other [*depending on how much mediation is needed for balance. Hebrew is the balancing vehicle of linguistic emanation that allows the sacred to unfold in a balanced way through the chain of being; otherwise, the inchoate stirrings of divine wisdom in Chokhmah remains stranded in a realm of inarticulation*].[254]

[*From explicating why Qodesh (Sacred) is aligned with the sphere of Chokhmah (Primordial Point) as the restraint of light into the form of letters, the homily now shifts now into explicating why Hebrew is Lashon haQodesh (Holy Tongue). Da'at is the meditating force that permutates the letters into words and from that processes Hebrew as Lashon haQodesh, thus enabling an articulate form. Making space for giving form requires the restraint of zimzum.*] And behold it is known through the [*esoteric*] teaching: **"Through Torah did the blessed Holy One create the world."**[255] The Aramaic translation of the verse **"In the Beginning created Elohim"**[256] for it is "with Wisdom the world was created," so that Wisdom is Torah, and Torah is its letters [*then the world is created through letters*].[257] Letters are a form of restraint [*as a product of this process, in their capacity to delimit undifferentiated light of the Limitless, to give it form, expressing that light in specific, delimited, and thus restrained ways*]. The principle at work here is that the world is created through letters, but there are higher levels of consciousness than the letters. There is no limit to the number of restraints [*the letters being just one type*], so much so that there is no limit to phenomenal worlds. However it is impossible to really apperceive how many restraints there really are, **"for one higher than the high watches** [and there are higher than they]."[258] It goes without saying, that these restraints

254. In German, *Lasche*; in Hebrew, *lashon ha'moznaim*. The tongue has to line up with midline of the scale. Language is the mediating point, much like the midline of the scale, between the ethereal spheres of *Chokhmah* and *Binah*.

255. Zohar I:161a.

256. Genesis 1:1.

257. Conventionally letters are associated with the lowest of the four categories of *TaNT"A*, like *Malkut*, the *Tagin* associated with *Zeir Anpin*, *Binah* with the vowels, and *Chokhmah* with the cantillation notes, but what the Vitebsker is suggesting in his reading which is novel is that the letters themselves have degrees of contractions, distinguishing between written and oral letters.

258. Literally, "[If you see the oppression of the poor, and the violent perverting of

and stages of manifestation in the phenomenal world are simply impossible to apperceive. It is evident [*that there are other levels of restraint that exist and precede the letters as*] in the realm of *TANT"A* remains higher.[259] The world constituted by letters is dependent on the higher and prior restraints that give vitality to it and affect their operation. But this is not the place to investigate the issue, for the infinite is exulted and well beyond our grasp, as Scripture states: **"The secret of YHVH is for those who are in awe of the One"**[260] so that a wise person will understand the matter.

This is why we perceive the phenomenal world through the letters, and we call these letters primary building blocks that our minds experience, even though there are higher worlds than the letters. As explicated in the Zohar—**"and lay down [*VaYiSH"KaV*] in that place"**[261]—there are twenty-two letters [*which compose the universe and keep the cosmic energy alive*], as discussed therein.[262] For every single matter that a sentient being knows through phenomenal experience is created by the letters and sustained through its vitality. [*Firstly,*] here the written letters are [*the most external form that provides an entry into*] the palace and vessel, so that the letters are pronounced by the mouth. [*Secondly,*] the letters articulated are vessels to inner thoughts, while [*thirdly*] the [*most deeply imbedded are the*] unsaid letters inscribed in the heart; their vessel is the spoken one, which is known in the heart of mystics and explicated in fourfold mapping explicated in the *Pardes*.[263]

[*On concluding its explication of the letters, which are restrained*

justice and righteousness in the state, marvel not at the matter;] for one higher than the high watches, [and there are higher than they]" (Ecclesiastes 5:7).

259. Compare with the view of the phenomenal-noumenal world in the thinking of Arnold Schopenhauer (1788, Gdansk; 1860, Frankfurt), who suggests that the entire phenomenal world is infinite because it does not have true being; if so, then the number of worlds would be the same as the number of minds, not really limiting its numbers. The true eidos is to equate it with what Vedanta philosophy calls the "I am," not the "nonexistent self," but the "true self." Vedanta philosophy does not recognize a particular self, whereas Schopenhauer sees ideas mediating between noumena and phenomena which can only be known by way of our individuated self.

260. Psalm 25:14.

261. "He came on a certain place and stopped there for the night, for the sun had set. Taking one of the stones of that place, he put it under his head and lay down in that place" (Genesis 28:11).

262. The Vitebsker is conflating this passage in the Zohar I:148a, which describes how Jacob gathers twelve precious stones on which he lays his head, which becomes the resting place of *Malkhut*. There are twelve precious stones below (three stones in four directions), and ten with the *Shekinah* as the tenth sphere resting on this bed, so these levels totals twenty two. This is then alluded to through the word play in the verb VaYiSH"KaV, which also aids in understanding the teaching that the phenomenal world [VaYiSH] is apperceived through the twenty-two letters of the Hebrew alphabet [KaV=22].

263. R. Moses Cordovero, *Pardes Rimonim*, Gate 21.

manifestations of Chokhmah (Primordial) Point that is called Qodesh (Sacred), the homily now shifts to explicate the collocation of letters and their conjoining into words in order to compose a language. In this mapping of cosmic consciousness, the creation of this sacred language or Lashon haQodesh refers to Da'at (Intuitive Knowing). From the atomistic to its larger molecular structure, just as if the images of letters have meaning, how much more so when these letters are combined into structures as whole words.]

And, behold, the esoteric allusions imbedded within the very shape of the letters is known to the esoteric masters, a small fraction of which is explicated in *Sefer haTemunah*.[264] If the very shape of the letter can transmit spiritual energy, know then that when you join letters together to form words that there is tremendous spiritual power in that word. [*The spiritual reality revealed within a word composed of letters is greater than that of individual letters which stand apart from the conjoining that takes place within a word.*] For when letters are combined into words, they take on the energy of the ramified point of meaning [*that remains unexpressed*]. If there is only one letter [*standing alone and not conjoined with other letters*], one cannot feel the ramified point of meaning.

[*The homily now turns its attention to explicating the words that constitute a sacred language—the very roots of all sentient beings and their vitality. At the forefront of concern here is the divine name of YHVH in relation to all other sacred names. Once the sacred names begin to diversify and extend the spiritual energy, there is an extension from the infinite to the finite ramified points of meaning. Further reflection follows on the sacred language and the reality of its sentient beings, especially the supernal, spiritualized energy field that corresponds with the language human beings use in the terrestrial sphere*].

Just as existents [*as they manifest the many degrees of the divine name, YHVH*] and names [*that is, all the other divine names, except for YHVH*] are both conveyed in the secret of *A<u>z</u>ilut* (Unified Consciousness), only are they the manifestation of existents as the vitality of all other names. [*The manifestation of the infinite within the vessels of the finite letters that constitute the divine name, YHVH, is intimately related to its vitality. What allows for A<u>z</u>ilut (Unified Consciousness) to emerge thus unifying existents and names is implied here and elsewhere by the Vitebsker as Da'at (Intui-*

264. For the mapping of the twenty-two Hebrew letters, see R. Nehuniah ben Hakanah, R. Yishmael, *Sefer haTemunah*, Temunah Rishonah. For a more general contextualization of how Hasidism carries forward earlier Kabbalistic concepts of language as found in *Sefer haTemunah*, etc., see Rachel Elior, "The Hasidic Concept of Language: The Window in the Word," in *The Mystical Origins of Hasidism* (Oxford: Littman Library of Jewish Civilization, 2006), 41–58.

tive Knowing). It is the combination of letters into words that creates more powerful vessels to contain this unification. The analogy here is between an idea and its manifestation, between being and names, in the level of Unity, maintained below in the material objects and their names.] Whatever becomes manifest in materiality has its vitality imbedded in its given name within language. This is why whatever name is ascribed to something in Hebrew, it is that very name which is considered its root within the realm of the spirit. If the letters are manifestations of supernal forms, then when these letters are conjoined through a name, it is that name which manifests and channels its spiritual vitality.

Thus the name of everything in sacred language is an invocation below of its root above, as Scripture teaches: **"whatever Adam called each living creature that would be its name."**[265] The human mind is the mechanism through which something exists as a material object [*and it does not have an independent existence of the mind that experiences it*].[266] The name in its locus as idea consists in the combination of letters, which underlies as substrata whatever the material object may be. The very manifestation of things depends on the structure of the human mind itself. The sources of vitality sustaining these letters are inseparable from the experience, and one might even say, from the existence of material objects. The name of a thing applies to the entire chain of being, for it is received from the root of the letters themselves [*but there is something there, regardless of whether a human being calls them into reality*]. Ontologically, the letters are not the ultimate origin, because there remain further levels that are restrained.

Consider this example: the word composed of the letter *Yod* and *Dalet* materializing and causing the creation of the form of the human hand [*YaD*]. [*Therefore Hebrew helps one to recognize that every hand is a materialization of that specific spiritual energy of the alchemy of these letters. By using language, one is learning about the spiritual foundation of the language,*

265. "And YHVH God formed out of the earth all the wild beasts and all the birds of the sky, and brought them to Adam to see what he would call them; and whatever Adam called each living creature, that would be its name" (Genesis 2:19).

266. The percepts are part of the structure of the mind, which means there is a metaphysical locus for such things. Kantian metaphysics names that which cannot be known as the noumenon, but each category had a substrate in the noumenal. This leads to Schopenhauer's critique of Kantian metaphysics by bumping this down to the level of an intermediary between noumenal and the phenomenal. Within this *zeitgeist*, the Vitebsker, however, sees a metaphysical realm of ideal forms where the letters do exist which the human mind and spirit has access to, already beginning with Primordial Adam, who could know and see the metaphysical roots of each and every thing. This is why Adam knew how to name each thing in Hebrew. It is also possible that the Vitebsker is claiming here that the very manifestation of things depends on the structure of the human mind itself. The sources of vitality sustaining these letters are inseparable from the experience, and one might even say, from the existence of material objects.

thus augmenting a deeper awareness of the transformative power in collocating words]. It is not called *Ya"D* because of the body; rather, it is so named as an instantiation of a chain of being, which is its sustaining vitality. Any of the myriad of stages along that particular level in the chain of being is called *Ya"D*, because it is an emanation extending from its source, thus collocating the [*supernal energies embodied in the*] letters *Yod* and *Dalet*. So the anthropomorphic references to the divine in Torah [*which are the seemingly scandalous ways of describing the divine through human body parts*]—for example **"the divine hand [*Ya"D*]"**[267]—thus refer to the emanations of these letters from their infinite source in Limitless One. It remains beyond one's capacity to grasp the Limitless One certainly not through the letters themselves and even within the vital spiritual energies of the ramified point of meaning [*that remains unexpressed, that is, allowing for a connection to the powers rather than the essence*].

[*From this focus on the names for limbs of the body, which have their roots in the supernal realm of the ideational and noumenal, the homily now shifts to another example of names and their supernal roots through ancestral archetypes. The transition builds upon the mystical teaching that the ancestral archetypes themselves are the merkavah (vehicle) for channeling the Shekinah*]. Consider another example: human names, [*which represent the phenomenal, enabling the self to know the other, mediating intersubjective experiences*][268] like Abraham, Isaac, and Jacob represent three distinct supernal sources.[269] Vitality is refracted from supernal roots into vessels of

267. "Then the hand [*Ya"D*] of YHVH will strike your livestock in the fields—the horses, the asses, the camels, the cattle, and the sheep—with a very severe pestilence" (Exodus 9:3).

268. Exodus 9:3—ere consciousness arises, centered on an I-Am, serving as the bridge but not the absolute itself.

269. On the power of ancestral names and their collocations, compare with Philo's exploration of how the divine totality becomes manifest in adding an *alpha* to the name Abram and subsequently a *rho* to that of his wife Sarai, see Philo, "On the Change of Names," 60–62. Philo dismisses divine agency as absurd in the bestowal of these names on the human beings, for "letters, whether vowels or consonants and the parts of speech in general are not the gifts of God's grace" (63–64); rather, a change of name stands for a change of human nature. What emerges here for Philo is the awareness of "a moral change from the study of God's works to the study of God Himself, in fact from astrology to piety, and the text may be taken as a divine instruction that studies of the former kind are of no real value (66–67)." See F. H. Colson and G. H. Whitaker, *Philo*, Volume V (Cambridge: Harvard University Press, 1934), 132. Whereas the early mystical exegesis of this Alexandrian Jew contemplates the Greek letters of the Hebrew ancestors, by contrast, the Kabbalah of the Zohar and beyond contemplates the letters of the ancestors in Hebrew. For example, see Polish Kabbalist, and chief rabbi of Cracow, Rabbi Natan Neta Shapira (1585–1633), *Megale Amukot*, Parashah Lech Lecha. It is this latter trajectory of contemplating the Hebrew letters as vessels of divine energy more common to Eastern Europe that the Vitebsker is drawing from in the present homily.

the specific letters that make up that name of the person or thing. The name a person carries is in no way arbitrary; rather, this sacred name consists of the combination of the letters at their manifest level. The letters constituting the names of Reuben and Simeon compose vessels containing its given levels of light, which then serve as sources of refraction for other beings at levels below and beyond. Even a thousand generations later, whomever is ascribed one of those names draws on the chain of being linked to the supernal roots of that name. So the construction [*of one's soul*] bares the [*supernal root of that*] name imbedded in that specific combination of letters.[270] And this is the meaning of the verse: **"This one shall be called Woman ['*ishah*], / For from Man ['*ish*] was she taken."**[271] So her name comes from this [*supernal root and*] place of origin with its vitality within the body of Primordial Adam. This is in line with Rashi's commentary, which explains how the letters of the noun are responsible for its vital existence.[272]

And thus there is an understanding that after a wicked person dies, his/her name [*does not bring forth any further vitality, and in this way the name*] is forgotten.[273] The name only serves as that person's unique spiritual nomination only insofar as one's actions are aligned to the roots of the name, drawing down its vitality from that root. [*Real spiritual growth begins when one commits to working on aligning the supernal roots of one's name with one's actions in the world. To be truly aware of the divine source within existence means that one is living up to the root of their name, which is manifest in*] the "returning light"[274] that extends back through the various levels the vitality of that name becoming manifest in the world.

So if a person aligns his/her acts with the root of vitality of his/her name throughout their lifetime, then such a person would be remembered

270. The journey of individuation then is that a person is already something, namely, this vital soul energy which exists beyond one's apperception. Thus it is through the course of one's life and its incarnations, one ultimately is able to find out who they are by seeing what they do in the world.

271. "Adam said: 'This one at last / is bone of my bones / And flesh of my flesh. / This one shall be called Woman, / For from man was she taken'" (Genesis 2:23).

272. Rashi ad loc Genesis 2:23. "This one at last"—This teaches that Adam endeavored to find a companion among all the cattle and beasts, but found no satisfaction except in Eve (b*Yebamot* 63a).

273. "The evil person in Inferno no longer remembers their name" (*Zohar Chadash*, Ruth 103a).

274. "Returning light" ['*or hozair*] and "linear light" ['*or yashar*] are terms from Lurianic Kabbalah which describe the journey of illumination and gnosis reaching back all the way to Primordial Adam. "Returning light" is so called because it returns and ascends from the terrestrial realm to its supernal source, while "linear light" is so called because it is drawn downward from its supernal source as its descends into manifestation within the terrestrial realm.

forever by that specific name. If the person acts out of alignment with the supernal roots of the letters of their name [*that is then transmitted from below to above through the "returning light"*], then such a person is no longer empowered by the divine source to draw down vitality [*through the "linear light" from above to below*]. Instead, actions misaligned from their supernal root in one's name then empower the force of dissipating spiritual energies. Then such a person is not known by their original name; rather, s/he is known by another distorted name from the World of Distortion. It is this illusory reality of desire that ultimately distorts the supernal roots of one's real name, as is known in esoteric wisdom and will be explicated later.

And so [*this brings us to*] the commentary of *Yavetz*[275] on the teaching in tractate m*Avot*: **"If there is no flour, there is no Torah."**[276] There are so many well-off households without even a whiff of Torah [*despite the plethora of materiality*]. But what is intended here is that the "flour" [*namely, whatever materiality you possess*] is not manifest unless the energies of its letters from Torah are drawn forth from the source of their being. Through the path of letters, [*"flour" is thus able to become*] manifest from above to below until it is fully embodied. [*When one is attuned to the vitality of the letters then the "flour" of all materiality*] satisfies according to its being in the world [*namely, the path of sacred satiety of emanation from above to below, which does not desecrate the permissible. In making "flour" through the path of Torah so that one is able to embody its sacral deeds, then*] one separates the dissipating spiritual forces through laws of our holy Torah, making it appropriate and pure. [*For example, this separation of the opposing spiritual forces takes place*] through the laws of uplifting [*water to cleanse the hands before partaking of "flour" as manifest in bread*], whether by laws permissible or prohibited. Only then is the "flour" [*when it is processed through the sieve of Torah and Halachah have the vitality to be*] satisfying in and of itself [*freeing one from any distracting desires for other materiality*]. This is not the case [*when "flour" is not connected to its source in root letters, and thus unable to truly satiate; rather,*] **"the**

---

275. R. Yosef Yavetz, haHasid, haDarshan, *Sefer haYavetz* [Andripol, 1550] (Warsaw, Poland: n.d.), 78. R. Yavetz was a Kabbalist philosopher born in Spain, left with the Expulsion in 1492, and finally settled in Mantua, Italy. The positioning of this cluster should have been at the beginning of the Mishnah rather than at the end of the list. The preceding pairs are inextricably bound to each other. This positioning shows that the requirement for flour and Torah, as Elijah and Moses understood that each term in this cluster is independent whereas the others are complementary. Flour is merely a tool, like a ladder to reach the birdcage, to facilitate studying. The ultimate level sought is to study Torah without any flour.

276. m*Avot* 3:17.

belly of the wicked shall want"[277] "and satiating hunger,"[278] as is the way of all desires. For [*just as*] "one does not die with even half of one's desires satisfied,"[279] [*so*] is the path of oppositional spiritual forces whose vitality comes from multiplicity and separation [*never being satiated, always desiring more*]—the opposite of what is sacred, of undifferentiated unity [*and satiety is the apprehension of the simplicity of the sacred. The soul develops an awareness of receiving pure light*].

This is why: "If there is no Torah, there is no flour," so the name of "flour" satiates and vitalizes, thus manifesting a difference from the World of Distortion [*where there is neither satiety nor is the identity contingent rather than essential, depriving the flour of its own namesake. Its name is not sufficient so it continuously exchanged*]—after it has received its vitality from there [*in the World of Distortion*].

For it is known that [*regarding flour and all material things that*] **"God has made even the one as well as the other"**[280]—[*in the realm of the sacred there is only one language, Hebrew, whereas on the Other Side, there are*] seventy languages which are seventy streams that branch out from a single tree which is the Hebrew language, and the roots of these seventy languages are based in the 231 gates of permutated letters, through the rotating wheel. But Hebrew is in the center. In every other language there has to be a correspondence to its origin in Hebrew. One word that is identical to the Hebrew is the umbilical cord which is the life-giving connection to the Tree-That-Is-All. As the blessed Sages teach: "*Hen* in Greek corresponds to the Hebrew word for 'one'"[281] and "for the word *totafot* itself implies four, [*it being composed of*] *tot* which means two in *Katpi* [*possibly Coptic*] and *fot* which means two in *Afriki*."[282] [*These foreign languages adapt a corre-*

277. "The righteous eat to the satisfying of desire; but the belly of the wicked shall want" (Proverbs 13:25).

278. b*Sukkah* 52b.

279. *Ecclesiastes Rabbah* 1:13.

280. "In the day of prosperity be joyful, and in the day of adversity consider; God has made even the one as well as the other, to the end that one should find nothing after him" (Ecclesiastes 7:14).

281. b*Shabbat* 31b: "For R. Johanan said in R. Eleazar's name: The Holy blessed One has nought else in His world but the fear of Heaven alone, for it is said, And now, Israel, what does YHVH your God requires of you, but to fear YHVH your God? and it is written, And unto human he said, Behold [hen], the fear of YHVH, that is wisdom, and in Greek one is hen. [Thus translating: the fear of the Lord is one, unique (in God's affections)]. That proves it."

282. b*Sanhedrin* 4b: "Has it not been taught: *le'totafot* [frontlets] occurs thrice in Torah, twice defective and once plene, four in all, to indicate [that four sections are to be inserted in the phylacteries]. Such is the opinion R. Ishmael. But R. Akivah maintains that there is no need of that interpretation, for the word totafot itself implies four, [it being composed of] *tot* which means two in Katpi [possibly Coptic] and foth which means two in

spondence to allow for a flow of the sacred from the source of vitality from Hebrew.] That is the place from which it draws forth its vitality, and that is also that place from which the other language separates outwards and disperses, namely, **"forked tongue"**[283] **"destruction is decreed"**[284] because of the oppositional forces. The extending branches from the tree top of the Tree-That-Is-All lean toward to the realm of oppositional forces.

This is not the case with **"the devoted one who is satiated in the soul"**[285] as explained in the Recanati's commentary and the ensuing exegesis.[286] **"And they envisioned God and ate and drank"**[287]; their eyes were satiated from the sparkle of the *Shekinah,* and Rabbi Yohanan said: actually they eat, as Scripture states: **"In the luminescence of the living King."**[288]

As Ibn Ezra teaches, look at how wondrous is this teaching: if one is able draw from the chain of being, from its lowliest to its highest point, then imagine if one could return to the original pure essence, this would be real eating [*namely, spiritual sustenance whereby their eyes were satiated from the sparkle of the Shekinah*]. This is what is meant by the verse **"food is the very awe of those have of the divine"**[289]—namely, the awe is a kind of spiritual sustenance, which supercedes the need for physical sustenance. Recanati's commentary concludes that the point of eating is not to destroy the physical form; rather, the real essence of eating is to give more strength, pleasure, and vitality to the one who is eating. [*Eating is not merely chewing a piece of meat; it is the drawing forth of vitality from that flesh and elevating.*] That is what is meant by "true eating"—so the real joy here is the pleasure and glow from the *Shekinah*, as Scripture states: **"If you take pleasure in the divine,"**[290] and here concludes Recanati's comments. [*By contemplating and drawing the spiritual energy from material matter one fulfills the deeper purpose of eating altogether.*]

So, behold, everything we use in the world was only given for our enjoyment to penetrate to the thing's spiritual core. From this spiritual core did the material descend and manifest. However, it is forbidden to take from the material, which is the oppositional force; rather, we should progress beyond the physical manifestation to discern how it is part of the chain of the Endless Being. [*The point is not to stay with the external, physical aspect of what you are eating; rather, it is*] to return and reawaken the ulti-

---

Afriki [the language of North Africa or Phrygia in Asia Minor]?"

283. Jeremiah 9:7.
284. Isaiah 10:22.
285. Proverbs 13:25.
286. *Leviticus Rabbah* 20:7.
287. Exodus 24:11.
288. Proverbs 16:15.
289. Psalm 111:5.
290. Isaiah 58:14.

mate source of the joy.

This comportment is referred to [*not merely*] as speaking in the holy tongue; [*rather,*] it means that one is comporting oneself in accordance with the pathways of the letters, [*showing his brothers how this wisdom of inner Hebrew applies to the spiritual life*].[291] It is impossible to articulate in language what is taking place here, so this must suffice for those who understand the secret. If so, when we use the expression "speech" [*dibbur*], what emerges from the physical world is then explicated in Torah of truth applies even to the dead [*whose soul comports itself in certain directions*].[292]

This is general principle: the entirety of the human and its purpose is to comport one's life through the sacred, as Scripture teaches: **"in all of one's ways, apprehend *Da'at*—sense of how the divine flows through."**[293] For *Da'at* is called the Holy Tongue as described above. [*Nahmanides sees Hebrew as a pure, spiritual language that emanates from the holy source, whereas Maimonides suggests that language is conventional but Hebrew is holier than other languages in that it does not include profanity, highlighting the symptom of the essence. For the Vitebsker, Hebrew is*] as expressed in the *Guide for the Perplexed*[294] that all languages are not merely as a social construct; rather, language is the guide for how the ideal society should construct itself including the ideal within each person, [*proving that Hebrew does not concern itself with the coarseness of the manifest world*]. Compare this with the contrary view of Nahmanides,[295] and my view the more enlightened view is aligned with Maimonides, who follows the path of truth, but it is impossible to go into all the details here; instead, the enlightened will deduce it by themselves.

And so now it is possible to understand the teaching of the blessed Sages as to why "it is not permitted to pray in Aramaic."[296] For prayer is named after the experience of merging as Scripture teaches: **"I was en-**

291. b*Sanhedrin* 8a.

292. b*Berakot* 18b, which describes how the dead no longer have functioning lips or any of the other orifices of speech, so the reference is to comportment in life and its effect in the afterlife.

293. Literally, "In all your ways acknowledge the One, [and the One will smooth your paths]" (Proverbs 3: 6).

294. Maimonides, *Guide for the Perplexed* (II:30).

295. Nahmanides ad loc Exodus 30:13, where he examines why Torah is called "sacred language," bringing Maimonides's view from the Guide that it is so called, for in Torah one does not find the names of sexual organs, or urine, or feces, rather only by euphemism. By opposing the Maimonidean view of sacred language, what Nahmanides is doing here is suggesting that what makes Torah a sacred language is the degree to which all of Scripture is composed of sacred language of the divine conversing through this medium with the prophets and their sacred communities, so that within that kind of discourse originating in the divine, sacred names are applied.

296. b*Sotah* 33a.

twined [*naFToLi*] with God"[297] is a form of wrestling to merge [*devequt*] which is prayer [*TeFiLa*].

Thus, if one wants to be connected through this wrestling as a transformation toward Compassion of the One, it can only happen through the letters of the words. These letters are the vehicle for channeling the spiritual qualities into the manifest world. Whatever aspect of spiritual qualities you hold onto, you must nullify them before the blessed Holy One to recognize that you are standing before the infinite. You desire deeply in your soul to cleave to the divine source, and in that desire you must dissolve your identity altogether. In prayer, one has to cultivate the radical amazement for the source of all language, to try to get through these linguistic channels [*which are flowing downstream into the world of communication, whereas the aspirant is ascending upstream toward the source of transcendent language. The Jewish mystical tradition imagines pre-creation where the Creator begins to create the manifest world from the final letter Tav to the first Aleph. In the primordial moment before creation, the letters remained concealed within the divine mind, sitting in a simultaneity within reversability.*[298] *So, in prayer, the aspirant attempts to recapture the primordial moment of creation by going back to a state where the letters are ordered in the conventional manner now known and used*]. One attempts to tie one's essence into the form of the letters so as to get back to the primordial letters prior to speech, and this is the **"to and fro"** oscillation [*back to a disordering of the letters sequence, for their ordering is a product of emanation, but before that the letters exist in a simultaneous reversibility*]. And it is possible to depart from the letters completely, not being bound by their forms at all; if one is completely burning with this desire to merge with the divine, then one is able to reach that place. Letters are a delimiting delineation into forms of this original infinite power, whereby one needs to break through every delimitation by ascending and drawing down compassion with compulsion back down into world.[299] And also it is not just the one who tries

297. Genesis 30:8.

298. For example, see *Haqdamat Sefer ha-Zohar* I: 2b, tr. Matt, 11: "*Bereshit*, in the beginning. Rav Hamnuna Sava said: 'We find the letters backward: *Bet* first, followed by a *bet*: *Bereshit*, In the beginning, followed by *bara*, created. Then *aleph* first, followed by *aleph*: Elohim, followed by *et*. The reason is: When the blessed Holy One wished to fashion the world, all the letters were hidden away. For two thousand years before creating the world, the blessed Holy One contemplated them and played with them. As He verged on creating the world, all the letters presented themselves before Him, from last to first."

299. Gershom Scholem, "Abulafia and the Doctrine of Prophetic Kabbalah," in *Major Trends in Jewish Mysticism* (Schocken: NY, 1946), 154–55. While not explicitly referred to by the Vitebsker, the parallels to Abulafian contemplation are striking, insofar as it requires the aspirant to transcend the letters by skipping through their forms, so that as each word is abstracted through the contemplation of each letters, until "you force yourself so that you pass beyond the control of your natural mind and if you desire not to think, you cannot carry

to draw this energy down, but given this is the preliminary intention, it requires no extra willing. Once one is part of that communion, then one's will already takes effect.

So it is for this reason that "one should never pray in Aramaic," which derives from the teaching Raba transmitted to his son: "not to sleep on an Aramaic bed." This means "one should not go to sleep without the recitation of *Shema'*."[300] Thus "Aramaic" comes to symbolize the lack of sacred comportment according to the holy Torah.

And so too with regards to prayer, which is itself a kind of merging with the divine totality by drawing down the letters and its energies. One who merges with the divine vitality in prayer is then able to transform reality. Along this path, "if God can make oil burn, so too, with vinegar"[301] [*so that all natural law is subject to divine will, so as when surpasses the letters to the divine will, then the flow of compassion can be drawn down through the Hebrew letters*].

It is known that it is impossible to achieve pure prayer and full merging except after training the spiritual qualities for the inner vitality of each and every matter. Then, and only then, will the veil be rent wherein there is no longer any separation. This approach to Hebrew letters is the one that created its syntax and thinking. This is the meaning of the verse: **"you shall merge with the One"**[302]—namely, as the blessed Sages teach: "Merge with the divine qualia."[303] When such mindfulness is lacking—and there is not a connection to the core vitality of the divine totality through the letters—then one is unmoored, unable to answer the call of Torah, rather remaining [*mired in the materialism of*] "Aramaic language." [*This juxtaposition of Hebrew and Aramaic is between the symbolism of each linguistic system, whereby the former transcends and includes materiality within the spirit, whereas the latter remains mired in materiality without any transcendent capacity. This reflects the ritual reality that Hebrew remains reserved for prayer as Lashon haQodesh, whereas lingua franca like Aramaic or Yiddish are not considered as elevated; given that these other languages hover in the world of commerce and transactions.*]

As I have written above, the root of the Israelite seeker stems from the holy language of Hebrew, which [*through its interaction with the coarseness of materiality inevitably*] draws into itself oppositional forces **"after their families, after their tongues [in Aramaic], in their lands, in their**

---

out your desire. You then guide your thinking step by step, first by means of script and language and then by means of imagination."

300. b*Berakot* 8b.

301. b*Ta'anit* 25a.

302. Deuteronomy 10:20.

303. b*Sotah* 14a.

nations."[304] So it is the holy language of Hebrew that then brings forth vital awareness to these oppositional forces which [*not only*] then rule over them. [*But such negative control is not limited merely to subjugation of sovereignty; rather, these oppositional forces*] can even change one's name according to the collocation [*of names*] that exist in their [*foreign*] language.

It appears that it is possible if one's [*first*] name is Reuben, [*that if such a person*] was to draw the negative energy of oppositional force upon himself, then he would already have a different name, similar to idol worshippers and astrologers [*so then one is called by their foreign name, in this case Aramaic*].

This is not the case in comporting with conviction proper to the Israelite seeker, as our blessed Sages teach: "Prayer in any language [*is acceptable*]"—[*even Aramaic, which does not contradict the earlier statement that one should not pray in Aramaic for so long as one comports according to the pathway of the seeker, then already it is no longer considered to be in the category of Aramaic, even if it appears to sound and seem that way*].

If indeed the Talmud has offered a solution [*to this apparent contradiction of statements, namely, that one is forbidden to offer prayers in Aramaic while prayer in all languages are acceptable, the Talmud reconciles the matter as follows*]—this statement refers to private prayer [*one is forbidden to offer prayers in Aramaic*], while that statement refers to public prayer [*prayer in all languages are acceptable*].

Behold [*this*] straightforward [*resolution of the Talmud*] is as it appears in context, and the judgment is adjudicated with truth as explicated further in the codex of the *Shulchan 'Arukh* [*namely, that in private prayer one is forbidden to offer prayers in Aramaic, while in public prayer Aramaic is permissible*].

However, according to the esoteric interpretation [*and deep devotion to the divine*] it is possible to interpret the words [*of the blessed Sages and their resolution in the Talmud*] in accord with our interpretation: "this in private"—namely, that one intends [*the prayer*] toward matters of self-concern [*insofar as this is not the path of comportment for the Israelite seeker, of which it is stated "one should not pray in Aramaic"*]; "*that* in public"—namely, [*that the prayer*] follows the pathway of interconnecting multiverses [*and is not self-concerned, so that such a prayer follows the Israelite pathway comportment whereby prayer in all languages is accepted, even Aramaic*].

And so is the pathway of every truth seeker [*to reconcile the apparent Talmudic contradiction according to its contextual meaning explained above*], and in particular, in the writings of Lurianic Kabbalah [*so too does*

304. "These are the sons of Ham, after their families, after their tongues, in their lands, in their nations" (Genesis 10:20).

one find the contradiction reconciled]. So long as [*prayer follows*] the pathway of conviction [*and immersion in the divine*] extends divine energy from the Limitless [*then one is able to pray in any language, even Aramaic*].

[*When prayer is enacted along the pathway of conviction and immersion, it is not affected by its being offered through the linguistic frequency of Aramaic, but*] on the contrary, this [*devotional posture*] subdues the language [*of oppositional force manifest in Aramaic*] beneath the primacy of the holy tongue, [*so that the oppositional force then becomes*] like a slave that receives a reward and energy from the sacred source—**"and he shall serve him forever."**[305]

This is the totality of being human and the purpose of its creation— to elevate things from lower to higher realms [*from the place of oppositional force to the sacred*] and to subdue the exteriorities by channeling them towards the interiority—insofar as one realizes the divine in all of reality, such that "there is no place devoid of the One."[306]

And an even more simple way to understand [*this issue of prayer which should not be in Aramaic*] one should become enlightened so that it becomes embedded in memory. This is evident through the pathway elucidated in the Zohar: "And [*Rabbi Simeon bar Yohai*] cried like a crane over those who are praying for their own benefit, that all their compassion is self-serving, as they pray 'Give us life, give us sustenance' and so regarding them the verse states: **'But [they] mingled themselves with the nations, and learned their works'**[307]—[*and this self-serving prayer is what*] is called Aramaic."[308]

For this [*kind of self-serving prayer*] is not according to the pathway described by our blessed Sages: "One should always first recount praise of the Holy One, and only then engage in petitionary prayer."[309] [*Devotion begins in recounting praise of the Holy One*] which is a process of transcending the spiritual qualia of the divine by way of the letters [*embedded in the words of the qualia:*] *Chesed* (Lovingkindness) and *Rachamim* (Compassion). [*This means one should focus the mind to contemplate these letters of prayer which transcend the spiritual qualia of the divine*] "and only then engage in petitionary prayer." [*For now that prayer proceeds after such*

305. Exodus 21:6.

306. *Tiquney Zohar*, Tiqqun no. 70, 122b.

307. Psalm 106:35.

308. *Tiquney Zohar*, Tiqqun 6, 22a.

309. "R. Simlai expounded: One should always first recount [literally "order"] the praise of the Holy One, and then pray in a petitionary manner." See b*Berakot* 32a, b*Avodah Zarah* 7b. On the embodied choreography of salutation of praise preceding the petition in rabbinic liturgy follows the etiquette of approaching the sovereign power, see more recently Uri Erlich, *The Non-verbal Language of Jewish Prayer, Kol Ăaṣmōtay Tômarnā": Haś-śāfā Hal-Lô Mīllûlît Šel Hat-Tĕfīlā* (Jerusalem: Magnes, 1999).

contemplation it is no longer self-serving; rather, its focus toward] immersion [*in the divine without regard to the self*] by way of [*the letters*] of the holy language [*which are the*] words of prayer [*itself*].

[*So when prayer becomes a process of immersion of self as a droplet into the sea of the divine without being self-serving, then*] one way or the other they will become extended by way of the letters of prayer—an effulgence of goodness, compassion, life, and peace in the land.

This refers to the material designations as being elucidated in our pristine Torah: **"[If you walk in My statutes, and keep My commandments, and do them] then I will give your rains in their season"**[310] **"that you may gather in your corn"**[311]—for these [*material designations*] are not the rewards for the devotion. For how grand is Your goodness hidden[312] for the reverent ones [*the reward for devotion accords with what is written in Scripture*]: **"neither has the eye** [*seen a God beside You*]."[313] [*This is a very high spiritual level insofar as it is concealed for the reverent ones but hidden in plain sight from the rest of coarse humanity.*]

But [*this issue of material designations*] of which Torah speaks, one way or the other will have extended through all these material designations: **"If you walk in My statutes"**[314] [*for the moment that you walk through these pathways you shall become immersed in the divine sea, so that you will then*] be drawing down vital energy from above [*even when you do not intend it, all the designations drawn and extended forth will then come*] through the pathway of one's comportment and immersion in the letters.

[*Now the homily returns to elucidate the opening exegesis regarding the four factors leading to the preservation of identity in exile, which include: (1) not changing their names; (2) not changing their language; (3) not becoming ensnared in sexual immorality; and (4) not succumbing to gossip.*] So this is the issue regarding the redemption from Egypt as a function of these factors:

(1) "They did not change their names"—that is, they were not called a different name from the World of Distortion [*that is mired in materiality*]; rather, only names from Torah were designated [*to each soul*] even though Torah was yet be given [*as they were still in Egypt*]. It was already known as an esoteric tradition from Abraham our ancestor, *o.b.m.*, as we learn in the Talmud: "Abraham our ancestor, *o.b.m.*, even fulfilled the obligation regarding the legal continuity through shared dishes."[315] [*Given that*

310. Leviticus 26:3-4.

311. Deuteronomy 11:14.

312. See Rashi ad loc Deuteronomy 3:36.

313. Isaiah 64:3.

314. Leviticus 26:3-4.

315. b*Yomah* 28a, referring to the rabbinic legislation of a legal fiction that extends continuity of the boundary of one's courtyard together with a neighbor by sharing dishes so

the comportment of our ancestors in Egypt retained its integrity, and they did not draw down distorted, foreign names from the World of Distortion, thus] we find [*in Scripture*] that Reuben and Simeon descended [*to Egypt*] and ascended as Reuben and Simeon.

(2) "They did not change their language"—the holy language [*of Hebrew*] and its [*power to*] extend and draw down [*vital energy into each and every material designation*] remained intact as discussed above;

(3) "They did not become ensnared in sexual immorality and there were no informers among them"—namely, the covenant of the tongue and phallus are interconnected,[316] [*insofar as one is loyal to the letters of speech that affects comportment is purified, so too is sexual morality. This creates a continuum whereby the covenant of the tongue is associated with the sphere Da'at (Intuition), while the covenant of the phallus is associated with the sphere of Yesod (Nexus), so*] that these mediums can then both draw on and balance above and below [*thus it is called a 'brit,' which literally means ring. To cut out a ring then is the process whereby each party of the covenant enters the ring and agrees to its terms of fidelity. Such a covenant bridges two parties, thus enabling balancing. It is Da'at (Intuition) that provides balance between Chokhmah (Wisdom) and Binah (Understandin) in the higher realms of the spheres, while it is the sphere of Yesod (Nexus) the balances between Nezach (Endurance) and Hod (Splendor) in the lower realms of the spheres*].

[*Now the homily returns to the opening statement of Joseph and its exegesis,*] so this [*explains*] Joseph's comportment in saying: I am circumcised [*in terms of the spiritual comportment being tied to the circumcision of the phallus as explained above*] **"like you"** [*my brethren*] and precisely not like a Muslim, circumcised and damaged in its covenant. Joseph comports himself through the pathway of a sacred language: **"that it is indeed I speaking to you"**[317]—namely, he received from his sacred ancestors [*as Scripture states regarding Abraham*]: **". . . to the end that he may command his children . . . that they may keep the way of YHVH."**[318]

If Joseph pledged that he would never speak Hebrew in front of Pharaoh, then clearly what is at stake here is the language of sacred comportment [*for every action in the world is a stringing together of lower letters with upper letters, as an embodied language. Recall that the building blocks of creation are already an expression of this same divine pathway of*

that carrying is permitted from one household to another on the Sabbath.

316. *Sefer Yetzirah* articulates a vision of both these medial organs and thus interconnected as the culminating organs to bring together senses and comportment.

317. Genesis 45:12.

318. "[For I have known him,] to the end that he may command his children and his household after him, that they may keep the way of YHVH, to do righteousness and justice; to the end that YHVH may bring on Abraham that which He hath spoken of him" (Genesis 18:19).

stringing together of letters, as an expression of the Limitless. Each atom in the universe is a saying, expressions that refract the Limitless, and so one who walks in the way of YHVH embodies such sacred comportment].

[*The homily now shifts to rereading a rabbinic interpretation of the structure of the Sukkah that lies at the heart of the Feast of Booths known as Sukkot.*] This serves to explain the verse: **"And once you contemplate it, wickedness will just about disappear."**[319] As the blessed Sages teach regarding the *Sukkah*: "R. Abba said in the name of Samuel: '[*Bitter*] herbs concerning which the Sages said that a person fulfills their obligation [*by eating them*] on Passover,[320] [*if these same herbs are used for a Sukkah-covering as plant matter they*] carry[321] ritual defilement, [*if they form a horizontal partition between a ritually fit and an unfit object then they*] do not act as an interposition to ritual defilement,[322] and cause invalidity in a *Sukkah*-covering in the same manner as the empty space of ether.'[323] What is the reason?—Since they wither when they crumble and fall, thus they are regarded as though they were nonexistent."[324] [*By comparing vegetable matter used in the two different pilgrimage holidays of Passover and Sukkot, it emerges now that the legal status of bitter herbs are not equivalent to Sukkah-covering that invalidates only at four handbreadths; rather, in this case they would become invalid if used as Sukkah-covering because this vegetal matter invalidates at three handbreadths, for the status of bitter herbs is like ether. In the process of shriveling up, falling, and decomposing, this vegetal matter now takes on the category of ether. This rabbinic reflection on the category of ether deeply intrigues the Vitebsker. Recall the mystics envision the Sukkah through the lens of its construction details to reflect a state of consciousness in the shade of interior conviction grounding the ether of existence.*]

And so too regarding the wicked ones, Scripture states: **"For they shall soon wither like the grass, and fade as the green herb"**[325]—[*like the green herb above whose legal status is akin to ether*] for the wicked do not draw out the vital awareness from the divine totality, and therefore they

---

319. Literally, "And yet a little while, and the wicked is no more; yea, you shall look well at his place, and he is not" (Psalm 37:10).

320. As, for instance, bitter herbs, lettuce, or endives prescribed for the first Passover evening meal.

321. While they are still fresh.

322. This is a rabbinic restriction; whereas in Torah, they act as an interposition until they become dry.

323. The space they occupy is regarded as empty space of ether, and just as an empty space of ether of three handbreadths in the roof of the *Sukkah* invalidates it, so does a covering of these herbs.

324. b*Sukkah* 13b.

325. Psalm 37:2.

shall shrivel up like vegetables [*whose status is nonexistence*]. This is what is referred to earlier in the verse: **"yet a little while, and the wicked is no more"**[326]—as if they are non-[*ether-like*]. Even while the wicked may appear to be there, their existence is one of nonexistence [*remaining illusory*], if while alive they are actually living without awareness of this divine vitality. This explains the continuation of the scriptural verse: **"And once you contemplate"** refers specifically to this nonexistence of **"wickedness"** for even if by appearances **"you shall look well at his place"** [*even in this phenomenal appearance*] **"he is not."**[327] [*Rather, these wicked ones resemble those*] who while alive [*are already considered to be*] thus called dead.

[*There is yet another way of reading the verse*]: **"Then Judah came near unto him, and said: 'Oh my lord . . .'"**[328]—to mean that Judah presented his own heart [*overcoming his repugnance before an Egyptian*], as is taught in the *'Or Chayyim* commentary: **"As one face reflects back another, so too the heart of one reflects back another."**[329] [*If Judah shows love to Joseph, the Egyptian, then Joseph will open his heart to Judah.*] Wearing his heart on his sleeve was meant to arouse the heart of the other. It is this sense of forcing himself to truly love Joseph by presenting his own heart that will thus arouse the love of the other.

This remark [*of the 'Or Chayyim commentary*] is truly inspired—words of truth and conviction. However, [*the 'Or Chayyim commentary needs to be further elucidated insofar as*] Judah's perception that Joseph was an Egyptian—for were not the Israelites were warned: **"Have no pity on them"**?!?[330] That is, not to share any charm with them,[331] and yet Judah did not hold back his love, neither did he exclude them from prayer, sacrifices, and eating [*all of which are spiritual expressions of drawing the other nearer*].

Behold, as our blessed Sages teach:[332] "Evidently our ancestor Jacob descended to Egypt in iron chains, but that his merit saved him" [*so that*

326. Literally, "And yet a little while, and the wicked is no more; yea, you shall look well at his place, and he is not" (Psalm 37:10).

327. Psalm 37:10.

328. "Then Judah came near unto him, and said: 'Oh my lord, let your servant, I pray O, speak a word in my lord's ears, and let not your anger burn against thy servant; for you are even as Pharaoh'" (Genesis 44:18).

329. Proverbs 27:19.

330. Deuteronomy 7:2.

331. b*Avodah Zarah* 20a.

332. b*Shabbat* 89b: "R. Hiyya b. Abba said in R. Johanan's name: it was fitting for our father Jacob to go down into Egypt in iron chains, but that his merit saved him, for it is written, I drew them with the cords of a man, with bands of love; and I was to them as they that take off the yoke on their jaws, and I laid meat before them." Compare with *Genesis Rabbah* 86a. Notice the expression of "bands of love" used here in b*Shabbat* 89b and its parallels throughout *Ketem Paz*.

his descent was dignified]. And the parable [*of our blessed Sages teaches about the issue of Jacob's descent to Egypt as a dignified descent is likened to*] a beast being recalcitrant as it is led to its slaughter—one pulls it by a chord, see there [*that exegesis which more fully describes this drawing through human cords and bands of love*]. Behold, the exegesis is meant to teach that the descent of Jacob and his children to Egypt was for the sake of raising up the holy sparks of Egypt, as is known in the verse: **"And they despoiled the Egyptians,"**[333] as evinced in its interpretive translation: "and we emptied out [*all of the holy sparks*],"[334] to which the Sages commented: "like a fishing net without any fish."[335]

So behold, the whole point of eating is to raise up the sparks [*contained within the matter one is consuming*]. So that whatever realm one is eating from, the sparks from one realm are raised up to the next in the act of mindful consumption. How wondrous it is that by eating something physical, one is thus interconnecting the vitality of being with the body! One cannot live without eating, and there must be sparks of vitality within everything that is consumed so that the soul is nourished [*by elevating*] the sparks, while the body absorbs matter.

Notwithstanding [*the reality that the whole purpose of food is to elevate sparks imbedded in materiality*], still there is spiritual resistance on the part of any holy spark becoming dislodged to be replaced back in its divine source. As the blessed Sages teach: "Every blade of grass has its own angel assigned to it, prodding that blade to grow,"[336] so the holy spark is afraid that this process of ascent could be a disaster. What happens if a misaligned person eats this food [*from a place of creaturely appetites rather than attuned spirituality*]? Then the spark will descend rather than ascend. But this is the lot of being human—whether or not one will eat in order to elevate is a matter of free will. Only a human being can choose to [*consume with attuned spirituality*] or not.

For there is no real connection to this process of ascent unless a person wants to consume food [*in a spiritually attuned way*] from the house of the King, the blessed Holy One so as to draw nearer **"[by] eat[ing] and drink[ing]."**[337] This was the case with Rav Hamnuna Savah, whose level of intentionality enabled him to unite animal and human worlds and transcend them immediately all the way to the Will of the Limitless, but most people

333. "And YHVH gave the people favor in the sight of the Egyptians, so that they let them have what they asked. And they despoiled the Egyptians" (Exodus 12:36).

334. Aquilas's interpretive translation renders "And they despoiled" (Exodus 12:36) as "And they emptied out."

335. b*Berakot* 9b.

336. *Genesis Rabbah* 10:6.

337. "And on the nobles of the children of Israel He laid not His hand; and they beheld God, and did eat and drink" (Exodus 24:11).

are not at his level.[338]

[*The homily then shifts to the next spiritual typology, below Rav Hamnuna Savah, as the one yearning to draw nearer through consumption of food and raise the sparks in the process of eating. Such a person can raise the sparks at this moment of conscious consumption, even when it is not necessarily as immediate as the first typology.*] There is then a level below this first typology [*whose conscious consumption is like the sacrifice that immediately transforms the material offering into holy sparks*]. This next typology concerns one who is familiar with being in the divine presence [*even if the offering is not accepted immediately*], and is unable to immediately redeem the holy sparks from the food being consumed; still, such a person [*is able to elevate the redeemed sparks*] with the additional vital energy that emerges from the act of eating. [*Even though such a person does not draw nearer to the divine source immediately through conscious consumption, still*] the vitality [*redeemed from the food itself*] integrates into one's being, so that any act one undertakes following this [*conscious consumption*] takes place for heaven's sake and then elevates the vitality as well.

This is not the case [*with the third typology*], *perish the thought*, if a person has a material approach to consumption by merely satisfying such creaturely appetites, then such a person is taking the spark and causing it to descend in the realm of the oppositional forces. And this is precisely why the holy spark is apprehensive of being released from the outset.

In truth, the sacred spark that sees an open space for its ascension [*has no apprehension of descending into the realm of oppositional forces*] and thus undoubtedly will search for ways to ascend. This dynamic is already known, in the case of the lower waters weeping in their yearning to return to reunite with the higher waters, crying: "We too desire to be in the presence of the King."[339] Prayer is such a yearning for a safe passage back to one's source in the sacred. Sometimes a person wears their heart on their sleeve and comes forward from the place of deep truth in the heart. This

---

338. See Zohar I:7a: "Rabbi El'azar and Rabbi Abba fell before [Rav Hamnuna Sava]. Meanwhile they did not see him. They rose, looking in every direction, but could not see him. They sat down and wept, and could not speak to one another. After a while Rabbi Abba said: 'This is precisely what we learned: On whatever path the righteous walk, with words of Torah between them, virtuous ones of that world come to them. This indeed was Rav Hamnuna Sava, coming to us from that world to reveal these words to us. Before we could recognize him, he vanished!' They rose and tried to goad the donkeys, but they would not move. They tried to goad them, but they would not move. Frightened, they left the donkeys behind. Still today that spot is called Donkeys' Site." The Vitebsker is reading the "donkey" [*hamor*] as symbolizing "materiality" [*homraniyut*], such that Rav Hamnuna Sava represents the ideal aspirant who is able to transcend materiality completely through deep devotion.

339. *Tiquney Zohar* 80a.

was the case with Judah approaching Joseph [*in coming forward from the place of deep truth in the heart that is the posture of prayer*], so that [*at that very moment of prayer*] all the distracting thoughts and qualities are aroused. These distractions emerge because they sense a direct pathway is opening to the sacred, which is their desire to be restored to ascend by way of return, and serve their destiny in serving the sacred.

[*Now the homily returns to the exegetical episode concerning Jacob who descended to Egypt in iron chains, while his merit saved him so that his descent was dignified.*] And so it was with Jacob our ancestor, as he was fearful of descending to Egypt to raise up the sparks from there. Just as with the "blade of grass being prodded to grow" as well as "the animal that fears being slaughtered," so too Jacob was afraid that his descent into Egypt shackled in iron chains would cause the sparks to descend. Rather, Jacob's merit caused him to trust in the blessed Holy One [*in the divine proclamation revealed in Jacob's dream that*]: **"I will also surely bring you up again."**[340]

[*It is important to understand the nuance at play, whereby in the case of sparks imbedded in the vegetal and animal realms they are apprehensive about descent into the oppositional realm, whereas in the case of Jacob, the operative apprehension here is not of the spark per se; rather, it stems from a deeper fear on the part of the human being. The problem is that the vehicle for redemption—that being human—is not entirely trustworthy because of free will. However, due to the merit of Jacob, knowing that the divine would be with him, Jacob was mollified in his descent to ascent.*]

Behold, our Torah is a teaching of truth and conviction, but it is strictly forbidden for a person to purposefully descend into distracting thoughts [*in the realm of oppositional forces*] to ascend and raise up the sparks. For what happens if one fails like lion [*to vanquish the oppositional forces*] in overcoming such a descent? Do not go looking for such danger, *perish the thought;* rather, only if such a trial comes to you without seeking it out, then descend to ascend. Only accept what the divine totality places before you. In such a situation, when one has to truly overcome the inner drive, mustering all one's spiritual capacities, then it is possible to return and raise up the sparks in this process of ascent.

This was the case regarding King Solomon, *o.b.m.*, who declared: "I'll have many [*wives*], and my heart will not go astray [*because I am forewarned and know that danger*].[341] So what emerged is that [*as soon as he put himself into this situation rather than encountering it involuntarily is that*] King Solomon really thought himself able to raise all the sparks [*but*

340. "I will go down with you into Egypt; and I will also surely bring you up again; and Joseph shall put his hand on your eyes" (Genesis 46:4).

341. b*Sanhedrin* 21a.

without the proper attunement] he failed these trials.

[*What emerges now in the juxtaposition of these rabbinic teachings is an apparent contradiction that the homily must now redress*]. Therefore the blessed Sages say that there is a blessing for seeing anything beautiful, even a gentile, "that this is the wondrous ways of the divine world"—this does not contradict the scriptural dictum: **"nor show mercy unto them."**[342] There is no contradiction here; one should not seek out such an encounter on purpose, but if it happens by chance, then of course, in that moment, take the pleasure of the sight you just experienced and elevate it. This is like the story of Rabbi Akivah who encounters the beautiful Matron by accident so he raised the sparks of that moment "when he was cornered."[343] [*When one descends lacking attunement in the moment of such a trial in order to raise up the spark, it*] requires a surrender similar to falling on one's face during prayer, as is known.

The general principle regarding this devotion of elevating sparks: one needs to contemplate whatever one encounters, [*for*] in anything that takes place, there is always some residue, whether good or evil, so one must analyze how that moment is beckoning a response. [*This situational residue out there*] is aroused in finding its mate [*where one's interior life is reflective of what is out there. A spiritual person is not independent of the exteriority but attuned to everything inside and out*]. So when this event takes place, whatever the quality of the event, one must bind oneself to the blessed Holy One. For all vitality emanates from this source of divine totality.

[*So the devotional act of interconnecting everything within the divine totality as it emerges moment to moment in every encounter is an invitation to*] pay attention, as the prophet says: **"Did not the divine?"**[344] [*emerge for you in this particular encounter?*] As Scripture states: **"and the Sovereign rule is over all"**[345]—for the sovereignty that rules and vitalizes everything happens through interconnection. This interconnection is a process elevated by conjoining the sovereign ground of being [*Malkut*] through the array of interconnection itself [*Yesod*]. This [*interconnection*] is: **"a ladder set up on the earth, and the top of it reached to**

342. Literally, "and when YHVH your God shall deliver them up before you, and you shall smite them; then you shalt utterly destroy them; you shall make no covenant with them, nor show mercy unto them" (Deuteronomy 7:2).

343. b*Avodah Zarah* 20b.

344. "Who gave Jacob for a spoil, and Israel to the robbers? Did not YHVH? He against whom we have sinned, and in whose ways they would not walk, neither were they obedient unto His law" (Isaiah 42:24).

345. "YHVH has established His throne in Heaven, / and the Sovereign rule is over all" (Psalm 103:19).

heaven"[346] to be elevated, as is known, from **"the devoted one is a nexus between worlds."**[347]

Thus behold, here we find Judah in his situational residue with an attunement [*symbolizing the ground of being in Malkhut in need of its sparks being elevated*] that sees a confluence within of all these incidents culminating in this very moment before him, when one brother turned to the other and said: **"What is this that God has done unto us?"**[348] Then did Judah realize that this was indeed a confluence of incidents, so that the sparks were ready to be elevated. Thus, Scripture states: **"Then Judah came near unto him"**[349]—namely, that Judah drew himself closer by empathizing with Joseph, overcoming his resistance to this opposing force to see him as a beloved creature of the divine totality, ultimately throwing his entire self into the encounter. [*Every devoted one resists encountering oppositional forces until the moment of the true encounter emerges allowing a deeper embrace of the heart to throw oneself into it.*] Even if such an encounter is with a gentile, or an Egyptian, such an encounter holds within it the possibility of bridging heaven and earth. But the divine totality causes this encounter to happen, so that this person would need to elicit within this trial a deeper sense of compassion in the other to arouse it in one's self. Judah is the one who instantiates the overarching vitality from the divine totality, so he had to come closer to connect up the blessed Holy One even within a gentile, and even an Egyptian, to overcome this oppositional force. For by way of truth, Joseph is the nexus. This is at once the simple meaning [*that Joseph appeared to be a gentile to Judah*] as well as the deepest reading [*that Joseph was actually a hidden zaddik*] of the verse: **"the divine is within me [*then allowing me to recognize it within you*]."**[350]

[7.3]. *PARASHAH VAYIGASH* 1–2 (GENESIS 44:18–47:27)

QUESTIONS FOR REFLECTION:

1. How many names are you known by? Focus on your Hebrew

346. "And he dreamed, and behold a ladder set up on the earth, and the top of it reached to heaven; and behold the angels of God ascending and descending on it" (Genesis 28:12).

347. Literally, "When the whirlwind passes, the wicked is no more; but the righteous is an everlasting foundation" (Proverbs 10:25).

348. "And he said unto his brethren: 'My money is restored; and, lo, it is even in my sack.' And their heart failed them, and they turned trembling one to another, saying: 'What is this that God has done unto us?'" (Genesis 42:28).

349. "Then Judah came near unto him, and said: 'Oh my lord, let your servant, I pray O, speak a word in my lord's ears, and let not your anger burn against thy servant; for you are even as Pharaoh'" (Genesis 44:18).

350. Genesis 44:18.

name; notice the forms of each letter. In what way can each letter serve as a guide to engaging materiality to elicit deeper awareness of your interior life?

2. What is the nature of your spiritual practice? How does it relate to your daily comportment? How much of your practice is head-centered? How much of it is heart-centered? How much of it is embodied? What might your spiritual practice look like if it flowed more integrally as a language of comportment? In what ways do you find it challenging to embody spiritual practice in the material plane and in the mundane world? How do spiritual mentors, friends, and/or community empower or weaken your embodiment of spiritual practice?

3. How does your sense of empathy allow you to draw closer to others? How do you navigate overcoming your resistance to seeing opposing forces as a beloved creature of the divine totality? What keeps you from throwing yourself wholeheartedly into such challenging encounters?

Exodus

[8.1]. *Parashah Bo'* (Exodus 10:1–13:16)

INTRODUCTION TO HOMILY:

To truly appreciate what religion means by creation under divine providence, one must identify the underlying cosmology of such claims. After modernity, seekers of such truth find themselves turning to science to clarify the nature of human understanding of cosmology. Most quantum physicists hold that the universe was created from matter, tracing its beginning moment to the Big Bang. Yet the dissenters from this materialist position of Quantum Cosmology, like Stuart Hammeroff and Roger Penrose have something to contribute to the way the spiritual world looks at consciousness.[1] *This minority opinion is that the universe was created from something, but that something is not merely matter to be traced all the way back to the Big Bang. Rather, the universe was created from consciousness. This claim is proved by examining what they call Objective Reduction, which is a scheme that describes how consciousness occurs in any appropriately organized system. If conscious experience is intimately connected with the very physics underlying space-time structure, then Objective Reduction in microtubules and other biomolecules point to something remarkable—namely, that the universe was created from the stuff of consciousness, not merely matter. This means that consciousness and meaning are the raw materials from which the universe was created. So, it is not by chance that humans are hardwired with a consciousness for meaning-making in a universe that mirrors such wiring. Yet the tendency in much of the exegesis to the first chapter of the book of Genesis is to read a concreteness of Creation to ensure a dualism that one does not find in a thoroughgoing non-dual system. The myth of cosmogenesis in Genesis does not question the concreteness of Creation, as opposed to seeing the world of experience as illusory. Although the homilist is concerned with the narrative of Exodus, it cannot be extricated from concerns of consciousness in Genesis. When self-consciousness is conjoined through devequt with divine consciousness, there is an overflow of the divine glory, such that the devoted one then becomes the site from which creation flows forth. Such an extension of consciousness*

1. See Stuart Hameroff, and Roger Penrose, "Conscious Events As Orchestrated Space-Time Selections," *Journal of Consciousness Studies* 3.1 (1996): 36-53.

emerges through the song of creation itself. The homily focuses on cultivating the ultimate level of 'emunah. This involves a kind of empowerment of the efficacy of the zaddik—here exemplified by rereading Talmudic lore concerning R. Pinchas ben Yair and R. Eleazar ben Pedat—whereby the laws of nature can be overwritten. This suggests a transcending of devotion by assuming for one's self this empowerment. By bringing one's self within the entire innermost point of creation, then the melodious extension of divine consciousness can then channel its song. The only way that the divine mind is open to change in the natural world is through the truly devoted ones, for these devoted ones are one of a kind and fulfill the spreading of divine glory but incorporating the divine glory within themselves they affect a change. This gives devoted ones the ability to affect change beyond themselves with the potential for new creation.

[8.2]. *Parashah Bo'* (Exodus 10:1–13:16)

HOMILY:

The inquiry is made about R. Shlomo Yitzhaki's commentary on **"its neck"**[2]—If the priest loses his redemption fee, then you lose your animal by breaking its neck.

The Vitebsker addressed the inquiry [*above*] through the teaching of our blessed Sages: The command of redeeming is preferred to breaking the neck, and so the command of levirate marriage is preferred over the ritual

2. "But every firstling ass you shall redeem with a sheep; if you do not redeem it, you must break its neck. And you must redeem every firstborn male among your children" (Exodus 13:13), see Rashi ad loc. "break its neck"—"one breaks its neck with a hatchet from behind and so slays it. The reason is: he [the owner of the ass] has caused it a loss to the possessions of the priest [by not giving him the lamb], therefore must he suffer loss in his own possession (b*Bechorot* 10b)."

The firstborn offspring of a kosher animal is sanctified meaning it is designated, while the donkey has an intermediate status. The command to redeem the firstborn of a donkey alludes to the reality that even among the impure and the wicked, who seemed to be ruled by base instincts and manifest no external devotional signs are pure at heart and can be redeemed. the donkey has neither cloven hooves nor chews its cud and hence has no signs of ritual purity. Even the firstborn itself is not intrinsically holy but still has the potential to be redeemed in devotional service. Lurianic Kabbalah builds upon the legal ruling (*Shulkhan 'Arukh, Y.A.* 321) to further suggest the original sanctification did not apply to the *'erev rav* (the mixed multitude) of Jews and non-Jews who left Egypt together with the Children of Israel. However, eventually the divine acceded to Moses' wish for the inclusion of the *'erev rav*. So redeeming the firstborn donkey also symbolizes this expansive mystical reading of holiness to include even what is not yet holy at all (Zohar II: 41b).

The status of the firstling ass is unique in that it is not ritually pure and thus needs to be exchanged for a sheep; while if it is not exchanged, then "its neck" must be broken.

of release [*halizah*];[3] but this is really difficult to realize and complete that service selflessly for the sake of heaven, thus the ritual of release is preferable just as is the case of breaking the animal's neck.[4]

Behold, Torah says: **"Go to Pharaoh"**[5] where R. Shlomo Yitzhaki then comments: "Go and admonish him—**'for I have hardened his heart.'"**[6] The reason for this is known, given that Pharaoh responded: **"I do not know YHVH nor will I let Israel go"**[7]; he refused to recognize that God has any control over the world and is actively involved in the particularities of all human affairs.[8]

While he indeed admitted and acknowledged a god [*Pharaoh*] that created the word, as would any theist, he is persuaded that once the Creator created the world he abandoned it, as is the belief of other heretics. So, instead of God ruling the world, it is left up to the constellations to direct the world. This explains why other nations were caught up in idolatry of the constellations.

This is why Moses says: **"For since I came . . . in Your Name,"**[9] which refers to particular providence in the name of YHVH, **"he has dealt ill with this people"**[10]—as is known, once there is a challenge to oppositional forces it becomes strengthened with the intention that the denial of providence will prevail: **"And the Egyptians made the children of Israel to serve**

---

3. *Halizah* is the "ritual of release by removing the shoe," which is derived from Deuteronomy 25:7-10. The defunct ceremony functions to "release" the widow of a man who died childless to marry someone other than her brother-in-law. Although the union with a brother's wife is incestuous and prohibited by Torah, in order to avert the extinction of the family line, the brother of the deceased is obligated to marry the widow in a *Yibum* or "levirate marriage." In the case of the brother refusing to marry the widow, Torah provides for this "release ritual." If the woman refuses to cohabit with the brother-in-law, then Jewish law requires the surviving brother to exercise his right to refusal to then release his sister-in-law, so she is "free" to marry someone else. Prevention of levirate marriages was a moral imperative of the Rabbis.

4. The implied question: How is it imaginable that one would forgo the command and appear to break the animal's neck rather than redeem it through the priest?

5. "Then YHVH said to Moses: 'Go to Pharaoh. For I have hardened his heart and the hearts of his courtiers, in order that I may display these My signs among them, and that you may recount in the hearing of your children and of your children's children how I made a mockery of the Egyptians and how I displayed My signs among them—in order that you may know that I am YHVH'" (Exodus 10:1-2).

6. "And the YHVH said to Moses: 'Go to Pharaoh"—Rashi ad loc—"and warn him."

7. "But Pharaoh said: 'Who is YHVH that I should heed Him and let Israel go? I do not know YHVH nor will I let Israel go'" (Exodus 5:2).

8. See Zohar I:195b.

9. "For since I came to Pharaoh to speak in Your Name, he has dealt ill with this people; neither have You delivered Your people at all" (Exodus 5:23).

10. Exodus 5:23.

with rigor"[11] in order to strengthen this denial, but in truth they do not understand that their resistance is all part of the divine economy and was a gift of God—for in the augmenting the oppression of enslavement, Pharaoh actually catalyzed the redemption.

This is the meaning of **"Go to Pharaoh"—"Go and admonish him"—"for I have hardened his heart";**[12] namely, this redemption is a function of particular providence that Pharaoh's heart is hardened through the reach of the divine providence.

Behold, in truth it is impossible to believe that there is such a direct involvement in every single micro-phenomenon as a decree from the Holy One, to believe that everything from the slightest accident in the world—whether a blade of grass withering or a stone being thrown—is all part of the divine choreography, as Scripture teaches: **"the place where the tree falls, there shall it be."**[13]

There is no movement, large or small—from the original filtering to the most microlevel of earthly existence, that does not stem from the Wisdom of the Holy One. In the Name is the dual purpose of revealing the divine glory of and wisdom of the One "whose attributes are Compassion and Mercy"[14] and for **"creating the environment"**[15] in which Israel could serve the divine **"and the devoted ones are the foundation of the world."**[16]

So that everything that exists in the universe is mirrored within the constitution of the human being—one who has the power and grandeur at hand to grow, strengthen and ultimately change the order of the universe. So this alteration of the natural world is possible through the spirit of one's words, so long as one's spiritual qualities and cognitions remain uninterrupted, in a pristine and extended conjunctive *devequt* with the Holy One.

Understand this through Wisdom![17] ***Aleph*-*Chokhmah*—"'The Wondrous One [*PeLeH Yoez*] is planning grace; / The Eternal Father, a peaceable ruler'"**[18] without any apperception or categorization except for the Limitless One, as Scripture states: **"but you saw no form";**[19] but it is

11. Exodus 1:13.

12. Exodus 10:1-2.

13. "If the clouds be full of rain, they empty themselves on the earth; and if a tree fall in the south, or in the north, in the place where the tree falls, there shall it be" (Ecclesiastes 11:3). Compare with Maimonides, *Guide* III:51: "everything in the hands of heaven."

14. b*Shabbat* 133b.

15. Literally, "In the beginning God created the heaven and the earth" (Genesis 1:1).

16. Literally, "When the whirlwind passes, the wicked is no more; but the righteous is an everlasting foundation" (Proverbs 10:25).

17. *Sefer Yetzirah* 1:4.

18. "For a child has been born to us, / a son has been given us. / And authority has settled on his shoulders. / He has been named / 'The Mighty God is planning grace; / The Eternal Father, a peaceable ruler'" (Isaiah 9:5).

19. "And YHVH spoke unto you out of the midst of the fire; you heard the voice of

through the form of the letters one sees the imperceptible through the unfurling of the divine, which is the **"*ALePH*"** as is known to be **"wondrous"** [*PeLeH*].[20]

So it is the case with all the letters—through which the entire universe was created, as is known[21]—and surely these [*primordial*] letters are not to be mistaken for the current letters as glyphs. For it is only by way of these latter forms that the spiritual energy was able to extend forth, but these forms themselves are not the primordial powers of creation; rather, these forms are a kind of garbing at the most basic level for the person who learns to read the aleph bet. For it remains merely a tool for the beginning of literacy.

So too with Torah and spiritual practice[22]—these forms all derive from the process of emanation and its thickening into materialization. This is what constitutes the name and spiritual attributes of the Holy One—all emanating forth from that deepest point within the heart [*which is intangible*]. It is this formless mind of the divine, an essence beyond essence [*to which our devotion yearns to connect*]: "Imitate the divine, just as God is compassionate."[23]

Regarding the matter of spiritual practice in the act of social justice or **"Love"**[24]—these devotional actions are extensions of the divine essence. Yet this essence beyond essence then takes on garbed forms that are tangible expressions of the ineffable through the very letters of the command **"Give to him readily"**[25] and **"Love your fellow as yourself."**[26] Then the aspirant sees the letters [*describing the devotional act in Torah itself*] as an incarnation of the emanative process.[27]

And this [*completion of the emanative process*] applies to all the commands of spiritual practice and are a thickening of the essence beyond essence in material form. This takes place moving our limbs or even **"The spirit of YHVH spoke has spoken through** [*him*], **/ and the word of**

---

words, but you saw no form; only a voice" (Deuteronomy 4:12).

20. Isaiah 9:5.

21. See *Peri haAretz*, Parashah Vayigash.

22. Another form of encoding the ineffable into the effable.

23. b*Shabbat* 133b.

24. "You shall not take vengeance, nor bear any grudge against your countrymen. Love your fellow as yourself: I am YHVH" (Leviticus 19:18).

25. "Give to him readily and have no regret when you do so, for in return YHVH your God will bless you in all your efforts and all your undertakings" (Deuteronomy 15:10).

26. Leviticus 19:18.

27. The aspirant is not commanded to complete a devotional act; rather, each devotional act is an ontological act put into communicable form, so that when the aspirant acts on that form, a person is completing the next step of extending forth the flow of the Holy One into the material world.

the One was on [*his tongue*]"[28]—all of which are deeply intertwined with the world's creation anew, constantly creating more tangible forms or even causing a change in the natural order and divine desire.

For behold the entirety of existence is meant to manifest Compassion and Mercy, to reveal the divine glory: **"Every one that is called by My name, / Whom I have created, / Formed, and made for My glory—.'"**[29]

From the first step of the original filtering all the way down the emanative process, everything points to divinity reaching the point of song.[30] Why did Joshua, who said **"Stand still, O sun,"**[31] think he would then recite the song in its place?[32]

To be a surrogate for the sun, the human being is the microcosm that contains within all of creation from the Crowning Consciousness of *Keter* to the Primordial Point of *Chokhmah*, through all these interconnections of the worlds.

And after all, divine glory that fills the human, within the innermost vital point within the depth of the heart—whereby the extension to all limbs of this inner vitality is utterly selfless for YHVH—so in becoming so emptied, then one becomes that central point from which all of creation emanates forth. For the sake of revealing the divine glory for every human is a **"microcosm."**[33]

Therefore now no one can complain or challenge the intervention of a devoted one who is completely selfless [*and emptied to become a focal point*] for the sake of becoming a divine microcosm, for such a person is acting as a conduit for the divine, so that the singing of the universe shines forth like no other in the universe. Just as Scripture states: **"Then the moon shall be ashamed, / and the sun shall be abashed. / For YHVH of Hosts will reign"**[34] so that afterward the devoted one will be filled with divine glory, sovereignty, and transparency illuminating further which sings the song in its place.

And similarly with the story of the Ginai River that boasted to R. Pinchas ben Yair: "I am forever flowing and thus undoubtedly fulfilling

---

28. "The spirit of YHVH spoke has spoken through me, / and the word of the One was on my tongue" (2 Samuel 23:2).

29. Isaiah 43:7.

30. Zohar I:123a.

31. "On that occasion, when YHVH routed the Amorites before the Israelites, Joshua addressed YHVH; he said in the presence of the Israelites: 'Stand still, O sun, at Gibeon, / O Moon, in the valley of Aijalon!'" (Joshua 10:12).

32. *Midrash Tanchuma*, Parashah Acharey Mot, no. 9.

33. *Tiquney Zohar*, Tiqqun, no. 70:130b.

34. "Then the moon shall be ashamed, / and the sun shall be abashed. / For YHVH of Hosts will reign / On Mount Zion, and in Jerusalem, / And the Presence will be revealed to His elders" (Isaiah 24:23).

the divine desire whereas you are uncertain." And so R. Pinchas ben Yair only responded as follows: "I decree that your flow shall be stopped up forever!"[35] On the one hand, a normal human lets the river flow. But R. Pinchas brought within himself the entire innermost point of creation, so he stood in the river's stead, so that the melodious flow of the river could more clearly channel its song.

While there is a reluctance to change anything in nature as it already expresses the divine glory, the only way that the divine mind is open to change in the natural world is through the truly devoted ones, for these devoted ones are one of a kind and fulfill the spreading of divine glory; by incorporating the divine glory within themselves they affect change. This gives devoted ones the ability to affect change beyond themselves with the potential for new creation.

And this is just as our Sages, *o.b.m.*, have taught regarding the response from the heavens to R. Eleazar ben Pedat's [*questioning his own suffering*]—"Even if the entire world would be recreated, there is no guarantee of things being different."[36]

The divine glory would be crystal clear to the beholder [*through the devoted one*] even though there are obvious signs of some mutability in the natural order. Clarity emerges for the one who listens to another imbued with the divine spirit. Yet [*on a regular basis*] the truth is that [*there is still*] the natural order that is the source recounting the wonders of the divine. For whose power is this limitless expanse of the cosmic glorification if not the divine through nature? Flowing since the six days of creation until the end of the world, **"The heavens declare the glory of God,"**[37] **"Their voice carries throughout the earth,"**[38] and each day **"The sun arises, and the sun sets,"**[39] as King David, *o.b.m.*, teaches: **"When I behold Your heavens, the work of Your fingers."**[40]

---

35. b*Hulin* 7a.

36. b*Ta'anit* 25a, where it recounts how R. Eleazar ben Pedat was in straits and attempted to break through. First he attempted bloodletting, then fasting, and then took garlic only to faint into a stupor. The Sages came to visit him and by now he was crying and laughing while a flame was coming out of Pedat's nose. When asked what happened, Pedat explained that he was sitting with the Holy One. I asked, "What is going on here? How much longer will I suffer?" So the Holy One responded: "My son, Eleazar, what would you prefer? That I recreate the world? Maybe then your fortune would change and you would be assured of living in a more prosperous situation!?!"

37. "The heavens declare the glory of God, / the sky proclaims His handiwork" (Psalm 19:2).

38. "Their voice carries throughout the earth, / their words to the end of the world. / He placed in them a tent for the sun" (Psalm 19:5).

39. "The sun arises, and the sun sets— / And glides back to where it rises" (Ecclesiastes 1:5).

40. "When I behold Your heavens, the work of Your fingers, the moon and the stars

The most remarkable manifestation of the limitless cosmic expanse is experienced in the grandeur of nature, and so it is paradoxically apprehended through the continuous existence of nature without change rather than in human nature. All materiality is limited in its power—for it is impossible for anything to remain static in the material as realm everything is always changing from moment to moment, **"perchance he is asleep and will wake up."**[41]

This is not the case with the blessed Limitless One, for **"See, the guardian of Israel / neither slumbers nor sleeps!"**[42]—that eternal power to keep matter in an unchanging way. The cycles of nature are unchanging even though the cosmos is full of transient material. It is that pristine divine desire that begins creation in an unbounded manner and keeps the world running in an unbounded way, even though it remains physical: **"One sees it, then it is gone; / it grows wings and flies away."**[43]

How good for one with the capacity to truly see and understand from the prosaic sense of nature that the world is ever-changing, yet its cycles are unchanging. Those cycles are overseen by the ever-seeing eye, forever dependent upon the divine vitality, akin to **"the creatures dashing to and fro"**[44]—so it is in every place and with every person.

The only way possible to truly receive this divine vitality is through the condition of **"to and fro."**[45] For [*in a moment of ascent into that*] endless flow of vitality the receiver is utterly nullified of corporeality. Thus it is [*the very material world of*] descent that is the vehicle for its ascent—for everything emanates from the Holy One and that divine vitality enlivens all sentient beings. In addition, the descent is an eclipse of the divine vitality—while the ascent is its revelation.

After contemplating this [*descent as a divine eclipse*]: [*one realizes*] the mundane cycles of nature are the greatest manifestation of the Limitless One precisely where the divine remains concealed within these cycles. This divine concealment within the mundane is actually the rhythm which reveals even more of the divinity than one could imagine. But someone who is shortsighted cannot see such depth within these cycles; rather, all is viewed as accidental and chaotic.

---

that You set in place" (Psalm 8:4).

41. "When noon came, that Elijah mocked them, saying: 'Shout louder! After all, he is a god. But he may be in conversation, he may be detained, or he may be on a journey or perchance he is asleep and will wake up'" (1 Kings 18:27).

42. Psalm 121:4.

43. "You see it, then it is gone; / it grows wings and flies away, / like an eagle, heavenward" (Proverbs 23:5).

44. "Dashing to and fro [among] the creatures was something that looked like flares" (Ezekiel 1:14).

45. Ezekiel 1:14.

And so it is with the case of Pharaoh and others who take up his theistic understanding of the world—this thinking does not take into account how the force that begins the process also sustains the process through particular providence.

However, these theists claim that after creation, the natural order was abandoned by the particular, continuous providence of the Creator and left under the control of the constellations, thus only operating through the **"to and fro"**[46] from moment to moment. This suggests there is a concealment simultaneous with the divinity present in the natural cycles. So that everything is in the hands of the spiritual seeker: **"Let all that breathes praise the YH—Hallelujah,"**[47] wherein the blessed Sages teach that **"each and every breath"** is a matter of **"to and fro."**[48]

This is true regarding the trials of the heart—like an alchemist's stone against which all other stones can be measured—or the **"to[ward]"** that tests whether the heart is ready to accept and allow the divine energy to abide within it; if not, then it retreats **"fro"** as an alternating current. This is the cosmic rhythm of life.

For [*if*] one who understands **"to[ward]"** [*as the implicit presence of the divine that humans make explicit*]—it is also the **"fro"** which is a descent [*of sensed divine energy*], [*then*] one needs to ascend to **"Let all that breathes praise the YH—Hallelujah."**[49] This is in opposition to the person who is numbed to the sensation of the divine feeding energy, such a person will not experience the extraordinary already embedded in the moment—not simply another aspect of the accidental reality of nature—rather, this moment is meant to show us how God has made such a moment, [*allowing the seeker to*] be filled with the reverence for each such moment and elevate it to its source.

And this is what the Holy One says to Moses: that he is the intellect as is known.[50] **"Go to Pharaoh"—which is the "neck"** [*ORePH*] as is known, which is forgetfulness, descent, and disconnectedness from the divine energy.

"Go to Pharaoh"—"for I have hardened his heart"[51]**—"for I"** re-

---

46. "Dashing to and fro [among] the creatures was something that looked like flares" (Ezekiel 1:14).

47. Psalm 150:6.

48. Ezekiel 1:14.

49. Psalm 150:6.

50. Zohar II:116b.

51. "Then YHVH said to Moses: 'Go to Pharaoh. For I have hardened his heart and the hearts of his courtiers, in order that I may display these My signs among them, / and that you may recount in the hearing of your children and of your children's children how I made a mockery of the Egyptians and how I displayed My signs among them—in order that you may know that I am YHVH'" (Exodus 10:1-2).

fers to the *Shekinah* as is known[52]—this refers to the *Shekinah* in the terrestrial realm, which is the eclipsed presence within the prosaic cycle of nature that courses through everything. And in truth **"I, I am the One"**[53] refers to the Limitless—only while in eclipse. The descent is needed for the sake of ascent—it is only possible to take effect through the process of **"to and fro,"** and the intention is as follows: in order to elevate the **"fro"** towards the **"to."**

This applies to the verse **"in order that I may display these My signs among them"**[54]—namely, the letters of the divine names that sustain all sentient beings, which are all letters in Torah. These letters elevate; so that the descent is for the sake of ascent.

This then refers to the teaching: "One should always order one's praise before the Place—and then pray"[55] to see that all of the created world of sentient beings are created for the sake of the Holy One. And if so, then there is nothing but the prayer of **"Let all that breathes praise the YH—Hallelujah"**[56] that will transform consciousness into true prayer—for everything then is in the uninterrupted and unified state of true *devequt*.

This now explains the issue at hand: the redemption of the firstborn ass with the goat really refers [*symbolically*] to distracting thoughts amid connected, constructive thoughts. The reason for this interruption is that these distracting thoughts want to join the elevation that comes from prayer. It refers to the exile of Egypt—which was exilic love, as explained in the Zohar and Lurianic Kabbalah.[57]

After the redemption from those **"whose members were like those of asses"**[58]—exile here is "materialism" of physical building materials, so the Holy One has commanded us to redeem the "asses"—referring to its prime essence, which is love. This love is first of the months [*when this command is given*], and the seven days of creating the world—and Israel is called "eldest"—which is Compassion, to elevate the energies of love and compassion—nothing but this divine presence.

---

52. Zohar III:276a.

53. "See, then, that I, I am the One; / There is no god beside Me. / I deal death and give life; / I wounded and I will heal; / None can deliver from My hand" (Deuteronomy 32:39).

54. "Then YHVH said to Moses: 'Go to Pharaoh. For I have hardened his heart and the hearts of his courtiers, in order that I may display these My signs among them'" (Exodus 10:1).

55. b*Berakot* 32a, b*Avodah Zarah* 7b.

56. Psalm 150:6.

57. R. Hayyim Vital, *Sefer Torat Hakham*, 116a, 147b.

58. "[S]he lusted for concubinage with them, whose members were like those of asses and whose organs were like those of stallions" (Ezekiel 23:20).

"[I]f you do not redeem it, you must break its neck"[59]—and if this command is to be completed with the proper intention, then it may necessitate completion by not completing it at all by way of "breaking the neck," which is the way of the oppositional force. This is akin to the issue of "command of levirate marriage in extremis"[60] to be a fulfillment of the command to know the divine in all pathways.

"Since this has caused a loss in the Priest's donation" in carrying forward the exterior energies of love, "thus he loses"[61] all of which may be a fulfillment of the command to know the divine in all ways.

Or perhaps there is another way to read this: "redemption" of the firstling [*material*] donkey! Imagine the true cleaving of *devequt*: when a person looks at their body as being a sparkling entity rather than merely being composed of materiality—through this path, luminescence is restored to the original light of the Limitless One, giving up all claims of self entering into the innermost point within one's heart, which is divinely endowed and thus filling with that divine point. So the divine essence emanates through one's body so that one is fully overcome by the divine.

When a person becomes such a microcosm of the divine, that person then includes within the self all sentient beings—that inclusion of all sentient beings as its redemption, liberating everything from its material servitude. This alternation of the divine takes place through inclusion, as we read about Joshua who said: **"Stand still, O sun,"**[62] which is the glory, and the shining of the sun's radiance.

And if one cannot redeem all sentient beings by attaining this giving up of selfhood, then one must respect the spiritual inertia of natural cycles; this explains why **"if you do not redeem it, you must break its neck,"**[63] then one succumbs to appreciating the wonder of these natural cycles. The ordering of one's praise is to acknowledge and celebrate the natural world as it stands, as Scripture states: **"When I behold Your heavens, the work of Your fingers."**[64]

59. "But every firstling ass you shall redeem with a sheep; if you do not redeem it, you must break its neck. And you must redeem every firstborn male among your children" (Exodus 13:13).

60. b*Yebamot* 122b, ad loc *Arukh laNeir*.

61. See above Rashi ad loc Exodus 13:13.

62. "On that occasion, when YHVH routed the Amorites before the Israelites, Joshua addressed YHVH; he said in the presence of the Israelites: 'Stand still, O sun, at Gibeon, / O Moon, in the valley of Aijalon!'" (Joshua 10:12).

63. "But every firstling ass you shall redeem with a sheep; if you do not redeem it, you must break its neck. And you must redeem every firstborn male among your children" (Exodus 13:13).

64. "When I behold Your heavens, the work of Your fingers, the moon and the stars that You set in place" (Psalm 8:4).

[*The question arises then as to why this command is given here at the moment of Exodus?*] The reason that this command was placed here at the moment of Exodus is because it was part of the earlier oath in the theophany, **"And when you have freed the people from Egypt, you shall worship God at this mountain."**[65] This is the revelation of Torah at Sinai where the "tablets are inscribed with freedom," liberated from the Angel of Death[66] and liberation from foreign sovereignty,[67] free to serve the divine completely.

So after the Exodus from Egypt, when the Israelites were enslaved to slaves—it follows R. Shlomo Yitzhaki's comment on **"the firstborn of the maidservant,"**[68] leading to the receipt of Torah—from which the heavens and the earth and the entire world were created, integrating the unfolding of all worlds, from the beginning until the lowest of levels. All this being suffused with the glory of the divine, and thus purified. This is what enabled the Exodus from Egypt to happen in the first place—by overcoming nature. Liberation is thus contained in the national-historical model as well as in this spiritual model, all contained within the aforementioned readings of the redemption of the firstling donkey.

[8.3]. *Parashah Bo'* (Exodus 10:1–13:16)

QUESTIONS FOR REFLECTION:

1. How does a comprehensive, general divine providence—knowing your species is provided for—affect you and your sense of being cared for in the world?

2. How might the natural rhythm, flow, and development of creation allow you to uncover the song of your soul? In what setting might you explore this natural rhythm, flow, and development of creation?

3. Why is the uplifting of fallen energies and emotions to the

65. "And He said: 'I will be with you; that shall be your sign that it was I who sent you. And when you have freed the people from Egypt, you shall worship God at this mountain.'" (Exodus 3:12).

66. *Song of Songs Rabbah* 8:3.

67. See m*Avot* 6:2; *Peri haAretz*, Parshah Shelakh

68. "And every firstborn in the land of Egypt shall die, from the firstborn of Pharaoh that sits on his throne to the firstborn of the maidservant who is behind the mill; and all the firstborn of cattle" (Exodus 11:5). Rashi ad loc. "the firstborn of the captive"—[these words are used in 12:29 instead of "unto the firstborn of the maidservant" in this verse]—Why were the captive smitten, for they had not enslaved the Israelites? In order that they might not say that their god had claimed satisfaction for the humiliation imposed on them and had brought this punishment on the Egyptians."

divine totality only achieved without ulterior motives or ego-centricity? Why is this such a challenge for each of us to live by?

[9.1]. *Parashah Beshalach* (Exodus 13:17–17:16)

INTRODUCTION TO HOMILY:

There are distinctive levels of ʻemunah that constitute a discipline that involves ascending degrees. The degrees of ʻemunah correspond to increasing degrees of clarity concerning the nature and perception of reality, particularly in regard to the apparent relationship between the person on the path and the divine goal. In this sense, reaching the ultimate level requires a gradual path of spiritual development. The dynamic of the paths are common in that each person follows some kind of gradual spiritual path. What characterizes ʻemunah at the initial stages ceases to have validity at the higher level; nevertheless, approaching the higher level generally requires ascending through the lower stages. At the ultimate level, the Vitebsker postulates a condition of empowerment for the zaddik which enables that person to influence and overturn the laws of nature, as seen already in Parashah Bo'. The flow of energy in time and space—what happens—is extended through the powers of YHVH. This extends as all the worlds built out of the divine personae of parsufim turn into spheres through sefirot. What maintains it is the very flow of shefa, whereby YHVH is the divine totality and its own source, being sui generis like the shell of the tortoise. The mistake of the ego is thinking that one is an independent doer, but it is all part of what is happening. But when the consciousness identified with a particular ego and retraces its path to what it really is, it then finds itself identical with YHVH—this marks the ultimate self-transcendence or bittul. The consciousness of that zaddik has become aware of and a part of the source itself through their mind and body. Within that space of such experience, the zaddik can then manifest this Will as the source of everything that is happening. At the ultimate level of ʻemunah, there is a realization of nonseparation or identity with all that exists. In that realization, a kind of empowerment is manifested by virtue of which the zaddik can miraculously change what is happening.

[9.2]. *Parashah Beshalach* (Exodus 13:17–17:16)

HOMILY:

“Then Moses will sing”[69]—it does not say “sang” [*in the past tense*] but “will sing” [*in the future tense*]—from here we learn that [*the futurity of*] resurrection [*alluded to in this future conjugation embeds it as described*]

69. “Then Moses and the Israelites sang this song to YHVH. They said: ‘I will sing to YHVH, for He has triumphed gloriously; / Horse and driver He has hurled into the sea’” (Exodus 15:1).

from Torah.[70]

[*Now there is a need to explain why Torah alludes to the futurity of resurrection here within the context of the Song of the Reed Sea, namely, why are these distinct temporal moments interwoven?*] The verse [*regarding the splitting of the Reed Sea*] reads: **"and the sea returned to its steady flow,"**[71] and so our blessed Sages interpreted **"its normal state"**[72] as **"its condition"** since it was an implicit condition within creation itself that the sea would be divided before the Israelites. [*And now in the moment of splitting the Reed Sea, the sea has fulfilled and realized its normative state.*] This raises difficulties [*for interpreters*], for according to this Scripture should have mentioned something [*about the implicit condition surrounding*] the moment of the Reed Sea's parting [*rather than at the moment when the sea returned to its normative state*], for, behold, the verse reads: **"and at daybreak the sea returned to its steady flow"**[73] [*but rather than "steady flow" it should really read "implicit condition"*]. Behold, Scripture also states: **"and at daybreak the sea returned"** [*which is not addressing the moment of the sea's splitting; rather, it focuses on its return to "steady flow" and still further it states "steady flow" instead of "implicit condition" of creation before the splitting*].

[*Furthermore, it now becomes necessary to explain the*] utterance [*of God to Moses the precedes the splitting of the sea*]: **"Why do you cry out to Me? . . . to go forward"**[74]—which means there is no reason for such an outcry, but the [*ironic*] condition is that the Israelites have the sea in front of them and the Egyptians surrounding—thus it is logical to **"burst into wild and bitter sobbing"**[75] [*but in truth this is no simple matter at all*] given their predicament of being closed in. [*In any event, they cried out, given that they were terrified and desperate.*]

[*Now there is a need to understand the implicit condition that the Creator made with the sea, and from there many of the interpretive difficulties should be answered.*] But in truth the matter is made known by our blessed Sages,[76] who teach that on the second [*day of creation, the formation of*] water was not yet completed, which is why it does not say **"it was good"**[77]

---

70. b*Sanhedrin* 91b.

71. "Moses held out his arm over the sea, and at daybreak the sea returned to its normal state, and the Egyptians fled at its approach" (Exodus 14:27).

72. Perhaps also means returning to the nature of water, which is to descend.

73. Exodus 14:27.

74. "Then YHVH said to Moses, 'Why do you cry out to Me? Tell the Israelites to go forward'" (Exodus 14:15).

75. "When Esau heard his father's words, he burst into wild and bitter sobbing, and said to his father, 'Bless me too, Father'!" (Genesis 27:34).

76. *Genesis Rabbah* 4:8.

77. "God called the dry land Earth, and the gathering of waters God called Seas. And

until the third day. At that time, Scripture states: **"Let the water below . . . be gathered . . . that the dry land may appear'"**[78] [*which signifies that the waters were completely formed*]. The twofold repetition of **"it was good"** [*first relating to the formation of water completed on the second day, and then secondly relating to the final formation on the third day itself*].

[*And so just as the production of water is divided into two distinct days, so too the implicit conditions which God ratified with the sea and the water are divided into twofold expectations regarding*] the two conditions involving the water [*namely, regarding the two stages of production for the water over two distinct days*]. The original state of the water at creation [*on the second day which had not yet involved a gathering into one place so that the dry land may appear; rather, there was only*] a spreading [*of the water without any limitation to delimit such spreading forth into a specific place. This quality of spreading is intrinsic to the identity of water,*] as is known that the "waters" [*which symbolizes the spiritual quality of Compassion that flows, relate to the first stage of its production concerned with flowing and spreading so that*] **". . . there was water overall the earth."**[79] Only afterward [*comes the second stage of its production, whereby there is a gathering together of the water to a singular place. This force of restraint holds the natural flowing of water. Furthermore, in this gathering together of water*] as is known, the land is lower than the sea as implied in the verse: **"Who summons the waters of the sea / And pours them out on the earth"**[80] [*from the sea to the earth*]—so that the word **"pours"** implies movement from a higher to a lower [*place. Thus, the gathering of the waters in the act of creating the world, whereby these waters that were initially flowing and spreading over the lower places of the earth are then restrained and gathered from there toward the higher plane of the sea. This again is contrary to the flowing nature of water, which tends to flow from higher to lower planes, and not to flow from lower to higher planes*].

[*This concludes reflections on the production of water in its twofold stages, so that what follows here now returns to the issue of the splitting of the Reed Sea, which realizes the two sets of conditions implied in the twofold stages of the production of water.*] Behold, the blessed Sages teach: **"In the beginning when God began creating"**[81]—creation of the universe

---

God saw that it was good" (Genesis 1:10).

78. "God said: 'Let the water below and the sky be gathered into one area, that the dry land may appear.' And it was so" (Genesis 1:9).

79. "But the dove could not find a resting place for its foot, and returned to him to the ark, for there was water over all the earth" (Genesis 8:9).

80. "Who made the Pleiades and Orion, / Who turns deep darkness into dawn / And darkens day into nigh, / Who summons the waters of the sea / And pours them out on the earth—His name is YHVH!" (Amos 5:8).

81. Genesis 1:1.

and its conditionality, in a certain sense, is for the sake of Israel, so that the entire world was conditional until the Israelites accepted Torah.[82] Nothing should stand in their way to receive and accept Torah, as Scripture states: **"when you have freed the people from Egypt, you shall worship God."**[83] All the miracles and alterations in nature were implicit in the narrative of creation itself.

So when it comes to the parting of the Reed Sea, it was implicit in the conditions of the second day[84] **"that the firmament would appear."**[85] When it comes to the return of the water to its **"its steady flow"**[86] in the morning, this refers to the first condition [*in the first stage of production of*] water and its capacity to spread over the Israelites' passageway.

Thus from the very beginning of the Reed Sea's parting [*that enabled the Israelites to journey forward to receive Torah*], it is self-evident the waters would part before the Israelites, for this was part of the order of creation at the outset [*wherein miracles were already inscribed within nature. This inscription is a function of creation being an act that emerges from forethought on behalf of the Creator, so that all the miraculous moments were for the sake of enabling the Israelites' receipt of Torah at Sinai*]. This does not imply any change in [*the divine Original Will which is eternal; rather, all these miraculous moments were inscribed in the original thought of creation*].

This is why [*Scripture then states*]: **"Why do you cry out to Me? . . . to go forward."**[87] This was not the case as the waters were returning near dawn upon the Egyptians [*to drown them and then move on*] according to their first alignment, in spreading out [*of the waters towards the place where dry land would emerge at the moment of the sea's parting, and this*] was a miracle, namely, that the waters should return [*now to the sea*] to spread out [*the water to the place where dry land will appear*] according its first condition. Behold, [*in the production of the waters in the midst of creation*], all the waters [*which originally covered the dry land initially*],

82. From the perspective of planetary consciousness, this refers to that moment until humanity would be guided by divine wisdom and higher consciousness to ensure the stability of the world.

83. "And He said, 'I will be with you; that shall be your sign that it was I show sent you. And when you have freed the people from Egypt, you shall worship God at this mountain'" (Exodus 3:12).

84. Thus, it is not necessarily a "miracle" but implicit within creation's plan and capacity for water itself.

85. See *Orakh Chayyim* on Genesis 1:9.

86. "Moses held out his arm over the sea, and at daybreak the sea returned to its normal state, and the Egyptians fled at its approach" (Exodus 14:27).

87. "Then YHVH said to Moses, 'Why do you cry out to Me? Tell the Israelites to go forward'" (Exodus 14:15).

after the dry land was seen [*and the waters gathered into their place, still*] they did not return [*namely, the waters where they were initially, thus here became the site of the Reed Sea splitting. Where the waters returned to their initial position covering the dry land—this was the miracle*].

[*Now there is an explication of a rabbinic teaching at hand regarding the lack of acknowledging the good on the second day of creation, given that the production of waters remained incomplete.*] This matter is addressed by the words [*in Scripture*]: **"And God saw that this was good"**[88] [*in the condition of water's creation on the second day which was not mentioned regarding the spreading out of the waters, which was the first stage in its production on the second day*]. Akin to the teaching of our blessed Sages regarding the splitting of the Reed Sea, the ministering angels wanted to sing [*as the Egyptians were drowning*], so the blessed Holy One interceded, saying: "But my handiwork is drowning in the sea and you want to sing songs!" So the singing of the song [*that remained unsung by the angels*] here is compensated for by the absence of the divine utterance **"this was good"**[89] on the second day.

[*It appears as though the unsung song over the return of the waters that drowned the Egyptians is a function of the spreading of the waters as a completion of its production on the second day of creation, which was still missing the divine utterance "this was good." And if the song was to be sung—it was after the splitting of the Reed Sea for the Israelites—which really comes from the gathering of the waters realized on the third day of creation, which is then marked by the doubling of "this was good." Indeed, what ensues through further explication is the opposite, that the singing of the song—namely, over the return of the waters that drowns the Egyptians, and the consequent interrupted song—takes place at the splitting of the Reed Sea for the Israelites.*]

Torah did not use [*negative*] language [*that celebrates through singing a song over the death of others*]: **"[the wicked] abandoned among the dead, / like bodies lying in the grave"**[90]—behold, this refers to the Egyptians who drowned in the sea, for behold [*these wicked ones which were likened to bodies in the grave; there is no longer a need for remorse in general over their drowning and loss, rather, on the contrary*] **"when the wicked perish it is a source of uplift"**[91] and then **"I will sing to YHVH, for He**

88. "God called the dry land Earth, and the gathering of waters He called Seas. And God saw that this was good" (Genesis 1:10).

89. Genesis 1:10.

90. Literally, "released among the dead, / like bodies lying in the grave / of whom You are mindful no more, / and who are cut off from Your care" (Psalm 88:6).

91. Literally, "When the righteous prosper the city exults; / When the wicked perish there are shouts of joy" (Proverbs 11:10).

has triumphed gloriously."[92] [*The question at hand is whether the Song at the Reed Sea relates primarily to the fall of the Egyptians or to the salvation of the Israelites. While Scripture portrays Moses as recounting the inspiration of the song as the former: "and what God did unto the army of Egypt, unto their horses, and to their chariots; how God made the water of the Red Sea to overflow them as they pursued after you, and how YHVH has destroyed them unto this day"(Deuteronomy 11:4), while the problematics of singing the Song as portrayed by the rabbinic exegesis aligns with the latter, namely, that all redemption has a human price.*]

As far as Israel is concerned, [*the rabbinic teaching of God interrupting the angelic chorus, decrying "But my handiwork is drowning in the sea and you want to sing songs!"*] they were judged through water [*so that the Egyptians were drowned by water in the final judgment. The rendering of this final judgment through water is strongly influenced by*] the case presented by the archangel of Egypt who claims "that both [*the Egyptians*] and [*the Israelites*] are idolatrous."[93] [*If both peoples are guilt of idolatry, then why are only Egyptians judged to drown in water?*]

This quandary is addressed in the verse **"and the one came not near the other all the night"**[94]—as the Zohar teaches this refers to the angels who cry out to each other, chanting antiphonally, and who are interrupted while the Israelites were passing through the sea, for at that moment [*at night*], the Israelites were being judged through water [*as to whether they would perish or not. After explaining that the singing of the Song of the Reed Sea appears to be inspired by the vanquishing of evil as manifest in the Egyptians through their judgment and drowning in the waters, the homily continues to explain, if so, why was "this was good" not included in the second day of creation? For the singing of the song, which is an expression of "this was good," comes from the returning of the waters to their natural levels that cover the Egyptians, which is a condition of the production of spreading waters that was realized on the second day of creation*].

This explains why **"this was good"**[95] was not uttered [*by the Creator*] on the second day [*of creation*]—since the [*creative production of the*] water was not fully formed in all its goodness, as explained by R. Shlomo

92. "Then Moses and the Israelites sang this song to YHVH. They said: 'I will sing to YHVH, for He has triumphed gloriously; / Horse and driver He has hurled into the sea'" (Exodus 15:1).

93. *Yalkut Shimoni* Exodus 240.

94. ". . . and it came between the camp of Egypt and the camp of Israel; and there was the cloud and the darkness here, yet gave it light by night there; and the one came not near the other all the night" (Exodus 14:20).

95. "God called the dry land Earth, and the gathering of waters He called Seas. And God saw that this was good" (Genesis 1:10).

Yitzhaki in his commentary.[96] [*And so despite the fact that the singing of the song was truly on account of the condition of the expansive flow of the waters as produced on the second day of creation, even so, since the waters were not fully formed in all their goodness, therefore "this was good" was not uttered. Recall the above challenge was raised: Why does Scripture use the language of the sea "returning to its normal state" when it would have been more logical, in light of these reflections, to use the language "restoring the waters to its implicit conditions" at the splitting of the Reed Sea? The resolution here is that this restoration of the waters drowning the Egyptians is also a condition of the sea's creation on the second day. Restoration of the waters is an act of Chesed (Grace) that extends, becoming more fully formed in all its goodness.*]

"[A]nd at daybreak the sea returned to its normative state"[97]—this quality of **"daybreak"** referred to here is Abraham's **"early morning,"**[98] as taught in the Zohar,[99] which is flowing grace and extension. [*Namely, the expansive flow of the waters in the morning that covered over the Egyptians in the Reed Sea and drowned them, these waters were Chesed (Grace), in keeping with the spiritual dynamics of this sphere of divine consciousness that is expansive and unlimited in its flow.*]

[*This is the issue of "morning" symbolizing Chesed (Grace), which reflects the*] truth that everything [*flowing from the non-manifest into manifestation within the created world*] is really about the hidden dimension of the spheres of divine consciousness and [*the unfolding of these*] worlds. However, when this flow [*of the limitless from the non-manifest into manifestation within the created world*] reached this lowly world [*then it has to become engarbed in the materiality of*] **"[d]arkness shall cover the earth."**[100] [*One then tends to see in every sentient being its material mani-*

96. Rashi ad loc Genesis 1:10. "He called Seas"—But does it not form one great sea? But it speaks of seas because the taste of fish which comes up from the sea at Acco is not the same as the taste of fish which comes up from the sea at Aspamia. "Consequently each division of the ocean has its special characteristics and therefore one may say the ocean is made up of different seas." See *Pentateuch with Targum Onkelos, Haphtaroth and Prayers for Sabbath and Rashi's Commentary*, vol. 1, trans. Rosenbaum, Blashki, Joseph (London: Shapiro, Valentine & Co., 1946), 257n2. The point here being that it was not a miracle given that the nature of creation itself was conditional at the moment of the Israelite's crossing the Reed Sea, given that the ocean is made up of different seas, each with their own impulses and qualities.

97. "Moses held out his arm over the sea, and at daybreak the sea returned to its normal state, and the Egyptians fled at its approach" (Exodus 14:27).

98. "And Abraham rose early in the morning, and saddled his ass, and took two of his young men with him, and Isaac his son; and he cleaved the wood for the burnt offering, and rose up, and went unto the place of which God had told him" (Genesis 22:3).

99. Zohar II:170b.

100. "Behold! Darkness shall cover the earth, / And thick clouds the peoples; / but on

festation rather than its spiritual qualia.]

[*Since "[d]arkness shall cover the earth" and this manifest world is indeed the place darkened through the coarseness of its material garbing in its concealment, thus*] it is called **"night"** [*and it is thus possible to use its scriptural referent of*] **"overnight"** that **"which appeared overnight and perished overnight."**[101] Meanwhile [*by contrast*] **"With the first of morning—light"**[102]—the time of the flow of illumination—and **"the men were sent off"**[103] [*namely, the Israelites who went forth at night into the sea*] so that in the morning they crossed into dry land **"as the sea reverted to its natural state at daybreak"**[104]—crashing down upon the Egyptians—then, at that moment, [*the angels*] sang the song [*over the restoring of the waters to their normative state*].

For behold, [*the verse reads*]: **"Then . . . will sing"**[105] [*in the future tense, namely, not at the moment when the Reed Sea split for the Israelites, rather*] after the full formation of goodness intended for water is actually realized [*that is, after the waters returned to their normative state, fulfilling the condition of their creation. This song was sung after the waters had fulfilled their conditions from creation and that is why*] **"this was good"**[106] was repeated on the third day of creation, after production of the waters was completely finished in the full formation of goodness. The repetition [*of "this was good"*] is a function of the poetic form of doubling in songs in general. [*Doubling within a song happens in one of two ways*]: either through doubling words, like "highly exalted"[107] or by doubling themes, [*so that even though there is multiplicity through doubling, still it all resolves itself in a*] disclosure of unity, as R. Shlomo Yitzhaki explained elsewhere.[108] [*This disclosure of such unity is manifest in the following twofold manner: first, in the essence of unity; secondly, in the manifestation of unity. Thus it takes duality to reveal non-duality.*]

[*The homily now shifts to address the cry that precedes the splitting of*

---

you YHVH shall shine, / And the Presence shall be seen over you" (Isaiah 60:2).

101. "Then YHVH said: 'You cared about the plant, which you did not work for and which you did not grow, which appeared overnight and perished overnight'" (Jonah 4:10).

102. "With the first of morning, the men were sent off with their pack animals" (Genesis 44:3).

103. Genesis 44:3.

104. "Moses held out his arm over the sea, and at daybreak the sea returned to its normal state, and the Egyptians fled at its approach" (Exodus 14:27).

105. Literally, "Then Moses and the Israelites sang this song to YHVH. They said: 'I will sing to YHVH, for He has triumphed gloriously; / Horse and driver He has hurled into the sea'" (Exodus 15:1).

106. "God called the dry land Earth, and the gathering of waters He called Seas. And God saw that this was good" (Genesis 1:10).

107. Exodus 15:1.

108. Rashi ad loc Exodus 15:1.

the Reed Sea and how it leads to the realization of the song that eventually will emerge. The cry in a moment of distress is what allows the broken heart to become more open to the spiritual support of 'emunah that deepens in relation to the rupture. As one enters into a state of merging into the spiritual support of 'emunah, one is not overcome by the distress at hand; rather, all focus of consciousness is aligned with the divine, to the point where the merging of devequt is the song itself which was finally sung. This Song at the Reed Sea was an inversion of the initial cry of distress that emerged at the beginning of the episode of redemption from Egypt.]

Behold, the exegesis on this verse [*teaches as follows*]: **"God did not lead them by way of the land of the Philistines, although it was nearer"**[109]—[*so the exegetical question that emerges in examining this verse is why use the subordinate conjunction "although"?*] The exegesis explains that the Holy One wanted the Israelites to encounter a danger so they would cry out—**"and God has brought to pass that human beings revere the One"**[110] [*which is the cry from distress that emerges from a place of existential fearfulness and vulnerability being confronted with something that is powerful enough to arouse the Kelippat Nogah, that is, the chance to make the conscious choice for deeper spiritual transparency*]. And if God would have led the [*Israelites*] **"by way of the land of the Philistines"**[111] [*there would not have been sufficient awe to elicit an inner cry of distress as a response to existential challenges. So "although it was nearer"*] and the [*Philistines would have*] already had the [*awesome*] experience [*of witnessing*] all ten plagues overwhelming the Egyptians, [*how could the Philistines then confront them? Given that no oppositional force remained before the Israelites, then they would be proceeding forward in their journey without any deeper sense of awe that would lead to an inner cry of distress and thus having the Israelites*] becoming overconfident. Without the challenging encounter, the Israelites would have fallen into a lower state of consciousness of **"Beware lest you forget."**[112] The Israelites needed the shock to wake up and remember divine consciousness.[113] Thus [*rather than having a direct divine route*] **"So God led the people roundabout, by way of**

---

109. "Now when Pharaoh let the people go, God did not lead them by way of the land of the Philistines although it was nearer; for God said, 'The people may have a change of heart when they see war, and return to Egypt'" (Exodus 13:17).

110. "I realized, too, that whatever God has brought to pass will recur evermore: / Nothing can be added to it / And nothing taken from it— / and God has brought to pass that human beings revere the One" (Ecclesiastes 3:14).

111. Exodus 13:17.

112. "Beware lest you forget YHVH, your God, in not keeping His commandments, and His ordinances, and His statutes, which I command you this day" (Deuteronomy 8:11).

113. *Tanchuma Exodus*, BeShalah 1.

the wilderness at the Sea of Reeds."[114] And so [*by way of that indirect route that took the Israelites through the Sinai desert amid its vulnerability toward the Reed Sea*], there at the precipice of the Reed Sea about to split [*when they had to jump into the water*] they encountered Amalek [*in the desert battling against them. So that after the Israelites experienced all these traumatic events along the way, only then*] **"the Israelites cried out to YHVH."**[115] In this way were the Israelites then gradually brought into serving the divine totality. So it follows there is this explanation of the verse: **"[they] may have a change of heart . . . and return to Egypt"**[116] [*namely, that the divine desire for the Israelites' cries of distress so that they would want to return*] teaches that they were already crying out in Egypt. [*Insofar as it was spiritually advantageous for Israel to have conditions that would be conducive to further spiritual evolution, they did not take the route of the Philistines; rather, as the Vitebsker writes in one of his letters of spiritual direction, there is a general principle that challenging times and economic conditions create the opportunities for strengthening and clarifying 'emunah.*[117] *This sense of deeper conviction and consciousness emerges in surrendering to the divine totality and the source of empowerment that is beyond what can be seen in the phenomenal world. It is a process of falling back into the totality and the field that supports everything that exists. 'Emunah then is the wisdom of letting go of what appears to be rationally and intuitively the source of one's own power. The irony in the narrative is that Pharaoh and the magnitude of his challenge is what draws the Israelites into deeper 'emunah. The path to the divine is away from the ego, but it takes a gradual shift in the mind so as not be vanquished by returning to Egyptian consciousness.*]

But what if the crying out [*of the Israelites over all the traumatic events they had experienced along the way*] was due merely to the fear of physical harm, which is the lower form of awe [*namely, the fear of vulnerability*]? There are different types of fear, as the Zohar explains,[118] wherein the highest level is a self-effacing awe in the face of overwhelming reality emerging from the essence and root of all worlds [*in its process of manifestation from the non-manifest*]—so the **"divine power can be recognized and dis-**

114. "So God led the people roundabout, by way of the wilderness at the Sea of Reeds. Now the Israelites went up armed out of the land of Egypt" (Exodus 13:18).

115. "As Pharaoh drew near, the Israelites caught sight of the Egyptians advancing on them. Greatly frightened, the Israelites cried out to YHVH" (Exodus 14:10).

116. "Now when Pharaoh let the people go, God did not lead them by way of the land of the Philistines although it was nearer; for God said, 'The people may have a change of heart when they see war, and return to Egypt'" (Exodus 13:17).

117. See *'Igeret* no. 12 in the forthcoming third volume in this series.

118. *Tiquney Zohar*, Tiqqun no. 30:73b, Zohar I:11b.

closed for all to see"[119] even under the material conditions of this world.

[*Behold, despite the cry of distress from the Israelites, which truthfully was due to fear of bodily trauma*] nevertheless, the first step and the beginning of one's [*spiritual*] path is still the lower, instinctual level of fear from the threat to one's well-being. Under such circumstances, one cries out to the divine source [*for in such a state of urgent existential fear there emerges the reality of a higher source of all that exists*]. One instinctively knows, beyond all reasoning and analysis, that such a higher power exists and holds the possibility of liberating, saving, and hearing that individual cry out. [*The conditions of danger and challenge motivates and compels one to experience some quality of 'emunah.*] As our blessed Sages teach: "the one who gives a selah to charity so that their child can live [*which appears to be inspired by an ulterior motive, even so*] that person is completely devoted," as the teaching suggests—such a person is completely devoted in their *'emunah* [*to their heart-center that has the compassionate nature to save lives*].[120]

Behold, it is a principle of tradition that our ancestors were redeemed as a reward for truth and *'emunah* [*as that instinctive trait of the heart-center exemplified by the crying out to a salvific force*] and **"the devoted one lives from that instinctive knowing of** ***'emunah.*****"**[121] So this is the right-hand pillar on which Torah is supported, so "Torah is said to rest upon a single support."[122] This is the principle of both lower and higher *'emunah,* enabling a kind of **"a stairway [that] was set upon the ground and its top reached to the sky."**[123] [*'Emunah is the foundation in reaching the lowest to the highest levels.*]

[*'Emunah is not merely the pillar upon which Torah is supported; rather, 'emunah is the ultimate reality and purpose of Torah*], for, behold, the entire Torah then is nothing but this instinctive *'emunah.* For the ultimate "purpose of knowing is *un*knowing."[124] [*This is what is meant* by *'emunah; namely, that is not cognitive and thus*] it is not conceptual [*and cannot be processed cognitively by the intellect. Rather, 'emunah exceeds cognitive capacities and knowledge, which is why the "purpose of knowing through Torah is unknowing" that is beyond the limitations of cognition. Just as*

119. Literally, "The Presence of YHVH shall appear, / And all flesh, as one, shall behold— / For YHVH has spoken" (Isaiah 40:5).

120. b*Pesachim* 8a.

121. Literally, "Lo, his spirit within him is puffed up, not upright, / But the righteous one is rewarded with life / For his fidelity" (Habakuk 2:4).

122. As the heathen demanded from Hillel, seeking conversion to Judaism.

123. "He had a dream; a stairway was set on the ground and its top reached to the sky, and angels of God were going up and down on it" (Genesis 28:12).

124. Ba'al Shem Tov, *Keter Shem Tov Hashalem*, ed. E. Shohat (New York: Kehot Publications, 2004), 3:7–8.

there are lower and higher levels of 'emunah, so too there are lower and higher degrees of parable relating to Torah. In the deepest sense Torah refers to the primordial, gnostic wisdom of the most Ancient One. The Wisdom that undergirds such a primordial Torah thus emerges from this foundation of 'emunah, as Scripture states]: **"True *Chokhmah* (Primordial Point) comes from No-Thing."**[125] [*Namely, the higher level of 'emunah cannot be perceived cognitively, and thus requires a turning of the mind toward a dissolution of the ego in contemplating No-Thing. This is not nonexistence or nihilism, for the mind recognizes that there remains hope—that it is a miracle. The miracle here is the possibility of gnosis whereby the mind can be healed and transformed from tainted existence and false belief. The self has to reformat its recognition of what was already hidden in plain sight*].

This [*Wisdom of Torah which is at its core 'emunah*] can only be obtained from the mouth of the master, whereby the receiving itself is [*more aligned with*] instinctive *'emunah.* By using the discursive mind, that ability to infer one matter from another [*which is not the same relaxed state of receptivity of Chokhmah (Primordial Point) transmitted by the master who is awakening consciousness in the disciple; rather*] what emerges [*in one's self*] is the [*capacity for*] *Binah* (Understanding). [*If somehow there is not any transmission of the higher level of 'emunah, it cannot be figured out merely by analysis. The sane mind on the level of nonconceptual 'emnuah is spontaneously extended by the mind that possess it, thus serving as the source of healing for others. Such consciousness is already extending love everywhere without exception, rather than projecting, which creates illusions of fear, vulnerability, and separation*].

[*Returning now to the matter of 'emunah based on the fear of punishment, this is the first step in spiritual growth toward a deeper divine service.*] In reality, **"the beginning of wisdom"**[126] [*of a deeper divine service which originates in*] *Chokhmah* (Primordial Point) and *'emunah* [*namely, emerging from the fear of retribution*] wherein **"the divine hand has wrought this"**[127] so that the Holy One would never be suspected of administering judgment without justice.[128] [*To have enough clarity of the sane mind requires the miracle of actually hearing and recognizing divine inspiration being broadcast continually.*]

[*Given that one is convinced "that the divine hand has wrought this,"*] thus [*such a person then*] returns to the One who administers the blow

125. Literally, "But where can wisdom be found; / Where is the source of understanding?" (Job 28:12).

126. "The fear of YHVH is the beginning of wisdom; a good understanding have all they that do thereafter; His praise endures for ever" (Psalm 111:10).

127. "Who knows not among all these, that the divine hand has wrought this?" (Job 12:9).

128. b*Berakot* 5b.

[*indicting the Holy One in the guise of*], **"YHVH roars from on high."**[129] [*This means that one cries out to God, which is a cry from bodily trauma, a feeling of vulnerability, and an awareness of a higher power, which can then bring one closer to divine service.*]

[*The conviction of 'emunah "that the divine hand has wrought this" compels one to such conviction, seeing that all sentient beings, their causes and events, all fall under the providence of their Creator and Provider.*] The individual is compelled to have *'emunah* in light of the expansive flow of all causal aspects of creation emanating from the divine source alone. This is an *'emunah* in precisely how the Holy One bestows life upon every sentient being and there is no other bestowing source present, extending into all causes, experiences, and effects of all such creatures. [*This homily is pointing to the higher 'emunah of extension that is more monist than non-dual, because without a critique of consciousness one cannot discover that awareness itself is non-dual; namely, a formless awareness. This divine inspiration is an extension of deeper love.*]

Even from the level of the four composite elements [*which encompasses all physical, material, and embodied sentient creatures and*] which are the enlivening sources of all these material elemental particles as the name YHVH. Yet this is deeply concealed in the four letters, as is known. [*The letters are symbols of these elements that appear in the lower worlds and are manifestations in subsequent stages beyond phenomenality. This gives a spiritual basis for the existence of everything.*] The deep concealment [*of these four elemental letters within material bodies*] leads to a loss and privation [*of vitality of existence that is present in the metaphysical realm of the four letters. Just as all sentient beings, except for their elements, have divine vitality that sustains them, so too is this the case*] in every human being. The human is composite of the elemental levels of embodiment and impulse [*while ruah (spirit) and neshamah (soul) levels are vital energies extending from that expansive divine source*]. This recognition itself of how much **"the self is intertwined returning to its source"**[130] within the Holy One is enough to cleave in truth to the divine. How could someone then [*go to the trouble of*] pursuing the King to simply pour out one's heart in vain, through the fear of punishment, mortality, and the fear of a painful afterlife, as well as other external forms of awe? [*This disposition seems counterproductive once*] one has *'emunah* in the divine vitality that is compounded

129. "You are to prophesy all those things to them, and then say to them: / YHVH roars from on high, / He makes his voice heard from His holy dwelling; / He roars aloud over his abode; / He utters shouts like the grape-traders, / Against all the dwellers on earth" (Jeremiah 25:30).

130. "If He set His heart on the human, if the One gather unto self one's spirit and breath" (Job 34:14).

within all things and has unlimited power,[131] as Scripture states: **"Raise up from the lowest possible."**[132] [*If a person has this consciousness characterized by non-dual gnosis, s/he cannot be led astray into those lower forms of 'emunah that remain in the realm of projection rather than extension. Its presence in creation is not eternal, but its nature is eternal.*]

[*Once one knows that the only reality is divine,*] if a person with such *'emunah* were to perish [*and die in the realm of extension and the nature of the mind is then withdrawn*], then only the divine vitality perishes. The root of this divine vitality, however, is immortal, eternal, and present in all things. When one reasons in this way, the only way to approach life is to support immersion [*of the mind*] within the presence of this divine reality. This transparency of divine reality is realized through the emanation of Torah even while embodied spiritual practice [*even if the material manifestation of the body is merely a garb. As long as the mind is embodied, it offers its own further extension. When the body dies, that extension is retracted, even though the mind in its pure form and in its very nature is extension*].

"For the commandment is a lamp"—namely, the materialization [*of enacting the sacral deed, which is illuminated by its source*]; whereas **"the teaching is a light"**[133]—that is, the illuminating source within the sacral deeds of spiritual practice [*namely, that Torah illuminates divine spiritual vitality within the very sacral deed itself*]. The divine letters and names [*Torah and sacral deeds*] animate [*and exist as true spiritual realities*] beyond any representation,[134] abstracted from any image. [*The divine source extends through the power of the forms of the letters in the divine name, but the name is merely the medium of the extension of the formless. This spiritual reality extends through Torah to sacral deeds, thus enabling these deeds to serve as a technique for maintaining immersion in the divine totality.*] Even though certain mind-states can be dropped and higher ones can be taken on without any image, there still remains a formlessness beyond conception. [*Thus when one performs an embodied, sacral deed, then one is actually conjoining the supernal light of Torah with its divine source. Behold, the divine names that are spreading into expansiveness have numerous degrees*], but the way such words are spoken orally are unlike their written form. [*This is because words that are spoken are expanded in their*

131. This *'emunah* can take one beyond the conventional sense and extent of justice according to the limits of consciousness. What is ultimate is not necessarily limited, so it has the capacity to free the individual from the soul's fate.

132. "YHVH deals death and gives life, / Casts down into Sheol and raises up" (1 Samuel 2:6).

133. "For the commandment is a lamp, / the teaching is a light, / And the way to life is the rebut that disciplines" (Proverbs 6:23).

134. b*Pesachim* 50a, regarding the nominations of Adonai is oral whereas YHVH is written. Beyond the phenomenal realm pointing to the noumenal realm.

oral articulation. Behold the divine names that are flowing forth are] even an expansion of "thinking" [*which tends to be even more expansive than an oral reading through the lips. In ascending each level*] thinking removes its form and then takes on a higher form [*for the higher the form, the more expansive it is*], wherein such elevated forms are beyond being written or spoken, except through [*the divine spiritual reality*], which is imperceptible. [*There is a hierarchy in the chain of being articulated here, so that the degree of concealment is proportional to its degree of manifestation. The point here is the extension reaches all the way through the ultimate degree of descent, but its presence there is not in the same quality that it is at higher stages in the extension process.*]

[*Now there is a return to the issue of 'emunah in the fear of retribution that leads to crying out. It is from this crying out that a person enters more deeply into the spiritual support system of 'emunah whose vitality sustains all sentient beings. This immersion is so deep that it reaches the point where one no longer focuses on the fear of retribution and instead focuses attention only upon immersion within the divine.*]

So then if one cries out for whatever the soul desires [*normally, such crying out relates to bodily, material, and worldly losses*], understand its connection to the name YHVH. This is the sustaining name, the four elements that bestows vitality on all material existence and everything thus far stated about *'emunah*. So now while engaged in prayer, one cleaves to the Holy One through the formless letters amid the oral expression and concentration of the heart, enabling one to surrender to the divine presence. This then is the only true portion that results through all of the effort.[135]

Once this reality becomes habituated within one's heart, then as one becomes capable of really transforming prayer at that level, immersion within the divine presence is the entire focus [*no longer distracted by fear of retribution*]. And in regard to the divine Original Will, there is nothing that stands in opposition to it, for everything from the beginning of creation was for the sake of this Original Will. [*As long as one's soul is caught up in anything other than the divine extension, then that particularistic point of view conditions what a person desires, and for that reason, nothing can come of it. To then reach the point where one is no longer limited by particular concerns, one needs to cultivate immersion that feedbacks the particular extension of the collective unconscious, inspired and empowered,*

---

135. This marks a radical monism (approaching non-dualism) which immerses in the vitality of all reality which underlies all phenomenality, thus transcending it toward beyond conception to the formless. When it comes to prayer on this level, then the aspirant merges with the reality which underlies all phenomenality [*hiyyut*].There is a contemplative method being prescribed here which is a contemplation of the four letters of YHVH, which are the four elements, compounded in the reality which underlies all phenomenality [*hiyyut*].

so that nothing can block it. This is possible only once the mind becomes sane, realizing that the only reality is the divine vitality. Prayer in its purest form is an extension of the divine totality when there is such clarity. When the mind is extending and not projecting, that is prayer—manifesting love, not judging others; including and not excluding others. Prayer in this case is a co-creative extension, that is, extending its inherent goodness through the very nature and purity of its own soul taking the form of the sane mind.]

This whole matter of *'emunah* [*and realizing the higher degree of this graduated path depends upon*], the mind-state by beginning with the fear of retribution [*through prayer that is a crying out in times of distress. This crying out is what then cracks open the heart, cultivating the conviction that everything is rooted in the divine*]. It is thus necessary to extract one's attention away from the construction of reality that is rooted in the creaturely appetites, preventing one from immersing in the reality that underlies all phenomenality. The more one habituates a discipline to this mind-state, the more one is able to cultivate *'emunah,* to the point where one realizes the very root of *'emunah* as Torah and **"wisdom preserves the one who possesses it."**[136] [*The play here in this verse from Ecclesiastes focuses upon the "enlivening vitality" of the letters in Torah that extend this light. Once the mind establishes a higher degree of 'emunah, then all is one, emerging through prayer. There is a necessity being articulated here for a gradual path toward the sanity of the pure mind, creating a space inside the heart. At some point down that graduated path, one begins to realize what this 'emunah really means.*]

This is [*the meaning of the teaching*]: "Torah was only given to the manna-eaters [*given that devoted ones can sustain themselves on the root of 'emunah*],"[137] because of the aforementioned *'emunah* beyond mind-concepts includes trust [*that is, the conviction that there would always be something to eat even after today's portion of manna was finished*]. Since the source is responsible for everything and is the ultimate power, implied in the verse: **"Descending to raise oneself up from even the lowest possible predicament,"**[138] as well as in the verse: **"his right hand on the rivers."**[139] The significance of the manna-eaters is that they consumed everything on the day it was given without storing any of it, for the One that

136. "For to be in the shelter of wisdom is to be also in the shelter of money, and the advantage of intelligence is that wisdom preserves the life of him who possesses it" (Ecclesiastes 7:12).

137. *Mechilta,* Beshalach 17.

138. "YHVH deals death and gives life, / Casts down into Sheol and raises up" (1 Samuel 2:6).

139. "[My faithfulness and steadfast love shall be with (David); his horn shall be exalted through My name.] I will set his hand on the sea, / his right hand on the rivers" (Psalm 89:25-26).

gives life is the One who gives sustenance.[140] On a daily basis, it is the vitality and sustenance, for everything is contained within it.

Behold, this aforementioned *'emunah* [*of vitality that sustains everything*] is also represented by the **"Torah"** [*because its purpose is*] to demonstrate and disclose the divine existence and how its sovereignty exists in all things. So it is obvious that Torah could only be given to manna-eaters, the ones who had a trusting *'emunah* [*to the point where they would not store away any manna for tomorrow but eat their portion each day, trusting in the knowledge that tomorrow there would always be more sustenance. This deep sense of trust comes from recognizing the reality of the divine vitality as reality, whereby one is no longer concerned with what appears to be real but actually depends upon this same divine reality. This deep trusting 'emunah of the manna-eaters enables action and extends in the mind to be fully present, pure, and sane rather than trusting in magical strategems, all of which are part and parcel of lower stages of religion*].

[*The homily now shifts from the deep trust of the manna-eaters to the lower level mind-state symbolized by Pharaoh.*] The meaning of the word **"PhaRAoh"** [*which symbolizes the enemy*] actually allows for something real to be disclosed [*the denotative meaning of the root, PRA*]—entrance-level fear of *yirah*. So that instead of dealing with one's enemies as oppositional forces without resolution, a trusting *'emunah* sees a more holistic perspective. Instead of being stuck in a permanent dialectic of opposition, one reorients by relating to an integration of both, leading to the disclosure of awe [*in the final letter of the Tetragram, namely, PRA"Heh, which represents the entrance level fear of Yirah to then realize more graduated levels of 'emunah*].

So this is [*the meaning of the verse*]: **"Now when Pharaoh let the people go"**[141]—namely, those that had been mired in exile as they began experiencing persecution, which is then how the purification process all began. For it is proper that one who begins such a process of spiritual purification receives aid. As the blessed Sages teach: "if you can open yourself just the eye of a needle [*and drop the tyranny of the egocentric mind*], then I will open a gate wide enough [*mephulash*] for chariots and wagons to pass through."[142] [*The widening of the gates of the egocentric mind needs to be pierced, so that it can move beyond projection to extension. By glimpsing a piece of the totality, the mind can then escape the prison of projection into*

---

140. b*Ta'anit* 8b.

141. "Now when Pharaoh let the people go, God did not lead them by way of the land of the Philistines although it was nearer; for God said, 'The people may have a change of heart when they see war, and return to Egypt'" (Exodus 13:17).

142. "Open up for me no more than a needlepoint, I'll make such a wide opening that horses and carriages can enter through it" (*Song of Songs Rabbah* 5:3).

an extension of divine love.]

Behold, [*even though the Israelites began their process of spiritual purification, and it was only fitting that divine aid would come through to open a widening gate of the mind, still*] the verse continues: **"God did not lead them by way of the land of the Philistines [*PHeLiSHtim*]"**[143]—which is "a path wide open" [*mePHuLaSH, which is a spiritual support system of 'emunah rooted in the vitality sustaining all sentient creatures; this is an 'emunah wide enough to encapsulate everything until the end. But as beginners,*] the Israelites were still not used to the work, and thus were still in need of sufficient repetition to habituate themselves in this trusting *'emunah* [*in the fear of retribution to cry out from a place of distress. This is the devotional service of ejecting the projection and choosing the projection of divine love. This is what opens the heart to trust that everything is sustained through its interconnectivity with the divine totality*]. Through such a trial, they become habituated by an even deeper trusting *'emunah*, especially in transition from the time of their exilic captivity in Egypt [*which exemplified this earlier level of 'emunah in the fear of retribution, and its accompanying cries of persecution, then graduating to the next level of 'emunah that comes with*] liberation. That is why the One exposed the Israelites to such trying situations and skirmishes in order to strengthen them with the experience they needed to then rest securely in a more trusting *'emunah.* [*There is a tension between the gradual path and the immediate path. Grasping initial stages of the gradual path is crucial, otherwise one cannot be truly qualified for the immediate path of 'emunah.*]

So [*this sentiment is then further*] expressed in the verse: **"God said, 'If the people are not tested, they may backslide to 'Egyptian consciousness' and have a change of heart in being exposed to war"**[144]—as the aforementioned exegesis suggested, [*that God purposefully exposed the Israelites to inner war in order to encourage returning to core values in teshuvah, causing them to cry out in distress*] so that if the Israelites traversed the roundabout route, they would not be in a position for cultivating that trusting *'emunah.*

Or [*the verse*] can be interpreted as follows, regarding the word **"PHaRAoh"**—namely, the evil impulse embodied as the "nape of the neck" [*ORePH*].[145] This is known from the teaching of our blessed Sages regarding "the great sense of remorse of evildoers"—when the evil impulse leaves them alone and is no longer inciting them, only then does remorse set in

143. "Now when Pharaoh let the people go, God did not lead them by way of the land of the Philistines although it was nearer; for God said, 'The people may have a change of heart when they see war, and return to Egypt'" (Exodus 13:17).

144. Exodus 13:17.

145. Shmuel Vital, *Sha'ar haPesukim*, Parashah Vayeshev.

[*and they wonder why they are not growing*]. So they falsely represent themselves with a purified heart, emptied of the evil impulse, yet, as our blessed Sages teach, "when strength fails the thief, he assumes the guise of a pacifist [*uninterested in thievery*]."[146] [*One is still bound here by the mind of projection, notwithstanding moments of reprieve from intense disturbance.*]

[*Given that the hearts of the Israelites appear emptied and nullified,*] the evildoers are then surprised at not having reached a more graduated level of maturity just because they are no longer feeling tested. But in reality they have yet to defeat the evil impulse. It is only through exposure to war that they are likely to flee [*back to being mislead by the evil impulse*]. This is what is meant by the verse: **"Now when Pharaoh let"**[147]—the evil impulse; **"the people go"**[148]—the enslaved spiritual attributes [*incited by the evil impulse*]; then it should come as no surprise that **"God did not lead them by way of the land of the Philistines"**[149] [*which is a wider opening, MePHuLaSh for 'emunah*]—being led around in a more roundabout way, as indicated in the verse: **"God said, 'If the people are not tested, they may backslide to "Egyptian consciousness" and have a change of heart in being exposed to war.'"**[150] [*Thus, it was premature to walk through the wider opening that is MePHuLaSh for 'emunah*] until they had habituated themselves to an *'emunah* that was more firmly fixed in their hearts[151] [*and thus it will not be dislodged when exposed to war*]. The graduated path [*HeRgeL*] is derived from the language of "leg" [*ReGeL*], namely, that one proceeds step by step, until one reaches the spiritual destination. Once one has chosen to establish this *'emunah* to be firmly fixed in their heart, there is nothing that stands in the way. [*Their ability to recognize the reality beyond their phenomenal world, while it did give the Israelites a basis for 'emunah, did not eradicate the structure of their egocentric minds. The whole basis of creation requires the agency of those with 'emunah to serve as the extension into the manifest world.]*

And this is meaning of the aforementioned verse: **"'Why do you cry out to Me? . . . to go forward.'"**[152] As R. Shlomo Yitzhaki's comment

146. b*Sanhedrin* 22a.

147. "Now when Pharaoh let the people go, God did not lead them by way of the land of the Philistines although it was nearer; for God said, 'The people may have a change of heart when they see war, and return to Egypt'" (Exodus 13:17).

148. Exodus 13:17.

149. Exodus 13:17.

150. Exodus 13:17.

151. Literally, "like a nail that is hammered in."

152. "Then YHVH said to Moses, 'Why do you cry out to Me? Tell the Israelites to go forward'" (Exodus 14:15).

suggests,[153] do not stand in one place, rather venture forward [*into higher levels of*] *'emunah*, even right into the sea [*that is, in true cleaving with the force which sustains and animates all sentient beings*]. What is the sea compared to divine being? What then is the meaning of their awareness of divine presence? So that if they would perish and drown, then what would be the meaning of their perishing? In reality, there is no such perishing, seeing that the divine vitality is eternal [*coursing through all sentient beings at all times. The vitality is what extends from the source of the divine totality through all levels of manifestation. It is not what appears to exist, but what really exists is the divine totality, which can be concealed, but it cannot be eliminated or damaged in any way for it remains imperishable*].[154]

Once [*the Israelites*] had *'emunah*, they cried out to the divine from the depth of the heart—all *'emunah* boils down to one thing—that life and death, **"Raising up from the lowest possible point"**[155]—it all comes from the divine. Once a person looks deep enough inside their heart, it is possible to go beyond all manifestation to connect with the [*non-manifest*] Wisdom that is *'emunah*, which precedes creation itself. [*The miracle here is that a person would experience the fearlessness of freedom, rather than being trapped in the identification with the perishable.*]

This is what is behind R. Shlomo Yitzhaki's explanation: "The *'emunah* they had in Me was strong enough to break through the sea"—if the Israelites are holding fast to *'emunah* governing everything, which is Torah, and the creative force itself [*so that*] creation could be renewed [*to redeem them*]. [*Rabbi Shlomo Yitzhaki's explanation is more in line with the rabbinic theology of the divine as a being beyond the world that can come to one's aid through conviction, whereas the Vitebsker sees the spiritual vitality as the only reality.*]

Therefore our blessed Sages taught that Nachshon and the tribe of Judah were the first to jump into the Reed Sea [*even before it had split*], and for this [*act of 'emunah*] their tribe would become the royal Davidic lineage

153. Rashi ad loc Exodus 14:15. "'Why do you cry out to Me?—[*There is no mention that he prayed to God concerning this, but*] this teaches us that Moses stood in prayer. [*Whereon*] the Holy Blessed One said to him, 'It is no time now to pray at length, when Israel is placed in trouble.'"

154. There is a clear tension here between the ethnocentric suffering of the Israelites and the suffering of all sentient beings, which includes the Egyptians. If the Egyptians are in peril, would they not also cry out to the divine? If prayer is a universal need, then surely it applies to the Egyptians as well as the Israelites.

155. "YHVH deals death and gives life, / Casts down into Sheol and raises up" (1 Samuel 2:6).

"and the Sovereign rule is over all,"[156] even over Israel's sovereignty.[157] [*The act of 'emunah is empowering, as the Vitebsker discusses elsewhere in Parashah Bo' relating to its cultivation in the deeply devoted one.*] This is expressed in the exegesis: "Judah has Sovereign holiness over all of Israel,"[158] for it is by way of messianic consciousness perceiving the divine will that spontaneously jumping into the sea is viable.

[*This homily now returns to the matter of supernal 'emunah, such that*] everything regarding *'emunah* finds its beginnings in that outcry and fear of loss [*so foundational to the human condition*] and the feminine quality of being human—from this [*vulnerable and open point*] flows the song, thus declined grammatically as feminine, namely: **"This song."**[159] [*From this vulnerable, feminine point is 'emunah integrated through the higher masculine point of 'emunah.*]

Notice how [*in relation to the Song at the Reed Sea*] the verse does not say **"sang"**; rather, it says **"shall sing"**[160] [*which reflects a deeper heart center*]. According to R. Shlomo Yitzhaki, it arose in [*Moses's*] heart that he shall sing, thus the letter *Yo"D* [*of Chokhmah (Primordial Point)*] was added from the heart.[161] This is the *'emunah* which begins to emerge in the depth of the heart [*from the vulnerability of the feminine. So the letter Yo"D of Chokhmah (Primordial Point) is*] **"Torah light"**[162] [*which sustains "the commandment is a lamp," for the former light is immersion in the divine, through which the human enters into foundational 'emunah*].

It is also the **"anointing dew"**[163] [*of Torah, with its unique*] capacity to revitalize the dead and bring about all forms of transformation [*like the splitting of the Reed Sea, which is all done through the power of Torah's luminous capacity encapsulated in its Yo"D of Chokhmah (Primordial Point), which is the root of 'emunah*].

This then is the real source [*for the teaching of our blessed Sages which began in interpreting "then shall sing," which opens the Song at the Reed*

156. "YHVH has established His throne in Heaven, / and the Sovereign rule is over all" (Psalm 103:19).

157. This could also be read to suggest that the rule of Israel and all similar ethnocentrisms is superseded by the evolving messianic consciousness that recognizes that the center of divinity is everywhere.

158. *Yalkut Psalms*, no. 799.

159. "Then Moses and the Israelites sang this song to YHVH. They said: 'I will sing to YHVH, for He has triumphed gloriously; / Horse and driver He has hurled into the sea'" (Exodus 15:1).

160. Exodus 15:1.

161. See Rashi ad loc Exodus 15:1.

162. Literally, "For the commandment is a lamp, / The teaching is a light, / And the way to life is the rebuke that disciplines" (Proverbs 6:23).

163. "O, let Your dead revive! / Let corpses arise! / Awake and shout for you, / You who dwell in the dust!— / For Your dew" (Isaiah 26:19).

Sea] for revitalizing the dead from Torah [*through the source of its vitality that is not perishable*]—and it is precisely from Torah [*and its luminous capacity within its Yo"D of Chokhmah (Primordial Point)*] which is *'emunah* itself. [*This higher level of 'emunah has creative power, in the place of the divine; such a devoted one can override any specific set of conditions in the natural world.*]

[9.3]. *Parashah Beshalach* (Exodus 13:17–17:16)

QUESTIONS FOR REFLECTION:

1. Given the cynicism and doubt that plagues you so often in your quest for connecting to your spiritual life, will the fear of punishment help or hinder your search for deeper convictions?

2. In what context do you feel most open to experiencing the root of *'emunah* in the vitality that enlivens and renews everything?

3. How might you explore entering into the rootedness of *'emunah* by confronting your concern over mortality, the abyss and privation when visiting someone who is terminally ill? Or when witnessing a new birth?

Leviticus

[10.1]. *Parashah Acharey Mot* (Leviticus 16:1–18:30)

INTRODUCTION TO HOMILY:

One of the characteristics of all forms of wisdom is the sense of dissatisfaction with the state of being within which we find ourselves and the recognition of the need to improve this state through some form of "meta-programing," which involves a transformation of energies through certain conscious practices. Through Rei'YaH, one can recognize the robotic nature of untransformed human consciousness and personality—which requires a transformation of energies through certain conscious practices. Who a person is depends upon a particular nature and form of energy that enlivens them at any given moment. This energy is known in Hasidism as 'hayyut.' To the extent that a person can learn to draw to himself/herself finer qualities of energy, then one can ameliorate his/her state of being, and this capacity is known as "meta-programming." In the terminology of Kabbalah, the cosmological term 'qelipot' is appropriated by the Vitebsker to represent confused states of consciousness that are poorly programmed. The initial step is the awareness that one is embedded in a poorly programmed form of consciousness. At the very moment that a form of poorly programed energy enters the mind, it already characterizes this person's state of consciousness. But the poorly programmed state only becomes actualized when it is outwardly expressed in action. To envision the taxonomy of the soul, there is a tendency in early Hasidism to shift into language of 'nefesh habehami,' literally, "animal soul" and the nefesh hasikhli, literally, "divine soul," which are based in kind of mind-body dualism that can be improved through meta-programming. The shift away from anthropocentrism within contemporary spirituality suggests that there are higher states of spiritual involution, so that nefesh habehami suggests "surface-soul" and the 'nefesh habehami' suggests "deeper-soul" in which the powers of reflection have become activated, in both cases corresponding to developmental stages. What is "surface" in the soul is imprinted first, and then supplemented by what is next and imprinted afterward and thus deeper. The greater the development, the greater the depth. The radical amazement of YiRaH is then also to be understood within these developmental stages. The conventional stages of human development are mediated by the experience of being an animal on the earth, but the human being has the potential of more evolved forms of angelic consciousness known as extraterrestrial. The potential to actualize forms of consciousness are not limited to the immediate needs of being an embodied creature on earth, and actually go beyond the immediate needs of being an earthbound creature. These higher forms of being are generally subsumed by what the Vitebsker as 'nefesh hasikhli,' which is more generally known as 'nefesh haElohit.' The fight and flight of the reptilian brain represents the YiRaH of the "surface-soul" and early stages of development, whereas the next stage in YiRaH of the "surface-soul" is when the warmer qualities of the mammalian brain are actualized. The former makes one wary, while the latter bonds, but are still surface or terrestrial levels of the 'nefesh habehimi.' Tempering the impulses of YiRaH and Compassion (Ahavah) comes with the deeper reflectivity that brings them under the auspices of deeper forms of consciousness that serve higher goals than mere physical survival. The energy that reaches a person has to pass through a series of veils. So then the construction of human experience is mediated by the seven veils that determine the quality of energy. These are a series of stages of veiling which mediate the intensity of this pure unlimited light, which manifests in a particular form of experience that human beings can have. Human experience results from a process that simultaneously limits and extends the pure, unlimited light—this diluted form of light as the emanation of the world. This very process produces surface levels of consciousness in which, from a higher perspective, there is a great deal of confusion and lack of clarity concerning the reality of one's self and the cosmos. For further spiritual evolution to occur, a return trip through these series of veils must take place, in order for any such meta-programming to be possible. Liberation from a constricted state of consciousness requires returning to an earlier state of nonexistence that can be understood as a gap—that is, a gap between the present and subsequent states. In this "transitional gap" (z̲imz̲um), what is regained is a state characterized by the fundamental plasticity of human potential. It is out of such "human plasticity" (homer ha'yuli) that new forms can emerge through meta-programming. Thus the recognition of what Gurdjieff called "the terror of the situation"—that is, the world is run by people who are asleep, limited, and controlled by superficial stages of consciousness—becomes beneficial to the aspirations of a human being who wishes to evolve further, or it stimulates and motivates one to disengage from the limits of one's present formation and regain access to the meta-programmer. This all points to the quest for inner freedom to recreate oneself.

[10.2]. *Parashah Acharey Mot* (Leviticus 16:1–18:30)

HOMILY:

[*The Vitebsker was asked a*] question regarding the following teaching: **"Pray for the welfare of the regime."**[1]

The master opens [*in response by interpreting*] the verse: **"YHVH spoke to Moses after the death of the two sons of Aaron . . . when they drew too close to the presence of YHVH,"**[2] and the interpretation proffered by R. Shlomo Yitzhaki, *o.b.m.*, is explained [*regarding why this verse is especially cautionary in terms of mortality*] by the parable of the latter doctor who was more effective with the patient than the former.[3]

And he goes on to explain the matter: **"Akavia b. Mahale'el said: Reflect on three things and you will not come into the grip of sin. Know where you came from,"**[4] and he further offered this explanation of **"Know where you came from"**—this is the way people normally speak by separating ideas into two sections. In the beginning the *Tannah* teaches that it is typical to ask a visitor on first greeting them: Where are you coming from and what do you need? It is not sufficient to merely realize that a person is but a visitor, rather the whole basis of existence is of lowly origin—from the moment of birth to burial. In [*the course of existence*] one takes on a serious attitude[5] [*despite being lowly*] to give an accounting to the Supreme King of kings, the Holy One. [*First, notice that every person is merely traveling through existence and impermanent; secondly, all things that appear most meaningful and attractive are actually illusory, thus there is an urgent*

---

1. "Rabbi Hanina, Deputy High Priest, said: Pray for the welfare of the regime; but for fear of it people would swallow one another alive. . ." (m*Avot* 3:2). This mishnah may have been chosen as a function of its commonplace study between Passover and Feast of Weeks when each week is dedicated to one chapter of m*Avot*.

2. "YHVH spoke to Moses after the death of the two sons of Aaron who died when they drew too close to the presence of YHVH" (Leviticus 16:1).

3. Rashi ad loc Leviticus 16:1—"What is this [*statement*] intended to tell us? [*Namely, why is it at all stated when God spoke this to Moses?*] R. Elezar b. Azaraiah explained this by way of a parable: [*It may be compared to the case of*] a sick person whom the doctor visited. The doctor said to him: 'Do not eat cold [*things*] nor sleep in a damp place!' Another doctor, who was more punctilious than the first, came and said to him: 'Do not eat cold [*things*] nor sleep in a damp place so you do not die as so-and-so died!' [*Certainly*] this [*the latter doctor's advice*] put him on his guard more than the former [*with a stronger warning*]; that is why Scripture states: 'after the death of the two sons of Aaron'."

4. "Akaviya b. Mahale'el said: Reflect on three things and you will not come into the grip of sin. Know where you came from, where you are going, and before whom you must give account. Where you came from: a fetid drop. Where are you going: to a place of dust, worm and maggot. And before whom you must give account: the Supreme King of kings, the Holy One" (m*Avot* 3:1).

5. Literally, "peeks into the great mountains."

need to separate oneself from such manifestations.]

From the structural repetition present in this aforementioned *Mishnah,* a moral lesson emerges—when one is born "accustomed to finery,"[6] regarding Akaviya b. Mahale'el the blessed Sages teach: **"for the Temple Court was never shut against the face of any man in Israel so wise and God-fearing as Akaviya b. Mahalale'el."**[7]

What the fear of the misdeed refers to is the misdeed itself rather than the punishment that may come from it. As is often explained, punishments are healing for the soul and they scour away the harmful effects of misdeeds. Surely, one should be more in fear of the cause of the damage itself rather than the remedy [*namely, the suffering that may be required for healing*].

And indeed anyone can understand that **"a living one should take it to heart"**[8]—that the core of a human being is their interiority and vitality, so once the vitality departs then the body is merely an inert corpse. And from this principle one can infer that wherever a person's awareness is located that is where a person actually is and what the person is identifying with. [*The divine vitality is not perishable but takes on difference forms; rather, it is only the embodied nature of reality.*]

[*If it all takes place in the awareness of consciousness*] as one contemplates a transgression, then one is already identifying and responding a misguided energy that consumes them, as the blessed Sages teach: "a person would not commit a transgression unless under acting on a corrupting influence."[9] Whenever a sacred mind-state is absent, then a distorted mind-state takes its place. The unwise energy that taints it emerges through such identification. There is no emptiness in the world—a pure mind-state is pure, and an impure mind-state is impure. [*It is the behavior that results from an impure, unwise, distorted or ignorant mind-state, which is the 'qelipot' or oppositional force. If you are contemplating a misdeed then you have already fallen into the 'qelipot' through that very identification. This is the descent that concerns the Vitebsker. One can be mindful and still act*

6. b*Shabbat* 10b.

7. "Akaviya b. Mahalale'el testified to four opinions. They answered: 'Akabya, retract these four opinions that you have given and we will make you Head of the Tribunal of Israel.' He said to them: 'Better that I be called a fool all my days than that I be made a godless creature before God even for an hour; for they shall not say of me, he retracted for the sake of the office' . . . whereon they laid him under a ban: and he died while he was yet under the ban, and the court stoned his coffin. R. Judah said: God forbid that it should be Akaviya that was put under the ban!—for the Temple Court was never shut against the face of any man in Israel so wise and sin-fearing as Akaviya b. Mahalale'el . . ." (m*'Eduyot* 5:6).

8. "It is better to go to a house of mourning than to a house of feasting: for that is the end of every human, and a living one should take it to heart" (Ecclessiastes 7:2).

9. b*Sotah* 3a.

in distorted ways, so that deeper discernment is necessary to cultivate as part of the spiritual practice.]

Every embodied being is dependent upon aspects of consciousness for its existence that enlivens them. So the energy present within a misdeed is given as a test for those aspiring toward righteousness [*as well as impeccability that includes devotionality*]. Throughout all the worlds created for the sake of the righteous ones, the energy of the misdeed challenges a person by benefiting or enjoying it. Even in merely thinking about the transgression actually descends to the point of actually identifying with that corrupting influence [*given that a person is defined from moment to moment through their deeds. What embodies a person's mind is the body, whereas the inner experience is the form, the sense of opportunity to be drawn to the energy and desirability of transgression. The sensitivity to avoid and feel repulsion by the vitality of the transgression is necessary; there is a mental process of acknowledging its pleasure, which is the contamination itself. This marks a shift from the sane mind to the insane mind. Ultimate knowledge, while unconventional, does not then give license to unwise or unethical behavior. The zaddik must continue to act with impeccability*]. Every act is formed by consciousness and enlivened by it, even the transgression, so that this damaging energy becomes the very person.

In reality, the negative forces have their roots in the very process of creation and become necessitated by divine restraint. From this restraint something new is initiated if creation is to occur. [*The cause of oppositional forces themselves extends all the way back to creation, which requires withdrawing the extension of the holiness of Limitless Light. This is the moment between the withdrawal of Limitless Light and the extension of the middle line where oppositional forces find their origin within the residual light.*]

Confusions and distortions emerge from these restraints within creation, which conceal the nature of reality. [*And were it not for the confusion, then there would be no separation between self and the divine.*] This is rooted in the very first moments of manifestation and self-concealment of the absolute within creation. From this spontaneous self-concealment of the absolute, then creation begins [*to unfold*] through the appearance of objects. All of manifestation and the appearance of all objects springs forth in a manner similar to the way[10] a plant emerges from its seed, and the way that "a chick emerges from the egg."[11] For the process of becom-

10. Involution is the way the divine descends into hylic matter, which is a spiritual evolution of consciousness.

11. See parallel in R. Dov Baer (Maggid) of Mezeritch, *Maggid Devarav leYa'akov*, ed. Rivah Schatz-Uffenheimer, nos. 56, 60, 78, 178, 180. Compare with the reiterations of the Maggid's teachings in a disciple of the Zlotchover Maggid, R. Meshullam Feibush Heller of Zabarzah, see Miles Krassen, *Uniter of Heaven and Earth* (New York: SUNY Press, 1998), 169–70. Consider also the correspondence between R. Meshuallam Feibush

ing, involving change from one form to another, cannot take place until the earlier form completely transcends and disappears.[12] The seed is compelled, at first, to perish, and similarly in the case of the egg, subsequently the remaining primordial matter that has the potential to change takes on a new form in the creation of the chick and the plant.

In the intermediate stage [*like the space between thoughts, or causal body, in one's mind-stream*], in that gap between its old and new form, where neither form exists it is called, **"No-thing,"**[13] which is the condition of emergence [*in the chain of being*] as alluded to in the verse:[14] **"Wisdom from within No-thing"**[15] as in the beginning of the chain of creation. [*Creation is a binary process, whereby the nature of reality is pulsating in and out of this duality, which is z̲imz̲um itself.*] The space that once was and the form that will be is then No-thing. Nothing new or different can emerge unless is it preceded by this gap; thus, it is seen to be returning to this continuous condition of No-thing.[16] As I have explained elsewhere,[17] a person can bring about miraculous transformations by descending into a condition self-effacement and No-Thing, which is *Chokhmah* (Primordial Point). [*There is an assumption here that the creative power of the miraculous happens when such a person will shape the conditions of existence once emerging from this gap. The will of the zaddik has the power to shape and form their own return to No-Thing.*]

[*In contrast to the state of pure consciousness of the zaddik who can return to No-Thing,*] the unconscious nature of the human mind is, unfortunately, like [*the glamor that attracts the mind known as*] **"the ceaselessly gleaming fiery sword"**[18]—so that the natural state of holiness [*without confusion*] is then rendered profane, purity becomes impure, negative forces cause harm to the human condition [*as a result of the glamor that attracts the mind to confusion*]. For once the holiness and reverence of heaven slip away, one is no longer present in human consciousness and returns to its

---

and R. Joel in Tiberias between 1777–81, see ibid., 3.

12. There has to be a gap between the original and new form, (what neo-Darwinists call a "missing link") and that gap is found in hylic matter. It is paraphrased in: "Fool! The seed that you plant will not live unless it dies" (1 Corinthians 15:36).

13. Literally, "But where can wisdom be found; / Where is the source of understanding?" (Job 28:12).

14. Involution here is to be understood as form of contraction [*z̲imz̲um*] whereby pure formless divinity involves itself in primordial matter.

15. Job 28:12.

16. "No-Thing" it is to be understood as primordial matter which can take on any form.

17. See *Peri haAretz*, Parashah Vayeshev, Parashah Vayigash 1.

18. Literally, "God drove Adam out, and stationed east of the garden of Eden the cherubim and the fiery ever-turning sword, to guard the way to the tree of life" (Genesis 3:24). This "fiery ever-turning sword" represents the ceaseless mental characteristics of the mind carelessly thinking

state of the emerging chain of being. Then the human subjectivity changes and is taken over by negative energies.[19] When energy and subjectivity lack holiness, then the body is subject to the negative impulses. And then that body in such a condition can do more harm. The body being more coarse than the subjective energies, and consequently may cause harm. In this mental condition, the "fear of transgression" becomes the impulsive cause of harmful actions. The very moment an aspirant loses focus of divine consciousness, then one's condition slips away, which is a greater blemish than the punishment it incurs. And this punishment itself is a form of healing. [*For a transgression to occur, the mind has to have become saturated by the distorting energy of the transgression. So that when one transgresses, one becomes the oppositional force itself.*]

So this spiritual virtue known as "weariness of transgression" derives directly from *Chokhmah* (consciousness). Whoever is so wise as to assume the condition of No-thing in relation to the divine vitality, one then becomes self-aware of being a new creature every day,[20] as Scripture states: **"'You are my child, / [at this very moment] I have birthed you this day'"**[21]—thus one will be very wary of the "fear of transgression." Therefore a wise person knows that whatever form s/he has assumed, is only an appearance that occurs because of divine veiling. The basis of this fear then is [*that one can deal with the changes so long as one has the knowledge that everything that appears does not have any independent existence; rather, it is dependent upon the constant pulsation of the absolute continuously and concealing itself. The creation makes one forget the source; but if every moment of appearance is linked to the No-thing. then one does not become confused*].

This is what our blessed Sages had in mind [*in mishnah 'Edoyut*] regarding Akaviya b. Mahalale'el: [*he had these levels of*] *Chokhmah* (consciousness) leads to "fear of transgression" wherein one follows from the other—and so [*here in mishnah* m*Avot this is precisely what he is referring to when he*] repeats the teaching, where [*Akaviya*] begins with the contextual meaning and afterward [*Akaviya*] then goes on to explain the matter: you have come **"from a decomposing droplet."**[22] Namely, the droplet [*has to shed its pure form as a drop, so that in*] becoming something new; it has to pass through a gap, where it is not what it was and not what it shall be-

19. Literally, "the harmful spirit of impurity."

20. Constantly renewing the self.

21. "Let me tell of the decree: / YHVH said to me, / 'You are my child, / I have fathered you this day'" (Psalm 2:7).

22. "Akaviya b. Mahale'el said: Reflect on three things and you will not come into the grip of sin. Know where you came from, where you are going, and before whom you must give account. Where you came from: a fetid drop. Where are you going: to a place of dust, worm and maggot. And before whom you must give account: the Supreme King of kings, the Holy One" (m*Avot* 3:1).

come. **"And where are you going"**[23] refers to the second condition of non-existence, which is a subsequent transformation of form, which involves a shift from pure being to a state of impure, devolving form. [*Before each transformation being read here in the Mishnah, there has to be a gap of no-thingness, before becoming an embryo, and then there is another transformation passing through another gap.*]

The way to understand the distinction here between the original loss of form [*from the droplet to the human form*] is called "effacement" [*'ayin, which is transformation into a pure form*]; while the subsequent loss of pure form to its devolving form, is called "to where" [*'AN, which is transformation into an impure form*]. The latter theo-linguistic form is lacking the mediating letter *Y"oD*,[24] which symbolizes the element of holiness[25] that is present in the transformed state. In the case of devolution, the sparks of divine energy symbolized by the aleph emanate through the emergence of the final *N"uN*, which descends lower into the realms of inconscient decomposition. [*When the seeker is in a pure mind state of Chokhmah, there is a cognizance of the divine vitality, the very energy within an enlightened state of awareness, where there is not only a transcendence of objects, but also there is an awareness of this divine life force that becomes all objects. This is an empty state, which is a holy state, through its knowledge of the divine. When there is a state of confusion, the sparks of divine vitality manifest through extension into the manifest objects themselves, without a sense of the divine presence.*]

Our Sages teach: **"So then you will never fall into the grips of diminishment"**[26]—for "hands" [*that latch onto the behavior, which*] are the sacred effects of love and reverence. [*One will not stray if one understands the difference between the two forms of nothingness.*]

As far as reverence is concerned, there is still a fear of punishment and death, as our blessed Sages teach: "There is no death without transgression"[27]—this fear [*of death*] is called an external reverence and applies universally to all human beings. As the blessed Sages teach: **"Those among Pharaoh's courtiers who revered YHVH's word"**[28]—this reverence is a fear of punishment—a fear losing one self [*which is egocentrism. This is the mind-state of 'qelipot' consciousness*].

---

23. m*Avot* 3:1.

24. R. Hayyim Vital, *Sefer 'Etz Ha'Da'at Tov*, Parashah Ki Tissa.

25. Literally, "the holy *shekel*" that has to be redeemed. Without this mediating letter, which represents the consciousness of holiness, the involution of the divine energy in Aleph is not redeemed, thus there is no spiritual evolution possible.

26. m*Avot* 3:1.

27. b*Shabbat* 55a.

28. "Those among Pharaoh's courtiers who revered YHVH's word brought their slaves and livestock indoors to safety" (Exodus 9:20).

But at its core, reverence comes from the consciousness that [*divinity is*] **"the core and root of all worlds,"**[29] which is indicated in the verse that states: **"and the divine dominion of the One extends over all"**[30]—so that all forms of awe and reverence include the painful punishments and death that eradicate the diseases of the soul. These consequences that scour the self from the soul are forms of healing and spiritual medicine for the soul. It can heal the soul from every affliction. [*It is that sense of recognition that there are painful rectifications that must be traversed as part of the refinement process is what leads to fearfulness. This is a wise type of fear.*]

For a [*wise*] person whose good lies in the divine presence is not embittered by the external forms of fear. As the blessed Sages teach about the verse: **"and found it very good"**[31]—"this is death."[32] As the Zohar explains how frequently a person is shocked into awakening so as to return to have the consciousness of the divine presence because of this external reverence, thus it was very good.[33] [*Rather than becoming embittered by 'qelipot'-consciousness, when one is connected to the pure mind-state, then the suffering experienced in life draws one closer to the source of the divine vitality. From the descent, one is motivated to ascend and uplift oneself from the impure mind-state to the root of the pure mind-state of wisdom.*]

Even in the case of the greatest devoted ones, they are not always holding at this higher level. Sometimes one cannot reach the true form of reverence except by first cultivating the external realm to reflect and contemplate its implications. Since all forms of reverence derive from a single root, from there one can uplift higher and higher [*into an advanced state of merging through Chokhmah-consciousness*], ultimately tasting the pleasantness of awe and becoming energized. The external form of reverence is bitter, while the supernal form is sweet.

Thus, the devoted ones are [*wise in their expression of*] gratitude, blessing the source for the creation of all these punishments whose consequence is suffering. As opposed to someone who is so brazen as to have never experienced external reverence and fears mortality—then for such a person, suffering and death are extremely distressing.

But in reality it should be called **"the well-being of the material man-**

---

29. Zohar I:11b.

30. "YHVH has established a throne in heaven, and the sovereign rule of the One is over all" (Psalm 103:19).

31. "And God saw all that God had made, and found it very good" (Genesis 1:31).

32. *Genesis Rabbah* 9:12.

33. See Zohar II:149b.

ifestation of divinity,"[34] for it **"imposes peace in His heights,"**[35] which arouses a return to divine consciousness as discussed earlier. Also **"this well-being is all embracing, / Well with the far and the near"**[36]—this is what bestows life and healing; therefore, it would be worthwhile for all people to maintain awareness of reverence. If one will be mindful of reverence, then one can discern between true sovereignty [*higher, internal reverence*] and [*lower, external reverence*]; if not, perish the thought, at very least, any modicum of reverence will guard such a person from misdeeds.

This is [*then the meaning of the mishnaic dictum*]: **"Pray for 'the well-being of the material manifestation of divinity'"**;[37] namely, at the very least, to maintain this form of lower, external reverence—**"but if it were not for this fear then people would swallow one another alive."**[38] For the soul is called a friend, in accord with the verse: **"your friend and your father's friend"**[39] so that a person will not become lost in impure consciousness.

For there is a distinction between the inner soul and outer soul.[40] The latter involves the vital soul that is concerned with the functions of nourishment, fostering growth and craving, all of which exists for the sake of the body. These forces constitute the basic life force of the body, as Scripture teaches: **"then the vibratory expression of the sensual soul descends to the lowest level"**;[41] however, through its evolutionary ascent of the body, these qualities [*of vitality, nourishment, growth and craving*] also can ascend. [*Namely, just as the body is elevated so too is the soul elevated.*]

---

34. "Rabbi Hanina, Deputy High Priest, said: Pray for the welfare of the regime; but for fear of it people would swallow one another alive. . ." (m*Avot* 3:2). This mishnah may have been chosen as a function of its commonplace study between Passover and Feast of Weeks when each week is dedicated to one chapter of m*Avot*.

35. "Dominion and dread are His; He imposes peace in His heights" (Job 25:2).

36. ". . . heartening, comforting words: / It shall be well, / Well with the far and the near / —said YHVH—" (Isaiah 57:19).

37. m*Avot* 3:2.

38. m*Avot* 3:2.

39. "Do not desert your friend and your father's friend; / Do not enter your brother's house in your time of misfortune; A close neighbor is better than a distant brother" (Proverbs 27:10).

40. *Nefesh habehimi* and *nefesh hasikhli* are generally translated as "animal soul" and "intellectual soul." If soul is the medium, which connects creation to its source, then it can look out and look in. Rather than impose an ascetic discipline on the *nefesh habehimi*, it invites the possibility of seeing all the world as sacred. The functions of consciousness enable it to be aware of all sources of phenomenality. In terms of the manifestation of divine consciousness, consider these levels of the soul: the "causal" (*Keter*), "subtle" (from *Chokhmah* to *Yesod*) and "gross" (*Malkhut*) levels of the soul. The subtle level is inner-soul whereas the gross level is outer-soul.

41. Literally, "Who knows if a human's life-breath does rise upward and if a beast's breath does sink down into the earth?" (Ecclesiastes 3:21).

This inner soul was not created to serve the body; instead, the body and the supporting spiritual elements that pertain to it, were created to serve this inner soul, and to act according to its influences in order to be elevated by it and evolve through its guidance. As soon as a person degrades his/her inner, guiding soul through immersion in the creaturely desires, that person becomes identified with and lost in the confusion of that outer soul. As such, the person is no longer fulfilling his/her human potential to be a higher animal, which **"would swallow one another alive"**[42]—the energies available in this inner level are appropriated off and misused by the outer influences. [*The inner soul can be overwhelmed by the allure of the world to the extent that s/he ceases to be functioning intentionally.*]

All of the reductive and limiting factors and sources of grace come into play by way of the initial restraint—except through some kind of involution, creation is not possible. Consequently all apparent limitations, the chastising powers of death, and the death of body and soul are all essentially divine grace and goodness. Were it not for this sense of weariness of others, **"but for the fear of it people would swallow one another alive"**[43] [*such a condition separates us from our source*]. The potential evolutionary elements are for the *inner soul*. Through the fears of the consequences, we are able to draw closer to the divine. [*In being fearful, the human avoids becoming totally immersed in the mind-state of confusion and oppositional forces of the qelipot.*]

All this change in form is a form of grace, which then explains the opening verse: **"after the death of the two sons of Aaron,"**[44] so that every form of death is a form of blessing: **"when they drew too close to the presence of YHVH."**[45] Thus, according to R. Shlomo Yitzhaki's comment, the doctor who instills fear in the patient is likely to be more effective in changing the patient's behavior.[46] The highest chance of survival comes by taking on the suggested healing regimen.

Furthermore **"Pray for the welfare of the regime"**[47]—namely, [*for either level of reverence*] is a means of connecting one to the Holy One and His *Shekinah*, as is known.

Now we understand the saying of the blessed Sages—**"Torah is only fulfilled through someone who experiences death"**[48]—by constantly re-

42. "Rabbi Hanina, Deputy High Priest, said: Pray for the welfare of the regime; but for fear of it people would swallow one another alive . . ." (m*Avot* 3:2).

43. m*Avot* 3:2.

44. "YHVH spoke to Moses after the death of the two sons of Aaron who died when they drew too close to the presence of YHVH" (Leviticus 16:1).

45. Leviticus 16:1.

46. Rashi ad loc Leviticus 16:1.

47. m*Avot* 3:2.

48. Zohar II:158b.

flecting upon death within oneself and contemplating the various forms to strengthen their reverence and enactment. The aspect of putting [*Oral*] Torah into practice is known through the spheres of **"Perpetuity and Grace"**[49]—[*fulfillment of the act is through this dying unto self as with*] **"the two sons of Aaron who died [in order to] draw too close to the presence of YHVH."**[50]

As explained further with regard to this verse: **"look at the birth-stool [*'ovnayim*]"**[51]—regarding the word *'ovnayim*, our blessed Sages alludes to the stiffening restraints of the birth mother's thighs becoming rigid like stone, simulating death for the sake of ensuring the existence of the embryo.[52]

This then is the meaning of the verse: **"YHVH spoke to Moses"**[53]—referring to the inner soul; **"after the death of the two sons of Aaron in the tent"**[54]—after the contemplation and simulation of death; **"when they drew too close [*in reverence*] to the presence of YHVH"**[55]—which is Written Torah as is known [*symbolized by the Holy One and Oral Torah symbolized by Shekinah in their unification*].

[10.3]. *PARASHAH ACHAREY MOT* (LEVITICUS 16:1–18:30)

QUESTIONS FOR REFLECTION:

1. When have you felt the effects of misusing the over-soul for the sake of the under-soul? What were the consequences?

2. If renewal of creation requires filtering, how might you practice such filtering in your creative endeavors?

3. Why is it so difficult for you to recognize the goodness in spiritual intimacy? What would enable you to become more comfortable and habituated in recognizing this goodness in your life?

---

49. *Tiquney Zohar,* Tiqqun, no. 70.

50. "YHVH spoke to Moses after the death of the two sons of Aaron who died when they drew too close to the presence of YHVH" (Leviticus 16:1).

51. "When you deliver the Hebrew women, look at the birth-stool: if it is a boy, kill him; if it is a girl, let her live" (Exodus 1:16).

52. b*Sotah* 16b.

53. Leviticus 16:1.

54. Leviticus 16:1.

55. Leviticus 16:1.

[11.1]. *Parashah Behar* (Leviticus 25:1–26:2)

INTRODUCTION TO HOMILY:

Although this homily is launched by an exegetical puzzle, its implications transcend the puzzle, entering into the larger challenge of integral spiritual living. In the book of Leviticus, the locus is the Tabernacle and Tent of Meeting, so why at the end of this book is the reader referred back to Mount Sinai? Exegetes like Northern French commentator Rashi attempt to respond to this seeming chronological disorder, but his response is the doctrinal commitment that the entire Torah emerges from Sinaitic origin. However once this exegesis on rigid doctrinal discourse, reaches the hands of the Hasidic homily, Sinai transforms into a concern about elevating consciousness through the spiritual practice of sacral deeds. Sinai is the symbol of revelation par excellence, but revelation is never separate from creation and redemption—rather, each spiritual milestone is integrated within the other. When we are mindful of our interconnectedness with all sentient beings of creation, only then are we called to act redemptively by elevating our integrated consciousness of creation. The telos of creation is to recognize our complete embeddedness within all created sentient beings with those lines of filiation running most directly through the human being. Sinai then serves more as an ontological compass in our journey toward the inner spiritual origin rather than a theological explanation of sacral deeds. The spiritual practice of sacral deeds is a process of elevating consciousness toward the Limitless.

[11.2]. *Parashah Behar* (Leviticus 25:1–26:2)

HOMILY:

The question was asked [*of the Vitebsker to explain*] the teaching: "Whoever appraises [*ha-sam*] his ways of comportment [*in this life*] becomes privileged to behold the salvation of the blessed Holy One, for Scripture states: **'[And to him] who orders his way.'**[56] Read not [*we-sam*] who sets [*his way*], but [*we-sham*] who appraises the worth [*of his way*], him will I show the divine salvation."[57]

[*The Vitebsker*] opened his remarks as follows on Rashi's comment: "What has the matter of the sabbatical year [*shemittah*] to do with Sinai?

56. Psalm 50:23 is being read in this way: whoever arranges their life in alignment with divine aspiration in this life will see divine salvation.

57. b*Moed Qatan* 5a: "Said R. Joshua b. Levi, Whoever appraises [*ha-sham*] his ways [*in this life*] becomes privileged to behold the salvation of the blessed Holy One, for it is said: '[*And to him*] who orders his way.' Read not [*we-sam*] who sets [*his way*], but [we-sham] who appraises the worth [of his way], him will I show the divine salvation."

Were not all commandments revealed on Sinai? But this statement is intended to suggest the following comparison: how it is in the law of *shemittah*—its general and particular prescriptions were ordained at Sinai. [*So too were all rules with their general and particular prescriptions taught on Sinai.*]"[58] And the matter at hand is expressed in the teaching: "By ten separate utterances was the world created. And what does Scripture teach thereby? Could the world not have been created by one utterance? But this [*requirement of ten utterances to be uttered with creation*] was to require the ungodly which destroy the world that was created by ten Sayings, and to give the godly reward which sustains the world that was created by ten Sayings. There were ten generations from Adam to Noah, to show how great . . ."[59] [*This Mishnah is puzzling, for it appears as though God is attempting to gratuitously and deliberately increase punishment of the wicked as retribution, which is a troubling theology.*] It sounds like God could have created the word with one utterance, but used only ten to increase the punishment of the evil, which is not consistent with divine compassion. What sense does it make to suggest that the divine capriciously rules with such a tyrannical wielding of power to punish the wicked? However, the ten sayings raise the stakes and may then create the misperception of a cruel and capricious divine force controlling the universe.

But [*this aforementioned theology of tyrannical divinity wielding power for greater retribution*] in truth is that the ten sayings[60] are the ten times that Scripture records **"And God spoke"** in the creation narrative.[61] Each utterance described by **"And God spoke"** is attached to a particular, explicit facet of creation that becomes manifest [*whereas there are implicit, mystical elements that remain beyond manifestation*]. This is known to us from the contextual reading of Scripture here [*notwithstanding the mystical readings*].[62] Finally, the human being is created as a creature that comprises all of prior creation. All the cosmos participated in the creation of an integrated human being; otherwise, the human would have only been from the earth, but the divine spirit comes from above.[63]

---

58. Rashi ad loc Leviticus 25:1.

59. m*Avot* 5:1–2.

60. There are only nine references to "And God spoke" [*va'yomer Elohim*] in the creation story of Genesis 1, while the Talmud counts ten.

61. The ten Sayings, which are actually nine, occur as follows: Genesis 1:3; 1:6; 1:9; 1:11; 1:14; 1:20; 1:24; 1:26; 1:29. Furthermore, in reading Zohar on Genesis, it then becomes apparent in this theosophical view that everything is part of an endless mystical cascade of interpretation that is highly esoteric.

62. This tension is evinced in the statement: "The secret things belong unto YHVH our God; but the things that are revealed belong unto us and to our children for ever, that we may do all the words of this law" (Deuteronomy 29:28).

63. Rashi ad loc Genesis 2:7, ". . . Consequently on the sixth day there had to be creat-

Behold, the blessed Sages teach that **"the end of creation was inscribed in its beginning,"**[64] given that accordingly the position of humanity's creation makes it the purpose of creation,[65] so then this is why Scripture teaches that human beings control the growth of all created, sentient beings. **"[A]nd have dominion [*u'RDu*] the fish of the sea"**[66] and in line with King David, *o.b.m.* [*who writes*]: **"You have made [human] master over Your handiwork, / laying the world at the feet of the human being."**[67] Just as the lower worlds [*are created through guidance*] so the upper worlds have been created, and the position of humanity's creation makes it the purpose of creation, as the blessed Sages teach: "every blade of grass in the terrestrial sphere has an angel in the supernal world . . . saying grow, grow."[68] It follows from the position of humanity's creation that the human rules over them all, even guiding the angels. If human beings fulfill their calling in the terrestrial sphere, so that "when the human ascends, it elevates the whole universe, and when the human descends [*yoRedD*], s/he brings the whole universe down."[69] The human being comprises a sympathetic affinity with all worlds,[70] including this material world, thus conducting [*the music*] of all creation.

We share creaturely appetites with the animals [*which means that humans are responsible to conduct this music as well*]; thus, just as we share

---

ed [*a being composed of*] heavenly and earthly matter, for otherwise there would have been envy (lack of harmony) among the works of Creation, in that there would have been devoted one class of them one day more of the creation than to the others." Compare with *Genesis Rabbah* 12, where the exegesis is creating a scenario of comparison where the three-three tie of the days of creation, so as to create the human being composed of the heavenly spirit in a vessel composed from the dust of the earth. The notion that humans have embedded within an integral microcosm of creation, which is another layer, starting from the Zohar onwards. The mystical reading goes beyond the dualism of the exegesis whereby the human creature is seen as a non-dual microcosm, see Meir ibn Gabbai, *'Avodat haQodesh* 2:23; ibid., *Sitrai Tefillot ha'hol v'Sodan*.

64. Yehudah HaLevi, *Kuzari* III:73.

65. b*Berakot* 6b, the pinnacle of creation here is actually for *yirat shamayim* [heavenly awe] rather than the human being as the pinnacle of all creation as suggested by the homily.

66. "[God blessed them and said to them: 'Be fertile and increase, fill the earth and master it';] and rule the fish of the sea, [the birds of the sky, and all living things that creep on the earth]" (Genesis 1:28).

67. See Psalm 8:7. This is a foundational concept in Kabbalistic thought; given the human is a microcosm of creation, there is responsibility to contribute to the greatness of creation and vice versa. See Matt, "Mystic and the Mitsvot," *Jewish Spirituality*, ed. Arthur Green (New York: Crossroad, 1986), 367–404; Moshe Idel, *Kabbalah and New Perspectives* (New Haven, CT: Yale University Press, 1988), 370n122.

68. *Genesis Rabbah* 10:7.

69. Zohar III:10a, compare with its gloss from Ecclesiastes 3:21.

70. Worlds likely alludes to the great chain of being in which there are multiple worlds, physical through the spiritual, incrementally stacked influencing each other.

bodily appetites with the animals, so are there points of commonality with all of creation. If we go too far in following our creaturely appetites, then that is the way of comportment to be rectified. The mystical overlay of the rabbinic teaching holds that the modality of rectification must retrace and elevate the modality of transgression.[71] There is a much deeper spirituality to understanding the sacrificial system to explore, but our main point here is more of an exoteric approach, namely, that the animal offerings are meant to redress the creaturely appetites which we share with larger, domesticated animals, and thus serve as a metonym for raising ourselves, bringing all those elements back to their divine source through the spiritual agency of the priests. Given that we are integrated with the totality of creation, if our creaturely appetites are misdirected, then it degrades all of creation; therefore, we are invited to elevate with the rest of creation with which we are intertwined.

Further along this line, whatever spiritual quality is activated within us by the way we walk, think, and feel through the world, in each and every moment we are constantly shifting and changing **"like an arrow flying,"**[72] so that sometimes when we think of compassion that can **"vouchsafe attentive caring."**[73] Yet this is merely one state that inhabits our minds, and so according to the emotional states that inhabit the human mind-stream, so are supernal reverberations aroused. As the Zohar teaches,[74] Abraham activates Compassion as Scripture calls him: **"Abraham, the one who arouses love cosmically,"**[75] and so it is with all the devoted ones and their spiritual

71. See b*Sotah* 14a, as we learn in the *Sotah* offering, so that the offering itself is from animal feed. And so it is with all the offerings made from animals, [notice they are only made] from sheep and cattle, for the creaturely appetites are the explicit and external, whereas the "hidden meaning is to now turn toward the eternal." This is precisely the issue, [*that the rectification, for example, is normally wheat flour but in this case the minha offering is barley flour to rectify the animal soul*]. On an external level, the sacrifice allows for a mending of one's bestial actions through the agency of the priestly offerings. By bringing this offering, one mends one's own error as well as uplifting all sentient beings from their place amid the oppositional forces within the depths of the material world that have been damaged. The rabbinic thinking here is more of a measure for measure, whereas this homily extrapolates the mystical contours beyond measure for measure, for example, as articulated in Nahmanides's Commentary to Leviticus 1:9. It is when s/he realizes internally how much s/he has distanced himself/herself from the eternal source of his/her soul and through this turning of one's heart, only then the explicit sacrifice is possible. The ritual is insufficient without this internal intentionality; it becomes all simply mechanical as a kind of religious behavioralism, so that when s/he turns to the divine then everything comes with him/her.

72. Literally, "You need not fear the terror by night, or the arrow that flies by day" (Psalm 91:5).

73. "By day may YHVH vouchsafe attentive caring, / so that at night a song to the One may be with me, / a prayer to the God of my life" (Psalm 42:9).

74. Zohar 1:87a.

75. "But you, Israel, My servant, / Jacob, whom I have chosen, / Seed of Abraham

attributes [*so by loving the divine, Abraham draws down this love into the world*]. And so it is with each devoted one who enhances the world through the spiritual qualities they keep in mind. If, however, a negative emotional impulse arises, then ask yourself: "What is this about? Where is it coming from?" [*which is really more of an epistemological analysis rather than an ethical one*]. At such a moment, you should be ashamed before the divine [*that is, discordant with your divine self*] so that you re-evaluate your basic assumptions to a reconstitution of your higher self, so that once again **"the sacred dwells amid the negative,"**[76] beckoning you to a more noble and clear way of thinking and being in the world. Whatever the errant impulse, precisely there dwells something sacred energizing that impulse. That desire needs to be surrendered from the entanglement of egocentric thinking toward a reorientation of self.[77] By confronting, contemplating, and being critically self-reflective about this impulse, one is then able to cleave deeper to the divine through that very sacred energy in its elevation. Through such critical self-reflection about this impulse, the individual's own ascent is augmented by the ascent of all the created, sentient beings now redirected within otherwise [*distracting*] thoughts and spiritual qualities, all the way through to the supernal worlds.

[*The homily now returns to the opening question that arose in the Mishnah, where it appears as though God is attempting to gratuitously and deliberately increase punishment of the wicked as retribution, which is a troubling theology. In this classic rabbinic theology, the calculus is one of reward and punishment as per the Mishnah. God could have created the word with one utterance, but used only ten to increase the punishment of the evil, which is not consistent with divine compassion. It is not this calculus of reward and punishment that is operative on a deeper level; rather, what emerges here is his/her subjective experience of redirecting his/her own energy from the impulse.*] This then is the recompense vouchsafed for the devoted ones, that is, the hidden good animating all sentient beings. For the root of *ma'amarot* is not merely to be understood as "speaking" but it also means "beckoning" and a contemplative evocation of inner vitality [*'amirah*], namely, this critical

---

my friend" (Isaiah 41:8).

76. Leviticus 16:16.

77. First, one acknowledges through a "subduing" of self; secondly, there is "distinguishing" of awareness that emerges through the act of "subduing"; and thirdly, this allows for the elevation of this spark into a "sweetening" of the desire that is redeemed. This is akin to the tripartite path of praxis that includes "subduing-distinguishing-sweetening" [*hakhna'a-havdalah-hamtakah*] in the earliest layer of Beshtian Hasidism; see Ba'al Shem Tov, *The Pillar of Prayer: Teachings of Contemplative Guidance in Prayer, Sacred Study, and the Spiritual Life from the Ba'al Shem Tov and His Circle*, trans. Menachem Kallus, ed. Aubrey L. Glazer (Louisville, KY: Fons Vitae, 2011), #95: 113–14; #95:2; 115–18; #96:119; #143.1:178; #148.9:198–99.

reframing [*at that moment where s/he becomes disentangled, reframed and re-energized, thus bringing into reality a new*] inner direction of the heart as alluded to in the Zohar.[78] God did not have to speak to Moses, but Moses was "beckoned": **"ascend the mountain."**[79] Thus these are the ongoing ten calls to guidance for us all. **"Unto Moses he said: go up to God"** is a strange locution [*for who then is the speaker here in this verse?*]. The strange construction belies a hidden level of beckoning, whereby Moses is being called by an inner voice, a level beyond his current attainment, to ascend Mount Sinai.[80] [*As we rise and grow spiritually, we are constantly beckoned by a higher level which we have not yet attained but which we can nevertheless hear beckoning us.*] It is known that each person comprises all of creation as a microcosm.[81] Certainly, the Creator could have created all of creation in a single *ma'amar*, but instead the Creator created all sentient beings with a tenfold inner guidance of the heart, so that each and every inner direction [*ma'amar*] was intended to serve in the capacity of compositional gratitude of the human being comprised of all creation. [*Insofar as we are comprised and interconnected with creation in an ongoing way, then when we act nobly and when we response to this inner direction*] not simply to get reward, then not only is the human being ascending alone but elevating with [*b'aloto*] all of [*creation*]. So as the blessed Sages teach that the whole permission to eat meat is [*meant*] to elevate the animal, but if a person is not involved in elevating the world, such a person is either evil or an ignoramus [*and therefore*] has no right to eat meat.[82] The process of transforming soul-energy from its animal state onward, requires mindfulness in the process of executing human free will. If as a human being I am not truly mindful of elevating the soul-energy of the pure animal, then I am denigrating the animal through my negligence.[83] Consumption means that one is collecting all the preceding soul-energy, cleaving in its own capacity to the divine. When we mindfully use that spiritual energy embedded within that sentient being, then the human can see the pristine spiritual energy from the primordial light from the six days of creation hidden [*within the world of sentient beings*] for the deeply devoted ones. [*What such mindfulness allows to emerge is pristine energy of that sentient being by uplifting nobly such energy so that one is responding to that inner direction and revealing anew that pristine*] light of **"And there was a beckoning"**—which is the vitality of that created, sentient being. [*Thus, when we are mindful of our interconnectedness with all sentient beings of creation, only then are we*

78. Zohar II:17a.

79. Exodus 24:1.

80. Zohar II:125b.

81. *Tiquney Zohar*, Tiqqun 70, 130b.

82. b*Pesachim* 49b.

83. b*Baba Metzia* 100a, where the transactional nature of tort law is extrapolated here to spiritual exchange.

called to elevate. The whole purpose of creation is to recognize our complete embeddedness in all created sentient beings with those lines of filiation running most directly through the human being.]

This then is the deeper meaning of the verse in the opening teaching: **"when I align my being with all of creation"**[84] in this world, in each and every moment, in everything I relate to and come into contact with in creation, each and every spiritual intention, until I reach the point of redemption [*influencing all of creation to move into that selfsame space. As a human being I have the capacity to mindfully clarify the spiritual genomes that include creaturely appetites within me so as to*] uplift all of creation and participate in this beneficence—which is the cosmos itself. So too Noah and Abraham required [*such mindfulness of*] the generations that preceded them. There is an incremental accumulation of the human being that is continuous with the rest of the all sentient creation and emergent—therefore it is all completely interconnected. All of sentient creation is nullified and nonexistent, thus accumulating through its negation within the human being; therefore, we are responsible for creation. This then is our call to elevate all of sentient creation. So too in the case with the Sabbatical year, in that all the bounty from the six preceding years incrementally accumulates and is thus embedded in the seventh year, so that all possessions and ownership claims lead to freedom [*rather than negating what preceded, this is a process of transformation, integration, and uplift. Recall now the opening question—why are we mentioning Sinai here at the end of the book of Leviticus? Sinai is more about the ontological inner spiritual origin rather than any theological concern*]. Everything then comes from Sinai. A return to origin, to No-Thingness—this is Sinai, which is Wisdom, seeing from that place of the seventh [*the place of beckoning all of creation to a more noble place, requiring his/her surrender and awareness of his/her inner calling that lies ahead*]. According to numerology, from the seventieth is the precipice of Wisdom, which is No-thingness—a type of contemplative seeing from the seventh which is apprehended within the super-structure of all sacral deeds. All sacral deeds come from Sinai, which is a spiritual practice of surrendering self to the inner calling. Once a sacral deed is elevated through its completion from Sinai, then that ultimate purpose of all devotion is about dissolving the self before the Limitless, opening one to a more sublime horizon atop the mount of spiritual ascension, so that **"Moses received Torah from [the openly naught consciousness of origin known as] Sinai."**[85]

84. Psalm 50:23.
85. m*Avot* 1:1.

[11.3]. *Parashah Behar* (Leviticus 25:1–26:2)

QUESTIONS FOR REFLECTION:

1. How does this integrative approach to Sinai change our lives, our spiritual practice? Is that a joy? Is that a burden?

2. If the human being is no longer viewed as superior or dominant, but rather is deeply emerged and involved in what preceded us, then how does that change our relationship to the animal world? To the resources of the earth?

3. The ten commands are here transformed to ten invitations to uplift the diverse lines of filiation—how is this an inner call to celebrate diversity of sentient beings?

4. Is the shift to deeper spiritual reflections concerned with the earth in this homily—and throughout this book, *Peri haAretz*, namely, Fruit of the Earth—somehow inspired by the context of the Land of Israel and the need to connect to the earth in a way that was not possible in the climes of Eastern Europe?

Numbers

[12.1]. *Parashah Shelach Lecha* (Numbers 13:1–15:41)

INTRODUCTION TO HOMILY:

Breaking through the character armor of the repressed and transcending the structures of personality are formed by external influences. There is often a childish tendency to be stultified by the overarching influence of environment, parents, and the way one was programmed in childhood. The process of overcoming the containing energy of embodiment requires great degrees of conscious suffering. The Land of Israel, which is nourished by the heavenly effluence, is the destination to which Israel is guided by the heavenly source, and thus requires similar efforts of conscious suffering to become conscious of our endlessness. Torah is the expression of the teaching from the source beyond that materializes in the realm of the sensible qualia that elucidates the pathways to the Land of Israel and the world-that-is-coming. The Land of Israel is the enlightened state of consciousness within which one is directly nourished by the flow that comes from beyond the spiritual qualia. The world-that-is-coming is the evolutionary possibilities of the future that one can become aware of through the conscious suffering of freeing oneself of the limitations of the spiritual qualia. The renouncing of the commanding self's control is painful, but by virtue of that kind of conscious suffering, access to higher being states becomes possible. The experience of being in the condition of embodiment, in which the presence of the divine source is obscured so that a person, in contrast to an angel, is unaware of its dependency. The level of being that is characterized by the experience of the world that seems to independently exist is bounded by these lower six spheres or middot. The world of sensibility is always known and expressed by these lower six energetic qualia, from Compassion (Chesed) to Grounding (Malkhut). The dynamic mode of the integrated field is bounded by these six energetic qualia that also unite and interact as the basis for everything that is experienced as appearance. And yet that realm of experience is not the entire integrated field. To extricate oneself from this limited view, what is beyond these six energetic qualia can be experienced only through conscious suffering. These treasures of the spiritual path are associated with the unified field beyond these six energetic qualia. If a person is motivated by Torah, then such a person will make an effort to detach from the limited consciousness of the lower six energetic spheres. This detachment of limited consciousness bounded by the lower six energetic spheres enables the energy of consciousness to reach higher levels of being. This conscious suffering is a function of the ego being attached to these lower six energetic spheres. The one who becomes unbound then overcomes the limitations of the boundary of these lower six energetic spheres; such a person becomes free from the overwhelming influence of the attraction of the world of appearances. This process of suffering for the sake of gaining access to the divine gifts transforms that being state of the person who intentionally takes them on and refines that state of being, including the personality and the character.

[12.2]. *PARASHAH SHELACH LECHA* (NUMBERS 13:1–15:41)

HOMILY:

"Send forth."[1] R. Shlomo Yitzhaki, *o.b.m.*, explains the verse as follows: the Holy One did not exactly agree; rather ,the Holy One merely refrained from objecting and said [*to Moses*]: "If you wish to do so**, send them**."[2]

The issue at hand is further explained by our blessed Sages: "The Holy One gave three precious gifts through [*conscious*] suffering to the Israelites—[*the divine guidance of*] Torah, the [*point of spiritual orientation of the*] Land of Israel, and the [*future that is coming through the*] world-that-is-coming,"[3] and they support each claim through Scripture.

So the issue comes down to what our blessed Sages teach: "The Holy One created the world by [*looking at*] Torah"[4]—and these are the letters of Torah as is known.[5] This is further explained in *Sefer Yetzirah*, namely, through the oral articulation of the letters[6] that humans were given the power of the building blocks of creation. It is the articulation of these letters that arouses all those worlds. These worlds are constituted from spiritual values and the crystallization of something more abstract [*namely, the six spheres of divine consciousness of primal forces making up the world,*

1. "Send forth men to scout the land of Canaan, which I am giving to the Israelite people; send one man from each of their ancestral tribes, each one a chieftain among them" (Numbers 13:2).

2. Rashi ad loc Numbers 13:2: "Send thee (more literally, for thyself)—i.e., according to your own judgment: I do not command you, but if you wish to do so send them." Furthermore, the interpretive challenge arises—whatever Moses needed know in advance of the conquest that could be ascertained through espionage is redundant to an omniscient divine power.

3. b*Berakot* 5a.

4. Zohar I:47a, 204a.

5. Zohar I:5a.

6. *Sefer Yetzirah*, II:3.

ranging from Chesed (Compassion) to Yesod (Nexus)] but also transcends what is below. [*The world is created through speech acts; thus, these six forces meld together in various combinations throughout time and space. When a person engages in an intentional act that utilizes some concentration of the primal energies, this also shakes up this energy, uniting this person with the divine field.*]

[*This oral articulation of the letters*] marks the beginning moments of revealing the worlds—by way of **"Your Compassion builds all worlds."**[7] [*Chesed (Compassion) is the uppermost of the aforementioned spiritual modalities of the cosmos as the first sphere from which all lower spiritual worlds are constructed.*] There is nothing desired [*in the world*] that would transcend these spiritual qualities [*and the letters*] expect the [*desires that lead to*] "scream." It is from a person's essence rather than their fantasy of self to then be in a state of the highest depth [*transcending all the aforementioned spiritual qualities*], according to the Zohar.[8] [*It is this screaming from*] the highest realm, transcending linguistic shrouding, that is found in the depth of one's heart. [*Given that this screaming emerges from the depth of the heart, it transcends language and thus it transcends the spiritual modalities of the personality through the qualia of 'middot,' which are housed in language.*]

Lo and behold, it is known that the truth and nature of all sentient beings is their desire to draw its vitality from its root for everything, yearning to return to its source [*a kind of evolutionary pull*][9]—in the way that the inanimate sphere yearns to blossom and elevate to the [*vegetative*] realm above it; in the same way that the vegetative sphere then yearns to evolve and enter into the animate sphere, and so on, as the animate sphere yearns for the linguistic sphere. [*The chain of being is defined by the following dynamic—the lower the being, the higher its aspiration.*] While each state is not conscious of this yearning to return to its roots, nonetheless, it is imprinted within the rhythms of nature.

It certainly follows that the one pronouncing these [*same*] words of Torah through which the world was created yearns to return to the root of language which is Torah. This primordial grounding immeasurably beyond creation preceding manifestation [*which relates to the spheres of Chokhmah (Elastic Wisdom) and Binah (Directionality)*][10] is composed of the measured spiritual qualities from which everything then flows. Ultimately, there is nothing within the created realm that does not harken back

7. "I declare, 'Your steadfast love is confirmed forever; / to all generations I will proclaim Your faithfulness with my mouth'" (Psalm 89:3).

8. Zohar II:19b.

9. On the parallel expression to "being drawn back to its root," see "they are enticed by themselves," in b*Sanhedrin* 61b, 112a.

10. *Genesis Rabbah* 8:2, literally two thousand years, but this is mythic numerology, where time does not even apply.

to its root in these spiritual qualities [*which are the vehicles of the divine becoming manifest into creation*]. The result of this flowing emanation is that the creation of these grounded material bodies, once imbued with vitality, seek ascent. [*This contemplation moves from embodiment to spirituality, which implies dualism. Yet there is no way to escape the subtle, élan vital that is always one, just with different degrees of density depending on the vibrational level and how close it remains to the surface of perception.*]

There is nothing that creates more suffering than this expansion[11] of vitality from the embodiment, this yearning to return to its root, to the point where sensory experience is transcended and left behind, as is known to the philosophers. All sufferings in the material body are perceived through the agency of the intellectual center through the experience of the moving center[12]—whereby any two things which are fused together experience pain from this disparity. And any suffering, *perish the thought*, is then felt in that sense of separation. This is especially the case when the soul expands from the body, which is one of the "seven decrees" [*that apply to a person from death through the process of judgment*].[13]

Even though we can learn from these aforementioned seven decrees about death, a permanent separation, then—in our case, of the "subtle body experience"[14] where the body is still vivified, there remains a vital trace of the spiritual within the material body.[15] The higher potentialities

11. Literally, "separation."

12. Literally, "from the power of the heart center" though here what seems to be implied is the more medieval philosophical understanding that the mind is the center of sensations, thus "heart" is euphemism for "mind." The three centers of an integrated being combines the intellectual, heart, and the moving center.

13. Zohar II:199b, see also Zohar III:127a, Pritzker edition, 311: "How many courts of law must a person pass through when he departs from this world! One is that judgment on high that we have mentioned, when the spirit leaves the body. One is the judgment when his actions and his words precede him and heralds proclaim about him. One is the judgment when he enters the grave; one is the judgment of the worm; and one is the judgment of Hell. And one is the judgment of the spirit that goes wandering through the world, finding no place until its actions have been requited. Surely, 'seven periods will pass over him' (Daniel 4:13)."

14. It is a semantic and spiritual question, regarding "subtle body" versus "out of body experiences," the soul is in something like an "astral body," but this is not when the body is asleep or when it is deprived of its senses, but there is something more than anxiety that leads to a kind of suffering from disorientation; see Jonathan Garb, *Shamanic Trance in Modern Kabbalah* (Chicago: University of Chicago Press, 2011). Consider from a neuroscience perspective how the subtle body is referred to as "people also see their 'double' in extra-personal space but it is difficult for them to decide whether they are 'disembodied,'" Moshe Idel and Shahar Arzy, *Kabbalah: A Neurocognitive Approach to Mystical Experiences*, 2015, 39; Whitley Strieber, *The Super Natural: A New Vision of the Unexplained*, 2016; compare with John C. Lilly, *Simulations of God: The Science of Belief* (New York: Simon and Schuster, 1975).

15. On the "trace" [*reshimu*], see for example, Zohar I:3b, 13a, 21a, etc.

of being disappear under these conditions, but the potential for them to return still remains.[16] This case is known from the prophets of how Daniel **"languished,"**[17] where those who are conscious in an astral body, like those afflicted with prophetic impulses so that all the sense becomes disengaged [*as in the case of out-of-subtle-body experience*].

[*The homily now shifts to bring our awareness to the reality that Torah itself is received in an out-of-body experience that comes with some form of conscious suffering.*] As the blessed Sages teach about [*the opening matter of the sufferings of Torah through*] this verse: **"Happy is the one is pained [in seeing the separation of the name] O YH"**[18]—all human malfunctioning is related to the separation of the letters of the tetragram [*that is, separating YH from VH, which manifests when one corporealizes the spiritual work of devotionality. This sense of divine suffering is a function of deep sensitivity and empathy on the part of the seeker. The true feeling of separation here comes from an awareness within oneself of wounding the divine*].[19]

Behold, there are some people who are so coarse in their attachment to materiality [*and are not able to fully elevate and emerge with spirituality*]—that they do not feel pain unless they are beaten [*because their spiritual senses are so dulled*], along the lines of **"A rebuke works on an intelligent man / More than one hundred blows on a fool,"**[20] whereas others [*who are more spirituality sensitized*] feel pain on a psychic, subtle body level, as Scripture teaches: **"A slave cannot be disciplined by words."**[21] [*While a person with a slave mentality will not be affected whatsoever by words of admonishment; by contrast, those who are more spirituality sensitized will be greatly affected by mere words.*]

By contrast, one who is spiritually sensitized and cultivates freedom from the material body [*that is, a state of being with a conscious aspect that is beyond the hypnotic, unreflective state that is coarseness and a victim of their programming*], which embodies the "freedom inscribed on the

16. Ba'al Shem Tov experiences this descent of spiritual consciousness [*histalkut ha-madreigot*] in his journey to the Holy Land via Istanbul. On *histalkut ha-madreigot*, see *Pillar of Prayer*, tr. Kallus, #37-56, pp. 29-50; ibid, Glazer, "Imaginal Journeying to Istanbul, *mon amour*," pp. 213-216, 227-230, esp. 244-245.

17. Literally, "So I, Daniel, was stricken, and languished many days. Then I arose and attended to the King's business, but I was dismayed by the vision and no one could explain it" (Daniel 8:27).

18. Literally, "Happy is the man whom You discipline, O YHVH, / the man you instruct in Your teaching" (Psalm 94:12).

19. Zohar III:225a.

20. Proverbs 17:10.

21. "A slave cannot be disciplined by words; / Though he may comprehend, he does not respond" (Proverbs 29:19).

tablets"[22] [*embedded in the deepest depths of consciousness which is the normative yet concealed set*]—which is known as the World of Freedom [*that is, freedom from the hypnotic, unreflective state that is coarseness as a condition of programming, as well as coarseness of intellect and emotion, and a dominance of creaturely appetites*]. Such a person who has a sensitized conscience can cultivate deep understanding and wisdom when they contemplate their roots in Torah [*in the depth of consciousness formed through the spiritual modalities of Chokhmah (Wisdom) and Binah (Understanding)*]; they are thus sensitive enough to be **"disciplined by words,"**[23] which are the very letters of Torah. So our blessed Sages teach: this liberated consciousness transcends all contingencies,[24] understanding a rootedness in Torah, two thousand years before the world was created through spiritual modalities.[25] [*Namely, the world was created from spiritual qualities beginning with Chesed (Compassion), whereas Torah emerges from more ancient spheres of Chokhmah (Wisdom) and Binah (Discernment) that precede the sphere of Chesed (Compassion) and transcend all lower spheres that flow from it. Thus, Torah is understood mystically to precede the world by two thousand years, which refers to the more ancient spheres of Chokhmah (Wisdom) and Binah (Discernment).*] One who has cultivated such wisdom and understanding connects through its roots in Torah whose letters are drawing the consciousness to re-establish the connection with the sources above the spiritual qualities.[26] [*The letters have the capacity to awaken the sensitized seeker into an expansive consciousness through the very efficacy of the reception of the letters and be reminded by them of their source. This liberates a higher being energy from its confinement in the habitual state bound by spiritual qualities of middot.*]

Behold, our blessed Sages offered this interpretation of the scriptural verse: **"learn from [the awakening discipline of] Your Torah"**[27]—in the case of the archetypes of injury, for example, when one knocks out [*a slave's*] tooth, then, *de minoris, ad majoris*, with the awakening discipline that a sensitive person can receive then frees them from the slave condition of their automatic state of consciousness.[28] [*Whereas the original Talmudic teaching focuses on how Torah is meant to teach the one who suffers, the Vitebsker is shifting the emphasis toward a yearning for one to learn*

22. See Exodus 32:16 and compare with m*Avot* 6:3.

23. "A slave cannot be disciplined by words; / Though he may comprehend, he does not respond" (Proverbs 29:19).

24. *Pirkai deRabbi Eleazer* 45.

25. *Genesis Rabbah* 8:2.

26. See Parashah Vayigash in this volume, regarding the root letters of existence.

27. Literally, "Happy is the man whom You discipline, O YHVH, / the man you instruct in Your teaching" (Psalm 94:12).

28. b*Berakot* 5a.

and understand more deeply from Torah that suffering is actually moving toward freedom from the limitations of embodiment.] When the mind is awakened and freed from its unconscious state, then the body is refined from all previous convolutions at the same time, attaining a higher state of being. For that moment there is a change of state in which all of the negativity is nullified through this refinement, and even though it may not be permanently eliminated, it will not return in the same condition. This process of separating out negativity and dissolution follows the earlier analogy, whereby, just as the original slave's eye or tooth knocked out will not return, so too the evil that undergoes self-purgation will never return. [*In losing human limbs, like the eye and the tooth, the enslaved one achieves liberation, so too every spiritually sensitized human that may become enslaved to corporeal contingencies has the capacity to realize ultimate liberation. By extending the spiritual capacities of the self to extend beyond the body, one can realize ultimate liberation from prior enslavement to the coarse nature of being states, which too often obstructs one from realizing more subtle realms. Just as limbs like the eye or tooth do not return, so too the evil that has been purged through spiritual cultivation cannot return. Only a particular aspect of negativity is nullified in this refinement through the disciplined awakening by way of the letters of Torah.*]

And through this understanding one can then resolve the perplexities the world over of how the body seems to return to its original vigor upon healing from sufferings. [*Even though the body returns to its original vigor, nonetheless the evil purged from the spiritual qualities does not return to its original state once the coarseness has been refined.*] Behold, the person who has cultivated this deeper understanding will be **"disciplined by words,"**[29] reaching the awareness that any transgression then separates the letters of the divine name, *perish the thought*. [*Namely, the awareness of how inextricably the divine name is intertwined throughout all of existence as cultivated by deeper understanding is what allows for a change of course and programming through words alone.*] Such a sensitized self-discipline is implied in the verse: **"Happy is the one pained [and disciplined in seeing the separation of the name] O YH"**[30]—namely, such a person's Wisdom [*Yo"D*] and Discernment [*H"eH*] are then reflected in the divine attributes [*which are the ground of one's spiritual being, such that when they are separated, then one immediately feels it and then feels intimately how to*]: **"instruct in Your teaching."**[31] The body and very substance of Torah itself

29. "A slave cannot be disciplined by words; / Though he may comprehend, he does not respond" (Proverbs 29:19).

30. Literally, "Happy is the man whom You discipline, O YHVH, / the man you instruct in Your teaching" (Psalm 94:12).

31. "Happy is the man whom You discipline, O YH, / the man you instruct in Your

[*is in realizing that Torah emerges from more ancient spheres of the yod of Chokhmah (Wisdom) and the Heh of Binah (Discernment). Such spheres of gnosis that are the foundation and root of Torah, preceding the creation of the world by two thousand years, and serve to instruct and discipline one to transcend any enslavement to the source that is transmitting which is rife with its own coarseness of corporeality. When a person associates the pangs of consciousness with a responsibility for having separated YH, then that is enough to reconnect oneself to one's roots and thereby come to the senses. Inner recognition of this condition is what awakens the shift in consciousness so long as one is already initiated into this awareness of the Name. Such awareness is thus the sense of disciplining by being pulled back to the primordial condition of YH, and divested of the veiling of the six lower boundaries of one's spiritual persona or middot.*][32]

So along this path of thinking: [*of those three aforementioned gifts given through conscious sufferings, we now turn to*] the gift of the Land of Israel through sufferings which requires some explanation. [*But before these afflictions are explained, the Vitebsker first turns to explicate how the manna could serve as spiritual sustenance given that it was desired by the mixed multitude, those who did not have the capacity to be initiates without any interest in divestment leading back to the primordial Torah.*] Behold, it is known that the manna was bread from heaven, such that this spiritual sustenance was at a higher level than the land upon which it then came to settle. And so, given the elevated nature of such spiritual sustenance, it raises a problem—how could the seeking of spiritual sustenance be motivated by selfish drives and creaturely appetites? [*Namely, how does the coarse desire wound the subtle spheres of divine consciousness?*] After all, spiritual sustenance should be immune from the allures of coarseness of constricted consciousness, completely freed from any convolution with evil whatsoever. [*If the mixed multitude are being fed from YH, how could they be desiring VH? Why are they not divested of all desires if they are not being fed the food that does not arouse such desires?*]

But this matter [*of convoluted spirituality*] is already addressed in the Zohar [*as follows*]: any spiritual form that descends into manifestation in this world, even an angelic form, must undergo a transformation of its qualities appropriate for this world.[33] The formal, physical qualities are not simply extraneous, but every vessel shapes the spirit that flows through it. We know this is the case from water, while formless, once poured into a container, will then take on the shape of its container, be it rounded or squared.

And so too, with regard to even the purest and most pristine spirituali-

---

teaching" (Psalm 94:12).

32. m*Hagiga* 1:8.

33. Zohar III:152a.

ty—when the spirit descends into embodiment, it takes on the formal qualities, shape [*and persona*] of the individual. So if a person is good, then the spirit takes on a good form; so too, with an evil person does the spirit then take on an evil form. So too, with regard to the process of materialization of spiritual sustenance in the manna for each person: it takes on the qualities of appearances of the person who collected it. If one was rebellious and devoid of reverence, then the effect of the manna would increase the negative tendencies within that person. This is because within the oppositional force itself, there is this added power of the pristine spiritual vitality [*that has entered into it. Due to its origin in divine grace and greater vibrational quality, there is a higher dose of vitality which becomes corrupted in the oppositional force of the 'qelipah,' actually strengthening the coarseness of such convoluted consciousness*]. The oppositional force now will only corrupt further even though it is emerging from the spiritual vitality. [*Manna does not appear to be different from bread, which emerges from the laws of nature; rather, manna is manifested by divine grace. This miraculous presence of manna nevertheless has the formal qualities of physical manifestation, which is why it arouses creaturely appetites.*]

[*This brings the homily back to its opening statement by Rashi that divine guidance did not fully support sending spies to reconnoiter the Land of Israel, but it permitted it nonetheless. The evil itself does not descend from the heavens, but it is permitted as a choice.*] Behold, the divine intention of the Holy One in giving the Land of Israel to the Jews was to provide spiritual sustenance through this land [*which looks like the rest of the earth but it is not*], which is at the same spiritual level as the manna that **"soaks up its water from the rains of heaven."**[34] [*If one has not already overcome the coarseness in one's spiritual nature, then the appropriation of the sacred exacerbates the obstacles to one's transformation, especially in the Land of Israel. So for a person with very exulted spiritual goals on earth, those boundaries then define the Land of Israel. Those boundaries within which that spiritual being is comporting itself are being directly sustained by the Holy One and not the laws of nature, even though it appears to be sustained by such laws.*]

The Holy One gives this directly without and mediation, as explained in *Chesed le-Abraham*,[35] so that **"On that same day, when they ate of the produce of the land,"**[36] then the manna ended, because [*from the per-*

---

34. "[B]ut the land you are about to cross and possess, a land of hills and valleys, soaks up its water from the rains of heaven" (Deuteronomy 11:11).

35. R. Abraham Azulai, *Chesed le-Abraham* (Vilnius: 1877), 3:21.

36. "On that same day, when they ate of the produce of the land, the manna ceased. The Israelites had no more manna; that year they ate of the yield of the land of Canaan" (Joshua 5:12).

spective of spiritual synergy] the produce from the land also comes from a spiritual source [*even from below*].

As we have explained already, embodied spirituality will take on the persona of the individual—the spiritual energy takes on one's physical energy. Everything is dependent on the preparation of spiritual energy to be received upon the material plane, "in whatever way you are prepared."[37] It all depends upon one's intention on consuming this energy; if one is eating this spiritual produce of the land in order to be cleansed and purged of any base drives, then it will have an extra effect; but if one consumes this spiritual produce of the land in order to be more materially oriented, then that same spiritual produce will merely enhance the very same materiality. As the blessed Sages teach "two people ate their paschal offering,"[38] just as it devolves upon these aspirants [*so too for all commands*]. In regard to these [*two spiritual personae*], Scripture states: **"The righteous can walk on them, / While sinners stumble on them."**[39] [*For the devoted one's intention is to uplift, thus the consumption itself raises spiritual energy.*]

So notice if a person's intent is to self-purge from all base desires and physical limitations, then every such intention enacted for cultivating this spiritual life force will flow and expand. Whereas if all intent is merely for creaturely appetites and desires, then all that ultimately matters to such a person is the taste and fulfillment of desires. Thus, the Holy One says: "With free will, the life I give you is a series of choices that includes the ability to falter"—certainly then free will has been given, "so all who want to contaminate themselves, the door is open."[40]

In this way it is possible to explain through the teaching of the blessed Sages[41] this verse: **"Indeed, it shall be said of Zion, / 'Every person [*with proper spiritual intention then has the capacity to be re*]born there [*and as if one is living in the Holy Land*].'"**[42] The one born **"there"** [*is the master of return in the diaspora*] and there is also someone [*a truly devoted one*

37. b*Sanhedrin* 48b, Rashi ad loc, *Tosafot* ad loc.

38. The paschal offering was to be eaten as the final course of the evening meal when the guests had already eaten their fill. So in the midst of this Talmudic discussion, the situation of "two people who roast their paschal lambs" arises whereby one eats the offering with the intention of fulfilling the precept, while the other eats it to merely have an ordinary meal. According to Resh Lakish, even the seemingly transgressive act of the latter has value for "at least he has carried the passover rite" regardless of intention, see b*Nazir* 23a.

39. "He who is wise will consider these words, / He who is prudent will take note of them. / For the paths of YHVH are smooth; / The righteous can walk on them, / While sinners stumble on them" (Hosea 14:10).

40. b*Shabbat* 114a.

41. b*Ketubot* 75a.

42. "Indeed, it shall be said of Zion, / 'Every man was born there.' / He, the Most High, will preserve it" (Psalm 87:5).

and/or Zionist is] whose intention remains focused on hoping for [*Zion*].[43] As our blessed Sages teach: "Even devoted ones cannot withstand the same place as the masters of return."[44] [*This exemplifies the power of intentional focus upon Zion from wherever one may be positioned in the world*].

The true measure of remorse within the master of return, as explained by Maimonides,[45] is that the feeling of regret is for existing in the world at all. By looking deeply within, I feel that it is better not to exist in the world lest I may cause any harm. If I cannot be completely immersed in the purely spiritual, then I would prefer to be completely nullified, ultimately transcending all the construction of the personality. [*Even if one is integrated, there are still flaws in the personality. The contrition has to come from beyond the spiritual qualia from the heart. And so in a non-defensive way, one can experience contrition in the essence of one's being beyond the construction of the personality and one's habitual nature*].

This explains: **"of Zion"**[46] [*u'leZion*] all the "marked" [*mezuyanim*] by these letters, as Scripture teaches: **"by still higher ones"**[47] **"it shall be said . . . 'Every man.'"**[48] Namely, these [*references refer twice to "man," whereby the*] devoted one remains at the spiritual level of the letters, while the master of return transcends language. For even the truly devoted one [*is too static, having been born into this state of devotion but without having suffered consciously for it and thus*] is unable to ascend to Zion [*the heart of the Land of Israel which is the spiritual reality prior to the spiritual qualia*] and elevate the oppositional forces into the spiritual heights of the master of return except by completely abandoning and surrendering one's soul to the source. The suffering of the pangs of conscience to the degree that one would rather die than do harm is what purifies the entire landscape of the entire body. Through utter dissolution of self—without even a speck of the dust of the apparent reality[49]—it is all about reaching the ultimate level of the spirit. [*The Land of Israel here is the test case that one would rather die than do harm. That awareness is located beyond the spiritual qualia in the state of true being which merits receiving Torah, the Land of Israel and the World that is Coming.*]

---

43. b*Ketubot* 75a.

44. b*Berakhot* 34b.

45. Maimonides, Laws of Return, *Mishne Torah* 2:2.

46. "Indeed, it shall be said of Zion, / 'Every man was born there.' / He, the Most High, will preserve it" (Psalm 87:5).

47. "If you see in a province oppression of the poor and suppression of right and justice, don't wonder at the fact; for one high official is protected by a higher one, and both of them by still higher ones" (Ecclesiastes 5:7).

48. Psalm 87:5.

49. Literally, "leaving nothing even a mustard seed."

[12.3]. *PARASHAH SHELACH LECHA* (NUMBERS 13:1–15:41)

QUESTIONS FOR REFLECTION:

1. When was the last time that the Spiritual Torah of Judaism has made an impression in your life? Was it during a moment of great joy or immeasurable loss? Why is it that more often than not you are open to that Spiritual Torah in times of loss rather than in moments of joy?

2. How might you take the spiritual lessons that are often garnered through the inevitability of loss and how it afflicts your heart toward a regular spiritual practice? What would such a practice look like? How would gratitude figure in to such a practice? How might your Torah study and Zionist activism also be transformed through conscious suffering?

[13.1]. *Parashah Korach* (Numbers 16:1–18:32)

INTRODUCTION TO HOMILY:

There is much to contemplate in reading and practicing this third-generation Tiberean Hasidism as a radically monistic philosophy of religion (akin to the radical monism of Hindu philosophy based on the Upanishads, called Vedanta). The process of deepening monistic consciousness is itself getting into the light of the spiritual qualia or middot, which means the one has the authentic and powerful experiences of Love (Ahavah) and Awe (Yirah). By turning one's attention away from the distraction of the sensibles, which fill the mind with images and thoughts, then one will experience more and more bliss—this marks the shift from gross to subtle levels of consciousness. By getting into the light of the spiritual qualia of the middot is to become more aware and more intimate with the source. The pioneering spiritual master of hasidism, the Ba'al Shem Tov already posited this in his renowned parable of the adept who wants to be intimate with the king in all its subtle levels, but there remains deeper attractions to the treasure troves along the way. And so, this immersion and distraction is the very dialectical nature between Grace (Chesed) and Rigor (Gevurah). The pathway of comportment is grounded in spiritual practice whereby it becomes second nature and a means of transformative transportation. All individuals are vessels ready to receive light, so that there is a differentiation of Endless light, holding that light from which all material that all individual creations are made then merge. Recall that the Great Mother as Lower Shekinah collects and receives the Endless light through refraction through the upper spiritual qualia, whereas the Great Mother as Upper Shekinah, also known as Binah, is the source of this very light. The precondition to be immersed in a state of integration with the light on the level of spiritual qualia is to merge with the Lower Shekinah. This merging requires a kind of deferring the commanding self without ceasing to exist and belittling oneself. In order to integrate with the Lower Shekinah, one must die before one dies (akin to "fana" in Sufism) to enter into the inner light of the higher spiritual qualia, which are Love (Ahavah) and Awe (Yirah). The lower spiritual qualia, which are coarse, do not retain this subtlety. The source of joy that results from this process should come from the source rather than from the elements of experience that accompany the recognition of the source.

[13.2]. *Parashah Korach* (Numbers 16:1–18:32)

HOMILY:

The commentary of R. Shlomo ben Yitzhaki teaches that **"Now Korach**

made a bad bargain for himself"[50]—for as our blessed Sages teach in tractate m*Avot*: **"Any controversy . . . Which controversy was for heaven's sake? . . . Which controversy was not for heaven's sake? This is the controversy of Korach and his faction."**[51]

It is known that there is a core intention in creating the world. After the unfurling of divine consciousness as human consciousness [*this intention is then realized*] once the human is able to choose between good and evil through free will. The human being was created to directly know **"to reject the bad and choose the good"**[52] so that all sentient beings are permeated with the divine glory, from the most towering being to the most insignificant microbe, even to the oppositional forces, as evinced by Scripture: **"You enliven all beings."**[53] For the universe needs all of it [*nevertheless, there will be a choice to reject some of it as evil*].

This is the core human condition—to refine the precious from the coarse—as is known esoterically: **"and the divine dominion of the One extends over all"**[54] so as to cast off the thorns [*of oppositional force*] and choose [*this spiritual*] life[55] in every moment. [*This choice allows one*] to be more mindful in knowing [*through this pair of scriptural verses*]: **"what this thing is about** [*phenomenal inquiry*] **and what that thing is about** [*nou-*

50. Literally, "Now Korach, son of Izhar son of Kohath son of Levi, betook himself, along with Datan and Abiram sons of Eliab, and On son of Peleth—descendants of Reuben—to rise up against Moses, together with two hundred and fifty Israelites, chieftains of the community, chosen in the assembly, those of repute" (Numbers 16:1). Compare with *Da'at Zekeinim Ba'alai haTosafot* ad loc. "'Now Korach, betook himself'—This section is beautifully expounded in the exegesis of Rabbi Tanchuma. 'Now Korach, betook himself'—He betook himself on one side with the view of separating himself from out of the community so that he might raise a protest regarding the priesthood [to which Moses had appointed his brother, Aaron]. This is what Onkelos [means when he renders it by] 'he separated himself' from the rest of the community in order to maintain dissension." Rashi ad loc Numbers 16:1.

51. "Any controversy that is for heaven's sake shall in the end be of lasting worth, but any controversy that is not for heaven's sake shall not in the end be of lasting worth. Which controversy was for heaven's sake? This is the controversy of Hillel and Shammai. Which controversy was not for heaven's sake? This is the controversy of disagreement of Korach and his faction" (m*Avot* 5:17).

52. "By the time he learns to reject the bad and choose the good, people will be feeding on curds and honey" (Isaiah 7:15).

53. Literally, "[You alone are the Lord. You made the heavens, the highest heavens, and all their hosts, the earth and everything on it, the seas and everything in them.] You keep them all alive, [and the host of heaven prostrate themselves before You.]" (Nehemiah 9:6).

54. "YHVH has established a throne in heaven, and the sovereign rule of the One is over all" (Psalm 103:19).

55. Namely, a spiritual awareness that recognizes the entire world is contingent upon the rooted spiritual energy of all sentient beings being enlivened and spiritually sustained from the One.

menal inquiry]"[56]—[*and through this pair of scriptural verses*]: **"'Because YHVH your God granted me good fortune' [*phenomenologically*]"**[57] and **"Who created these [*noumenally*]?"**[58] For [*these pairs of verses then beckon the question:*] is it not the animating force of YHVH that constitutes, encompasses, and permeates all sentient beings? For Who has endowed the cock to discern between phenomenal matters?—[*and by extension Who has endowed the human being with*] good spiritual counsel, knowing good from evil?

Once one becomes mindful, then why cleave to evil? "Substitute for the evil the good" hidden within it, which elevates and energizes all phenomenality as the enlivening force of existence. Therefore the devoted one **"makes restitution"**[59] of the soul by extracting the precious from the coarse, which is the offering to YHVH **"a pleasing aroma"**[60]—spiritual delight before "the One Who Spoke and we fulfill that desire." This allows the devoted one to realize the divine desire in creating the world precisely in spiritualizing the physical—so that "**the presence of the One fills all the earth.**"[61] This awareness resides even in the place of free will wherein one extracts the precious from the coarse—which is the realm of oppositional forces. This is what is meant by verse: **"a pleasing aroma"**[62]—namely, [*an aroma*] derived from the shells of embodiment and oppositional forces.[63]

---

56. Literally, "Thereon Esther summoned Hathach, one of the eunuchs whom the king had appointed to serve her, and sent him to Mordekhai to learn the why and wherefore of it all" (Esther 4:5). While elsewhere the thrust of the verse can be translated idiomatically as: "Isaac said to his son, 'How did you succeed so quickly, my son?' And he said, 'Because YHVH your God granted me good fortune'" (Genesis 27:20), the force of *ma zeh* as philosophical is only possible when translated hyper-literally as: "What is this?" By asking this kind of foundational question of existence, one comes to discover different realms of consciousness that emerge from the phenomenal and noumenal realms. This explains why the first level of questioning existence is in relation to the phenomenal realm of the senses, while the oppositional realm in this dialectic is the noumenal realm of the spirit.

57. Genesis 27:20.

58. "Who created these? He who sends out their host by count, / Who calls them each by name: / Because of His great might and vast power, / Not one fails to appear" (Isaiah 40:26).

59. "The one responsible for the pit must make restitution; he shall pay the price to the owner, but shall keep the dead animal" (Exodus 21:34) is here being read in the hyper-literal sense that everything is pre-owned by the divine, so that recognition of the divine origin of anything through spiritual practice then "makes restitution" possible it to its original divine owner.

60. "Its entrails and legs shall be washed with water, and the priest shall turn the whole into smoke on the altar as a burnt offering, an offering by fire of a pleasing aroma to YHVH" (Leviticus 1:9).

61. "And one would call to the other, / Holy, holy, holy! YHVH of Hosts! The presence of the One fills all the earth" (Isaiah 6:3).

62. Leviticus 1:9, where *ishai* (pleasing aroma) is being read as *'ishah* (woman) leading to the interpretation as *nukbah* (feminine).

63. Often times the Zohar likens this to the "rose surrounded by thorns." For ex-

This refers to "the One Who Spoke and we fulfill that desire"—the One Who Spoke the world into existence through ten speech utterances, for the sake of unfurling divine desire in matter, even so "we are fulfilling the divine desire," to fulfill the prophetic vision: **"For the land shall be filled with devotion . . . as water."**[64] What this means [*esoterically*] is that the **"land"** refers to matter, the greatest restraint of the blessed Infinite One as it enlivens the dust of the earth and all which contains it, so as to encompass it and permeate it. This is the [*condition embodied in the scriptural verse*] **"For the land shall be filled with devotion . . . as water"**[65]—an expansion [*of the spiritual within the physical realm*].

We find that in the creation of the world the restraint itself is expressed as follows: "The blessed Holy One created the world through Torah"—with twenty-two "letters"[66] so that our blessed Sages then teach that Holy One contemplated Torah to create the world, as Scripture states: **"I [*i.e.Torah*] was with the Holy One as a confidant,"**[67] for Torah was revealed through the [*containing*] mouth of the divine,[68] which is the restraint which our blessed Sages described as "a black fire engraved on white fire."[69]

To elucidate the matter: as is known esoterically, the divine restraint that took place is by way of the divine indwelling upon earth as divine pathos. Namely: to entirely elevate the sacred vitality in the lower world is a real need of the divine, which our blessed Sages teach: **"Israel provides sustenance to their Father in heaven,"** as is known.[70]

This is further explicated: "*Abram* is not generative—rather *Abraham* is generative,"[71] as is known: *Abram* symbolizes extension and spreading forth, so that if there was only this extension then there would be no restraint—then it would be impossible to have any spiritual lineage. But *Abraham* is the last letter of the Name YHVH, so once the *Shekinah* is in the lower realm which is the generative for the sake of then elevating Her again to face YHVH.

As is known: by preparing the lower realms to be receptive, every generative action [*of a new spiritual reality embodied in*] the terrestrial world

ample, see Zohar I: 1a; I: 137a; II:185b; III: 37b, etc.

64. "In all of My sacred mount / Nothing evil or vile shall be done; / For the land shall be filled with devotion to YHVH / As the water covers the sea" (Isaiah 11:9).

65. Isaiah 11:9.

66. Zohar I:204a.

67. "I was with Him as a confidant, / A source of delight every day, / Rejoicing before Him at all times" (Proverbs 8:30).

68. *Yalkut Shimoni*, Deuteronomy, ch. 3:821.

69. *Midrash Tanchuma Genesis* 1.

70. Zohar III:7b.

71. Literally, Abram does not give birth—rather Abraham gives birth (*Genesis Rabbah* 44:10).

creates bliss. This is analogous to the love shared between husband and wife—which is called a "concealed love."[72] This is not the case regarding "brotherly love"—which is an extending love that derives from the same root—a revealed love, as Scripture states: **"If only it could be as with a brother . . . When I met you in the street, / And no one would despise me"**[73]—for constant bliss is not real bliss. This, however, is not the case for concealed love [*which is erotic, albeit intermittent*], which nourishes the *Shekinah* in the terrestrial realm. The greatest bliss is experienced in overcoming the distance [*separating the terrestrial and supernal realms from each other*].

So our blessed Sages teach: "Each of these matters are words of the living God—even though these prohibit and those permit."[74] The matter is as follows: "these" refer to the light of the seven days of creation which are the spiritual attributes, which are five attributes against five—five attributes of Compassion against five attributes of Restraint. So our blessed Sages teach: "the Tablets were constructed with five utterances in opposing columns."[75]

In opposition to the flow of extension, there needs to be restraint, to the point where the *Shekinah* in the terrestrial realm comes to light.[76] In coming to light, it reaches this lowly, empirical world where everything divine cloaks itself in materiality, including Torah and spiritual practice. For ex-

72. This love is considered concealed.

73. "If only it could be as with a brother, / As if you had nursed you had nursed at my mother's breast / When I met you in the street, / And no one would despise me" (Song of Songs 8:1).

74. b*Gittin* 6b.

75. j*Shekalim* 6:1.

76. Compare the Vitebsker's expansive term here of "*Shekinah* in the terrestrial realm" [*Shekinah ba'takhtonim*] with R. Shneur Zalman's more narrowly focused term in the *Tanya'* of "a dwelling place in the terrestrial realm" [*dirah ba'takhtonim*]. On the usage of the latter, see R. Shneur Zalman of Liady, *Tanya'*, I:33, I:36, I:37, I:44, *Igrot haQodesh* 6, Quntrus 'akharon 'al kama perakim. R. Shneur Zalman's linguistic focus on a circumscribed place for the divine presence, rather than allowing for what the Vitebsker's teaching proposes as a more ethereal and perhaps ecstatic hovering of the divine presence. Was this subtle shift in terminology a reaction to Shneur Zalman's sensitivity to the controversy between Hasidim and Mitnaggedim from that winter in 1772, when he went to Vilna with Menachem Mendel of Vitebsk to convince the Vilna Gaon that the Hasidic heresies were groundless? Did this sensitivity to perceptions of overtly ecstatic language increase after the Gaon refused to receive them? Regardless, the term dirah ba'takhtonim takes on new meaning in light of his own experience in enclosed spaces, as in 1798, when R. Shneur Zalman was imprisoned for fifty-two days in the Peter-Paul Fortress in St. Petersburg. While the publication of the *Tanya'* in 1796 remains an important date on the Ha"BaD calendar, the anniversary that is most celebrated as a time for deep spiritual renewal is the nineteenth of Kislev (1798), the date on which R. Shneur Zalman was released from Czarist imprisonment within his own delimited dwelling space that likely affected his own emerging theosophy..

ample, [*consider the cases of*] the *Sukkah* and *Lulav*, etc.[77]

And so it is the case with spiritual values: the spiritual nature of compassionate values is to flow beyond the self—whereas the spiritual nature of rigorous values is to contract. And even these qualities are **"immanent derivations of the one divine source that created them,"**[78] given by one Shepherd. Divinity thus enshrouds itself in these spiritual values without any change to divinity as is known, except insofar as there is an unfurling of the supernal desire—to move from potentiality to actuality.

One spiritual value unfurls and enshrouds itself in material forms, so that Torah, the Holy One, and Israel are one, as is known.[79] [*How is this manifestation possible?*] Consider [*the ephemeral nature of the material bodies which house the spirit*] be it the 600,000 letters of Torah corresponding to the 600,000 souls standing at Sinai, which derive from the world of Compassion, allowing for a spreading of the these spiritual qualities to flow forth and intersect, revealing the divine presence, whereas whatever is forbidden in the world of Rigor is manifest by way of restraint and setting boundaries by way of the divine.

All this pertains to the realm of divine illuminations and not to the vessels. For the purpose of the divine illuminations and the vessels is to prepare the latter to receive the lights [*so the charge can be contained*]. Thus: "They did not refrain themselves from lending each other these vessels, whether they were forbidden or permitted."[80]

"The halachah follows the School of Hillel—because of their humility"—which means "Halakhah" is the composed of the letters of "containment" [*HaKaLaH*]—symbolizing the *Shekinah*, for the School of Hillel is lenient, which embodies compassionate spiritual values. For She is not *sui generative* in and of Herself as is known: just as the moon does not illuminate on its own [*only extrinsically*] but from the light of the sun which illuminates within it [*which is intrinsic to it*].

The meaning of "Halakhah" is walking—to instruct others on **"the way they are to walk"**[81] the divine path. Torah and the spiritual practice serve as 613 counsels for walking the divine path, as Scripture states, **"Walk in My ways."**[82] As is known, both the 248 limbs as well as the 365 sinews of the

77. All ritual implements can be viewed as garments of light; for example, see R. Hayim Vital, *Sha'ar haKavvanot*, Derushai Hag haSukkot 3, 4, 5, 8.

78. Literally, "Have we not all one Father? Did no one God create us? Why do we break our faith with one another, profaning the covenant of our ancestors?" (Malachi 2:10).

79. Zohar III:73a.

80. b*Yebamot* 13b.

81. "[A]nd enjoin on them the laws and the teachings, and make known to them the way they are to walk and the practices they are to follow" (Exodus 18:20).

82. "When Abram was ninety-nine years old, YHVH appeared to Abram and said to him, 'I am *El Shaddai*! Walk in My ways and be blameless'" (Genesis 17:1).

body have to be purified and sanctified. Every organ in the body has the potential to draw holiness to it by way of its vital spiritual bond and truly nullifying the physical sensibilities of materiality [*through a prosaic routine*].

So after a few times, this "walking" [*as a prosaic routine*] becomes habitual [*hergel*]—which comes from the word "leg" [*regel*], so that step after step one is enriched in this practice, until the habit becomes "second [*spiritual*] nature." So that second spiritual nature is [*the point of the original creation of the human being*] derived from the language of "the framework that the Sages enacted"[83]—that such generic forms [*of blessing*] simply reflect an initially created form.

As in the verse: **"And He created God** [*Elohim*]**"**[84] wherein it is known that "God" [*Elohim = eighty-six*], "the nature" [*hateva = eighty-six*], and "the throne" [*ha'kisse = eighty-six*] all share the same numerology.[85] It is thus fitting for the divine throne to be clustered there at the beginning of creation and nature, given its connection to the Original Will. [*For it is through the throne*] then that the divine presence dwells on an individual in the forms of a tabernacle and temple. These forms of tabernacle and temple symbolize respectively the supernal and terrestrial *Shekinah*—which [*dwell within the individual*] by binding one's soul within them.

And it is known: binding one's soul verily with the terrestrial *Shekinah* is a process of unification and integration with Her. There is a singular spiritual intention here—to become a vessel through one's soul, **"[*then*] one can integrate [*the soul*] back into the divine spirit and breath"**[86] so as to receive **"the sun/for light by day"**[87]—by cleaving to YHVH through these spiritual attributes as is known.

In any event, not everyone is spiritually prepared to reach this state; only those who are prepared to traverse the path of true death. The terror and torment with which death bursts into your [*being*],[88] without any change [*in the eternality of the divine nature*], is known as **"The Tree of Death."**[89]

83. b*Berakot* 40b, which discusses the need to adhere to the framework of blessings enacted by the Sages.

84. Literally, "And God created human in the divine image, in the divine image God created the human being; male and female God created them" (Genesis 1:27).

85. Zohar III:223a.

86. "If the Holy One but intends it, / He can call back the divine spirit and breath" (Job 34:14).

87. "No longer shall you need the sun / for light by day, / Nor the shining of the moon / For radiance by night; / For YHVH shall be your light everlasting, / Your God shall be your glory" (Isaiah 60:19).

88. b*Shabbat* 32a, referring to those situations in which death bursts into one's being, i.e., etiology of death in women emanates from transgressions relating to neglecting candle-lighting, menstrual purity, and bread-making.

89. Zohar III:120b.

After having walked through this pathway [*of death*], one will surrender the soul to be put to death and then suffer through deep sorrow and death. If then one will receive the compassion of divine illumination then **"In two days God will make us whole again."**[90] As the sun shines through darkness [*just like passing through a dark night of the soul happens by way of*] cleaving to the divine attributes and cultivating love for the divine that leads to deeper presence of illumination. **"And all the peoples of the earth shall see YHVH's name is proclaimed over you"**;[91] namely, the divine name, blessed be, in its essential and known core.

For **"the heavens belong to YHVH, but the earth is for humankind"**[92]—for it is impossible to reach those spiritual affects symbolized as the **"heavens"** except by way of the **"earth."** It is precisely this going the way of [*all flesh*] which is the way of walking the **"earth"** that is death, and only from there does one ascend to the **"heavens."** For there is no other way of ascent to the heavens except going through the route of **"the human who relinquishes the self inside the tent [*of the Shekinah*]"**[93] which is the tabernacle—symbolized by the *Shekinah*—and the Land of Israel.

As is known in the Zohar[94] regarding the spiritual matter of prostrations in prayer—whereby one surrenders the soul to this place of the *Shekinah* as is written it requires abundant desire in the truest sense of the heart—in cleaving and interconnecting complete desire and yearning; if soul surrender is not done completely, then it is dangerous [*leading toward true death*]. For after one surrenders the soul to this place of [*spiritual*] death, it will not be a complete wholeness and there is the risk of remaining there, in order to become a vessel to receive the Compassion, there are the spiritual attributes that enliven such a seeker.

This is what is meant by the verse: **"And they die, without Wisdom [*Chokhmah*],"**[95] as explained in the following verse: **"He established the heavens with Understanding [*Binah*]"**[96]—for *Chokhmah* (Primordial

90. In two days God will make us whole again; / On the third day God will raise us up, / And we shall be whole by God's favor" (Isaiah 6:2).

91. "And all the peoples of the earth shall see YHVH's name is proclaimed over you, and they shall stand in awe of You" (Deuteronomy 28:10).

92. Psalm 115:16.

93. Literally, "This is the ritual: When a person dies in a tent, whoever enters the tent and whoever is in the tent shall be unclean for seven days" (Numbers 19:14). Compare with R. Dov Baer, Maggid of Mezeritch, *Maggid Deverav leYa'akov, Liqqutai 'Emarim* (New York: Kehot Publications, 2003), no. 267:70a.

94. Zohar III:120b.

95. "Their cord is pulled up / And they die, without wisdom" (Job 4:21).

96. "YHVH founded the earth by wisdom; / He established the heavens with understanding" (Proverbs 3:19).

Point) is that most supernal mind-state, which is the point of truth and the beginning of the root, and if one does not surrender the self and insert the beginning of the root and truth which is *Chokhmah* (Primordial Point) to be integrated within the *Shekinah*, then one will die.

And if one were to say: why bother with such suffering—namely, to serve in this [*process of spiritual emptying*] that is so threatening and terrifying—as the verse states: **"How terrifying is this place!"**[97]—why not just appreciate the divine fullness that fills the earth revealed in all the particulars and generalities of time-space-soul continuum? This continuum of holy vital energy is nourished by the seven days [*symbolizing the*] lower spheres of divine consciousness,[98] as alluded to by the verse: **"Your steadfast Love is confirmed forever."**[99]

Nothing in the world escapes the general field of [*providential*] divine vision, [*whose range is so far-reaching that it is akin to*] a sevenfold seeing [*through the loving fullness of the lower spheres of divine consciousness*] that range **"over the entire earth."**[100] It is known that the entire Torah and the commands are included in and through [*this sevenfold field of loving, providential vision*], thus **"it grows as high as the sky"**[101] through these channels to enjoy divine illumination—to cleave to these spiritual attributes, [*as well as cultivating*] love and awe for the One.

Behold **"it should never escape one's attention"**[102]—namely, be steadfast so that **"one shall walk the royal path,"**[103] for there is no room for any other service—so **"This is the gateway to YHVH—the devoted ones shall enter through it"**[104] and **"Thus only shall [*one*] . . . enter the sacred state,"**[105] for it is impossible to really penetrate the [*deeper*] level

97. "Shaken, he said, 'How awesome is this place! This is none other than the abode of God, and that is the gateway to heaven'" (Genesis 28:17).

98. Akin to the seven spiritual attributes from *Chesed* to *Malkhut*. The question being asked rhetorically here is why not just remain content in practicing *Chesed* (Compassion) and avoid the confrontation with death in the dissolution of *Chokhmah* (Wisdom)?

99. "I declare, 'Your steadfast love is confirmed forever; / there in the heavens You establish Your faithfulness" (Psalm 89:3).

100. "Those seven are the eyes of YHVH, ranging over the entire earth" (Zechariah 4:10).

101. "Though he grows as high as the sky, / his head reaching the clouds" (Job 20:6).

102. "Mordekhai had this message delivered to Esther: 'Do not imagine that you, of all the Jews, will escape with your life by being in the king's palace'" (Esther 4:13).

103. "Allow us, then, to cross your country. We will not pass through fields or vineyards, and we will not drink water from wells. We will follow the king's highway, turning off neither to the right nor to the left until we have crossed your territory" (Numbers 20:17).

104. Literally, "This is the gateway to YHVH—the victorious shall enter through it" (Psalm 118:20).

105. "Thus only shall Aaron enter the Shrine: with a bull of the herd for a sin offering and a ram for a burnt offering" (Leviticus 16:3).

of Written Torah except by way of Oral Torah, which is also known as the *Shekinah*.[106]

This is explained through the parable: "If one only has the inner keys and has no outer keys, it is impossible to enter."[107] Unless one goes through pathway [*of Oral Torah and its rigorous devotion of limitations*], it is not then possible to elevate and reach the state of *devequt*, love and awe of the divine source—rather, one will fall into deep descent.

This explains [*the verse*]: **"One that makes worldly use of the crown of Torah shall perish"**[108]—This crown refers to Written Torah itself, **"where one's Wisdom exceeds one's deeds [of Compassion] . . . [*whose roots are*] few [*so that Compassion will be*] overturned."**[109]

"What real value is there for a human being / in all the deeds one does beneath the sun?"[110]—in seeking an experience where one is fully in the revealed light, one cannot reach such a state without a whole heart, so **"Prepare [*your heart*] to meet your God, O Israel!"**[111] For **"the Merciful One desires the heart"**[112] and realizing [*this kind of*] radical amazement is only possible after one will review what is absent from one's core—which is confronting one's mortality and surrendering the soul, as discussed above.

If you imagine having attained all the love and fear of the divine without going through this pathway of confronting death through the knowing heart—then surely this is an illusion and nothing but fantasies. In deluding oneself that this is spiritual, one is actually being carried away by materialist passions. For the evil that abides in the Tree of the Knowledge of Good and Evil occludes the good one that thinks is being performed, so that all the devotional deeds done are egocentric and completely self-serving for ulterior motives.

By way of parable: any person who is conscious of his/her own status to that degree of self-awareness is then estranged from being with the Sovereign. To truly serve the Sovereign, means abandoning concern for one's own status, given that the Sovereign is overseeing everything, even in one's personal life.

By way of another parable: Why do I need to have security, be it fi-

---

106. Rabbi Natan Neta Shapira (1585–1633), *Megale Amukot*, Parashah VeEtchanan 82:1.

107. b*Shabbat* 31b.

108. m*Avot* 4:5.

109. m*Avot* 3:18.

110. "What real value is there for a human being / in all the gains one makes beneath the sun?" (Ecclesiastes 1:3).

111. "Assuredly, / Because I am doing that to you, / Even so will I act toward you, O Israel—Prepare [your heart] to meet you God, O Israel!" (Amos 4:12).

112. Zohar II:162b.

nancial, political, professional, or in terms of knowledge? Is there anything lacking in my life? My life is guarded and the attempts at security are inconsequential, if that is how I am measuring my value base, then my life is guarded and the attempts at security are inconsequential.

The reality is understood and necessary: whatever status you feel you have is considered a part of you, so long as you continue in that mind-state, you are separated from this Sovereign. Those superficial markers of status are meaningless in the face of the Sovereign.

The danger is that if you are completely devoted to this sovereign mind-state, in that moment of hesitation when you do not respond immediately, are you not then guilty? Only a devoted one in this sovereign mind-state without any ulterior motives is guilty of treason. Betraying that devotion takes but a moment's hesitation. If you are not ready to be deployed without a moment's hesitation, then do not immerse yourself in this degree of proximity. However, someone who is completely devoted to this immersion and ready to be deployed without any hesitation will surely be considered trustworthy by the sovereign.

Behold, the Zohar teaches[113] regarding [*the generative power of gnosis as alluded to in*] the verse: **"When the woman saw that the tree was good,"**[114] and in the following verse: **"Hence a man leaves,"**[115] see there at length as well as at the end of the entire zoharic section where it states: **"Come and see: 'For YHVH your God is a devouring fire' . . . Whoever desires [to penetrate the wisdom of holy unification should contemplate] . . . a flame ascending [with its] two lights: one, a white light, radiant; the other, a light tinged with black or blue. The white light is above, ascending unswervingly, while beneath it is the blue or black light, a throne for the white, which rests on it, each embracing the other, becoming one . . . here lies the mystery of the thread of blue . . . This is grasped in two directions: above, by that white light; below, by what lies beneath, by which it is fueled, primed to glow. This constantly consumes anything cleaving below, anything it rests on, since by nature it consumes and devours. One depends on destruction and death of all."**[116] [*Namely, the mind-state of the ascending white flame is achieved by dissolving the ego, while the mind-state fueled by ulterior motives is a destructive flame, thus encapsulated in the blue-black flame.*]

113. Zohar I:3b.

114. "When the woman saw that the tree was good for eating and a delight to the eyes and that the tree was a desirable as a source of wisdom, she took of its fruit and ate. She also gave some to her husband, and he ate" (Genesis 3:6).

115. "Hence a man leaves his father and mother and clings to his wife, so that they become one flesh" (Genesis 2:24).

116. Zohar I: 50b–51a, Zohar: Pritzker Edition, vol. I, trans. Daniel C. Matt (Stanford University Press: Stanford, 2004), 282–83.

In order to explain the reasoning here, the matter is expounded upon in *Sefer Liqqutai 'Emarim*:[117] namely, it is impossible to enact any change [*be it through renewal or expansion*] in the created world, unless it is elevated to its divine source. For example: sowing seeds [*in the earth*] adds abundance [*through expansion of the seeds*]. It is impossible for the seeds themselves to grown into wheat unless they nullify themselves [*by decomposing*] in the earth, and become one with the earth's soil. So too in the case of insemination within a woman [*in order for something to grow, it must return to its root*].

The matter is as follows: generative power [*for vegetation lies in potentia*] within the earth itself. Should one say: if so, then the earth should blossom without any sowing; it is a matter of the earth, and its internal generative power is really limitless in this regard, to the point whereby it is impossible for anything to expand and disseminate unless a species is sown within the earth [*becoming one with its already self-contained generative powers*]. Once [*the given seed's*] form is worn out in the earth only then will that species become aroused enough to sprout forth from its generative root. From there it has the capacity to expand so profoundly.

So the root is the intermediary between the branches and the supernal powers that stem from it in the unfurling of the chain of being. It is not possible for such unfurling to take place from a higher to lower level, unless it has some means to do so—and this is the aforementioned root.

For this root integrates all the supernal forces, and from that integration all other branches spread forth. The root itself is merely a preparatory means and should not be considered in isolation [*from this integral system*]. So in relation to the supernal realm, [*this capacity*] integrates all sentient beings; whereas in relation to the terrestrial realm, [*this capacity*] is the root of all sentient beings.

Therefore one cannot argue with the necessity [*of the dark side of mortality*]: namely, it is impossible to cross over into a state of divine consciousness over there unless by way of the *Shekinah*, and in so doing one tastes real death. Self-effacement within Her is real, so that afterward one becomes awakened on the return to human consciousness. This is why the *Shekinah* is called **"that which lacks anything of Her own"**[118]—rather it is only [*that causative capacity*] that reaches Her by way of the luminescence of spiritual qualities.

It is known: **"Dashing to and fro [among] the creatures,"**[119] thus one who becomes integrated within the *Shekinah* surrenders to a real death [*of*

117. R. Shneur Zalman of Liady, *Sefer Liqqutai 'Emarim*, aka *Tanya'* (1796).

118. Zohar I:181a.

119. "Dashing to and fro [among] the creatures was something that looked like flares" (Ezekiel 1:14).

the commanding self]. So [*through this dynamism*] She is called a "vessel" [*that has the capacity to collect and hold things even while utterly emptied in form*]—denoting integration, whereby integrating the reception of all the supernal energies, then "wearing out" the [*separating form of the*] terrestrial realm that are self-contained within Her.

This is what was meant by our blessed Sages in their reading of the verse: **"and cleaving to the One"**[120]—which beckons the question of whether it is possible to cleave to the *Shekinah*? After all, She is an all-consuming fire. Rather cleave to the spiritual qualities of the One, namely: after one has nullified [*the commanding self, by dying unto self*] and become completely integrated within the *Shekinah*, then one returns and is reawakened by way of cleaving. For it is known: by way of interconnection and cleaving, the *Shekinah* also receives. This interconnection is called *Yesod*, so that She receives influx from these spiritual attributes.

This is the meaning of "cleave to the spiritual attributes of the One"—for in these spiritual attributes there is cleaving which is not present [any longer] in the *Shekinah*—for the spiritual attributes are a nonconsuming **"white fire"** that ride on the **"blue fire,"** as described in the aforementioned Zohar passage.[121] [*Recall that the mind-state of the ascending white flame is achieved by dissolving the ego, while the mind-state fueled by ulterior motives is a destructive flame, thus encapsulated in the blue-black flame*].

Thus in **"gliding back to where it rises"**[122] Moses was in no way weakened; rather, he spoke face-to-face to the Holy One [*thus his ascent precluded any crossing over through the Shekinah*].

This explains the matter: **"any controversy . . . that is"**[123] within every human being is a microcosm **"for the heaven's sake"**—which means an inner struggle regarding spiritual affects, as discussed earlier, that influences the degree to which one acts with compassion or rigor, [*relating to what is*] permitted or forbidden, even in regard to insights and awe. The principle at work is to keep this intention of integrating the self into the **"[*manifest*] name of the [*non-manifest*] heavens"**—namely, that it is the root of one's soul, which is the *Shekinah*. This inner struggle is concerned with how inte-

120. "If, then, you faithfully keep this Instruction that I command you, loving YHVH your God, walking in the ways of the One, and cleaving to the One" (Deuteronomy 11:22).

121. Zohar I: 50b–51a.

122. "The sun rises, and the sun sets— / And glides back to where it rises" (Ecclesiastes 1:5).

123. "Any controversy that is for heaven's sake shall in the end be of lasting worth, but any controversy that is not for heaven's sake shall not in the end be of lasting worth. Which controversy was for heaven's sake? This is the controversy of Hillel and Shammai. Which controversy was not for heaven's sake? This is the controversy of disagreement of Korach and his faction" (m*Avot* 5:17).

gration into the *Shehkinah* takes place—how to dissolve [*one's commanding self*] into Her, alongside the Holy Blessed Name.

So the act of self-abnegation is understood through the verse: **"This is the day YHVH has made— / let us exult and rejoice on it."**[124] As our blessed Sages teach:[125] "To have the capacity to rejoice with the divine at that moment [*and every particular controversy within each moment*]—thus we are taught: **"YHVH has made— / let us exult and rejoice on it"**[126]—so one should rejoice in the divine.

[*Regarding the aspects of uncertainty whether one rejoices in the moment or in the divine totality*] this means: wherever and whenever that illumination alights upon a person it is called **"day"**[127] and any of these spiritual affects are known as the secret of the divine essence [*even though they appear as plural the secret is they are all one*]. This is why the verse states: **"upon it"**[128]—namely, rejoice on the divine totality, so that one realizes this illumination is actually the divine essence. [*And so one's rejoicing emerges in immersing with the divine essence rather than rejoicing in the illumination that one feels and enjoys.*]

As is known, the divine qualia of *middot* are understood esoterically as the essence [*namely, these qualia are the illumination of the divine essence itself*]. If so, it as is if the King suddenly arrives to stay with you [*that is, the divine light transcends the qualia from which it shines*], then one opens up and makes one's entire house along with all its vessels available [*that is, all the sensibles*]. The one who welcomes such royalty must have undergone self-abnegation [*insofar as one has become integrated into the Shekinah*]. For behold the King is not embodied, *perish the thought*, rather if one truly is open like a royal space for dwelling, then one becomes fully integrated into the *Shekinah.*

This explains: **"Which controversy was for heaven's sake? This is the controversy of Hillel and Shammai,"**[129] which are the spiritual affects, **"for heaven's sake?"**—commitment to a path through spiritual practice and learning [*HaLaKaH which is reconfigured at the KaLaH (bride) of the Shekinah through self-abnegation, and She is referred to as Shem ("sake of")*].

124. Psalm 118:24.

125. *Song of Songs Rabbah* 1:32.

126. Psalm 118:24.

127. Psalm 118:24.

128. Psalm 118:24.

129. "Any controversy that is for heaven's sake shall in the end be of lasting worth, but any controversy that is not for heaven's sake shall not in the end be of lasting worth. Which controversy was for heaven's sake? This is the controversy of Hillel and Shammai. Which controversy was not for heaven's sake? This is the controversy of disagreement of Korach and his faction" (m*Avot* 5:17).

This was precisely not the case in regard to the **"disagreement of Korach and his faction"**[130]—insofar as Korach disagreed with Moses over [*whose spiritual disposition was to draw from and shine forth the luminosity of the Shekinah, from the place of self-abnegation and No-thing, whereas Korach saw the distribution of spiritual energies differently*]. In saying: **"For all the community are holy,"**[131] Korach was claiming that they already realized the spiritual state of Moses [*even though none of them had yet cultivated any sense of self-abnegation near what Moses had acheived*]. He was caught in the spheres beyond the *Shekinah*, as discussed above in the explication of the Zohar.[132] [*This means that Korach was caught in the spiritual qualia of the "white fire" of divine luminosity, and not through the pathway of "dark fire" that is the Shekinah, the state of self-abnegation into No-thingness; rather, he was hovering in qualia beyond it.*]

As is known: [*to be hovering in a spiritual state beyond the Shekinah*] is the place of the Tree of Knowledge and Good and Evil [*where the spiritual qualia that emerge for the aspirant without self-abnegation fully integrated into the Shekinah are susceptible to corruption, and so*]—**"from there separation ensues"** [*getting lost in the World of Separation*], *perish the thought*. Thus when Korachites wanted to draw nearer [*to the divine by way of the qualia of "white fire" without following the path of spiritual affects present in the "black fire"*] to bring forth the offering—then the consuming fire devoured them [*namely, the very black fire they skipped over*]. As the blessed Sages teach: "for Torah is black [*consuming*] fire on white [*illuminating*] fire."[133] This is the path of Torah you must traverse, which is through the black fire—if you do not go through this fire, it will go through you.

[13.3]. *Parashah Korach* (Numbers 16:1–18:32)

QUESTIONS FOR REFLECTION:

1. What kinds of spiritual habits have become second nature to you? What kinds of spiritual habits do you yearn to become second nature to you? What keeps you from cultivating these spiritual habits?

2. The process of traversing and transcending our mortality can be harrowing and illuminating; how has this journey affected your

130. m*Avot* 5:17.

131. "They combined against Moses and Aaron and said to them, 'You have gone too far! For all the community are holy, all of them, and YHVH is in their midst. Why then do you raise yourselves above YHVH's congregation?'" (Numbers 16:3).

132. Zohar I:50b–51a.

133. *Tanchuma Genesis* 1.

ability to integrate within the embodied Sovereignty [*Malkhut*] of your spiritual practice?

3. In confronting, traversing, and transcending your mortality, what kind of illumination of the spiritual qualities have you experienced? How has this experience of insight and illumination affected the spiritual constitution of your emotions, like Love [*Ahavah*], and Reverence [*Yirah*]?

4. Why is it important to focus the rejoicing of spiritual practice in your encounter with the divine self (however fleeting) and not merely in the blissful sensation of illumination from it? What spiritual pitfalls can be avoided by returning to rejoice in your encounter with the divine self?

[14.1]. *Parashah Pinchas* (Numbers 25:11–30:1)

INTRODUCTION TO HOMILY:

The only place human beings can live is on this planet, according to Steven Hawking and other quantum cosmologists. The earth then is the only place of cohabitation for the human species. Critics like Naomi Klein proffer a strong critique of climate change and degeneration, but like many environmental activists, what is missing is any appeal to higher power. This leads to some suffering to begin with. What then is the basis of morality? Philosophers like Arthur Schopenhauer in his "On the Basis of Morals" (1840) interrogated with regards to this question of the basis of morality amid the hopelessness of humanity. There must be some ultimate ground for compassion within reality. The Vedanta axiom claims "Tat Tvam Asi" (तत्त्वमसि), a Sanskrit phrase, translated variously as "You are That," suggesting that every person is sacred energy known as 'hayut' coursing through the world that generates compassion—namely the Shekinah. This recognition evokes compassion in saints and artists, who attain salvific enlightenment by sharing in conscious suffering with the Shekinah through an inquiry into the nature of martyrdom. Without a sense of transcendence amid deep immanence, to get beyond the illusion that people act independently, there is a need for spirituality. Sacred energy known as 'hayut,' which enlivens creation, dwells within the earth's atmosphere, which itself is probably an effect of the psycho-chemistry of the entire cosmos. This élan vital or 'hayut' is the intelligence that enables the cosmos to be what it is within the earth's magnetic field and we should live with this.

[14.2]. *Parashah Pinchas* (Numbers 25:11–30:1)

HOMILY:

The question is asked in the Talmud: From whence do we learn that a priest who is less than whole is ineligible for ritual duty? As Scripture states: **"I grant him My pact of peace."**[134] Namely, when the priest is whole and less than whole, and the answer is that "whole" [*shalem*] is teaching us that this is a broken peace.[135] [*Rather than reading this condition as maimed, the homily here is reading this as a spiritual condition of being less than whole, not fully integrated. In the Hebrew word for wholeness, the scribal tradition is to break the vav to embody this state of being less than whole.*]

Our blessed Sages teach on the verse[136] **"Pinchas stepped in to**

134. "Say, therefore, 'I grant him My pact of peace'" (Numbers 25:12).
135. b*Qiddushin* 66b.
136. b*Sanhedrin* 44a.

judge"[137] by noticing it does not say **"he prayed,"** rather **"stepped in to judge"** with his Creator.[138]

The issue at hand can be explained through the Zohar's interpretation of this verse: **"Swear to me . . . If you find . . . you must tell him**."[139] The Zohar then interprets this verse to mean:[140] given that all souls are a deep part of the *Shekinah,* She is pleading and adjuring these souls with their direct connection to the divine to feedback to the divine source itself which is **"in the fever of love."**[141] [*Shekinah is telling all the embodied souls to tell its source of Her longing. She is that element in embodied consciousness that expresses longing for its transcendental source.*]

In order to understand this further, the Zohar teaches elsewhere that "whoever is awakened [*to his/her real purpose here as a servant of the divine power*], nothing is lacking; about this person in such a state, Scripture states: **"for those who revere God lack nothing."**[142] [*The issue of wholeness is now understood to be related to the being state of yirah, such that one in this state is lacking nothing, thus whole to make an independent judgment.*]

Now to understand this further, it is necessary to turn to the following teaching: "Ben Zomah saw a mass of people on the Temple Mount, so he was moved to recite this blessing: Blessed is the One who created all of these to serve me [*for the sake of fulfilling my true purpose which is to intervene and save the divine*]!"[143] This should really bring a person into a deep sense of awe, in recognizing that "the whole world exists for one's own sake!"[144] and then one realizes how the manifestation of divinity [*Shekinah*] is present in all things and all people without exception. Perhaps such a person will be aroused to do what is good and what is right from the divine perspective, and all the more so when the *Shekinah* has to garb

137. Literally, "Pinchas stepped forth and intervened, / and the plague ceased" (Psalm 106:30).

138. Making an assessment of the integral system as it exists and how one then who is awakened wants to then intervene within the system. Here Pinchas makes a judgment on the divine judgment about to take place.

139. "Swear to me, daughters of Jerusalem! / If you find him now / you must tell him / I am in the fever of love" (Song of Songs 5:8).

140. Zohar I:122a.

141. Song of Songs 5:8.

142. "Revere YHVH, you His consecrated ones, / for those who revere God lack nothing" (Psalm 34:10).

143. b*Berakot* 58a: "Our Rabbis taught: If one sees a crowd of Israelites, one says, Blessed is the One who discerns secrets, for the mind of each is different from that of the other, just as the face of each is different from that of the other. Ben Zoma once saw a crowd on one of the steps of the Temple Mount. He said, Blessed is the One that discerns secrets, and blessed is He who has created all these to serve me."

144. b*Berakot* 6b.

Herself in an instrument of divine judgment in order to subdue one's heart. [*In the dialectic of experience, what happens in time and space, there are moments when the Shekinah and Her presence is truncated, and so under those conditions discord and suffering is magnified.*] As a result, [*such a compassionate*] person will be [*awakened*] in awe of the divine presence—feeling the divine presence in a way that arouses one to take on the mantle of responsibility for the totality. [*Shekinah as the totality exists as one's own support and opens the challenge of what it means to be deployed and responsible.*]

When one is engaged in real prayer, the main thing to take to heart is the diminished condition of the *Shekinah*, who should be completely unimpeded in all worlds, then that conscious power used in prayer is "resonating and affecting everything in its totality"[145]—everything that is created, formed, and made, as evident in exemplars like King Solomon, *o.b.m.*, and Moses our teacher, which is implicit in creation itself, as seen in the verse concerning the human: **"and rule the fish of the sea,"**[146] not leaving out anything from this all-inclusive embrace of all that exists. [*Rather than dominion over the created world, one is called on to feel responsible for the totality, not to exploit it.*]

But if a person's consciousness is limited and lacking in this field of prayer for all-inclusive embrace of all that exists, then the *Shekinah* by necessity has to invest Herself in a limited form and diminished condition of judgments for Her own sake. Such a limited prayer will be shocked to the depths of their heart for the divine. *Shekinah* is not empowered by the divine field in it totality if She has to invest Herself in truncated forms of judgment. [*The sense of truncation is a goad to clarify one's relationship to the Shekinah and to recognize Her suffering in one's own suffering. There is a shift here from the focus on the individual to expand toward the totality, shifting from the personal to the transpersonal, in the intentional sense of recognizing the existence of the Shekinah as the omnipresent reality. Her wholeness depends upon a responsible person's recognition of their place within the totality, so that where one stands is interconnected to all levels of existence without distinction and hierarchy.*]

Behold, it is known: every person truly engaged in prayer is an emissary of the *Shekinah*, which is implied in the verse: **"Swear to me"**[147] such that the *Shekinah* is initiating and swearing that person in as an emissary

145. b*Sotah* 5a.

146. "God blessed them and God said to them, 'Be fertile and increase, fill the earth and master it; and rule the fish of the sea, the birds of the sky, and all the living things that creep on earth'" (Genesis 1:28).

147. "Swear to me, daughters of Jerusalem! / If you find him now / you must tell him / I am in the fever of love" (Song of Songs 5:8).

able to enter into deep state of awareness of the divine presence and one's relationship to it while being moved to be a servant. When a person is engaged in prayer with this awareness of the divine presence, then the *Shekinah* is pleading that this emissary should express Her being **"in the fever of love"**[148] for the divine self. As we explained before, one engaged in true prayer should clothe themselves in the divine suffering of the *Shekinah*, who is lacking the full empowerment from the divine source. And such a person engaged in true prayer will be freed of egocentrism and their own personal needs.

So now we understand what the Zohar means by this awareness of the divine in merging with the *Shekinah*, "lacking nothing"[149]—when one is cleaving to the *Shekinah*, taking on the consciousness of the totality and feels its pain, one feels no personal shortcoming and is not attending to personal needs whatsoever. All of those concerns no longer have any value in comparison to the *Shekinah*'s needs, when his/her care is for Her.

Nothing worldly really matters to the person truly engaged in prayer, in comparison to Her suffering and through the magnitude of one's great empathy, until one feels Her suffering to be unbearable. Such a person would infinitely prefer any form of death to life with such divine suffering. It is nothing for this person to sacrifice himself/herself completely in martyrdom because in that person's state of divine love is so blissful.

When a person is thus empowered, s/he is not held back or subject in any way to the roots of judgment, having transcended the law of Torah. It is impossible for such a person to focus his/her mind, given his/her overwhelming state of being **"in the fever of love."**[150]

This was the case with Pinchas in his deep empathy for the divine suffering—in his receiving the diminishment of the *Shekinah*, as the Ba'al Shem Tov teaches that everything a person experiences in the world is there to fulfill his need [*to be an emissary for the Shekinah*]. And Pinchas was aroused and released himself from the laws of Torah, and even if he would have consulted with a sage whether he was obligated to allow himself to go among 24,000 people to kill Zimri, it would not have been permitted. But Pinchas could not stand to remain alive any longer thinking of the laws of Torah as a function of the magnitude of his empathy for divine suffering.

And this explains the verse: **"and he intervened"**[151]—namely, Pinchas made his own judgment, making his own **"leap beyond the limits"**

---

148. Song of Songs 5:8.

149. *Tiquney Zohar* 5b.

150. Song of Songs 5:8.

151. Literally, "Pinchas stepped forth and intervened, / and the plague ceased" (Psalm 106:30).

[*pelilim*][152] because he was **"in the fever of love"**[153] driving him mad. And this madness is a form of sweetening the judgment. [*Pinchas is willing to leap beyond convention, transcending the need to defend his own well-being to thus act for the sake of the totality of the Shekinah.*]

This explains: "[*How do you know if your prayer was answered?*] If prayer is fluent on your lips,"[154] that is, coming from one's state of deployment, as in "being sent to you [*whereby everyone was sent to you to make peace*]."[155] For the prayer that one is reciting is an emissary for the *Shekinah* as a part of Her. One who truly engages in this intensely empathetic prayer has to dissolve into Her, and offer the prayer in the greatest state of intimacy.

This is the sign that R. Shlomo Yitzhaki[156] offered regarding the expression "prayer is fluid"—that the prayer flows from the heart, so that a person speaks without any **"barrier,"** without **"cohesion,"** without any **"tearing,"** as explained in the Zohar.[157]

Behold, the Zohar also teaches[158] regarding this verse: **"Provide me with a reliable sign"**[159]—a Mosaic sign which is the whole letter *Vav*, which represents a complete and unbroken empowerment from above. The emissaries answered Rahab and said: No. For Moses has passed on and Joshua has taken over and this is his way that: **"you tie this length of crimson cord."**[160]

As is known in the case of the whitening of the scarlet cord,[161] which is a sign of the sweetening of judgment,[162] **"Your lips are like crimson thread"**[163] if my prayer is a sign of spiritual deployment."

---

152. "When men fight, and one of them pushes a pregnant woman and a miscarriage results, but no other damage ensues, the one responsible shall be fined according as the woman's husband may exact from him, the payment to be based on arbitration/intercession/mediation" (Exodus 21:22).

153. "Swear to me, daughters of Jerusalem! / If you find him now / you must tell him / I am in the fever of love" (Song of Songs 5:8).

154. b*Berakot* 34b.

155. m*Kallah*, no. 3.

156. R. Shlomo Yitzhaki ad loc b*Berakot* 34b.

157. *Raya Mehamna*, Zohar III:228a.

158. Zohar I:241b.

159. "Now since I have shown loyalty to you, swear to me by YHVH that you in turn will show loyalty to my family. Provide me with a reliable sign" (Joshua 2:12).

160. "[Unless,] when we invade the country, you tie this length of crimson cord to the window through which you let us down. Bring your father, your mother, your brothers, and all your family together in your house" (Joshua 2:18).

161. *Raya Mehamna*, Zohar III:228a.

162. Zohar II: 69b

163. "Your lips are like crimson thread, / Your mouth is lovely. / Your brow behind your veil / [Gleams] like a pomegranate split open" (Song of Songs 4:3).

So in regards to the question of the ritual fitness of the maimed priest, the verse reads: **"I grant him,"**[164] and then the question is raised if there is a *Vav*, there can be no brokenness or anything lacking. This is not the case here, however, where Pinchas is deployed as an emissary of the divine suffering, which implies a place of judgment. And they answer [*in the Talmud*] that it is a sign in the diminished *Vav*—A broken peace.[165]

[14.3]. *PARASHAH PINCHAS* (NUMBERS 25:11–30:1)

QUESTIONS FOR REFLECTION:

1. How does the spiritual reality of divine suffering affect your spiritual practice, especially when you experience some lack?

2. How can your prayer life be uplifted by divine suffering to repair the growing lacks in the world?

3. How does the spiritual reality of divine suffering amid your own suffering open you to a deeper practice of empathizing with others who are suffering?

164. "Say, therefore, 'I grant him My pact of peace'" (Numbers 25:12).
165. b*Qiddushin* 66b.

[15.1]. *Parashah Matot-Massey 1* (Numbers 30:2–36:13)

INTRODUCTION TO HOMILY:

Although some suggest that young children before the age of four years typically lack a theory of mind, it is difficult to agree they are not sentient. To be human is to be fully aware of the self in the context of all sentient beings in creation. Imagine living a life marked by the awareness that everything is deeply interconnected, that all sentient beings in the world reveal divine glory and spiritual grandeur, that every detail in creation uniquely reveals divine glory, and that all details of sentient beings from the planetary perspective are encompassed within the human macrocosm. Such interconnected consciousness leads to a devotional posture where all acts are for the sake of the One. Given that human spiritual qualia are endlessly divided, it is possible to realize that so too are the qualia of sentient beings. By expanding our awareness to encompass all sentient beings, whether material or spiritual, they become manifest in the human being through spiritual qualia and cognition. This has implications for the expansive nature of the mind-stream, so when thoughts cross a person's mind, one must subdue the evil within each thought. This process of subduing and channeling the inner impulse requires one to draw on the interconnectivity to the divine totality. For the human mind, this interconnection with this divine totality is most common through cognition. For cognition remains that highly specific facet of human creation, enabling us as human beings to even envy the thoughts of others. And yet, the reality of the rectification that emerges in returning to the intrinsic awareness of our interconnectivity within the divine totality can only but extend goodness and blessing. This goodness expands exponentially to the point where messianic consciousness of non-dual reality will once again become the truth. What the Vitebsker argues here is that unification is only enabled through the meditation of Da'at (Intuitive knowing). For Da'at (Intuitive knowing) encompasses the seven lower spiritual qualia, which in turn encompass all sentient beings. The focus on this spiritual cognition as a process of unification of Da'at (Intuitive knowing) happens through the mediation of all sentient beings which come to mind.

[15.2]. *Parashah Matot-Massey 1* (Numbers 30:2–36:13)

HOMILY:

"Moses spoke to the heads of the Israelite tribes, saying: This is what YHVH has commanded . . . "[166] and the end of the book [*of Numbers then*]

166. Numbers 30:2.

states: **"These are the commandments and regulations that YHVH enjoined on the Israelites, through Moses, on the steppes of Moab, at the Jordan near Jericho."**[167] [*In juxtaposing these opening and closing verses of the weekly reading*] the following issue emerges [*and is encapsulated in this*] teaching, as the blessed Sages said: **"Do not despise any person . . . any sentient being."**[168] And so [*we learn this principle from*] an incident in the life of Rabbi Eleazar in the name of Rabbi Simeon, where it happened that there was an unseemly person, who turned out to be Elijah [*greeting Rabbi Eleazar who spurned him, and instead said to him, "Good for nothing, how ugly you are*]. Are all your fellow citizens as ugly as you are?" Afterward Elijah chastised Rabbi Eleazar [*for being so learned and yet being so full of himself that he is unable to respect another human being*] but forgave him on the condition that he would not act in the same manner in the future.[169]

This issue we are examining is [*analogous to the aforementioned incident and relates to*] this renowned verse: **"YHVH made everything for a purpose,"**[170] **"All who are linked to my Name, / Whom I have created"**[171]—even the most minute creature in the ocean is all necessary for the universe, for the greatness of the Creator is revealed through these

167. Numbers 36:13.

168. "[Ben Zoma] used to say: Do not despise any person, / Do not deem anything impossible, / For there is not any person / That has not their moment, & there is not a thing / That has not its place" (m*Avot* 4:3).

169. b*Ta'anit* 20b: "There chanced to meet him an exceedingly ugly man who greeted him, 'Peace be on you, Sir.' He, however, did not return his salutation but instead said to him, 'Good for nothing, how ugly you are. Are all your fellow citizens as ugly as you are?' The man replied: 'I do not know, but go and tell the craftsman who made me, "How ugly is the vessel which you have made."' When R. Eleazar realized that he had done wrong he dismounted from the ass and prostrated himself before the man and said to him, 'I submit myself to you, forgive me.' The man replied: 'I will not forgive you until you go to the craftsman who made me and say to him, "How ugly is the vessel which you have made."' He [R. Eleazar] walked behind him until he reached his native city. When his fellow citizens came out to meet him greeting him with the words, 'Peace be on you O Teacher, O Master,' the man asked them, 'Whom are you addressing thus?' They replied, 'The man who is walking behind you.' Thereon he exclaimed: 'If this man is a teacher, may there not be any more like him in Israel!' The people then asked him: 'Why?' He replied: 'Such and such a thing has he done to me.' They said to him: 'Nevertheless, forgive him, for he is a man greatly learned in Torah.' The man replied: 'For your sakes I will forgive him, but only on the condition that he does not act in the same manner in the future.'" b*Ta'anit* 20b, ad loc *Tosafot s.v. Nitdamin lo adam ehad* already made the claim that this ugly creature is actually Elijah, as identified in bDerekh Eretz.

170. "YHVH made everything for a purpose, / Even the wicked for an evil day" (Proverbs 16:4).

171. "All who are linked to my Name, / Whom I have created, / Formed, and made for My glory—" (Isaiah 43:7).

minutiae rather than through their eradication. Since revealing divine glory is the purpose of existence, then every created minutiae in all its biodiversity is reflective of this glory. The majestic divine being is present in everything, in the secret of the verse **"the divine sovereignty is revealed in every minutiae of existence,"**[172] and this further explains the verse that teaches **"And You are the vitality in every living thing,"**[173] and finally the verse **"How grandiose is Your Wisdom present in all created things."**[174] So the divine glory that is revealed from this particular sentient being cannot be revealed in any other one.

[*Just as there is such diversity amongst all sentient beings, so too there are*] all sorts of diverse manifestations of the divine qualities [*like Awe*], for example, [*whether we are considering*] Fear of punishment, Fear of shame, and Awe from grandeur, so too with degrees of Love, all these [*permutations of the divine qualities*] are ways of awakening the human being and constitute its being. So we see that there are many layers to each divine quality, whether within Awe, within Love, and so within each and every spiritual quality and its endless scales of minutiae and interconnection. It is precisely these variations that constituent elements of divine glory manifest in each minute creature; the **"human being is the microcosm"**[175]—the field of experience is constantly changing and flowing as a collection of the divine qualia. [*These divine qualities require dynamism in order to be unified within the One, whereas in stasis there is a loss of unity.*] Human consciousness is the means by which all this introspection and interconnectivity between the upper and lower levels is possible. Every impulse and impression arises within consciousness to remind a person of the source. A conceptual event like the occurrence of a thought can arouse qualia of [*repulsion in*] Awe and [*attraction in*] Love. These qualia should act as stimuli to a greater awareness of the presence of the source in the totality. Each and every spiritual qualia is interconnected [*through a realignment*] leading to gratitude.[176]

See how King Solomon understood the diversity of sentient beings through inner contemplation of his various capabilities and inherent variations; he could then identify those variations in all other sentient beings. Given that King Solomon was paying attention to the constant changes

---

172. Literally, "YHVH has established His throne in heaven, / and sovereign rule over all" (Psalm 103:19).

173. Literally, "You are alone YHVH. You made the heavens, the highest heavens, and all their host, the earth and everything on it, the seas and everything in them. You keep all alive, and the host of heaven prostrate themselves before You" (Nehemiah 9:6).

174. "How many are the things You have made, O YHVH; / You have made them all with wisdom; / the earth is full of Your creations" (Psalm 104:24).

175. *Tiquney haZohar*, Tiqqun 70, 103b.

176. m*Sotah* 1:7.

through the appearances in the mind, so he knew the language [*as the essence*] of all sentient beings. And so too every moment is unique, so time is not a series of undifferentiated moments; there are twenty-eight moments,[177] and the change that emerges from moment to moment is infinite. This flux in the appearances within the mind is found even with the great saints in terms of the sacred dynamism of their consciousness, as with the typologies of archetypal consciousness of Moses and its shadow in Balaam [*da'at haqelipot as a complete immersion in the world appearances and being lost in it*]. There is a correspondence between what is inside the divine macrocosm and its shadow outside. This is where we encounter the first allusion to a further incorporation of the parallel outside to what is inside. The dynamism of the sacred moves through the stasis of the truncated view of Balaam consciousness, namely, where Mosaic consciousness of the sacred within himself and through himself has to embrace and subsume that which is outside. **"The one no less than the other corresponding to God's doing."**[178] [*Notwithstanding this dialectic, it does not preclude transformation of consciousness.*] As Mosaic consciousness enters into the shadow, then gradually it subdues negative influences, transforming into a purified mode of consciousness. According to the teaching of the BeSh"T, people suspected the Mosaic view as also containing the shadow side of Balaam [*given that that shadow element is part of self-consciousness, and thus will bring the self under suspicion*]. Such purified consciousness itself overcomes the shadow, until the messianic era when the husk will be annulled and **"death will be swallowed up by eternity"**[179] so that the very process of ascent to the *Shekinah* depends on the confrontation with its shadow. Dealing with such a confrontation within the mind-stream allows one to utilize the presence of opposition within one's own mind as a motivating and energizing factor to draw closer to such a self-creating ideal. The fuel for the ascent of a person equipped to make the journey is the oppositional elements themselves, and their transformation constitutes this ascent [*so that the only ascent for Moses is through Balaam*]. This dross becomes a springboard to ascend higher to the Creator. These are internal challenges, whereby the nature of existence is a process of overcoming of darkness through the light, as our blessed Sages have taught.[180] This is also mentioned numerous times in the Zohar. So when a person attempts to

177. Ecclesiastes 3:2-8.

178. Literally, "So in a good time of fortune enjoy the good fortune; and in a time of misfortune, reflect: The one no less than the other was God's doing; consequently no one can find fault with the divine" (Ecclesiastes 7:14).

179. Idiomatically, "He will destroy death forever. / My Lord God will wipe the tears away / From all faces / And will put an end to the reproach of His people / Over all the earth— / For it is YHVH who has spoken" (Isaiah 25:8).

180. b*Shabbat* 77b.

subdue the shadow in the presence of truth [*before the divine source*] from that within the very evil residing within oneself, it is a process of nullifying the evil and sweetening the judgment to then bring it into the outer world.

This is why the verse states in this order: **"bring [interiority] of my soul closer to redemption"**[181] first by recognizing the root of distracting thoughts of the external enemies within my own interiority [*so perceiving these forces as exterior is already getting trapped in the evil itself*]. In order to be truly freed and redeemed from the oppositional forces, getting past the seven lower spheres, **"so that I am freed of any adversaries."**[182] The first capacity is a detachment from what is arising in the thought stream being caught up in outer-directed consciousness that requires redemption. The moment one breaks that hypnotic state of enchantment, it follows that one will be redeemed from one's enemies. This act of detachment nullifies the power of the oppositional force.

This shift in consciousness is a messianic moment, which happens in turning away your outer-directed consciousness to rather focus on a more inner-directed consciousness. By going higher than *Da'at*, then it is possible to reach the realm beyond distinctions. *Da'at* then serves as the stitching that keeps the seven lower spheres together, so that redemption has to happen from the seventy nations of the world rooted in the seven lower spheres. But the ultimate purpose is to push oneself off alienated consciousness [*Da'at*], so that there is no longer any obstacle between human and divine consciousness. Any other lower level still reveals the stitching of consciousness [*Da'at*], so the purpose is to get beyond any such stitching. This is what our blessed Sages explain when they say that "the messiah only emerges in the interstice between thoughts."[183] This means that redemption is an active effort whereby your electromagnetic force of spiritual intuition [*Da'at*] to transcend, witnessing the world creation of seven lower spiritual qualities abiding and uniting with the upper *mokhin* (view of the higher self) [*Keter-Chokhmah-Binah rather than Chokhmah-Binah-Da'at*]. Israel will be united with blessed Holy One in messianic consciousness. When the qualia play out and are expanding in time and space, they will populate the world through seven qualia as seventy nations. Redemption requires the transcendence of *Da'at*, so there is no barrier between self and the divine totality, identifying with "I am" [*yichud 'amiti*] rather than the subjective self [*Da'at takhton*] identified with the personality.

181. Literally, "Come near to me and redeem me; / free me from my enemies" (Psalm 69:19).

182. Psalm 69:19.

183. b*Sanhedrin* 97a speaks about the advent of the Messiah that will happen in the moment between thoughts. The Vitebsker, however, rereads this Talmudic section whereby the totality of the mind in *Da'at* comprehends all the spiritual qualia of *middot*, whereas the messianic consciousness that transcends it emerges from the view of the higher self through *mokhin* (consciousness).

This is what our blessed Sages mean in teaching that "Celestial throngs are reciting the doxology in the presence of Israel rather than to the presence of the divine totality,"[184] because in that state of being, the collective is fully identified with the creative source itself.[185] However, in the present condition, prior to the emergence of messianic consciousness, it happens through the sphere of *Da'at* that mediates and aspires to unite all creatures to their source, and neutralize the sources of conflict that separate them, so as to bestow good upon them. [*It is a matter of refining the personality that precedes messianic consciousness, so that one becomes a support for uniting all of creation with its source and neutralizing and overcoming all the causes of evil that separate them, gracing them with beneficence.*]

The issue at hand: a person is much more than merely a body and his/her immediate environment, but actually when the spiritual being is integrated, such a person is an entire world and they are responsible for that entire world. [*This integral being of 'qomah shlaimah' is fractal in nature and should not be confused with the cosmos itself, because the cosmos itself is not contiguous with any particular form of human consciousness. Accessibility requires the multi-perspectival view of every soul, leading to a devotional view, where the individual is not lost in feeling identical; rather, one is an integral part of the totality. From this perspective, the awesomeness of the totality becomes an object of devotion.*] Then such a person will turn consciousness toward aspects of created *realia*, thus elevating these elements, offering these refractions to constitute the source of divine totality: **"in the fullness of human consciousness [*Da'at*] the depths are pierced."**[186] From the depths this devotional posture is aroused, and in the condition of such consciousness one purifies everything, in accord with the teaching of the Zohar: "all of them are refined through Wisdom,"[187] and after this elevation to their root—then such elevated human consciousness is showered with goodness and blessing.

As the blessed Sages teach:[188] "the role of clarified human consciousness [*Da'at*] is to serve and hover as the collective medium between two divine names of ***'El* [*symbolizing the sphere of the Shekinah creating a lower vector*] *De'ot YHVH* [*symbolizing the sphere of Tiferet creating an upward vector*].'"**[189] *Da'at* then is that spiritual energy connecting the leaf

184. b*Baba Batra* 75b.

185. This is a similar conception developed in depth by the rereading of the doxology in the *Ketem Paz,* a forthcoming volume in this series.

186. Literally, "By knowledge of the One the depths burst open, / And the skies distilled like dew" (Proverbs 3:20).

187. Zohar III:10b.

188. b*Berakot* 31a.

189. Literally, "Talk no more with lofty pride, / Let no arrogance cross your lips! / For YHVH is an all-knowing One; / By the One actions are measured" (1 Samuel 2:3).

to the root that is the blessed Name as discussed above, so that **"All [sentient beings] linked to My Name / manifest My Glory."**[190] [*The divine totality manifests in the realm of appearance so that*] all sentient beings are imbedded with the holiness of the Name, for the Limitless One encircles and **"fills all worlds of consciousness,"** as is known.[191] So **"in the depths of one's consciousness,"** the status of all the objects of consciousness are elevated in those very same [*worlds of consciousness*] to their roots, then unifying those [*worlds of consciousness*] with the Limitless One [*not disappearing but recognized as inseparable from the infinite*].

[*The fullness of expanded human consciousness is responsible for all the objects of manifestation; there is an analogy with the miqdash as will now be elucidated.*] In this way, the sanctuary is thus [*seen in light*] of the blessed Sages' teaching,[192] namely, that the sanctuary was given between divine names, as Scripture states: **"Your hands have established O YHVH, / The sanctuary ADoNaI."**[193] Structurally there is an equivalency between **"sanctuary"** [*miqdash*] and **"consciousness"** [*Da'at*], both residing between the two divine names, so that the holy temple was the source of blessing to sustain all sentient beings of the entire world,[194] uniting the upper and lower. It was through the locus of worship from which light emanates now accomplished through one's *Da'at* smelting through the husk and uplifting the sparks to their source. Had the seventy nations understood the spiritual channeling of the *miqdash*, they would not have destroyed it. Now that there is no temple, its substitute is the integral topography of the spiritual being [*enabling the unification of upper and lower worlds*]. So too a person is stimulated by the contents of their own expanded consciousness, and then the world itself becomes a stimulus of one's devotion to the divine source. If we were in the condition of messianic consciousness, we still could not identify with the divine totality and so we are dependent on everything that exists within our experience to achieve this. This is a function of *Da'at* [*a conductivity of bliss as both the medium and its mitigation through its spheres, so that Da'at both unifies and separates for purposes of protection. We are dependent on everything in existence, and everything in existence is dependent on us*]. Pure bliss is the condition of expanded human consciousness in its fullness and is not possible until the realization of messianic consciousness; only then is unmediated joy possible and pres-

190. Literally, "All who are linked to My Name, / Whom I have created, / Formed, and made for My Glory" (Isaiah 43:7).

191. Zohar III:225a.

192. b*Berakot* 33a.

193. Literally, "You will bring them and plant them in Your own mountain, / The place You made to dwell in, O YHVH, / The sanctuary, O YHVH, which Your hands have established" (Exodus 16:17).

194. b*Sukkah* 55b.

ent. [*Under the present conditions, complete merging is not yet possible, because there is too much suffering amid all sentient beings, so*] until then, bliss is conditional on the recognition of the divine nature of all that exists and upon the elevation of all sentient beings through *Da'at*.

It is a general principle that each and every devoted person has to survey everything through the mind, from everything below right up to the individual's spiritual stature. And what if a person claims to be so devoted to have overcome and transcended all materiality, emotions and desire, thus there is nothing left to purge? Do not think this way, for you are oblivious to sensing your true spiritual composition. The foolish one [*lacking mindfulness*] does not sense this reality; just because you have worked through one specific sphere of mind-stream, there is work that remains in another. [*You may have gotten beyond certain corrupting tendencies that afflicted you in the past, but that does not mean you have overcome all corrupting tendencies. The higher your development level, the greater the potential for deeper corruption.*]

When one is mindful in this way, then the corrupting thought becomes **"chagrined and unwelcomed in one's eyes."**[195] Be careful not to bring this idolatrous attitude inside one's inner temple, wherein the heart is the palace of love. [*The danger here is excluding the affect of the heart, which would feel this chagrin emerging from shame, lest one become too intellectual in contemplation. It is this affect which serves to awaken such a seeker.*] What follows from this awareness in one's mind-stream that something is embarrassing is an arousal that connects to the elevation to remind one of the divine nature of one's soul filled by the energy of the *Shekinah*. This uplifting from the dust of this divine energy is contingent upon being awake, continuing the process of spiritual journeying from one station to the next, from one moment with the potential for awakening to another, from one evolutionary level to the next. [*Being affected by what comes to you changes the nature of reality. The information that is passing through the mind-stream is the creation of the world itself, because the world is created by that information rather than energy and matter.*[196] *Reality is thus co-creative, insofar as a person can feel ashamed by the information and that affects the nature of reality; thus every human being is a co-creator of creation.*]

These then are the forty-two stations written about in Torah, which the Israelites had to pass through to be liberated from materiality of bricks and mortar within Egypt to the Holy Land, which is the Community of Israel, the forty-two letter Divine Name. The wandering of Israel is not some hap-

195. Psalm 16:4.

196. According to quantum cosmologist Jude Currivan in *Cosmic Hologram: In-formation at the Center of Creation.*

penstance event; rather, [*the letters of this forty-two letter Divine Name*] are necessary steps of purification along the journey to elevate from below to above. [*In order to reclaim the fullness of one's consciousness, one needs to journey through these forty-two stations in order to reclaim one's wholeness.*] Sometimes devoted ones experience a descent, appearing to go backward on their journey. [*Sometimes conditions appear in the mind-stream that are retrograde; what one is responsible for is not the content but how one reacts to it.*] But the descent is necessary for the next ascent.

In terms of navigating through the content of our minds, there are moments that appear to be regressions rather than progressions, so that many times we appear to be moving backward. This movement from a progressive to a regressive state is part of the **"integral process"**[197]—but more of a retrenchment for the sake of a further launching forward. And this dynamic dialectic will continue ad infinitum, until redemption—may it come speedily in our day. And in that vision of the future perfection that is always coming, the dream is of a process without any descent, so that the *Shekinah* is lifted upward through an integral path. [*There is a sense of progression by privileging the good amid the shadow, but it is dialectical to the point of creating momentum. The sublime construction of the human being centers around the intervention of the affective sphere of Da'at that integrates the cognitive spheres of Chokhmah and Binah. This affective sphere of Da'at serves as the course-correcting conscience*]. Therefore [*the angels supporting the redemptive aspirations*] are singing the doxology to the Community of Israel, which is a taking leave of complacency. [*The angels here are encouraging forces within the integral field, giving power to those who are making an effort to move closer to the sublime madness of redemption*].

[*Returning to the opening verses under examination here, pointing to*] this as the meaning of: **"And Moses spoke"**[198] [*is a kind of speech which*] is a matter of the mind directing [*those who trust that there is a counsel for this moment that integrates the illumination and the vessels*], as in **"He subjects people,"**[199] for Mosaic consciousness is *Da'at*. And **"to the heads of the Israelite tribes,"**[200] [*where the "heads"*] refer to the aspects of change which are cardinal points defining the limits of space through the twelve directions of the outward spokes [*of space that is occupied by all phenomenon symbolized by a dodecahedron*], **"of Israel"**[201] [*as the wings*

197. Based on the intrinsic process of this verse, "When the House was built, only finished stones cut at the quarry were used, so that no hammer or ax or any iron tool was heard in the House while it was being built" (1 Kings 6:7).

198. "Moses spoke to the heads of the Israelite tribes, saying: This is what YHVH has commanded . . ." (Numbers 30:2).

199. "He subjects people to us, / Sets nations at our feet" (Psalm 47:4).

200. Numbers 30:2.

201. Numbers 30:2.

of the Shekinah] which is the spiritual support [*serving as the open-hearted receivers of the transmission of Mosaic consciousness*]; all of these matters **"are plighting their troughs"** as two become one in their blending of love from one divine source, united through love. *Da'at* has to serve as the deep source of awareness whose presence unites everything that arises within the mind at its source, serving as intelligence of the unified field composed of information.

This explains the entire verse: **"These are the sacral deeds,"** which means they are fused together,[202] whereas **"statutes"** are the consequences of practicing awareness with regularity of the unifying presence of *Da'at* through just comportment. [*So*] **"[t]hat YHVH commanded through Moses's hand"** [*means*] through the unification of the Limitless with the mind's control center of Mosaic consciousness of *Da'at* by means of the channel of transmission through *'emunah* gathered together as founded in Community of Israel. **"And Plains ['*Aravot*] Moab"** explains that *'emunah* is a mixture of [*confusion and conflict in the mind-stream*] of thoughts leading to a union whereby that "all sentient beings are taken notice of by the divine in order to bestow them life"[203] **"for you bestow them all life"**[204] as they all come from the Limitless blessed be. [*There is no separate self that is producing its own thoughts, so that everything that manifests gets its existence from a transcendental source. What the apparent individual can do is place themselves in a condition of unification with the appropriate spiritual support, aware that it all comes from the transcendental source. The implication is that such a person in this condition then is blessing all creation which emerges from a consciousness of non-dual totality.*] This is the meaning of **"Moab, through Jordan to Jericho,"** whereby Jericho was the outer limit point from which the voice of the high priest, and the sounds of snorting goats and other devotional moments [*like the aroma of incense that*] could be apperceived from the Holy Temple in Jerusalem. And there are other examples elsewhere that show how "Jordan" [*YaRDeN*] is a "descent" [*YeRiDah*] for the sake of ascent to apperceive the Temple [*which is higher consciousness of Da'at*]. The spiritual practice through religious behavior of sacral deeds allows a comfort to emerge in consciousness where there is a practice of unifying all convoluted mixtures by multiplicity as real from the descent into Jordan, and even though it is a descent, it is ultimately an ascent into Jericho. [*The Temple is a symbol of unified consciousness which emerges from a consciousness of non-dual totality. From the place of distance which represents descent it is still connected through awareness of Temple consciousness.*]

---

202. b*Berakot* 6b.

203. *Rosh Hashanah* Liturgy.

204. Nehemiah 9:6.

Or one can say this differently, namely, that sacral deeds are connected to candles, as Scripture teaches: **"for deeds are candles, and the teaching is light of conscious awareness"**[205] and the verse: **"The candle of the divine is the soul of the human, searching through the visceral nuances of the mind"**[206]—as the essence of preparing for each sacral deed is a kind of scanning of one's present condition in order to see if it is worthy of the state of unification as embodied in every limb. [*It is condition of alignment between the source of everything and the individual appearances in the mind.*] It is a matter of taking that minute amount of light from the deed to see if that light of conscious awareness can be held, and as the light grows it is all consuming. So **"These are the conscious commandments"**[207] [*which are opportunities for surrendering to self-judgment and spiritual accounting, so that one should be ready to undergo trials to*] completely give oneself over [*to this abiding light. In rightness of alignment to this state, there is a surrendering to conscious suffering as an expression of divine energy. If, for example, anger is righteous, then it might be an awakening energy from the source, arousing us to righteous actions. Recall the Ba'al Shem Tov's tripartite practice: (1) Surrender – (2) Separation – (3) Sweeten*[208] *– revealing the constant realignment of energy and information. In order to prepare for the unification of the object of experience, the awareness of the object and the source, the first step is Surrendering to divine nature of what one is experiencing from its divine root; next is Separation as an extraction process of choosing the holy aspect of the given energy that reminds him/her of the divine source to allow for realignment; so that the final Sweetening is the divine grace that descends if the person qualified as a process of reception, rather than something that one produces; it is something that one is touched and blessed by. To be a qualified vessel to receive, this process must be experienced*].

Further reflections on this weekly reading: [*after reflecting on the Temple as a metaphor for the mind-stream and its interdependence between embodied consciousness and everything that appears within that consciousness and how there is a mutuality of influence, now the homily turns to the Temple as a dwelling for the Shekinah and the meaning of Her tears emerging from weeping*].

"And Moses spoke to the heads of the tribes."[209] Rashi is pointing out that in contradistinction to all the other prophets who approximated the

205. Proverbs 6:23.

206. Proverbs 20:27.

207. "These are the commandments and regulations that YHVH enjoined on the Israelites, through Moses, on the steppes of Moab, at the Jordan near Jericho" (Numbers 36:13).

208. See Ba'al Shem Tov, *Pillar of Prayer*, tr. Kallus, #95:113-114; #95.2: 115-118; #96:119; #143.1:178; #148.9: 198-199.

209. Numbers 30:2.

message they channeled by using the language of analogy ["*God is saying something like this" in the language of 'ko 'amar'*], whereas Moses spoke precisely with demonstrative articles ["*this is the matter*" *in the language of 'ze ha'davar'*]. So the Vitebsker taught: **"If you shall listen,"**[210] where Rashi teaches that "first you understand what you already heard and then you shall hear something new."[211] The blessed Sages teach that "when you have an empty vessel it can be filled, but if it is already full it cannot be filled; whereas when it comes to encountering divine wisdom, one has to have already devoted oneself to filling it with learning."[212] [*There is a real contradistinction that this prophetic language is pointing to, between the particularity of the human mind-stream and the universal wholeness of the divine. Even though the drop loses itself in the sea of consciousness, and thinks that there is nothing but the sea, in fact, the drop can never really know the totality of what the sea knows. Individual consciousness can never be contiguous with the totality of consciousness. The presence of the old conditions the potentiality of the new. Something new can come through because of what is already there. From the perspective of transmission, it has the capacity to transmit more. But from the point of view of the receiver, there needs to be an emptying to receive something new.*]

[*Now the homily transitions into the weeping over the destruction of the Temple, and then the homily returns to bring these two concepts together for an innovative reading*].

So this matter is addressed in the verse: **"Because YHVH has [thought to] afflict her,"**[213] and the exegesis of our blessed Sages, which teaches: "'Is this all suffering for naught?' Therefore Scripture states: **'For her many transgressions'**"[214] [*Is the suffering just deserts or not?*] There is an explanation of this exegesis in the literature, the core of which is seemingly surprised at the suffering and affliction that is in the straits, so was all this affliction for naught? If this was an event that happened in the past which is

210. Deuteronomy 11:13.

211. Rashi ad loc Deuteronomy 11:13. "And it shall come to pass if you will hearken"—If you hearken to the old [if you hear again what you have already learned, i.e., if you repeatedly study the previous lessons], you will hearken to the new [you will more easily gain new knowledge] (b*Sukkot* 46b, Rashi ad loc Exodus 19:5). Similar is the meaning of "If you have begun to forget," your end will be that you forget all of it. So too, is written [in a certain Essene Scroll]: "If you forget Me on that day, I will forget you two days (*Sifre* v. 22; end of j/b*Berakot*). My commandments which I] command you this day"—[*this suggests*] that they should [ever] be to you as new [commandments], as though you had heard them [for the first time] on that day (*Sifre* v. 32).

212. b*Sukkah* 46b.

213. "Her enemies are now the masters, / Her foes are at ease, / Because YHVH has afflicted her / For her many transgressions; Her infants have gone into captivity / Before the enemy" (Lamentations 1:5).

214. *Lamentations Rabbah* 1:33.

over, then why would one continue to be afflicted by the destruction of the Temple in the future? [*Weeping over the destruction of the Temple is really over the future rather than being limited to the past. Namely, one should forever remain anxious of what will come in the future, for what happened in the past cannot be changed*] in accord with the verse: **"Happy is the one who is anxious always"**[215] wherein anxiety is directed toward the future. [*Namely, being caught up in the past has no value if it merely remains nostalgia. It is important to understand that there are consequences for one's actions and transgressions, but the destruction of the Temple demonstrates a lawful rolling over of spiritual energy, so that the future receives some of that past energy. Thus, making room for the new comes from older traditions, but to receive something new, there is a letting go necessary. The weeping might be seen as a kind of purgation in this process of letting go.*] This is in accord with the verse stating that:[216] **"It is superfluous to be sullen"** and therefore **"It is better to go to a house of mourning,"**[217] which then explains its reasoning: **"for that is the end of every being, and a living one should take it to heart,"**[218] which is future-oriented. So by understanding that the past is past, there emerges a capacity to focus on the future. David was crying out until the sick boy died, then he stopped, "I was fasting until now hoping the divine would hear, but now what is the point?" Being sullen [*'ATZev*] is akin to being idolatrous [*'ATZabeyheim*]. If one has a divine connection, then there is no need to be sullen. If one is aligned to the divine, there is only dazzling light and uplifting energy, so why mourn the destruction of the Temple? [*There is a tension here between exterior expressions of depression and internal alignment with joy, whereby the exterior is an oppositional force and the interior is aligned with the divine totality.*]

Let us consider this teaching of the blessed Sages: "*This* [*joy*] refers to the inner chambers; *whereas that* [*divine weeping*] refers to the outer chambers."[219] But this is not the place to expand on it comprehensively.

215. "Happy is the one who is anxious always, / But the one who hardens their heart falls into misfortune" (Proverbs 28:14).

216. Literally: "From all toil there is some gain, / But idle chatter is pure loss" (Proverbs 14:23).

217. "It is better to go to a house of mourning than to a house of feasting; for that is the end of every being, and a living one should take it to heart" (Ecclesiastes 7:2).

218. Ecclesiastes 7:2.

219. b*Hagigah* 5b: "If you will not listen, My soul will weep in secret because of the arrogance (Jeremiah 13:17) . . . But is there weeping before [i.e., on the part of] the blessed Holy One? Look, Rabbi Papa has said: 'There is no sadness before the blessed Holy One, as is said: "Splendor and majesty are before Him, power and joy in his place" (1 Chronicles 16:27)!' There is no contradiction: this refers to the inner chambers; that refers to the outer chambers." Matt comments: "The last sentence is usually taken to mean 'This [the weeping] refers to the inner chambers; that [the joy] refers to the outer chambers.' However, Hananel

The general principle here is that the oppositional force of the husk exists on the outer layer of the fruit, which is referred to as "the outer chambers" as Scripture states: **"YHVH, Lord of Hosts, called forth . . . weeping and lamenting,"**[220] and as Scripture also states: **"for YHVH has called forth a seven year famine."**[221] Through this **"calling,"** [*these verses both point to the divine*] as a marshaling of the oppositional forces and so empowering them. So this is the meaning behind the verse: **"and so the divine called its heart to be saddened."**[222] [*For there is no chronology from the divine perspective, which would produce regret about the past or anxiety about the future; rather,*] all time—past and future—is one. As the Zohar teaches, it is for the sake of inclining **"to his heart."**[223] Sadness is the oppositional husk itself which **"can only ensnare sinners, while one who is pleasing to God escapes its web."**[224] Then, **"the content one is a feast without end."**[225] This is also the case for anxiety, which is part of sadness, wherein precisely **"those anxious ones in Zion can only be sinners."**[226] It is then by way of jesting that it is possible to explain this aforementioned exegesis on the verse **"Because YHVH has afflicted her,"**[227] for this is not a sadness of regret; rather, it is an empowering the realm of sadness, which is the realm of sin. It is not that God is upset *for* the sins of Zion, rather being upset comes *from* the sins themselves.

But the commentators have explained the teachings of the sages dif-

---

ben Husiel (on the passage in b*Hagigah* 5b) adopts the reverse interpretation: 'This [the joy] refers to the inner chambers; that [the weeping] refers to the outer chambers' which accords with Rabbi Yose's view here." Matt, *Zohar Pritzker Edition*, Zohar III: 15bn293, 96.

220. Literally, "YHVH, Lord of Hosts, summoned on that day / To weeping and lamenting, / To tonsuring and girding with sackcloth" (Isaiah 22:12).

221. Literally, "Elisha had said to the woman whose son he revived, 'Leave immediately with your family and sojourn somewhere else; for YHVH has decreed a seven year famine on the land, and it has already begun'" (2 Kings 8:1).

222. "And YHVH regretted having made human beings on the earth, and so the divine called its heart to be saddened" (Genesis 6:6).

223. See Zohar I:57, also Zohar III:15b: "The blessed Holy One is ready: if they return, He returns; if not, all ceases and judgments are executed. Then, He was grieved to the heart (Genesis 6:6)—He was grieved in the outer chambers."

224. Literally: "Now, I find woman more bitter than death; she is all traps, her hands are fetters and her heart is snares. He who is pleasing to God escapes her, and he who is displeasing is caught by her" (Ecclesiastes 7:26).

225. Literally: "All the days of a poor person are wretched, / But contentment is a feast without end" (Proverbs 15:15).

226. b*Berakot* 60a on the verse: "Sinners in Zion are frightened, / The godless are seized with trembling: / 'Who of us can dwell with the devouring fire: / Who of us can dwell with the never-dying blaze?'" (Isaiah 33:14).

227. "Her enemies are now the masters, / Her foes are at ease, / Because YHVH has afflicted her / For her many transgressions; Her infants have gone into captivity / Before the enemy" (Lamentations 1:5).

ferently: "as long as the Holy Temple was not built in that generation, it is as if it was destroyed in that generation."[228] Therefore, the divine weeping is appropriate as it derives from being separated from dwelling with the *Shekinah*. If it happened, it happened. Rather, so long as return is not taking place, that is, so long as the Holy Temple is not seen to be rebuilt in that generation, it is as if it was destroyed in that generation. In both cases, weeping is appropriate. Transgressions are impediments to rebuild the Temple, and so Scripture states: **"For her many transgressions."**[229] An unrepentant generation and the rebuilding of the Temple can coexist.

This is why they say: "[*weeping*] for the loss as nonexistence"; rather, Scripture states: **"For her many transgressions."**[230] That is the transgressions that are impeding the rebuilding of the Temple as future-oriented, insofar as they are destroyers of the [*future*] Temple. Only through introspection of *teshuvah* can one go forward into the future, rebuilding the Temple.

In order to now expand the teaching: "as long as the Holy Temple was not built in that generation, it is as if it was destroyed in that generation,"[231] we need to turn to the Zohar: **"And Abraham was old, well stricken in age."**[232] Abraham and David were elevated beyond the consciousness of the spiritual qualia. Their aging refers to this transcendent state whereas spiritual qualia is childishness. The days of the week are the spiritual qualia of the divine [*from the qualia of Grounding (Malkhut) to Compassion (Chesed)*]. So when Abraham aged, he elevated the spiritual qualities [*Ancient of Days (Atik Yomin)*]. This is the meaning of "so long as the Holy Temple is not seen to be rebuilt in that their days, it is as if it was destroyed in those days." Those days are the spiritual qualia which built the Temple. Every spiritual seeker is a Temple in miniature known as a Tabernacle, as the Prophet teaches: [*lest you think the fetish over the building as bricks and mortar, rather the concern is about the spiritual constitution of the individual ready to carry the divine within*] **"The Temple of YHVH, The Temple of YHVH, The Temple of YHVH."**[233] *Shekinah* is called "Palace" [*Heikhal= Heh + Kol*], which is "all" [*Kol in numerology* is *fifty*]. *Shekinah* is the final *HeH* [*of the Tetragramaton of YHVH, and thus She is sixty-five in numerology*], containing the five spiritual qualities that are collected in *Yesod* [*fifty*]. This is the site of the unification of Indwelling Presence [*Shekinta*] and Holy One [*Qudsha Brikh hu*].

And so: "Palace" [*Heikhal*] also relates to "sound" and "speech."

228. j*Yomah* 1a.
229. Lamentations 1:33.
230. Lamentations 1:33.
231. j*Yomah* 1a.
232. See Genesis 24:1, in Zohar I:129a.
233. Jeremiah 7:4.

"Sound" is the vibration of silence, whereas "speech" is the final level of all those above it. "Speech" is a form of communication that allows for two separate people to commune through such a medium. This is how each of the worlds above connects to the lower one, by this link of "speech" which connects one realm to the lower one. However, from the perspective of the lower worlds, the "speech" is considered to be "thought"; that is, the person who is listening to the one talking, their speech becomes thought that is enshrouded as letters embodying that interlocutor's thought. When the speaker speaks, the listener is trying to comprehend the speech.

In this sense, the speech becomes the listener's thought. If s/he can train himself/herself to pay attention to this, then look inside as to what are his/her thoughts and the forms that they take, and s/he will see that whatever his/her thoughts are, they are the result of hearing divine speech. His/her thoughts are a channeling of a supernal speech. *Shekinah* is talking to him/her through your throat, which composes his/her thought through the mind-stream, as She is a channel known as the sanctuary. All good that is inside his/her thought is the blessing of "undifferentiated sound" [*qol*] that is filtering down from the blessed Holy One as you process, taking shape in whatever form it does as "speech," which is *Shekinah*.

Any differentiation in speech is a process of thought being broken into different forms of letters as consonants and patterns of speech. The vowels are the energy of the "soundless sound" [*qol*], not written but are the invisible inflections that enliven the words of speech. S/he as speaker is the first differentiator of speech from thought.

For any iterations of thought that are expressed, even the most prosaic and clichéd, these thoughts are actually the lower waters, which are yearning to ascend and return to their source in the "soundless sound" [*qol*]. This is symbolized by the sphere of *Tiferet*, which is the blessed Holy *Shekinah* housing whom his/her speech is yearning to reunite. This is a low-energy output needing to be amplified spiritually. What appears as independent objects within the consciousness of the individual human being is the result of a process of emanation that links all the way to the root, through these particular stages.

The energy of devotion is what elevates the letters back to their source. The qualia of Awe and Love are the two wings that allow these letters to elevate and fly back to their source in thought. [*Here the emphasis is on the mindful attentiveness to the content of the mind*] as constituting the union of the Indwelling Presence—what one *says*—and the blessed Holy One—and what one *thinks*. The one who is wise will be contemplating constantly an awareness [*yitbonen*] through a deconstruction as it appears through the concept letters [*as the crystallization of energies from the divine source*]. This immediately produces the qualia of Awe and Love, which emerge from an acceptance of a divine source by renouncing and disidentifying ownership of your own thoughts [*recalling the Ba'al Shem Tov's tripartite practice: (1) Surrender – (2) Separation – (3) Sweeten – revealing the constant realignment of energy and in-formation*].[234] The Joy that emerges is called "face-to-face." [*This non-dual state reveals itself so that the presence of the source from which the energy of speech emerges is part of awareness in the midst of prayer, speaking both orally and resounding within the mindstream and bringing on a blissful state. That is, the face of the Indwelling Presence is Awe, while the face of the blessed Holy One is Love which come together in union.*]

So this is really an elevation of the conditions of consciousness through these two wings of Awe and Love [*like attractive forces when elevated to a non-dual level of consciousness*] which restore this face-to-face unification. [*The lower worlds are actually emanations from a higher source, even though the consciousness within them does not include the recognition of their nature as emanation. It is a matter of human experience, so that the conditions of consciousness include both the multiverses as well as the Indwelling Presence. Claiming that You are the universe is a rectification of anthropocentricity, not of the human as the center of the universe but that the universe is within human consciousness. But there are actually a locus on a continuum, so that this is an elevation of consciousness that descends and can return to arise again to a point where the separation is no longer a factor, actually reaching a complete unification between the source and its emanations. The devotion or Yirah (Awe) that emerges is of the Shekinah (Indwelling Presence) worshiping through the Ahavah (Love) of the blessed Holy One, all caused by the mind of the aspirant. Ahavah is coming down and Yirah is the force that is rising up to meet it, which allows this wing analogy to be seen like the upper and lower Kundalini in Kasmir Shaivism*]. One then cleaves with the descending force of Love as a contemplative experience.

[*In the unitive state, it is not merely ecstatic absorption but prophetic empowerment so that*] the deeply devoted one has fully actualized human powers so that what he decrees is fulfilled. So that one ascends beyond the world taking on the power of the creative force of the *Shekinah*, **"[t]his is nothing but the house of the divine"** such that the space of one's mind becomes a vessel that holds blessing. [*Instead of being absorbed in the content of one's own mind, one needs to become the witness of it, thus emptying it and revealing its spaciousness so that when such awareness is cultivated then the mind can become a house of the divine. Instead of the mind becoming filled with angelic or demonic influences, the deeply devoted one with*

234. See Ba'al Shem Tov, *Pillar of Prayer*, tr. Kallus, #95:113-114; #95.2: 115-118; #96:119; #143.1:178; #148.9: 198-199.

this Yirah becomes the agent of the Shekinah and then channels angelic influences.] The more one brings awareness to the content of the mind, the more it becomes the space that can hold blessing power.

"A woman cannot make a covenant, unless it is someone who makes her into a vessel,"[235] and here the vessel is the *Shekinah*. For the feminine water is the vessel, while the children are the feminine water to the vessel [*meaning that Shekinah is the feminine waters in relation to the Holy One arousing the masculine waters; so by analogy, the human is the feminine waters in relation to the Shekinah making Her into a receptive vessel capable of holding the masculine waters. She is either a vessel or unformed matter channeling blessing depending on the state of the mind*]. The blessing that emerges from the *Shekinah* depends on the good mind-state [*of detachment from their content*], and if that is continuous then it renders the mind into a vessel that can hold blessing power.[236]

This is the ascent of the worlds by way of the wings of Awe and Love, which returns the blessed Holy One and the Indwelling Presence to being face-to-face [*as a divine self-seeing*]. When the mind [*instead of becoming lost in its theorizing recognizes its non-dual nature, it*] acts to join blessed Holy One and the Indwelling Presence. [*In the two elements which are non-dual there is the presence of*] fear of the divine [*which precludes the mind being lost in the glamor of phenomenality and the reality of its own thoughts, which leads to a shock of recognition*] of the splendid glory of pure light. The mind-awareness of subjectivity itself energizes a connection with the sacred web with the Indwelling Presence. [*This is an awareness that emerges*] after its ascent into a recognition of non-duality in such intensity that it is beyond all the worlds [*of conscious experience*]. "You shall also decree a thing, and it shall be established"[237] so that a person whose mind has merged completely with the mind of the field of reality, as Scripture teaches: "the deeply devoted one reigns through" (2 Samuel 23:3).

By making the mind into a vessel that holds blessing power, [*one can realize what*] the blessed Sages meant when they referred to "a woman can

---

235. b*Sanhedrin* 22b: "R. Samuel b. Unya said in the name of Rab: A woman [*before marriage*] is a shapeless lump, and concludes a covenant only with him who transforms her [*into*] a [*useful*] vessel, as it is written: For your maker is your husband; the Lord of Hosts is his name."

236. b*Qiddushin* 40a: "Good intention is combined with deed, for it is said: Then they that feared the Lord spoke one with another: and the Lord hearkened, and heard, and a book of remembrance was written before him, for them that feared the Lord, and that thought on his name. Now, what is the meaning of 'that thought on his name'?—Said R. Assi: Even if one [*merely*] thinks of performing a precept but is forcibly prevented the Writ ascribes it to him as though he has performed it. Evil intention is not combined with deed, for it is said: If I regarded iniquity in my heart, The Lord would not hear."

237. "You shall also decree a thing, and it shall be established unto you, and light shall shine on thy ways" (Job 22:28).

only make a covenant by becoming a vessel"[238] to hold blessing. This refers to the *Shekinah*. [*The mind in its pristine source can either be channeling angelic or demonic flow of thought*] so the mind must be rendered into the condition of a vessel where it is longing to receive the power of blessing. The children refers to the lower mind, stimulating the Mother (*Shekinah*) who then nourishes their longing through Her bestowal of blessing power. [*In this homily the Mother (Shekinah) is not seen as part of the mind. Even though the psycho-spiritual element is present, there is not a relinquishing of the overtly cosmological view. Below is Mother (Shekinah) whereas above is the Holy One, or lower human and Mother (Shekinah) above. The good thinking takes place in the lower human longing for flow from Mother (Shekinah)*]. Letters of the thought rather than the thought itself [*namely, the condition in which something deeper is awareness of the content of the mind-stream*] act as vessels on both levels [*the cosmological and the psycho-spiritual level*].

Whomever does not have this contemplative state of the unification of the Holy One and *Shekinah* within one's thoughts [*namely, the condition in which something deeper is awareness of the content of the mind-stream*], then this condition of unification does not exist. [*This unification is a psycho-spiritual condition rather than a non-dual cosmology. It is a being state which is not constant; rather, it depends on the contemplative action and practice*]. If so, what capacity will such a person have to communicate once the body is perishing and corrupting? For if one's consciousness is dependent upon the physical body to function as receiver for the transmission from the high intelligences, then how would such consciousness be possible once the body ceases to exist? To make matters worse, it is not merely lacking consciousness of this unification, but the fact that the content of the mind created a coarsened experience, given over to self-interest and pleasures—whereby that condition is "damned as contaminated."[239] [*This reiterates the potentiality for a soul without assuming one already has one. Coating the higher energy-body is what allows such a soul to exist beyond the lower food-body that eventually decomposes.*]

The point here: one should strive during one's mortal existence to direct one's inner resources to fulfill and realize one's divine obligation [*and opportunity*] to understand the purpose for which human beings are here to accomplish. [*If one does not make the effort to be contemplative, then one remains an empty, mechanical material body. Freedom from the mechanical nature of human existence is a potentiality that requires a knowledge and will apply that technology.*] All this effort is for the sake of being,

238. b*Sanhedrin* 22b.

239. Leviticus 13:45.

called a completely integrated human being [*that has fulfilled of its potentiality in a normal condition of objective reason by controlling one's insurmountable subjectivity*]. After the disappearance of the material body, there is a survival of consciousness that continues [*likened to the higher energy-body*]. But the continuation of such consciousness is contingent upon the development of contemplative power while in the body. [*No state is as precious as the condition of human birth, because through it can one truly realize the quality of one's being state.*] The condition of the soul in the Garden of Eden in a spiritual body state functions on another level in its capacity to carry, give, go forth, speak, think and see—all by way of the spiritual qualia of the mind-stream. [*If the cultivation of the inner qualia is meant to be the essential focus of the devotional work in this world, then one is cultivating an awareness of the eternal so that consciousness survives beyond the material body, enabling a beatific, eternal experience.*]

[*Now the homily returns to the opening queries surrounding the issue of the doubling of the verb enabling one to now see*] the meaning of the verse: **"And it shall come to pass"**[240] from the necessity of becoming unified in the mind. [*The word 'assifah' suggests a collecting and assembling of the disparate focii of thought within the self that need to be brought into an abiding witness state*] as referred to in the verse: **"And Saul summoned the people"**[241] that is, all of one's disparate parts, which enables that person to participate in the condition of integration of the divine in the human. The basic contemplative practice [*is that*] of maintaining an awareness of the presence of something deeper within the letters of one's own thought, like the ingression of feminine waters into a pool. The hearing of the old [*traditions*] is the recognition of the already divine presence within one's own thoughts; whereas, the hearing of the new [*insight*] is conditioned by maintaining that state of participating and connecting to the condition of integration of the divine in the human. [*Establishing the witness state is a necessary precondition for deeper integration of the human mind-state within the divine. Then there is an integration of the senses and powers, so that one becomes a unified, integrated being, with effects upon the embodied state as well. This is a deeper dimension of the subconscious; it is the source which is now accessed if and when a person is unified.*]

This means: from the human side, there is a need to clear the mind

240. "And it shall come to pass, if ye shall hearken diligently unto My commandments which I command you this day, to love the YHVH your God, and to serve Him with all your heart and with all your soul" (Deuteronomy 11:13).

241. "And Saul summoned the people, and numbered them in Telaim, two hundred thousand footmen, and ten thousand men of Judah" (1 Samuel 15:4).

of old thoughts that had been filling it, so that new thoughts can arise in the form of feminine waters. That is, when the human mind is full it cannot contain more, but rather there needs to be an openness in order to be receptive. From the divine side, however, the opposite applies here, in the divine effluence coming into the vessel of the human mind to be filled. These feminine waters are the energy of longing for the source one's vitality, which is what transforms the mind into an appropriate vessel for holding the holy blessing power. These letters are not transformed into vessels that hold blessing power; rather, they are the content of the mind. Unless the letters as thoughts are emptied, they will not be able to contain the holy blessing power.

This is the matter at hand: all the prophets who prophesied with **"like this"** [*koh*] as in the verse **"and something like this shall you speak"**[242] and **"you speak"**[243]—[*indicates*] there is this contemplative awareness added to the mere content of the mind-stream. Moses is not approximating meaning of the divine instruction as something "like this"; rather, he is pointing demonstratively pointing the divine presence, to the very vitality by virtue of the contemplative practice. That direct recognition of the very divine presence is of the utmost importance for transformation of the person in such a state.

Moses was separated from his wife, Zipporah, which means that his awareness was in the position of the witness which is detached from the content of thought, thus able to observe it in an objective stance. Moses could indicate demonstratively "this is what is real, where it all comes from," rather than the content itself that he accesses the source of the vitality within the vessel itself. "This" whose numerology is twelve, then splits into six and six [*namely, Moses is focusing on the integration of the letter source of vitality of the Vav (=6) within the Heh (=5) of the vessels of thought*].

As mystical literature teaches it another way: *Olam-Shana-Nefesh*; *Olam* is the surface which is the vessel as letters; *Nefesh* is the vitality within the letters of thought; *Shana* is the coordinate of time, so that in any given moment there is a particular integration of thoughts and vitality, whereby *Olam* is dynamic, given that the thoughts are constantly in flux.

Behold, the apportioning **"like this"** of this vitality into various quantities. When asked "What is *really* there?" one responds demonstratively: "This is the source of vitality." When asked: "What is content of the mind?" one responds, "It is 'like this'."

This is why all the prophets were answering the question "What are

242. Numbers 23:5.

243. Exodus 4:22.

our thoughts telling us about the world and how is the divine speaking to us?" One responds, "It is 'like this'." Moses goes beyond this and prophesies, not interpreting through analogy but goes straight to the source, "this is the source of vitality" [*davar*] as the *Shekinah*.

Thus: **"mouth to mouth shall I speak to It,"** which is the source of the vitality within it, so that Moses sees the presence clearly, rather than seeing it peripherally, like the prophets who then have to represent this peripheral vision—**"Not through analogy."** The vitality is composed of Love and Joy, which is the direct vision of Mosaic consciousness which can be demonstratively pointed to, whereas the prophetic indication is peripheral. All the prophets were not fully present, given they had to work through the ego, whereas Mosaic consciousness is fully realized, taking a stand in Eternal Love [*Ahavah*] rather than as the other prophets do in Surrender within Time [*Yirah*]. By realizing this, Moses stands his ground and is not effaced but eternalized, whereas all other prophets are annulled and relinquish the fuller vision.

Or: "mouth to mouth" refers to the prophets are receiving from the lower level of apperception being from the *Shekinah*, whereas the higher station of manifestation as Mosaic, is speaking from the source of the divine totality proximate to his own mouth.

And this is the meaning of the rabbinic dictum: "Moses is asking and answering with the divine voice as his own," "Moses will speak and God will answer."[244]

"And when the voice of the horn waxed louder and louder, Moses spoke, and God answered him by a voice" (Exodus 19:19) of Moses.

[15.3]. *Parashah Matot-Massey 1* (Numbers 30:2–36:13)

QUESTIONS FOR REFLECTION:

1. What experiences in your spiritual journey allow for an opening to the objective witness stance of Mosaic consciousness and what obstructs it most?

2. What is the spiritual sensation of channeling Mosaic consciousness when you can clearly see the mind-stream is "like this"? How does the clarity of "like this" mind-state described by the Vitebsker compare with the "like this" mind-state of a medieval Sufi mystic like Jelaludin Runi, who writes of his experience: "If anyone wants to know what spirit it is,/or how divine fragrancc smells,/lean your head toward him/Keep your face there, close. Like this." Why is such clarity hidden in plain sight

244. b*Berakot* 45a

so often experienced as a surprise, as Rumi writes: "When Shams comes back from Tabriz,/He'll put just his head around the edge/ of the door to surprise us. Like this." Compare this notion of being surprised by God with Garb's essay in this volume.

Deuteronomy

[16.1]. *Parashah VeEtchanan* (Deuteronomy 3:23–7:11)

INTRODUCTION TO HOMILY:

Life can easily become untethered and driven by apathy, indifference that eventually leads to becoming overwhelmed by oppositional forces. To realize the awareness "that there is no-thing else" as Deuteronomy 4:35 claims is more than mere confessional as it might appear at first blush in its biblical context—to a Hasidic mystic like the Vitebsker, this is a matrix for devotional life. But with this degree of radical monism comes the challenge of true spiritual freedom. In a world dominated by the horrors of "altruistic evil"—acts of terror committed in the name of religion—how can one maintain the expansiveness of mind to envision a place beyond the possibility of anger and hate? What does it mean to extend such expansiveness of mind to the Sinaitic moment of revelation? Such spiritual freedom is the place beyond the possibility of hatred and anger, where compassion flows even upon the wicked, all flowing from and returning to its origin point in the womb of Binah (Contemplative Discernment). This homily then suggests it is possible through preparation, contemplation, and deep devotion to cultivate such a mind-state of freedom that transcends the spiritual spheres. Returning to the primordial womb of BiNah through contemplation [hitBoNenut] allows for missed moments and their ensuing heartbreak to be transformed into a deeper divine love lived in life.

[16.2]. *Parashah VeEtchanan* (Deuteronomy 3:23–7:11)

HOMILY:

The verse: **"that you might know."**[1] Rashi comments on **"you have been shown"**—[*by asking*] when? It was at the time of Sinaitic revelation, when the seven heavens were opened, tearing open those veils of the netherworlds, revealing that there was one deity alone.[2]

---

1. "Unto you it was shown, that you might know that YHVH, He is God; there is none else beside Him" (Deuteronomy 4:35).

2. "'Understand this as the Targum has it: 'You have been shown.' When the blessed Holy One gave Torah, He rent open to them the seven heavens, and just as he rent open the higher regions so did He rend open the lower, so that they saw that God was alone the One. On this account it is stated, 'Unto you it was shown, that you might know that YHVH is

Behold, the Vitebsker opened his discourse: **"And I besought YHVH at that time, saying:"**[3] and Rashi explicates this verse: "This is a gift that can only be a freely given gift" [*not contingent upon his merit but still seeking permission to enter the Land of Israel*]. Devoted ones do not want to depend upon their merits rather divine gifts freely given.[4]

This is the meaning of the verse: **"Console, console, My people, says your God."**[5] "Sinning doubly, punishing doubly, therefore consolation is redoubled."[6]

What is *teshuvah* all about? It is the site of *Binah*, which is also associated with shofar and Jubilee in the Zohar[7] [*announcing a reversion back to the source in freedom*]. The exterior force is known as a freedom of being untethered as a dissipation [*that does not allow spiritual work or progress or meaningful application of the self*]. As our blessed Sages teach: "Inferno is completely untethered in its dissipation."[8] And the reasoning behind this is expressed in the Zohar in various places such that the person becomes possessed by the spirit of untethered dissipation. [*In lacking spiritual preparation for each moment, one experiences an infernal state of consciousness of untethered dissipation from the presence of spiritual bounty. That perceptive capacity to notice such spiritual bounty requires preparation.*]

For the hovering of the sacred in consciousness, one needs to focus through the occlusion of clarity, which is experienced in the oppositional-*qelipot* and emerges from a lack of preparation of focus and clarity to expe-

---

God; there is none else beside the One.'" Rashi ad loc Deuteronomy 4:35, compare with b*Hagigah* 12b: ". . . Resh Lakish said: [There are] seven, namely, *Wilon, Rakia', Shehakim, Zebul, Ma'on, Makon, 'Araboth*. Wilon serves no purpose except that it enters in the morning and goes forth in the evening and renews every day the work of creation, for it is said: 'That stretches out the heavens as a curtain, and spreads them out as a tent to dwell in.' *Rakia'* is that in which sun and moon, stars and constellations are set, for it is said: 'And God set them in the firmament [*Rakia'*] of the heaven.' *Shehakim* is that in which millstones stand and grind manna for the righteous for it is said: 'And He commanded the skies above, and opened the doors of heaven; and He caused manna to rain on them for food' etc. *Zebul* is that in which [*the heavenly*] Jerusalem and the Temple and the Altar are built, and Michael, the great Prince, stands and offers up thereon an offering, for it is said: 'I have surely built You a house of habitation [*Zebul*], a place for You to dwell in forever.' And how do we derive that it is called heaven? For it is written: 'Look down from heaven, and see, even from Your holy and glorious habitation.' *Ma'on* is that in which there are companies of Ministering Angels, who utter [*divine*] song by night, and are silent by day for the sake of Israel's glory, for it is said: 'By day YHVH does command His lovingkindness, and in the night His song is with me.'"

3. Deuteronomy 3:23.
4. Rashi ad loc Deuteronomy 3:23.
5. Isaiah 40:1-2.
6. *Yalkut* 545.
7. Zohar I:79b.
8. b*Eruvin* 19a.

rience the sacred presence within each moment.

Intellect and good thoughts per se are not enough to bring the focus that *qedushah* requires, or to avoid dissipative energy of the *qelipot*. [*Clearly, this is in opposition to the developing devotional thinking of R. Shneur Zalman of Liady, where intellect becomes the focal point of devotion in the Tanya'.*] Sometimes one just does not have enough power within the intellect alone to stay away from the pull of this dissipative energy of the *qelipot*. Or as the blessed Sages teach: if someone repeats an offensive behavior, it eventually becomes permissible and causal in one's life. It is not just that this behavior is prohibited, and it makes no logical sense to be involved in these transgressions, yet the intellect still justifies such errancy. One must sanctify the body, for the intoxication of the dissipative energy can otherwise be overwhelming. Under the throes of the dissipative energy, where is such a person and their hope to take a different direction? One drags the divine vitality into the dissipative energy of the *qelipot*; therefore, it is a double transgression taking place here as is known. As the blessed Sages teach: one can force the divine vitality in to places it does not belong.[9] As Scripture teaches: **"The two sins of the people: first, they sinned; secondly, in dragging the divine vitality into the dissipative energy."**[10] It is a kind of aimless wandering that is taking place here, so that when one finds oneself in the same place again, it is necessary to turn in *teshuvah*. The whole thrust of *teshuvah* is a call to confront the dissipative energy and the aimless wandering head on. It is by way of mindfulness [*rather than by way of the intellect*] that one is able re/turn in *teshuvah* back to the womb of *Binah* (Discernment). One's downfall begins through staggering like a drunkard, into a deeper kind of aimless wandering [*lacks the focus of mindfulness*]. It is through the process of contemplation that one is able to transform the dissipative energies of the seven oppositional nations that are identical with the negative modalities.

Teshuvah is also called Shofar, for as one is searching for freedom from the clutches of these negative modalities, freedom can be heard through the call of the Shofar, which is the Jubilee. Then one begins to wonder: Where was his/her dignity when s/he was in the throes of aimless wandering and addiction? It is not only his/her own dignity; rather, it extends to the realm of the sacred as well as the divine that s/he represents. The bitterness that emerges from descending into such dissipative spiritual energies is real, notwithstanding the awe of Eden and Inferno.

When a human being is able to truly contemplate how much this descent into such dissipative spiritual energies affects a deep bitterness, then this very embitteredness itself weighs more heavily on the sensitive spiri-

9. b*Avodah Zarah* 54b.

10. Jeremiah 2:13

tual being than any plethora of punishments, in this moment and beyond. For all punishment serves eventually as an elixir for healing from descending into such dissipative spiritual energies.

"How disappointing that my deep love for the divine has been dragging through the mire."[11] Self-awareness of one's shortfalls elicits bitter disappointment and understanding of dragging to the divine through the mire, who in divine love will follow him/her wherever s/he wanders. Nevertheless, the divine must undergo constriction in these narrow places.

This is the case of Pinchas whose self-awareness leads him to be disappointed with his behavior that is more painful than all punishments. He realizes his life in one moment.[12] While punishment is painful, it is much more about missed opportunities;[13] double bitterness leads to double inner transformation..

This is the meaning behind the verse: **"Speak about Jerusalem"**[14]—speak with tough love into the heart with perfect abashedness and with internal awareness, **"and call out to Her"**[15]—so from the embitteredness there is **"calling out one to the other,"** a loving call with a deep precious affection that emerges [*in an inner dialogue of love between his/her present self with his/her aspirational selves*].

"Iniquity transforms into desire,"[16] so one's heart is roused for the divine limitless love despite all his/her personal shortcomings and the missed opportunities for connection with divine totality. [*This is an ever-deepening process of self-awareness which is at once very painful, seeing how much time s/he has wasted, while at the same time, the intensity of that regret is very bracing and positive insofar as it motivates refining his/her acts and propelling him/her in a focused way.*] The sin is now propelling his/her forward spiritual motion.

And this is the meaning of the verse: **"And I besought,"**[17] for the way of the deeply devoted in their humbled state and even "*Keter* is darkened in the presence of the Cause of all Causes,"[18] for the desire and yearning of the deeply devoted is about bonding.[19]

Such deeply devoted ones do not pay any mind to the good deeds

---

11. "Hatred stirs up strife; but love covers all transgressions" (Proverbs 10:12).

12. b*Berakot* 7a.

13. b*Berakot* 34b.

14. "Bid Jerusalem take heart, and proclaim unto her, that her time of service is accomplished, that her guilt is paid off; that she has received of the YHVH's hand double for all her sins" (Isaiah 40:2).

15. Isaiah 40:2.

16. Isaiah 40:2.

17. Deuteronomy 3:23.

18. *Tiquney Zohar* 135b, Tiqqun 70.

19. Zohar I:171a.

[*which are darkened in relation to the divine totality and*] are still based in the physical world notwithstanding their sacrality: **"for sacral deeds are candles, [and Torah is light]."**[20] Untramelled spirituality breaks forth in illumination without any physical constraint. Simplex luminosity, symbolized by Torah, is completely transcending all corporeality.

This is the desire of the deeply devoted to ascend to the most elevated spiritual levels. And from that apex, there is descent, channeling the luminosity back in to the terrestrial world for the sake of the world. This is also the way of the prayer for deeply devoted ones, unfocused on their own good deeds, luminous as they are, because in comparison to the infinite, it never measures up. Just as the divine gives light to the oppositional forces, so too deeply devoted ones yearn for light.

And the verse continues: **"in that moment,"**[21] which refers to any of the twenty-eight moments[22] [*all the changing scenarios of human experience*] so that whatever the time may be, the deeply devoted one wants to channel love.

"To say"—refers to speech that is not the actual words but the origin of speech itself, the internal source of the voice itself, beyond the diversity of human emotion and spiritual disposition, thus dissolving any emotional turbulence.

"As you began"—returning to the point of origin.

"Your grandeur"—the overflow of Compassion.

S/he is praying for his/her own lack. Contemplate that everything comes from the divine totality. Even though s/he is lacking, it is actually a concentration of divinity. Embittered about how much one falls short, one realizes that "Wisdom at the beginning and the end."[23]

The core teaching at hand: the main purpose of the spiritual life is to channel compassion to all sentient beings, especially the wicked. For who really knows what resides in the heart of another human being? Perhaps such a wicked person will reach the highest point of return that even a deeply devoted one may never reach. [*Even if the wicked person has not yet re/turned, since s/he does not know where they stand, that person could re/turn at any instant to become the highest spiritual being.*]

Thus never speak negatively about any person. One should never judge another person, given that we have lost the right to prosecute another person with corporeal punishment even with two witnesses, and given that there is no longer a Sanhedrin. Now one simply cannot judge another person in the

20. Proverbs 6:23.

21. Deuteronomy 3:23.

22. Referring to those twenty eight instances of temporal contingency that demarcate existence as described in Ecclesiastes 3:2-8.

23. R. Moses Cordovero, *Pardes Rimonim* 15:1.

heart. That prosecutorial proclivity to infect the innermost chambers of our hearts. And if s/he wants to be zealous for the divine, then be zealous about himself/herself—putting himself/herself under that kind of scrutiny.

So this is the meaning of the verse: **"that you might know . . . that there is no-thing else"**[24] refers to the [*true spiritual freedom to envision a place beyond the possibility of anger and hate in the*] Sinaitic moment. The freedom here is the place beyond the possibility of hatred and anger, where compassion flows even on the wicked all flowing from its origin point. This mind-state of freedom transcends the spiritual spheres, which are called the seven heavenly firmaments.[25] These spiritual qualities are spreading and veiling [*in that the rending of the veil itself acknowledges that every modality is both a revelation of the divine as well as an expression of restraint, which is the case for any form of manifestation, especially the spiritual spheres. This opening of the seven firmaments is transcendent, leading to total freedom, being free even from the constraint of holy judgment, Elohim, which is still restrained. Freedom is about reaching the mind-state of Chokhmah (Primordial Point) and Binah (Womb) all returning to its origin. In its origin, it is all divine compassion without even a hint of Restraint and Judgment. Restraint is absorbed back into Compassion at this transcendent Sinaitic state of freedom*]. For the divine totality of YHVH is Compassion, while Elohim is Restraint, which is the restrained aspect of the divine in any kind of lack. To return to the divine [*which is a channeling of compassion and negating the restraint and lack*] so the One has [*nothing but*] mercy.

[16.3]. *Parashah VeEtchanan* (Deuteronomy 3:23–7:11)

QUESTIONS FOR REFLECTION:

1. What keeps you from experiencing the true spiritual freedom to envision a place beyond the possibility of anger and hate? Are the obstacles and oppositions to this spiritual freedom happening on an interpersonal level? On a communal-tribal level? On a national level? On a cosmic level?

2. How might cultivating a practice of deep-seated compassion for integrating the divine totality into my life elicit a loving return?

---

24. "Unto you it was shown, that you might know that YHVH is God; there is none else beside the One" (Deuteronomy 4:35).

25. Rashi ad loc Deuteronomy 4:35, and compare with *Pesiktai Rabbati*, both describing the Holy One opening the seven heavenly firmaments in giving Torah. Sinaitic revelation is read here as non-dual, reiterating the monism of the Holy One.

[17.1]. *Parashah Eqev 2* (Deuteronomy 7:12–11:25)

INTRODUCTION TO HOMILY:

What role do Fear and Awe play in the religious life? There is a difference in degree and in direction when "yirah" is translated and practiced as an either/or rather than an integration of Fear and Awe. The Hasidic tradition already knows the distinction between fear of reward and punishment ('yirat sekhar v'onesh') in contrast to awe before the immensity ('yirat ha'romemut'). But what is explored that is so unique here is a kind of elemental, foundational, even one might say, radical 'yirah' within the eternal life that is a vantage point of the creation that is anterior to it, as if poised at the cosmological Big Bang. What our homilist attempts to innovate here is what the texture of awe is like, that very awe that the divine self feels at the threshold of creation? For the seeker, the task is to return and plummet higher and deeper into the origin of being—to be present right before creation has taken place! The implications of such a devotional posture are immense, for example, especially philosophically, insofar as any presence after creation is contingent, but anything preceding is noncontingent. The homily is envisioning a nuanced, supple texture of awe that ultimately has nothing to recoil to or from, in contradistinction to contemporary neo-Hegelians like Slavoj Zizek, who affirm a certain divine recoil. Rather, the Hasidic posture seeks an originary point even prior to humility—for humility is a spiritual qualia that is only possible after creation. However, to be standing at the place before creation is to only be in the awe of absorption into divinity. And so, as the homily unfolds, pay attention to how a third category of 'yirah', or more accurately a primordial, non-dual origin of yirah emerges here, so as to allow these binary categories to dissolve. By precluding the sense of separation that the derivative, binary forms will inevitably inculcate, here the Vitebsker's proposed vision of yirah is a radical call to complete immersion in the divine infinitude that erases any sense of a separate, commanding self. This is even higher than Love-Ahavah, which requires dyadic awareness of lover-beloved. Beyond Awe, this sense of 'Yirah' conveyed in this homily, which becomes then the highest mystical state attainable, because it is absorption in the divine.

[17.2]. *Parashah Eqev 2* (Deuteronomy 7:12–11:25)

HOMILY:

"Everything is in the hands of heaven, except for *yirah* of heaven,"[26] as Scrip-

26. Rashi ad loc b*Berakot* 33b. He comments that the divine decrees physical qualia rather than moral qualia. For Moses *yirat shamayim* was a small request given that he was immersed in this qualia.

ture states: **"And now, Israel, what does YHVH your God require of you, but to have *yirah* of YHVH your God, to walk in all these ways . . ."**[27] And similarly, Rabbi Simeon bar Yohai has said: "the blessed Holy One has in His treasury nought except a trove of the fear of heaven."[28] As Scripture states: **"fear of YHVH which is His treasure."**[29] [*This juxtaposition of these statements on yirah leads to a third statement for potential resolution.*] And [*the Vitebsker*] said: As the Zohar teaches: "One who possesses *yirah* lacks nothing."[30] As we have already interpreted elsewhere,[31] the Zohar speaks about radical *yirah* as a qualia prior to all worlds [*of separation, whereas this more foundational, elemental, radical form precedes it as unified consciousness*]. This is [*as Scripture refers to it*]: **"radical *yirah* within the eternal life,"**[32] which is the ultimate *devequt* (immersion). [*Radical 'yirah' within the eternal life is a vantage point of creation that is anterior to it, as if poised at the very cusp of creation. This is the awe that God feels at the threshold of creation, but present right before creation has taken place. Any presence after creation is contingent, but anything preceding is non-contingent; thus,*

27. "And now, Israel, what does YHVH your God require of your, but to have *yirah* of YHVH your God, to walk in all these ways, [and to love the One, and to serve the YHVH your God with all your heart and with all your soul]" (Deuteronomy 10:12).

28. b*Berakot* 33b: "R. Hanina further said: Everything is in the hand of heaven except the fear of heaven, as it says, And now, Israel, what does YHVH your God require of thee but to fear. Is the fear of heaven such a little thing? Has not R. Hanina said in the name R. Simeon b. Yohai: The Holy One, blessed be He, has in His treasury nought except a trove of the fear of heaven, as it says, The fear of the Lord is His treasure?—Yes; for Moses it was a small thing; as R. Hanina said: To illustrate by a parable, if a man is asked for a big article and he has it, it seems like a small article to him; if he is asked for a small article and he does not possess it, it seems like a big article to him."

29. "And the stability of thy times shall be a hoard of salvation—wisdom and knowledge, and the fear of YHVH which is His treasure" (Isaiah 33:6).

30. *Haqdamat Tiquney Zohar* 5b.

31. See above, *Peri haAretz*, Parashah Pinchas, 14.2 in this edition.

32. Literally, "The fear of YHVH tends to life; and he that has it shall abide satisfied, he shall not be visited with evil" (Proverbs 19:23). Being completely absorbed in the divine without any recoil, so that even the more lofty awe before the immensity and its recoil is not at play—this is a fear that participates in the divine life itself. See Zohar I:11: "At the site where holy awe dwells, below is evil awe, beating, striking, accusing. It is a lash to whip the wicked. Whoever fears the punishment of flogging and accusation, as mentioned—that awe called 'awe of YHVH leading to life' (Proverbs 19:23) does not hover over him. Who then hovers over him? Evil awe. So that lash deploys above him—evil awe, not awe of YHVH." What is implied in the phrase, "Below is evil awe" that is below *Shekinah*, holy awe, lies the demonic realm, the Other Side, who accuses human sinners and is then empowered to punish them, see Matt, vol. 1, p. 78. Fear of the right object is a key concern for the Zohar, but the *Peri haAretz* is concerned with reading chayyim as *devequt*, that is, life is immersion within the divine. Compare with the later Hasidic re-reading of the *Peri haAretz*, see R. Shalom Noah Barzovsky, *Netivot Shalom*, vol. 4, Parashah Eqev (Jerusalem: Emunah v'De'ot, 1997), 67a–69b.

the quality of such awe has nothing to recoil from. Humility is only possible after creation. But standing at the place before creation, it is only the awe of absorption into divinity.]

This **"radical *yirah* within the eternal life"** [*as a participation in the divine life through a state of devequt (immersion) therein*] is contrary to the natural inclination for *yirah* as fear that causes separation from such *devequt* (immersion). This is known from the esoteric reading of the verse describing the celestial creatures: **"dashing to and fro"**[33]—namely, that in confronting fear the natural reaction is to cringe and be repelled a bit, as Scripture states: **"I would exult in pain,"**[34] like someone whose hand touches the fire and his/her hand retracts from the fire. [*And not only is there a separation from devequt (immersion) through yirah (fear of punishment), but*] even with *yirah* [*ha-romemut (awe) before the immensity does this emerge*] whereby one is in a more expanded mind-state through this radical, foundational *yirah* in the multiverses of consciousness [*there is also an effect on the overall 'devequt' (immersion)*]. Even in this state of *yirah* as reverence that emerges from the *mysterium tremendum* before the immensity of the Great Sovereign as the First Cause there is a sense of embarrassment [*that comes from the self-consciousness of unworthiness*].

But **"radical *yirah* of eternity"**[35] is a state of *devequt* (conjunction) that transcends all devotional expressions of love and all spiritual-emotional qualia. [*This radical 'yirah' of eternal life is accessed*] when one is invested in the *Shekinah* [*by dawning Her garment which is the interface of the divine and human realm through language*], and is so intended [*to be part of this integral rung of all sentient beings immersed in the flow of the divine. From the root of one's spiritual apperceptions, however abstract the apperceptions may be, from the letters shedding and reformulating their form, to the point of incalculability, then one begins to realize the grandiose reach of receiving all these aspects of receptivity and the consciousness of such receptivity*]. And so, by entering into states of ethereal, contemplative possibility, [*one feels*] the contours of the letters of thought [*and conceptual states preceding language*], and are thus exceedingly supple. This is the state where forms recede and emerge ceaselessly. When one becomes aware that this is a gaze from the divine origin, then one becomes awestruck; insofar as one is having this experience, it is a gift of effulgence from the divine origin. One then surrenders in awe to this originary moment of the gaze. Precisely in one's surrender, there is an integration within the source of effulgence and with-

33. "Dashing to and fro [*among*] the creatures was something that looked like flares" (Ezekiel 1:14).

34. "Then should I yet have comfort; yea, I would exult in pain, though He spare not; for I have not denied the words of the Holy One" (Job 6:10).

35. See above n31.

in the divine source itself. [*Contemplating the cognitive letters of creation from which thoughts arise is what then allows one to reimmerse in the divine ocean. This is a non-attached gaze, contemplating how one's own thoughts are divine thoughts arising. One enters into the divine perspective by gazing at the moment before and above the thoughts, becoming co-terminus with the origin of all thought. More than merely dissolving the ego, here the purpose is dissolution of self that is directed towards its source in the divine, which is a kind of apotheosis.*]

[*Thus yirah*] transcends and precedes all qualia, as Scripture states: **"Wisdom** (*Chokhmah*) **emerges from a primordial root,"**[36] whereby efflugence itself precedes the very quality of Wisdom (*Chokhmah*), preceding and extending even the letters yet to be formed [*so that one is observing thought from the place above where it arises*]. Even those matters already thought through, like this kind of cognitive *yirah* of the heavens, which is a conjoining of two separate qualia [*that still transcends and precedes all qualia*]. As is known, *yirah* is a single word [*and qualia given the expression is in apposition, which receives*] while the "heavens" [*the next qualia*] transcend it through its effulgence. [*Both qualia, 'yirah' and 'shamayim' build on each other, so that 'yirah' is emerging from the place of divine origin-'shamayim'.*]

[*The homily returns to resolve the opening question surrounding the tension between the Talmudic dictum that "Everything is in the hands of heaven, except for yirah of heaven" as juxtaposed with the Zoharic dictum that "One who possesses 'yirah' lacks nothing." 'Yirah' has its analogous sphere with the ground of being or Malkhut that directs and guides the universe.*] So *Yirah* is aligned with the sphere of *Malkhut* (Grounding),[37] for *yirah* is only possible with a force above it that allows for reception, as "sovereignty is only possible with subjects."[38] Awareness of such dependency on this guiding power is *malkhut*, as Scripture states: **"and this kingdom rules over all."**[39] [*R. Ezriel of Gerona calls the sphere of Keter "Afisat haMahshava" or the place where thought arises which stands as the consummation of thought.*]

Behold, when one has adopted this radical *yirah* of the heavens as a completely immersive experience, then one turns the tables becoming the *influencer* rather than *being influenced*. Instead of *being ruled by* nature, rather one *rules* nature. One who has this attunement of primordial *yirah*, when so immersed in the divine, then one has all the powers within one's hand.

This explains the blessed Sages' surprise at the teaching [*which responds to the question "What does the divine ask of you?"*]: "*Yirah* is a small word-

36. Psalm 111:10.

37. *Haqdamat Tiquney Zohar* 6b.

38. *Kad haKemakh, Rosh Hashanah* 2a.

39. "YHVH has established His throne in the heavens; and this kingdom rules over all" (Psalm 103:19).

thing," and so they also commented that: "yet for Moses this word is no small thing," which means that for Moses who was the zaddik of the generation who has complete power over all realms, hovering in the primordial *yirah* of the heavens, he is in control of the natural world prior to the unfolding of the divine totality. As a result, Moses is in control of all unfolding, which for him is insignificant, given that he is the partner of the *Matronita.* So what does God want from him? So much more.

The devoted one is the spiritual being who possesses . . . "what" [*MaH*] can be investigated, the *yirah* before any concealment whatsoever . . . what else is needed. **"Only"** [*ki im*] becomes **"Only the Mother"** [*ki 'em*] ;[40] nothing remains externally to be revealed. Once s/he is absorbed in the divine, s/he is the heart of it all.

"Such a person is a co-creator known as 'the partner of the *Matronita*' [*or the Shekinah*], She who rules all the worlds. This is the meaning of the teaching: 'One who possesses *yirah* lacks nothing,'[41] and is also the meaning of the teaching: 'everything is in the hands of heaven, except for *yirah* of heaven.'"[42] [*If one has primordial 'yirah', then one has control of all the worlds of consciousness, and the power to transform physical reality through contemplative magic.*]

As the blessed Sages teach: "the devoted one has the capacity to rule over *yirah* of Elohim [*Shekinah*]." *Binah* is where s/he asks questions, but before that there is not even the concept of a question. . . .

Regarding this teaching, the blessed Sages are astonished: "the blessed Holy One has in His treasury nought except a trove of the fear of heaven"[43]—for nothing remains except awe, and it if it here then everything is here, which is the purpose and directionality of all integration into the divine, so that nothing else remains. [*Moses does not see this demand for yirah as being much of a request, given his predisposition. Going deeper, the homily is suggesting that Moses is positioned in a divine pre-positioning in the place of origin, which is most astonishing here. Living quotidian life from a place of 'yirah' is*

40. Esther 2:14.

41. *Haqdamat Tiqquney Zohar* 5b.

42. Rashi ad loc b*Berakot* 33b. He comments that the divine decrees physical qualia rather than moral qualia. For Moses *yirat shamayim* was a small request given that he was immersed in this qualia.

43. b*Berakot* 33b: "R. Hanina further said: Everything is in the hand of heaven except the fear of heaven, as it says, And now, Israel, what does YHVH your God require of thee but to fear. Is the fear of heaven such a little thing? Has not R. Hanina said in the name of R. Simeon b. Yohai: The Holy One, blessed be He, has in His treasury nought except a trove of the fear of heaven, as it says, The fear of the Lord is His treasure?—Yes; for Moses it was a small thing; as R. Hanina said: To illustrate by a parable, if a man is asked for a big article and he has it, it seems like a small article to him; if he is asked for a small article and he does not possess it, it seems like a big article to him."

hardly trivial, so in the case of Moses, when you possess a trait like primordial 'yirah', it is a state beyond psychology or ontology, rather it is an ontic, primordial reality—a situatedness before the emergence of being, united with divine, looking at the world before its very emergence. This is a profoundly transformative mystical perspective.] This is the astonishment of the blessed Sages in their teaching: "a parable regarding one who asks for a gold vessel, then you give it; but if one asks for a copper vessel and does not have it, that is a great ask." [*The reason that Moses had this divine perspective, akin to the gold vessel, was his ability to channel and transform everything.*]

Everything emerges from primordial awe, rather than reading it as an exception. The hands-on control of all reality happens when one is channeling this awareness into all levels of creation. [*Certainly in a contemplative mode as well as in an embodied mode, the zaddik has the capacity to transform reality by being immersed in the primordial 'yirah'.*]

Another way of reading [*that Talmudic dictum*]: "in the hands of heaven"—is that in the universe everything is under divine control while the hands are agents of motion in the world, except with the *yirah* of the heavens which is the active and dynamic force. Then hands are not even needed, above *assiya (embodiment)*, prior to *aztilut (unitive consciousness)*, which is primordial. [*While the contextual reading of the Talmud is focusing on yirah as an exception, here in the homily there is no exception, so that everything emerges from this yirah because it has been redefined by this absorption in the divine, in the place anterior to creation, out of which emerges this 'yirah'.*]

[17.3]. *PARASHAH EQEV* (DEUTERONOMY 7:12–11:25)

QUESTIONS FOR REFLECTION:

1. Given that *yirah* is to be afraid of what you know or what you expect, standing before creation, *yirah* is not the fear of what you know or expect, because nothing has happened yet. It is the sense of responsibility for being in the place of total potential. But what are the real underlying fears of surrendering? Do you hold on to that or preclude such an absorption into the divine?

2. If you are able to position yourself prior to creation, renewal becomes possible however supple. Amid the extraordinary suppleness of this state of infinite possibility, what does it really mean to position yourself prior to creation?

[18.1]. *Parashah Shoftim* (Deuteronomy 16:18–21:9)

INTRODUCTION TO HOMILY:

Every sentient being is an expression of divine love and manifests this in the created world. And so, of all the stations of the spiritual journey, it is the love that emerges from the divine totality that allows for a deeper interconnectivity with all sentient beings. In principle, this homily displays a great sensitivity in its interrogation into the expansiveness of divine love to the dangers inherent in exceptionalism, namely, that receiving Torah is just an expression of heavenly grace that remains a gift rather than a mark of intrinsic difference that would somehow distinguish one creature from another. By contemplating the inner dimensions of the Golden Rule, what emerges is that love is a metaphysical identity of all human creatures regardless of their moral and spiritual attainments. 'Emunah as the aligning principle here is the realization that everything derives from the divine totality, so that whatever excellence one appears to have realized is not one's own doing but merely a bestowal of divine grace. Given that everything emanates from the divine totality, no human being is entitled to spiritual arrogance over another, no matter how great the apparent disparity. Aligning oneself to this principle of 'emunah underscores how a humanity that is bound by such commonality is reinforced by a deeper and abiding metaphysical love that is inescapable.

[18.2]. *Parashah Shoftim* (Deuteronomy 16:18–21:9)

HOMILY:

[*The Vitebsker was asked regarding*] the teaching about sequence of exemptions from war as presented and taught by our blessed Sages: **"'Who has built a new house . . . who has planted a vineyard . . . who has betrothed a wife . . . Who is there that is fearful . . . ?"**[44] There is a lesson here [*in the sequencing of war exemptions, beginning with shelter to economic sustenance, and then building a family so it is*] about etiquette and how to run a life. Regarding the one who is afraid, the Sages explain that this is a fear of

44. "And the officers shall speak unto the people, saying: 'Who has built a new house, and has not dedicated it? Let him go and return to his house, lest he die in the battle, and another man dedicate it. And who has planted a vineyard, and has not used the fruit thereof? Let him go and return unto his house, lest he die in the battle, and another man use the fruit thereof. And who has betrothed a wife, and has not taken her? Let him go and return unto his house, lest he die in the battle, and another man take her.' And the officers shall speak further unto the people, and they shall say: 'Who is there that is fearful and faint-hearted? Let him go and return unto his house, lest his brethren's heart melt as his heart'" (Deuteronomy 20:5-8).

being killed for one's transgressions, [*namely, that one will not be protected by divine providence in battle. All of the other exemptions are not really legitimate, and are there only to preclude embarrassment for an admission to such transgression and any accompanying existential fear*].[45]

[*The Vitebsker*] opens his discourse [*to address these questions with the beginning of the weekly reading, which states*] **"Judges and officers . . . tribe by tribe."**[46] How is it that the First Pietists had such an intimate connection with the divine totality, notwithstanding they only learned the Order of Torts? In the epoch of Rabbi Yehudah the Prince, it was the case that as soon as one of them would take off their cloak to pray, the rain would come [*answering their prayers immediately*]. Yet we go through so much more study than the First Pietists by completing thirteen study sessions alone on Tractate *'Uktzin* in the Order of Purifications, [*suggesting that our studies are a more comprehensive curriculum than those of our predecessors*], yet when we pray the rain never comes!?! So the Talmud responds: the First Pietists had extreme passion, to the point of surrendering their souls to sanctifying the divine name[47] [*by contrast with the time of Rabbi Yehudah's study circles our study simply lacks that same intensity thus the lack of rain answering our prayers*].

In order to understand this teaching, we need to return to another Talmudic story, this one about the proselyte who comes to Hillel to be converted [*to the devotional pathways of Judaism*] on the condition of being taught the entire Torah standing on one foot. So Hillel taught him: "What is despicable to you, do not do unto others."[48] Rather than being facetious, this proselyte seeking conversion was yearning to be genuinely righteous and authentically engaged in his search for a solid article of spiritual support of balance, integrity, and firmness of *'emunah* that would allow him to base his life "on one foot." From the balance and integrity of this one solid pillar, he would be stronger to climb spirituality and rise up the ladder of ascension to align with the divine. [*The proselyte is asking to be given a religion that will bring together all the disparate elements of his being with such steadfastness and seamlessness that he will never worry about toppling because of the balance and integrity. This standing the proselyte sought*] "on one foot" is that search to align with a steadfast article of spiritual support of *'emunah*. [*Why did the proselyte ask for this?*] For fear of descending by means of trials and the exigencies of life which blindside and destabilize us,

45. b*Sotah* 44a.

46. "Judges and officers shall you make for yourself in all your gates, which the YHVH your God gives to you, tribe by tribe; and they shall judge the people with righteous judgment" (Deuteronomy 16:18).

47. Rashi ad loc b*Berakot* 20a indicates that he was willing to overcome ego and limitations of self-image.

48. b*Shabbat* 31a.

and thus losing this spiritual support of *'emunah* that can serve as a lifeline to stand in good stead during those moments of life that might tempt or shake us. [*The proselyte is deeply aware of the contingencies of human life, being blindsided by any number of circumstances that can be destabilizing. If the seeker yearns for a religion that brings together the disparate facets of one's being, destabilization has no affect upon the steadfastness of balance and integrity.*]

[*Hillel*] answered the proselyte: the principle at stake here is that it is impossible to really begin to engage in devotional service without firmness of spiritual support of *'emunah*, if there is **"but a glimmer of inner conviction from the beginning [that] is a divine gift"**[49] within spiritual practice [*setting up an ever deeper spiral of 'emunah in this pleonastic expression. The first step in inner conviction is the self-aware reflection that even that first step emerges from the divine totality, which is a recursion relationship, that is, a function defined in terms of itself that is enfolding*].[50] Namely, that miniscule, sprouting point of spiritual support comes from the divine [*and not from human will or agency*], so that it is the divine totality which acts as the trusted caretaker, giving him/her the tools to use for such spiritual support. [*'Emunah grows to the extent that one surrenders. While one has to take the initiative into 'emunah, then part of the surrender is the realization that even one's initial glimmering is a response to the divine calling. By attributing that first glimmer to the divine, it leads to firmer, more stable, balanced, and integrated levels in a virtuous circle of ascent, whose center of spiritual gravity is more firmly established.*] **"Hear, you deaf, and look, you blind, that you may see"**[51]; **"A new heart also will I give you, and a new spirit will I put within you; and I will take away the stony heart out of your flesh, and I will give you a heart of flesh."**[52] [*These verses suggest that it is a gift to receive that very sensibility embedded within all senses which is the beginning of "emunah' which does not come from one's initial work. Rather the initial work itself is a priori a divine gift. Otherwise, one has a heart of stone and remains tone deaf to the religio-spiritual sensibility. It is very hard to explain this disposition to someone who does not have this sense. Therefore the first step of 'emunah' is for it to be recognized as a divine gift.*]

And even though the blessed Sages taught "everything is determined by the heavens, except for the awe of the heavens,"[53] [*which suggests that*

49. Literally, "O YHVH, You are my God, I will exalt You, I will praise Your name, for Your has done wonderful things; even counsels of old, in steadfastness and truth" (Isaiah 25:1).

50. *Genesis Rabbah* 1:1.

51. Isaiah 42:18.

52. Ezekiel 36:26.

53. b*Berakot* 32b.

such a solid spiritual support is realized through human agency], this only refers to his/her own arousal from below into a state of awe that is in his/her hands to be catalyzed, preparing one for the divine to experience its arousal from above [*following one's own cue. The work of the aspirant to make space—clearing a space in the heart to invite the divine presence. The sensation itself must come from above. So then divine grace which is arousal from above is always prior to human agency, which is an aspect of our creatureliness, being created by God out of God from God. What this Talmudic dictum suggests to the homilist is that even though divine grace is a gift, the human mandate is to clear the space for that prior grace to settle in. To be an ample receptacle for grace requires preparation*]. For supernal blessing cannot abide in an **"unreceptive vessel"**[54] [*namely, the receptor of this flow needs to be aligned and aroused toward the source in order to receive*], as the teaching of Elisha shows [*in asking the widow*]: **"[*Tell me,*] what do you have in the house?"**[55] [*Two modalities are taking place here for the homilist: first, the widow needs at least one receptive vessel; secondly, in order to receive the blessing emerging from that single flask, there must be numerous other vessels to receive the overflow. In that narrative, divine grace is embodied in finding that single flask that remains with the widow, while the human agency is how the widow captures the divine overflow without it being fully received. The contribution of the widow is creating transparency of receptive space for the prior divine grace in the presence of the prophet and the single flask.*]

Without the wherewithal for spiritual support from the divine [*and feeling the angelic tap upon the shoulder guiding us to wiser choices*], one would not be able [*to have such sustenance*], as the blessed Sages teach: "if you can open yourself [*to this possibility of spiritual support*] just the eye of a needle [*and drop the tyranny of the egocentric mind*], then I will open before you a gateway [*wide enough*] for chariots and wagons to enter."[56] By arousing the self into such a state of awe [*by clearing the path*] **"then the windows of heaven open"**[57] [*and emanate toward the seeker*] so that

54. While rendered here contextually as "unreceptive vessels", by contrast, the scriptural verse describes more literally "empty vessels", see: "Then he said: 'Go, borrow your vessels abroad of all your neighbors, even empty vessels; borrow not a few'" (2 Kings 4:2).

55. And Elisha said unto her: 'What shall I do for you? Tell me; what do you have in the house?' And she said: 'Your handmaid has not anything in the house, save a pot of oil'" (2 Kings 4:3).

56. "Open up for me no more than a needlepoint, I'll make such a wide opening that horses and carriages can enter through it" (*Song of Songs Rabbah* 5:3).

57. "Bring the whole tithe into the storehouse, that there may be food in My house, and try Me now here, says YHVH of hosts, if I will not open you the windows of heaven, and pour you out a blessing, that there shall be more than sufficiency" (Malachi 3:10).

"the great waters overflow"[58] **"with unstoppable love"**[59] whereby everyone receives this overflow according to their own capacity—not everyone has the same capacity [*of opening to receive the overflow of this love. The concern here is that the intense rush could possibly quench the love, but it does not because the love is more intense than this overwhelming rush. This does not overwhelm the thirst, but intensifies it in a virtuous spiral of ascent. So that love continues with ever greater intensity, creating the ever-virtuous circle of awareness of divine love that prompts the individual to an even greater movement of surrender of self and opening up the self, opening the gates further, greater love and so on. This is what the proselyte is asking for: a religion that is firm and rooted enough that it is not overwhelmed even by the initial rush of intensity that sometimes overwhelms beginners*].[60]

And were you to say: such an apportioning [*of receptive spiritual capacities for divine grace*] betrays a kind of favoritism [*rest assured that*] "these matters are mysterious and remain incomprehensible."[61] **"The spiritual garments you wear not entirely of your choosing are what make space for grace"**[62] "[a]fter all, what do you have to do with the mysterious ways of the Merciful One?"[63] **"Who knows the human spirit whether it ascends"** with the alacrity of an eagle [*to great spiritual heights*]—**"and the creaturely spirit whether it descends"**[64] into the deepest depths of entangled husks, perish the thought. [*It would be human arrogance to feel that one could actually foresee who matters yet unseen will unfold, which is both exciting and frightening.*]

[*Behold, it is forbidden to denigrate, castigate, or judge someone else's relatively lower level of spirituality or the degree to which their creaturely spirit brings about descent, given that it remains the mysterious ways of the Merciful One.*] Or look deeper inside, perhaps you transgressed [*and this caused your fellow to be distant from the divine totality*]. If "everyone

58. "For this let every one that is godly pray unto You in a time when You may be found; surely, when the great waters overflow, they will not reach unto him" (Psalm 32:6).

59. "Many waters cannot quench love, neither can the floods drown it; if a man would give all the substance of his house for love, he would utterly be contemned" (Song of Songs 8:7).

60. Compare with the to and fro of waters in Parashah Noach.

61. b*Hagiga* 13a.

62. Literally, "The lambs will be for your clothing, and the goats the price for a field" (Proverbs 27:26).

63. b*Berakot* 10a, which describes King Hezkiyahu and his relationship to Isaiah the prophet who prays for his health which is extended for fifteen years. The king did not want children, as he foresaw that Menasseh would become an idolatrous leader. Isaiah responds to the king that he has no business with the concealed plans of the divine.

64. "Who knows the human spirit whether it goes upward, and the creaturely spirit whether it goes downward to the earth?" (Ecclesiastes 3:21).

who struggles with the divine totality is intertwined in responsibility for the other,"[65] then at their root all beings are intertwined and completely composed from one root soul—so his/her transgressions could have a deleterious effect upon someone else. Or because many circumstances **"are turned round about by divine guidance"**[66]—so **"never judge someone else until you reach their place."**[67] Or perhaps if s/he was standing in that very place, s/he may have fallen even further and made worse choices. [*There is a humility that emerges from radical surrender of the possibility of rationalizing life's course rather accepting that it is not a level playing field with regard to spiritual capacity. Even if every person has different opportunities and challenges, the divine light is still everywhere. Life is not meaningless or arbitrary, even if the divine will is beyond rationalization. Therefore s/he must feel whatever s/he has is not a result of his/her wisdom or piety; rather, it is a function of divine grace, and s/he should then refrain from judging others.*]

And were s/he to say: [*Still*] why does the divine test [*this same person so*], throwing s/he into situations of such negative dissipation, filled with these kinds of tribulations? [*Know that*] the ways of the divine are mysterious. The divine totality desires to be revealed in the public sphere even in the most entangled fields of opposition and dissipative energies [*which would explain why certain people find themselves navigating tribulations present in such fields—in order to sanctify the divine name precisely in that realm of descent*]. But this is not his/her lot, [*for s/he was not thrown into such entangled fields of opposition and dissipative energies, rather*] **"YHVH your God has been with you"**[68] **"and shown you mercy"**[69] as a loved one, so that **"divine awe may be before you."**[70]

This is the core principle: it is not a question of human agency when

65. Literally, "Everyone in Israel is responsible for one another" (b*Shavuot* 39a). My rendering reflects the etymology of Israel, as the one who struggles with God. The homilist reads this rabbinic dictum to suggest that taking credit or assigning blame for the diminished state of spirituality of the other as irrelevant and reprehensible. Any comparisons between individuals as to their moral-spiritual standings destroy the singularity of each soul that is created in the divine image.

66. "And they are turned round about by His guidance, that they may do whatsoever He commands them on the face of the habitable world" (Job 37:12).

67. m*Avot* 2:4.

68. "For YHVH, you God has blessed you in all the work of your hand; the One has known you walking through this great wilderness; these forty years YHVH your God has been with you; you have lacked nothing" (Deuteronomy 2:7).

69. "And there shall cleave nothing of the devoted thing to your hand, that YHVH may turn from the fierceness of His anger, and show you mercy, and have compassion on you, and multiply you, as He has sworn unto your ancestors" (Deuteronomy 13:18).

70. "And Moses said unto the people: 'Fear not; for God is come to prove you, and that His fear may be before you, that you do not sin'" (Exodus 20:16).

it comes to sacral deeds, and even cleaving to the divine totality; rather, the realization of any spiritual path is contingent upon divine endowment, bestowing, and withholding.

"But if God were to say: I have no delight in you,"[71] [*and thus withhold the flow of divine love and awe from him/her*], then [*nothing in the world, not even*] **"the rams of Nebaoth"**[72] [*that one would bring as offerings*] would help one to become sanctified. For the human being cannot impose oneself upon the Almighty. **"If God does not beckon us with a prior spiritual sensibility, we could not self generate our religious stature?"**[73] One's devotion is simply insufficient and does not avail.[74] How then can divine holiness rest upon us and cleave to the One without prior awareness of divine grace? It is only by virtue of divine compassion and lovingkindness for all created beings [*that divine holiness flows forth allowing one to cleave to the One*], as Scripture states: **"and the tender mercies of the One [extend] over all created works of the One"**[75] such that **"You cannot even do the things deserving of reward without grace."**[76]

Therefore, first one should praise the divine totality [*to recognize that human devotion itself is only by divine grace*] so as to ensure receptivity of the request. [*Such recognition requires one to*] get into the proper perspective, understanding one's insignificance as a human being. Composed merely of base material and dirt from the ground, not hearing, not seeing, not even understanding something within the heart. [*Whatever can be heard, seen or understood is a divine bestowal for*]: **"The One that planted the ear, shall the One not hear? The One that formed the eye, shall the One not see?"**[77]

The human capacity for speech and language is by divine bestowal, as Scripture states: **"O Lord, [who] opens my lips [as] I utter praise to the One."**[78] Is not your love and awe then anything but a manifestation of the divine totality? Who is the lover spreading in your soul? After all, what is love? [*Is it not that that subject who loves, the object of love, and the love*

71. "But if He were to say: I have no delight in you; behold, here am I, let Him do to me as seems good to Him" (2 Samuel 15:26).

72. "All the flocks of Kedar shall be gathered together unto you, the rams of Nebaoth shall minister unto you; they shall come up with acceptance on My altar, and I will glorify My glorious house" (Isaiah 60:7).

73. "Can a human be profitable unto God? Or can one that is wise be profitable unto God?" (Job 22:2).

74. "If you be righteous, what gives you God? Or what does God receive of your hand?" (Job 35:7).

75. "YHVH is good to all; and the tender mercies of the One are over all created works of the One" (Psalm 145:9).

76. Psalm 62:14.

77. Psalm 94:9.

78. "O Lord, open my lips; so my mouth shall declare Your praise" (Psalm 51:17).

itself are actually all really textures of the divine totality?] Love itself is all carved out from the divine totality. It is the divinity totality [*whose reality is love*] that extends, embraces, and unites everything condensed by restraint within the human microcosm.[79] [*So that even reaching out to the divine is a yearning from the divine to the divine. Thus, the first step of sacred service is to acknowledge that one stands within divinity.*]

In every place the human being stands [*as a microcosm*]; the divine totality is standing within that person, for the divine is the place of the human. "The divine totality transcends and fills all worlds."[80]

The more one is seized by this love, the more such love really is limitless, beyond any other valuation, even **"If anyone wants to pay you for your love, such a person would be utterly contemned."**[81] For even this love for the divine emerges from the divine totality. [*The love itself is an eruption of divinity flowing through the human lover.*] Before being lovestruck by the divine, everything else is meaningless [*such that the human being cannot ultimately generate the love of the divine, one is simply seized by it*]. But the more the lover gets excited and enflamed [*with the love of the Beloved*], the more one's heart comprehends [*divine*] truths that are not merely a byproduct of one's own soul. For what can such a lover really accomplish [*as far as this divine love is concerned*], being so basely comprised of materiality? Rather, it is **"the divine spirit [*that*] is speaking through him,"**[82] so that [*such a love*] is a **"firebrand plucked from the [*divine*] fire."**[83] [*This very awareness creates a further virtuous intensification of the enthusiasm in love. The more one recognizes this love is not sui generis, the more one is seized by it. Only because of this divine bestowal*] can the ecstasy of the lover be further aroused, so that this feeling cannot be captured in the written word, neither are parchment [*broad enough*] nor ink [*fluid enough*] nor days [*long enough*] to capture the available chambers of the heart filled with such a love.

[*It is from the power of this recognition that love is the divine spirit speaking through the lover, one realizes there is no difference between the self and the other; thus, one is intertwined through love with all sentient beings*]. And through this expansive love, one becomes necessarily bound to all people and sentient beings who share this experience of attunement with the divine. "The ultimate knowledge is knowing that one is unworthy."[84]

79. *Tiquney Zohar*, Tiqqun 70, 130b.

80. *Tiquney Zohar*, Tiquun no. 57; compare with Zohar III:225a.

81. "Many waters cannot quench love, neither can the floods drown it; if a man would give all the substance of his house for love, he would utterly be contemned" (Song of Songs 8:7).

82. 2 Samuel 23:2.

83. Zechariah 3:2.

84. "The purpose of knowing is unknowing." Compare with Ba'al Shem Tov, *Keter*

[*Once you are a lover, you love everything. The lover soon realizes that love is not a personal achievement but is the overflowing effluence from the source of supernal blessing.*] Such deep love is not something a human being can acquire or create by oneself. Rather, such love emanates through the desirous bestowal of the blessed Holy One. And if the divine had given this gift of love to another friend, then your friend would have also been ecstatic. In what way then can one ever claim to be better than his/her friend?

So too, when this love ceases to flow through the material world, there is nothing to distinguish him/her from other embodied beings. [*This becomes most evident when one observes material matters which emerge in the course of life that a human being might encounter, so*] whatever s/he is involved in, wherever s/he is outside [*in nature*] or out in the street, [*this arousal which arises perpetually in the mind without even blinking*] **"like the arrow that flies by day"**[85] [*so that even the devoted one is as susceptible as an ordinary person; rather,*] s/he realizes how much s/he shares in common with all others—such thoughts [*also pass through the minds of*] thousands [*of others*], through each and every devoted one. The realization here is that [*as a devoted one on the material level*] there is really nothing that separates him/her from others who have completely succumbed to distracting desires [*except for this grace*].

Thus, through such love, [*the devoted one*] has a desire to raise up others as part of an expansive whole, so the differentiation should not be divisive but allow identification with other particularities. Such a mind-state leads the [*devoted one*] to feel that s/he is that *other*, even if that *other* may be an ordinary glutton. [*Once one realizes that without these moments of grace that one is no different than anyone else,*] therefore, through this process one becomes bonded to others [*deflating one's exaggerated self-image so as to be able*] to love every person who struggles with the divine, even the wicked ones. [*These shifts in mind-states are really an indication of the degree to which the individual is not ultimately in control. Whereas for Tanya', the state of the devoted one (zaddik) is completely unwavering, but here in Peri haAretz there is a willingness to contemplate changing moods or mind-states and how they are modulated by grace.*] Through this awareness so one truly understands that **"one is answered in the storm"**[86] [*such that even the bountiful grace of the devoted one is also undeserved*] and becomes bound up intimately with all other sentient beings, thousands upon thousands, where no one is superior to the other. It is precisely this

Shem Tov Hashalem, ed. E. Shohat (New York: Kehot Publications, 2004), 3:7–8.

85. "You shall not be afraid of the terror by night, nor of the arrow that flies by day" (Psalm 91:5).

86. Job 40:6, recalling that the human being does not understand the divine ways of creation.

humility and sober self-awareness that allows one to elevate other sentient beings in this way. [*Paradoxically, the self-recognition emerging from this deep humility of the devoted one allows such a person to bond with many people, elevating them, and not necessarily vice versa.*]

Whatever spiritual qualities one has garnered are but a gift of grace from the blessed Holy One. [*There is a great sensitivity here to exceptionalism, so that receiving Torah is just an expression of heavenly grace. It is a gift rather than a marking of intrinsic self-worth. And the grace is not a result of effort. The contrast to R. Shneur Zalman's Tanya' is striking, insofar as it focuses upon the exceptionalism of the Jewish soul, intellectual effort, and human arousal through works. Notice just how divergent are the lines of mystical praxis found in Peri haAretz from Tanya'.*]

When a spiritual person ascends to greater and greater heights of love in the divine totality, then such a person will consequently raise up everyone, even in the thousands, alongside, for all are but one soul. [*The inherent challenge to such a theology of grace is that*] the person who thinks s/he has done this work to achieve spiritual elevation will then look at others with contempt [*possibly*] then even becoming an atheist [*leaving no place for the divine*].

This aforementioned [*state of being lovestruck into expansive consciousness*] is unavailable to someone who imagines that: **"My power and the might of my hand has gotten me this [*spiritual*] wealth [*in my devotional service of the divine*]."**[87] One who may be open to learning, spiritual practice and devotional deeds that comprise Torah, [*but understands neither what it means to experience this expansive love nor that it flows from the divine rather than from the self*], such a person is considered to be an enemy of those who struggle with the divine, as if bereft of God. Such a person is even more spiritually devolved and diminished than all **"the wicked [*who*] are like the troubled sea,"**[88] augmenting even more negative, dissipating energy, descending deeper and deeper.

Such a person is **"a whisperer separating familiar friends"**[89]—one is working through a self-generated assumption of piety based on a lower *Yirah* (fear) [*which is the Shekinah Herself*] being thus separated from the Life of Lives. [*This separation happens when*] one proclaims oneself as the unique source of all this spiritual capacity, divorced from the real source.

[*This is precisely the opposite situation in the case of*] Hillel [*who*

87. ". . . and you say in your heart: 'My power and the might of my hand has gotten me this wealth'" (Deuteronomy 8:17).

88. "But the wicked are like the troubled sea; for it cannot rest, and its waters cast up mire and dirt" (Isaiah 57: 20).

89. "A forward man sows strife; and a whisperer separates familiar friends" (Proverbs 16:28).

completely recognized that all of his spiritual realizations were nothing but divine bestowal and beyond that he was no different than any other human being], who was so remarkably humble, and would say: "If I recognize that I am here [*only by virtue of grace and that my work has done nothing and without it I would be sunk in obtuseness*], then [*when I do feel the divine grace, I can bring everyone in ascent for*] with me everybody is here."[90] Hillel feels a deep interconnection with all of creation through this expansive sense of cosmic self, wherein all sentient beings are intertwined within him. [*Just as such a spiritual being will elevate others attuned alongside to this frequency, so too, one needs to elevate everything towards the divine totality.*]

[*This awareness is captured in the scriptural verse*] **"Everywhere I see the divine presence of YHVH always before me"**[91] means s/he equates everything with the divine awareness, even oppositional forces that s/he encounters, sees, or knows. [*The way one is able to equate everything with the divine totality is by*] aligning with the scriptural verse that teaches: **"And you enliven them all,"**[92] which the Zohar then interprets to mean: "Upper and lower waters are crying and yearning to return before the divine totality and reunite."[93] These waters [*namely, the lower waters which embody the lowliest manifestation of reality, thus causing all the oppositional force to emerge, are precisely what are*] yearning to reunite through ascension [*with the upper waters*] at the moment when the divine totality cherishes them most. For it is the Divine Name, YHVH [*the divine totality*] that elevates everything.

In regard to the Divine Name [*as referenced above in the scriptural verse: "Everywhere I see the divine presence of YHVH always before me"*[94]] YHVH is composed of: *Chokhmah* (Primordial Point) [*as the first Yod of YHVH*] and *Binah* (Discernment) [*as the first Heh of YHVH*]—the place of inner contemplation returning to the divine source. This positioning [*of the Divine Name also extends to include*] *Ahavah* (Love) [*as the Vav of YHVH*] and *Yirah* (Awe) [*as the final Heh of YHVH*] as is known. [*The allusion here is to the Divine Name of YHVH as constituting a fusion of Chokhmah (Primordial Point) with Binah (Discernment) with Ahavah (Love) and Yirah (Awe). From the fusion of all these four spiritual qualities, it is understood*

90. b*Sukkah* 53a.

91. Literally, "I have set YHVH always before me; surely God is at my right hand, I shall not be moved" (Psalm 16:8).

92. Literally, "You are YHVH, even You alone; You have made heaven, the heaven of heavens, with all their host, the earth and all things that are thereon, the seas and all that is in them, and You preserve them all; and the host of heaven worships You" (Nehemiah 9:6).

93. *Tiquney Zohar* no. 5, 19b.

94. Literally, "I have set YHVH always before me; surely God is at my right hand, I shall not be moved" (Psalm 16:8).

then that the divine has the capacity to uplift and elevate everything.]

For it is from a true state of Awe, which is the final *Heh* [*of YHVH*] and *Shekinah* [*known to be the root reality of all sentient beings, which is the quality of Yirah (Awe). A true state of Awe overtakes one's consciousness from the Shekinah as the root reality of all sentient beings*]. One trembles in this state, overcome by the recognition that one is standing in the root reality of all sentient beings. [*This attentiveness is a spiritual commitment; more than just awareness, it is an abiding awareness of Presence. When one is motivated by being in the Presence of the immensity then that intensifies the breathtaking nature of Awe. Mindfulness alone will not suffice. And thus one recognizes how much*] the Community of Israel and Adonai serve as an abode and a voice of the living divinity that emerges from one's mouth and speaks. [*One abides within the gravitas of this supernal rootedness that is the Ground of Being (Malkhut). At this point one falls prostrate in fear and awe, until one becomes*] terrified to return. [*This signifies the completion of the Yirah (Awe) stage, so that in what continues in the homily, there is a shift to the emergence of Ahavah (Love) and how it ascends from this previous Yirah (Awe) stage.*]

And one cleaves to the Voice [*which is a mode of speech, since Malkhut (Ground of Being) is the mouth, that is divinely guided, so that the cognitive mind is not speaking*]—this is the Love which flows and enlivens all articulations, flowing from the realization of Awe, which is the human disposition to yearn for what is lost.[95] [*Since s/he is in a state of mysterium tremendum, s/he becomes the thought-out love object of the divine that wants exactly that kind of receptivity.*] This causes the effulgence after the receiver, so that with eyes of the soul opening through true Awe, then one fills with Love. [*Rather than wanting to respond to it, one goes with this flow, allowing oneself to be absorbed into the divine voice of Love.*]

[*Now that one has reached a state of Awe, then Love begins to hover in the mind-stream, for Love and Awe are the*] path of a "man" returning lost objects [*namely, the "woman"*], for this is the model of effulgence [*and it is the way of*] the receiver [*which is "woman," akin to Love which flows and Awe which receives*] so that true Awe is what begins the flow of Love.

[*Following the realization that this awakening is also powered by the divine ascending higher and higher, whereby Awe embodies the final Heh of the Tetragram ascends to the Vav of the Tetragram, thus channeling all the way back to Binah (Discernment), which is the first Heh of the Tetrgram and from there to the first Yod of the Tetragram, which is Chokhmah (Primordial Point).*] Once one has achieved this realization [*that Love as Binah (Discernment) flows*] from a "Life and Master of the Universe of Source of Life," then there is an ascent to a higher, divine power. [*And from*

95. b*Qiddushin* 2b.

Binah (Discernment), it continues to flow and ascend] to No-thing which is *Chokhmah* (Primordial Point), the mini-*Yod* [*of the Tetragram, which is small considering it symbolizes No-thingness*]. It is from [*this first marking of the Yod*] that all the letters emanate into forms [*given that Yod is a primal point and all other letters are extensions of this point into various forms*], and from this *Yod* it ascends into the [*silent, unknown*] Chief of the World—which is *Aleph.*

This is the form of *Aleph:* [*composed of these three conjoining letter forms*] *Yod-Vav-Dalet,* as is known which is the Chief of the World—moving from the infinite through its expansive manifestation in three columns and their extension. The middle [*column which is composed of the supernal Chokhmah (Primordial Point) and Binah (Discernment)*] is the tower hovering in the ether, which elevates that secondary extensions [*of the left and right side of the Tree of Life*]—the spiritual modalities of Love and Awe [*all ascending towards the infinitude of Aleph*]. The tower itself is [*shaped like*] the letter *Lamed,* which leads to the permutation [*of Aleph and Lamed, which creates 'EL—the Primal Divine*].

[*From this juncture, the homily now returns to the issue of being mindful of the divine at all times in a more general fashion.*] The reality is that before the creation of the multiverses, the One was singular and so was the name alone [*for sentient beings were not yet created*].[96] And after everything [*namely, all sentient beings were created*], notwithstanding, in the deeper realm of contemplation, there is nothing that exists in the world aside from the One—for all is within the One, and the One is within all, creating and sustaining all things, such that "the One and the name stand alone." The divine gives it form so that there is still only the divine and its Name as one, nothing changes. For behold, [*all of creation*] is only for the sake of manifesting divine grandeur, so that everything is called through the Name and for the glory of the divine, even oppositional forces.

So that even before one transgresses and after one transgresses—it is all one [*divine manifestation*] elevated through [*the divine name of*] *'EL.*[97] From the beginning to the end, all is divine. [*If all is divine, from sentient beings to the human being, then these creatures have no independent existence, and if so, then*] how can a person approach sovereignty [*and consider*] humans in this way or that? [*For they have no independent existence from the divine totality.*]

[*Now the homily returns to its initial thrust that the level of spirituality of the human being is contingent upon the divine totality, so that a person is only able to elicit arousal from below by arousing one's self towards a deeper conviction.*] For the human being is only meant to prepare the order

96. *Genesis Rabbah* 21:5.

97. b*Rosh Hashanah* 17b.

of praising the divine totality [*namely, arousing one's self towards a deeper conviction from below. If one contemplates the omnipresence of the divine as well as its apparent opposition, then that contemplation enables one to realize anything*]. In any case, it shall be made part of the totality [*which hovers above the one whose conviction is Awe and Love*].

[*Given that there is a priority to divine grace at all times, even if one has divine works, so as we have learned elsewhere there is value in cultivating virtue.*] As Moses our teacher, *o.b.m.*, explicates in Parashah VaEtchanan: **"You have begun to show your servant,"**[98] for You have infused the beginning of Awe within me from You. [*Namely, at the beginning of the spiritual relationship, even the Awe one feels before You emerges from You to You. Once the seeker surrenders all selfhood to the divine totality then that person receives the expansive flow of beneficence in return.*]

So that after [*the first stage of Awe it follows with the rest of the flow through the verse*] **"Your greatness, and Your strong hand,"**[99] namely, [*supernal*] spiritual qualities of unbounded love. In any case, [*this Love extension*] begins [*through Awe, as mentioned previously, namely, that the path of Love's extension returns after Awe and dwells upon it. And so, in this manner do one's spiritual qualities become more expansive and unbounded*].

So it is all [*encapsulated in the verse*] **"And I besought YHVH"**[100]—a gift of grace [*which is*] only the majestic desire, without any connection to works whatsoever.[101] As Scripture states: **"Not for your righteousness, or for the uprightness of your heart do you go in to possess their land"**[102] [*which symbolizes the Shekinah and the spiritual quality of Awe from which divine service first emerges. Even this initial state of Awe does not emerge within the seeker because of righteousness or uprightness of heart, rather it all emerges from the divine totality*].

This is the meaning of: **"And I besought YHVH"**[103]—a gift of grace, **"Let me go over, I pray, and see [*the good land*] . . ."**[104]—[*which symbol-*

98. "O YHVH God, You have begun to show Your servant Your greatness, and Your strong hand; for what god is there in heaven or on earth, that can do according to Your works, and according to Your mighty acts?" (Deuteronomy 3:24).

99. Deuteronomy 3:24.

100. Deuteronomy 3:23.

101. This is a gift that can only be a freely given gift [*not contingent on his merit but still seeking permission to enter the Land of Israel*]. Devoted ones do not want to depend upon their merits but divine gifts of grace freely given, see Rashi ad loc Deuteronomy 3:23.

102. "Not for your righteousness, or for the uprightness of your heart, do you go in to possess their land; but for the wickedness of these nations YHVH your God drives them out from before you, and that He may establish the word which YHVH swore unto your ancestors, to Abraham, to Isaac, and to Jacob" (Deuteronomy 9:5).

103. Deuteronomy 3:23.

104. "Let me go over, I pray, and see the good land that is beyond the Jordan, that

izes the Shekinah. Even though the contextual reading suggests that Moses did not receive an answer to his petition, however, on a deeper level Moses did receive a vision of the Land of Israel which is Shekinah—an alignment of his own personal will with the higher Will].

[*The homily continues to explicate the matter of degrees through a parable about human beings and that the flow of inspiration is not contingent upon one's deeds.*] It is a well known folk tale [*which illustrates the matter at hand concerning*] the endurance of an earthly [*king*], where the king deploys the simplest [*and most expendable*] of his foot soldiers on the ground in the heart of the battlefield, whereas his [*important*] advisors are deployed close to the king at a distance [*from the battlefield, taking pleasure in his company. Meanwhile, the ground soldiers are in the thick of things in the battlefield and they are vanquishing the enemy in accord with their performance in battle rather than sitting at a distance, taking pleasure in the king's company*]. And notwithstanding [*this disparity*], after the battle is won, it is the advisor [*who*] sits beside the king and takes pleasure in his company [*not the foot soldiers on the ground who vanquished the battle through their deeds in the field*]. And this entire [*disparity between the advisor taking pleasure in the king's company and foot soldier on the ground in the thick of the battle*] is but the majestic desire—without being suited to specific deeds, for one who is able to withstand being deployed as a foot soldier on the ground in the thick of battle—such a person is deployed [*by the king to the battlefield, and those with other capacities are so deployed by the king elsewhere*] accordingly. [*So it is with spiritual capacities of human beings, which are from the divine and not necessarily contingent upon one's works, rather divine flow emerges through the gift of grace.*]

From this reality [*that human beings have markedly unique spiritual capacities that are not contingent upon their deeds*], it does not however nullify [*the calculus*] of reward and punishment. **"Far be it from God, that He should do wickedness; and from the Almighty, that He should commit iniquity"**[105] rather everything [*that emerges in reality is a function of*] justice [*being rendered in its own time and space, such that just deserts are served, all in due time according to one's works*]. For all [*sentient beings*] are [*interconnected through the web of creation*] to the divine name, for who knows [*how*] all these [*beings are part of this web*] of serving the divine totality. [*Behold, even though human beings have varying spiritual capacities, each person is deployed to work toward the truer purpose of life, of revealing the divine name and essence, everyone according to their capacity and degree of development. The human mind cannot really distin-*

goodly hill-country, and Lebanon" (Deuteronomy 3:25).

105. "Therefore hearken unto me, those of understanding: Far be it from God, that He should do wickedness; and from the Almighty, that He should commit iniquity" (Job 34:10).

guish between challenging spiritual work or the person who seems to be born as a zaddik. Rather, every person serves with his/her given capacities.]

And through this [*a human being recognizes that everything is a divine name and all sentient beings have been created in order to serve the divine totality according to its intrinsic capacity, so that*] all of Israel will be beloved to the One. [*Once one realizes that one's spiritual stature is not within one's power, then one is able to realize a genuine detachment from spiritual grandeur to a place of deeper humility.*]

For if all things are [*an extension of*] the divine name [*so that all the letters are necessary in its constitution, and every sentient being was created*] according to the divine desire [*then it follows that*] according to the teaching of our blessed Sages: "The creation of all sentient beings is an extension of the divine desire."[106] And [*notice*] Rashi's comment on this teaching: "They asked everyone whether the divine desire is embedded within creation,"[107] which is so deep it is explored at length in the sacred literature.

The general principle is as follows: whoever serves the divine totality in this manner [*namely, recognizing that the service itself emerges from the divine totality, and from the human perspective, one person is no more elevated than his/her fellow, so then*] one loves all sentient beings [*partnering with them*] and [*from that universal love then*] elevates all those interconnected with their specific spiritual level. [*If his/her embrace of the world as it is remains contingent upon his/her self-understanding of not having reached his/her position of spiritual virtue by any particular virtue on his/her part, rather, it has been scripted from the divine author, therefore with that comprehension, there is a limit to the circumferential inclusion that s/he can reasonably assert to bring into his/her awareness. One's compassionate inclusion is fueled by this process of divine grace and not works, so that even one's yearning is not his/hers own. The radius and circumference of his/her circle of compassion is circumscribed by those who deny the totality of the divine name.*] And the inverse [*also holds, namely that even if*] one hates the wicked [*insofar as one feels that the wicked are not interrelated to their spiritual value*] in any case, this means [*as it appears within*] that one's devotion and support [*renders this wicked person as not also emerging from the divine totality*] and thus one becomes haughty, making one more wicked than anyone [*in thinking that this personal devotion is somehow more elevated than anyone else*]. So that if one is self-righteous [*namely, one forgets how all devotion emerges from the divine totality rather than from the self*] and that the divine is divorced from any of it [*then such a person is not deeply devoted but rather is*] coarse [*and deeply disconnected*] from everything.

106. b*Rosh Hashanah* 11a.

107. Rashi ad loc b*Rosh Hashanah* 11a.

[*The homily now returns to the opening query of the proselyte beckoning Hillel for a steadfast path on one foot, so equipoised that this spiritual support system would not falter. So Hillel taught the proselyte, "What is despicable to you, do not do unto others," which is the Golden Rule just rendered in the negative.*]

This is precisely what Hillel taught in his humility, namely, that "the entirety of Torah could be taught on one foot," which is a steadfast support system [*and that everything emerges from the divine totality, even the individual's own convictions. From this divine perspective, one needs to constantly serve as co-creator with all sentient beings and love it all, which is what Hillel told to the proselyte:*] **"Love your fellow as yourself."**[108] As Scripture states: **"Do not I hate them, O YHVH, that hate You?"**[109] [*so it appears that one should hate the wicked, but the mandate applies only to*] those whose weakness emerges from the negation of the divine totality and oppose the flow of inspiration, but [*not any hatred whatsoever toward*] the weakness of impulse-driven creatures or boundary-crossers [*for it is forbidden to hate them. The question lingers in this homily about the place of righteous indignation versus zealotry in a teaching so concerned with the expansiveness of divine grace that permeates the spiritually sensitive being. As such, the sensitive reader should also take into account the last two verses of the aforementioned psalm, which now beckon an even deeper introspection, specifically, this hatred that emerges from righteous indignation also has the potential to become haughty and self-righteous: "Search me, O God, and know my heart, try me, and know my thoughts; And see if there may be any way in me that is grievous, and lead me in the way everlasting" (Psalm 139:23-24). It is this cycle of expansiveness of heart emerging once again after the constriction of judgment that suggests the thrust of this homily resurfaces with a mandate to love all sentient creatures within the web of the divine totality*].

For who really knows one's spiritual makeup and whether one shall ever be in the position [*of the same unrefined impulse. So then love all co-creators in the web of the divine totality, doing one's part to uplift such unrefined impulses*]. It is known that there is nothing in the world [*even coarse desires*] which transcend the seven spiritual modalities that construct reality [*from the spheres of Chesed (Compassion) to Malkut (Grounding)*] and allow for its elevation [*which includes all particularities and contingencies composing the world*].

So, the human being an integration of all these [*seven spiritual modali-*

---

108. "You shall not take vengeance or bear a grudge against your countrymen. Love your fellow as yourself" (Leviticus 19:18).

109. "Do not I hate them, O YHVH, that hate You? And do not I strive with those that rise up against You?" (Psalm 139:21).

ties that construct reality], thus necessitating their elevation to their roots in the divine totality as is known and discussed elsewhere.

For example: even the most elevated fear [*of the divine still*] remains at a most basic level of all [*the spiritual modalities, given that fear is the entry into all the more elevated manifestations of divine consciousness through its spheres*]. It is from this most primal level of fear [*of the divine totality*] that an external reverence emerges [*which is the fear and trembling one experiences over one's own physical well-being, sustenance and other corporeal concerns*].

So if one encounters [*this sense of external reverence*] then one needs to engage introspectively, [*by asking oneself*]: What am I really fearful of? From which spiritual modality is this fear being drawn from? Is this nothing but the fear of the Holy One [*from which it is all emerging and drawn forth this very external reverence which I am encountering in this moment?*]

[*And so one is invited to contemplate deeply*] what is the source of my fear? After all is not the entire world full of divine glory and nothing but this One? [*Namely, if there really is no one to fear but the Holy One,*] then what is my life [*that I should be fearful of physical well-being, sustenance, and other corporeal concerns?*] And where am I really headed [*with any such privation in life that I fear*] except towards the divine totality? If this is really so, then what am I really [*and what point is there in fearing over anything in my life given that*] I have nothing to fear except from the divine glory [*which elevates this primal fear that is external to its internal root*]*?*

So one comes to truly discern and realize that in the bonding, indeed the awe, which is a fear of the divine, actually also emerges through the divine totality. This spiritual quality of reverence is created by the divine totality and is not possible without such integral vitality.

And so if this vitality is drawn from a higher realm [*toward Awe*] then Love is actually contracted within it [*for Love is the animating vitality within all things*]. For the vitality that extends and interconnects in any matter is this Love. [*Then*] one way or the other, divine love is shed upon such a person, and the cord of compassion extends with bountiful blessing [*as this all flows from Love. So from the Compassion of bountiful blessing*] then one encounters the waters which will never be illusory [*for waters are the qualia of Compassion as is known*].

[*The homily now returns to its opening investigation of why it is that the First Pietists had such an intimate connection with the divine totality. By comparison with the time of Rabbi Yehudah's study circles, the Vitebsker is inquiring why his own study simply lacks that same intensity, thus the lack of rain answering his own Tiberean circle's prayers. Moreover, there is a reason for excluding those who deny the divine name and its totality. There is a certain destabilization the Vitebsker is inviting, so that on one level the denier of the divine name could also be destabilized and brought into the circumference of inclusion, but only one with deeply expansive, messianic consciousness can redeem all.*]

This is the meaning behind the teaching: that in "the time of Rabbi Yehudah, they only knew the Order of Torts"[110]—[*for their devotional work was focused upon not harming their fellow*] which is the real work of [*Hillel's dictum that*] "what is despicable to you, do not do unto others." This is interpersonal ethics of **"Love your fellow as yourself."**[111]

As so the blessed Sages taught: "As soon as Rabbi Yehudah took off one of his shoes," [*meaning that as soon as one removes the gross corporeal expression of the higher spiritual modes of the seven emotional spheres*], the bonding one then feels in Awe towards the divine totality [*is actually Love*].

[*So that*] "the rain then comes"—this is the extension and vital flow [*of the blessing imbedded within the coarseness of the spiritual modality*] so that **"many waters cannot quench love."**[112]

And they explain [*further in that Talmudic passage*] the reason why that generation was so successful in drawing down the rains: "By surrendering any preconceptions of what it means to be human for the sake of the divine name."[113] This really means a descent to the lower levels [*of spiritual qualia, like raw fear*], and then finding the sublime spark [*of higher reverence imbedded within that qualia*] to uplift it as an expression of awareness of the divine totality.

Therefore this [*totality of surrender of attachment to self*] is a devotional expression of disentanglement of concern over one's own destiny. Whatever s/he has is one expression of the divine name, for everything is an expression of the divine name, so that ultimately it is the transpersonal element that expresses and unites all these divine names, "so that the rain will come."

[*Now the homily returns to the opening verse at hand,*] **"Judges and officers shall you make for yourself"**[114]—meaning how one views **"yourself"** [*in having committed to deep spiritual work; it might lead one to*

---

110. b*Berakot* 20a ad loc Rashi indicates that he was willing to overcome ego and limitations of self-image.

111. "You shall not take vengeance or bear a grudge against your countrymen. Love your fellow as yourself" (Leviticus 19:18).

112. "Many waters cannot quench love, neither can the floods drown it; if a man would give all the substance of his house for love, he would utterly be contemned" (Song of Songs 8:7).

113. Zohar III:260a.

114. "Judges and officers shall you make for yourself in all your gates, which the YHVH your God gives to you, tribe by tribe; and they shall judge the people with righteous judgment" (Deuteronomy 16:18).

become self-centered]. The path of **"judges"**—whereby the interpersonal is the touchstone of the most sublimely spiritual, according to the teaching "what is despicable to you, do not do unto others." For it all comes from the divine which means "whatever YHVH has given to you and your tribe" [*in all its diversity*], therefore **"love your fellow as yourself"** [*because with this awareness of one's stature as not one's doing, then s/he can accept others as s/he accept oneself, within one's circumference*].

Or one can say: **"Judges"**[115]—the place of *Binah* (Discernment) [*which is the upper mother on the side of judgement*]; whereas, the **"officers"**[116] are the development of a true realization of the fear [*of the lower Mother of Malkut as a lower level of fear and executing judgement. The task is to elevate the lower level of fear to the higher Mother's level*]. This realization that even fear emerges from the divine totality allows one to see that there is also vitality there [*insofar as it all emerges from its source in Love*].

"And you shall choose life"[117]—that is, there is life within it [*and be aware of the source of life in any circumstance, even in the place of fear. So choose to perceive the life, that is within any circumstance, even the most terrifying*].

"[W]hich YHVH your God gives to you"[118]—it is known that this is the origin of change and extension [*in the sphere of the ground of being, called Malkut*] as the gates of entry into any human bonds of affiliation of the Promised Land of Israel. [*Out of this ground of being emerges a deeper appreciation of the diversity of all sentient beings.*]

[*Now the homily returns to the opening verse at hand and its rabbinic exegesis that sees 'yirah' as a foundational form of comportment, recalling the three cases of exemption, the one who has built the house without dedicating it, the one who has planted the vineyard without tasting the fruits, and the one who has betrothed without the privilege of marriage.*] So in order to truly understand what constitutes a human being, there presides the military chaplain-priest with his announcement of those going to battle who should turn back, namely, that within every person there is an internal voice that is calling to victory over the battle with the inner impulse. This fear before the immensity of life and transgression is symbolized by the **"house"**; and love is the **"vineyard"** as the Tree of Life; and the unification of partners of both Fear [*as feminine*] and Love [*as masculine*] through **"betrothal"** which is the comportment that Torah is teaching.

---

115. Deuteronomy 16:18.
116. Deuteronomy 16:18.
117. Deuteronomy 30:19.
118. Deuteronomy 16:18.

[*If you have gone through this process of Fear and Love but feel there are still some unresolved transgressions,*] **"[then] the officers shall speak further unto the people"**[119]—[*as the blessed Sages teach*]: the one who fears transgressive acts should return to his **"home"** [*that is, a higher place where sin has no hold and where the internal anointing oil of Compassion is beyond Compassion, sweetening all*]. Namely, that [*the home here is*] the point in the palace [*referring to the point of Chokhmah (Wisdom), the point marking the tiny Yod. The home symbolizes fear which ascends to awe through the point of Chokhmah (Wisdom), as explained above in relation to the four letters constituting the divine name. The tetragram itself then begins with fear in the final Heh, so that from there a process of ascent through the spheres takes place, eventually realizing Awe through the point of Chokhmah (Wisdom). After reaching that point of Chokhmah (Wisdom) in the first Yod of the tetragram, one needs to ascend further, drawing towards the root itself in Aleph as the Master of the Universe, which requires stretching*] to reach that place of ascent into their roots.

[*This homily concludes with a lofty vision about higher and higher stages of realization. When one achieve great virtue, it is not oneself. This requires a real surrender of attachment of self, then the rain comes. The interpersonal is the most spiritual, so one needs to disentangle concern with self by expanding one's circumference of compassion. Even the drama of one's own entanglement in ego must be surrendered. This is a deeper level of ego, insofar as it refers to any sense of concern with destiny and personal distinctiveness. Once one recognizes that what s/he has comes from the divine totality, then it is a giving back to God that which is divine—and that is everything. Reaching that level is an expression of ultimate transparency where total surrender brings one to the divine and total absorption therein.*]

[18.3]. *Parashah Shoftim* (Deuteronomy 16:18–21:9)

QUESTIONS FOR REFLECTION:

1. Often in spiritual growth, there is a period of searching that can lead to "spiritual window shopping"—trying this or that practice based on the human desire for pleasure and ecstasy without requisite rootedness in the selfsame tradition. How is your spiritual practice a reflection of your own needs, desires, and pleasures? How might I begin the process of "trying" your spiritual

119. "And the officers shall speak further unto the people, and they shall say: 'What man is there that is fearful and faint-hearted? Let him go and return unto his house, lest his brethren's heart melt as his heart'" (Deuteronomy 20:8).

practice toward a more selfless spirituality whose roots are divine rather than human? What obstacles might you face with such a re-orientation?

2. In confronting the terrors of life, especially in facing your own mortality, it is natural to be fearful. But how do you then acknowledge this fear from external threats to your mortality and transform them into an internalized awe of the divine totality?

[19.1]. *Parashah Ki Teizai 1* (Deuteronomy 21:10–25:19)

INTRODUCTION TO HOMILY:

As a human being, our lives are full of oppositions. Seeing ourselves in constant self-opposition is common in many modes of analysis that impact the ways that we live religious lives. From the psychoanalytic perspective, in his analysis of the ego, Jacques Lacan presents a subject in a state of "primordial Discord" torn between unity and anarchy, organization and chaos, integration and fragmentation. While much of this worldview is seen through the dyadic relation between mother and child, Lacan argues that there is also the question of the mother's desire. This suggests a symbolic lack whereby she is not entire and omnipotent. The question of desire means that the imaginary unity of the ego amid its oppositional relations abides in a symbolic relation of difference. While Lacanian analysis is resigned to living in the fissures of such difference, the religious seeker yearns for recovering that lost unity. From the Zen Buddhist perspective, for example, the subject stands opposed either to the outer world of nature or to the inner world of the psychē), or both, which thus again promotes an oppositional mode of thinking. Zen philosophy seeks an experiential dimension that goes beyond the oppositional thinking of the everyday standpoint. Along this line of yearning for the transcendent but that is seen as the divine totality, the Jewish mysticism that undergirds the Hasidic thinking of the Vitebsker suggests that the core of oppositional forces and judgments hovers in exposed places of our lives. Oppositional forces are exterior in the sense of hovering in those fragile moments of disclosure that come with the devotional life that demands transparency. In opposition to this disclosure in the most vulnerable parts of human life, the divine is called the hiding place of the world, as well as the private domain. Prescient of these Lacanian concerns so prevalent in psychoanalysis for the symbolic nature of linguistic signification, here the Vitebsker envisions a divine vital energy that is drawn forth from the letters of speech. This divine vital energy is drawn forth from the holy language of Hebrew, and from there to all other seventy universal languages. Speech itself arouses the spiritual qualities of a human being, from the side of vitality that draws forth from within. Moreover, all desires of the material world have divine vitality within, such that spiritual qualities within everyone can be aroused from the place of inner speech. Spiritual qualities of the one engaged in spiritual practice are aroused from a deep desire for the divine. This suggests that one can grow coarse from abiding in the apparent oppositional relations of difference in material perception and carnal bliss. Rather, the Hasidic approach of the Vitebsker is to advise how spiritual qualities can emanate forth ultimately from the divine self, which is limitless. Given that spiritual qualities emanate from such an infinite source, these qualities cannot ultimately be grasped through rational perception or any kind of cognitive analysis. Rather, we see throughout this homily how the commands of spiritual practice of unifying these oppositional forces can paradoxically be enacted in the material world, necessitating constriction and boundaries. The Vitebsker is suggesting a contemplative practice that relies on vessels to delimit spiritual qualities to come into perception. Returning to the unified self is a willingness to see the self prior to any primordial Discord, whereby the Vitebsker's take on spiritual practice thus enables a transformation from divided materiality to a more integrated spirituality.

[19.2]. *Parashah Ki Teizai 1* (Deuteronomy 21:10–25:19)

HOMILY:

"When you take the field against your enemy . . . deliver them."[120] The explanation of R. Shlomo Yitzhaki is as follows: "The Torah refers here to one thing only—the libidinal impulse."[121]

The master opened his teaching with the different techniques for the self-transformation of *teshuvah* as envisioned by the blessed Sages[122]—[*which includes changing of one's behavior, name, and domicile*] as further elucidated in the [*Tiquney*] *Zohar*.[123]

The way to really explain these [*different techniques for the self-transformation of teshuvah*] is by way of knowing, as Scripture teaches: **"For the command is a lamp, / The teaching is a light"**[124]—referring to the 248 commands that are like candles to illumine the light of Torah. These 248

---

120. "When you take the field against your enemy, and YHVH your God delivers them into your power and you take some of them captive" (Deuteronomy 21:10).

121. Rashi ad loc Deuteronomy 21:11: "'And you delight in her, that you would take her for your wife'—Scripture is speaking (makes this concession) only in view of one's evil inclinations (namely, one's carnal desires, see b*Qiddushin* 21b). For if the blessed Holy One would not permit her to him as a wife, he would nevertheless marry her although she is forbidden to him. However, if he does not marry her, in the end he will hate her, for Scripture writes immediately afterwards (verse 15) 'If a man have two wives, one beloved, and another hated' and ultimately begets a refractory and rebellious son by her (verse 18). It is for this reason that these sections are put in juxtaposition."

122. b*Yomah* 86b, compare with b*Baba Kama* 66b, 93a which proffers a theory of identity and loss of identity of physical objects and substances, whereby the material is transformed and therefore does not need to be returned. A firm commitment to change is the nature of *teshuvah*.

123. *Tiquney Zohar* 124b, Tiqqun no. 70.

124. "For the commandment is a lamp, / The teaching is a light, / And the way to life is the rebuke that disciplines" (Proverbs 6: 23).

commands are the [*spiritual*] channels of subjectivity[125]—the *Shekinah* by which a person becomes illumined by means of Torah [*and then connect*] with that illumination within the channels of one's soul.[126] Such [*enshrouded illumination of the commands*] **"supports and uplifts"**[127] [*one's soul*] "amid the perennial battle that divinity has with the Oppositional Forces of *Amalek* that impede it in every generation"[128]—which is the Oppositional Force of "the libidinal impulse that overpowers a person's psyche daily."[129] So the divine influence aids a person through this spiritual practice [*to overcome this opposition*] by offering refuge [*in aligning with the channels in one's psyche*] that is the **"shelter"** of those wings and **"abide in the refuge of *Shaddai*"** [*such that the emanation of divinity supports all that exists*][130] as concealed within all the concealments of the world.[131] When a person is immersed in the divine energy field taking refuge in these psychic channels, no goads of judgment lead one astray.

It is known: "A [*divine*] blessing [*is not quantifiable and*] can only be found in something that is hidden from sight [*a qualitative spiritual texture that requires internal perception attuned to the concealed dimension*]"[132] in a place where the libidinal impulse no longer holds sway over a person, **"No eye has seen [them], O god, but You, / Who act for those who trust in You."**[133] The jurisdiction of the oppositional forces and judgments exists in the realm of the external senses; so the greater [*the degree of manifestation to the senses*], the greater [*the oppositional forces can take hold of it. This is less a concern for the revelation of esotericism but more a concern for the workings of the ego that may overtake the charismatic person in this public forum, whereby the larger the movement, the greater the oppositional forces*]. Consider the first tablets which given in a very public celebration of manifesting the concealed, [*being revealed to such an extent to the oppositional forces that*] they were shattered.[134] [*Perhaps this is an allusion to the spiritual leadership of the court-centered rebbe in the Hasidic milieu*

125. Literally, "limbs of"; compare with R. Nahman of Bratzlav, *Liqqutai Moharan*, No. 29.

126. For more on the 248 spiritual limbs and 365 spiritual sinews, see R. Chaim Vital, *Shaarei Kedusha*, I:1 on the verse: "You clothed me with skin and flesh / And wove me of bones and sinews" (Job 10:11).

127. Isaiah 63:9.

128. *Pirkai deRabbi Eleazer*, no. 43.

129. b*Sukkah* 52b.

130. Captured in our own subjectivities, religion allows the seeker to take refuge in a transcendent structure of meaning and significance along with embodied practice.

131. "O you who dwell in the shelter of the Most High and abide in the protection of *Shaddai*" (Psalm 91:1); on "concealed of most concealed," see Zohar II:89a.

132. b*Ta'anit* 8b.

133. "Such things had never been heard or noted. / No eye has seen [*them*], O god, but You, / Who act for those who trust in You" (Isaiah 64:3).

134. *Midrash Tanchuma,* Parashah Ki Tissa 31a.

and its pitfalls. The growing public face of Hasidism and its mass revelation of teachings may have been what inspired this spiritual master of this homily to emigrate to Tiberias.]

So the [*verse captures this teaching, where Jacob is telling his sons after having been to Egypt with a troubling encounter with the viceroy. They are told not to come back unless they bring back their youngest brother, Benjamin*]: **"Why would you make a self-display in pubic [*titra'u*]?"**[135] And so the [*verse captures this teaching as well*]: **"They shall be overexposed leading to the shame [*dai'ra'on*] / of all flesh"**[136] and thus the [*the oppositional forces*] are called "externalities" [*referring to this act of self-display*]—the more one relies on the externality of the senses, the more one becomes subject to the qualitative experience of the senses [*which then creates aversions, attractions, and temptations*] of the powers of enchantment. [*There is even a specific libidinal impulse for self-display which compromises the intimacy of esoteric teachings made public.*][137] This stands in real contrast to the divine: also known as the hidden place of the world,[138] interiority,[139] the private "realm."[140] Even Torah is called **"The gold of your thigh"**[141]—namely, just as a thigh is concealed, so too is a word of Torah [*meant to be concealed and not revealed in public gatherings*].[142] So it follows: "If you have been attacked by the libidinal impulse [*that brigand, known as the powers of enchantment to self-display in teaching Torah in public*] then draw [*that attack on your quest for mindfulness*] into the House of Study"[143] to find shelter in the refuge [*in the hidden reality*] of Torah

---

135. "When Jacob saw that there were food rations to be had in Egypt, he said to his sons, 'Why do you keep looking at one another?'" (Genesis 42:1).

136. "'They shall go out and gaze / On the corpses of the men who rebelled against Me: / Their worms shall not die, / Nor their fire be quenched; / They shall be a horror / To all flesh. / And new moon after new moon, / And Sabbath after Sabbath, / All flesh shall come to worship Me' / —said YHVH" (Isaiah 66:24).

137. Within human subjectivity there is a level of consciousness that is more real and true, which is divine consciousness, which cannot be seen externally. That is why the powers that can enchant us are "external forces."

138. "R. Nahuniah ben Hakana said: 'One verse states: "And now they do not see light, it is brilliant in the skies round about God in terrible majesty"' (Job 37:22). Another verse, however states: 'He made darkness his hiding place' (Psalm 18:12). It is also written: 'Cloud and gloom surround Him' (Psalm 97:2). This is an apparent contradiction. A third verse comes to reconcile. It is written: 'Even darkness is not dark to You. Night shines like day—light and darkness are the same.' (Psalm 139:12)" (*Sefer HaBahir* 1:1).

139. *Tiquney Zohar* 136b.

140. *Tiquney Zohar* 12a.

141. "How graceful your steps in those sandals, / O nobleman's daughter. / The gold of your thigh / shaped by a master craftsman" (Song of Songs 7:2).

142. b*Moed Qatan* 16a.

143. b*Qiddushin* 30b.

[*by dragging those forces of enchantment into the interiority of intimate display*].

The term "*adam*" [*which is more intimate*] stands as more valiant rather than "*ish*"[144] [*which is more on self-display*] and relates to different levels of spiritual evolution [*whereby 'adam' is the ascendant divine name whereas 'ish' is descendant. This hierarchy reflects the spiritual evolution from 'enosh' (mortal) to 'ish' (dignified person) to 'adam' (cosmic being)*]. Why then does Scripture [*use such a descendant description as*]: **"YHVH, [*as*] the 'man' of war"**[145]—such a description applies during the descendant moment of external battles. To shatter the oppositional force, divinity must descend into baser forms of a call to arms with an outstretched arm, to then assert its power precisely where it is concealed to defeat the power of enchantment. The intervention of divinely informed consciousness must enter into the very place where one is entrapped by enchantment within manifestation in order to undermine it.[146] *Perish the thought* that one should apply the higher name of divinity to the realm where the oppositional forces have jurisdiction [*whereby "adam" is the ascendant name whereas "ish" is descendant divine*].

This then is in line with what the blessed Sages teach: "When the King arrives the court falls into a respectful silence, so too when the divine influence arrives it is in silence rather than in a great trembling and tumult. For whatever is known about supreme, earthly powers enters into manifestation, so too with the advent of supreme, heavenly powers."[147] Thus, the one who is aware of this arrival must understand the subtle stature of supreme, heavenly powers. [*Everything in the spiritual life is about being sub rosa and not on self-display lest one fall into the clutches of the ego.*]

And it is known:[148] even the oppositional forces in the most manifest aspect of the world are contingent upon the verbal directive of the King—so that even these [*oppositional forces*] are enlivened by the most **"faint flicker"** from the holy source.[149] This is the esoteric meaning of the verse: **"and Its jurisdiction extends into every domain."**[150] [*There is a yearn-*

144. Literally, "adam" means human and "ish" means man; here these are technical terms of the divine name as will be explained.

145. Literally, "YHVH, the man of war— / YHVH is the Name" (Exodus 15:3).

146. b*Sukkah* 12a, the idiom of "until an axe is swung at it" means to refute or disprove something, but here it refers to divinely informed consciousness for the sake of defeating the powers of enchantment.

147. b*Berakot* 58a, even though he was blind, Rav Sheshet knew when royalty arrived everything quiets down in the court.

148. *Tiquney Zohar*, no. 69:108b.

149. Zohar II:69b.

150. Literally, "YHVH has established His throne in heaven, / and His sovereign rule is over all" (Psalm 103:19).

ing to engage in self-display, whereby the public sphere is always ready for making its surfaces and services available to holiness.] Thus, what motivates the powers of enchantment is to pursue holiness in order to get a grip on that vitality in order to maintain their own energy needs. But once the sparks of holiness have been refined and liberated from the powers of enchantment, they are powerless **"to destroy death forever."**[151] [*While it is true that the oppositional forces are nourished by the flickers of holiness, it does not mean that one should accept this. One needs to extract the sparks and leave behind its darkness, then the dark lights will be eviscerated. This is a warning not to take the route of self-display.*]

Behold: Torah and the blessed Holy One are a single unity,[152] so too, the words and the letters of Torah gesture and arouse their inner light; [*through their own vibrational levels, they are transmitting divinity into the manifest world*]. Take for example, the word "Beneficence"—that all the beneficence manifest in the world is encapsulated within the "letters" for the word "beneficence" and the same is true in regards to "joy"—all the joy in the world is encapsulated within the "letters" for the word "joy." [*Harkening back to Sefer Yetzirah, this Kabbalistic view of language assumes the essential character of language is not just semantic content; rather, the vehicle of the letters in their deepest atomization conveys spiritual truth. The information being conveyed is only the tip of the iceberg, which means the joy that one yearns for is actually encapsulated energetically in the vehicle of these very specific letters themselves.*]

So all the seventy [*earthly*] languages are energized from the holy language of Hebrew, but the language of Torah is unique, as Scripture teaches: **"and Its ground of being extends into every [linguistic] domain."**[153] How is this possible in all domains? Through the vibrations of the letters of Torah. This is akin to the matter: "so Greek language, the number one is referred to as *hen*"[154]—this is the source of unique nourishment from Torah, as is the case for all other languages. [*This Kabbalistic posture evinces an essentialist view of language here, whereas the Vitebsker is suggesting that it is not limited to Hebrew. Given the expansive nature of sacred ground of being, Malkut, the Vitebsker's essentialisation of language here is able to be the much more expansive view, namely, that all languages have a vibrational quality to all phonemes regardless of whether it is Hebrew or Greek. This means that there is no language in the universe that is merely*

151. "He will destroy death forever. / YHVH my God will wipe the tears away / From all faces / And will put an end to the reproach of His people / Over all the earth— / For it is YHVH who has spoken" (Isaiah 25:8).

152. Zohar III:73a.

153. "YHVH has established His throne in heaven, / and His sovereign rule is over all" (Psalm 103:19).

154. b*Shabbat* 31b.

conventional.]

Consequently, the expression of human affects in personality are aroused in response to forms of speech in all languages. For example, the affect of joy is aroused whenever one hears [*words of*] good news. And so too, anguish is aroused from oppositional [*and thus negative*] speech. When one hears something antagonistic, then the emotions of pride, splendor, grace, and the endless words praising a person apply to [*and arouse*] all spiritual qualities.[155] [*Not just semantic content but the actual vibrational qualities of language arouse the spiritual qualities.*]

As far as the spiritual affects and expression of emotions themselves, their expression is not recognizable within the words and letters of their name in any language. For example, "Compassion" [*CHeS"eD*]—in the letters of "Compassion" [*CHS"D*] the spiritual affect is manifest through the concealed divinity. From there the divine energy that expresses these spiritual affects drawn forth by Torah's language and letters extends to all other languages. [*If not for this higher level vibrational origin of language that is being channeled into the manifest level of being, then one would not be able to experience compassion. So it is the divine desire to channel this vibrational origin into spoken language.*]

And this is the case regarding the verse: **"And God saw that this was good"**[156] to see is to channel [*the spiritual affect*], as Scripture states: **"And all the nations/shall flow to it"**[157]—related to the language of "illumination" [*nihora*], which is the light of the eye as well as attraction. [*The cognition of the affect is dependent upon it.*] The eye of emotional cognition is the eye of the heart, as Scripture states: **"and my heart sees wisdom."**[158] This echoes what was taught regarding the one who secretes: [*Before one has*] three sightings [*one must have*] two—this is the logic that draws down the secretion.[159] [*Thus this tropism of seeing implies both*

155. In every language there is divine spiritual vitality, so the energy of particular affects are therefore aroused by speech.

156. "God called the dry land Earth, and the gathering of waters God called seas. And God saw that this was good" (Genesis 1:10).

157. "In the days to come, / The Mount of YHVH's House / Shall stand firm above the mountains / And tower above the hills; / And all the nations / Shall gaze on it with joy" (Isaiah 2:2).

158. Literally, "I said to myself: 'Here I have grown richer and wiser than any that ruled before me over Jerusalem, and my mind has zealously absorbed wisdom and learning'" (Ecclesiastes 1:16).

159. See b*Megillah* 8a, where the mishnah states: "[*There is no difference between one who secretes and makes*] two sightings [*on a single day or two successive days*] and one who makes three [*on one day or three successive days, or two on one day and one on the next*] except in the matter of bringing a sacrifice." Further on in the Talmud, R. Simlai raises the hypothetical question regarding two versus three sightings as to whether two sightings bring uncleanness but do not entail a sacrifice, while three entail a sacrifice but no uncleanness.

light and attraction].

In each case [*of spiritual dispositions*], "like identifies its own kind and awakens it,"[160] so too according to the internal landscape that one has cultivated in the heart is one's spiritual affect aroused.[161] So if one is crude and materialistic—then their spiritual affects are only aroused in very corporeal forms to reach their roots. For example: silver, gold and delicacies, and human pleasures, even though the vessels that express the spiritual affects in these cases are coarse and highly materialized, still [*for the spiritually evolved person*] the concealed spiritual affects are aroused in the mystery of: **"and His sovereign rule is over all."**[162]

The viability of the spiritual affects depends on the capacity and sensitivity of the vessel through which it is being expressed. The spiritual affect expressed through an insensitive person will be a weak and fleeting expression of that divine energy, as Scripture states: **"the physical conditions cease, then the [*spiritual affect of*] Love also ceases."**[163] This is not the case for divine Love [*which is eternal and unchanging as exemplified in scripture*]: **". . . For Love is fierce as death . . . Vast floods cannot quench . . . If one offered all their wealth for love, / One would be laughed to scorn."**[164]

The Talmud then answers R. Simlai that before one has three sightings, one must have two, namely, that one category of sightings flows or continues from the other. The reason why rabbinic literature refers to this seminal emission as "sighting" because one is not merely seeing but also channeling.

160. The expression is recontextualized from the halachic principle that "like identifies its own kind and awakens it." b*Eruvin* 9a already first appears in Ba'al Shem Tov, *Keter Shem Tov*, no. 194. The divine name in the food is not aroused unless there is a deeper spiritual intentionality linked and embodied in the food.

161. Taking his cue from the Ba'al Shem Tov's reading here on intentionality while in the midst of eating to extend into a much wider ambit, to apply to an embodied practice, so that everything that exists is an emanation from the divine source without exception. It is a spiritual practice that demands what is preoccupying the seeker from moment to moment, given that a person is a receptacle with limited sensitivities. So these spiritual affects will come through even the coarsest of forms, nevertheless they are expressions of the concealed emanation of divine effluence that expresses that affect.

162. "YHVH has established His throne in heaven, / and His sovereign rule is over all" (Psalm 103:19).

163. "If love depends on some [transitory] thing, and the [transitory] thing passes away, the love passes away too; but if it does not depend on some [transitory] thing it will never pass away. Which love depended on some [transitory] thing? This was the love of Amnon and Tamar. And which love did not depend on some [transitory] thing? This was the love of David and Jonathan" (m*Avot* 5:16).

164. "Let me be a seal on your heart, / Like the seal on your hand. / For love is fierce as death, / Passion is mighty as the netherworld; / Its darts are darts of fire, / A blazing flame. / Vast floods cannot quench love, / Nor rivers drown it. / If one offered all their wealth for love, / One would be laughed to scorn" (Song of Songs 8:6-7).

Thus, it is the case [*in transforming this ethical teaching to a cosmological principle*]: **"the inner reflection is not as essential as the active expression"**[165]—for the letters are imbedded in the mystery of materialization, while the crowns, vowels, and tropes align as manifestations of higher metaphysical levels at earlier stages of *spiritual* evolution, through manifestation (*nefesh*)—spirit (*ruah*)—soul (*neshama*).[166] This is what is meant by the teaching: "The Holy One created the world through Torah,"[167] for through six days, God was involved in emanating the material world, and on the seventh day—these are the seven [*words and the twenty-seven*] letters.[168] [*Thus, there is a high spiritual value placed upon the materialization of the world.*]

This is the raison d'etre of a human being's creation: to embody the spiritual affects and make use of them through the letters of Torah and the light of divine commands. Through the apperception of a single command that is given to carry out, the spiritual affect of joy will be aroused in the same way it could be aroused by some physical pleasure in an object. Much like this case: one who rejoices in the commands, and then "a smile did not leave his lips the whole day."[169] [*The divine words are the embodied practice of the ineffable in a very specific, concrete way.*]

For the core practice is to adhere to the divine affects through enacting the commands. Were it not for the limiting quality of the divine command—the spiritual affect would be unbounded, as they emanate forth from the Limitless source. For the spiritual affects emanating from the Holy One that is Without End—and there is no way to perceive it—thus restraint is necessary [*for any perception*]. Once there is a restraint the light of the affect can flow through a bounded channel, without being overwhelming, lest the vessel receiving it become insufficient. This is the function of the initial restraint. Rather, in a proportionate measure is it enable to function as a vessel. Then in this contracted form is it possible for apperception of this spiritual affect resulting in the vessel.

Thus, all filterings serve the purpose of manifesting the Divine Glory and Compassion for the contracted vessel in its diminished form. After this

165. "Simeon his son said: All my days have I grown up among the Sages and I have found nothing better than silence; and not the expounding [of the Law] is the key thing rather following through; and one that multiplies words occasions sin" (m*Avot* 1:17).

166. *Tiquney Zohar*, Tiqqun no. 19:39b.

167. Zohar I:47a, 204a.

168. Namely, a composite of twenty-two letters including the five final forms.

169. "R. Ela said to 'Ulla: When you go up there, give my greeting to my brother R. Berona in the presence of the whole college, for he is a great man and rejoices to perform a precept [*in the correct manner*]. Once he succeeded in joining the closing signature of redemption [*geulah*] with the central prayer [*tefillah*], and a smile did not leave his lips the whole day" (b*Berakot* 9b).

filtering, the Divine Love of a "miracle" [*NeS*] can be revealed through the experience of a "trial" [*NiSayon*], and this is encapsulated in the teaching: "In midst of suffering does one find redemption."[170]

In every case where a command involves a restraint of acting into a material way, it constitutes a **"lamp"** that is illuminated by the **"light of Torah."**[171] This inner illumination is the joy of enactment, and similarly in the case of all divine affects, were it not for delimitation there is no way possible to apperceive it for the divine affect is Without End. It all depends upon the human capacities. If the person is spiritually insensitive—then the boundaries within which the spiritual affect would be aroused then are limited to material forms, whereas if the person is spiritually sensitive—then their love is expressed on a higher spiritual level.

And thus [*now it is possible to understand the rabbinic statement*]: "In the place where masters of return stand, even completely devoted ones cannot stand,"[172] for the specific command in turning oneself in direct alignment with the divine is higher than all commands. After the master of return has worked on and attained these spiritual affects in the realm of the corporeal—whether conforming to the commands of the permissible or forbidden—at the very least one has apperceived a bit of the divine affect in being connected to these commands. So now [*as one turns into alignment with divinity*] the higher realm of spiritual affects, [*in the process are then*] transforming subsequent stages of perceptions through commands to more evolved apperceptions of divine cognition involved in this turning.[173]

While commands involving materiality are embodied, the arousal of divine affects in carrying out these commands is lesser than what the master of return experiences in the act of turning.

Lo and behold, after mastering this re-turning [*from perception to apperception*] to strengthen one's access to divine affects beyond their dependence on material forms, one's joy and sadness are no longer reactive to the diminished, contracted state of materiality. Thus, [*after truly re-turning from perception to apperception*] immersion in materiality no longer conflicts with the spiritual affects. Rather, [*there is a more expansive capacity of spiritual affects upon turning to be conditioned*

---

170. See *Midrash Tanchuma,* Parashah Meiqez no. 3.

171. "For the commandment is a lamp, / The teaching is a light, / And the way to life is the rebuke that disciplines" (Proverbs 6:23).

172. b*Berakot* 34b.

173. This points to a hypernomian practice wherein turning to this apperception is the highest form of devotion. This often opens the door to a kind of radical supranomianism transcending the commands. This type of "transmoral pietism" is always hovering in mysticism in general, and Hasidism in particular. On this paradoxical pietistic stance that transgresses the law as its fulfillment, see Elliot R. Wolfson, *Venturing Beyond: Law and Morality in Kabbalistic Mysticism*, (Oxford: Oxford University Press, 2006), esp. 235-7, 262-3, 272-3.

completely by] divine love and grace.

This is what is meant by "changing one's behavior"—really! [*There is a shift from perception of materiality to the apperception of spiritual affect beyond the light of commands*]; as well as "change of place"—in retreating from conventional realm to re-turn to the individual realm; and "changing one's name"—really! The collocation of divine names then differs from its subsequent usages. The re-turning now stands as the source of light. At this present moment [*following this threefold process of return*], one is now [*called by a new name*] using the holy language [*of Hebrew*] and this facilitates [*the apperception of spiritual affects as symbolized*] through **"the command is a lamp, / the teaching is a light."**[174] At first [*as one facilitates the aforementioned shift from physical perception to spiritual apperception*], one uses a derivative and diminished name from the seventy languages as described above.

This is what is meant by [*re-turning to change*]: "through [*the constricted*] action [*of commands*], through location [*of the finite to the infinite*] and through relationship [*with the divine names*],"[175] which again allows for transformation encapsulated in the three realms of "space-time-soul" matrix.[176] For any transformation in action is drawn from the ephemeral to the eternal.

This is what is meant by [*returning*]: **"When you take"**[177]—by entry into the public arena to express and receive deeper love, there is a revelation of the higher level of the spiritual qualia holding limited forms of light.[178] Surely **"the field against your enemy"**[179]—in the state where multiplicity exists there is duality, implying the oppositional force pursues holiness wherever it can be found. Were it not for the divine aid available [*against the oppositional forces of distraction*] which is the unveiling of the *Shekinah* as **"YHVH, the master of war"**[180] [*the buzzing, blooming confusion of the world known as qelipot*]. Now we can understand what is meant by the rabbinic teaching: **"Pray for the welfare of Sovereign [*divine aid that supports the pursuit of oppositional forces*]"**[181]—which is the *Shekinah*,

174. "For the commandment is a lamp, / the teaching is a light, / And the way to life is the rebut that disciplines" (Proverbs 6:23).

175. b*Yomah* 86b.

176. *Sefer Yetzirah* 6:1.

177. "When you take the field against your enemy, and YHVH your God delivers them into your power and you take some of them captive" (Deuteronomy 21:10).

178. *Tiquney Zohar*, Tiqqun no. 21:60a.

179. "When you take the field against your enemy, and YHVH your God delivers them into your power and you take some of them captive" (Deuteronomy 21:10).

180. Literally, "YHVH, the man of war— / YHVH is the Name!" (Exodus 15:3).

181. "Rabbi Hanina, Deputy High Priest, said: Pray for the welfare of the regime; but for fear of it people would swallow one another alive . . ." (m*Avot* 3:2).

"were it not for the awe She inspires then people would swallow one another alive."[182]

[*Now we can understand the opening verse*]: **"and YHVH your God delivers them into your power and you take some of them captive"**[183]—this refers to the pre-transformational level of material values used at first [*in perception that tend to be commandeered into distraction*].

"And you see among the captives"[184]—this refers to the drawing down of **"a beautiful woman"**[185]—known as "feminine waters"; for the material values first perceived and used at the pre-transformational level transform into "feminine waters" so that their arousal enables [*the transformation that elevates the corporeal through spiritual values to be drawn down and*] then return [*to flow forth*] therefrom. This is the meaning of **"and would take her to wife"**[186]—namely, taking the limited light that is present in a material vessel used for a commanded act, transforming her [*i.e., that limited vessel*] to then reveal higher forms of light.

Certainly a fully integrated spiritual being can immediately access the higher form of unlimited light and has no need for this [*embattled process of return, shifting from perception of corporeal forms to apperception of spiritual forms*]. Given that there is no one singular path, everyone needs to follow his/her own path. The application of this teaching depends upon one's spiritual strength and sensitivity, so that the apperception of the higher forms of unlimited light in spiritual entities manifests in the stepped down form of the corporeal. People vary in terms of their capacity mediated by their sensitivity to spiritual forms and corporeal forms to apperceive higher light. Each person has a certain degree of power to effectively stand in this place of [*inner*] struggle to elevate their capacities to hold and receive higher and greater degrees of divine light.

This explains [*R. Shlomo Yitzhaki's opening comment that*]: "Torah is speaking here of one thing only—the libidinal impulse"[187]—for "only speaking" is an act of filtering, being refracted into distinct letters [*as phonemes*] into sounds in order to draw down and reveal the undifferentiated

182. See (m*Avot* 3:2), wherein given that the *Shekinah* is synonymous with "regime," the symbolism suggests that through the encounter with fear the *Shekinah* is revealed and thus battles the oppositional forces. For these oppositional forces pursue holiness swallowing their sparks.

183. "When you take the field against your enemy, and YHVH your God delivers them into your power and you take some of them captive" (Deuteronomy 21:10).

184. ". . . and you see among the captives a beautiful woman and you desire her and would take her to wife" (Deuteronomy 21:11).

185. Deuteronomy 21:11.

186. Deuteronomy 21:11.

187. Rashi ad loc Deuteronomy 21:10.

voice into one specific instantiation of infinitude.[188] This is the flow of the divine vitality into speech, as is known:[189] the uniting of word and sound is the unification of the Holy One and his *Shekinah*. For if a person is unable to undergo simple restraint of spiritual forms [*to shift from material perception to spiritual apperception through unlimited means*] then a deeper restraint [*through more delimited perception of materiality into the realm of spiritual entities is necessary*]. This is akin to the rabbinic teaching:[190] "If one subdues [*the libidinal impulse*], well and good. If not, let that person be reminded of the day of death [*namely, death as a more delimited form of restraint, and to use that very restraint of materiality as a vessel*] until [*such time as the contracted forms of light can stimulate the elevation of one's own capacity and draw down higher spiritual forms until*] **"[transcending as] dying the very contracted form of the vessels [from the ephemeral to the] eternal."**[191] [*Whereas the rabbinic teaching is focusing the libidinal impulse within the same person at different points of development, this homily recontextualizes these encounters to speak to diverse and unique spiritual capacities, and so different techniques are suggested for different soul types, no matter how sublime or depraved.*]

[19.3]. *Parashah Ki Teizai 1* (Deuteronomy 21:10–25:19)

QUESTIONS FOR REFLECTION:

1. When was the last time your inner voice aroused you to return to spiritual practice? Could you discern such an inner voice from other white noise clouding your conscience? Once discerned, did this call from the inner voice inspire a sustained spiritual practice? Why or why not?

2. While your heart may grow coarse from material perception

188. The lower the level, the energy of the higher level becomes more limited in its forms and vessels; the higher the level, the energy of the higher level becomes more unlimited.

189. Zohar III:228a.

190. b*Berakot* 5a: "R. Levi b. Hama says in the name of R. Simeon b. Lakish: One should always incite the impulse for good within the soul to do battle against the libidnal impulse. For it is written: Tremble and sin not. If one subdues the libidnal impulse, well and good. If not, let that person study Torah. For it is written: Commune with your own heart. If one subdues it, well and good. If not, let that person recite *Shema'*. For it written: Upon your bed. If one subdues it, well and good. If not, let that person be reminded of the day of death. For it is written: And be still, Selah." Compare with *Eyn Ya'akov* ad loc b*Berakot* 5a.

191. "He will swallow death forever. / YHVH my God will wipe the tears away / From all faces / And will put an end to the reproach of His people / Over all the earth— / For it is YHVH who has spoken" (Isaiah 25:8). It must be recalled in conclusion that the purpose of this spiritual process of return is not to remain in withdrawal; rather, withdrawal is merely a vessel to reach the path of interior, spiritual vitality.

and carnal bliss, do you find there is a need for striking a balance in your life? Does your spiritual practice support such a balance? What happens to your life when your spiritual practice does not support such a balance?

3. To what degree do the commands of your spiritual practice enacted in the material world necessitate constriction and boundaries? Do you find that your spiritual practice is helped or hindered by a regimen of constriction and boundaries? What happens to your spiritual practice when you are freed from such constriction and boundaries?

[20.1]. *Parashah Ki Tavo 1* (Deuteronomy 26:1–29:8)

INTRODUCTION TO HOMILY:

This world is a place of transitions, given that this world is a passageway. It affords the opportunity to make repairs because we are in transit. Human beings have the capacity to construct meaning with compassion. Thus, all spiritual qualia need to be harnessed to elevate the material to its roots and to be used wisely. True value is as a conduit for the next level of spiritual evolution. This is HaG"aT-emotionally based Hasidism, which begins here but is not limited to it. Emotional intelligence leads to higher states of consciousness rather than suppressing emotions. This is about getting on the emotional train, but not stopping at any one station, eventually leading into transcendent realms. While it may be a long journey replete with stations and hiatuses along the way; nevertheless, the first impulse to self-improvement includes everything. So nothing is more important than getting on the train for the journey itself. Arrivals are pleasurable, while beginnings are always fraught. This world is the staging area for the spiritual developmental process to unfold. Music is an apt metaphor for this journey through cantillation trope. This homily attempts to reframe the terror of anguish imbedded in the scriptural chastisements by juxtaposing them with bliss of first fruit offerings. This juxtaposition is meant to show that the negativity of the year can be transmuted and left behind. Part of the journey is realizing is that there is the baggage of negativity that can indeed be left behind. What makes this transition possible is when we navigate from the place of deep compassion, for ourselves, for the world, and for the process of being. It is also motivated by bliss, an affect common to Hasidism, therefore do not see the chastisement as motivation from the place of fear, rather re-orient this recoiling from fearful admonition. The spiritual work here is to feel the attraction of the spiritual bliss at the end of the journey. There is something beyond transition once one has completed the process of teshuvah, whereby one can chose to overlook the slights against oneself. To overlook this moment of potential resentment, one can still be off put inside. But overlooking the slight is itself transitional; once one sees that the goal is transcendence, then arriving in that bliss allows one to let go of any potential present baggage. Even the partial state of letting go allows one to dwell in the bliss of transcendence. The curses are transformed into blessing, by letting go and leaving them behind.

[20.2]. *Parashah Ki Tavo 1* (Deuteronomy 26:1–29:8)

HOMILY:

"Raba said: the one who overlooks slights against oneself [*and is expected to take umbrage*] such a person is forgiven all his iniquities [*when that accounting comes before the celestial tribunal, they will give one a pass*], as it says, **'Forgiving iniquity and passing by transgression.'**[192,193] Behold, in this reading section [*of Parashah Ki Tavo*], there are many commentators who interpret this as the supernal Land of Israel being described in the continuation of the verse: **"when you come into the land . . . take the basket [*TeNA*],"**[194] but the Land of Israel does not mean the physical world, but the *time-that-is-coming*. The basket refers to the acrostic of mystical linguistics of *TN"A* [*Cantillation Notes-Vocalization-Letters insofar as language is likened to a sonic basket containing and conveying all these aspects of signification*].[195]

[*The homily now shifts into a prolonged introduction to distinguish between this-world and the world-to-come.*] The issue that emerges here is found in the teaching of R. Yaakov: **". . . Prepare yourself [*hatkein*] in this-world, which is a corridor to enter into the banquet hall, the world-that-is-coming."**[196] [*It is necessary to "prepare yourself (hatkein)," for*] even though the antechamber is a passageway that marks transition from place to place before the entrance to the banquet hall; nevertheless, the very passage is the opportunity for transformation. [*If this world is an antechamber, it does not diminish its significance.*] It is in the very passage through the antechamber itself that the act of rectifying oneself takes place, so that this world is one transit camp.[197]

[*From here, the homily moves to explicate the passageway in the antechamber of this-world, which functions as a preparation for the world-that-*

---

192. Micah 7:18.

193. b*Rosh Hashanah* 17a: "Raba said: He who forgoes his right [to exact punishment] is forgiven all his iniquities, as it says, Forgiving iniquity and passing by transgression. Who is forgiven iniquity? One who passes by transgression [against himself]."

194. "And it shall be, when you come into the land which YHVH your God gives you for an inheritance, and does possess it, and dwell therein . . . And the priest shall take the basket out of your hand, and set it down before the altar of the YHVH your God" (Deuteronomy 26:1, 4).

195. *Toldot Yaakov Yosef* and *Degel Mahene Efraim* ad loc Parashah Ki Tavo.

196. m*Avot* 4:21.

197. This challenges an approach to analysis of the Vitebsker as seeking to completely transcend the corporeal realm, see Rivkah Shatz-Uffenheimer, *Hasidism as Mysticism* (Jerusalem: Magnes Press); for a critique of this position, see Seth Brody, "Open To Me the Gates of Righteousness: The Pursuit of Holiness and Non-Duality in Early Hasidic Teaching," *JQR* LXXXIV, nos. 1–2 (July–October 1998): 3–44.

is-coming]. The purpose of this-world is completely oppositional to the world-that-is-coming, a spiritual state that is difficult to fully apprehend, given its heightened spirituality [*such juxtaposition leads to incommensurability*]. If so, then how can this-worldly temporality serve as a preparation for the world-that-is-coming? How can this passage on the world of materiality relate to and prepare one for the world of spirituality? [*Given that we are all in transit in this world.*] The truth is found in Scripture that teaches: **"Happy is the one whose strength is in You; whose heart is on the pilgrim highways."**[198] The issue then emerges in the verse: **"the world is created With Compassion"**[199] [*given that we are in transit in this world, our capacity to make meaning in this world is constituted by the application of our moral-emotional disposition. The first and foremost of our moral-emotional disposition manifest in the seven lower spheres, which is Chesed (Compassion) to Malkhut (Grounding) so that*] there is no creature that exists in the universe, except through the lower spiritual qualities from which the world was constructed. The human being is thus a microcosm through the seven spiritual qualities of creation. Even though this entire world is material, it is built from the spiritual quality of Compassion. Whatever qualities of *Chesed* (Compassion) have been translated into the human being should not be overwhelmed by materiality [*so that when one applies Compassion to one's interactions in the world, one realizes its purpose is to elevate oneself in the cosmos, rather than merely using this sense of Compassion in a selfish way*]. Rather, God put all this materiality before the human being for him/her to recognize and recall [*in that spiritual capacity his/her connection to*] the divine name, reconnecting everything and one's self back to its divine root in the Limitless. [*The moral-emotional qualia of the middot are valuable only insofar as they provide us with the vehicle for transition to more transcendent spiritual modalities, but realize even if this path begins with emotional layers it does not end there*].

[*The constructive path for engaging one's spiritual capacities so as to elevate them amid any material context is through remembrance of the divine name*] for in following such a path of knowledge [*one comes to realize just how much*] these forces, thoughts, motivations, and reactions constituting the expressions of being alive in one's soul as supernal lights. As human beings, we have **"no concept of this measure"**[200] **"[s]eeing it is hidden from the eyes of all living"**[201]—how **"great is the goodness"**[202] hidden in

198. Psalm 84:6.

199. Psalm 89:3.

200. Literally, "Human knows not the price thereof; [neither is it found in the land of the living]" (Job 28:13).

201. Literally, "Seeing it is hidden from the eyes of all living, and kept close from the fowls of the air" (Job 28:21).

202. Literally, "O how abundant is Your goodness, which You have laid up for them

every human being and these [*moral-emotional*] capacities [*recognized in the most elevated and mature expression then are considered*] **"so divine, none compares to You, who works for the waiting one."**[203] [*This is the opposite of an unthoughtful emotionality. But once one realizes such remarkably elevated values and goodness concealed in their spiritual capacities,*] then how could one really apply such capacities merely to creaturely appetites and evanescent existence?

As the parable of the precious pearl teaches, even if one was starving one would not waste the pearl, given its elevated status, by trading it for something as insignificant as a morsel of food, unless one was a fool. [*So it is with one's spiritual capacities, once s/he really knows their value and elevated status, why would s/he squander them on momentary self-indulgence of evanescent existence, even if one is starved and one's passions overtake him/her? In contrast to the pietistic ethics of Mussar, which would focus more upon the castigation of one's indulgence on sin, here the homily is castigating the misuse of higher emotional faculties for lower purposes. The homily continues with a scriptural citation, which will explain how the passage in the antechamber of this-worldly materialism can serve as a preparation to entering the spiritual world-that-is-coming.*]

This is [*all explained in the verse*]: **"Happy is the one whose strength is in You"**[204]—for the seven spiritual qualia [*each sphere contains a tenfold mapping of the spheres is actually*] **"seventy"** [*spelled the same as "strength" above with the letters 'Ayin-Zayin, signifying the numerology of seven below in the terrestrial realm and seventy above in the celestial realm*]. It is known that the lower [*numbers, which are of course letters in Hebrew, from the first to the ninth are considered to be a*] single digit, [*and once these single digits increase and ascend*] to double digits [*from the eleventh to ninetieth*] they are expanding, [*so too the seven spiritual qualities in this worldly, terrestrial realm are single digit and then in their ascension into the world-that-is-coming, they expand into double digits, thus from seven to seventy*]. All these capacities [*of spiritual strength intertwined within the material as symbolized by the letters 'Ayin-Zayin*] that allow one to experience the material world do not stop there; rather, these material capacities serve as **"pilgrim highways"**[205] in opening up to another pathway [*to the root of spiritual qualia*] **"in You,"**[206] leading all the way back to the Limitless.

---

that fear You; which You have wrought for them that take their refuge in You, in the sight of the children of humankind!" (Psalm 31:20).

203. "And whereof from of elders have not heard, nor perceived by the ear, neither has the eye seen a God beside You, who works for him that waits for the One" (Isaiah 64:3).

204. Psalm 84:6.

205. Psalm 84:6.

206. Psalm 84:6.

[*Given that the material qualia are grounded in this time, they are able to serve as "pilgrim highways" that connect their pathways to the spiritual qualia of the time-that-is-coming. Thus passing through the antechamber of this time is a passageway that marks preparation and transition into the time-that-is-coming. What follows in the homily at length now is the process of rectifying and refining these spiritual qualia, and how to ensure these qualia do not become a means to and end that is merely materialist; rather, the qualia remain directed towards the divine totality. This now allows for a fuller*] reconsideration of the opening teaching and its explanation that: "He who forgoes his right [*to exact punishment*] is forgiven all his iniquities," whereby at the beginning of one's spiritual formation, one's spiritual qualia are simply the tools that allow one to experience the world as it is, sweet and tempting, wanting to take in this experience. At that moment—the first inkling of return—one must attempt to overcome those qualia drawing one to a specific experience, changing the direction of initial impulse in the process of turning around and returning to the pathways of the Limitless. [*Those pathways of the emotional qualia, when elevated and mature, are not a final destination where one gets stuck; rather, it is a process. By not following the seemingly irresistible impulses of emotional reactiveness; then one is more open to transformation of 'teshuvah'. This is the process of returning to the root of the spiritual qualia which is the ability to catch oneself becoming overwhelmed by emotions.*] This is the first inkling of returning [*to the awareness of the transitional nature of all mind-states. It is just that—a first inkling and not the fuller return that transforms action in the manifest world*]. This first inkling still marks a beginning and receptivity in the heart to return, even though s/he may have not yet reached that place where the connection is full and good. Those initial reactions emerge from these emotional qualia and are still assertive and pushing him/her in a certain direction [*that can spiral out of control, but s/he has the capacity to be mindful and return to the root of the qualia*].

We have discussed elsewhere[207] the core issue—to habituate a spiritual practice so that one's capacities are transitional and can be guided back to be redirected toward the divine alone [*embedding them in that root*]. The matter is addressed by our blessed Sages who teach the one who uproots the direction of those impulses, **"lest there should be among you a root that bears gall and wormwood [*of idolatry*]."**[208] For every [*emotional qualia*] lies in the **"root"**—all the branches spread from that root. In the regard, our blessed Sages teach: "If you take a stick and throw it into the air, it will

207. R. Menachem Mendel of Vitebsk, *Peri haAretz*, Parashah Ki Tissa.

208. ". . . lest there should be among you man, or woman, or family, or tribe, whose heart turns away this day from YHVH our God, to go to serve the gods of those nations; lest there should be among you a root that bears gall and wormwood" (Deuteronomy 29:17) .

come back down to the ground and become rooted back in its source."[209] [*It is easier to throw something untethered into the air, which always returns to its ground of existence which is inescapable, for its root extends from this rootedness, even while currently untethered.*]

The general principle here: "if one is a robber, one is not a scholar" [*which suggests a dialectic between spirituality and corporeality*], namely, that there is no divinity that can be apperceived through the coarseness of materiality.[210] So long as one is preoccupied with the materiality, there is no possibility of elevating to divine apprehension. [*For these qualia to bridge and connect to the spiritual, they must no longer see materiality as a means to an end.*]

But the truth is that the very beginning of contemplating that first impulse of return already encompasses everything within it wherein the end of returning is inscribed in this very first impulse of its beginning.[211] The act of contemplation itself transforms you into a deeply devoted one. As the blessed Sages teach: "Behold you are consecrated to me [*because on the occasion of the wedding, one transforms into the state of becoming a deeply devoted one*]" so that this completely wicked person is transformed in that first impulse to return. This impulse emerges from that inner point. This is the beginning of all the letters, leading them along in the process of manifestation. In the same way, spiritual development begins with a singular point as the beginning that has already within it all the future unfolding potential.[212] This is why it is not difficult, except in the beginning moment [*especially as related to the process of returning through teshuvah*], as the blessed Sages teach: "All beginnings are challenging."[213] Once you are able to navigate through the beginning through the power of the first impulse, then there is a great pleasure in fulfilling one's original intent.

This issue of the beginning is akin to birthing [*in the process of returning through 'teshuvah' which*] is in the cellular constitution of the fetus that then leads to the birthing of the human being. All is hidden in potential within that point. Just as the physical body of the human being has to undergo untangling and distinguishing each of our physiological faculties, so too, in the soul's usage of its spiritual qualia, there is a need for untangling and distinguishing to channel them from what is in potential to what can be actualized.

---

209. *Genesis Rabbah* 53:20.

210. b*Avodah Zarah* 17b: "When they brought up R. Eleazar b. Perata [for his trial] they asked him, 'Why have you been studying [Torah] and why have you been stealing?' He answered, 'If one is a scholar he is not a robber, if a robber he is not a scholar, and as I am not the one I am neither the other.'"

211. *Sefer Yetzirah*.

212. *Tiquney Zohar*, Tiqqun 5, 20b.

213. *Mekhilta Yitro* 19:5.

Even though everything is contained in this first point, without learning and spiritual practice, this spiritual stem cell will not be realized. [*As the qualia emerge and are extended through spiritual practice, then*] this spiritual stem cell can turn into any letter it wants. Rather, only through prolonged discipline will this point take on a specific spiritual identity in its fullest stature.

So the first impulse for self-improvement through *teshuvah* includes everything that is to come. This moment of the beginning is a point within the heart. It encompasses all facets of return [*which are the spiritual qualia whose direction is always toward the divine totality*]. Even by contemplative awareness [*the impulse of return encompasses all facets within, it still remains a beginning point, therefore an inkling is never enough, rather*] from there it must be ramified and unpacked, until it grows into great spiritual qualia. [*Although these began as material qualia, now they are spiritual, thus allowing a*] transforming of this inner point [*of the impulse of return, namely, the greater spiritual qualia that have been drawn and extended from that point*] into the externalization [*which is akin to what are*] called letters. [*By analogy, in the same way that the scribe begins a Hebrew letter from the point that contains the entire letter's shape in its entirety, albeit in contracted form, so that*] from the letter, moving the quill back and forth, which then leads to the next stage in the development of external communication of the concentrated inner point, allowing for the possibility of bliss in completion. [*By way of another analogy*] when a person is born, the roots of faculties are already imbedded within the fetus, just not fully manifest or differentiated. Rather, these faculties remain in potential, included in a singular point. It takes work and practice to differentiate the various faculties of the individual, to take the unified potential into actuality, differentiating into such faculties of a fully developed person. Even though everything is contained in that point, without the learning that comes from experience and practice in the world, there is no growth and plasticity to emerge embodied in the world. Emergence is a process of differentiation, so that each of the spiritual qualia creates a platform for the expansion of self for the purposes of completing a well-rounded human being.[214]

[*The matter at hand is explained*] according to the verse in Scripture, which teaches: **"And the rib, which YHVH had built up"**[215]—whereas the **"fierceness of one's countenance"**[216] does not display plasticity once

214. The narcissicism of small differences is being re-appropriated from the Talmudic literature, *kol echad bone bama l'atzmo*, so that it shifts from being derogatory critique of religious sectarianism to positive, insofar as the individual inolution of spiritual qualia should develop their own platforms and fields of expression.

215. Literally, "And the rib, which YHVH had taken from the man, made He a woman, and brought her unto the man" (Genesis 2:22).

216. "A nation of fierce countenance, that shall not regard the person of the old, nor

it is actualized into a stable identity, these spiritual qualia are more fluid in their potential at the beginning. [*It becomes more difficult to change personality as you grow older in contrast to the fluidity of beginnings at birth.*]

So it is within the first stirring impulse of return at the beginning, which is the point in the heart that integrates everything. [*Following the inner point of the vowel that extends into consonantal letters, which are the spiritual qualia built on the impulse of return, now*] certainly the point [*which is the first impulse of return at the beginning*] is already integrated within the joy that was already there, concealed in the first stirring [*so that afterward when the point extends into letters and cantillation notes, it is then that revealed bliss of musicality which emerges from concealment*]. "To engender joy of spiritual realities to the Creator—as it says 'We shall do the work of the Will of the One.'"[217] But this joy cannot yet be felt [*for such joy of the sacral deed within that inner point is the inkling of return as if sensed*] as with the more mature spiritual qualia [*of the letters and tropes*]. The apperception of joy from these [*qualia*] is a matter of perception and etiquette in using these [*qualia*], all the more forcefully in the time-that-is-coming, transcending materiality.

[*Alas, this work of return through teshuvah, an overturning of material qualia into spiritual qualia, this*] is a matter [*that was addressed by our blessed Sages, who taught:*] **" . . . Prepare yourself [*hatkein*] in this-world [*of materiality*], which is a staging area for the developmental process of emerging into a full spiritual personality as one enters into the banquet hall, the world-that-is-coming [*of spirituality*]."**[218] [*This happens when the person*] **"shifts in what generates pleasure"**[219] from the sensorial modalities not to sense the materiality whatsoever.

So this is the issue at hand as explained by what the blessed Sages teach: "Ezra made a regulation for Israel that they should read the curses in Leviticus preceding Pentecost [*as we read in Parashah Bechuqotay*], and those in Deuteronomy preceding New Year [*as we read in Parashah Ki Tavo*]."[220] [*This is the reasoning behind reading Torah pericopes of Para-*

---

show favor to the young" (Deuteronomy 28:50).

217. Rashi ad loc b*Zevakhim* 46b.

218. m*Avot* 4:21.

219. "[A Psalm] of David; when he changed his demeanor before Abimelech, who drove him away, and he departed" (Psalm 34:1).

220. b*Megillah* 31b: "It has been taught: R. Simeon b. Eleazar says: Ezra made a regulation for Israel that they should read the curses in Leviticus before Pentecost and those in Deuteronomy before New Year. What is the reason?—Abaye—or you may also say Resh Lakish said: So that the year may end along with its curses. I grant you that in regard to the curses in Deuteronomy you can say, 'so that the year should end along with its curses.' But as regards those in Leviticus—is Pentecost a New Year?—Yes; Pentecost is also a New Year, as we have learnt: 'On Pentecost is the new year for [*fruit of*] the tree.'"

shah Ki Tavo and Parashah Bechuqotay, which read:] "Let the year be finished with all its curses,"[221] for "assembly on pilgrimage is also the new year of the tree."[222] [*The homily then continues reflecting on the incipience related to the New Year known as Rosh haShannah as opposed to the New Month of Rosh Hodesh.*]

In the celestial worlds above time [*in terms of duration*], *shanah* then refers to "change" whereas *chodesh* refers to "a state of renewal" [*hiddush*], moving from one state of consciousness to another [*otherwise it will all be reified in a steady state*]. [*Primordial*] Torah precedes [*duration*] and presides over two thousand transformations [*which means that there were states of being in flux*]. We understand from our blessed Sages that the curses "begin with the snake as the first animal to be cursed"[223]—for it is the root of all the curses [*as the snake symbolizes separation from the divine totality*]. All curses are developments that cause separation from the divine totality. So when one engages in self-transformation, then one is returning their root, transmuting one's very nature from curses back to blessings [*thus inverting the snake's curse of separation from non-dual origin*], to the point that aspects of one's existence are radically changed, working only for sake of the divine totality. By engaging in this turning of *teshuvah*, then all of the curses of this world will be transformed into goodness, extending the stream that flows from its original source. This transformation will extend the snake into a staff, [*for the staff is the form of divine extension from above to below*] drawing out blessing rather than evil.[224]

[*This brings the homily to now elucidate why the chastisements are ordered into Torah readings during the closing of the season, namely, to wear them off and nullify them.*] The whole transformation of the year [*recalling that SHaNah (Year) means SHiNui (Change)*], with all its curses, all ends up culminating with the act itself of reading Torah [*as ordered by Ezra*] presiding over **"two thousand transformations"** from one state to another, so that the flow of *Chesed* (Love) extends through all these states. [*By bringing the negative energy to light, it is not only eliminated but it is transmuted from negative to positive in line with transformative capacity of temporality of the season of Shavuot (Pentecost), which is its own return to origin. This is a real reversal of energies. Thus, the curses are transformed into the primordial compassion which preceded creation.*]

This explains the opening of the verse: **"And so let it be"**—denotes hap-

221. *Moed l'Kol Hai* 13.

222. m*Rosh Hashanah* 1:2.

223. b*Eruvin* 18a, so that the curse follows in a causal chain from the snake to Eve and then to Adam, and all of humanity.

224. R. Hayyim Vital, *Sha'ar haKavvanot*, Derushai haPesach, Derush 12, wherein the birthing waters of the hind is contaminated at the moment when snake bites the opening of her womb.

piness [*as a promise of what shall be*], **"when you come into the land"**[225] which is the supernal land, the joy of sacral deeds happens when one comes back to the impetus for change in the pristine point of origin. [*The time-that-is-coming is a modality of spiritual apperception through joy of the sacral deed which incorporates spiritual qualia and the bliss that ensues from them. The way of reaching these spiritual qualia of merging with the divine is by way of return, as the verse continues to explicate*]: **"Take the basket [*TeNA*]"**[226]—the taste of joy demands that one go through the whole process of unpacking the undifferentiated point [*into smaller extensions, becoming the differentiated world as we know it*]. The act of reading this chastisement text aloud with all of its *TeNA*—cantillations, vocalizations, and letters [*which symbolize the three stages of return*]—extends the point [*which is the inkling of return that extends from potential to actual*] until it reaches the spiritual qualia [*namely, the letters*] and from there one apperceives joy [*of the sacral deed*] and the bliss of the cantillations.

[*Although in return one reaches the cantillations last, still from the place of truth*] in any case the cantillations even precede vocalization points, and all the more so letters [*which preceded them according to TeNA*]. Yet it is known according to our blessed Sages: "The end is inscribed in the beginning"[227] [*namely, whatever is finally enacted remains forefront in the mind, and thus despite the fact that cantillation precede letters and vowels, being forefront in the mind, in reality, they settle in at the end after vowel and letter. The pleasure may be the highest and added last to human experience*].

[*After having explained the opening of the verse: "And so it shall be when you come into the land," then the homily continues by linking this back with another Talmudic teaching concerning one who forgos his right to exact punishment and is forgiven all his iniquities.*] This is what our blessed Sages teach: "One who forgoes his right [*to exact punishment*] is forgiven all his iniquities."[228] So it follows in this language of "forgoes" first and foremost, [*namely, forgoing all other iniquity, but*] "the transgression itself is not erased" [*and neither is it deracinated from its root, for the human*] still has being that [*only*] begins to "forgo" the spiritual qualia, not enacting their acts, rather it is still the spiritual quality itself which is not erased [*nor uprooted*] from the same root after it. [*This is an endless se-*

225. "And it shall be, when you come into the land which YHVH your God gives you for an inheritance, and does possess it, and dwell therein . . . And the priest shall take the basket out of your hand, and set it down before the altar of the YHVH your God" (Deuteronomy 26:1, 4).

226. Deuteronomy 26:1, 4.

227. b*Kiddushin* 82a.

228. b*Rosh Hashanah* 17a: "Raba said: He who forgos his right [*to exact punishment*] is forgiven all his iniquities, as it says, Forgiving iniquity and passing by transgression. Who is forgiven iniquity? One who passes by transgression [*against himself*]."

quence of the second sin becoming the first, but when does one ever exhaust the sequence? One is thus always not intending to follow the transgressive act.] The commitment is to enter into the very root of the spiritual quality always for the divine sake. This is what is meant by *teshuvah* in returning to the same time, place, and circumstance and acting differently. The physical desire is tracked back to its root so that one offers it up to the divine. One has such passionate love of the divine love that it actually extinguishes the fire of the impulse for evil. Even in the same tempting circumstance, now divine love extinguishes the impulse for evil. [*The only way to remove the residue of transgression is to transmute it all.*] When a sacral deed is enacted from the state of deep love, then the sin itself is actually erased. This is what transmutes the energy at its very source.

[20.3]. *Parashah Ki Tavo* (Deuteronomy 26:1–29:8)

QUESTIONS FOR REFLECTION:

1. What moments in your life when you are challenged in letting go of baggage so as to return obstacles and oppositional forces to their original source in deep love?

2. Which spiritual station do you need to be in order to overlook the negativity of oppositional forces in your life?

3. How do you make the goal of spiritual transcendence so already meaningful and attractive that it already has an energetic, transformative propulsion even when you are not there yet? Is that process of spiritual formation something that happens individually or can it be fostered in conscious community? What is the nurturing framework of a communal context that can support you in work?

Glossary of Hebrew Terms

Aleph-Bet — alphabet of 22 Hebrew letters.

'Ahavah — Love as the quality that counterbalances Fear (see *Yirah*, *middah*).

ahd, ahid, itahid — embrace (= grasp and unite), link, grasp, clasp, seize, grab, clutch, latch on, snatch, attach, adhere, graft, connect, join, adjoin, band (together), hold, hold together, hold fast, hold firm, take hold, handle, tie, possess, unite, merge, splice, catch, grip, fasten, cling, intermingle, weave, interweave, intersect, interlink, compose, constitute, comprise, intertwine, blend; 1:152b *itaheid be-ilana*; 193a: *ahidan be-ilana* — joined to the Tree of Life.

'akhdut hapashut — different modalities of the divine reality can open spiritual beings to deeper awareness of the undifferentiated oneness, in contradistinction to the filtering process of (see *Tzimzum*). This undifferentiated oneness of the limitless primal reality is referred to more commonly in philosophical theology as "simplex."

'amn – omana — artistry, craftsmanship, worksmanship, skill; artisan; art, craft; handiwork all meanings associated with the root *AMN*.

'emunah — often rendered as "faith" within the universal spiritual context of the West under great Christian influence, this translation remains insufficient for the application to this particular path of Tiberean Hasidism. Starting with the frequent invocation of its shared root *AMN* in the response to a blessing with *Amen*, it denotes "faithfulness" which is more than creedal faith, as in the expression *ne'emanut.* What is connoted, moreover is an abiding sense of "conviction" that underlies "truthfulness". Recalling that root *AMN* denotes the ability to strengthen or to fortify, so one responds *Amen* as a demonstrative sign of confirming the blessing just articulated. In this sense, the term connotes conformation, affirmation, corroboration as part of its nuance. But *'emunah* is more complex than "blind faith", more nuanced than forcing oneself to believe something unreal or untenable. Total integration of the self in symmetric balance, without being skewed or fixated on any one state or emotional disposition so one can ascend to the infinite with clarity and transparency. Firmness, alignment and integrity. There is no commandment for *'emunah* as it stands as the basis of all religious life. *'Emunah* is an ability to realize that what you believe in is not contingent upon the way you explain it, rather you have a direct and clear relationship with that which cannot be apperceived. The mind is not the absolute arbiter of the spiritual relationship, for the purpose of knowing is unknowing. In contrast to "blind faith", this is a knowing that is not-knowing, enlightened agnosis, which is key for *'emunah.*

'Ayin — The state of No-thingness whereby the self is dissolved amidst the mystical experience of merging (see *Devekut*).

bittul — Nullification in general, often of the ego or shell of self in particular that needs to be shed in order to enter into a trance state leading to non-dual mystical apperception.

brit milah — refers both to the ritual ceremony of circumcising a male child on the eighth day as well as to the circumcised *membrum.*

Da'at — Literally, intuitive knowing, or eruption of consciousness, *Da'at* often remains concealed form the ten manifest spheres of divine consciousness (see *Sephirot*). As a nexus point between emotional states and cognition, this concealed sphere stands in opposition to Cartesian bifurcation of mind and body, or the demarcation of emotion and cognition. Unlike many philosophers who held that emotion is the enemy of cognition, one needs to work through the emotional centers of one's being in order to enable one to authentically reach cognition. Emotions are not superfluous but essential to integral being. Thus when emotions are balanced, leading to cognition, then a unified, organic, meaningful integrity for the human being emerged as *Da'at.* (see ***sephirot***)

dbq — cleave, cling, join, adjoin, conjoin, unite, adhere, attach, overtake, fuse; merge.

itdabbaq, itdevaq, le-adbeqa — grasp, apprehend, comprehend, fathom, seize, absorb, attain, get hold of.

devekut — a cultivated state of deep attunement that leads to the experience of merging, which could be brought on by a trance state whereby the self is emptied as in *bittul* (see above). A pure and simple reaching out and surrendering without any ground of being which thus requires *'emunah*. The spectrum of mystical experience being described ranges from sympathetic alignment to total absorption.

dibbuk haverim — "mystical companionship" that builds on the aforementioned state of *devekut* at its core. This experience of *devekut* is more horizontal than vertical in that the collective *communitas*, albeit a relatively small confraternity is what facilitates this deeper attunement, attachment and merging of *devekut*.

'eruv/ai tavshilin — a shared cooked dish that is used as part of a legal fiction to permit cooking on the holiday for a purpose beyond the day's usage, namely for a Sabbath immediately following.

glgl – gilgel gilgulim — rotate rotations (Zohar 110b), spin schemes (Zohar 158b, 199a, 19; 201b, 4), put someone through ordeals; intrigue; tortuousness, tortuosity, convolution; permutation of letters; roll, revolve, spin, rotate, turn.

galgal — (rolling) wave;

gilgul — rolling, whirling, revolving, revolution, rotation, turning, cycle, cycling, migration, transmigration, reincarnation;

gilgulin de-mitgalgelan — cycles revolving;

glgl be-gilgul — revolving in (many) convolutions;

glgl ha-hozer v'sovev — cycles of constellations revolving and returning;

glgl ha-mazalot — Zodiac wheel of the constellations organized according to astrological signs.

halitza — the "ritual of release by removing the shoe," which is derived from Deuteronomy 25: 7-10. The defunct ceremony functions to "release" the widow of a man who died childless to marry someone other than her brother-in-law. Although the union with a brother's wife is incestuous and prohibited by Torah, in order to avert the extinction of the family line, the brother of the deceased is obligated to marry the widow in a *Yibum* or "Levirate marriage". In the case of the brother refusing to marry the widow, Torah provides for this "release ritual". If the woman refuses to cohabit with the brother-in-law, then Jewish law requires the surviving brother to exercise his right to refusal to then release his sister-in-law, so she is "free" to marry someone else. Prevention of Levirate marriages was a moral imperative of the Rabbis.

Hanukkah — festival of lights commemorating the Maccabean victory over the Seleucid Greeks in 167BCE. This commemoration has a dual focus, at once upon the rededication of the desecrated Jerusalem Temple [*HaNuKat haBayit*] as well as upon the miraculous single cruse of oil that lasts for eight days. The commemoration lasts eight days, each night of the festival lights are kindled in the eight branched candelabra [*Hanukiyah*].

hayyoth — literally "animals" as well as more generally "living creatures" to denote the wondrous nature of the ecstatic vision as described in Ezekiel 1: 5.

ẖbr – ithabbar — joins, conjoins, unites, converge, merge, connect, attach, combine, compose, collaborate, associate, participate, fraternize;

meHaBeR — the connector, conjoiner, merger.

hitkashrut — bonding or interconnecting between spheres, people, community. In the same way that chemical bonding occurs, materials exchange electrons, so too does the spiritual interconnection take place.

hitlabshut — enshrouding the divine presence personnified typically as a feminine. Assuming the guise or the role of or manifested in.

hishtalshelut — unfolding of the chain of being.

hiyyut — vitality that is imbued by the divine.

homer ha'yuli — *hylic* matter is the way the divine descends into the manifest world of materiality, which then serves to enable a spiritual evolution of consciousness. The material body that has utterly decomposed, still retains within it *hylic* matter, from which a new form may emerge. There has to be a gap between the original and new form, (what neo-Darwinists call a "missing link") and that gap is found in *hylic* matter.

hsd – hasid — saint, devotee, pious, pious devotee, devout one, faithful one (see *Hesed*).

hsg – hasagah — literally, perception or grasp; also connoting apperception, in the sense, that perception is limited to the somatic frame of senses in the phenomenal, whereas apperception can also refer to abstract realities or concepts in the realm of the noumenal.

ila'ah — transcendent, supernal, lofty, superior, supreme, superb, upper, high, on high, higher, highest, noble, ultimate, utmost, finest, paramount, eminent, esteemed, sublime, exalted, elevated, soaring, towering, magnificent, splendid, intense, heavenly, celestial;

'alma ila'ah — higher world (or upper world, supernal world), heavenly, celestial; sublime mystery.

Ilan d'kol Hai — the cosmic Tree-that-is-All. This *'Ilan* likely makes a veiled appearance early on in Ancient Israel, with a more sustained symbolic rendering in early medieval Jewish mystical literature of Provence. Jewish mysticism in relation to its more theosophic iterations shift back and forth in referring to this cosmic tree as either the *'Ilan* or the '*Etz Hayyim*.

iqqar — root, essence, principle, source, essential element, main object, foundation, taproot.

kofer b'iqqar — idiomatically, heretic. Interpreted here as a state of unawareness whereby one is in denial of a deeper spiritual reality.

kll – kelal — total, totality, sum, summation, whole, entirety, entire amount, consummation, sphere, realm, assemblage; in general, general rule, (essential) principle, category, class, state, generalization, generality; together; overall, all-inclusive, universal, comprehensive.

kelala de-khola — totality of all, principle of all (principle encompassing all)

kelil — inclusive (all-inclusive), include, enclose, encompass, contain, combine, integrate, incorporate, merge, coalesce, fuse, blend, mingle, absorb, comprise, compose, compound, embrace, enfold, envelop, engulf, brought him under the aegis, imbue; complete;

kelil be — composed of.

itkelil mi — comprises, composed of;

itkelilan — same as above, plus interwoven, interlaced, intertwined, intermingling, integrated, crowned;
le-akhlala — encompassing, to include, etc. (see ***kelil***)

lshn – lishana — tongue, language, speech, term, phrase, expression, version.

ma'amar — teaching, speech utterance, the latter related often times to the Creator's creation of the world in a single utterance. It also comes to symbolize each and every inner direction created within all sentient beings.

maqor — spring, fountain, source.

middah – middot (pl) — spiritual attributes, *qualia*, or values that imbue human consciousness with divinity and allow for an awareness of the process of spiritual refinement.

mokhin — it emerges from the view of the higher self through, the perspective that witnessing in a detached way the view of the "I am", it transcends totality of the mind in *Da'at* comprehends all the spiritual qualia of *middot*, which is still not representative of ultimate reality which has no "I" at all.

mi'darga l'darga — "*in*volution" rather than mere evolution suggests an internal form of spiritual evolution or interior progress along the path of formation. Oftentimes this is measured through distance (ascending the divine mountain) or time (i.e. from day to day, moment to moment).

mikal l'homer — *de minoris, ad majoris,* drawing analogies from the minor to the major case.

mishnah — Oral Law redacted by Rabbi Judah the Prince, circa 2nd century CE.

mitzvah — While often translated as commandment. More accurately, a sacral deeds that informs broader spiritual practice. It is traditionally enumerated as 613, with positive and negative deeds.

mshkh — draw, draw to, toward, conduct, channel, flow, stream, continue, convey, proceed, emanate, transmit, derive, extend, expand, stretch, pull, attract, prolong, persist, spread, drag, lure, seduce, allure.

Mussar — "self-refinement" treatises that promote a regular review of *middot* (see above). By mistranslating such treatises as merely "ethical" cordons off any layers of "mystical" experience present in the modern corpus of *Kabbalistic Mussar*. Key figures who promulgated this work of self-refinement within the context of *Kabbalistic Mussar* include the circle of R. Moshe Hayyim Luzzatto, Gaon of Vilna, etc.

nissayon — the principal trial(s) once experiences along the path of life.

nivraim — all creatures fashioned in the process of creation by the Creator, referred to here as sentient beings. What the expression sentient beings allows for is a more globalized view of the ongoing impact of the creative force within the universe, ranging from all levels of existence, from inanimate and animate matter, from the vegetal to the animal kingdoms, reaching all the way to the human kingdom. The recognition of everything that we think is external to ourselves is actually present in the same unifying field of existence that includes us as well — such that inter-being exists without any single center.

'olam — literally, world, universe. The cosmological implication for the mystic is akin to the Multiverse of Consciousness which refers to mind-states that are part of spiritual evolution. Literally, "world" or "universe" the mystical import of the term refers to the four-world matrix of divine consciousness, namely, *ABY"A.* It also is used generically in relation to the spiritual attributes or *middot*.

'Olam ha'Atzilut — unified consciousness;

'Olam ha'Beriyah — cognitive consciousness;

'Olam ha'Yetzirah — emotional consciousness;

'Olam ha'Assiyah — embodied consciousness.

'Olam haTemurot — World of Distortion or Distorted Mirrors is an approximate translation of this phantasmagoric image in kabbalah. While in *mishnaic* terms, *Temurah* denotes a kind of substitution or replacement wherein the human being can be substituted by an animal sacrifice, its extrapolation in to the kabbalistic tradition suggests however, that the replica of a given spiritual reality reproduces, at best, the distorted reflection of a flawed mirror. Just like an ape resembles a human being, much of what appears in such a an external comparison of mirroring may show much in common between the exterior *qualia* but that parallel dissolves upon reflection of the interior *qualia*.

'ophan/im – those "spinning creatures" rotating on wheels of concentric circles to denote the wondrous nature of the ecstatic vision as described in Ezekiel 1: 16.

'orah – way, course, path; property.

'or — light, luminescence;

'or yashar — "Linear Light" is the attribute of Compassion [*Hesed*] whereby the upper realm flows forth towards receptive, lower sphere. *Hesed* is the Love that is directed by haste and running so that it overflows all limits and restraints, leading the situation whereby one can become completely annihilated from reality with overwhelming merging of Love.

'***or hozer*** –"Returning Light" is the attribute of Restraint [*Din*] whereby the lower realm flows forth as a more limited force. *Din* restrains and limits the otherwise overwhelming predilection of light to merge through the force of *Hesed*.

plsh – mePHuLaSH — literally, a path wide open. It connotes is a spiritual support system of rooted in the vitality sustaining all sentient creatures, wide enough to encapsulate everything (see *'emunah*).

PHeLiSHtim — archenemy tribe of Philistines as the archetype of evil (see *Sitra Akhra*).

parsuf/im — holy configurations of divine energy in the form of countenances: *Atika Kadisha*; *Zeir Anpin*; *Yisrael Sabbah*. The flow of divine love from its unmitigated source is a descent in the following stages:
(1) ***'Atika Kadisha*** — "Holy One of Ancient Days", this is the first stage of flow from the source of divine love emanating from a pure white beard of the divine persona so called;
(2) ***Zeir 'Anpin*** — "Young Impatient One", this is the second stage of flow from this previous source of pure white descends into the black beard as the intermediate hypostasis of the divine persona so called;
(3) ***Yisrael Sabbah*** — "Elder", this is the flow of the divine love from its unmitigated source symbolized as the dark beard turning white (pure love), causing the young dark beard to appear as if aging.

pra — what allows for something real to be disclosed as the entrance level fear (see *Yirah*);
PhaRAoh — the Egyptian demagogue who represents the archetype of evil (see *Sitra Akhra*).
ORePH — nape of the neck, symbolically associated through shared assonance with Pharaoh.

psht – itpeshat — spread, extend, expand, stretch, disperse, distribute, diffuse, scatter, disseminate, emanate, ramify, branch, permeate; strip; straighten, smooth, smoothen (Zohar 2:84b, 1).

pt<u>h</u> – pt<u>h</u> qera — opened with a (the) verse, explained the verse as referring to, in connection with; unraveled a verse.

ptq – pitqa — slip, decree, letter, note, list, record; *pitaq* "slip, memorandum, name slip carried by the Angel of Death" (derived from Greek *pittakion*). See *Qohelet Rabbah* on 3:2; *Zohar* 3:15a, 156b.

qdm — anticipate, precede, preface, prepare, ahead of time, in advance, advance, intercept (zp 2:372), do early, do before, before its time, beforehand, prematurely, previously, do already, arise early, come early, arrive early, hasten, do or be first, be the first to, put or place or mention first, begin (with), initiate, introduce, attain first, set out, forestall (prevent by prior measures), take precaution, foresee, be zealous, take precedence, give preference to; (hasten to) intercede; (spoke) up; soon, quickly, immediately; do in time.
qadma'a — previous, preceding, former, original, first, earlier; primary, primal;
qadma'ei — ancients;
mi-le-qadmin, kidbeqadmita — as before, as originally, as previously, at first;

qdsh – qaddishei elyonin — holy ones of the Highest (Most High) (Daniel 7:18); (or occasionally "supernal holy ones");

qudsha — holiness, realm of holiness, sanctuary.

qshr — bind, link, link up, join; connect, attach, fasten,nexus, bond, knot, tie, weave, braid, wreathe, cluster, joint, intermingle, interlink, concatenate (adj.); catch, entangle; See ***qtr***.

le-qashra qishra — to bind the bond, to tie the knot, forging links;

qshr — sorcery; see ***qshr*** (Liebes, *Peraqim*, 397); entangle, bound in bonds; 2:25a, 37b-38a, 52b, 69a.

qelipah — literally, "husk" or "obstruction", so that within a dualistic cosmology there is always this oppositional form of divine personification.

qtrg — denounce, accuse, prosecute, incriminate, assail, attack, provoke, incite, antagonize, contest, contend, harass, bring charges, level accusation; persecute, hostile, object, oppose.

ratzon — desire or ultimate will of and within the divine.

ratzon 'elyon — supernal desire or original, primordial will of and within the divine. This Original Will is the most benevolent, pristine, bountiful impulse of divine desire to move to creation and playful, creative bounty. The human seeker is trying to access something that is always there. The kabbalah states that such a state is ongoing, that the seeker needs to access in all of its sublimity and deep originality (see ***Keter***).

Rgl- ReGeL— denotes "leg";

HeRgeL — connotes through associative assonance the graduated path that one proceeds step by step, until one reaches the spiritual destination.

Ruah haQodesh — literally, "Holy Spirit" or "Divine Spirit". The thrust of this expression connotes deepest in-spiration, as if, the divine source was breathing spirit, as it were, into the moment, into the circumstance, in the seeker.

reishith — primal point of beginning, as opposed to eternal origin.

seder — most often used to refer to the Passover Symposium, reflecting its meaning of order, chronology or flow of events. Also relates to the ordering of the cosmos in a chain of being.

sephirot — spheres or vessels of divine consciousness that make the infinite manifest to consciousness. There are ten explicit, main spheres of divine consciousness, from the most refined of *Keter* through to the most coarse of *Malkhut*. Implicit to this system is a pseudo-sphere that oscillates in and out of consciousness known as *Da'at*, representing Intuitive Knowing.

(1) ***Keter*** — the crown of consciousness, a state of no-thing, the first glimmer of possible manifestation into spheres; a most subtle and refined state;

(2) ***Hokhmah*** — whereas "Wisdom" in the West refers to a growing process of sagacity, in Kabbalah this archetypal Father refers to a flash of insight, that primordial point from more extensive knowledge can

grow into categories of cognition, then captured and nurtured through the archetypal Mother of Discernment of *Binah*. Often *Hokhmah* is referred to by its requisite process of ego-nullification known as *Bittul* or more simply as '*Ayin* or No-Thing. Sometimes referred to as the beginning of everything, that Original Point of *Hokhmah*;

(3) ***Binah*** — Discernment that refers to the process of spiritual involution within the system of spheres (see ***Sephirot***). Such Discernment refers to the components of accrual, from acognitive luminal apperception to *un*knowing in the heart] constitute the forty nine gateways of Discernment. Discernment all way to the root of their origin, reaching to the Infinite Without End;

(4) ***Hesed*** — Love, loving-kindess, kindness, faithful love, steadfast love, grace, faithfulness, goodness, graciousness; loyalty;

(5) ***Gevurah*** — Rigor, judgment, restraint;

(6) ***Tiferet*** — Harmony, mediating point;

(7) ***Netzakh*** — Perpetuity, eternality;

(8) ***Hod*** — Splendor, humility;

(9) ***Yesod*** — Connector, erotic center (whether phallic or janic);

(10) ***Malkuth*** — Ground of being, embodiment.

S"M — mnemonic acrostic for the fallen angel, *SaMaEL*, symbolizing the opposing, demonic force (see ***sitra akhra, qtrq***).

seraphim — literally, "fiery serpents" originally mythically conceived serpent deities embodied, but here used to denote the wondrous nature of the ecstatic vision as described Isaiah 4:29, 30:6.

Skl-haskeil — this is a different modality which is the aspect of intellect that can grasp spirit, on *haskeil* see "You gave also Your good spirit to instruct them, and withheld not Your manna from their mouth, and gave them water for their thirst." (Nehemiah 9: 20), but the reading here is the gift of "en-spirited cognition".

shv – teshuvah — returning to God, return, turning back, turn (back) in order to transform self;

ba'al teshuvah – one who returns to God, master of returning.

Shekhinah — Indwelling Presence also known as the immanent, feminine divine presence. In the kabbalah, it is the symbolic interface of the divine realm with the human phenomenal realm. It is the personified area where heaven and earth meet (see *Malkuth*).

shemitah — the sabbatical year where the land lays fallow.

shna – ishtenei — mutated, deteriorated.

shanah – year as the accumulation of mutations in time;

shinui — change as the nullification of the natural reality in its ascent beyond the lower nature.

shleimut — integration, wholeness.

sitra — side, dimension, realm, direction, aspect (astrological influence), facet, flank, angle, page, corner, respect, perspective; mode (*mopsik*); (*terein* — twofold); inclination, intention, tendency, characteristic, type, species, way; *teẖum* (Tishby); realm (Goldstein); piece (Goldstein, *Matoq mi-Devash*); segment; in terms of;

sitra akhra — other side, the realm of distortion, contamination, evil;

sitra d'qedusha — holy side, the realm of the sacred, wholeness, integrity.

skl – istakkal — gaze, contemplate, meditate, reflect, consider, ponder, speculate, envision, envisage, imagine, observe, notice, regard, investigate, examine, see, look, look into, look out for, behold, has an eye for, be watchful, careful, scrutinize, perceive, realize, glimpse, infer, foresee, oversee.

Soul, levels of:

Nefesh — Literally, soul, life, being, essential being, essential self, inner nature, breath, life breath. It connotes the libidinal impulse in the lowest grade of soul;

Nefesh ha'sikhli — literally, intelligent soul, rendered here as over-soul;

Nefesh ha'behemi — literally, animal soul, rendered here as under-soul;

Ruah — spiritual level of the soul;

Neshama — pneumatic level of the soul;

Haya — vital energy of the soul;

Yehida — unitive consciousness of the soul absorbed in ultimate oneness.

ta'am — reason, incentive, sense, motivation, meaning, exegesis, argument, rule, law, taste, basis, intonation. Also refers to cantillation note.

T"aNTA — a mystical mnemonic mapping of trope [*Ta'amim*], vowels [*Nekudot*], letters [*'oTiyot*] which serves as the embodiment of the infinite within the finite scroll of Scripture in particular, and in the Hebrew language more broadly.

ta'anug — often translated as joy, pleasure, but the depth of this pleasure is best rendered as *jouissance.*

tefillah — refers to conventional prayer. On the hand it is the fixed liturgy of the synagogue. On the other hand, it refers to personal, petitionary prayer. It can also refer to a surrender or emptying of self.

tehiyat hameitim — refers to the doctrine of resurrection that finds its most sustained articulation in post-biblical literature of the rabbis from the 2nd to the 6th centuries CE.

tqn – tiqqen — mend, repair, recast, refound (glass), refine, enhance, improve, prepare, ready, brace oneself, cultivate, tend, prime, enable, correct, proper, put (oneself) right, precise, rectify, perfect, restore, align, realign, straight, order, set in order, configure, arrange, array, adorn, embellish, decorate, ornament, design, weave, deploy, equip, furnish,

establish, set, set up, place, make firm, confirm, harmonize, symmetrize, ripen, mature, remedy, amend, straighten, pave, smooth, make fit, qualified, suited, suitable, convenient, make up for, compensate, intone (song), poise, mold itself, attend (Soncino: maintain, uphold, sustain, renew, reinforce, cosmic reconstruction) *Mopsik*: reparation; ensure;
ittaqan al tiqquneih — restored to perfection, perfectly mended;
taqin — Onq: *ve-taqin la-hada* (*ve-hinneh tov me'od*);
atqin — prepare, ordain, arrange, array, equip, attune, prime, invent, compose, innovate, institute, invest (someone with), establish, enact, inaugurate, install, erect, introduce, prescribe (array, ordain, institute evening prayer), affix, provide;
atqin orha qaman, orha mittetaqna qaman — has paved the way for us; the way before us is paved, smooth; our path is made straight before us, auspicious.
ad la itqan — not yet revealed.
tiqquna — preparation, equipment, ritual, rite, restorative rite, restoration, reintegration, mending (of one's being), (make) amends, correction, remedy, reparation, enhancement, refinement, harmony, perfection, adorning, adornment, array, arraying, arrayal, arrangement, adjustment, finishing touch, configuration, maintaining; administration (of justice); institution; well-being, (bodily) constitution; trappings, fixtures, accoutrements; procedure; weapon;
be-tiqquna — refinedly;
atqin tiqqun — restore perfection…
tiqqunin of the beard — enhancements, curls;
tiqqun olam — social order, welfare; 1:38a: rearranged the world for them; working the earth, preparing the soil, cultivate; restoration, mending, enhancement, harmony, harmonizing, adorning, arraying, maintaining, perfection of the world.

Torah — literally, the sacred teachings revealed at Mount Sinai, often referred to as the Ten Commandments and transmitted as the Five Books of Moses or the Pentateuch or Five Books. A more expansive connotation refers to all of Jewish knowledge, both Written Torah and Oral Torah.

TZDK – tsaddik/im — literally, a "righteous one" that refers to a state of deep devotion; those exemplary figures who can maintain a condition of unicity in being bound or connected with divinity even under the conditions of exile, dispersal, and plurality;
tzaddik v'ra lo — literally, the one devoted to a life of righteousness experiences evil and suffers. The quandary that emerges here is also referred to as theodicy, namely, that the moral assurances of the Torah as constructed by the rabbinic imagination or any other forsaken belief about "divine retribution measure for measure".

tzedakah — the righteous act of social justice, whereby one rebalances the scales of injustice in the world by reaching out to the other in need.

tzimzum — derived from the primordial creation story of the world (cosmogenesis), where the mystical account, especially in Lurianic Kabbalah, reveals facets of the divine hidden in plain sight. The creative act of generating a new world comes through a process of the divine Creator entering deeper into a state of *jouissance*, whereby all of divine consciousness that can manifest does as the divine totality. Self-revealing (or theophany) is meant to enable a connection between the human and divine. This process of squeezing the divine self through the strainer is what then reveals aspects not yet manifest. The real "I" of the human spiritual being cannot exist until there is a form to receive it. The meta-programming, which is the self-assertion of the essence is a manifestation of the real "*Anokhiyut*". Life is only real when "I am" — "*Anokhi*". True spiritual progress demands that one has to work on the commanding self "Ani" to evolve into a unified self or "*Anokhi*" in order to connect to the divine "I". It is this scrutiny of practical consciousness that leads to more mindful living. The world becomes real when "I" become real; but too often the human remains a prisoner of its pre-programmed persona. Squeezing the divine self through the strainer is what then reveals aspects not yet manifest.

yegiah — the engagement of serving the ultimate reality through a form of agency.

yetser ha-ra — evil impulse.

yh̲d – le-yah̲ada yih̲uda — effecting, actualizing unification (union, unity) (fittingly); unite, unify; *be-yih̲uda h̲ada* — in unison.

Yirah — literally, fear including terror, but also awe. awe, reverence, fear; revere, be in awe (of). Once one realizes the enormity of what is crystallized in the physical, then the *mysterium tremendum* emerges, ultimately leading to transparency of self before the divine.

פרי הארץ

פרי הארץ (קאפוסט תקעל ד"ה)
פרי הארץ (ז'יטומיר תרל"ד)
לקוטי אמרים (לבוב תרע"א)

הרב הקדוש **מנחם מנדל מויטבסק** זכותו יגן עלינו

(ת"צ— יום ב', ראש חדש אייר, תקמ"ח)

בראשית

[א]. פרשת נח

(ממצוה עצמה שנעשה דרך הולדה)

אֵלֶּה תּוֹלְדֹת נֹחַ נֹחַ אִישׁ צַדִּיק תָּמִים הָיָה בְּדֹרֹתָיו וכו' (ו,ט) ופירש"י ז"ל למדך שעיקר תולדותיהם של צדיקים מעשים טובים. הענין הוא דרשת חז"ל (ב"ר כ"ו, א עיי"ש) אשרי האיש זה נח אשר לא הלך בעצת רשעים זה דור המבול ובדרך חטאים זה דור הפלגה:

ושורש הדברים דאית יראת מצוה כשהאדם מתבונן להיות מעשה המצוה ענין אלקות כידוע (עיי' זח"ג רכח ע"ב) וכשהוא מתחיל לעשותה באבריו הגשמים ותשמישי מצוה ג"כ גשמיים, הוא מתבהל ומתפעם רוחו איך הוא מגשם ענין אלקות וכי אלקים הוא גשמי חלילה. ואחר התפעמו כפעם בפעם אעפ"כ הוא מתחזק באמונתו ית' שהמצוה הוא התקשרות ודברי אלקים חיים מן הרצון העליון שאמר ונעשה רצונו עד סוף השתלשלות מדריגת השפלים, ומבין ענין התלבשות השכינה באותה מצוה כידוע שכל מצוה הוא ענין השכינה (עיי' זח"א כד ע"א). והתלבשות השכינה בגשמי זה הוא עבור התקשרות כל הגשמיים השפלים ע"י אבריו העסוקים במעשה המצוה ומתקשרים דרך השתלשלות המדות ודעת בינתו שורש מוצאם והגעתם עד אין סוף ב"ה:

וזהו (משלי ו כג) **נֵר מִצְוָה** שהמצוה הוא נר ע"י **הַתּוֹרָה אוֹר** כי החכמה ובינה נקרא אור תורה, ופי' שע"י חכמה ובינה שהאדם מכניס במצוה להאירה שהוא פי' **תּוֹרָה אוֹר** ע"י כן המצוה נר ומאירה ג"כ אבל בלאו הכי המצוה היא גשמיות ונפרד, ובמה הוא התקשרות בו ית' על ידה שנקראת מצוה לשון לצוות לזה (ברכות ו ע"ב) שהוא לשון התקשרות אבל הוא ע"י השכל ובינה שמכניס במצוה מחמת הפחד ורתת שאחזתהו שלא לגשם ענין אלקית ובאותו פחד לא הניח אמונתו שממשיך אהבה ושמחה שהוא ענין המדות והתבוננות בגדולתו ית' וחסדיו הגדולים להיות משלח פארותיו מאין סוף ב"ה ורצון העליון התלבשות שכינה בתחתונים לקשרם וליחדם אתו ונעשה לאחדים בדביקות הגמור:

אבל כל זה לא תחול אלא אחר היראה והפחד תחלה כנזכר לעיל מפני שכל המדות והשמחה שהאדם מביא על עצמו בהסכמה שרצונו באותה מידה אינם אמתיים כי אינם מתדמים בדמיונו אם לא שקדמה אותו פחד ה' והוא מתחזק באמונתו ומה שנמשך אח"כ מן האמונה איזה אהבה או שמחה או כל מדה ומדה המה אמתיים שהוא רוח הקודש. וזהו שמוזכר בזוהר כמה פעמים (ח"א ז ע"ב ועוד) ובש"ס (שבת לא ע"ב) שצריך להקדים היראה ובלתי קדימת היראה הכל הבל ורעות רוח ולא רוח הקודש. וזהו שאמרו רז"ל (עה"פ ויקרא יב א) **אִשָּׁה כִּי תַזְרִיעַ** וכו' ופי' הזריעה הוא ענין היראה והאהבה כידוע שבשעת הזריעה חלים על האדם שני מדות אלו היראה והאהבה יחד ומתפעם רוחו כמבואר בזוהר (ח"ג מג) **וּמִבְּשָׂרִי אֶחֱזֶה אֱלוֹהַּ** (איוב יט כו) ופי' **אִשָּׁה** הוא המצוה שהיא שכינה (עיי' ת"ז ת' כ"ב סח. ושם ת' לט עט ע"ב). וזהו **אִשָּׁה כִּי תַזְרִיעַ וְיָלְדָה זָכָר** שאם הפחד חלה על האדם מן המצוה שהוא מגשם אותה כנזכר לעיל עד שמן הפחד מגיע אל המדות והשמחה בו ית' שאמר ונעשה רצונו רצון העליון שהוא עולם הזכרים והזכרון והחיים והברכה והשפעה, כי ברצון ברא העולם ומחדש בכל יום תמיד מעשה בראשית ומשם הוא ההולדה שמוליד דבר שלא היה בעולם כלל כי הרצון הוא קודם הבריאה שהרי ברצונו ברא:

וזהו עיקר תולדותיהם של צדיקים מעשים טובים שמשם הוא מוליד גשמיים ג"כ שהרי מצות פריה ורביה גם כן מצוה והיא ראשונה שבמצות, ואחר היות צדיקים עוסקים במצוה זו על דרך הנזכר ועולה למעלה מסדר הבריאה משם ממשיך החיות והתולדה לולד הנוצר בגשמי, מלבד ממצוה עצמה שנעשה גם כן על דרך הולדה מלבד שהוא דבר קיום ונצח לעולם וחי בהם מעולם ועד עולם. ודבר זה אי אפשר להיות כי אם על ידי שפלות ודכות רוח כשמסתכל ומתבונן שפלות עצמו ופחיתתו מזה מתבהל שלא לגשם המצוה, מה שאין כן המתחסד בהתגלות בקול רעם ורעש מפני היותו עוסק במצות ה' ומתגדל על

ידה בגדלות יותר ממה שהיה בו תחילה, כל המדות והשמחות שיגיעו הם אינם אלא דמיונות כנזכר לעיל וכל מצותיו הם גשמיים כולם וגופים בלי שום חיות בהם. וזהו (בראשית ט ב) **וּמוֹרַאֲכֶם וְחִתְּכֶם יִהְיֶה עַל כָּל חַיַּת הָאָרֶץ** הכתוב אחר מצות פרו ורבו, והענין כשתעסקו במצות פריה ורביה כתיקון סדר המצות להקדים היראה והפחד של מצוה כנזכר לעיל ומן היראה זו תגיעו אל הרצון העליון והחיות שקודם הבריאה שממנה נברא העולם ומשם יתמשך חיות לולד הנוצר ומוראו על כל הנבראים, וכן הוא בעצמו בהגיעו למעלה מן הבריאה ביראתו, מה נורא המקום הזה על כל הנבראים כמאמר (שמות כג ב) **אַחֲרֵי רַבִּים לְהַטֹּת** והצדיק הוא הרבים כי הוא מקורם ושרשם. ועד"ז חיות הולד כי מפני היות חיות הולד ומוראו קודם ולמעלה מן כל הנבראים שהוא מן הרצון שקודם הבריאה וזהו ומוראכם וחתכם שמפרש רש"י ז"ל וחיותכם יעו"ש. ומה שאין כן כשלא הקדים המורא והמשכות חיות הולד כנזכר לעיל למה יהיה חתתו ומוראו על כל חית הארץ:

וזהו שאמרו חז"ל (עירובין יג ע"ב) נוח לו לאדם שלא נברא ועכשיו שנברא וכו' והקשו התוס' הא אמרו חז"ל (ע"ז ה ע"א) בואו ונחזיק טובה לאבותינו שאלמלא הם לא באנו לעולם דמשמע יותר טוב לו לאדם שנברא ומתרצו בצדיקים ורשעים. והענין עפ"י דברינו הנ"ל יובן שאפילו עכשיו שנברא אין טוב לו לאדם בעמלו שיעמול תחת השמש כי אם שיגיע למעלה מן השמש וקודם הבריאה, ובמה יגיע לשם שיפשפש במעשיו שעברו להיות ממארי דחושבנא ויכיר פחיתותו ויתבהל בעשותו מצות ה', וימשמש במעשה המצות דהשתא והמישמוש הוא התחזקות באמונתו אחרי פחדותו, וממילא יחול על ראשו רוח הקודש והשמחה ויגיע אל הרצון שקודם הבריאה שהוא שלא נברא. וזה פי' נוח לו לאדם שלא נברא שיגיע לכך ועכשיו שנברא יגיע אל שלא נברא ע"י פשפוש ומשמוש כנ"ל ולא קשה מידי מבואו ונחזיק טובה לאבותינו והוא שתרצו התוס' בצדיקים וכו':

וזהו פי' **אֵלֶּה תּוֹלְדֹת נֹחַ** פירוש שלא נברא ממקום רצון העליון וזהו סוד **נֹחַ אִישׁ צַדִּיק תָּמִים הָיָה בְּדֹרֹתָיו** שהם מעשים טובים ופירוש **בְּדֹרֹתָיו** הוא מקום רצון העליון שהוא סדר הדורות. או יאמר **בְּדֹרֹתָיו** פירוש במצות פריה ורביה היה איש צדיק תמים גם כן שהגיע במעשה המצוה אל קודם הבריאה. ועל דרך זה אפשר לומר בכל המצות שהרי כל המצות נקראים **תּוֹלְדֹת**, וזהו שאמר אח"כ ויולד נח שלשה בנים שמן סדר עסק מצות פריה ורביה כנ"ל הוליד שלשה בנים בגשמי כנ"ל:

ועל דרך זה אפשר לומר פירוש השמות והוא חם הוא הגשמי של מצוה שהוא הקטן כפירש"י ז"ל באמצע הסדר (ט. כד) ומן **חָם** שהוא שם הגשמי נתבהל והגיע לשם שהוא השכינה (עיי' זח"ג ערה ע"ב) כמאמר (שמואל ב' ח יג) ויעש דוד שם ומן השכינה הגיע ליפת שהוא הגדול שהוא האהבה כמאמר (בראשית ט כז) **יַפְתְּ אֱלֹהִים** ליפת שאהבה היא המדה והשמחה כנ"ל וכסדר הנ"ל. וזהו שאמר אחר כך (ט כ) **וַיָּחֶל נֹחַ אִישׁ הָאֲדָמָה וַיִּטַּע כָּרֶם**, פירוש כשנח נעשה חולין כפירוש רש"י ז"ל ונעשה איש האדמה שהוא מגושם ויטע כרם היינו מעשה המצות כמאמר (שה"ש א ו) **כַּרְמִי שֶׁלִּי לֹא נָטָרְתִּי** והמצות ג"כ מגושמים, וזהו **וַיַּרְא, חָם [אֲבִי כְנַעַן] אֵת, עֶרְוַת אָבִיו** פירוש בזיון **אָבִיו** שבשמים להיות אלקים גשמי כ"כ **וַיַּגֵּד לִשְׁנֵי-אֶחָיו, בַּחוּץ** פירוש ויגד לשון המשכה כמאמר (דניאל ז י) **נְהַר...נָגֵד**, כי הדיבור הוא המנהיג את כל הרוחניות שמעוררים והגשמיות ג"כ כידוע ולכן נקרא דיבור לשון הנהגה וכתרגומו של (בראשית ב ז) **וַיְהִי הָאָדָם לְנֶפֶשׁ חַיָּה** ת"י לרוח ממללא כי הדיבור הוא החיות. וזהו **וַיִּקַּח שֵׁם וָיֶפֶת אֶת הַשִּׂמְלָה** שהוא התלבשות הנ"ל ופניהם אחורנית שהוא השפלות והיראה שנסוג אחור וירא מגשת אליו ובזה ואת ערות אביהם לא ראו:

כללא דמילתא התקשרות אדם השפל ברצון העליון ע"י השפלות והיראה וממנה מגיע אל התבוננות ועיונית השכל והחכמה להכניס בכל מצוה שהוא עוסק בה כנ"ל, אבל בלתי התבוננות והשגה המצוה ג"כ גשמי, וכן להיפך בלתי המצוה עסק הגשמי אין ההתבוננות והשגה מקשר את האדם להבורא ית"ש, והראיה לזה שלמה המלך ע"ה שנאמר (מלכים

א' ה יא) **וַיֶּחְכַּם מִכָּל הָאָדָם** כיון שרצה להתחכם בלא המצוה על אזהרת (דברים י"ז: ט"ז, י"ז) **רַק לֹא יַרְבֶּה לּוֹ סוּסִים וְלֹא יַרְבֶּה לּוֹ נָשִׁים** שאמר (סנהדרין כא ע"ב) ארבה ולא אסור ואעפ"כ נכשל:

זהו שדרשו חז"ל אשרי האיש זה נח אשר לא הלך בעצת רשעים זה דור המבול פירוש להשתמש בשכל עצמו בלא עסק מצות, כי רבוי ההשגה נקרא מבול כמאמר (תהלים כט י) **יְהֹ-וָה לַמַּבּוּל יָשָׁב וַיֵּשֶׁב יְהֹ-וָה מֶלֶךְ לְעוֹלָם** וכמוזכר בזוה"ק (ח"א נו ע"א) על (פסוק בראשית ז, ו) בשנת **שֵׁשׁ מֵאוֹת שָׁנָה וְהַמַּבּוּל הָיָה** וכו' עיי"ש. (תהילים א, א) **וּבְדֶרֶךְ חַטָּאִים לֹא עָמָד** זה דור הפלגה שהיה להם יראה חיצוניות כמאמר (בראשית יא ד) **פֶּן נָפוּץ** וכו' וגשמיות הוא בלא התקשרות האמונה והשכל. וה' יתן בלב כל חכם לב חכמה ודעת אלקים בציון אמן:

[ב]. פרשת לך לך

(תפילה היא אמונה פשוטה)

ארז"ל (שבת קח ע"א) מילה באותו מקום מנין שנאמר (יז,י) **הִמּוֹל לָכֶם כָּל זָכָר** מקום שהוא זכר וכו', הענין הוא ע"ד הפסוק (לעיל טו,ו) **וְהֶאֱמִן בַּיהֹ-וָה וַיַּחְשְׁבֶהָ לּוֹ צְדָקָה**. והוא ע"ד ארז"ל (ע"ז ז ע"ב) לעולם יסדר אדם שבחו של מקום ואח"כ יתפלל, כי השכינה היא הנקראת תפלה (זח"א כד ע"א) שהוא הדבקות האמתי ברצון העליון ע"י האמונה בלי שום טעם. ודקות הענין יתבאר בהמשך הדברים כמאמר (קהלת א, ז) **כָּל הַנְּחָלִים הֹלְכִים אֶל הַיָּם וְהַיָּם אֵינֶנּוּ מָלֵא אֶל מְקוֹם שֶׁהַנְּחָלִים הֹלְכִים שָׁם הֵם שָׁבִים לָלָכֶת**. והוא כי השכינה **לֵית לָהּ מִגַּרְמָהּ כְּלוּם** כי אם הנמשך אליה דרך המדות שהם שבחו של מקום כידוע (זח"ב ריח ע"ב). לכן כשהאדם חפץ לדבקה בו ית' אי אפשר כי אם על ידי תפלה שהיא השכינה שהיא היראה **בְּזֹאת יָבֹא...אֶל הַקֹּדֶשׁ**, אבל מדלית לה **מִגַּרְמָהּ כְּלוּם** צריך תחלה לסדר שבחו של מקום כנ"ל בכדי לעורר אליה והשכינה אומרת **חָמֵי בְּמַאי בְּרָא אֲתֵינָא לְקָמָךְ** (זח"ג יג ע"א). וכשמגיע אל הדבקות יבין את זאת באמונתו כי עדיין לא השיג לא טעם ולא הריח בהשגה שמץ מנהו ואפס קצהו ולא נכנס בה כלל, וכבודו הוא אמונתו לבד להתדבק בו ית' ע"י האמונה אחר כל העיונית והשכלים שהשיג, שכל השגותיו אינם יכולים בו ית' שהרי הוא א"ס ב"ה. אבל כל השגותיו אינם רק פעולת התחזקות האמונה. וחוזק האמונה מגדיל מנהיר ומזהיר סידור שבחו ית' יותר שהרי **לֵית לָהּ מִגַּרְמָהּ כְּלוּם**, וגדולת סידור שבחו של מקום במופלא ממנו יותר מביאו אל הדביקות ותפלה יתירה **וְהָאָרֶץ לְעוֹלָם עֹמָדֶת** (קהלת א, ד) שהיא אמונה בלי שום השגה בו ית' והאמין בה' כנ"ל וכן הוא לעולם. וזהו לעולם יסדר אדם שבחו של מקום, וזהו **כָּל הַנְּחָלִים הֹלְכִים אֶל הַיָּם...אֶל מְקוֹם שֶׁהַנְּחָלִים הֹלְכִים שָׁם הֵם שָׁבִים לָלָכֶת**, כנ"ל:

והנה איתא במדרש (ב"ר ל, י בשינוי) החילוק שבין נח לאברהם הוא עפ"י משל, נח דומה לאוהבו של מלך שיושב באפילה והמלך בא ומאיר לו ואברהם דומה לאוהב שבא להאיר למלך ואמר המלך עד שאתה מאיר באפילה תלך ותאיר במקום אור עיי"ש הלשון צח וזהו שאמר **לֶךְ לְךָ**. והענין הוא כי נח היה צדיק באמונתו בלי שום השגה עיונית והיה תמים במעשיו והשי"ת האיר לו. אבל אברהם בן שלש שנים הכיר את בוראו (נדרים לב ע"א) ע"פ עיון והתבוננות והיה הולך וגדל בדעה בינה והשכל ואחר כל זה היה תמים במעשיו שהיא האמונה לבד. כמאמר (בראשית יז א) **הִתְהַלֵּךְ לְפָנַי** שהוא למעלה מן המדות **וֶהְיֵה תָמִים** אח"כ, כי ההשגה בו ית' הוא אין סוף וההתקשרות והדביקות האמתי בו ית' הוא ע"י אמונה זו לבד. ע"ד משל התקשרות כל העולמות זה בזה המה ג"כ ע"י אמונה, ואפי' בעולם השפל דרך משל אדם יש לו נחת רוח כשבנו הקטן מכיר שהוא אביו בטרם שידע הנער שום שכל אעפ"כ יש לו נחת. וכן עד"ז היתה בריאת העולמות כולם כמאמר (פס"ז בראשית א,א) **בְּרֵאשִׁית בָּרָא** בשביל ישראל שנקראו ראשית שידעו לפאר ליוצרם ויקראו לפניו אבינו מלכנו (רמב"ן סוף פר' בראשית ע"ש). וזהו כל שעשועיו ית' כמאמר (פסחים קיב ע"א) יותר ממה שהעגל רוצה לינק פרה רוצה להניק וזהו ההתקשרות שבין כל עולם לעולם שכל הגדול מחבירו

רוצה להשפיע לשתחתיו ובהשפעתו מקבל תענוג יותר מהתחתון בקבלתו. אבל אין המשל דומה לנמשל כלל שהרי כל אלה נבראו באופן וסדר זה וטבע הבריאה היא התקשרות זה, משא"כ הוא ית' עילת כל העילות אין סוף ב"ה הבורא את הכל וגם טבע הבריאה הנ"ל אין שייך בו שום תענוג והתקשרות הנ"ל כלל, שהרי הוא ברא הטבע ומקיים אותה בכל רגע, כי בלתי חפץ קיומה בכל רגע ברצונו ית' כאילו לא היתה וממילא בטילה, א"כ מה הוא ההתקשרות מאתו ית' להשפיע זה אינו כי אם חפץ ורצון פשוט, כמאמר (עץ חיים בפתיחה ע"ש) כשעלה ברצונו ית' המוזכר ברצונו ברא תחילה וברצונו מקיים ומשפיע תמיד ומתענג, אבל אין שום השגה יכולה ההתקשרות זה:

והנה הרמב"ם ז"ל (מורה נבוכים חלק ג' פרק מט) כתב טעם למצות מילה להתיש כח המתאוה, והאמת כי הוא ז"ל הוציא מפיו קדוש דברים אמתים העומדים ברומו של עולם אע"פ שלא כיון בהם. וכמו שהכוונה והטעם בחיתוך ערלת המילה כן הוא בכרם ערלה תחלה ומצות בכורים. והענין כמאמר (ישעיה כח ד ע"א) **כְּבִכּוּרָהּ בְּטֶרֶם קַיִץ** וכו' כי הראשית והתחלה הוא דבר חביב והחביבות הוא רק מפני היותו ראשית לבד שכן דרך לכל ראשית להיותו חביב ואהוב מאד, שהוא התענוג וההתקשרות שבין עולם לעולם, מן הראשית אל שלאחריו וממנו אל שלאחריו נקרא הוא ראשית וכן לעולם. אבל עיקר העבודה וההתקשרות בו ית' להשיג הדביקות האמתי שאחר כל השגות, שאין ההתקשרות השגה בו ית' שהרי הוא ית' חוץ מכל הנבראים וחוץ מכל החביבות והאהבות וחוץ מטבע ההתקשרות הנ"ל שהרי הוא הבורא את הכל. אבל הדביקות בו הוא באמונה לבד בלי שום טעם אהבה חיבה ותאוה. וזהו שכתב להתיש כח המתאוה כי מצות מילה שאנו חתומים בה באבר המוליד ומוציא נשמות שהוא הדביקות צריכה להיות להתיש כח המתאוה כי אם ע"י האמונה לבד. ובמצות מילה שהתיש כח המתאוה חותמו אמת ואמונה בו ית' לדבקה בו בלי שום השגת טעם, כדרך ההתקשרות כל העולמות מעילה לעלול מחמת טבע תענוג ההשפעה כנ"ל שהרי א"ס הוא ית' אדון הטבע ולא שייך בו טבע תענוג הנ"ל. אבל הדביקות וההתקשרות השפעתו ית' מאתו אינו כי אם האמונה ברצונו הפשוט להשפיע בלי שום טעם. וזהו החילוק שבינו ית' לכל הנבראים המשפיעים שהרי כל המשפיעים מקבלים בהשפעתם התענוג היותם משפיעים כטבע הבריאה. משא"כ הוא ית' אדון הטבע אינו מקבל כלל רק משפיע:

וזהו שאמרו (בראשית יז, י') **הִמּוֹל לָכֶם כָּל זָכָר**, ממקום שהוא **זָכָר**, רק משפיע ואינו מקבל כלל בהתיש כח המתאוה ותענוג ההשפעה כלל בלי שום טעם כלל ובזה הוא מתקשר בחכמה עליונה שהיא יו"ד (ת"ז ת' יח לב ע"א). וכמאמר (איוב כח, יב) **וְהַחָכְמָה מֵאַיִן תִּמָּצֵא** שהוא מאין ואפס בלי שום טעם. ומילת זכרים כזה הם חותמו אמת ואמונה:

וזהו שאמר **וְהֶאֱמִן בַּיה-וָה וַיַּחְשְׁבֶהָ לּוֹ צְדָקָה** שכל האמונה שהשיג אחר כל העיונים והשכלים לא חשב לשום השגה כי אם למדריגה התחתונה שהוא אמונה צדקה שהרי כל ההשגות בטלים כנגדו ית'. ומה שהשיג אח"כ הוא שאמר (בראשית יח כז) **וְאָנֹכִי עָפָר וָאֵפֶר**, שהוא התקשרות בחכמה עליונה שהוא השפלות כאפס ואין כמאמר **וְהַחָכְמָה מֵאַיִן תִּמָּצֵא**. והשגת אמונה גדולה כזו שאחר כל השכלים והעיונית והשגות הדביקות שמשיג יאמין באמת ואמונה מחמת שפלות עצמו להיותו בעיניו עפר ואפר בודאי כל השגותיו אין בו לא טעם ולא ריח ולא שום דביקות כלל ובאמונתו יחיה לדבקה בו ית', אמונה זו היא הנקראת **אָמְנָה אֲחֹתִי בַת אָבִי הִוא אַךְ לֹא בַת אִמִּי** (שם כ יב). כי אמונה זו אינה נשפעת כי אם מאתו ית' בעצמו בלי שום עולמות אמצעים שמקבלים תענוג בהשפעתם כמאמר יותר ממה שהעגל רוצה כנ"ל והמבין יבין. ולכן באמונה זו הוא הדביקות בו ית'. ולכן מוזכרים בתורה המדריגות כסדר תחלה פסוק (בראשית טו, ו') [**וְהֶאֱמִן בַּיה-וָה**] **וַיַּחְשְׁבֶהָ לּוֹ צְדָקָה** ואח"כ אנכי עפר ואפר ואח"כ פסוק **וְגַם אָמְנָה אֲחֹתִי בַת אָבִי הִוא אַךְ לֹא בַת אִמִּי** עיי"ש:

[ג]. פרשת וירא

(ההתנגדות היא עצמה העזר)

במדרש (תנחומא וירא א) פתח ר"י נפחא כתיב (שמות כ כא) **מִזְבַּח אֲדָמָה תַּעֲשֶׂה לִּי וְזָבַחְתָּ עָלָיו** וכו', אדם עושה מזבח וזובח עליו עולות ושלמים נאמר עליו (שם) **בְּכָל הַמָּקוֹם אֲשֶׁר אַזְכִּיר אֶת שְׁמִי אָבוֹא אֵלֶיךָ וּבֵרַכְתִּיךָ**, אברהם אבינו שזבח את עצמו לא כ"ש, זהו שנ' **וַיֵּרָא אֵלָיו יְהֹ-וָה**. אך יתפרש הענין בהקדים תרין תמיהי דמדכר דכירי המפרשים, א' למה הוזכר נסיון העקדה על שם אברהם ולא הוזכר הנסיון ע"ש יצחק שמסר את נפשו אליו ית' וכפרש"י ז"ל (בראשית כב,א) **אַחַר הַדְּבָרִים** הם דבריו של ישמעאל (ע"ש) והשיבו יצחק שימסור א"ע לשמו עיי"ש. ב' למה לא הוזכר במקרא נסיון אברהם באור כשדים:

אבל הענין ידוע מאמרם ז"ל (סוכה נב ע"א) כל הגדול מחבירו יצרו גדול ממנו. ואמרו (שם ע"ב) יצרו של אדם מתגבר עליו בכל יום ואלמלא הקב"ה עוזרו לא יכול לו שנאמר (תהלים לז לב-לג) **צוֹפֶה רָשָׁע לַצַּדִּיק וּמְבַקֵּשׁ לַהֲמִיתוֹ... יְהֹ-וָה לֹא יַעַזְבֶנּוּ**. והנה מאמר בעל עקידה על פסוק (בראשית ב יח) **אֶעֱשֶׂה לּוֹ עֵזֶר כְּנֶגְדּוֹ** יש שההתנגדות הוא העזר, שאלמלא התנגדות **אֶת זֶה לְעֻמַּת זֶה עָשָׂה הָאֱ-לֹהִים** (ע"פ קהלת ז יד) היה ביטול הבחירה שכר ועונש או לפי דברינו במ"א (פרשת קרח ע"ש) היה ביטול התענוג כידוע, או שלא היה יכול לסבול תענוג של השגה אם לא **בְּרָצוֹא וָשׁוֹב** שהיא ההתנגדות. כללא דמלתא לפי ערך גודל ההשגה והעבדות **אֶת זֶה לְעֻמַּת זֶה עָשָׂה** עשה הביטול ומחשבת חוץ מהיפוך להיפוך הקטן לפי קטנו והגדול לפי גדלו בכדי שיבא אל העזר הנ"ל. אבל במה הוא נעזר מנפילתו בהתנגדות ח"ו העיקר הוא ע"י האמונה הגדולה ופשוטה בלי שום טעם וסברות כלל. שהרי באותה השגה והעבדות שהשיג כבר נפל לשכנגדו, לכן יראה להתחזק באמונה הגדולה ופשוטה בחזקה. וזהו העזר שהקב"ה עוזר לכל אדם בכל יום נגד היצה"ר בהשפעתו לאדם את האמונה זו להתחזק בו ית' ועל ידה יקום על משענתו:

ובזה יתורץ קושית צדיק וטוב לו צדיק ורע לו (ברכות ז ע"א) שהרי **בֹּחֵן לִבּוֹת יְהֹ-וָה** (משלי יז ג) יודע לפעמים התנגדות את זה לעומת זה של השגה ועבדות שלא יוכל לעמוד בה ולא יוכל קום מנפילתו באותו התנגדות ולהתחזק באמונה כנ"ל, מקדים לו רפואה למכתו להרע או להטיב וע"י אותה סיבה תתחזק האמונה. או שההתנגדות עצמה לא תחול עליו בפרך כל כך מחמת היסורים או העוני שהם בעצמם סיבת יראת ה' ובטול התאות ואמונות הכוזבות. והנה אחר ידיעתנו באמת שהעבירה והתרחקות מאתו ית' הוא רע ומר ממות ויסורין, שהרי היסורין והמיתה ממרקין העבירות והמה רפואות המכה, ממילא ידוע שהמכה גרוע מיסורי הרפואה. ומעתה צדיק ורע לו אפשר לומר שהרעה והיסורין המה טובתו ורפואת מכתו שהוא התנגדות עבודתו והשגתו את זה לעומת זה, אולי הוא באופן שלא היה יכול לעמוד נגדה ובנפלו לא יוסיף קום אם לא ע"י היסורים והדלות שמתיש כח ההתנגדות כנ"ל. וצדיק וטוב לו הוא כי את זה לעומת זה שכנגד שכלו ועבודתו ודרך הלוכו אינו צריך חיזוק היסורים ובלתם יכול לעמוד כנגדם. וזהו דבר שאין שום בריה יכול לשער שהרי כל א' נכוה מחופתו של חבירו (ב"ב עה ע"א), אבל לפניו ית' גלוי וידוע **הַיֹּצֵר יַחַד לִבָּם הַמֵּבִין** וכו' (תהלים לג טו). וכן ארז"ל (תענית כה ע"א) על גודל העניות של ר"א בן פדת, שהשיבו לו בספיקא קמי שמיא אפילו ע"י חזרת בריאת עולמות מחדש אולי יתרמי בשעתא דמזוני, והענין הוא כדברינו שכנגד השגת רבי אלעזר בן פדת שכלו ועבודתו ההתנגדות מזה אשר את זה לעומת זה, אם אפשר לעמוד כנגדה בלי יסורין או אולי שאי אפשר להיות אם לא על יסורי עוני:

והנה נסיון העקדה הובא במדרשים (ב"ר נו יב) ורש"י ז"ל (בראשית כב יב) שהי' לו לאברהם להרהר אחר מדותיו והוא שאמר ר' אבא אמר אברהם אפרש לפניך את שיחתי אתמול אמרת לי (שם כא יב) **כִּי בְיִצְחָק יִקָּרֵא לְךָ זָרַע** וחזרת ואמרת (שם כב ב) **קַח נָא אֶת בִּנְךָ** ועכשיו אתה אומר לי (שם יב) **אַל תִּשְׁלַח יָדְךָ**. שהוא שנוי רצון אצל הבורא ית' ח"ו שהוא שורש הכפירה ח"ו. וכן כל הקושיות צדיק ורע לו היפך מן

הראוי והבטחת התורה או שאר קושיות ואמונות הכוזבות אשר את זה לעומת זה עשה אלקים נגד כל דביקות והשגת אמיתותו בחכמתו, וכמאמר רש"י ז"ל (שם ג א) אצל **וְהַנָּחָשׁ הָיָה עָרוּם מִכֹּל**, ארור מכל, לפי ערמתו וגדולתו היתה מפלתו. אבל אברהם אבינו ע"ה עמד בנסיון ולא הרהר אחר האמונה בהשגתו את דבריו ית' שהמה מהופכים והתחזק באמיתות האמונה הגדולה והחזקה מרצונו הפשוט ית' כי לא מחשבותיו מחשבת השי"ת ולא דרכיו דרכו ואינו מבין דבריו ית' והנהגתו כלל. וכל הרעות המתדמים מאתו ית' הם טובות אמתיים כנ"ל וכל דבריו הנראים מהופכים הכל אל מקום א' הולך והן המה בלי שום שנוי ותמורה ח"ו. ומה שאין מובן **דָבָר רֵק הוּא מִכֶּם** (ע"פ דברים לב מז), שאין שום השגה יכולה להשיג דבריו ית' ופירוש מלותיו (ישעיה ה כ) האומרים **לָרַע טוֹב וְלַטּוֹב רָע** וכ"ש שאינו מובן מחשבותיו וכ"ש רצונו הפשוט. ובאמונה זו התחזק אברהם אבינו ע"ה ולא סמך על השגתו ועמד בנסיון שלא להרהר אחריו ית':

כללא דמלתא עיקר הנסיונות הם באמונה, כמאמר (דברים ח ב) **לְנַסֹּתְךָ לָדַעַת אֶת אֲשֶׁר בִּלְבָבְךָ**, וכל הנסיונות שהיו לאברהם אבינו ע"ה היו על דרך זה כמו הרעב שאמר בתחלה **לֶךְ לְךָ** ואח"כ מתדמה שינוי רצון בהביאו רעב למקום זה כפרש"י ז"ל (בראשית יב י) וכן כולם. אבל נסיון המסירות נפש עבורו ית' אחרי הידיעה כי הוא הבורא הוא אמר ויהי הוא צוה למסור נפשו ולזבוח עצמו עבורו ית' מי לא ישמע ומי לא יאבה לו ית', אם אמנם גם הוא נסיון אבל לא לפי ערך אבותינו הקדושים, וכן קושית העולם אפילו כל דהו אם השי"ת היה אומר לו בעצמו שיזבח את עצמו עבורו והיה יודע שהם דברי הש"י בוודאי היה שומע לו. ולכן לא הוזכרו בתורה שני הנסיונות הנז"ל.

כארז"ל (ילקוט שמות קפז ע"א) שלא היה צריך להתחיל את התורה אלא מ**הַחֹדֶשׁ הַזֶּה לָכֶם** (שמות יב ב) אבל **כֹּחַ מַעֲשָׂיו הִגִּיד לְעַמּוֹ** (תהלים קיא ו). כי התורה לעולם עומדת ונוהג בכל דור ובכל אדם ע"י הסתכלותו והתבוננותו במעשה הכתוב בתורה מדותיו ית' והנהגתו בעולם השפל בחכמה העליונה ליתן טהור מטמא ומרע טוב, וכל הגבורות הם חסדים ו**הַכֹּל הוֹלֵךְ אֶל מָקוֹם אֶחָד** ושורש כולם רצונו הפשוט באמונתו הפשוטה הגדולה והחזקה. ובזה מתמתקים כל הגבורות בחסדים שהרי באמונה זו נוקב עד התהום ומשלב כל המדות ליחד לאחד ומשם מתברך ונשפע אמונתו ית' החזקה ואח"כ מבין דבריו ית' בהתגלות שאינם מהופכים, כמו שהשיב השי"ת לאברהם אבינו שם (כ"ב יב) כפרש"י ז"ל. וממקור הברכות ממילא מתברכים כל העולמות עד עולם השפל ושלשול קטן שבים:

וזהו פתיחת ר"י נפחא שאמר **בְּכָל הַמָּקוֹם אֲשֶׁר אַזְכִּיר אֶת שְׁמִי**. כידוע שמלת שם הוא נוקבא ושכינה (זהר ח"ג רעה ע"ב) ומלת **אַזְכִּיר** הוא לשון זכר. ופי' **בְּכָל הַמָּקוֹם** שמתייחדים השמות הנוקבא בזכר והגבורות בחסדים **אָבוֹא אֵלֶיךָ וּבֵרַכְתִּיךָ** ברכה והשפעה בהשגה והגשמיות ממילא מתברך. ומה שהזכיר לשון אברהם שזבח א"ע הוא פי' נסיון האמונה כנ"ל הגרוע ומר ממות וזביחה, וזהו שאמר **וַיֵּרָא אֵלָיו יְהֹ-וָה** בהתגלות והבנת קצת דרכיו ית':

[ד]. פרשת תולדות

(המצוות והחוקים בשורשם בטלים)

וְאֵלֶּה תּוֹלְדֹת יִצְחָק בֶּן אַבְרָהָם (כה יט). פירש"י ז"ל יעקב ועשו האמורים בפרשה. הענין הוא על דרך (שבת לא ע"א), תשובת הלל להגר שבא להתגייר על מנת שילמדנו כל התורה על רגל אחת וקבלו ולמדו מה דסני לך לחברך לא תעביד פרש"י ז"ל שהוא מצות **וְאָהַבְתָּ לְרֵעֲךָ כָּמוֹךָ**. עיי"ש במהרש"א שמקשה למה לא אמר לו בלשון שנצטוינו בתורה ואפי' בלשון תרגום עכ"פ בלשון עשה ותרחם לחברך כוותך ואמר בלשון שלילה ובלשון לא תעשה מה דסני לך לחברך לא תעביד:

אבל הענין הוא ארז"ל (אבות ה א) **בַּעֲשָׂרָה מַאֲמָרוֹת נִבְרָא הָעוֹלָם** והם כנגד עשרת הדברות כארז"ל (ב"ר א ב) שהסתכל בתורה וברא את העולם. והנה ענין בריאת העולם ידוע שהיה מתחלה הוא ושמו אחד אחדות פשוט בלי שום

תפיסה השגה וגבול שהוא אין סוף וכשעלה ברצונו הפשוט לברוא צמצם את עצמו כידוע (עץ חיים בפתיחה). והנה ענין אחדות פשוט וא"ס הוא דבור **אָנֹכִי** (שמות כ ב) וכל המצות עשה, והצמצום שהוא הגבורות הוא הלא תעשה ודבור **לֹא יִהְיֶה לְךָ** עם כל פרטי הלא תעשה שבכל התורה כולה מעילה לעלול בפרטי פרטים. הנה כל השרשים והענפים כללים ופרטים שיש להם שורש למעלה עשו פרי למטה במעשה המצות. וזו היא תורתנו הקדושה עם כל מצותיה חקותיה ותורותיה:

והנה ארז"ל (יומא כח. עה"פ בראשית כו, ה) **עֵקֶב אֲשֶׁר שָׁמַע אַבְרָהָם בְּקֹלִי וַיִּשְׁמֹר מִשְׁמַרְתִּי** וכו' מלמד שקיים אברהם אבינו ע"ה אפילו ערובי תבשילין, אשר לכאורה תמיה מנא ידע, ואם נאמר שהשיג מעשה המצות והמשפטים שהשכל מחייב אעפ"כ יקשה האיך השיג החוקים שאין להם טעם ואין שום שכל מחייב, כמו פרה אדומה ושארי חוקים. אבל לפי דברינו יובן, כאשר אמרו רז"ל (במדבר רבה יט ד) שאמר למשה לך אני מגלה טעמי פרה ולאחרים חוקה שכל החוקים יש להם טעם ושורש למעלה בסדר הבריאה כי הבריאה היתה ע"פ התורה רק כי לאו כל מוחא סביל דא לכן לאחרים חוקה. אבל לא דברה תורה בגדולים כמשה ואברהם אבינו ע"ה שאין לך דבר עומד בפניהם להיות חוקה, אבל כל החוקים הם אצלם מצות לידיעתם והשגתם טעמם ושרשם:

אבל דבר זה אי אפשר להיות שיתהפכו החוקים למצות לפניו אם לא בהתבטל המצות מפניו ואינם נוהגים אצלו על דרך משל כל הל"ת **לֹא תִרְצָח תִּנְאָף לֹא תִגְנֹב** שאין האזהרות אלו ראוים לפניו מחמת שבירת תאותו עם כל המדות גשמיות שאינו משתמש עמם לצרכו כלל בלתי לה' לבדו, וכל עשיית צרכיו הם מאוסים אצלו, כלכלוך הטיט והצואה שאינם צריכים להזהיר לשום אדם שירחק מהם כי בלא"ה יעשה מפני המיאוס. ועל דרך זה אמר דוד המע"ה (תהלים קט כב) **וְלִבִּי חָלַל בְּקִרְבִּי**. הנה לאדם כזה שאין המצות נוהגים אצלו מגלים לו טעמי החוקים ונעשים לו החוקים למצות. וזהו ארז"ל (נדה סא ע"ב) שיתבטלו המצות לימות המשיח, **כִּי מָלְאָה הָאָרֶץ דֵּעָה אֶת יְהֹ-וָה** (ישעי' יא ט), ויהיה להם תורה אחרת מן החוקים יהיו מצות. וכשהולך מחיל אל חיל והיה רק למעלה למעלה עד שיגיע אל שורש כל התורה והמצות שהוא **אָנֹכִי יְהֹ-וָה אֱלֹ-הֶיךָ** אחדות פשוט ואין סוף בעמדו שם תרפינה כנפי כל המצות והחוקים וכולם בטלים שהרי הוא ביטול היצה"ר להיותו עומד למעלה וקודם התחלת הבריאה והיצה"ר מנין:

והנה באמת שבתחילת וקודם הבריאה הוא העשה **אָנֹכִי יְהֹ-וָה אֱלֹ-הֶיךָ** ואח"כ הל"ת, אבל בהשגת המצות צריך להיות להיפך בתחילה **סוּר מֵרָע** ואח"כ **וַעֲשֵׂה טוֹב** שהרי האדם בתחילה **פֶּרֶא אָדָם יִוָּלֵד** (איוב יא יב) ומדרגתו למטה מטה וצריך להוסיף מחול על הקדש למעלה מעלה עד **אָנֹכִי יְהֹ-וָה אֱלֹ-הֶיךָ**. וזהו שהגר שבא להתגייר רצה ללמוד כל התורה על רגל פי' קיום והעמדה אחת. והנה באמת למדו אם אמנם שורש הכל הוא **אָנֹכִי יְהֹ-וָה אֱלֹ-הֶיךָ** כנזכר, אבל הגר לא היה יכול להבין השגת **אָנֹכִי** אם לא בדרך שלילה תחילה, **לֹא יִהְיֶה לְךָ**, מפני היות מדריגתו תחילה מטה מטה וזהו שאמר ואידך פירושא זיל גמור. כי מצות **וְאָהַבְתָּ** והשלילה מה דסני לך לחברך לא תעביד הוא מצות **אָנֹכִי** ו**לֹא יִהְיֶה לְךָ**. וכהבנת פרש"י ז"ל:

וזהו **וְאֵלֶּה תּוֹלְדֹת יִצְחָק בֶּן אַבְרָהָם** שהוא סדר הבריאה ופי' יצחק שהוא צמצום וגבורות בן אברהם שהוא חסדים ואחדות פשוט (עיין זח"ג שב ע"א) ומאלה נפצה כל הארץ. זהו שפירש"י ז"ל **תּוֹלְדֹת** הם יעקב ועשו האמורים בפרשה וכפירש"י ז"ל (כה, כה) על עשו שנעשה ונגמר בשערותיו ביום הוולדו וכמאמר הזהר (ח"ג צא ע"ב) על פסוק (ויקרא כב, כז) **שׁוֹר אוֹ כֶשֶׂב אוֹ עֵז כִּי יִוָּלֵד** תיכף ביום הולדו נקרא שור בן יומו מפני היותו נגמר ביום הולדו מה שאין כן אדם. אבל באמת אדם במדותיו הגשמים ביום הוולדו נגמר כמאמר (בראשית ד, ז) **לַפֶּתַח חַטָּאת רֹבֵץ**, **מִמֶּלֶךְ זָקֵן וּכְסִיל** (קהלת ד, יג). ולכן ביום הולדו נקרא עשו. ואח"כ **וְיָדוֹ אֹחֶזֶת בַּעֲקֵב עֵשָׂו**, ופי' ידו היא התפיסה שלו שהיא חכמה תתאה שהיא יו"ד (עיין ת"ז ת' מ, פ ע"ב) וזהו ידו ואחר כך ממנה יגיע

לחכמה עילאה ומצות **אָנֹכִי** שהוא אחדות פשוט. והמבין יבין:

[ה]. פרשת וישלח

(היפוך המאורע לטובה ע"י האמונה)

במדרש (ב"ר עו א. בשינוי) אמר ר' פנחס בר' ראובן מצינו בחור שבאבות בחור שבנביאים שהיו מתייראים שנאמר **וַיִּירָא יַעֲקֹב מְאֹד** וכתיב (תהלים קלה, ד) **כִּי יַעֲקֹב בָּחַר לוֹ יָ-הּ** וכו' ומשה רבינו ע"ה כתיב (שם קו, כג) **לוּלֵי מֹשֶׁה בְחִירוֹ עָמַד** וכו' ונאמר (במדבר כא, לד) במלחמת סיחון ועוג **אַל תִּירָא אֹתוֹ** משמע שהי' מתיירא. הנה במדרש הזה מניח כל הקושיות ומסלק כל התמיהות שכנגד הבטחת התורה על צדיק ורע לו (עיין ברכות ז ע"א), שהרי הן המה שהבטיחם הקב"ה בעצמו (בראשית כח, טו) **וְהִנֵּה אָנֹכִי עִמָּךְ וּשְׁמַרְתִּיךָ בְּכֹל אֲשֶׁר תֵּלֵךְ** וכן משה רבינו ע"ה בכמה הבטחות (שמות ג, יב ועוד), ונתייראו שמא יגרום החטא, כמו שמביא רש"י ז"ל (בראשית לב, יא):

והנה ענין שמא יגרום החטא בכדי להבינו על ענין העבודה האמיתית היא שכל צדיק וצדיק עיקר תוכן כוונתו בכל מעשי רצוניו בכדי לעשות נחת רוח לבוראו שאמר ונעשה רצונו, ואפי' אם הקב"ה מבטיח לו כל הטובות והשמירה מעולה מתיירא שמא יגרום החטא, גסות לבו בהבטחה זו בעצמו ויתרחק מאתו יתברך, ממילא יסתעפו שאר היראות התחתונות להתעורר אליו. ומעתה יש להתיירא לעולם יותר שהוא צדיק ובטוח מאתו ית' פחדתו אליו נאום ה' והבטחתו שלא ירחיקוהו. והנה על ענין **וַיִּשְׁלַח יַעֲקֹב מַלְאָכִים לְפָנָיו אֶל עֵשָׂו** ומבואר בזוה"ק (ח"א קסו ע"א) גודל החכמה והתחבולה בכוונת מעשה זו. ובמדרש (ב"ר עה, ב) משמעותו איפכא שהי' לו לילך לדרכו ובזה [ששלח] הי' **כְּמַחֲזִיק בְּאָזְנֵי כָלֶב עֹבֵר מִתְעַבֵּר** וכו' (משלי כו, יז):

אבל תוכן הענין הוא **עֵדוּת יְהֹ-וָה נֶאֱמָנָה מַחְכִּימַת פֶּתִי** (תהלים יט ח) שעיקר עסק התורה והמצות צריכות כוונה להבין פחיתותו ופתיותו איך קשור בחומריות. אדם מאדמה הולך אחר ההבל ויהבל גשמי חומר מעוכר בכל השגותיו ורצונותיו ומדותיו ונח"ר שלו הכל הבל אחר הידיעה גודל הא"ס מאתו וכל מאויו וחפצו ורצונו להתדבק בו ית'. ואינו יכול בהבינו גודל ההרחק מאתו והשגתו כי הוא פתי חסר לב באין מבין חכמתו יתברך ויתעלה העליונה, לכן כל מגמתו להתחבט בעסק התורה והמצות שהם מועצות ודעת אלקים **פֶּן יִרְאֶה בְעֵינָיו...וּלְבָבוֹ יָבִין** ע"י עסק המצות שהם **עֵיטִין [טָבִין]** כמובא בזוהר (ח"ב פב ע"ב). ובאמת כי עסק מצות כזה היא הנותנת חיים לעושיה **וִיהֹ-וָה יִתֵּן חָכְמָה מִפִּיו דַּעַת וּתְבוּנָה** (משלי ב ו) להבין ולהשכיל **שֵׂכֶל טוֹב לְכָל עֹשֵׂיהֶם**. וזהו **עֵדוּת יְהֹ-וָה נֶאֱמָנָה מַחְכִּימַת פֶּתִי**, פתי דייקא, מי שמחזיק את עצמו לפתי בעיניו ודורש ומבקש עצות לנפשו שהם המצות שישכילו אותו **וְהַמַּשְׂכִּלִים יַזְהִרוּ כְּזֹהַר הָרָקִיעַ** ויודע דעת עליון. וזהו **עֵדוּת יְהֹ-וָה נֶאֱמָנָה** שהם אותיות דעות ה' כי המצות הם הדעת שמחבר מחברת הקודש. משא"כ מי שהוא חכם בעיניו אין המצות מחכימות אותו, שאינם מחכימות רק מי שהוא פתי בעיניו ומבקש חכמה אבל מי שהוא חכם וצדיק בעיניו ואינו חסר מכלום א"כ אינו מבקש בעסק התורה והמצות להאירו מסכלותו כי לאורו ילך, וא"כ מה תאיר לו ומה העצה היעוצה ע"י המצוה אם אינו שואל בעצה מה יתן ומה יוסיף לו המצוה שאין נותנין עצה אלא למי ששואל כהוגן:

והנה הענין יעקב ועשו האמורים בפרשה הם על דרך זה כי ענין עשו הוא ענין התנגדות שעומד כנגד כל **קִרְבַת אֱ-לֹהִים** יחפץ להפיר עצתו בגדלות הפסולה כמאמר (בראשית כז טו) **עֵשָׂו בְּנָהּ הַגָּדֹל**, ואח"כ כשמפילו בגדלות נוקם הוא ובעל חימה אח"כ להנקם ממנו. וזהו שצוה יעקב לאמר לעשו (שם לב, ד) **כֹּה תֹאמְרוּן לַאדֹנִי לְעֵשָׂו...עִם לָבָן גַּרְתִּי וָאֵחַר עַד עָתָּה** ואחר עד עתה ופירש"י ז"ל ותרי"ג מצות שמרתי, פי' שכל המצות ששמרתי **עִם לָבָן** הי' שהוא היצה"ר שרציתי להנצל ממנו ויהי לי שור וחמור צאן ועבד ושפחה שהם הויות עולם ככל האדם ולא נעשיתי שר וחשוב כפירוש רש"י ז"ל. והנה להיות (ברשאית כה, כז) **וְיַעֲקֹב אִישׁ תָּם יֹשֵׁב אֹהָלִים** היה משמעות היותו מלאך אלקים

וחשוב גדול, לכן השפיל עצמו והי' שפל בעיני עצמו כי לא הגיע עד עתה אל המנוחה, אבל **עִם לָבָן גַּרְתִּי** שכל מה ששמר ועשה ולמד הכל עם לבן עדיין להנצל ממנו ולשית עצות בנפשו. ובזה ניחא תמיהת המפרשים ששלח יעקב ועשו דברים מהופכים הכנעה וגדלות שהוא עם לבן גרתי ולפי זה הכל אחד:

והנה ידוע היות יעקב בחיר שבאבות וכן משה בחיר שבנביאים. והנה ענין בחור הוא דבר הממוצע ומכריע בין תרי הפכים הזה או זה ובא השלישי והכריע בנתים והוא הבחור, והוא הנקרא דעת המחבר ומייחד הכל אל אחדות פשוט. כי באמת מאתו ית' (איכה ג, לח) **לֹא תֵצֵא הָרָעוֹת** כי טוב הוא ומטיב אבל כל הרעות המתדמים או מדות הנמדדות הכל אל מקום אחד הולך לתכלית הטובה, רק האדם אינו מבין וגולה מבלי דעת, כי הדעת הוא המחבר הנהגת המדות ע"י החכמה העליונה. וכן תנאים הראשונים היו יודעים ומחברים כמו (תענית כא ע"א) נחום איש גם זו לטובה. וכמעשה רבי עקיבא (ברכות ס ע"ב) שכל המאורע היה לטובתו, כי הידיעה שהיא התקשרות או האמונה באחדות הפשוט בכל סיבות המתהפך הוא המתקת הדינים. לכן יעקב ומשה שהיו נקראים בחור שהוא הדעת המחבר היו מתייראים שהרי הוצרכו ללכת בזה וגם בזה כדרך המכריע ומחבר גבורות בחסדים. ובאמת שאם היו חסדים לבד ולא הי' שום יראה בודאי היה הולך לבטח דרכו כדרך המדרש על **וַיִּשְׁלַח יַעֲקֹב** אבל באמת יעקב הי' בחור שבאבות שהוא אוחז בשני הקצוות כנזכר לעיל. לכן חכמה גדולה עשה ב**וַיִּשְׁלַח יַעֲקֹב** כמבואר בזוה"ק שהי' מתיירא והמתיק והעלה היראה למעלה למעלה שהוא היראה שמא יגרום החטא כנ"ל ובזה הכניע הגבורות והיראות חצוניות. וכן משה רבינו ע"ה שהי' בחור ודעת המחבר הוכרח להתיירא אבל היראה היא היתה סיבת הכנעה יראת השפלות. וה' יזכנו להיות מן היראים השלמים אמן:

[ו]. פרשת מקץ

(להתחזק באמונה במדרגה שפלה)

אמר רב חמא בר מניומא אמר רב נר חנוכה שהניחה למעלה מעשרים אמה פסולה כסוכה וכמבוי (שבת כב ע"א) הענין הוא על סדר הבנת הפסוק (מא, א) **וַיְהִי מִקֵּץ שְׁנָתַיִם יָמִים וּפַרְעֹה חֹלֵם** וכו'. והענין הוא מדריגה השמינית מן הבטחון המבואר בספר חובת הלבבות (שער הבטחון) הוא כי זה כל האדם שהוא במדריגה היותר שפלה ותחתונה, **יִבְטַח בְּשֵׁם יְהֹ-וָה הַצּוּר תָּמִים פָּעֳלוֹ** כי הוא הפועל הכל צופה ומביט עד סוף תכלית הכל. כמאמר (ישעיה מב, כד) **מִי נָתַן לִמְשִׁסָּה יַעֲקֹב** וכו' **הֲלוֹא ה' זוּ**, הפועל אמת ואמונה בו ית' כי הוא הטוב הגנוז כי מאתו (איכה ג, לח) **לֹא תֵצֵא הָרָעוֹת**, ואף כי אין שום שכל מחייב ומשיג שום טובה מסבה זו, הוא מחמת העדר השגת חכמתו יתברך, כי **הַחָכְמָה מֵאַיִן תִּמָּצֵא** (איוב כח, יב) שאינו מושג לשום גוף ואינו גוף (על פי איוב כח, כא) **וְנֶעֶלְמָה מֵעֵי[ן] כָל חָי**, גם צריך להאמין בהשגחה פרטיות מאתו יתברך על כל מה שבעולם קטן וגדול, ואין שום דבר בלתו. וע"י בטחון כזה, שהוא האמונה בהשגחתו ית' ברור, ופעולתו אמת ואמונה כי טוב הוא, מעלה סיבה זו ומקשר אותה בחכמה העליונה. שהוא מידת צדיק המקשר כל העולמות וסוד **יוֹסֵף הוּא הַשַּׁלִּיט...הוּא הַמַּשְׁבִּיר** (בראשית מב, ו) כי בהגיעו אל החכמה העליונה היא מקור הברכות משם מתברך ומשפיע שולט ומשביר לכל:

והוא ענין התפילה שיהיה עיניו למטה ולבו למעלה (יבמות קה ע"ב) וענין עיניו למטה הוא האמונה בהשגחתו ית' והסתכלות עיניו ויורדים מטה מטה מקרני ראמים עד ביצי כינים. שבדרך אמונת האדם והסתכלות בהשגחתו יתברך כן ממשיך על עצמו השגחתו, אם מאמין השגחתו בפרטות, מושגח בפרטיות, עד נוקף אצבעו ממש שהוא מאתו ית' ואם מסיר עינו מהשגחתו יתברך ואינו מאמין ניתן תחת הטבע ונקרא כופר. לכן ענין התפילה שהוא ההתקשרות, צריך ליתן עיניו למטה שישים עיניו בהשגחתו ית' מטה מטה וממילא תהיה לבו למעלה ויהיה קשור למעלה משבעת ימי הבנין, שהיא החכמה שהיא למעלה מן ההשגה. שהרי אינו יכול להשיג חכמתו

יתברך בכל סיבה, וא"כ יותר שהאדם נופל בשפל סתר המדרגה ממילא משיג ומבין **הלא ה' זו**, שהרי אינו משיג ומבין טובת הסבה מה שאין כן כשהולך וטוב אינו משיג כל כך חכמתו ית' שהוא נעלמה שהרי סבותיו מושגים לטובה. וזהו יוסף הוא הצדיק, הניתן **בַּבּוֹר** שהוא בעמקי הקליפות וכל זמן שתלה בטחונו **בשַׂר הַמַּשְׁקִים** שאמר כי אם זכרתני אתך **וַיִּשְׁכָּחֵהוּ** שכל ענין הטבע הוא עיקר השכחה אבל מקור הזכרון הוא למעלה מהטבע, וכיון שתלה בטחונו בשר המשקים שיוציאו מן הבור על דרך הטבע לכן **וַיִּשְׁכָּחֵהוּ**:

ואם אמנם יוסף צדיק היה, **שֹׁמֵעַ** אף **כִּי הַמֵּלִיץ בֵּינֹתָם**, הוא הטבע שהרי הטבע ג"כ מאתו ית' ורצה לקשר הטבע בו ית' ובאמת דבר זה קיום הטבע להעמידה על מכונה ולקיימה ולהחיותה. אבל אין דרך נס בכך שהרי הנס הוא ההשתנות ואין השתנות שייך כי אם למעלה מן הטבע בלי שום שיתוף טבע כלל, שהוא חוץ מן הטבע בלתי לה' לבדו, ויוסף היה צריך שינוי הטבע להעלותו, מן הבור השכחה ולבוא למעלות הזכירה לכן וישכחהו שהרי בזה אדרבה קיום הטבע. **וַיְהִי מִקֵּץ שְׁנָתַיִם** ימים שהם שני דרגות ושני שינוים כי שנה לשון שינוי כמבואר בזוה"ק (בראשית קצג ע"ב), **וּפַרְעֹה חֹלֵם** מלת פרעה פי' ההתגלות שהוא הטבע, חלם הוא **עָלְמָא דְאִתְכַּסְיָא** ופי' מקץ ג"כ כמבואר בזוה"ק (בראשית קצג ע"א) שהוא **קֵץ שָׂם לַחֹשֶׁךְ** (איוב כח, ג). ופי' הוא **מִקֵּץ** מחמת קץ וסתר המדרגה התחתונה השיג (ישעיהו מ"ב: כ"ד) **הֲלוֹא יְהֹ-וָה זוּ** (קהלת ח, א) **וּמִי כְּהֶחָכָם וּמִי יוֹדֵעַ פֵּשֶׁר דָּבָר** כי אם אלקים (תהילים קלו, ד) **הָעֹשֵׂה נִפְלָאוֹת גְּדֹלוֹת לְבַדּוֹ** והוא הטוב הגנוז ובזה התקשר בחכמה העליונה שהוא למעלה מן הטבע ב' דרגות שהם חכמה ובינה, שנתיים ימים שהם למעלה מן הטבע, מכל זיי"ן ימי בנין, שנפלו בטבע. וזהו השבעה פרות ושבעה שבלים היפות שנבלעו ברעות **וְלֹא נוֹדַע כִּי בָאוּ אֶל קִרְבֶּנָה**, שהיא מקום השכחה וכיון שהעלה הכל, הי' עליה גם לזה ויזכור שר המשקים אותו לפני פרעה וכיון שהגיע למקור הברכות משם נתברך הכל וזהו (מא, כח) **אֲשֶׁר הָאֱלֹהִים עֹשֶׂה הֶרְאָה אֶת פַּרְעֹה** שהוא בהתגלות:

כללא דמילתא כל זמן שהוא מצטער מן השפלות הירידה אל המקום אשר הוא חונה שם ורוצה להנצל ממנה הרי הוא מלובש בגוף ואינו יכול להשיג חכמתו, ואין לו שום שייכות עם החכמה שהוא למעלה מכל טבעי הגוף והשגתו. מה שאין כן כשמקבל היסורים באהבה אמיתית, בהשגתו (ישעיהו מ"ב: כ"ד) **הֲלוֹא יְהֹ-וָה זוּ** הטוב הגנוז כנזכר לעיל וא"א להשיג טובתו, אז טוב לו להיות מתקשר בחכמה שהרי כשאינו מצטער מהיסורים יצא מכלל הגוף ונתקשר בחכמה. וזהו שאמרו רז"ל (ברכות סב ע"א) סמא דיסורים שתיקותא, כי השתיקה הוא התקשרות החכמה כמאמר (אבות ג, יג) **סְיָג לַחָכְמָה, שְׁתִיקָה** וזהו ענין גם זו לטובה (תענית כא ע"א), וזהו ענין קיבול היסורים באהבה:

והנה ענין החכמה הוא נקראת שמן כמאמר (קהלת ט, ח) **וְשֶׁמֶן עַל רֹאשְׁךָ אַל יֶחְסָר**, וזהו ענין החנוכה כשנכנסו יונים להיכל וטמאו כל השמנים שהוא ענין כל השכליים שנטמאו בקליפה ונפלו בתוכה. חוץ מפך אחד שהיה בחותם הכהן הגדול, שהוא ענין ההשגה השגחה פרטיות הכל מאתו יתברך וחותמו אמת ואמונה כי הוא הטוב שאינו מושג, אם אמנם אין בו אלא כדי יום אחד שהוא מדת החכמה אבל ממנו מתברכים כל השמונה שכליים שלמטה ממנו ומדליק שמונה ימים. ולכן נר חנוכה שלמעלה מעשרים פסולה כי כ' הוא הכתר דלא שלטא בו עינא (עיין זח"ג רמג. ות"ז ת' נה. פח ע"א) כי אם בחכמה ע"י השגה בהשגחה פרטיות שהוא ענין ד' אל יראיו כידוע, וכדרך שהוא נותן עין יפה בהשגתו משם הוא ממשיך שפע וברכה, מה שאין כן בכתר דלא שלטא ביה עינא. והנה פליגי בזה חכמינו ז"ל (שבת כא ע"ב) אם להדליק כנגד הנכנסים או כנגד היוצאים ואלו ואלו דברי אלקים חיים. שהרי באמת **כֻּלָּם בְּחָכְמָה עָשִׂיתָ** (תהלים קד, כב) מוכרח להיות כולם נכללים בו שהרי כח הפועל בנפעל ולכן היה אפשרות הויות כולם ע"י, וכן למטה הימנו מוכרח להיות כלול כל עלול בעילתו הקודמת לו, שאם לא כן הוייתו מהיכן הוא אם לא כח הפועל בנפעל. ולכן באמת מן הראוי הי' להדליק ביום א' כל השמונה להיות כולם כלולים שם וכן אח"כ ביום שני זיי"ן להיות כולם כלולים בו כידוע אבל אין

אנו יכולים להשיג בהיותם בכללות, כי אם על ידי התפשטות והתגלות, לכן אין אנו מדליקין אלא כנגד היוצאין שכל מה שיצא נתגלה יותר מוסיף והולך השגתינו להשיג ולפרסומא ניסא קא אתינא:

[ז]. פרשת ויגש א'

(הבריאה נבראה מא"ס בלי גבול)

וְהִנֵּה עֵינֵיכֶם רֹאוֹת וְעֵינֵי אָחִי בִנְיָמִין כִּי פִי הַמְדַבֵּר אֲלֵיכֶם (מה, יב). ופרש"י **עֵינֵיכֶם רֹאוֹת** שאני מהול ככם ועוד כי פי המדבר אליכם בלשון הקודש. ועליו הקשה הרא"ם הרי נשבע יוסף לפרעה שלא לגלות לשון הקודש כדאיתא במס' סוטה (לו ע"ב) והמהרש"א תירץ אצל אחיו שאני:

ולדעתי יובנו באופן אחר בלי שום חילוק בין אחיו לאחרים והוא דהנה ידוע זכות גאולת מצרים על ד' דברים שלא שינו את שמם ואת לשונם וגדורים מעריות וכו' (ויק"ר לב, ה). ובכדי להבין יתבאר מענין הרל"א שערים צרופי אותיות והמשכתן (עיין ספר יצירה פ"א) מלבד (דברים לב, ט) **חֵלֶק יְהוָ-ה עַמּוֹ יַעֲקֹב חֶבֶל נַחֲלָתוֹ** שהוא פנימית הגלגל וחיותו נקודתו ומרכזו כידוע שמרכז הגלגל הוא חיותו וכן תנועתו בלתי אפשרי כי אם דרך המרכז, לכן נקרא לשון הקודש וישראל עם קדוש בשם גופו של אילן שהוא הנקודה הפנימית וכל צבא השמים וכל הברואים כולם נקראים בשם ענפים המסתעפים מן האילן ונקרא עולם התמורות וכן כל השבעים לשונות והעכו"ם שרשם מעולם התמורות וסוף כל התמורות המה הקליפות. אשר לכן אין שום שייכות לאומה ולשון בתורה הקדושה שהיא הנקודה פנימית המחיה את הגלגל מה שאין כן העכו"ם הם חיצונית הגלגל ואין שום שייכות לפנימית כי גבול נתן ה' להבדיל בין הקדש והחול. ולכן עכו"ם שלמד תורה חייב מיתה (סנהדרין נט ע"א), וכן (ירמיהו ב, ג) **קֹדֶשׁ יִשְׂרָאֵל לַיה-וָה רֵאשִׁית תְּבוּאָתֹה כָּל אֹכְלָיו יֶאְשָׁמוּ** כדרך זר שאכל קודש וכן כל הנקרא ראשית אסור לזרים כענין תרומה וחלה. כידוע שראשית הגלגל הוא נקודת המרכז וממנו מסתעף כל הגלגל, לכן אין התורה מיוחדת כי אם לישראל ושניהם נקראים ראשית וענין אחד להם כמאמר (עי' זח"ג עג ע"א) אורייתא וקוב"ה וישראל כולא חד:

והנה רש"י פירש על מאמר (בראשית ב, כג) **לְזֹאת יִקָּרֵא אִשָּׁה כִּי מֵאִישׁ לֻקֳחָה זֹּאת** מכאן שנברא העולם בלשון הקדש. ולהסבירו יפה נדרשת על מאמר חז"ל (מובא ברש"י בראשית א, א) **בְּרֵאשִׁית בָּרָא אֱלֹהִים** מתחילה עלה במחשבה לברא העולם במדת הדין ואחר כך שיתף מדת הרחמים. והענין ידוע שתחילת הבריאה מאין סוף הפשוט בלי גבול בהבראו להיותו מוגבל בלתי אפשר כי אם על ידי הצמצום הבלי גבול בעצמו אז יגביל הגבול והצמצום הוא שרש הדין. כידוע שכל המוגבלים יותר המה גופים הגשמיים וחומרים עבים כלים ונפסדים שכל מה שהוא יותר רוחני הוא רחוק מן ההפסד ועיקר שם הכליון וההפסד הוא ענין קליפה ורע ודינין, הרי שם הגבול והצמצום שרש הדין:

והנה כללות הצמצום המה האותיות, **וּמִבְּשָׂרִי אֶחֱזֶה אֱלוֹהַּ**, כאשר יתבונן האדם בתחילת מחשבתו המשוטטת ואינה נחה כלל **וְהַחַיּוֹת רָצוֹא וָשׁוֹב** פושט צורה ולובש צורה הכל המה צורת אותיות. כי בלתי אפשרות השגת מחשבה מבלי אותיות כי בלי אותיות המחשבה פשוטה ואינה מושגת כלל מגודל פשטותה ואינה נקראת מחשבה כי אם אחרי צמצום הפשיטות פושט צורה ולובש צורת אותיות אחרים. כי מצרף לחכמה אחר כך מבין דבר בבינה ומתגלה הדעת שהיה בהעלם מכריע בין חכמה לבינה. ואחר התגלות הדעת יוצאים המדות אהבה ויראה ומתגלה יותר להכריע ביניהם בתפארת. וכן עד סוף כל המדות. שכל עיקר הדעת להיותו מכריע ומחבר שנים כאחד לכן נקרא הדעת לשון הקודש להיותו מכריע בין חכמה הנקרא קדש כידוע (זח"ג רצז ע"א). והמכריע נקרא לשון כעין קנה המשקולות של מאזנים שמתבונן ההכרעה מן הלשון היוצא מן הקנה ומכריע לאיזה צד. וכן נקרא בלשון אשכנז מה שיצא למעלה מן הקנה בשם לשון:

והנה ידוע מאמו (זח"ב קסא ע"א) **וּבְאוֹרַיְיתָא אִתְבְּרֵי** [קודשא בריך

הוא] **עָלְמָא** וכן התרגום על **בְּרֵאשִׁית בָּרָא**, בחוכמתא ברא כי החכמה היא התורה והתורה היא האותיות. כללא דמילתא שהעולם נברא באותיות שהוא ענין הצמצום. אם אמנם כמה צמצומים לצמצומים יש עד אין מספר. וכל שכן שאין להשיגם כי **גָבֹהַּ מֵעַל גָּבֹהַּ** שומר ועולמות אין מספר כידוע מענין הטעמים, נקודות, תגין, שלמעלה מן האותיות. והמה חיותם והנהגתם שאין אנו עתה בבאורם. והשכלתם מאד נעלה ונעלמה מעין כל חי כי אם **סוֹד יְהֹ-וָה לִירֵאָיו** וחכם מבין מדעתו. ולכן אנו מכנים כאן לאותיות בשם ראשית (ההמשכה) [המחשבה]. כמבואר בזהר (חלק א' קמח ע"א) על פסוק **וַיִּשְׁכַּב בַּמָּקוֹם הַהוּא** יש כ"ב אתוון עיין שם. כי אין שום דבר שנברא כי אם על ידי אותיות והן הנה חיות אותו דבר וקיומו. והנה אותיות הנכתבות המה גוף והיכל אל המוזכרים בפה. והמוזכרים בפה הם גשמיים לערך המחשבה שהוא בלב ואותם שהם בלב הם האצילות ידוע בלב המשכילים כמבואר בפרד"ס:

והנה תמונת האותיות ברמיזתן ממש ידוע למשכילים ועל כל פנים שמץ מנהו מבואר בספר התמונה, ואז תדע דמכל שכן בהתחברות אותיות הקדושים ונעשים מהם תיבה שרוחניות התיבה הוא ענין גדול. מפני שכבר נתגלה בה חיות של נקודה כי באות א' אין מרגישין הנקודה וד"ל. וכמו שההויות והשמות הם סוד אצילות רק השמות הם ההתפשטות ההויות וההויות הם חיות של השמות, כך כל תיבות לשוננו הקדושה התיבות הם למעלה וכל הנקרא בשם זה למטה בגשמיות המה התפשטות והשתלשלות השפע מלמעלה רבבות מדרגות עד שנתגשם, ואותו שם דבר הוא חיות של הדבר ההוא. לכן כל שם דבר מלשון הקודש הוא שמו באמת למעלה בשרשו, כמאמר (בראשית ב, יט) **וְכֹל אֲשֶׁר יִקְרָא לוֹ הָאָדָם** הוא שמו שכל עיקר המשכה והתפשטות הוא ע"י אדם. כי השם דבר במקורו הם אלו אותיות והבורם רק שכל חבל השתלשלות נקרא בשם זה מפני חיותו וקיומו שמקבל משם דרך משל יד נקרא מקור השם למעלה צירוף **יַ"ד** הוא כח וחיות של **יַ"ד** האדם והוא יורד ומשתלשל עד שנברא גוף **יַ"ד** אדם ונקרא גם כן י"ד. לא מפני הגוף כי אם מפני חבל השתלשלות כח וחיות של היד נקרא הגוף על שמו. אם אמנם מראשית ההשתלשלות עד סיומו בגוף יש כמה רבבות מדרגות, כולם נקראים יד על שם ראשית ומקוי החיות. והן הנה הכנויים שבתורה (שמות ט, ג) **יַד יְהֹ-וָה** וכו' הם כחות עליונים שנאצלו מאתו יתברך. כי האין סוף אי אפשר לתפוס אף בנקודה וכל שכן באותיות. וכן בשמות האדם דרך משל אברהם, יצחק ויעקב, הם ג' מקורות ושרשים, אשר מהם מתפשט החיות עד גוף האדם למטה והוא נקרא על שם מקור שרשו וחיות קיומו. וכן ראובן ושמעון הם מקורות ושרשים אחרים בערך כמה מדרגות למטה מהם. ואם אחר כך נקראים אפילו אלף אנשים אברהם או ראובן בנו על שם זקנו אפילו עד אלף דור. כל אלו נקראו מפני חבל השתלשלות שנתפשטו משם. וזהו מאמר (בראשית ב, כג) **לְזֹאת יִקָּרֵא אִשָּׁה כִּי מֵאִישׁ לֻקֳחָה זֹּאת** שנקראת על שם מקום לקיחתה וחיותה משם. וזהו שפירש"י מכאן שנברא העולם בלשון הקדש פירוש שנברא ממש באותיות שם דבר ההוא: והנה לכן מקובל אצלינו שכחת אדם רשע את שמו אחרי העדרו (עיין ז"ח רות ק"ג ע"א). כי אין השם מיוחד אליו לקרוא בשם זה אלא אם כן הוא דומה לו בפעולותיו להמשיך כחותיו וחיותו משרשו באור חוזר ונעור לעבודתו יתברך שמו ולדבקה בו דרך אור הישר שנתפשט השתלשלותו והויותו שהם אותיות שמו לעולם, וזה זכרו לנצח אחרי העדרו. מה שאין כן אם אינו דומה בפעולותיו לשמו, שאינו ממשיך כוחותיו וחיותו והנאתו מאתו יתברך שמו ומגביר על נפשו החומריות והקליפות, אין נקרא בשם הראשון כי אם שם אחר מעולמות התמורה שנמשך אחריו וקיבל חיותו משם ונהפך שמו לשם אחר וד"ל. ועוד יתבאר לקמן:

והן המה דברי היעב"ץ בפרקי אבות במאמר (פ"ג יז) **אִם אֵין תּוֹרָה, אֵין קֶמַח.** והנה עינינו רואות כמה בתים מלאים כל טוב ואין בהם אפילו ריח תורה. אבל הכוונה שאין הקמח נקרא בשמו כי אם על ידי המשכת התורה המה אותיות הוויתו. כי על דרך אותיות נשתלשל מלמעלה למטה עד

גשמיות הקמח שלמטה ומשביע על דרך שנתהווה. ומפריד הקליפות ממנו על פי דיני תורתנו הקדושה הן דיני נטילה הן דיני איסור והיתר אז נקרא קמח ומשביע כדרכו ואינו רוצה במותרות. מה שאין כן **וּבֶטֶן רְשָׁעִים תֶּחְסָר** (משלי יג, כה) ומשביעו רעב, כדרך כל התאוות שאין אדם מת וחצי תאוותו בידו (קהלת רבה א, יג). כדרך הקליפה שכל חיותה הוא הרבוי והפירוד, היפך הקדושה שהוא אחדות פשוט. לכן **אִם אֵין תּוֹרָה, אֵין קֶמַח** נקרא בשם **קֶמַח** המשביע ומחיה כי אם שם אחר מעולמות התמורה אחרי שהוא מקבל חיותו משם כידוע כי **אֶת זֶה לְעֻמַּת זֶה עָשָׂה הָאֱ-לֹהִים** (קהלת ז, יד) שבעים לשונות שהם ע' ענפים המסתעפים מאילן א' שהוא לשון הקדש. ושרשם של הע' לשון הם הם הרל"א שערים צרופי אותיות עולם התמורה על דרך גלגל החוזר. אבל לשון הקדש הוא מרכזם ובכל לשון מוכרח להיות מלה א' שוה ללשון הקדש. ואותה המלה הוא חיותם ודביקותם באילן כמאמרם ז"ל (שבת לא ע"ב) שכן בלשון יווני קורין לאחת וכמאמר (סנהדרין ד ע"ב) ט"ט בכתפי שתים. שהוא מקום חיותו מלשון הקדש ומשם יפרדו, והיה **חֵץ שָׁחוּט לְשׁוֹנָם מִרְמָה** (ירמיהו ט, ז). כליון חרוץ מפני הקליפה ונופה נוטה למקום טומאה:

מה שאין כן כשהצדיק אוכל לשובע נפשו מבואר בס' רקאנט"י מדרש רבה (ויק"ר כ, ז) על מאמר (שמות כד, יא) **וַיֶּחֱזוּ אֶת הָאֱלֹהִים וַיֹּאכְלוּ וַיִּשְׁתּוּ**, שזנו עיניהם מן זיו השכינה ור' יוחנן אמר אכילה וודאית דכתיב (משלי טז, טו) **בְּאוֹר פְּנֵי מֶלֶךְ חַיִּים.** וכתב החכם אבן עזרא ז"ל ראה החכם איך הפליא לדבר, כי המאכל השפל שהוא בא מסיבה אחר סיבה המקבל זו מזו זן את האדם ומפרנסו, על אחת כמה וכמה הדבק ורואה בעין הלב סיבת הסיבות שהוא ניזון ומענג והיא האכילה הוודאית והעיקרית וכו' וזהו (תהלים קיא, ה) **טֶרֶף נָתַן לִירֵאָיו** וכו'. ומסיים הרקאנט"י, ודע שאין כוונת האכילה להפסד דבר הנאכל אלא להוסיף כח ותענוג וחיים לאוכל, על זה נקרא אכילה וזהו אמרם אכילה וודאית שהרי התענוג הוא עיקר שם האכילה. וכן היה אצלם שמחת הנפש ותענוג זיו השכינה, כמאמר (ישעיהו נח, יד) **אָז תִּתְעַנַּג עַל יְהֹ-וָה** עד כאן לשון הרקאנט"י ז"ל. והנה על דרך זה צריכין להיות כל ענייני הגוף ותשמישי עולם הזה שלא נתן ליהנות לבני אדם כי אם מן הפנימית שהוא הצורה ושרשו של אותו דבר והויתו, אשר משם נשתלשל ויצא החומר, אבל אסור ליהנות מחומרה של מקום שיצא משם. כי אם להתדבק (ובמצוה) [בצורה] דרך השתלשלותו, עד אין סוף ברוך הוא, להיות חוזר ונעור אליו יתברך, דרך התענוג ההוא שמקבל מאותו דבר. והנהגה זו נקראת מדבר בלה"ק, ופירושו מתנהג ע"ד אותיות לשון הקדש של שם דבר תשמישו. כי הדבור נקרא ע"ש הנהגה לשון (סנהדרין ח ע"א) דבר א' לדור, והדבור הוא מנהיג את הכל כידוע. ואין רצוני להאריך בזה כי אי אפשר להעלות על הכתב דברים שעומדים ברומו של עולם. כי אם זה נקרא דבור מה שמדברים בה' מוצאות הגשמיים הא מבואר בתורת אמת שלנו (ברכות יח ע"ב) כי המתים מדברים ועת לקצר ודי למבין ברמיזה:

כללא דמילתא כי זה כל האדם ותכליתו להתנהג על דרך אותיות לשון הקדש שהוא מאמר (משלי ג, ו) **בְּכָל־דְּרָכֶיךָ דָעֵהוּ** כי הדעת נקרא לשון הקדש כנזכר. ויכול לפרש דעת הרמב"ם בספר המורה גם כן על דרך זה ועיין ברמב"ן ז"ל פ' [כי] תשא (שמות ל, יג) שרוצה לסתור דבריו ולדעתי שפתי חכם חן דברי הרמב"ם ז"ל ע"פ אמת וא"א לבאר מחמת האריכות והמבין יבין לעצמו:

ואפשר לומר טעם זה למאמרם ז"ל (סוטה לג ע"א) שלא להתפלל בלשון ארמית כי התפלה נקראת על שם הדביקות כמאמר (בראשית ל, ח) **נַפְתּוּלֵי אֱ-לֹהִים** וכו'. ודביקות התפלה כדי להמשיך השתנות ברחמיו צריך להיות באופן זה לצאת בדבוריו מן המדות שהתחיל בהם, שהרי תחלה כשמתחיל להתפלל על איזה דבר בוודאי הוא מאחת המדות אם חסד או גבורה וכו', אבל כשמדבר דבריו העיקר הוא להתבטל מן המדות מפני פחדו יתברך העומד לפניו וכלות נפשו אליו לדבקה בו. והדביקות הוא להתקשר עצמותו באותיות דבורו היוצאים מן הפה

ולהגיע בהם עד אותיות המחשבה, שהם ב**רָצוֹא וָשׁוֹב**. ואפשר שיצא מן האותיות אל שרשם מגודל ההתלהבות. ואחר שיצא מן הצמצום אז יכול לעשות השתנות והמשכה אחרת מאתו יתברך בחזירתו דרך הרחמים כידוע. וגם שממילא נעשה רצונו בהגיע למעלה מן הצמצום. ועל פי דרכנו יוכל לפרש אמרם ז"ל שלא להתפלל בלשון ארמית כדרך הלשון שצוה (רבי יהושע בן לוי) [רבא] לבנו (ברכות ח ע"ב) אל תשב על מטת ארמית ופירושו שלא תיגני בלא קריאת שמע עיין שם. הרי שקרא להעדר הנהגה על פי דת תורהנו הקדושה בלשון שם ארמית. וכמו כן בענין התפלה שהוא הדביקות אליו יתברך דרך המשכות התיבות שם דבר ההוא שמתפלל וכשמתדבק לפנימית חיותו אפשר לשנות. ע"ד (תענית כה ע"א) מי שאמר לשמן וידלוק יאמר לחומץ וידלוק וכו'. וידוע שבלתי אפשרות תפילה זכה ודביקות שלם, כ"א אחרי הרגל כל מדותיו השתמשם ברוחניות וחיות פנימי של כל דבר ודבר אז לא יהיה מסך מבדיל דביקותו ית' והוא הנהגה ישראלית דרך דת תוה"ק כמאמר (דברים י, כ) **וּבוֹ תִדְבָּק** ואמרו חז"ל (סוטה יד ע"א) הדבק במדותיו. מה שאין כן בהעדר (הדת) [הדעת] ובלי שום דביקות אל שרש פנימיות החיות אז נקרא על שם לשון ארמית. כמו שכתבתי לעיל, כי שרשו של אדם הוא מלשון הקדש והוא ממשיך על עצמו מחמת תאותו קליפות ועמים אחרים וכבר הוא תחת לשונותם בארצותם ובגוייהם, ובלשון הקדש (ב"מ) מביא חיות לאומות והקליפות והם מושלים עליו. ומשנים שמו אפילו כפי הצירוף שיש בלשונם, נמצא יכול להיות שבהיות שמו ראובן כפי שהמשיך על עצמו חיות מהקליפה כבר יש לו שם אחר ושמו כשם עכו"ם ב"מ מה שאין כן כשהוא מתנהג [על] דרך אמונה הישראלית. אמרו רז"ל תפלה בכל לשון. אם אמנם תירץ הגמרא (סוטה לג ע"א) הא ביחיד והא בצבור הנה הפשוט כפשוטו והדין דין אמת כמבואר בשלחן ערוך (או"ח סי' קא. סעיף ד) אבל על דרך האמת אפשר לפרש דבריהם כדברינו, הא ביחיד פירוש כשמכוון לעניני עצמו הא בצבור כשהוא על דרך התקשרות כל העולמות. וכן דרך כל בעלי אמת ובפרט בכתבי האר"י ז"ל. ובלבד שיהא דרך אמונה והמשכת החיות מאין סוף ברוך הוא אדרבא בזה מכניע הלשון תחת הקדושה כעבד המקבל פרס וחיות מהקדושה ועבדו לעולם. כי זה כל האדם ותכלית בריאותו להעלות כל הדברים ממטה למעלה ולהכניע החיצונית אל הפנימית במציאת אלהותו יתברך בכל דבר ולית אתר פנוי מיניה (ת"ז ת"ע קכב ע"ב) [והבן זה מאד]:

ודרך היותר פשוט להבנת למען ישכילו להיות לזכרון. הוא על דרך המבואר בזהר (תקו"ז תיקון ו' כב ע"א) וצוח ככרוכיא על המתפללים לשם הנאתן כל חסד דעבדין לגרמייהו עבדין הב לנא חייא הב לנא מזוני ואיתמר בהון (תהלים קו, לה) **וַיִּתְעָרְבוּ בַגּוֹיִם וַיִּלְמְדוּ מַעֲשֵׂיהֶם**. זהו הנקרא בלשון ארמית. כי אינו כדרך שאמרו ז"ל (ברכות לב ע"א) לעולם יסדר אדם שבחו של מקום שהמה התפשטות מדותיו יתברך דרך האותיות חסד ורחמים ואחר כך יתפלל לדבקה דרך לשון הקדש תיבות תפילתו. וממילא ימשכו דרך אותיות תפלתו השפעה טובה ורחמים וחיים ושלום בארץ. וזהו ענין יעודים הגשמיים המבוארים בתורתנו התמימה, (ויקרא כו, ד) **וְנָתַתִּי גִשְׁמֵיכֶם** וכו' (דברים יא, יד) **וְאָסַפְתָּ דְגָנֶךָ** וכו'. לא זהו שכר העבודה כי מה רב טוב הצפון ליראיו **עַיִן לֹא רָאָתָה** וכו' (ישעי' סד, ג). אבל התורה אמרה שממילא יומשכו כל היעודים האלה **אִם בְּחֻקֹּתַי תֵּלֵכוּ** ממשיכים החיות מלמעלה למטה בדרך אותיות הנהגתו ודביקותו:

וזהו ענין גאולת מצרים מפני הד' דברים. שלא שינו את שמם להקרא בשם אחר מעולמות התמורה אף על פי שלא קיבלו התורה עדיין רק בקבלה מאברהם אבינו עליו השלום כמאמר הש"ס (יומא כח ע"ב) קיים אברהם אבינו עליו השלום אפילו ערובי תבשילין. נמצא ראובן ושמעון נחתי וראובן ושמעון סלקי וכו'. ושלא שינו את לשונם לשון הקדש והמשכתו כנזכר לעיל. וממילא שהיו גדורין מעריות ושלא היה בהם דלטורין שהוא ענין ברית הלשון וברית המעור (עי' ספר יצירה א, ג) המשכות ומכריעין בין עליונים ותחתונים. וזהו דברי

יוסף הצדיק עיניכם הרואות שאני מהול ככם, ככם דייקא ולא כערבי מהול ופגום בברית כי פי המדבר אליכם שהיה הנהגתו על דרך לשון הקדש שכן קיבל מאבותיו הקדושים. כמאמר (בראשית יח, יט) **לְמַעַן אֲשֶׁר יְצַוֶּה אֶת בָּנָיו...וְשָׁמְרוּ דֶּרֶךְ יְה-וָה** וגו'. ועתה אין אנו צריכין לומר שדבר לשון הקדש מפני השבועה. וזהו פי' הפסוק (תהלים לז, י) **וְעוֹד מְעַט וְאֵין רָשָׁע וְהִתְבּוֹנַנְתָּ עַל מְקוֹמוֹ וְאֵינֶנּוּ**, על דרך אמרם ז"ל בסוכה (יז ע"א) אויר פוסל בג' וסכך פסול בד'. (ושם יג ע"ב) אמר ר' אבא אמר שמואל ירקות שאמרו חכמים אדם יוצא ידי חובתו בפסח פוסלים בסוכה משום אויר מאי טעמא כיון דלכי יבשי נפלי ופרכי כמאן דליתנהו דמי. וכן הרשעים כתיב בהם (תהלים לז, ב) **כִּי כֶחָצִיר מְהֵרָה יִמָּלוּ וּכְיֶרֶק דֶּשֶׁא יִבּוֹלוּן**. מפני שאינם ממשיכין חיות פקחיות מאתו יתברך. וזהו ועוד מעט ואין רשע נמצא יבשי פרכי ונפלי וכמאן דליתנהו דמי וזהו והתבוננת אפילו כשהוא על מקומו ואיננו ובחייהם קרויים מתים (ברכות יח ע"ב):

פרשת ויגש ב'

עוד מפרשה זו:

וַיִּגַּשׁ אֵלָיו יְהוּדָה וַיֹּאמֶר בִּי אֲדֹנִי (מד, יח). הנה בספר אור החיים מובא לפרש מלת **וַיִּגַּשׁ** מאי הגשה ופי' הוא כראוי לו שהגשה היה בלב להיות ידוע **כַּמַּיִם הַפָּנִים לַפָּנִים כֵּן לֵב הָאָדָם** לאדם (משלי כז, ט). ובדברים אלו היה רצון יהודה לעורר רחמי יוסף לכן הגיש בלבו להתקרב ליוסף ולאהוב אותו באמתות הלב בכדי לעורר אהבת יוסף אליו לעורר רחמיו. והנה יצא מפה קדוש דברי פי חכם חן אמת ואמונה, אבל אם אמנם לפי דעת יהודה שהיה סבור על יוסף שהוא מצרי שהוזהרו ישראל (דברים ז, ב) **לֹא תְחָנֵּם** שלא ליתן להם חן (ע"ז כ ע"א), לא נמנע יהודה מלקרב לבו לאהוב אותו ע"ד הידוע בתפלה וקרבנות ואכילה:

הנה ארז"ל במדרש (ב"ר פו, א) וש"ס (שבת פט ע"ב) ראוי היה יעקב אבינו לירד בשלשלאות של ברזל למצרים אלא וכו' ומשל בהמה שמוליכין אותה למקולין ואינה רוצה לילך מושכין אותה בחבל ע"ש. הנה המשל הוא הוראת ענין ירידת יעקב ובניו למצרים בכדי להעלות נצוצות הקדושות ממצרים כידוע על פסוק (שמות יב, לו) **וַיְנַצְּלוּ אֶת מִצְרָיִם** כתרגומו ורוקינו, ואמרו רז"ל (ברכות ט ע"ב) כמצודה שאין בה דגים. והנה ענין האכילה של אדם ג"כ לצורך זה בכדי להעלות הנצוצות מדרגא לדרגא מדומם לצומח הראוי לאכילת אדם ושאינו ראוי עולה מצומח לחי עד שמגיע לאכילת אדם. והחוש מעיד שלכאורה דבר פלאי להיות המאכל הגשמי סבה להתקשרות הנפש בגוף שאינו יכול לחיות בלא אכילה ומוכרח להיות במאכל ניצוץ חיות הקדש אשר הנפש ניזון ממנה והגוף מן הגשמיות. ואף על פי כן אין רוצה שום ניצוץ הקדוש לזוז ממקום שהוא בסתר המדרגה ולעלות, כארז"ל (ב"ר י, ו) שכל עשב יש לו מלאך הממונה ומכה אותו ואומר לו גדל, כי הניצוץ הקדוש מתיירא ממקרה בלתי טהור אולי יזדמן לפני אדם בליעל שיפילו יותר באכלו משהוא עכשיו אף כי זה כל האדם עומד על הבחירה ומי יודע אם יבחור בטוב להעלותו. כי אין שייכות לשום עלוי אלא אם יחשוב האדם לזון ממזוני דמתיהיב מבי מלכא קודשא בריך הוא בתוך המאכל ויאכל וישתה ויחזה את האלהים להתקרב אליו ע"י המאכל, כמעשה דרב המנונא סבא שהוא מתעלה תיכף כמעשה הקרבן ומתייחדים כל העולמות מן השפלים התחתונים עד רצון עליון אין סוף ברוך הוא ע"י יחוד אדם ובהמה באכילתו אותה. ולמטה ממנו אדם שטוב לפני אלהים ואינו מעלה תיכף באכילתו עכ"פ התוספת חיות שקבל באכילתו והחיות הגיע ג"כ לזאת תורת האדם וכל מעשה שיעשה אח"כ לשם שמים מתעלה החיות ג"כ. מה שאין כן ח"ו כשהאדם מתגשם מן האכילה ויאכל וישבע ותאוותו יבא לו הרי הוא מפיל לנצוץ הקדוש בתוך הקליפה יותר ויותר שהרי הוא נותן חיות ובורא קליפות ר"ל. זהו יראת הניצוץ להתעלות עד שמכים אותו כנזכר לעיל:

ובאמת ניצוץ הקדוש שרואה מקום מוכן לפניו להתעלות בלי ספק מבקש מאד כידוע מענין מים תחתונים בוכים גם אנן בעינן **לְמֶהֱוֵי קֳדָם מַלְכָּא** (עי' תקו"ז ת' ה' יט ע"ב) שהוא ענין התפילה שלפעמים כשאדם נגש אל

האלהים בנקודת לבו באמת כאמור ביהודה מתעוררים עליו מחשבות זרות או מדות זרות והוא שרצונם להתעלות, כי הנה מקום אתם מוכן להעלותם ע"י התשובה להיותו מוכן לשרת בקדש. וכן יעקב אבינו היה מתיירא מלירד למצרים להעלות הנצוצות כענין עשב המכים אותו לגדל ופרה שמוליכים אותה למקולין להעלותה בשחיטתה ואכילתה ראוי לירד בשלשלאות של ברזל, אלא שזכותו גרמה לו שהבטיח לו הקב"ה אנכי אעלך גם עלה:

והנה תורתנו תורת אמת ואמונה שבודאי אסור לו לאדם להביא את עצמו לידי נסיון להכניס את עצמו במחשבה זרה בכדי להעלותה ח"ו. כי מי יודע אם יתגבר כארי ויתנשא או אולי ירד מטה מטה ולא יעמוד בנסיון ח"ו. אם לא כשהנסיון נזדמן לפניו בלא מתכוין בודאי מן ה' לנסותו וצריך להתגבר בכל כחו ומסירת נפשו על התשובה והוא העליה. וזה היה ענין שלמה המלך ע"ה שאמר (סנהדריו כא ע"ב) ארבה ולא אסור ומתחילה יצא במתכוין בכדי להעלות נצוצות קדושות ולא עמד בנסיון. וזה ארז"ל (ברכות נח ע"ב) לברך על בריות נאות ברוך שככה לו בעולמו אפילו על גוי נאה ואינו סותר למאמר **לֹא תְחָנֵּם** (דברים ז, ב), כי שם מירי להכניס עצמו לראותו אינו רשאי בכדי לומר כמה נאה גוי זה, משא"כ כשכבר נזדמן לפניו בודאי צריך לברך להעלות הנאות הראיה. כמעשה דרבי עקיבא בההיא מטרוניתא שארז"ל (ע"ז כ ע"ב) קרן זוית הואי. ובתחילה ודאי אסור והוא מסירת נפש כענין נפילת אפים כידוע:

והנה כללא דמלתא מענין ההעלאה הוא שצריך האדם להתבונן על כל המזדמן לפניו שגם בו נמצא שמץ מנהו מאותו הדבר אם טוב ואם רע ואחר שמצא מין את מינו וניעור, לכן צריך תיכף להתקשר בו ית' מעין המאורע שנזדמן לפניו בשומו אל לבו (ישעיהו מ"ב: כ"ד) **הֲלוֹא יְהֹ-וָה זוּ** ואין דבר בלתו כמאמר (תהלים קג, יט) **וּמַלְכוּתוֹ בַּכֹּל מָשָׁלָה**, כי המלכות הוא המושל בכל **וּמְחַיֶּה** הכל (עי' זח"א קמט ע"ב) וע"י ההתקשרות בו ית' מתעלה עם המלכות אל היסוד שהוא ההתקשרות, והוא, (בראשית כח, יב) **סֻלָּם מֻצָּב אַרְצָה וְרֹאשׁוֹ מַגִּיעַ הַשָּׁמָיְמָה** לעלות כידוע מ**צַדִּיק יְסוֹד עוֹלָם** (משלי י, כה). לכן הנה יהודה כשראה כל אלו הסבות שנזדמנו לפניהם כאמרם (בראשית מב, כח) **אִישׁ אֶל אָחִיו...מַה זֹּאת עָשָׂה אֱלֹהִים לָנוּ** הבין יהודה להיות הדבר מתבקש מאתם להתעלות, לכן **וַיִּגַּשׁ אֵלָיו יְהוּדָה** בלב אפילו אם היה גוי או מצרי שהרי כבר זימן ה' לפניהם והקרה להיותם מוכרחים לרחמיו לבקש מאתו על נפשם. וזהו שאמר בי אדני להיות יהודה היה מלכות בית דוד **וּמַלְכוּתוֹ בַּכֹּל מָשָׁלָה** והכל כלול בו ויגש להתקשר עמו אליו יתברך וע"פ האמת להיותו יוסף הוא היסוד ומתקשר עם המלכות וזהו בי אדני ע"פ פשוט גם ע"פ אמת:

שמות

[ח]. פרשת בא

(הבריאה היא אמירת שירה ליתברך):

שאל השואל מאמר רש"י ז"ל בד"ה **וַעֲרַפְתּוֹ** (שמות יג, יג) הוא הפסיד ממונו של כהן לפיכך יופסד ממונו:

פתח הרב בארז"ל (בכורות יג ע"א) מצות פדיה קודם למצות עריפה וכן מצות יבום קודם למצות חליצה אלא שזהו עבודה קשה שבמקדש לכוין לשם שמים בלתי לה' לבדו ביבום לקיום המצוה בלבד לכן נהגו בחליצה, וכן הענין כאן בעריפה:

הנה התורה אמרה (שמות י, א) **בֹּא אֶל פַּרְעֹה** פרש"י ז"ל והתרה בו, **כִּי אֲנִי הִכְבַּדְתִּי אֶת לִבּוֹ** וכו'. הענין ידוע להיות פרעה השיב (שם ה, ב) **לֹא יָדַעְתִּי אֶת יְהֹ-וָה וְגַם אֶת יִשְׂרָאֵל לֹא אֲשַׁלֵּחַ**, פירשו המפרשים (עיין זח"א קצה ע"ב) כי פרעה היה מכחיש בענין השגחה פרטית שהוא שם הוי"ה ב"ה המהוה **מְחַיֶּה אֶת כֻּלָּם** (נחמיה ט,ו). אם אמנם היה מודה באלהות כענין שאין העולם מחודש על פי מקרה כ"א על ידי כוונת המכוון אבל נמשך אחר אמונת שארי האפקורסין כי עזב ה' את הארץ אחרי עשותה תחת המזלות כוכבי השמים וכסליהם, ועל ידם הם כל הנהגות העולם, ולכן כל אומות העולם היו עובדי כוכבים ומזלות כידוע מעניינם ואין כוונתינו להאריך בביאורים. וזהו שאמר משה (שם כג) **וּמֵאָז**

בָּאתִי...לְדַבֵּר בִּשְׁמֶךָ שהוא בהשגחה פרטית שהוא שם הוי"ה **הֵרַע לָעָם הַזֶּה**, כידוע מענין התחזקות הקליפה לעמוד על נצחונה בכפירת ההשגחה פרטית **וַיַּעֲבִדוּ מִצְרַיִם אֶת בְּנֵי יִשְׂרָאֵל בְּפָרֶךְ** בכדי להתחזק בעניינם יותר, ובאמת לא ידעו כי גם זה מתת אלהים הוא שהרי קושי השעבוד היה משלים כמאמר חז"ל (עיין פרדר"א מח ע"א). וזהו **בֹּא אֶל פַּרְעֹה** והתרה בו **כִּי אֲנִי הִכְבַּדְתִּי אֶת לִבּוֹ** פירוש להסביר לו אופן ההשגחה פרטית כנ"ל כי אף גם זאת שהכביד עולו על ישראל לא מחמת חזקת ידו היא זו להורות על העדר ההשגחה אבל אדרבא היא בעצמה השגחה נפלאה כנ"ל:

והנה באמת רחוק מרשעים ויפג לבם להאמין השגחה פרטית כזו שאין אדם נוקף אצבעו (חולין ז ע"ב) ואין שום עשב יבש ונעקר ואין שום אבן נזרק כי אם בזמן ומקום הראוי לו כמאמר (קהלת יא, ג) **מְקוֹם שֶׁיִּפּוֹל הָעֵץ שָׁם יְהוּא**. ואין שום תנועה גדולה וקטנה מן הצמצום הראשון עד שפל המדרגות שבארץ ותחת לארץ הכל מאתו יתברך כפי חכמתו בשמו ולכבודו לגלות אלהותו והכמתו ומדתו יתברך מה הוא חנון ורחום (שבת קלג ע"ב), והכל **בְּרֵאשִׁית בָּרָא** בשביל ישראל **וְצַדִּיק יְסוֹד עוֹלָם** (משלי י, כה). שכל מה שיש בעולם יש באדם ובידו הכח הגדולה לגדל ולחזק לכל ולשנות סדרי בראשית במאמרו וברוח פיו ולבו לשמים בדביקות אחדות פשוט בלי שום הפסק מעורה ע"י מדותיו ודעתו הבן בחכמה, **[וְאִ]אַלֶּ"פְ[ךָ] חָכְמָה** (על פי איוב לג, לג) שהוא **פֶּלֶ"א יוֹעֵץ אֵל גִּבּוֹר אֲבִי עַד שַׂר שָׁלוֹם** (ישעיה ט, ה), בלי שום השגה ותפיסה כי אם אין סוף ב"ה כמאמר (דברים ד, יב) **וּתְמוּנָה אֵינְכֶם רֹאִים** אבל תמונת האותיות מה שהוא מדבר הם השתלשלות מאתו יתברך כענין **הָאָלֶ"ף** שהוא **פֶּלֶ"א** כידוע (עיין תיקו"ז ת' ע קלה ע"א). וכן כל האותיות אשר על ידם נבראו שמים וארץ וכל העולם כידוע (עיין לעיל פר' ויגש א) בוודאי לא מאותיות התמונה שהם עכשיו נבראו כי אם ע"י עניינם בהתפשטות התמונה מאתם. והתמונה שלהם לא באה כי אם להתלבש עצמם בכדי להבין ענין קריאתם לקטן המתחיל א"ב שאי אפשר להתחיל כי אם בהראותו תמונה א' וללמדו קריאתה:

וכן כל התורה והמצות שהם כל שמותיו ומדותיו יתברך בהתפשטות התמונה והגשמית מאתם כי אם נקודה שבלב הפנימית שבתוך תוכה שהוא מופשט מכל תמונה וגשם בלתי לה' לבדו והדבק במדותיו יתברך מה הוא חנון. כענין מצות צדקה, או מצות **וְאָהַבְתָּ** שהמדות הם רחמנות ואהבה, שהם מופשטים מן התמונה אבל מתלבשים בתמונת אותיות **נָתוֹן תִּתֵּן** (דברים טו, י) **וְאָהַבְתָּ לְרֵעֲךָ כָּמוֹךָ** (ויקרא יט,יח) ומתפשטים באברים גשמיים לעשותם. וכן כל המצות המורים הכל שמותיו יתברך ועניני הדביקות בו יתברך אם ע"י מעשה איברים או **רוּחַ יָהּ-וָה** אשר **דִּבֶּר** בו **וּמִלָּתוֹ עַל** לשונו (ע"פ ש"ב כג, ב) הקשורים והעטופים בו יתברך בורא שמים חדשים וארץ חדשה או משנה סדר הנהגת הבריאה אל רצונו, שהרי עיקר יסוד מוסד הבריאה כשעלה ברצונו הפשוט הוא למען הראות כוחו ומדותיו שיקרא רחום חנון מלך כידוע, ולמען התגלות אלהותו כמאמר (ישעי' מג, ז) **כֹּל הַנִּקְרָא בִשְׁמִי וְלִכְבוֹדִי בְּרָאתִיו**:

והנה מן הצמצום הראשון עד שפל המדריגות וכל עניני נבראים ונוצרים ונעשים שונים כולם מורים אלהותו יתברך ואומרים שירה הארץ ומתחת לארץ הכל לכבודו כידוע (עיין זח"א קכג ע"א). וענין יהושע שאמר **שֶׁמֶשׁ...דּוֹם** (יהושע י, יב) מלומר שירה כי הוא יאמר במקומה (תנחומא אחרי מות ט), וענין אמירתו במקומה הוא להיות האדם הוא התקשרות כל העולמות מתחילת הבריאה עד סוף ההרכבות ע"י גופו מכתר החכמה והתקשרותם כסדר השתלשלות העולמות. כולם וכל הנמצאים שבכל העולמות, ואחרי אשר כבוד ה' מלא את האדם בתוך תוכו של נקודת עצמית, מקום חיותא שבלבו שהוא המתפשט בכל האיברים, ואין שום פניית מחשבת עצמו בשום אבר והרכבת גופו ונפשו בלתי לה' לבדו בהפקרות אמיתי, נמצא הרי הוא עומד במקום כל הנבראים לכבודו יתברך שהרי כבודו מתראה באדם זה שהוא **עוֹלָם קָטָן** (תקו"ז ת' ע' קל ע"ב):

ומעתה אין שום טענה לשום נברא שרצון הצדיק לשנות סדרה איך יפסיק מהתראות כבודו יתברך על ידו באופן שהוא, שהרי הצדיק ממלא מקומו ומאיר לכל העולם יותר מן השמש בצהרים, כמאמר (ישעיה כד, כג) **וְחָפְרָה הַלְּבָנָה וּבוֹשָׁה הַחַמָּה כִּי מָלַךְ יְהֹ-וָה צְבָאוֹת**, ואחרי שהצדיק מלא כבוד ה' ומלכותו ויראתו הוא המאיר יותר והוא אמירת שירה במקומה. וכן (חולין ז ע"א) גינאי נהרא שפלג מימיו לר' פנחס בן יאיר שהשיב לר' פנחס אני הולך לעשות רצון קוני ובודאי עושה ואתה ספק וכו' אשר לא השיב ר' פנחס כלום על דבריו כי אם גוזרני עליך שלא יעברו בך מים לעולם, והרי לכאורה שפיר קאמר גינאי נהרא. אבל באמת כדברינו כן הוא להיות ר' פנחס היה ממלא מקום כבודו וא"כ מיותר הוא והיה יכולת בידו לגזור שלא יעברו בו מים כלל:

ולהיות כל עניני הבריאה והנמצאים כולם הם התגלות אלהותו יתברך וכבודו לכן קשה בעיניו לשנות ההנהגה והטבע כי אם על ידי צדיקים גמורים כנזכר לעיל הממלאים מקום כבודו באופן אחר שמים חדשים וארץ חדשה כנ"ל. שזהו ארז"ל (תענית כה ע"א) על ר' אלעזר בן פדת שהשיבוהו מן השמים אם רצונו לחזור ולברא העולם מחדש אולי יתרמי בשעתי דמזוני שהוא שנוי ההנהגה:

והנה אם אמנם שנוי הטבע מראה לעין כל אלהותו יתברך לשמוע ה' בקול איש אשר רוח אלהים בו, אבל באמת הנהגת הטבע היא היא שמגיד נפלאות ה' לבדו וכח מי יכיל שלא יפסוק מהנהגה וסדר א' מששת ימי בראשית עד סוף העולם **הַשָּׁמַיִם מְסַפְּרִים כְּבוֹד אֵ-ל** וכו' **בְּכָל הָאָרֶץ יָצָא קַוָּם** וכו' (תהלים יט ב-ה) ובכל יום **וְזָרַח הַשֶּׁמֶשׁ וּבָא הַשָּׁמֶשׁ** (קהלת א, ה) וכמאמר דוד המלך ע"ה (תהלים ח, ד) **כִּי אֶרְאֶה שָׁמֶיךָ מַעֲשֵׂה אֶצְבְּעֹתֶיךָ** וכו'. ומה שאינה משתנה ותמיד מתנהג על סדר אחד היא ההוראה על גדולת כח אין סוף ב"ה וכח אלהות שאינו משתנה כדרך כח האדם וכל הגשמים מוגבלים בכחם שאי אפשר להיותם ימים או עשור על סדר כח אחד כי אם משתנה מיום ליום ומשעה לשעה **וְכִי דֶרֶךְ לוֹ וְכִי שִׂיחַ** לו **אוּלַי יָשֵׁן הוּא** (ע"פ מ"א יח, כז). משא"כ כח אלהות יתברך כי **הִנֵּה לֹא יָנוּם וְלֹא יִישָׁן** (תהילים קכא, ד) ותמיד משגיח ושופע מהוה ומקיים ומחדש בכל יום תמיד מעשה בראשית, ברא ברצונו הפשוט וברצונו מקיים בכל עת תמיד ומהוה **הֶתָעִיף** עינו **בּוֹ וְאֵינֶנּוּ** (ע"פ משלי כג, ה):

והנה באמת אשרי משכיל ורואה ומבין מסדר ההנהגה הטבעית להבין ממה שאינו משתנה איך גודל השגחתו יתברך פרטית ועינא פקיחא, שהרי אין שום דבר נמצא בלתי חיותו יתברך, **וְהַחַיּוֹת רָצוֹא וָשׁוֹב** בכל מקום ולכל אדם. שאי אפשר לקבל חיותו יתברך כי אם ברצוא ושוב כי בהתמיד השפעת החיות יתבטל המקבל, לכן ירידה צורך עליה הוא וכל הדברים צריכים להתעלות והכל מאתו יתברך וחיותו **הַמְחַיֶּה אֶת כֻּלָּם** (נחמיה ט,ו), מלבד כי הירידה הוא חיותו בהסתר פנים והעליה היא בהתגלות. ואחרי ההתבוננות צמצום היותר גדול בהסתר פנים הרי זו גלוי שכינה והתגלות אלהותו יתברך יותר ויותר, אבל הכסיל לא יבין את זאת ואינו מבין מתמידות הנהגה טבעית השגחתו יתברך בפרטות ומניח אותם תחת המקרה:

וכן פרעה וכל הבוטחים כמוהו שלא ידעו ולא יבינו מתמידות ההנהגה השגחה פרטית אם אמנם האמינו כל מלכי ארץ להיות תחילת הבריאה ענין אלהות שאי אפשר לשום סדר הנהגה להיות על דרך המקרה כידוע ומבואר בטענותיהם. אבל אמרם שאחר הבריאה הנה הוא הניח על סדר ההנהגה כוכבים ומזלות ולא השגחה פרטית ב**רָצוֹא וָשׁוֹב** בכל עת ובכל רגע עד אשר יהיה הכל ביד האדם הישראלי ו **כֹּל הַנְּשָׁמָה תְּהַלֵּל יָ-הּ הַלְלוּיָ-הּ** שארז"ל (ב"ר יד, יא) על כל נשימה ונשימה שהוא ענין **הָרָצוֹא וָשׁוֹב** שהוא ענין נסיונות הלב כמו אבן בוחן שמבחינים עליו כל כסף שבעולם, כי **הָרָצוֹא** הוא בוחן את הלב אולי תוכל לחול עליו, ואם לאו **שׁוֹב** ותיכף חוזר ורצוא לנסותו לדעת את אשר בלבבו מה נשתנה אולי עתה תוכל לחול וכן לעולם. והנה מי שמבין **השׁוֹב** הוא ג"כ ענין הרצוא רק שהוא דרך ירידה וצריך להיות מטפס ועולה, הרי על כל נשימה תהלל יה. מה שאין כן מי שאינו נפגע ואינו מרגיש בדבר

שיצא מן הכלל לא ללמד על עצמו יצא במקרה וטבע כי אם אלהים עשה שיירא מלפניו להעלות גם זה לו לבדו:

וזהו אומר השי"ת למשה שהוא השכל כידוע (זח"ב קטז ע"ב עיי"ש) **בֹּא אֶל פַּרְעֹה** שהוא ענין עורף כידוע שהוא השכחה והירידה מחשבת חוץ, בא אל פרעה והתרה בו **כִּי אֲנִי הִכְבַּדְתִּי אֶת לִבּוֹ כִּי אֲנִי** הוא השכינה כידוע (עיין זח"ג רעו ע"א) שהוא ענין שכינה בתחתונים שהוא הטבע וההרגל והנהגה תמידית של כל דבר, ובאמת **אֲנִי אֲנִי הוּא** אין סוף רק שהוא בהסתר פנים והירידה צורך עליה הוא שאי אפשר לחול כי אם ב**רָצוֹא וָשׁוֹב** והכוונה הוא כדי להעלות גם את השוב אל הרצוא. וזהו **לְמַעַן שִׁתִי אֹתֹתַי אֵלֶּה בְּקִרְבּוֹ** פירוש למען האותיות ושמותיו של הקב"ה המחיה את כל הנבראים כולם על אותיות התורה כדי להעלות והירידה צורך עליה. וזהו (ע"ז ז ע"ב) לעולם יסדר אדם שבחו של מקום ואחר כך יתפלל כי הסידור שבחו של מקום הוא מכל הנמצאים בעולם להיכר שבחו והתגלות אלהותו ותפיסת השגתו מ**כֹּל הַנִּקְרָא בִשְׁמוֹ, וְלִכְבוֹדוֹ בָּרָא** (על פי ישעיהו מג, ז), ואם כן אין דבר בלתו והרי כל נשימה ונשימה תהלל יה ואחר כך יתפלל בודאי שהרי הוא הדביקות האמיתי אם אין שום הפסק בעולם:

והנה ענין פדיון פטר חמור בשה הוא ענין עליית מחשבות זרות ורעות מעין הטובות כי באו אל קרבנה ובאמצע מחשבה טובה עולה איזה מחשבה זרה ממינה שכבר הוריד אותה ורצונה להתעלות, כענין גלות מצרים שהיה על אהבה זרה כידוע בספר הזהר וכתבי האר"י בכל עניני שובבי"ם. ואחרי הגאולה מאתם **אֲשֶׁר בְּשַׂר חֲמוֹרִים בְּשָׂרָם** (יחזקאל כג, כ) וגלות חומר ולבנים צונו השי"ת בפדיון פטר חמור שהוא ראשית חמור שהיא האהבה שהוא ראשון לחדשים וז' ימי הבנין שבישראל הנקראים בכור (שמות ד, כב) ומצותה לפדותה בשה לכהן שהוא חסד (עיין זח"א רנו ע"ב) ולהעלות כל החסדים ואהבות בלתי לה' לבדו. **וְאִם לֹא תִפְדֶּה וַעֲרַפְתּוֹ** שהוא לכלות אותו שהוא דרך העורף והקליפה שלא להשתמש בו כלל אם אינו יכול לכווין לשם מצוה לבד ולא להנאת עצמו, כענין מצוה ביבום יותר וכו' לדעת את ה' בכל דרכיו משכיל כן יהי רצון אמן. ולפי שהוא הפסיד ממונו של כהן שהוא הכניס אהבות החוצה לפיכך יופסד וכו' וה' יורנו מדרכיו ונלכה באורחותיו **בְּכָל דְּרָכָיו דָעֵהוּ** (על פי משלי ג, ו):

או יאמר ענין פדיון **פֶּטֶר חֲמֹר** הוא ע"ד האמור לעיל (פרשה זו) בענין הדביקות אמיתי אשר אם יוכל איש לספור את עפר הרכבת גופו ספיר גזרתו ועל דרכיו נגה אור אין סוף ב"ה מגודל הזדכך חומרו ודביקות נפשו בהפקרות גמור מתוך תוכה של נקודת מקום חיותא דלבא וימלא כבוד ה' בהשתלשלות עצמותו כולו כליל לה'. הרי הוא עולם קטן הכולל כל הנבראים ופודה את נפש כל הנבראים מעבודתם לשנות ההנהגה כפי רצונו שהרי הוא ממלא מקומו כנזכר בדברינו, וכענין יהושע שאמר ל**שֶׁמֶשׁ...דּוֹם** שהרי הוא במקום השמש הוא הודה הוא זיוה הוא הדרה. מה שאין כן אם אינו יכול לפדותו מוכרח להתנהג על דרך הטבע והנהגה הקדומה זהו **וְאִם לֹא תִפְדֶּה — וַעֲרַפְתּוֹ** שיתנהג את עצמו דרך העורף והטבע ויסדר שבחו של מקום מהנהגת הטבע כמאמר (תהלים ח, ד) **כִּי אֶרְאֶה שָׁמֶיךָ** וכו':

ותלה הכתוב מצוה זו ביציאת מצרים להיות ידוע מאמרו יתברך בתחלת שליחות משה להוציאם אמר (שמות ג, יב) **בְּהוֹצִיאֲךָ אֶת הָעָם מִמִּצְרַיִם תַּעַבְדוּן אֶת הָאֱלֹ-הִים עַל הָהָר הַזֶּה** שהוא קבלת התורה חרות על הלוחות חירות ממלאך המות (שהש"ר ח, ג) וכל שעבוד מלכיות המסתעפים מאתו בלתי לה' לבדו אותו יעבדו. ואחר יציאתם משעבוד מצרים שהיו עבדים לעבדים כפרש"י ז"ל **בִּבְכוֹר הַשִּׁפְחָה** (שמות יא, ה) והגיעו לקבלת התורה שנברא בה שמים וארץ וכל העולם (עיין שמ"ר מז, ה), הרי הם כוללים כל השתלשלות העולמות מיום ברוא אלהים עד שפל המדריגות וכבודו יראה אליהם, לכן היה יכולת השתנות ההנהגה בענין יציאתם ממצרים כדברינו כנזכר לעיל בענין פדיון פטר חמור:

[ט]. פרשת בשלח

(כשנכנס באמונה השורשית, אינו חושש על מיתתו, אבדתו, והעדרו)

אָז יָשִׁיר מֹשֶׁה שר לא נאמר אלא ישיר מכאן לתחיית המתים מן התורה (סנהדרין צא ע"ב), בפסוק (שמות יד, כז) **וַיָּשָׁב הַיָּם לִפְנוֹת בֹּקֶר לְאֵ"יתָנוֹ**, ואמרו רז"ל (ש"ר כא, ו) **לת"נאו** הראשון כי תנאי התנה הקב"ה במעשה בראשית בתחילת הבריאה שיקרע הים לפני ישראל. והענין קשה לפי זה היה צריך המקרא לומר בשעת קריעת הים **לת"נאו**, והנה אמר וישב הים לפנות בוקר **לְאֵיתָנוֹ**. גם מאמר (שמות יד, טו) **מַה תִּצְעַק אֵלָי דַּבֵּר אֶל בְּנֵי יִשְׂרָאֵל וְיִסָּעוּ**, ומשמעו דבר פשוט הוא ואין שום מקום לצעקה, והלא הים עומד לפניהם ומצרים מאחריהם ולהיכן יסעו ויש לצעוק **צְעָקָה גְּדֹלָה וּמָרָה [עַד מְאֹד]**:

אבל באמת ידוע מה שאמרו ז"ל (ב"ר ד, ח) בשני שלא נגמר מלאכת המים ולא נאמר בו **כִּי טוֹב** עד יום שלישי שאמר (בראשית א, ט) **יִקָּווּ הַמַּיִם... וְתֵרָאֶה הַיַּבָּשָׁה** הוכפל כו **כִּי טוֹב** שני פעמים. נמצא שהיו ב' תנאים עם המים שתחילת בריאת המים היה התפשטות כידוע מענין המים והיה **מַיִם עַל פְּנֵי כָל הָאָרֶץ**, ואח"כ חזר הקב"ה ואמר **יִקָּווּ הַמַּיִם... אֶל מָקוֹם אֶחָד** נגד טבעם, כידוע שהים הוא גבוה מן היבשה, כמאמר (עמוס ה, ח) **הַקּוֹרֵא לְמֵי הַיָּם וַיִּשְׁפְּכֵם** ושפיכה היא ממקום גבוה לנמוך:

והנה אמרו רז"ל (ויק"ר לו, ד) **בְּרֵאשִׁית בָּרָא** בשביל ישראל שנקראו ראשית, וכל העולם תלוי עד שיקבלו ישראל את התורה (ע"ז ג ע"א), ואחר אשר תחילת הבריאה היה בשביל ישראל שיקבלו את התורה, אין לך דבר עומד לפניהם בענין לכתם לקבל את התורה כמאמר (שמות ג, יב) **בְּהוֹצִיאֲךָ אֶת הָעָם מִמִּצְרַיִם תַּעַבְדוּן אֶת הָאֱ-לֹהִים** וכו'. וכל הניסים והשתנות הטבע שנעשה אינו השתנות כי אם תחילת הבריאה היה על דעת כן:

והנה ענין קריעת ים סוף היה נכלל בתנאי השני שהיה עם המים שתראה היבשה וכו', וענין שוב המים לפנות בוקר היה נכלל בתנאי הראשון עם המים בתחילת בריאתם כסדר התפשטותם. ולכן מתחלה בשעת קריעת ים סוף דבר פשוט היא שיקרע לפני ישראל שהרי הוא סדר הבריאה מתחילה ואינו השתנות, וזהו **מַה תִּצְעַק אֵלָי דַּבֵּר אֶל בְּנֵי יִשְׂרָאֵל וְיִסָּעוּ**, משא"כ שישוב הים לפנות בוקר על המצרים כדרכו הראשון בהתפשטות היה נס שיחזור לתנאו הראשון בהתפשטות שהרי כל המים אחר שנתראה היבשה לא חזרו:

וזהו הענין **וַיַּרְא... כִּי טוֹב** שלא נאמר בשני בענין התפשטות המים, כדרך שאמרו רז"ל (מגילה י ע"ב) בקריעת ים סוף בקשו מלאכי השרת לומר שירה אמר להם הקב"ה מעשי ידי טובעים בים וכו', ואמירת השירה היא מאמר **כִּי טוֹב** שלא נאמרה בשני, ולא דברה תורה **בְּמֵתִים [רשעים] כְּמוֹ חֲלָלִים שֹׁכְבֵי קֶבֶר** (תהלים פח, ו) המה המצרים שטבעו בים שהרי **וּבַאֲבֹד רְשָׁעִים רִנָּה** (משלי יא, י) **וְאָשִׁירָה לַיהּ-וָה כִּי גָאֹה גָּאָה**, אבל על ישראל נאמר שהיו ישראל נדונים במים מטענות שר של מצרים הללו עובדי ע"ז והללו וכו' (עיין ילקוט שמות רלד, ובזוהר דלקמן). וזהו **וְלֹא קָרַב זֶה אֶל זֶה כָּל הַלָּיְלָה** המוזכר בזוה"ק (זח"ב קע ע"ב) במאמר שהמה המלאכים שקוראים זה אל זה לומר שירה לא קרבו לומר שירה כל הלילה שהיו ישראל עוברים את הים שהרי היו נדונים כנ"ל, וזהו שלא נאמר **כִּי טוֹב** בשני שלא נגמר בטובו ובמילואו כפרש"י ז"ל. **וַיָּשָׁב הַיָּם לִפְנוֹת בֹּקֶר** בוקרו של אברהם כמבואר בזה"ק (שם) שהמה חסדים והתפשטות, כי באמת הכל הם עולמות ומדות, רק כי בהשתלשל לזה העולם השפל החשך תכסה ארץ נקרא לילה אשר **בִּן לַיְלָה הָיָה** (יונה ד, י) והבוקר אור והחסדים והאנשים שולחו ועברו ליבשה וישב הים לפנות בוקר על מצרים, ואז אמרו שירה. שהרי **אָז יָשִׁיר** אחר שנגמר במילואו וטובו, וזהו **כִּי טוֹב** שהוכפל בשלישי שנגמר מלאכת המים, וענין הכפל כדרך כל השירות שהמה כפולים. או במלות כמו **כִּי גָאֹה גָּאָה** או כפל הענין במילות שונות וכולם לדבר אחד מתכונים והענין ידוע שהוא התגלות האחדות, וכן פרש"י ז"ל במקום אחר (שמות טו, א ברש"י ישן).

והנה אמת ואמונה היא שעמדה לאבותינו ולנו, בשכר אמונה נגאלו (ילקוט הושע תקי"ט) **וְצַדִּיק בֶּאֱמוּנָתוֹ יִחְיֶה** (חבקוק ב, ד), והוא העמוד הימיני שהתורה נשען עליו כל התורה כולה על רגל אחד שהוא המצב התחתון והוא העליון **סֻלָּם מֻצָּב אַרְצָה וְרֹאשׁוֹ מַגִּיעַ הַשָּׁמָיְמָה.** שהרי כל התורה כולה אמונתו ית' (עיי' זח"ג עג ע"ב) ואין אחר האמונה כלום, ותכלית הידיעה שאינו יודע (בחינת עולם יג. ע"ש). שהרי אינו מושג **וְהַחָכְמָה מֵאַיִן תִּמָּצֵא** (איוב כח, יב), ואינה נקנית כי אם בקבלת חכמה שהוא שומע מפי הרב שארז"ל, הקבלה הוא האמונה, הוא חכמה, והמבין דבר מתוך דבר הוא הנקרא בינה. נמצא שהראשית הוא החכמה והאמונה שמאמין בו ית' כי יד ה' היתה זאת ולא חשיד קוב"ה דעביד דינא בלא דינא (ברכות ה ע"ב עיי"ש) לכן שב עד המכהו **שָׁאֹג יִשְׁאַג עַל נָוֵהוּ** (ירמיה כה, ל), הרי הוא מוכרח להאמין באמונה זו איך התפשטותו ית' בכל הנבראים סיבותיהם ומאורעותיהם והוא ית' המחיה את הכל ואין דבר בלתו. אפילו בכל ד' יסודות המורכבים המחיה אותם הוא שם הוי"ה ברוך הוא וברוך שמו בארבע אותיותיו בהעלם גדול כידוע. וענין הפסדם הוא העדר החיות מאתם וכי זה כל האדם הרכבת יסודו גופו ונפשו רוחו ונשמתו אליו יאסוף, ובאסיפה בעלמא סגי אליו ית' לדבקה בו דבקות האמיתי. כי מה האדם שיבא אחר המלך לפנות את לבו לבטלה ליראת העונש ואבידת גופו ונפשו ועניני גיהנם ויראת חיצוניות אחרי אמונתו בחיות המחיה את הכל ובידו הכח והגבורה ומושל בכל כמאמר (ש"א ב, ו) **מוֹרִיד שְׁאוֹל וַיָּעַל**. אז יאמר אף אם יפסיד ויאבד לא יאבד כי אם מה שהוא העדר חיותו ית' אבל עיקר שורש החיות אשר מאתו ית' לעולם תעמוד וחי בהם, וא"כ אין לו בעולם כ"א לדבקה בו ית' וכבודו עליו יראה על ידי השתלשלות התורה והמצוה בעשותם באברי הגוף. **כִּי נֵר מִצְוָה** הוא הגשם **וְתוֹרָה אוֹר** המאור בתוכה ומחיה אותם ע"י האותיות, ושמותיו ית' המופשטים מכל תמונה, לא כמו שהוא נכתב הוא נקרא בפה (פסחים נ ע"א), אף כי התפשטות המחשבה הפושט צורה ולובש צורה מלמעלה ממנו בלי שום תמונה הנכתבת או נקראת כ"א שאינו מושג, והיה אם צעק יצעק לכל אשר תשאלנו נפשו ויבין את זאת כי גם זה הוא ענין שם הוי"ה המהוה את הארבע יסודות וכל הענין האמונה הנאמרת פה ועתה הנה הוא מתפלל ומתדבק בו ית' על אותיותיו הנ"ל, באמרי פיו והגיון לבו, וחיותו ומסירת נפשו לכבודו ית' שהרי זה חלקו מכל עמלו ומה לו עוד, ובאמת יכול לעשות השתנות בתפלתו אחרי היות ממשיל באמיתית לבו את כבודו ית' על הכל, ובכל ענין רצונו בכבודו ית' אין לך דבר שעומד נגדו, כי כן היתה תחלת הבריאה הכל לכבודו ית':

וכל ענין אמונה זו הכל תלוי בתחילת האמונה ביראת העונש וכו' ולהרגיל עצמו בזה, ואחר שיהיה זריז ורגיל בעבודה זו הכל כנ"ל להאמין בה' הנה כל ענין האמונה אחת היא עד שמגיע אל שורש האמונה כנ"ל שהיא התורה **וְהַחָכְמָה תְּחַיֶּה בְעָלֶיהָ** (קהלת ז, יב). וזהו (מכילתא בשלח יז ע"א) לא נתנה תורה אלא לאוכלי המן כי באמונה הנ"ל נכלל האמונה והבטחון להיותו מחיה את הכל ומושל בכל, **מוֹרִיד שְׁאוֹל וַיָּעַל**, ושם **בַּיָּם יָדוֹ וּבַנְּהָרוֹת יְמִינוֹ** (ע"פ תהלים פט, כו), וענין אוכלי המן הוא הבטחון שלא להותירו למחרתו כי מאן דיהיב חיי יהיב מזונא (עיין תענית ח ע"ב) וכל יום בעצמו הוא החיות והוא מזין לכולא ביה. והנה אמונה זו היא התורה הוראות והתגלות אלהותו ית' **וּמַלְכוּתוֹ בַּכֹּל מָשָׁלָה** ובוודאי לא נתנה תורה אלא לאוכלי המן שהם המאמינים ובוטחים כנ"ל. והיא הבנת מלת פרעה שהוא פרע ה' אחרונה שבשם הנקרא יראה, ומן היראה מתגלה אלהותו ית' כנ"ל:

וזהו **וַיְהִי בְּשַׁלַּח פַּרְעֹה אֶת הָעָם** שהיו משועבדים בגלות והתחילו לטהר ומן הראוי לבא לטהר להיות מסיעין לו כמאמר רז"ל (שהש"ר ה, ג) פתחו לי כחודה של מחט ואני אפתח לכם פתח מפולש שהעגלות וקרנות נכנסים בתוכה, והנה **וְלֹא נָחָם אֱלֹ-הִים דֶּרֶךְ אֶרֶץ פְּלִשְׁתִּים** שהוא דרך מפולש, והטעם **כִּי קָרוֹב הוּא** ועדיין לא הורגל בעבודה זו עד שמזדמן לו פעם ושתיים ותופס אומנתו להתחזק באמונתו שהיה לו בזמן השעבוד והיראה הראשונה בהיותו בגלות

מצרים וזהו שמזדמנים לו מלחמות וסבות הכל לחזקו ולנסותו אם יעמוד באמונתו, וזהו **כִּי אָמַר אֱלֹ־הִים פֶּן יִנָּחֵם הָעָם בִּרְאֹתָם מִלְחָמָה וְשָׁבוּ מִצְרָיְמָה** כפשט המדרש הנ"ל ושהוא מדתם ואמונתם שהחזיקו במצרים לצעוק אל ה':

או יאמר לפרש מלת **פַּ"רְעֹה** שהוא היצה"ר הנקרא **עֹ"רֶף**, כידוע מענין אמרם ז"ל הרשעים מלאים חרטות כשהיצה"ר מניחם ואינו מסיתם ומתחרטים מאוד וכמדומים הם שלבם חלל בקרבם ובטל היצה"ר מאתם כמאמר רז"ל (סנהדרין כב ע"א) כד חסרי לגנבא נפשיה לשלמא נקוט, ולכן המה מתמיהים על שאינם מגיעים למדרגה יותר גדולה ובאמת שעדיין לא נצחו את היצה"ר ובעת מלחמה קרובים לשוב, וזהו **בְּשַׁלַּח פַּרְעֹה** שהוא היצה"ר **אֶת הָעָם** שהם המדות המשועבדים, שאין לתמוה ש**לֹא נָחָם אֱלֹ־הִים דֶּרֶךְ אֶרֶץ פְּלִשְׁתִּים** לשון פתח מפולש כנ"ל, **כִּי אָמַר אֱלֹ־הִים פֶּן יִנָּחֵם הָעָם בִּרְאֹתָם מִלְחָמָה**. עד אחר ההרגל באמונה הנזכר והנקבע בלבו כיתד בל ימוט, ההרגל הוא לשון רגל, שפוסע והולך מעט מעט עד שמגיע לתכלית המבוקש, ואחרי אשר דרך אמונה בחר לקבוע בלבו אין לך דבר שעומד כנגדו. וזהו **מַה תִּצְעַק אֵלָי דַּבֵּר אֶל בְּנֵי יִשְׂרָאֵל וְיִסָּעוּ** כפרש"י כנ"ל אין להם אלא ליסע, וענין הנסיעה שלא לעמוד על מקום אחד אלא לילך באמונתו מכאן ואילך אפילו בים, כי מה הוא ענין הים להויותו או מה ענין יראתם ואם יאבדו ויטבעו מה הוא ענין אבדתם שהרי חיותו ית' הוא נצחיות. ואחרי אשר האמינו בה' ויצעקו אליו א"כ כל ענין האמונה אחת הוא, יְהֹ־וָה **מֵמִית וּמְחַיֶּה מוֹרִיד שְׁאוֹל וַיָּעַל** (ש"א ב, ו), שהרי אפשר להגיע באמונה זו מעומקא דלבא למעלה מן המדות והעולם להתקשר בחכמה שהוא אמונה, להיות קודם הבריאה:

וזהו דברי רש"י ז"ל כדאי הוא האמונה שהאמינו בי לקרוע להם הים, אחרי היותם מחזיקים ודבקים באמונה, שהוא התורה שבה נבהא העולם, ואם בריאה נברא מחדש שהרי האמונה הוא מושל בכל. ולכן נחשון ושבט יהודה שקפצו תחלה בים על אמונתו ית' אמרו רז"ל (סוטה לז ע"א) שבשביל זה זכו למלכות בית דוד **וּמַלְכוּתוֹ בַּכֹּל מָשָׁלָה** אפילו על ישראל המושלים בכל כמבואר במדרש (ילקוט תהלים תשצ"ט) היתה יהודה לקדשו ישראל ממשלותיו של יהודה מפני ששמע יהודה דבר קדשו ית' לכנוס בים תחלה:

(וכן) [וכל] ענין האמונה התחלתה הוא הצעקה ויראת ההפסד והתחתונה שהוא נוקבא, ומזה נסתעף השירה, לכן נאמר לשון נקבה **הַשִּׁירָה הַזֹּאת**. והנה שר לא נאמר אלא **יָשִׁיר** ופרש"י ז"ל (טו, א) שעלה בלבו שישיר, לכן ניתוסף היו"ד שהוא הלב שהוא המחשבה והאמונה. השרשית שהיא ה**תּוֹרָה אוֹר טַל אוֹרֹת טַלֶּךָ** (ע"פ ישעיה כו, יט) להחיות מתים וכל השתנות. וזהו מכאן לתחיית המתים מן התורה, התורה דווקא, שהיא האמונה:

[ו]. פרשת אחרי מות

(חיות העבירה ונפש הבהמי נכללים בנפש החיוני המגדל הזן והמתאוה)

נשאל מאמר (אבות ג, ב) **הֱוֵי מִתְפַּלֵּל בִּשְׁלוֹמָהּ שֶׁל מַלְכוּת** [שאלמלא מוראה איש את רעהו חיים בלעו]:

פתח הרב פסוק **אַחֲרֵי מוֹת שְׁנֵי בְּנֵי אַהֲרֹן בְּקָרְבָתָם לִפְנֵי יְהֹ־וָה** ופרש"י ז"ל משל לרופא וכו' זה זרזו יותר מן הראשון. ואמר הענין על דרך מאמר **עֲקַבְיָא בֶּן מַהֲלַלְאֵל** (אבות ג, א) **הִסְתַּכֵּל בִּשְׁלֹשָׁה דְבָרִים וְאֵין אַתָּה בָא לִידֵי עֲבֵרָה. דַּע, מֵאַיִן בָּאתָ מִטִּפָּה סְרוּחָה** וכו'. והוא דקדוק העולם על שכפל דבריו. ותשובתם שתחלת דבריו הם להזכיר את האדם שהוא אורח בעולם הזה שכן דרך השאלה לאורח בתחילת ראותו אחר נתינת שלום מאין בא ולאן הולך ומה ענינו והצטרכותו, אח"כ פירש לא די שהוא אורח אלא שכל ענינו הוא מאוס ונמאס מתחלת בואו עד שובו לאפרו ובין כך וכך מכניס ראשו בין הרים גדולים אשר עתיד ליתן את הדין לפני מלך מלכי המלכים הקב"ה:

אבל אפשר להבין מכפל דבריו וסדרם מוסר השכל כאשר מבטן מי יצא ומלתא אלבישייהו יקירא, שהנה עקביא בן מהללאל ארז"ל (עדיות פ"ה מ"ו) **שֶׁאֵין עֲזָרָה נִנְעֶלֶת בִּפְנֵי כָל אָדָם מִיִּשְׂרָאֵל**

בְּחָכְמָה וּבְיִרְאַת חֵטְא כַּעֲקַבְיָא בֶּן מַהֲלַלְאֵל. שהנה ענין יראת חטא הוא היראה מן החטא עצמו יותר מן העונש הבא עבורו כמבואר כמה פעמים שהעונשין המה רפואת הנפש ומירוקה מרעת החטא ובודאי יש לירא ולפחד מן המכה עצמה יותר מן הרפואה. וכן הוא מובן **לְכָל הָאָדָם וְהַחַי יִתֵּן אֶל לִבּוֹ** (ע"פ קהלת ז, ב) אחרי שעיקר האדם הוא הפנימית וחיותו והגוף הוא בשר האדם ולבושו כנראה שאחרי הפרדו החיות הגוף הוא פגר מובס (עיין לעיל פר' תצוה), ומכללו אתה שומע שבכל מקום שאדם מחשב ומהרהר ונותן נפשו עינו ולבו עליו שם הוא ועל שמו נקרא. הרי שאם מחשב בעבירה הרי הוא בעצמו הקליפה ורוח הטומאה המחיה אותה והשורה עליה, כארז"ל (סוטה ג ע"א) אין אדם עובר עבירה אלא אם כן נכנס בו רוח שטות, שתיכף בהפרד הקדושה ויראת שמים מאתו חלה עליו רוח הטומאה, כידוע שאין שום דבר ריק בעולם, אם אינו מקרי טהור הרי טמא טמא יקרא מן המזיקין ונגעי בני אדם (עיין זח"ג נא ע"ב ולעיל במאמר שבת שבתוך פסח). שהרי אי אפשר לשום גוף וחומר בלתי הצורה המצייר אותו ומחייהו, והחיות שבתוך העבירה לא נתנה כי אם לנסות בהם בני אדם הצדיקים בכל בריאת העולמות שנבראו בשביל הצדיקים, ומהו חיות העבירה וצורתה הרי היא אפשרית עשותה והנאתה. וא"כ האדם בעשותו אותה הרי הוא העבירה בעצמה או בחשבו שם הרי הוא חיות העבירה והנגע בעצמה מנגעי בני אדם שנתהפך מן הקדש לחול מטהור טמא:

והנה אמתת ענין התהוות הקליפות והטומאה עיקר שורשם מתחילת הבריאה מהכרח הצמצום והסתלקות התפשטות קדושת א"ס ומן הצמצום נתחדש דבר מעתה אם בריאה יברא. וכן דרך כל התחדשות תצמחנה כצמיחת הצמח מן הגרעין ובריאת האפרוח מן הביצה, שאי אפשר להתחיל התחדשות ההשתנות מצורה הראשונה אל החדשה עד שתפסד צורה הראשונה ותלך לה מכל ועיקר שהגרעין מוכרח להיות תחלה כלה ונפסד לגמרי וכן הביצה, ואח"כ על השארות חומר ההיולי שאפשר להשתנות חל עליו צורה החדשה בבריאת האפרוח והצמיחה. ובשעה שהדבר בטל משני הצורות נקרא **אַיִן** שהוא ענין הצמצום שהיא **וְהַחָכְמָה מֵאַיִן תִּמָּצֵא** (איוב כח,יב) כתחלת סדר הבריאה, שאי אפשר לשום התגלות חדש כי אם בחזירתו אל **הָאַיִן** תחלה, כמבואר במקום אחר (פרשת וישב ופרשת ויגש א') בענין. יכולת האדם לעשות השתנות ונסים בהגיעו אל השפלות והביטול **וְהָאַיִן** שהוא **הַחָכְמָה**:

וכן דרך האדם **לַהַט הַחֶרֶב הַמִּתְהַפֶּכֶת** ח"ו ואיתעביד מקודש חול ומטהור טמא וקליפה מזיק נגעי בני אדם, כי בהסתלק הקדושה ויראת שמים מאתו ואחרי צמצום הקדושה והתפשטותה משתנה ונעשה רוח הטומאה מזיק וקליפה וגופו נעשה גוף להקליפות. והרי הוא מזיק עם גוף שהוא יותר קשה ומגושם משאר מזיקין וקליפות רוחניות. וזהו יראת חטא שמשתנה להעשות חטא עצמו שהיא המכה היותר קשה מן העונש שהוא הרפואה:

והנה יראת חטא זה מסתעף מן החכמה מי שהוא חכם שמתבטל ונעשה אין נגד חיות הקודש להעשות בכל יום בריאה חדשה כמאמר (תהילים ב, ז) **בְּנִי אַתָּה אֲנִי הַיּוֹם יְלִדְתִּיךָ**, לכן מתירא מן החטא בעצמו אחרי ידיעתו שאחרי הביטול והסתלקות צורה הראשונה משתנה ולכן מתירא. וזהו ארז"ל על עקביא בן מהללאל שהיה לו מדריגת החכמה ויראת חטא שאחד נמשך מחברתה והן הם דבריו בכאן וכפל דבריו, שמתחילה הפירוש כפשוטו ואח"כ הסביר הענין שבא **מִטִּפָּה סְרוּחָה** שהוא אחרי הפסד וכליון בטול כח הטפה להעשות בריה כנודע, **וּלְאָן אַתָּה הוֹלֵךְ** שהוא אין השני להשתנות מבריה טהורה לטמאה וקליפה שהוא רמה ותולעה. והחילוק שבין הביטול והאין הראשון לאין השני שהמשתנה מקדושה לקליפה אינו נקרא אי"ן ביו"ד כי אם א"ן בלא יו"ד שהוא שקל הקודש, אבל מכניס ניצוצי חיות האל"ף דרך התפשטות נו"ן פשוטה אל המותרות וקליפה:

ואמרו **וְאֵין אַתָּה בָא לִידֵי עֲבֵרָה** כי ידים נקרא אהבה ויראה, והנה אית יראה ואית יראת העונש שהם העונשין והמיתה כארז"ל (שבת נה ע"א) שאין מיתה בלא חטא,

ויראה זו הנקרא יראה חיצונית נוהגת בכל באי עולם אפילו באומות העולם כמאמר (שמות ט, כ) **הַיָּרֵא אֶת דְּבַר יְהֹ-וָה מֵעַבְדֵי פַּרְעֹה** שהיא יראת עונש שהיא יראת הפסד עצמו. אבל עיקר היראה מפני **עִקָּרָא וְשָׁרְשָׁא דְּכֹל עָלְמִין** (זח"א יא ע"ב) היא הנקרא **וּמַלְכוּתוֹ בַּכֹּל מָשָׁלָה** (תהילים קג, יט) שכל היראות מסתעפין ממנה שהם העונשין יסורים ומיתה הממרקים חלאת זוהמת הנפשות כי רפאות הוא ומזור ותחבושת הנפשות מכל מכה וכל חלי:

והנה לאדם שטוב לפני האלהים אינו רע ומר עליו יראת החיצונים כארז"ל (ב"ר ט, יב עיי"ש) **וְהִנֵּה טוֹב מְאֹד** זה המות, כמבואר בזהר (ח"ב קמט ע"ב) כי הרבה פעמים אדם שב אל עושהו מפני יראה זו לכן טוב הוא מאוד. ואפילו לגדולי הצדיקים לאו כל עתים שוים שלפעמים אינו יכול להגיע ליראה אמתית כי אם ע"י התחלת היראה חיצונית לדמות בנפשו ואחרי שכל היראות הם משורש אחד ממנה מגיע מעלה מעלה וטועם נעימת היראה והתלהבות אליו יתברך. ולכן הצדיקים מודים ומברכים אותו יתברך על כל מה שברא מן העונשין והיסורין, כי אם מי שלא ראה מאורות מימיו שאין לו כי אם יראה חיצונית ויירא מהפסד גופו רע עליו המעשה יסורים והמיתה, אבל באמת היא הנקראת **שְׁלוֹמֹה שֶׁל מַלְכוּת** כי הוא **עֹשֶׂה שָׁלוֹם בִּמְרוֹמָיו** (איוב כה, ב) לשוב לפניו כנזכר וגם **שָׁלוֹם שָׁלוֹם לָרָחוֹק וְלַקָּרוֹב** (ישעיה נז, יט) היא הנותנת חיים ורפואה כנזכר, לכן עכ"פ ראוי לכל אדם שלא לסור מאחרי עיניו יראה זו שאם יזכה יבחין בין מלכות האמתי ובינה ואם לאו ח"ו על כל פנים יסור מרע ויעשה טוב מפני היראה:

וזהו **הֱוֵי מִתְפַּלֵּל בִּשְׁלוֹמָהּ שֶׁל מַלְכוּת** שהוא להתדבק ביראה זו עכ"פ, **שֶׁאִלְמָלֵא מוֹרָאָהּ, אִישׁ אֶת רֵעֵהוּ חַיִּים בְּלָעוֹ** כי הנשמה נקרא ריע כמאמר (משלי כז, י) **רֵעֲךָ וְרֵעַ אָבִיךָ** וכו' ובעודו בחיים יבלעוהו הקליפות כדברינו לעיל שלא יתהווה קליפה ומזיק כמותה בהמשכו אחריהם. כי החילוק הוא שבין נפש אדם השכלי ונפש הבהמי הוא כי נפש הבהמי הוא נפש החיוני והמגדל והזן והמתאוה כולם לא נבראו כי אם לצורך הגוף שהמה צורת וחיות הגוף, וזה מאמר (קהלת ג, כא) **וְרוּחַ הַבְּהֵמָה הַיֹּרֶדֶת הִיא לְמַטָּה** וע"י עליית הגוף המה מתעלים. משא"כ נפש האדם השכלי לא נברא בשביל הגוף אדרבא הגוף וכל הנפשות הבהמיים נבראו בשביל הנפש השכלי ולפעול על ידיהם ולהמשיך אחריהם ולעלות עמה, וא"כ תיכף בהמשיך האדם נפשו השכלי להנאת הגוף הרי הוא נעשה נפש הבהמי והרי הוא בהמה וזהו **חַיִּים בְּלָעוֹ** שמבליע החיות בתוכם. ומעתה הנה מתהוים כל הצמצומים (הגבורות עונשין וחסדים ע"ד הצמצום הראשון שלא היה שום אפשרות הבריאה כי אם ע"י צמצום וכן כל הצמצום והגבורות עונשין ומיתה מגוף ונפש הכל חסד וטוב **שֶׁאִלְמָלֵא מוֹרָאָהּ, אִישׁ אֶת רֵעֵהוּ חַיִּים בְּלָעוֹ** כנזכר וע"י מתקרב לפני ה':

וזהו **אַחֲרֵי מוֹת שְׁנֵי בְּנֵי אַהֲרֹן** שכל שנוי המיתות הם בני אהרן שהוא חסד (זח"א רס"ו ע"ב) **בְּקָרְבָתָם לִפְנֵי יְהֹ-וָה**, וזהו פרש"י ז"ל משל לרופא וכו' שכל מה שזרז השני שלא ימות כדרך שמת פלוני הוא היותר טוב ושלום **וּשְׁלוֹמָהּ שֶׁל מַלְכוּת** הוא יחוד קוב"ה ושכינתיה כנודע. וזהו ארז"ל (זח"ב קנה ע"ב) **אֵין הַתּוֹרָה מִתְקַיֶּימֶת אֶלָּא בְּמִי שֶׁמֵּמִית עַצְמוֹ בְּאֹהֶל** שמזכיר לעצמו כל המיתות ומדמה בעצמו אותם לחזק היראה והתורה. וידוע שקיום התורה נקרא **נֶצַח וָהוֹד בְּנֵי אַהֲרֹן בְּקָרְבָתָם לִפְנֵי יְהֹ-וָה וַיָּמֻתוּ** (תקו"ז ת' ע') כמבואר על פסוק (שמות א, טז) **וּרְאִיתֶן עַל הָאָבְנָיִם** ארז"ל (סוטה יא ע"ב) שמתקשים הירכים כאבנים שהוא מיתתם לקיום הולד. ופי' **וַיְדַבֵּר יְהֹ-וָה אֶל מֹשֶׁה** הוא השכל **אַחֲרֵי מוֹת שְׁנֵי בְּנֵי אַהֲרֹן** שהוא אחרי שהמית עצמו באוהל כנ"ל **בְּקָרְבָתָם לִפְנֵי יְהֹ-וָה** שהוא תורה שבכתב כנודע:

[י"א]. פרשת בהר

(האדם סוף מעשה במחשבה תחילה)

נשאל מאמ[ר] (מו"ק ה ע"א) כל השם אורחותיו בעוה"ז זוכה ורואה בישועתו של הקב"ה שנאמר (תהילים נ, כג) **וְשָׂם דֶּרֶךְ אַרְאֶנּוּ בְּיֵשַׁע אֱלֹהִים:**

פתח בדברי רש"י ז"ל (כה, א) מה ענין שמיטה להר סיני אלא מה אלו

נאמרו כללותיהן ופרטותיהן מסיני אף כל וכו'. והענין מאמר רז"ל (אבות ה, א-ב) בעשרה מאמרות נברא העולם והלא במאמר אחד יכול וכו' וליתן שכר טוב וכו', עשרה דורות מאדם וכו' עשרה דורות מנח עד אברהם וכו' וקבל שכר כולם. הנה תמיהת העולם על בעשרה מאמרות והלא במאמר אחד יכול אלא וכו' וכי הקב"ה בטרוניא בא עם בריותיו אחר שהיה יכול לברא במאמר אחד למה ברא בעשרה מאמרות כדי להפרע עונש עשרה מאמרות:

אבל באמת ענין העשרה מאמרות הם י' פעמים ויאמר ויאמר הכתובים בסדר הבריאה אשר בכל ויאמר היה בריאה פרטית כידוע לנו מענינים הידועים **וְהַנִּגְלֹת לָנוּ** כי **הַנִּסְתָּרֹת לַיהֹ-וָה אֱ-לֹהֵינוּ** (ע"פ דברים כט, כח) אבל המבואר בספר התורה (פר' בראשית) **וַיֹּאמֶר... יְהִי אוֹר וַיֹּאמֶר...יְהִי רָקִיעַ** וכן כולם בריאת שמים וארץ ומקוה מים ובהמות ועופות ואחרי כולם **וַיֹּאמֶר** נעשה אדם הכלול מעליונים ותחתונים כפרש"י ז"ל (שם ב, ז).

והנה ארז"ל (קידושין פב. עיי"ש) סוף מעשה במחשבה תחילה שכולם לא נבראו אלא בשביל האדם וכן אמרו ז"ל (ברכות ו ע"ב) כל העולם כולו לא נברא אלא בשביל זה, לכן כל העולם כולו מתנהג ע"י האדם כמאמר (בראשית א, כח) **וּרְדוּ בִּדְגַת הַיָּם** וכו'. וכמאמר דוד המלך ע"ה (תהילים ח, ז) **תַּמְשִׁילֵהוּ בְּמַעֲשֵׂי יָדֶיךָ כֹּל שַׁתָּה תַחַת רַגְלָיו** וכו'. וכענין התחתונים כן הוא בעולמות העליונים שנבראו ואדם על כולם שהרי ארז"ל (ב"ר י, ז) אין לך עשב מלמטה שאין לו מלאך מלמעלה וכו' ואומר לו גדל ואחרי היות האדם מושל בכל מלמטה כן הוא מושל על המלאכים והממונים עליהם והעולמות העליונים שנבראו בשבילו שהרי הוא מלך על כולם (עיין זח"ג י ע"א). ובהא **סָלְקֵי** ובהא **נָחֲתֵי** העולמות וכל הנבראים ע"י רוח האדם העולה מעלה מעלה לדבקה בו יתברך, או רוח האדם ובהמה היורד מטה מטה ח"ו, כן ממשיך העולמות וכל הנבראים אתו אחרי שכולם כלולים בו. כידוע מנפש הבהמית שבאדם שהיא נפש המתאוה וכן כל הנבראים כולם. ואם נמשך האדם אחרי נפש הבהמית שלו הרי הוא בהמה בצורת אדם, ובדבר שקלקל צריך שיתקן בו כמבואר בקרבן סוטה היא עשתה מעשה בהמה קרבנה מאכל בהמה (סוטה יד ע"א), וכן ענין כל הקרבנות **מִן-הַבְּהֵמָה, מִן-הַבָּקָר וּמִן-הַצֹּאן** (ויקרא א, ב) מלבד **הַנִּסְתָּרֹת לַיהֹ-וָה אֱ-לֹהֵינוּ** הוא עניינו שיתקן מעשה בהמית שלו וישוב אל ה' כאשר יורו אותו הכהנים מקריבי הקרבן, ועל ידו מתעלים כל הנבראים שלמטה מטה ומעלה מעלה הנוגעים במקום קלקלתו שהורידם מתחלה אל עומק הקליפות ע"י מעשיו הרעים:

ועל דרך זה כל מעשי האדם דרכיו ומחשבותיו בעוה"ז אשר בכל עת ובכל שעה ובכל רגע כחֵץ **יוֹמָם יְצַוֶּה יְהֹ-וָה חַסְדּוֹ** (תהילים מב, ט) או כל מדה ומדה שמתעורר עליו וכהתעוררות מדותיו כן הוא התעוררות העליונים כמאמר (עיין זח"א פז ע"ב) **אַבְרָהָם אִתְעַר** [חסד] **לְעָלְמָא** שקראו הכתוב (ישעיה מא, ח) **אַבְרָהָם אֹהֲבִי** וכן כל הצדיקים במדותיהם. ולכל אשר יעבור עליו מדה רעה או מחשבה זרה מסתכל הוא מה זה ועל מה זה ויירא בושת מלפניו יתברך עד שמתבטל ומתעלה ע"י חיות הקודש **הַשֹּׁכֵן אִתָּם בְּתוֹךְ טֻמְאֹתָם** ומאמרו יתברך אשר במאמרו ברא אותו הדבר והוא חיותו טוב הגנוז בתוכו, וע"י הסתכלותו בזה מתדבק אליו יתברך ע"י אותו החיות. וע"י עליתו מתעלה ג"כ אותה הבריאה שבאה לו במחשבתו ומדותיו וכן [כל] העולמות העליונים:

וזהו ליתן שכר טוב לצדיקים שהוא הטוב הגנוז בגוה המחיה אותה הבריאה שהוא הויאמר שנברא על ידו כי לשון אמירה הוא הנהגה וחיות פנימי כארז"ל (עי' זח"ב יז ע"א) אמירה בלב וכמאמר (שמות כד, א) **וְאֶל מֹשֶׁה אָמַר עֲלֵה אֶל יְהֹ-וָה** שהרי האומר הוא ג"כ ה' אבל הוא מדריגה נסתרת כמבואר בזהר (ח"ב קכה ע"ב). ולהיות האדם כלול מכל הנבראים הרי הוא עולם קטן (עיין ת"ז תיקון ע' קל ע"ב) ובודאי היה יכול להבראות במאמר אחד אבל ברא הקב"ה עשרה מאמרות כל מאמר בריאה פרטית והאדם אחרון מכולם הכולל כולם כדי לקבל שכר כולם בעלותו כנ"ל. וכן הרשעים כמאמר רז"ל (פסחים מט ע"ב) עם הארץ אסור לאכול בשר

כי מה מועיל שנעשה מבשר הבהמה גופו ובשרו והרי הוא ג"כ מעשה בהמה אחרת ואדרבה מחליף מבהמה טהורה לטמאה, שכל הטמאים ג"כ נכללים באדם אחרי היותו בעל בחירה ועתה באכילתו הנה הוא מחליף פרה בחמור. אבל זה כל האדם שצריך לשקול בפלס מאזני מדותיו שבודאי הם מסתעפים מן הבריאות שקדמוהו ובהתדבקו אליו יתברך ע"י החיות והאמירה של אותה הבריאה הוא מתבטל ומזדכך וזוכה לראות אותו האור של ששת ימי בראשית שנגנז לצדיקים שהוא האור של ויאמר שהוא חיות של אותה הבריאה:

וזהו כל השם אורחותיו בעוה"ז זוכה ורואה וכו' וכן בכל מדה ומדה שמתעורר עליו עד שמקבל שכר כולם וכן נח ואברהם קבלו שכר כולם. כללא דמילתא שבכל סוף דבר נכללים כל הסדר שקדמוהו והוא תכלית הכל והכל כאין בטל ומבוטל נגדו ונגרר אחריו וזהו ענין השמטה שכל הששה שנים נכללים בשביעית ומתבטלים נגדה לכן כל הקנינים מתבטלים ויוצאים לחירות, והכל מסיני שהוא הביטול והאין כי ענין סיני הוא הענוה והאין כידוע שגימטריא עין שהוא סוף חכמה שהוא האין וההסתכלות ומשביעית נלמד על כל המצות שמתעלים ע"י סוף המעשה מסיני שהוא הביטול והאין וזהו (אבות א, א) משה קבל תורה מסיני:

במדבר

[י"ב]. פרשת שלח לך

(התורה היא רוחנית למעלה מן המדות, וכן ארץ ישראל ועולם הבא):

בפסוק **שְׁלַח לְךָ** פרש"י ז"ל שהקב"ה לא הסכים רק שלא מיחה (בהם) [בו] ואמר אם תרצה שלח. והענין הוא על דרך שאמרו רז"ל (ברכות ה ע"א) שלש מתנות טובות נתן הקב"ה לישראל וכולן ע"י יסורים תורה וארץ ישראל ועוה"ב ודרשו הכל מהכתוב. הענין הוא ידוע ארז"ל (זח"א ה ע"א) באורייתא ברא קוב"ה עלמא והם אותיות התורה כידוע. ומבואר בספר יצירה (פ"ב מ"ג) וקבען בפה, שהאותיות נקבעו בקביעות באדם בפה, ובהברת האותיות מעורר כל העולמות שהם מן המדות ולמטה שהם התחלת העולמות והתגלותם ע"ד (תהילים פט, ג) **עוֹלָם חֶסֶד יִבָּנֶה**, ואין לך שום מבוקש שיהיה למעלה מן המדות רק צעקה מוזכר בזוהר (זי"ב יט ע"ב) עומק רום שהיא למעלה למעלה מפני שהיא מעומקא דלבא שא"א להתלבש באותיות:

והנה ידוע אמיתת וטבע הנבראים למשוך אחר שרשו ובתר עיקרא גרירא, כדרך הדומם להצמיח ולעלות יותר ממדריגתו ודרך הצומח לגדל בכדי לכנוס בחי וחי במדבר הגם שאין יודעים מאומה אך נטבעים בטבע. וא"כ בוודאי מן הראוי בהזכיר אותיות התורה שבהם נברא עלמא להתמשך אל שרשו שהוא התורה שהיא היתה אלפים שנה קודם שנברא העולם (ב"ר ח, ב) שהם המדות, והוא התפשטות כל הגשמיות מעיקרו שאין לך דבר שיהיה בלא מדות והוא בהעמיד הגוף מלמטה והחיות עולה למעלה. ופירוד החיות מן הגוף עד ביטול ההרגש שאין לך יסורים קשים מהם כידוע מהחוקרים שכל יסורי הגוף מכח הלב וכל דבר יסורים הם פירוד הדביקות וכן דרך וענין כל החולשות ר"ל כידוע. מענין פירוד הנשמה מן הגוף שהיא מן ה**שִּׁבְעָה דִינִין** ם כידוע (זח"ב קצט ע"ב), אם אמנם בנידון דידן אין הפירוד לעולם מפני שנשאר הרשימה כידוע מדרך הרוחניות והסתלקותם, אעפ"כ מובן גודל היסורים עד שהגוף נשאר מעמד בלי שום חיות כידוע מהנביאים וכתובים מדניאל (ח, כז) **וְנֶהֱיֵיתִי** שהיו חולים ממש בביטול כל ההרגשות:

והנה הוציאו רז"ל מן הכתוב (תהילים צד, יב) **אַשְׁרֵי הַגֶּבֶר אֲשֶׁר תְּיַסְּרֶנּוּ יָּ-הּ וּמִתּוֹרָתְךָ תְלַמְּדֶנּוּ**, ואפשר לפרש בכמה ענינים אחד ידוע הוא כי **יָּ-הּ** הוא חצי השם וכל הפגמים של אדם הוא בהפריד אותיות ה' כידוע ענינו מהו (זוח"ג רכה ע"א). והנה יש אנשים עבי הגופים שאינם מתיסרים כ"א בהכאה וביטוש על דרך (משלי יז, י) **תֵּחַת גְּעָרָה בְמֵבִין מֵהַכּוֹת כְּסִיל מֵאָה**, כי המבין מתייסר בדברים כמאמר (שם כט, יט) **בִּדְבָרִים לֹא יִוָּסֶר עָבֶד** שהוא עב. משא"כ בן חורין שהוא בעל תורה הנקרא חרות על הלוחות ודרשו רז"ל (אבות ו, ג)

חירות כידוע שהוא עלמא דחירות, שהוא המבין וחכם כידוע שהם אלפים שנה שהוא למעלה מן המדות, יוסר בדברים שהן אותיות כשמתמשכין אל שרשם שהיא התורה. והנה דרשו רז"ל (ברכות ה ע"א) בתיבות **וּמִתּוֹרָתְךָ תְלַמְּדֶנּוּ** בק"ו משן ועין שאדם יוצא בהם לחירות יסורין שממרקין כל גופו של אדם, והמירוק הוא הזדככות החומר וביטול הרע לגמרי שהיה מעורב טוב ברע בכל המדות ולא ישוב עוד כשהיה כמו שן ועין שאינן חוזרות, ובזה מתורץ קושית העולם על היסורים שהגוף חוזר לאיתנו. והנה אדם שהוא מבין מתיסר בדברים בהשיגו פירוד אותיות ה' על ידו ח"ו וזהו **אַשְׁרֵי הַגֶּבֶר אֲשֶׁר תְּיַסְּרֶנּוּ יָ-הּ** פירוש החכמה ובינה שלו שהם **יָ-הּ** וזהו **וּמִתּוֹרָתְךָ תְלַמְּדֶנּוּ** שהן הן גופי תורה:

ועל דרך זה הוא מתנת ארץ ישראל על ידי יסורים, אבל צריך מעט ביאור הנה ידוע מענין המן שהוא לחם מן השמים שהוא במדרגה למעלה מן הארץ כידוע שהוא רוחני ולכאורה קשה האיך אפשר למעול מעל בה' להתאוות תאוה ובהיות מזון רוחני כזה שהוא מופשט מהרע. אבל הענין הוא ידוע מאמר הזוהר (ח"ג קנב ע"א) אפילו מלאך כשרוצה להתראות בזה העולם צריך להתלבש במלבושי עולם הזה, וכן דרך כל הרוחנים הפשוטים שמשתנין בירידתן על אופן ודרך הכלי שמתלבשים בו כידוע ממשל המים שמשתנין להיות כצורת הכלי אם עגולה או מרובעת. ולכן אפילו הרוחני היותר פשוט ברדתו וכניסתו באדם משתנה אל מה שהוא אדם אם טוב ואם רע ומתגשם והמן היה מתגשם, הכל לפי מה שהוא אדם, והנה באדם בליעל היה הרוחניות פועל הרע ביותר מפני שהרבה חיות רוחני ודק בקליפה והאדם בליעל מתגשם ביותר ומתגשם יותר ויותר:

והנה כוונת השי"ת היתה בנתינת ארץ ישראל לישראל הוא לזונם ממזון א"י שהוא במעלת המן שהוא **לִמְטַר הַשָּׁמַיִם תִּשְׁתֶּה מָּיִם** (דברים יא, יא) שהוא הקב"ה בעצמו ולא ע"י שום שר וכמבואר בספר חסד לאברהם (מעין שלישי נהר כא) אשר לכן נפסק המן **בְּאָכְלָם מֵעֲבוּר הָאָרֶץ** מפני שלא היה מצטרך להם כי ענין אחד הוא. והנה כבר הקדמנו שהכל לפי מה שהוא אדם וחלילה אפשר להתגשם יותר כנזכר, כי הכל תלוי בהכנה והזמנה מילתא היא לשם מה שהוא אוכל אם להתמרק מתמרק ביותר ע"י הרוחני היותר דק ואם להתגשם מתגשם ביותר. וכמאמר (נזיר כג ע"א) שנים שאכלו פסחיהם שארז"ל עליהם נאמר (הושע יד, י) **וְצַדִּקִים יֵלְכוּ בָם וּפֹשְׁעִים יִכָּשְׁלוּ** בם. והנה אם כוונת האדם להתמרק כל מגמתו והסתכלותו הוא על כל החיות הרוחני שבתוכו משא"כ אם כוונתו לתאוותו כל מגמתו והסתכלותו על הטעם וגשמיות התאוה שממנו לכן אמר השי"ת חייך אני נותן להם מקום לטעות בוודאי שהרי הבחירה נתנה וכל הרוצה לטמא פותחין לו (שבת קד ע"א):

ובדרך זה אפשר לפרש פירוש ארז"ל (כתובות עה ע"א) על פסוק (תהילים פז, ה) **וּלְצִיּוֹן יֵאָמַר אִישׁ וְאִישׁ יֻלַּד בָּהּ**, אחד הנולד **בָּהּ** ואחד המצפה לראותה, שהוא ארז"ל (ברכות לד ע"ב) במקום שבעלי תשובה עומדים צדיקים גמורים אין יכולים לעמוד. כמבואר בהרמב"ם ז"ל שחרטת בעל תשובה צריך להיות על כל פנים באופן זה שמתחרט על היותו בעולם כלל ומחליט באמתות הלב כי טוב יותר שלא יהיה בעולם מלעשות רע, והוא מסירת נפש הגמור שהיא למעלה מהמדות. וזהו **וּלְצִיּוֹן** שהם הצדיקים המצויינים כידוע כל אחד ואחד באותיות שנאמר (קהלת ה, ז) **גָבֹהַּ מֵעַל גָּבֹהַּ** וכו' **יֵאָמַר אִישׁ וְאִישׁ**, שהוא אחד צדיק גמור ואחד בעל תשובה שהוא פירוש אחד המצפה לראותה ואחד הנולד בה, שאפילו צדיק גמור אינו יכול להעלות כ"א על ידי הפקרות ומסירות נפש ובוודאי ממרקין כל גופו. והכל אחד תורה וא"י וחיי עוה"ב שאי אפשר להיות שום נקודה גשמיות כגרגיר חרדל כי שלשתן למעלה מן המדות הם:

י"ג]. פרשת קרח

התכללות עם השכינה דרך תבטלות אליו יתברך)

רש"י ז"ל **וַיִּקַּח קֹרַח** שלקח מקח ע לעצמו, הנה ארז"ל באבות (ה, ז) **כָּל מַחֲלוֹקֶת... אֵיזוֹ הִיא חֲלוֹקֶת שֶׁהִיא לְשֵׁם שָׁמַיִם?... שֶׁאֵינָהּ לְשֵׁם שָׁמַיִם? זוֹ מַחֲלוֹקֶת רַח וְכָל עֲדָתוֹ**. הענין הוא ידוע עיקר כוונת בריאת העולם הוא ד שיגיע בהשתלשלות למקום בחירה ברע או בטוב אשר ברא ת האדם ישר לדעת **מָאוֹס בָּרָע כָחוֹר בַּטּוֹב** (ע"פ ישעי' ז, ט). כבוד ה' מלא כל הנבראים מגבוה ל גבוהים עד השלשול קטן שבים פילו הקליפות כמאמר (נחמיה ט, ו) **וְאַתָּה מְחַיֶּה אֶת כֻּלָּם** כי צורך עולם בהם. ועיקר מעשה האדם הוציא יקר מזולל בסוד **וּמַלְכוּתוֹ כֹּל מָשָׁלָה** (תהלים קג, יט) הכרית הקוצים ובחור בחיים כל אשר יפנה ישכיל ובכל דרכיו דעהו **מַה זֶּה וְעַל מַה זֶּה כִּי הִקְרָה ה-וָה אֱל-הֶיךָ לְפָנָי וּמִי בָרָא לֶּה** (ישעיהו מב, כד) **הֲלוֹא יְהֹ-ה זוֹ** המהוה כל הויות ומחיה ותם הסובב וממלא אותם ומי נתן שכוי בינה בין בדברים ועצה דעת טוב ורע. ועתה למה ירע בבו להתדבק ברע יחליפנו וימיר ותו רע בטוב הגנוז בתוכו המחיה ותו שהוא חי החיים. ובזה נפש דוניו **יָשִׁיב לִבְעָלָיו** בהוציא יקר זולל להקריב קרבן להוי"ה **אִשֵּׁה יחַ נִיחוֹחַ** (ויקרא א, ט) נחת רוח פניו שאמר ונעשה רצונו, כי צונו בבריאת העולם היה דוקא גשמי שיהיה **מְלֹא כָל הָאָרֶץ כְּבוֹדוֹ** ג"כ במקום שיש בחירה להוציא יקר מזולל שהם הקליפות. וזהו (ויקרא א, ט) **אִשֵּׁה רֵיחַ נִיחוֹחַ** לה' שהוא ממקום הנוקבא והקליפות. וזה שאמר ונעשה רצונו פירוש שאמר עשרה מאמרות בשביל השתלשלות הגשמי וחומרי כזה ואעפ"כ נעשה רצונו, **מָלְאָה הָאָרֶץ דֵּעָה...כַּמַּיִם** וכו' (ישעיה יא, ט) פי' כי הארץ הוא הגשמי והוא הצמצום היותר גדול בא"ס ברוך הוא להחיות עפר הארץ ומלואה ולהיות סובב אותה ולמלאות אותה וזהו **מָלְאָה הָאָרֶץ דֵּעָה...כַּמַּיִם** שהם התפשטות כידוע. נמצא בריאת העולם היה הצמצום וזהו באורייתא ברא קוב"ה עלמא וארז"ל (ב"ר א, ב) נסתכל בתורה וברא את העולם שנאמר (משלי ח, ל) **וָאֶהְיֶה אֶצְלוֹ אָמוֹן** כי התורה מפי הגבורה נתנה שהוא הצמצום וארז"ל (תנחומא בראשית א) שהוא אש שחורה חרותה על אש לבנה. ולבאר הענין הוא אחר שידוע שעיקר הבריאה הוא הצמצום שהוא שכינה בתחתונים צורך גבוה פי' החיות הקדושה שבתחתונים להעלות כולה כליל לה' וצורך גבוה פי' כענין ארז"ל (זח"ג ז ע"ב) **יִשְׂרָאֵל מְפַרְנְסִי לַאֲבִיהֶן שֶׁבַּשָּׁמַיִם** וכידוע. וזהו (ב"ר מד, יב) אברם אינו מוליד אברהם מוליד כידוע שאברם הוא התפשטות ואם היה רק התפשטות ולא היה שום צמצום אי אפשר להיות שום הולדה כנ"ל, אבל אברהם שהוא בה' אחרונה שבשם שהיא שכינה בתחתונים הוא המוליד בהעלתו אותה אל מול פני ה'. כידוע שכל הולדה היא מקבלת תענוג מתחתונים בהכנת התחתונים להיות מקבלים שהיא אהבת איש לאשתו הנקראת אהבה מסותרת, משא"כ מאהבת האחים שהיא אהבת ההתפשטות שניהם משורש אחד שהיא אהבה מגולה כמאמר (שה"ש ח, א) **מִי יִתֶּנְךָ כְּאָח לִי ... אֶמְצָאֲךָ בַחוּץ אֶשָּׁקְךָ גַּם לֹא יָבוּזוּ לִי**, כי תענוג תמידי אינו תענוג משא"כ באהבה מסותרת שהיא שכינה בתחתונים שהיה רחוק ונתקרב הוא התענוג הגדול:

וזהו ארז"ל (גיטין ו ע"ב) אלו ואלו דברי אלקים חיים אע"פ שאלו אוסרין ואלו מתירין, הענין הוא על דרך אור שבעת הימים שהם המדות חמשה מול חמשה ה' חסדים וה' גבורות, וזהו ארז"ל (ירושלמי שקלים פ"ו ה"א) שהלוחות היו ה' מול ה'. שכנגד כל ההתפשטות צריך להיות צמצום, עד שתצא לאור שכינה בתחתונים והגיע עד עוה"ז השפל והגופני וכולם נתלבשו בגופים אפילו התורה והמצות בדברים גופנים כמו סוכה ולולב וכיוצא בהם. וכמו שבדרכי המדות החסדים להתפשט והגבורות לצמצם הגם כי אב אחד לכולם ואל אחד בראם וכולם מרועה אחד נתנו והוא מתלבש בתוכם כידוע בלי שום שינוי כלל ח"ו כי אם השתלשלות רצון העליון להוציא מכח אל הפועל. כמו כן אחר ההשתלשלות והתלבשות בגופים ואורייתא וקוב"ה וישראל כולא חד (זח"ג עג ע"א) כידוע משִשים רבוא אותיות וששים רבוא נשמות וכו' אשר מעולם החסדים מתירים להתפשט

גם בזה נגלה כבוד ה' ממנו ג"כ ואשר מעולם הגבורה אוסרים ע"ד צמצום וגבול נתן ה' עד פה תבא. וכל זה אינו אלא באורות אבל לא בכלים שהרי כל כוונת שניהם אינו אלא לעשות כלים שהם גשמיות לקבל האורות, ולכן לא נמנעו מלהלוות כלים זה לזה אפילו שאלו אוסרים ואלו מתירין וכו' (יבמות יג ע"ש):

והלכה כב"ה מפני שענותנין הם (מפי) [ופירוש] ה"לכה שהיא אותיות ה"כלה שהיא השכינה כבית הלל שהם המקילין שהם החסדים מפני דלית לה מגרמה כלום, כידוע שאין הירח מאיר אלא מאור השמש המאיר בתוכו. ופירוש הלכה הוא הילוך להורות להם **הַדֶּרֶךְ יֵלְכוּ בָהּ** לה', כי התורה והמצות הם תרי"ג עיטין להתהלך לפני ה' (זח"ב פב ע"ב) כאמור באברהם (בראשית יז, א) **הִתְהַלֵּךְ לְפָנַי** כידוע (זח"א קע ע"ב) שהם כנגד רמ"ח איברים ושס"ה גידים לטהר אותם ולקדשם בכל מצוה לאבר המיוחד אליו להמשיך הקדושה על עצמו בקשר החיות וביטול ההרגש ממש. וההילוך הוא ע"י הרגל פעם ושתים שהוא לשון רגל ומקבל שכר על כל פסיעה ופסיעה, עד שמההרגל יעשה טבע שני שהוא מלשון (ברכות מ ע"ב) מטבע שטבעו חכמים שהוא תחילת בריאתו כך הוא. כמאמר (בראשית א, כז) **וַיִּבְרָא אֱל-הִים** כידוע (מזח"ג רכג ע"א) שאֱ"ל-**הִים** בגימטריא הטבע וגימטריא הכסא, להיות תחילת הבריאה והטבע כסא נכון אל רצון העליון

לשכון עליו משכן ה' ובית עולמים שהם שכינה עילאה ושכינה תתאה ע"י התקשרות נפשו בהם:

וידוע כי התקשרות נפשו באמת עם השכינה תתאה והתאחדו עמה להתכלל בה, והיינו שלא תהיה כוונתו אלא להעשות כלי בנפשו **רוּחוֹ וְנִשְׁמָתוֹ אֵלָיו יֶאֱסֹף** לקבל **הַשֶּׁמֶשׁ לְאוֹר יוֹמָם** ולהדבק בה' שהם המדות כידוע. על כל פנים אי אפשר להגיע לזה כי אם מידי עברו דרך המות ממש ויאחזוהו פלצות ויסורי בידקי מיתה ממש בלי שום שינוי כידוע שנקרא בזוהר (ח"ג קכ עיי"ש) **אִילָנָא דְמוֹתָא**. ואחרי עברו דרך הילוכו זה ויתן את נפשו למומתים ויסבול צער מיתה אם יאיר ה' חסדו **וִיחַיֵּנוּ מִיֹּמָיִם** אז יאיר כשמש אפילתו להדבק בה' ובמדותיו לאהוב אותו ויראת ה' על פניו, **וְרָאוּ כָּל עַמֵּי הָאָרֶץ כִּי שֵׁם יְהֹ-וָה נִקְרָא עָלֶיךָ** וכו' שהוא שם הוי"ה ב"ה בעצמו כידוע. כי **הַשָּׁמַיִם שָׁמַיִם לַיה-וָה וְהָאָרֶץ נָתַן לִבְנֵי אָדָם** וא"א להגיע אל השמים שהם המדות אם לא בדרך כל הארץ, וזהו הנקרא **הֹלֵךְ בְּדֶרֶךְ כָּל-הָאָרֶץ** (מ"א ב, א) שהיא המיתה ולהיכן הולך אל השמים שאין שום דרך אחר שיעלה השמים אם לא **אָדָם כִּי יָמוּת בְּאֹהֶל** (במדבר יט, יד) שהוא משכן שהוא שכינה א"י:

והנה ידוע הוא בזוהר (שם) בענין נפילת אפים שהיא מסירת נפש למקום הזה שהיא השכינה וכתב שם שצריך רעו סגי בנקודת אמיתת הלב בדביקות והתקשרות

חפץ ורצון גמור שאם לא כן סכנ הוא לפניו, שאחר שאמר שימסו עצמו למקום המות ולא יהי בשלימות גמור בכדי שיוכ להעשות כלי לקבל חסד ה' מעול שהם המדות להחיותו ישאר שם וזהו (איוב ד, כא) **יָמוּתוּ וְלֹא בְחָכְמָה** פירוש כידוע מפסו (משלי ג, יט) **יְהֹ-וָה בְּחָכְמָה יָסַ אָרֶץ** כי החכמה הוא העליו שבמוחין והוא נקודת האמ והתחלת השורש, ואם אינו מכני התחלת השורש והאמת שהו החכמה להתכלל בשכינה ולמסו עצמו אליו ימות:

ואם אמר יאמר מה לי ולצר הזאת לעבור בדרך זה כי הוא נור ואיום כמאמר (בראשית כח, יז) **מַה נּוֹרָא הַמָּקוֹם הַזֶּה**, הלא כ הארץ לפני ונגלה כבוד ה' בכ דבר פרטי וכללי בעולם שנה נפ שהם חיות הקודש מז' ימי הבני כמאמר (תהילים פט, ג) **עוֹלָ חֶסֶד יִבָּנֶה**. ואין לך דבר בעול שיצא מכלל השבעה עיני ה המשוטטות **בְּכָל הָאָרֶץ** (ע' זכריה ד, י) ומהם ובהם נכללו כ התורה והמצות כידוע שהוא תור שבכתב, לכן על ידם **יַעֲלֶ לַשָּׁמַיִם שִׂיאוֹ** (ע"פ איוב כ, ו ליהנות מאור ה' ולהדבק במדותי אהבתו ויראתו. הנה אל ידמ בנפשו להמלט באופן זה כי א **דֶּרֶךְ הַמֶּלֶךְ** ילך כי אין מקו לעבור בדרך אחר **זֶה הַשַּׁעַר לַיה-וָה צַדִּיקִים יָבֹאוּ בוֹ בְּזֹאת יָבֹא. אֶל הַקֹּדֶשׁ**, וא"א להגיע לתור שבכתב כי אם דרך תורה שבע" שהיא שכינה כידוע, והוא מש שארז"ל (שבת לא ע"ב) שמסר

לו המפתחות הפנימים והמפתחות החיצונים לא מסרו לו בהי עייל כי לא זה הדרך שיעלה ויבא ויגיע אל הדביקות אהבת ויראת ה' אבל ירד מטה מטה:

וזהו (אבות ד, ה) **וּדְאִשְׁתַּמֵּשׁ בְּתָגָא, חֲלָף** שהוא כתר של תורה שבכתב בעצמו כארז"ל (שם ג, יז) על **שֶׁחָכְמָתוֹ מְרֻבָּה [ו]מִמַּעֲשָׂיו...מֻעָטִין... וְהוֹפַכְתּוֹ עַל פָּנָיו**. כי **מַה יִּתְרוֹן לָאָדָם בְּכָל המעשים אשר יעשה תַּחַת הַשָּׁמֶשׁ** בהגלות נגלות אם אין לבבו שלם **הִכּוֹן לִקְרַאת אֱל-הֶיךָ** וכו' (עמוס ד, יב) כי **רַחֲמָנָא לִבָּא בָּעֵי** (זח"ב קסב ע"ב) וא"א בשום אופן שתחול עליו יראת הרוממות כי אם אחר שיעבור יראת העדרו מעיקרו שהוא המיתה ומסירת נפש כנ"ל. וכל האהבות ויראות ה' אשר ידמה האדם בנפשו בלתי עברו המעבר הל"ז בודאי שקר ענה בנפשו בעצמו וקנינים המדומים הם בנפשו מהתעוררות מדותיו הגשמיים כי ברע הוא מעץ הדעת טוב ורע ורחוק הוא מה' וכל מעשה המצות הכל הוא אינו אלא גדלות להיות לו לשם ולתהלה ולקבל פרס. על דרך משל מי שיש לו מעלה בודאי רחוק הוא מהמלך מפני שכל מי שהוא עם המלך יחד כלום חסר לו ואין צריך לו שום דבר, דרך משל עשירות למה לי כלום חסר וכו' תחבולות ערי בצורות ושמירה מעולה למה לי הרי שמור הוא חכמה מלאכה למה לי כנ"ל. נמצא ממילא מוכרח ומובן מי שהוא בעל מעלה שיש לו אותו מעלה בודאי רחוק הוא מן המלך שהמעלה נקרא מעלה אצלו ויש לו, כי בהתקרבו אל המלך ממש שאין לו אותה מעלה כי למה היא לו. אבל סכנה עצומה היא פן ואולי לא יבטל רצונו חיש ומהר לעשות רצון המלך ויתחייב בנפשו, אם לא שיודע בעצמו ואמיתת לבבו שלם ברצון גמור ומסירת נפשו לעשות רצון המלך תיכף קולע אל השערה ולא יחטא אז יכול להיות עמו תמיד בעת שמחתו ופחדתו כי בטוח הוא בעצמו ולאיש אשר אלה לו מגלה לו המלך מסתוריו וכל עניניו:

והנה בזוהר בראשית (דף ג ע"ב) על פסוק (ג, ו) **וַתֵּרֶא הָאִשָּׁה כִּי טוֹב הָעֵץ** הרשום אצל פסוק (ב, כד) **עַל כֵּן יַעֲזָב אִישׁ** וכו' עיי"ש כל המאמר ובסוף המאמר **תָּא חֲזֵי כִּי יהו"ה אלהי"ך אֵשׁ אוֹכְלָה הוּא... מַאן דְּבָעֵי... בְּשַׁלְהוֹבָא דְּסָלְקָא אִית תְּרֵין נְהוֹרִין, חַד נְהוֹרָא חִוְורָא דְּנָהִיר, וְחַד נְהוֹרָא דְּאִתְאַחִיד בָּהּ אוּכָמָא, אוֹ תִּכְלָא, הַהוּא נְהוֹרָא חִוְורָא אִיהוּ לְעֵילָא וְסָלְקָא בְּאוֹרַח מִישׁוֹר, וּתְחוֹתֵיהּ הַהוּא נְהוֹרָא תִּכְלָא אוֹ אוּכָמָא דְּאִיהוּ כָּרְסְיָיא לְהַהוּא חִוְורָא... וְעַל דָּא רָזָא דִּתְכֶלְתָּא...וְהַאי אִתְאֲחִיד לִתְרֵין סִטְרִין ... וְדָא אָכְלָא תָּדִיר וְשָׁצֵי לְהַהוּא... דְּהָא בֵּיהּ תַּלְיָא שֵׁיצוּ דְּכֹלָּא מוֹתָא דְּכֹלָּא** וכו' הרי דברינו בפירוש הנזכר:

וכדי לבאר טעם לדבר מבואר בספר לקוטי אמרים שא"א לעשות השתנות בעולם אם לא בהעלות הדבר אל שורשו, והמשל בזה הזריעה שזורעים חטים כדי שיתוספו ואי אפשר ליגדל אלא אם כן החטים הזרועים מתבלים בעפר ונעשים עפר הארץ כידוע וכן זרע אדם באשה. והענין הוא כי כח הצומח הוא בארץ. ואם תאמר א"כ תצמח הארץ בלי שום זריעה הענין הוא כי הארץ וכח הצומח המושרש בתוכו הוא ממש אין סוף בערך ההוא עד שאי אפשר להתפשט שום דבר אלא א"כ כשזורעים איזה מין וחוזר לעפרו אז אותו המין מתעורר לצאת ומפני שהגיע בהתבלותו בעפר אל שרשו כח הצומח יש בו כח להוסיף הרבה. והשורש הוא ממוצע בין ענפים ובין כחות העליונים ממנו בדרך השתלשלות כידוע שא"א להשתלשל מדרגא לדרגא אחרת אלא אם כן ע"י ממוצע והוא השורש כנ"ל. כי השורש ההוא הוא הכולל את כל כחות העליונים וממנו מתפשטים ענפים אחרים, אבל השורש בעצמו אינו אלא הכנה ולא שום דבר בפני עצמו כי נגד עליונים הוא כללות הכל ונגד התחתונים הוא שורש הכל. לכן מחוייבים דברינו שא"א לעבור אל מקום ה' שמה אא"כ דרך השכינה ולטעום טעם מיתה ממש להתבטל בתוכה ממש ואח"כ חוזר וניעור. ולכן השכינה **לֵית לָהּ מִגַּרְמָהּ כְּלוּם** רק מה שמגיע אליה מאור המדות. וידוע כי **הַחַיּוֹת רָצוֹא וָשׁוֹב** ולכן מי שנכלל בשכינה מוסר עצמו למיתה ממש ולכן נקראת רק כלי לשון כללות שכוללת קבלת כל כחות העליונים ומכלה התחתונים שנכללים בתוכה:

וזה דרז"ל (סוטה יד. עיי"ש) על פסוק (דברים יא, כב) **וּלְדָבְקָה בוֹ**

וכי אפשר לדבק בשכינה והלא אש אוכלה הוא אלא הדבק במדותיו, פירוש אחר שנכלל בשכינה ונתבטל לגמרי בתוכה אח"כ חוזר וניעור ע"י דביקות כידוע שגם השכינה מקבלת ע"י מדות הדביקות והתקשרות שנקרא יסוד ומקבלת מאור המדות. וזהו הדבק במדותיו כי במדות שייך דביקות משא"כ בשכינה כמבואר בזוהר בראשית הנזכר כי המדות הם **אֶשָּׁא חִוְּרָא** שאינו שורף ורוכב על **אֶשָּׁא דִתְכֶלְתָּא** כמבואר שם, לכן משה שהיה **מְקוֹמוֹ שׁוֹאֵף זוֹרֵחַ הוּא שָׁם** (ע"פ קהלת א, ה) פנים בפנים דבר בו בלי שום חלישות:

כללא דמלתא הרי בכל אדם מישראל כלולים כל המדות ושורש נשמתו אבר מהשכינה וכנסת ישראל הנקרא **שֵׁם שָׁמַיִם** כי המדות נקראים שמים והשכינה נקראת **שֵׁם שָׁמַיִם** שהשם הוא כללות הדבר ולא דבר בפני עצמו. וזהו **כָּל מַחֲלוֹקֶת... שֶׁהִיא** בכל אדם **לְשֵׁם שָׁמַיִם** פירוש מחלוקת מדותיו כנזכר איך יתנהג בחסד או בגבורה מותר או אסור אפילו בדבר תורה ויראה, העיקר צריך שתהיה כוונתו לכלול עצמו בשם שמים שהוא שורש נשמתו שהוא השכינה, וכל עניני מחלוקותיו הם איך להתכלל בשכינה ואיך להתבטל בתוכה נגד השי"ת ב"ה:

וענין הביטול אפשר להיות על דרך הפסוק (תהלים קיח, כד) **זֶה הַיּוֹם עָשָׂה יְהֹ-וָ֑ה נָגִילָה וְנִשְׂמְחָה בוֹ** וארז"ל (שהש"ר א, לב) יכול ישמח ביום ת"ל **זֶה הַיּוֹם עָשָׂה יְהֹ-וָה נָגִילָה וְנִשְׂמְחָה בוֹ** שישמח בה'. והפירוש הוא כי איזה הארה שבאה לאדם נקרא **יוֹם** מאיזה מדה שתהיה כי הוא הארה מהשי"ת, יכול שישמח ביום פירוש בההארה במדה שהוא מודד ת"ל **בוֹ** שישמח בה', פירוש שיבין שההארה הוא עצמות ה'. כידוע כי המדות הם הסוד הנקרא עצמות וא"כ כשהמלך בא פתאום להתאכסן אצלו צריך להניח לו כל ביתו וכל כליו ואם הוא מניח להמלך כל ביתו וכל כליו נמצא ממילא נעשה הוא כמי שאינו כלל שהרי המלך אינו גשם ח"ו בשום כח גשם ח"ו ואם הוא נעשה בית המלך **מָה הוּא** אז נכלל בשכינה:

וזהו **אֵיזוֹ הִיא מַחֲלוֹקֶת שֶׁהִיא לְשֵׁם שָׁמַיִם? זוֹ מַחֲלוֹקֶת הִלֵּל וְשַׁמַּאי** שהם המדות **וּמַחֲלוֹקֶת שֶׁהִיא לְשֵׁם שָׁמַיִם** פירוש לשם הלכה כדברינו וכנ"ל, משא"כ קרח ועדתו שחלק על משה ואמר **כִּי כָל הָעֵדָה כֻּלָּם קְדֹשִׁים** כמותו שהיה נאחז למעלה מהשכינה שהם המדות כמבואר בזהר הנזכר. וידוע הוא שהוא מקום עץ הדעת טוב ורע ומשם יפרד ח"ו ולכן כשרצו להתקרב ע"י הקטורת מדי עברם אש אוכלה אכלתם, וזהו דרז"ל כי התורה אש שחורה על גבי אש לבנה והוא דרך הילוכו של אדם אל התורה דרך אש שחורה שהיא השכינה אז יצליח:

[י"ד]. פרשת פנחס

(המרגיש בצער השכינה, כל העולם נחשב לו לכלום):

בגמרא (קידושין סו ע"ב) מנין לכהן בעל מום שהוא פסול שנאמר (כה, יב) **הִנְנִי נֹתֵן לוֹ אֶת בְּרִיתִי שָׁלוֹם** [כשהוא שלם] ולא חסר, ופריך והא **שָׁלוֹם** בו' כתיב ומשני ו' **דשָׁלוֹם** קטיע. הנה ארז"ל (סנהדרין מד ע"א) על הפסוק (תהלים קו, ל) "**וַיַּעֲמֹד פִּינְחָס וַיְפַלֵּל** ויתפלל לא נאמר אלא **וַיְפַלֵּל** מלמד שעשה פלילה עם קונו וכו':

הענין הוא ע"ד המבואר בזהר (ח"א קכב ע"א) ע"פ (שה"ש ה, ח) **הִשְׁבַּעְתִּי ...אִם תִּמְצְאוּ... מַה תַּגִּידוּ לוֹ** וכו', ודרש הזהר שהשכינה משבעת כל **נִשְׁמוֹת** היורדים בעוה"ז שיגידו להקב"ה **מחוֹלַת אַהֲבָה** השכינה אליו. ובכדי לפרש הענין הוא ידוע אמרו בזהר (תקוני זהר ה ע"ב) **מַאן דְּאִית בֵּיהּ יִרְאַת יהו"ה, לֵית לֵיהּ חוֹסֶר** כלל שנאמר (תהלים לד, י) **אֵין מַחְסוֹר לִירֵאָיו.** והענין ע"ד מאמר (ברכות נח ע"א) בן זומא ראה אוכלסא בהר הבית [וכו'] ואמר ברוך שברא כל אלו לשמשני. והוא מוסר ופחד גדול כשאדם נותן אל לבו שכל העולם לא נברא אלא בשבילו (שם ו ע"ב) ונתלבשה השכינה בכמה וכמה פרטים ובני אדם לאין קץ ומספר ובכמה מיני גשמים אולי יתפעל זה לעשות הטוב והישר בעיני ה', וכ"ש אם צריכה להתלבש בעונשין ח"ו ובאומות העולם כדי להכניע את לב זה

שיירא מלפני ה' ויעשה רצון קונו: נמצא כשאדם מתפלל לפני השי"ת על איזה דבר שחסר לו העיקר שישים אליו לבו על שפלות השכינה שמהראוי להיותה שלמה בכל העולמות, שיהיה האדם הישראלי מושל בכל מכל כל בכל הנבראים נוצרים ונעשים כשלמה המלך ע"ה ומשה רבינו ע"ה, שכן היתה תחלת הבריאה שאמר (בראשית א, כח) **וּרְדוּ בִּדְגַת הַיָּם** וגו' ולא יהיה חסר כלום. משא"כ כשהוא חסר ממילא נשמע שהשכינה הוצרכה בהכרח להתלבש בחסרון למענו בכדי שיתפעל ויתלהב לבו לה', לכן יאחזנו פלצות מאמיתת נקודת הלב ולא יכוין בתפלתו על מילוי חסרונו כי אם על חסרון השכינה שאינה נשפעת מהשי"ת בשלימות אם מוכרחת להתלבש בחסרון. והנה ידוע הוא שכל אדם מישראל הוא אבר מהשכינה ושלוחה כמותה, וזהו פירוש **הִשְׁבַּעְתִּי אֶתְכֶם** וכו' שהשכינה משבעת לנפשות ישראל שכל אחד אם ימצא את השי"ת יגיד לו מ **חוֹלַת אַהֲבָת** השכינה אליו כנ"ל שיתלבש בצער השכינה שאינה נשפעת מהשי"ת ולא יכוון על עצמו וחסרונו:

וזהו **מַאן דְּאִית בֵּיהּ יִרְאָה**, שהוא הדביקות בשכינה **לֵית לֵיהּ חוֹסֶר**, פירוש שהרי אינו חסר לנפשו כלום מכל ואינו מגמתו על חסרונו כלל, שכל זה אינו שוה לו נגד חסרון השכינה בקנאו את קנאתה. וכל העולם כולו אינו נחשב לו לכלום נגד הצער ומגודל הקנאה בצער השכינה עד שכלו כל כחותיו ואינו יכול לסבול, ויותר טוב לו אלף אלפי רבוא פעמים מיתתו מחייו, ומה לו לזה להפקיר עצמו ולמסור נפשו על קדושת שמו שהרי נחת רוח הוא לפניו בתכלית האהבה בתענוגים:

ובהיות האדם בכח זה אינו נאחז כלל בשרשי הדינים והוא למעלה מדין תורה וא"א לו לכוון דעתו לילך עפ"י ד"ת כי **חוֹלַת אַהֲבָה** השי"ת הוא. וזה היה פנחס בקנאו את קנאת ה' ית' בראותו את שפלות השכינה. כמאמר הבעש"ט שכל מה שאדם רואה בעולם לצרכו הוא, ונתפעל פנחס והפקיר עצמו נגד הד"ת, שאם היה שאלת חכם אם מוכרח להפקיר עצמו לילך בין כ"ד אלף ולהרוג את זמרי לא היו מתירים לו, אבל פנחס לא יכול לסבול לעמוד על חייו ולא עלתה על דעתו הד"ת מגודל קנאת שפלות השכינה. וזהו **וַיְפַלֵּל** שעשה פלילה עם קונו פי' פלילה לשון דיינא הנקראים **בִּפְלִלִים** (שמות כא, כב) ועשה דין אחר מחמת **חוֹלַת אַהֲבָת** השי"ת, ואופן זה הוא המתקת הדינין ואדם המתפלל באופן זה נענה על תפלתו שהרי הדין נמתק. וזהו (ברכות לד ע"ב) אם שגורה תפלתי בפי וכו' ופי' שגורה לשון שליחות כמו שגרני אליך כי תפלת פיו הוא שליח מהשכינה מפני היותו אבר מהשכינה וצריך להתלבש בשכינה ולהתפלל תפלתה אצל השי"ת. וזהו הסימן שנתן רש"י ז"ל (שם) על לשון שגורה תפלתי שהתפלה נובעת מלבו ומדבר בלי שום עיכוב שהוא סרכא שהוא **טְרֵפָה** כמבואר בזוהר ר"מ פנחס (דף רכח ע"א):

והנה מבואר בזוהר (ח"א רמא ע"ב) על פסוק הנאמר ברחב הזונה (יהושע ב, יב) **וּנְתַתֶּם לִי אוֹת אֱמֶת** שבקשה סימנא דמשה שהוא ו' שהוא המשכה שלמה שלא היה בה שבירה שהוא אמת כידוע, והשיבו לה השלוחים לא כי עתה מת משה וממשלת יהושע הוא שהוא **אֶת תִּקְוַת חוּט הַשָּׁנִי...תִּקְשְׁרִי** (שם, יח). כידוע מענין הלבנת לשון של זהורית שהוא המתקת **הַדִּינִין** (זח"ג קב ע"א). וזהו (שה"ש ד, ג) **כְּחוּט הַשָּׁנִי שִׂפְתֹתַיִךְ** כידוע והוא אם **שְׁגוּרָה תְּפִלָּתִי בְּפִי** וכו'. וזהו דרשה דכהן בע"מ פסול מפסוק **הִנְנִי נֹתֵן לוֹ** וכו' ופריך והא בו' כתיב והוא מקום שא"א להיות בו שבירה משא"כ הכא ופנחס שלוחא דשכינה הוא, ומשני ו' **דשָׁלוֹם** קטיע שהוא ו' זעירא:

[ט"ו]. פרשת מטות-מסעי א'

(בריות העולם מגלים כבודו וגדלותו)

וַיְדַבֵּר מֹשֶׁה אֶל רָאשֵׁי הַמַּטּוֹת לִבְנֵי יִשְׂרָאֵל לֵאמֹר זֶה הַדָּבָר אֲשֶׁר צִוָּה יְהֹ-וָה. ובסוף הספר (לקמן לו, יג) **אֵלֶּה הַמִּצְוֹת וְהַמִּשְׁפָּטִים אֲשֶׁר צִוָּה יְהֹוָה בְּיַד מֹשֶׁה אֶל בְּנֵי יִשְׂרָאֵל בְּעַרְבֹת מוֹאָב עַל יַרְדֵּן יְרֵחוֹ**. הענין הוא ארז"ל (אבות ד, ג **אַל תְּהִי בָז לְכָל אָדָם... לְכָל דָּבָר** וכן מעשה דר"א בר"ש (תענית כ ע"א) שנדמה לו אליהו ז"ל לאדם מכוער שאין

כמוהו עד שגינה אותו ר"א וכו', ואח"כ אמר לו אליהו מוסר עד שקיבל ע"ע שלא לעשות כן וכו':

והענין כי הנה ידוע מאמר (משלי טז,ד) **כֹּל פָּעַל יְהֹ-וָה לַמַּעֲנֵהוּ** ופי' (ישעיה מג, ז) **כֹּל הַנִּקְרָא בִשְׁמִי וְלִכְבוֹדִי בְּרָאתִיו** וכו', שכל הבריות שבעולם עד השלשול קטן שבים צורך העולם בהם וגדולת הבורא מתגלית בהם יותר מבלתם, שאם היה אפשרי ההתגלות בלתם לא היו נבראים. עד שאין לך דבר שבעולם אפילו הקליפות ואומות העולם ועונשין הכל לכבודו ית"ש וזהו סוד (תהלים קג, יט) **מַלְכוּתוֹ בַּכֹּל מָשָׁלָה**, וכן פי' (נחמיה ט, ו) **וְאַתָּה מְחַיֶּה אֶת כֻּלָּם**, וכן פי' (תהלים קד, כד) **מָה רַבּוּ מַעֲשֶׂיךָ יְהֹ-וָה כֻּלָּם בְּחָכְמָה עָשִׂיתָ**, וכבודו ית' שמתגלה מבריה זו א"א אותה ההתגלות מבריה אחרת:

והענין הוא אם יראת עונש, או יראת בושת, או יראת הרוממות, שמתעורר האדם על ידם ובכל אחד מיראות הנזכרות יש כמה וכמה פרטים עד אין קץ ומספר, וכמו כן מתחלקין האהבות וכן שארי המדות והתקשרות עד אין קץ כידוע. והן הן גופי הבריות בעוה"ז השפלי החומרי, וכן הוא באדם שהוא **עוֹלָם קָטָן** כלול את הכל בחילוף המחשבה והדמיונות והמדות וההתקשרות עד אין קץ (ת"ז ת"ע קל ע"ב), כידוע שהמחשבה היא קומה שלמה אם טוב ואם רע ח"ו מתעורר ממנה להשי"ת ב"ה אם ליראתו הנזכרת אם לאהבתו ית' או בכל מדה ומדה שהוא מודד הוא מודה לו ית'. ובזה היה יודע שלמה המלך ע"ה הלשונות מכל הבריות שבעולם בהסתכלותו על עצמו וחילופו וחילופי חילופיו, שהרי אין המחשבה עומדת אפילו רגע אחד אבל פושט ולובש צורה תמיד כידוע ולא כל העתים שוים כידוע מכ"ח עתים (קהלת ג, ב-ח) והשתנות לאין מספר. ודבר זה נוהג אפילו בגדולי הצדיקים ואפילו משה רבינו ע"ה כנגדו היה בלעם דעת דקליפה שהיה כולל כל הדעת ומחשבת חוץ ופסול המוקדשין, כמאמר (שם ז, יד) **אֶת זֶה לְעֻמַּת זֶה עָשָׂה הָאֱלֹהִים**, ואחרי שמשה רבינו ע"ה. היה דעת דקדושה בודאי היו מוכרחים כל אלו לעבור במחשבתו והוא גבר עליהם והכניע בעצמו כל הרע עד שהגיע להיות במדרגת דעת דקדושה כידוע. ומאמר הבעש"ט שכל מה שהיה בבלעם היו חושדין למשה רבינו ע"ה, מפני שכל זמן שלא נגמרה עלית השכינה כאשר יהיה בזמן (השכינה) [המשיח] וגואל צדק בב"א שהוא ביטול הקליפה ו**בִלַּע הַמָּוֶת לָנֶצַח** (ישעי' כה, ח), מוכרחים כל העליות להיות רק במחשבת אדם כשר. והאדם כשר א"א לו להגיע ולעלות אל שורשו כי אם ע"י שכנגדו שיעלו במחשבתו והוא יתעורר מהם לבוראו ית', והן הן הנסיונות כמארז"ל (שבת עז ע"ב) בברייתו של עולם מעיקרא חשוכא והדר נהורא והוא מוזכר בזוהר הרבה פעמים. לכן כשהאדם רוצה להכניע איזה דבר רע העומד עליו בתחילה צריך להכניע באמת לפני וכו' ב"ה מאותו הרע השוכן בעצמו וזהו ביטול הרע והמתקת הדינין. וז"ש (תהלים סט, יט) **קָרְבָה אֶל נַפְשִׁי גְאָלָהּ** ואח"כ **לְמַעַן אֹיְבַי פְּדֵנִי**, פי' בתחלה ביקש שתבא הגאולה לנפשו מכל אומות העולם שהם ההתקשרות במחשבת חוץ וממילא יהיה פדוי מאויביו שהוא ביטול הקליפה והמתקת הדינין. וזהו שארז"ל (סנהדרין צז ע"א) אין משיח בא אלא בהיסח הדעת פי' כי הדעת הוא כללות כל המדות מז' ימי הבנין ואינה מדה בפני עצמה, והגאולה שצריכה להיות מכל (השבעה) [השבעים] אומות העולם אשר שרשם ז' ימי הבנין א"א להיות כ"א שיגיע למעלה מן הדעת שיסח עצמו מן הדעת ולא יהיה שום אמצעי בינו לבין השי"ת ולא שום הפסק בעולם כ"א יחוד אמיתי. וזהו ארז"ל (ב"ב ע"ה ע"ב בשינוי) עתידין מלאכי השרת לומר קדושה לפני ישראל כמו שאומרים לפני השי"ת מפני שיהיו אחדות גמור עם השי"ת. אבל עכשיו קודם ביאת המשיח הדעת הוא המיחד את כל הברואים להשי"ת ומבטל הרע מהם ומשפיע טובה להם:

והענין כשהאדם כולל בדעתו כמה וכמה נבראים שעוברים במחשבתו שהוא קומה שלמה והוא מתעורר מהם אל הבורא ית"ש **בְּדַעְתּוֹ תְּהוֹמוֹת נִבְקָעוּ** (משלי ג, כ) ומעלה אותם ומבררם במחשבתו כמאמר הזהר (ח"ג י ע"ב) **כֻּלָּם בְּחָכְמָה...אִתְבְּרִיאוּ**, ואחרי עליתם אל שורשם נשפעים משם טובה וברכה. וזהו ארז"ל

(ברכות לג ע"א) גדולה דעה שנתנה בין שני אותיות שנאמר (שמואל א' ב, ג) **אֵל דֵּעוֹת יְהֹ-וָה**, כי הדעת הוא המיחד כל השמות ממטה למעלה ומייחד הענף אל השורש שהוא שם הוי"ה ב"ה כדברינו הנזכר. שהרי **כֹּל הַנִּקְרָא בִשְׁמִי וְלִכְבוֹדִי בְּרָאתִיו** ובכל הבריות כולם יש בהם קדושת שמותיו ב"ה כי אין סוף ברוך הוא סובב כל עלמין ו[איהו] **מְמַלֵּא כָּל עָלְמִין** כנזכר. **וּבְדַעְתּוֹ** ו מעלה האדם אותם אל שרשם ומייחד לא"ס ב"ה. ועד"ז היה המקדש כארז"ל (ברכות לג ע"א) כמו כן על מקדש שניתן בין ב' אותיות שנאמר (שמות טז, יז) **פָּעַלְתָּ יְהֹ-וָה מִקְּדָשׁ אֲדֹנָי**, כידוע שהמקדש היה משפיע ומחלק מזון וטובה לכל הברואים ואפילו לאומות העולם כמבואר בפרי החג (סוכה נה ע"ב) ושארי דברים המבוארים בזוהר, והוא ארז"ל (שם) אילו היו יודעים האומות גודל טובתם מן המקדש לא היו מחריבין אותו. ועכשיו במקום מקדש הוא האדם הכשר שע"י מתיחדים כל הברואים אל שרשם ונשפעים טובה. וכמו כן האדם מתייחד באמצעית הברואים (וכו') [כנ"ל], מפני שעכשיו קודם ביאת המשיח א"א להיות היחוד אמתי בלי שום אמצעי כי הדעת שהוא היחוד הוא הנקרא תענוג ועכשיו קודם ביאת המשיח א"א לשום אדם לסבול התענוג עליון כזה והיחוד אמתי בלי שום אמצעי:

כללא דמלתא שאצל כל צדיק וצדיק מוכרחים לעבור במחשבתו כל שכנגדו עד מקום מדריגתו, ואפילו אם יאמר המתחסד שכבר בטל כל הרגשותיו ותאותיו אין שוטה מרגיש שאם אין לו במדה זו יש לו במדות אחרות כיוצא בו. וכשבאה לו המחשבה צריך להיות נבזה בעיניו נמאס שהעמיד צלם בהיכל שהרי האדם הוא מקדש מעט כנזכר וכידוע שהמחשבה והמוח הוא קודש קודשים והלב הוא היכל האהבה ושאר דברים כמבואר בכמה מקומות. ואח"כ כשמתעורר מן הדבר אל הבורא יתב"ש הוא היחוד ועלית השכינה והקמתה מעפרא והאדם ג"כ מתעלה בזה והולך מדרגא אל דרגא ומנסיון לנסיון וממסע למסע:

וזהו המ"ב מסעות הכתובים בתורה שנסעו ישראל ממצרים שהיא עבודת פרך בחומר ולבנים שהוא מעשה הגשמיות והגופניות, וכדי לצאת משם ולהגיע אל ארץ ישראל שהיא כנסת ישראל ולעשות יחוד שלם צריך על כל פנים מ"ב מסעות וזהו שם של מ"ב הידוע ומכוון לעלות מעלה מעלה. והנה ענין המסעות היו כמה פעמים לאחור כידוע לכן לפעמים מזומן לצדיקים איזה ירידה ממחשבתו אבל באמת הוא כי הירידה צורך עליה היא **וּמַסָּע שְׁלֵמָה** כדרך כל המסעות. עד שתבא הגאולה בב"א ויהיה עלית השכינה בפועל ויחוד אמתי בלי שום אמצעי והפסק ולכן יאמרו קדושה לפני ישראל שענין הקדושה הוא פרישת המותרות מהם. וזהו **וַיְדַבֵּר** שהיא לשון הנהגה כמו (תהלים מז, ד) **יַדְבֵּר עַמִּים** ומשה הוא הדעת, **וְאֶל רָאשֵׁי הַמַּטּוֹת** הם שרשי ההשתנות שהם י"ב גבולי אלכסון, **לִבְנֵי יִשְׂרָאֵל** הוא האמונה, **לֵאמֹר** הוא לשון יחוד ואהבה כמו (דברים כו, יז) **אֶת יְהֹ-וָה הֶאֱמַרְתָּ**, והפירוש הוא שירגיל וינהיג הדעת את כל ההשתנות שיעלו בדעתו באמונה ליחד אותם לבורא ית"ש:

וזהו **אֵלֶּה הַמִּצְוֹת** שהוא פירוש ג"כ יחוד כמו לצוות לזה (ברכות ו ע"ב) **וְהַמִּשְׁפָּטִים** פירוש ע"י הרגל יהיה קל בעיניו וישר והדין נותן, **אֲשֶׁר צִוָּה יְהֹ-וָה בְּיַד מֹשֶׁה** פירוש יחוד אין סוף ב"ה עם הדעת, אל בני ישראל פירוש ע"י האמונה, **בְּעַרְבֹת מוֹאָב** פירוש להאמין שכל הערבוביא במחשבות וכל **בְּרִיּוֹת בּוֹ יִפָּקֵדוּ לַחַיִּים** כמאמר (נחמיה ט, ו) **וְאַתָּה מְחַיֶּה אֶת כֻּלָּם** – **כֻּלָּם** באים מאין סוף ב"ה. וזהו **מוֹאָב עַל יַרְדֵּן יְרֵחוֹ** כידוע שביריחו היה השגת המקדש כמשארז"ל (יומא לט ע"ב) ביריחו היה נשמע קולו של כ"ג ביריחו היו מתעטשים העזים וכו' וכמה דברים וזה שהירידה הוא לצורך השגת המקדש. או יאמר כי **הַמִּצְוֹת** כמו נרות כנאמר (משלי ו, כג) **כִּי נֵר מִצְוָה וְתוֹרָה אוֹר** וכמאמר (שם כ, כז) **נֵר יְהֹ-וָה נִשְׁמַת אָדָם חֹפֵשׂ כָּל חַדְרֵי בָטֶן** שעיקר הכנת כל מצוה לחפוש באבריו וגופו אם ראוי שתשרה עליו וזהו **וְהַמִּשְׁפָּטִים** שהוא מסירת נפש:

פרשת מטות-מסעי ב'

וַיְדַבֵּר מֹשֶׁה אֶל רָאשֵׁי הַמַּטּוֹת וכו' זה הדבר אשר צוה ה'. פרש"י

ז"ל כל הנביאים נתנבאו בכה אמר ה' מוסיף עליהם משה שנתנבא בלשון זה הדבר:

פתח הרב (דברים יא, יג) **וְהָיָה אִם שָׁמֹעַ תִּשְׁמְעוּ** פירש"י ז"ל מאמר חז"ל (סוכה מו ע"ב עיי"ש) אם שמוע בישן תשמע בחדש שלא כמדת הקב"ה מדת בשר ודם שמדת ב"ו כלי ריקן מחזיק מלא אינו מחזיק ומדת הקב"ה דוקא המלא מחזיק שנאמר אם שמוע תשמע וכו':

והענין הוא מאמר (איכה א, ה) **כִּי יְהֺ-וָה הוֹגָהּ עַל רֹב פְּשָׁעֶיהָ** ומדרש חז"ל (איכ"ר א, לג) יכול על מגן ת"ל **עַל רֹב פְּשָׁעֶיהָ**, ומבואר בספרים הבנת המדרש ותוכן דבריהם הוא אשר לכאורה תמוה ענין הצער ויגון להיות מיצר ודואג על חורבן בית המקדש מה שעבר אין. כי מאמר (משלי כח, יד) **אַשְׁרֵי אָדָם מְפַחֵד תָּמִיד** הוא על העתיד וכן מאמר (שם יד, כג) **בְּכָל עֶצֶב יִהְיֶה מוֹתָר** וכן (קהלת ז, ב) **טוֹב לָלֶכֶת אֶל בֵּית אֵבֶל** וכו' שהרי פירש טעמו **בַּאֲשֶׁר הוּא סוֹף כָּל הָאָדָם וְהַחַי יִתֵּן אֶל לִבּוֹ** על העתיד, אבל להיות עצב ומיצר ודואג על העבר מה זה ועל מה זה, כמאמר דוד המלך ע"ה אחרי מות הילד (ש"ב יב, כג) **לָמָּה זֶּה אֲנִי צָם הַאוּכַל לַהֲשִׁיבוֹ** וכו'. והעצבות היא הקליפה היותר קשה מכולם שהרי הע"ז נקראת על שמה (תהלים קטו, ד) **עֲצַבֵּיהֶם כֶּסֶף וְזָהָב** ומאמר (הושע ד, יז) **חֲבוּר עֲצַבִּים**, וכן אין לה שייכות עם השי"ת כמאמר (דברי הימים א' טז, כז) **הוֹד וְהָדָר לְפָנָיו עֹז** **וְחֶדְוָה בִּמְקֹמוֹ** ואין השכינה שורה אלא מתוך שמחה (שבת ל ע"ב):

והנה מאמר חז"ל (חגיגה ה ע"א) כאן בבתי גואי כאן בבתי בראי צריך הבנה ואין כאן מקומו כללא דמלתא שהקליפה הוא מחוץ לפרי נקראת בתי בראי, ומאמר (ישעיה כב, יב) **וַיִּקְרָא אֲדֹנָי יֱהֺ-וִה... לִבְכִי לְמִסְפֵּד** וכו' כמאמר (מ"ב ח, א) **כִּי קָרָא יְהֺ-וָה לָרָעָב** שקָרָא לקליפות ונתן רשות שליטתם, וזהו (בראשית ו, ו) **וַיִּתְעַצֵּב אֶל לִבּוֹ** שהרי העבר ועתיד שוין לפניו וכפירוש הזהר (ח"א נז. וח"ג טו ע"ב) למאן ל**לִבּוֹ** עיי"ש. ואחרי היות העצבות קליפה וטומאה אינה נמשכת כי אם למי שהוא מבחינתה **הַחוֹטֵא יִלָּכֶד בָּהּ וְטוֹב לִפְנֵי הָאֱלֹהִים יִמָּלֵט מִמֶּנָּה** כמאמר (משלי טו, טו) **טוֹב לֵב מִשְׁתֶּה תָמִיד**, שהרי אפילו בפחד שהוא מבחינת העצבות ארז"ל (ברכות ס. עה"פ בישעיה לג, יד) **פָּחֲדוּ בְצִיּוֹן חַטָּאִים** דוקא. וע"ד הלצה אפשר לפרש בזה דברי המדרש **כִּי יְהֺ-וָה הוֹגָהּ** למי שהוא ביגון יכול על מגן ת"ל על רוב פשעיה שאינה נמשכת אלא מן הפשעים מקליפות. אבל המפרשים פירשו המדרש על דרך ארז"ל (ירושלמי יומא א, א) כל דור שלא נבנה בית המקדש בימיו כאלו נחרב בימיו ועל דא ודאי קא בכה שפיר על רוב פשעיו וחטאיו מנעו הטוב שאין הוא עם הבהמ"ק יכולים לדור בעולם אחד. והוא דבריהם יכול על מגן להיות מיצר ודואג על חורבן בית המקדש כי מה שעבר אין, ת"ל על רוב פשעיה לכן העצבות נקרא על להבא עדיין שהיא התשובה באותו מקום שיבנה בית המקדש במהרה בימינו:

ובכדי להרחיב דבריהם ולפרש דברי בנין או חורבן ביהמ"ק בימיו הוא על דרך דברי הזהר (ח"א קכט ע"א) על (הפסוק בראשית כד, טו) **וְאַבְרָהָם זָקֵן בָּא בַּיָּמִים** וכן אצל דוד המלך ע"ה, כי הימים נקראים המדות והזקנה נקראת למעלה במקום שאין שם התחלקות הימים והמה הביאו והעלו מדותיהם למעלה למקום הזקנה, וזהו ענין בנין ביהמ"ק בימיו פירוש במדותיו. כי כל אדם מישראל מקדש אקרי משכן כמאמר הנביא (ירמיה ז, ד) **הֵיכַל יְהֺ-וָה הֵמָּה** והשכינה נקראת **הֵיכָל** כמספר אדנ"י (זח"א כג ע"ב) ובתוכה ה' לכן נקרא ה' כל (עיין זח"ג רפט ע"א) פירוש שהיא ה' אחרונה שבשם וכל המדות כלולים בה, כענין היסוד הנקרא כל שכלול כל החמשה מדות וכל אחת כלולה מי' כמספר כ"ל (עיין שם רנה ע"א). וזהו היכל שהוא ענין יחוד קוב"ה ושכינתיה, שהוא ענין קול ודבור שאין דבור בלא קול דלית לה מגרמה כלום אבל אית קול בלא דבור כמבואר בזהר (ח"ג רכח ע"ב). כי הדבור הוא הנקרא סוף כל דרגין בכל עולם ועולם, כענין הדבור שמיחדים שני בני אדם וגופים מחולקים לכוונה אחת, כן הענין בעולמות כי סוף כל דרגין מעולם עליון נקרא דבור המיחדו עם עולם התחתון ממנו כידוע (עיין לעיל פר' ויגש א'), אמנם נגד עולם התחתון אותו הדבור נקרא מחשבה כענין המדבר נגד השומע

שאצל השומע אותיות הדבור המה מחשבתו שכל מחשבה מוכרח גם כן להתלבש באותיות כידוע:

וכשירגיל האדם את עצמו לתת לב לדעת ועינים לראות ואזנים לשמוע כל מחשבתו ואותיותיו ויבן את זאת כי מחשבתו הוא דבור העליון הכללי כנסת ישראל שהיא השכינה הנקראת היכל וכלי מחזיק ברכה שלום, והברכה וטוב הגנוז בתוכה הוא החיות הנקרא קול. והוא הנקרא דבור כנגדו שכל התחלקות אותיות נקרא דבור וכלים, והנקודות המה החיות שבתוכם המנהיגים האותיות ונקרא קול. וא"כ כל אותיות מחשבתו אפילו מכל הדברים היגעים המה מים תחתונים ומיין נוקבין המ(ת)בקשים לעלות אל שורשם וחי בהם ע"י החיות ונקודת האותיות קול ודבור שהוא יחוד קוב"ה ושכינתיה. ובהצטרף היראה ואהבה מן המדות כי המה גדפין להעלות אותיות המחשבה, מי חכם ישמר אלה ויתבונן תמיד באותיות מחשבתו יחוד קוב"ה ושכינתיה מדברים מתוך גרונו ומחשבתו מיד יגיע אליו היראה וההכנעה ואהבתו יתברך והשמחה מזה הנקרא פנים בפנים. וזהו עליות העולמות ע"י גדפין יראה ואהבה להחזירם פב"פ מפני פחד ה' והדר גאונו ולדבקה בו ע"י המחשבה מחברתו הקדש עם השכינה, ואחרי עליתו למעלה מהעולם ויגזר אומר ויקם כמאמר (ש"ב כג ג) **צַדִּיק מוֹשֵׁל יִרְאַת אֱלֹהִים** אבל **אֵין זֶה כִּי אִם בֵּית אֱלֹהִים** אותיות מחשבתו שיעשה אותה **בֵּית אֱלֹהִים** וכלי מחזיק ברכה:

וזהו (סנהדרין כב ע"ב) אין אשה כורתת ברית אלא למי שעושה אותה כלי שהיא השכינה כידוע שהמ"ן הוא הכלי והבנים המה מ"ן לאמם שהוא מחשבה טובה המצטרף למעשה כלים המה אותיות המחשבה, מה שאין כן מי שאינו משגיח על מחשבתו ואותיותיו ונקודותיו במה ידבר אחרי התפשטו מגופו והעדר כלי הדבור מעמו הכלה ונפסד וכ"ש אם דבורו ג"כ מגושם וגופני להנאתו וטובתו **וְטָמֵא טָמֵא, יִקְרָא** (ויקרא יג, מה). כללא דמלתא שכל ימי חיי הבלו של אדם צריך להרגיל א"ע להשתמש בכל כחותיו הפנימים לשם שמים המה מדותיו ולבו ועין שכלו ומחשבתו בכדי שיוכל להקרא אדם שלם בכל דרכיו אחרי הפרד הגוף מעמו לשאת ולתת ולילך ע"י מדותיו ולדבר ולחשוב ולראות ע"י מחשבתו ועין שכלו. וזהו **וְהָיָה אִם שָׁמֹעַ תִּשְׁמְעוּ** שהוא לשון אסיפה כמו (ש"א טו, ד) **וַיְשַׁמַּע שָׁאוּל** ולשון יחוד כמו השמע לי, כי אם בקי ורגיל הוא בעבודת ה' לעשות יחוד קוב"ה ושכינתיה ע"י אותיות מחשבתו והחיות שבתוכו ישמע מחדש ע"י מ"ן חדשים הבאים במוחו ומחשבתו תמיד. וזהו שלא כמדת הקב"ה מדת בשר ודם שמדת בשר ודם ריקן מחזיק מלא אינו מחזיק משא"כ מדת הקב"ה המה הכלים הרוחנים אותיות המחשבה שאינם נעשים כלים אלא ע"י המלאם כבוד ה' ומ"ן המתבקשים לשורש חיותם הוא שעושה אותם כלי בית ה' כלי מחזיק ברכה וחיות הקודש:

והוא ענין כל הנביאים שנתנבאו בכה שהיא השכינה הנקראת דבור כמאמר (במדבר כג, ה) **וְכֹה תְדַבֵּר** **וְכֹה אָמַר ה'**, (שמות ד, כב) וכידוע (הקדמת ת"ז ב ע"ב), והוא על דרך הנזכר על ידי אותיות מחשבתו בהצטרף היראה, מוסיף עליהם משה שהתנבא בזה הדבר שהוא ענין החיות שבאותיות המחשבה והאהבה. כי משה היה פרוש מן האשה הנקראת כלי והיכל שהמה האותיות וכל דביקותו היה בחיות שבתוכו הנקרא זה במספר י"ב אות ו"ו. כמבואר בספרי המקובלים שבכל דבר יש עולם שנה נפש עולם הוא השטח וכלי המקבל, שנה הוא הזמן, נפש הוא החיות שבתוכו, והוא ענין שבכל דבר מהותו וכמותו ואיכותו, מהות הוא ענין העצמות והחיות איכות הוא ענין העולם, כמות הוא זמן. והנה המהות הוא החיות שבתוך האיכות והאיכות והאיך מתחלק לכמה שהוא ענין האותיות והחיות שבתוכם, והנה על שאלת מהות כשאומר מהו שייך לומר זהו, על שאלת האיכות שאומר איך שייך להשיב כה. לכן כל הנביאים נתנבאו בכה מוסיף עליהם משה שהתנבא בזה ממעלה למטה דרך כה כמאמר זה הדבר כי הדבר נקרא שכינה. לכן פה אל פה אדבר בו שהוא החיות שבתוכו האהבה והשמחה הנקראת פב"פ במראה ולא בחידות שהתנבא בזה כאדם שמראה באצבע, והנבואה בכה הוא ענין חידה וכל הנביאים היו

מתבטלים מפני היראה ומשה היה עומד על עמדו שמדתו היא האהבה. או ענין פא"פ הוא להיות הפה נקרא ע"ש דרגא התחתונה מן היה עומד על עמדו שמדתו היא האהבה, או ענין פא"פ הוא להיות הפה נקרא ע"ש דרגא התחתונה מן ההשגה שהוא הדבור, והנה כל הנביאים היה הפה העליון שהיא השכינה מחשבה אצלם משא"כ משה שהיה דבוק למעלה במחשבתו והפה העליון היה כנגד פיו ומדבר בדבר ה' וזהו (ברכות מה. עה"פ שמות יט, יט) **מֹשֶׁה יְדַבֵּר וְהָאֱלֹהִים יַעֲנֶנּוּ בְקוֹלוֹ** של משה:

דברים

[ט"ז]. פרשת וָאֶתְחַנַּן

(להמשיך רחמים על כל הברואים כי הוי' רחמים הוא ואלקים מדת הדין רק צמצום כבודו)

פסוק (ד, לה) **אַתָּה הָרְאֵתָ לָדַעַת**. פירש"י ז"ל כתרגומו איתחזיתא בשעת מתן תורה פתח להם שבעה רקיעים וכשם שקרע את העליונים כך קרע את התחתונים וראו שהוא יחיד וכו':

הנה פתח הרב בפסוק (ג, כג) **וָאֶתְחַנַּן אֶל יְהֹ-וָה** וכו' ופירש"י אין חנון אלא מתנת חנם אע"פ שיש להם לצדיקים לתלות במעשיהם הטובים וכו'. והענין הוא ע"ד הפסוק (ישעי' מ, א-ב) **נַחֲמוּ נַחֲמוּ, עַמִּי—יֹאמַר**, וכו' **כִּי לָקְחָה מִיַּד יְהֹ-וָה כִּפְלַיִם** וכו' והמדרש (ילקוט שם תמ"ה) הוא עיקר חטאו בכפלים ולקו בכפלים ונחמו בכפלים זהו **נַחֲמוּ נַחֲמוּ**. והענין הוא להבין מהו תשובה מבואר כמה פעמים בזוהר (ח"א ע"ט ע"ב וח"ג צט ע"ב עיי"ש) שהוא מקום בינה ושופר וחירות. הנה הוא מהיות ידוע מכמה מאמרי הש"ס והזוהר שהקליפה נקרא חנם כמארז"ל (עירובין יט ע"א) גיהנם על עסקי חנם ובזוהר בכמה מקומות (זח"ב קכח ע"א), והטעם להיותם מתדבקים באדם חנם ושורים עליו בלתי שום הכנה. כי להשראת הקדושה על האדם צריך תיובתא סגי וחילא תקיף ומסירת נפש אז ידבק במדותיו כי הלא אש אוכלה הוא, משא"כ הקליפה שורה מעצמה על האדם בהעדר הקדושה. כי האדם כלי מוכן הוא לקבל אם קדושה קדוש הוא והבא לטהר מסייעין לו ואם לאו ח"ו הקליפה מעצמה שורה וטמא טמא יקרא: והחוש מעיד אדם שאינו מרגיל עצמו בחיבת הקדש אף על פי ששכלו מחייב ואמונתו אתו לעשות הטוב והישר וכמה טענות נגד עשות הרע ובפרט בענין הגדלות אף על פי כן אין בידו לעשות או להכנע נגד הבורא ית"ש. ובודאי אין זה כי אם רוע לב והקליפה השורה עליו שאינה מנחת אותו, או כמו שאמרו רז"ל (יומא פו ע"ב) עבר ושנה בה הותרה וכו' אלא נעשה כהיתר וכו' הגם שיודע האיסור מן התורה והמושכל אעפ"כ הקליפה השורה עליו עושה לו הדבר כמו היתר ומי יודע באיזה אופן ר"ל מידיעה זו. ולכן כל מדה ומדה ואבר שבאדם שאינו מוקטר ומוגש ומוקדש לשמו ית"ש ממילא חל הטומאה (שם) והקליפה שם ועושה כל מה שעושה כשכור חטאים ועונות ופשעים בלתי הבין. ואחריתה מרה כלענה כשמתבונן בעצמו שכל מה שעשה עשוי ע"י הקליפה ואיה איפה הוא ותקותו מי ישורנה, ומלבד זה שנתרחק מהשי"ת בעצמו אלא שהטריח את קונו בצמצומים רבים להשפיע חיות אל הקליפה. כידוע (עיין זח"א קנב ע"ב ות"ז תפ"ד צה ע"ב) מהיות חיות האדם מחיות הקודש ואבר מהשכינה ובהתדבקו אל הקליפה מכניס ניצוצי הקדושה אל הקליפה, וזהו ארז"ל (ע"ז נד ע"ב) ולא עוד אלא שמטריחין אותו וכו' ומאמר הפסוק (ירמיהו ב, יג) **כִּי שְׁתַּיִם רָעוֹת עָשָׂה עַמִּי** וזהו (איכה א, ח) **חֵטְא חָטְאָה יְרוּשָׁלַם** והנה אחרי שהתבונן היותו כמתעתע ותועה בדרך צריך לחזור ולשוב בדרך אשר בא בה אל דרך הישר וזהו באותו מקום, אבל כל תשובותו הרמתה צריך להיות לסור ממוקשי מות אל דרכי החיים בכל מדותיו. לכן נקרא התשובה בינה וחירות שהרי ע"י התבוננות שב אל ה', ותחלת קלקולו הוא מהתעות כשכור והקליפה שורה עליו ממילא ועכשיו ע"י התבוננות מתחרט ושב ויוצא לחירות משבעה עממין שהם הקליפה שהם מדות הרעות. גם נקרא שופר שהרי כשמתבונן על כל מה שעברו עליו ממים הזדונים ואנה הלך ופנה הודו בהרחיקו מן הקדושה וחיי החיים והלביש שק ואפר שהיא הקליפה ולא על עצמו בלבד כי אם על

הקודש ועל המקדש ג"כ כנזכר אז תאחזהו פלצות ומרה תהיה לו מלבד יראת גן עדן וגיהנם:

והנה באמת כשהחי יתן אל לבו מרירות החטא בעצמו אחרי אשר כבר עשהו הוא יותר קשה בלבו של אדם מכל העונשים האפשרים להיות על חטא זה הן בעוה"ז והן בעוה"ב כפלי כפליים. והדין נותן שהרי אותם העונשין הם רפואה ומזור ומירוק אותו החטא בכדי להבריאו ומסתמא המכה היא הגריעות והחסרון והמרירות יותר ויותר מן הרפואה ולהכי הוא מתרפא ברפואה מן המכה. והנה ידוע ארז"ל (זח"א ה ע"א) באורייתא ברא קוב"ה עלמא שהוא באותיות התורה וכידוע מן הזהר (ח"ב קעט ע"ב) שכל מעשה האדם ותחבולותיו הכל הם אתוון, ואם חוטא ח"ו מכניס האותיות ברע ח"ו. ולכן נתקן הודוי על דרך א"ב בכדי שאח"כ כשמתבונן על התעוותו את מעשיו ותופס בלבו גודל מרירות החטא בעצמו כנ"ל שהוא כפליים מכל העונשים בודאי מתחרט וצועק על מה שעבר אשמתי וכל הודוי עד כלות כל כחותיו ובטול מדותיו. כי מגודל המרירות אש לא נופח אחזתהו (ע"פ איוב כ, כו) אשר אי אפשר להכניסו בדבור ואמירה כי אם בקול הברה גנוחי גנח וילולי יליל וצועק סתם אל ה', והאלקים יעננו בקול כי בזה מתעלים האותיות מן הרע שהרי הוא העלה הדבור שהם האותיות אל הקול שהוא למעלה מן הדבור (עיין זח"א פו ע"ב) וזהו שנקרא שופר. ומן ההתבוננות בדעתו יכנס בבינה ומשם אל החכמה שהוא האהבה: וזהו (משלי י, יב) **וְעַל כָּל פְּשָׁעִים תְּכַסֶּה אַהֲבָה** שהוא אהבת השי"ת שהגיע אליו מחמת קנאת ה'. צבאות שקנא לעצמו בגודל רחמנותו על השי"ת והכרח עוצם צמצומו ע"י חטאיו, ומן הרחמנות בא אל אהבת השי"ת בקנאו את קנאת ה' ועושה דין בעצמו עם מרירות לבו כפלים מכל העונשין ונעשה פנחס קנאה וקונה עולמו בשעה אחת, וזהו (ברכות ז ע"א) יפה מרדות אחת בלבו של אדם וכו' וזהו (שם לד ע"ב) במקום שבעלי תשובה עומדים וכו'. וזהו דברי הפסוק **נַחֲמוּ נַחֲמוּ** וכו' וכופל הנחמה שהפסוק מדבר בבעלי תשובה מחמת יראת חטא עצמו ולא מחמת יראת עונש שהוא כפל מן המרירות של עונשין. וזהו (ישעיהו מ, ב) **דַּבְּרוּ עַל לֵב יְרוּשָׁלַם** כי דברו הוא לשון קשה ומרירות על לב ירא שלם, וקראו אליה שהקריאה לשון חבה לשון שמלאכי השרת משתמשין וקרא זה אל זה כי מן המרירות יבא אל האהבה והחיבה. וזהו (שם) **כִּי נִרְצָה עֲוֹנָהּ** שהרי הוא שב מאהבה וזדונות נעשין לו כזכיות ומן העון נעשה רצון, ולמה כל זה כי לקחה מיד ה' כפלים בכל חטאותיה שהרי זה השב נתעורר בלבו על רחמנות השי"ת בכפלים על החטא בעצמו איך עשהו והטריח את קונו כל כך:

וזהו **וָאֶתְחַנַּן** וכו' כי דרך צדיקים שהם דכאי ושפלי רוח ונבזים בעיניהם עם כל מעשיהם הטובים שהוא פירוש מאורים, כידוע (ת"ז ת"ע קלה ע"ב) שאפילו כת"ר אוכם הוא קדם עילת העלות, ועיקר חשקם ותאותם הוא להדבק בה' כידוע (זח"א קעא ע"ב עיי"ש) שמדת הצדיק הוא התקשרות. ואינם שמים על לבם מעשיהם הטובים אשר אור לה' כי אוכם הוא מפניו יתברך וגשם גמור הוא, כמאמר (משלי ו, כג) **כִּי נֵר מִצְוָה וְתוֹרָה אוֹר** שהמצוה הוא נר שהוא אור הדבק בגשמי **ותוֹרָה אוֹר** שהתורה הוא אור פשוט ומופשט מכל הגשמיים, וזהו חשק הצדיקים להתדבק במקור העליון ומשם ממשיכים ומשפיעים רחמים לכל העולמות כדרך הצדיק שהוא התקשרות כל העולמות, וכן דרך תפלתם ג"כ שאין שמים לבם אל מעשיהם הטובים ומאירים כי במה נחשב להם נגד אין סוף ב"ה אבל מבקשים מתנת חנם שהוא כמו שהשי"ת ב"ה מחיה הקליפות כמאמר (נחמיה ט, ו) **וְאַתָּה מְחַיֶּה אֶת כֻּלָּם**:

וזהו שאמר **בָּעֵת הַהִיא** פירוש אם הוא באיזה עת שהוא מן הכ"ד עתים (קהלת ג, ב-ח) כן הוא דרך תפלתו להמשיך רחמים בתורת מתנת חנם בכל עת שהוא, וזהו לאמר שהוא מלשון לאמר לאחרים פירוש שהוא מוצא ושורש הדבור שהוא למעלה מן הכל שהרי אמירה בלב (זח"ב יז. עיי"ש) וכל שכן שהוא למעלה מן המדות וממילא מתבטלים המדות והדינין. וזהו (ברכות לב ע"א) לעולם יסדר אדם שבחו של מקום תחלה ואח"כ יתפלל ויבקש צרכיו פירוש שצריך להתקשר במקור העליון כמו שאמר אתה החילות להראות את עבדך שהוא מוצא

ושורש דבר ומשם להמשיך רחמים כסדר המדות גדלך וידך החזקה. ואח"כ כשמגיע אל מקום החסרון אשר חסר לו מכניס בלבו שהרי הכל מאתו יתברך ובכל חסרון מוכרח להיות צמצום ביותר של השי"ת ובודאי גרם איזה חטא ומקנא בלבו ומתמרמר ושב עד שחוזר אל שורש החכמה ואהבת ה' כנ"ל שהוא חכמה בראש וחכמה בסוף:

כללא דמלתא להמשיך רחמים על כל הברואים ואפילו על הרשעים כי מי יודע מה בלבו של אדם (או) אולי הגיע בתשובתו בשעה אחת מה שאין צדיק גמור יכול ושלא לקטרג על שום אדם, שכבר ניטלה מאתנו החכמה והמדע לדון את האדם אפילו על פי שנים עדים והשפעת שכל זה לא היה רק בזמן הסנהדרין וכל שכן בלא עדות וראיה, אין זה כי אם גדול דעה שהוא רב עלילות ומעשים טובים ומקנא לה' צבאות אם רוצה לקנאות יקנא לעצמו בלבו כנ"ל בכל אשר ימצא. וזהו אתה הראת לדעת וכו' כי בשעת מתן תורה היה לישראל חירות שהוא מקום התשובה שהוא למעלה מן המדות שהם נקראים רקיעים שהם מפריש ומסך, אבל ראו כי ה' שהוא הוי' רחמים הוא אלקים מדת הדין שהוא צמצום השי"ת בכל חסרון מחמת חטא (המעשה) [העושה] וכשישוב אל ה' וירחמהו:

[י"ז]. פרשת שופטים

(רוחניות האדם מאת הו"יה, שהוא עצמו החיים שעליהם מתיירא)

על מאמר רז"ל (סוטה מד ע"א) באזהרת משוח מלחמה וסדרו מי האיש אשר בנה וכו' אשר נטע וכו' אשר ארס וכו' ואח"כ מי האיש הירא וכו'. וארז"ל למדה תורה ד"א בתחלה יבנה בית וכו' כסדר ועל הירא וכו' ארז"ל (שם) הירא מעבירות שבידו:

פתח הרב בפרשת שופטים ושוטרים וכו' עד לשבטיך, והנה ע"ד מאמרם ז"ל (ברכות כ. עיי"ש) ותמיהתם על חסידים הראשונים באמרם דאלו בשני דרב יהודא כולי תנויי בסדר נזיקין הוה ואי הוה שליף חד מסאניה אתי מטרא ואנן תנינן י"ג מתיבתא בעוקצין וכו' ומשני ראשונים הוה מסרי נפשייהו על קדושת ה' וכו'. ובכדי לבאר מאמר זה נקדים לבאר מאמר (שבת לא ע"א) הגר שבא להתגייר לפני הלל ע"מ שילמדו כל התורה כולה על רגל אחת ולימדו מה דסני עלך לחברך לא תעביד. והענין הוא שהגר שבא להתגייר חפץ בהצדקו שיהי' לו העמדה וקיום באחת, שהיא איזה אמונה חזקה לא יפול הנופל ממנה ואדרבה יתחזק להיות מטפס ועולה כי האמונה חזקה נקרא רגל ונקרא אחת כמבואר במ"א (עיין לעיל פרשת תולדות ופ' ויקהל), ומפני יראתו שלא ירד מטה מטה לפעמים ע"י נסיונות ומאורעים בקש זאת. והשיב לו כזאת הנה כללא דמילתא שאין שום אפשרות התחלת אפס קצהו של עבודתו יתברך אם לא באמונתו אמונת אומן פי' שמיעוט נקודת אמונתו בו יתברך ג"כ מאתו יתברך כי הוא הנותן לו לב לדעת ועינים לראות ואזנים לשמוע, כמאמר (ישעיהו מב, יח) **הַחֵרְשִׁים שְׁמָעוּ וְהַעִוְרִים הַבִּיטוּ לִרְאוֹת** וכו', **וְנָתַתִּי לָהֶם לֵב בָּשָׂר** וכו' (יחזקאל לו, כו). ואם אמרו רז"ל (ברכות לג ע"ב) הכל בידי שמים חוץ מיראת שמים לא אמרו רק על אתערותא דלתתא לבד בכדי שיוכל לחול עליו אתערותא דלעילא, משום דברכתא דלעילא לא שריא על אתר ריקנא כמאמר אלישע (מ"א ד, ב) **מַה יֶּשׁ לָךְ בַּבָּיִת** מה יש לך בבית וכו'. אבל אלמלא הקב"ה עוזרו לא יכול לו (קידושין ל ע"ב), וכמאמר (שהש"ר ה, ג) פתחו לי כחודה של מחט ואני אפתח לכם וכו' כי באתערותא דלתתא ארובות השמים נפתחים בפרץ מים רבים לא יכלו לכבות את האהבה כל חד לפום שיעורא דיליה ולאו כל אפין שוין:

וא"ת וכי משוא פנים יש בדבר הן הם הדברים שהוא מופלא ומכוסה ממך (ע"פ חגיגה יג ע"א) וכבשים ללבושך (ע"פ משלי כז, כו) בהדי כבשי דרחמנא למה לך, מי יודע רוח בני אדם העולים למעלה קל כנשר, ורוח האדם ובהמה היורדים למטה בעמקי הקליפות ר"ל. או אולי שעונך גרמו לו וחטאתך מנעו הטוב ממנו מפני היות כל ישראל ערבים ומעורבים נפש אחת ממש בשורשם, או רובי הנסיונות והוא מסיבות מתהפך, **וְאַל תָּדִין אֶת חֲבֵרְךָ עַד שֶׁתַּגִּיעַ לִמְקוֹמוֹ** (אבות ב, ד), או אולי

במקום שהוא עומד אפילו צדיק גמור לא היה יכול לעמוד באמונתו והיה רק רע הרבה יותר ממנו. וא"ת למה השליכו ה' מעל פניו למקום הקליפות ונסיונות אלו כבשא דרחמנא היא ורוצה בהתגלות אלהותו גם שם ולקדש שמו ברבים שהם הקליפות, משא"כ אתה לא כן ה' אלהיך עמך נתן לך רחמים אהבתו **וְיִרְאָתוֹ עַל-פְּנֵיךָ** (שמות כ, טז):

עיקר ושורש הכל שאין ביכולת האדם בעצמו לעשות שום מעשה וחשבון מצות ומעשים טובים ולהדבק בדרכי ה' ית' כי אם על ידו ית' הבורא מאורי האש אהבתו ויראתו על פניו. ואם כה יאמר לא חפצתי בך כל אילי נביות (ע"פ ישעי' ס, ז) לא יועילו לו לקדש עצמו, וכי מה יועיל גבר עם אל אם יצדק מה יפעל לו (ע"פ איוב לה, ז) ובאיזה אופן תחול עליו קדושת ה' ודביקתו, אין זה כי אם רחמיו על כל מעשיו, וחסד אל כמאמר (תהלים סב, יג) **וּלְךָ אֲדֹנָי חָסֶד כִּי אַתָּה תְשַׁלֵּם** לאיש כמעשהו:

לכן לא תכון העבודה לאלקים כ"א אחרי סדור שבחו של מקום והסתכלות זכרון מיעוט ערך עצמו ועומק שפלותו, איך האדם קרוץ מחומר גשם עכור עפר מן האדמה בעיניו לא יראה ובאזניו לא ישמע ובלבו לא יבין כ"א אלהים עשה היום, (שם צד, ט) **הֲנֹטַע אֹזֶן הֲלֹא יִשְׁמָע אִם יֹצֵר עַיִן הֲלֹא יַבִּיט** וכו'. ואין כחו בפיו לדבר כ"א בדבר ה' כמאמר (שם נא, יז) **אֲדֹנָי שְׂפָתַי תִּפְתָּח**, גם אהבתו גם יראתו (ישעיהו מ"ב: כ"ד) **הֲלוֹא** **יְהֹ-וָה זוּ** כי מי האוהב אם לא חי ה' המתפשט בנפשו ואת מי אוהב לה', ומה היא האהבה הלא היא המוחצבת מעצמות אלהות המתפשט ומתקשר ומתאחד בעולם השפל ומתצמצם בעולם קטן הוא האדם (ת"ז ע' קל ע"ב) ובכל מקום שהוא עומד בתוכו ית' הוא עומד כי הוא מקומו של (אדם) [עולם] סובב כל עלמין וממלא כל עלמין:

ובשעה שתוקפו מדת האהבה לאדם אין אתו יודע עד מה (שיר השירים ח, ז) **וְכָל הוֹן בֵּיתוֹ בָּאַהֲבָה, בּוֹז יָבוּזוּ לוֹ** נגדה וכולא קמיה כלא חשיבא כי מאת ה' הוא, וכל מה שהוא מתלהב יותר ומשיג בלבו אמיתות הענין אשר לא מנפשו היא כי מה עשה ובמה יוכל לעשות ככה מגודל עכירות גשמיות גופו ומחשבתו, אבל (ש"ב כג, ב) **רוּחַ יְהֹוָה, דִּבֶּר-בּוֹ** ומלתו על לשונו ואהבתו הלא זה אוד מוצל מאש ה', אז יתלהב יותר ויותר בקול גדול ולא יסף לא תכיל היריעה ולא יספיקו ימים דיו לבאר עוצם וגודל חללה של לב האוהב אמיתי ונקודתו בזה והבל פיו בלהב השמימה:

ובאהבה זו ממילא יתקשר לכל באי עולם ובני אדם כיוצא בו, אחרי היות האהבה שפע ברכה עליונה בתכלית הידיעה כי לא זכה מנפשו אליו וא"א כלל לעשותה ולזכות בה אבל ברצונו הקב"ה נתנה לו, ואס היה נותן מתנה זו לחברו היה חבירו כיוצא בו מתלהב לשמו יתברך וא"כ במה נחשב הוא מחברו. והראיה באם העדר האהבה זו הרי הוא ככל האדם בעניני הגשמיים פעם במדות פעם בחרון פעם ברחוב כחץ יעוף יומם מחשבות כאלו לאלפים לכל צדיק וצדיק, והנה בהיותו במדה זו הרי הוא כאותו אדם ובמדה זו הרי כאותו בעל תאוה. וממילא אוהב כל ישראל אפילו לרשעי ישראל מפני אמיתות הבנתו וידיעתו שקרובים המה ויש לו שייכות עמהם והנה הוא כאחד האדם ואין לו לעצמו יתרון עליהם כ"א מה שענוהו בשערה מן השמים. ולכן בהיותו מתעלה באהבת ה' מתעלים כולם עמו לאלפים מפני שבהיותו במדות השייכים אליהם הרי הוא והם נפש אחת בכל מדה ומדה שהוא מודד הרי הוא מקושר עם אלפים ורבבות בני אדם לכן בעלותו עולים עמו:

משא"כ אדם המדמה בנפשו (דברים ח, יז) **כֹּחִי וְעֹצֶם יָדִי, עָשָׂה לִי אֶת-הַחַיִל הַזֶּה** ללמוד לשמור ולעשות ולקיים את כל התורה הרי הוא שונא ישראל וכמו שאין לו אלוה ממש, ובוודאי הוא כן ופחות וגרוע הוא מכל (ישעיה נז, כ) **וְהָרְשָׁעִים, כַּיָּם נִגְרָשׁ** ומוסיף כח בקליפה יותר מכל הרשעים ויורד מטה מטה, והוא (משלי טז, כח) **וְנִרְגָּן ,מַפְרִיד אַלּוּף** שהוא מפריד היראה שהיא השכינה מחי החיים באמרו כי לא מן השם הוא זה וידו עשתה זאת. כן הלל שהיה עניו מאוד אמר (סוכה נג ע"א) אם אני כאן הכל כאן שבכל מקום שמוצא את עצמו הרבה יש מאותו המין והרי הוא

כאחד מהם אבל לה' הישועה לכן כשעולה עולים עמו:

וזהו (תהלים טז, ח) **שִׁוִּיתִי יְהֹ-וָה לְנֶגְדִּי תָמִיד** פירוש שהוא משוה את ה' אפילו בכל התנגדות המזדמן אליו או ראה או ידע, מאמין במאמר (נחמיה ט, ו) **וְאַתָּה מְחַיֶּה אֶת כֻּלָּם** והם כמו מאמר (ת"ז ה, יט ע"ב) מים תחתונים בוכים גם אנן בעינן למהוי קדם מלכא שרוצים להתעלוה על פי ה' בזמן אשר יחפוץ ה' ביקרם, כי השם הוי"ה הוא המעלה את הכל. וענין שם הוי"ה הוא החכמה והבינה מקום ההתבוננות לשוב אל ה' והאהבה והיראה מפניו כידוע. כי מן היראה האמיתית שהיא ה' אחרונה ושכינה בעמדו מרעיד לזכרו היותו עומד בתוך שורש הכל, וכנסת ישראל ואדני מעון הוא לו, וקול דברי אלקים חיים יוצא מפיו ומדבר בדבריו נבהל להשיב. ומתדבק בקול שהוא האהבה המשפיע ומחיה את הדיבור שהוא היראה כדרך האיש לחזור אחר אבידתו (קדושין ב ע"ב) שהוא המשפיע אחר המקבל ועל היראה האמיתית ממילא חל האהבה. ואחרי ידיעתו שאף גם זאת כח ה' הוא וגבוהים עליהם אלהים חיים ומלך עולם חי החיים עולה הוא במעלה זאת ומשם אל האין שהיא החכמה שהיא יו"ד קטנה שממנה נעשים כל האותיות ומן היו"ד עולה אל אלופו של עולם שהוא אל"ף. כי צורת א היא יו"ד וי"ו דל"ת כידוע מן אלופו של עולם השתלשלות הג' קווים והתפשטותם, שהאמצעי הוא מגדל הפורח באויר המעלה התפשטות השניים שהם אהבה ויראה והמגדל הוא הלמ"ד (עיין זח"ב צא ע"א) וזהו הצירוף אל. נמצא שקודם בריאת העולמות היה הוא ושמו לבד, ואחרי שברא הכל אעפ"כ באמיתות התבוננות אין שום דבר בעולם בלתו והכל בתוכו והוא בתוך הכל ומציירו ומקיימו והרי הוא כאילו הוא ושמו לבד שהרי הוא רק למען הראות גדלו וכל הנקרא בשמו ולכבודו אפילו כל ההתנגדות. וזהו (ר"ה יז ע"ב) ה' קודם שחטא ה' אחר שחטא אל המעלה את הכל ומתחילה ועד סוף הכל הוא יתברך בעצמו, ומה לאדם שיבא אחר המלך למה זה הוא כך וזה הוא כך ואין לו לאדם כי אם לסדר שבחו יתברך לפניו כמו סידור בעלמא וממילא תעשה הכל. כמאמר משה רבינו ע"ה **בָּוָאֶתְחַנַּן** (דברים ג, כד) אתה החילות להראות את עבדך כי אפילו תחלת יראתי מפניך מאתך אני, ואח"כ את גדלך ואת ידך החזקה שהם המדות ההתפשטות והאהבה ממילא חלה עליו. והכל **וָאֶתְחַנַּן** במתנת חנם (רש"י שם) רק ברצון המלך לבד בלי שום כושר מעשה כלל כמאמר (שם ט, ה) לא בצדקתך וביושר לבבך אתה בא לרשת את ארצם וזהו **וָאֶתְחַנַּן** במתנת חנם אעברה נא ואראה וכו':

ומשל הדיוט היא בנצחונו של בשר ודם שהמלך מעמיד הפשוטים מחיילותיו בקשרי המלחמה הכבדה והשרים יושבים עם המלך ברחוק ומתענגים עמו, ואעפ"כ אח"כ שכבשו המלחמה השר יושב עם המלך ומתענג (עמו) עם המלך, וכל זה אינו כי אם רצון המלך בלי שום היותו ראוי במעשיו לכך, כי מי שיכול לעמוד בקשרי המלחמה מעמידו, ומי ששייך לשימוש אחר ממנהו ע"ז. ואי משום הא אינו ביטול השכר והעונש חלילה לאל מרשע ושדי מעול (א"פ איוב לד) אבל הכל במשפט שהרי הכל הוא שמותיו יתברך ומי יודע בכל אלה רק למען דעת את ה' ולעבדהו מודעת זאת שאין לכ"א רק לעבדו ית' באופן שהוא, שהרי לכך נברא ובכך נברא ומה לו עוד. ובזה יהיו כל ישראל כולם אהובים לו שהרי כל אחד הוא שמו יתברך באופן רצונו כמאמר (ר"ה י"א ע"א) כל מעשה בראשית לדעתן נבראו [ו]פירש"י ז"ל ששאלו מכל אחד אם רצונו בבריאה והענין לבאר הוא עמוק ומובא בספרים:

כללא דמלתא מי שעובד את ה' על דרך זה אוהב לכולם ומעלה את כל השייכים בערכו, ובהיפוך מי ששונא אפילו לרשעים ממילא משמע כי בצדקתו ובחזקתו ויגבה לבו ואם הוא הצדיק [ממילא כן] (בעינו ו)לא ה' פעל כל זאת ועקוב הוא מכל. וזהו שלמדו הלל בענותנותו כל התורה כולה על רגל אחד הוא האמונה כנ"ל **וְאָהַבְתָּ לְרֵעֲךָ כָּמוֹךָ** (ויקרא יט, יח), ומאמר (תהלים קלט, כא) **הֲלוֹא מְשַׂנְאֶיךָ יְהֹוָה אֶשְׂנָא** הוא לשונאי שמו ית' שהם המינין והאפיקורסין אבל לא לשום בעל תאוה ועובר לתאבון. כי מי יודע מה שהית והינך אם אתה תגיע למקומו, כידוע שאין לך דבר בעולם שיצא מגדר שבעת ימי

הבנין הצריכים להתעלות והאדם כלול מכולם וצריך להעלותם לשורשם אל ה' כידוע ומבואר במ"א (עי' לעיל פר' קרח). על דרך משל היראה העליונה שהיא התחתונה שבכולם שממנה נסתעף יראה החיצוניות, ואם היא מזדמנת לאדם צריך להתבונן מה אני ירא מאין נמשך לי מדה זו הלא מיראתו יתברך, ומפני מי אני ירא הלא מלא כל הארץ כבודו ואין שום דבר בלתו, ומה חיי הלא הוא יתברך ולאן אני הולך אליו יתברך א"כ מה אני ואין לו לירא כי אם מכבודו יתברך. וכשיגיע ליראת ה' יבין וישכיל אם אמנם היראה היא פחד ה' הלא גם זה המדה נבראת מאתו ית"ש ויש בה חיות מאתו יתברך שאי אפשר בלתו, ואם נמשך לה חיות ממקום גבוה ממילא מצומצם בתוכה אהבה שהרי חיות הנמשך ומתקשר בדבר היא האהבה, וממילא מתלהב עליו אהבתו יתברך וחוט של חסד משוך עליו בשפע ברכה ומשם אל מוצא המים אשר לא יכזבו לעולם:

וזהו דבריהם דבשני דרב יהודא כולהו תנויי בנזיקין הוה שהיא העבודה מה דעלך סני לחברך לא תעביד דברים שבין אדם לחבירו **וְאָהַבְתָּ לְרֵעֲךָ כָּמוֹךָ**. ואמרם וכי הוה שליף חד מסאני פירוש שאם פשט גשם אחד משבעת ימי הבנין ע"ד של נעלך וכו', כלומר שאם היה מקשר עצמו במדת היראה אליו יתברך הוי אתי מטרא פירוש המשכה ושפע חיות שמחיה היראה היא מדת האהבה שהיא שפע ברכה (שיר השירים ח, ז) **מַיִם רַבִּים לֹא יוּכְלוּ לְכַבּוֹת אֶת הָאַהֲבָה**, ואמרו הטעם מפני שאינהו הוי מסרי נפשייהו על קדושת השם כידוע (זח"ג רס ע"א) מענין נפילת אפיים שהיא ירידה צורך עליה לברר ניצוצות הקדושה מתוך הקליפה ולהעלותם בעלייתו הוא נקרא מסירת נפש על קידוש השם, לכן אחרי שאינם חוששים על עצמן כלל רק על שמו ית' כי הכל הוא ושמו לבד ואין סוף המתפשט ומיחד לכולם הוא המעלה אותם בעצמו ובכבודו מתראה עליהם וה' כברק יצא ואתי מטרא:

וזהו **שֹׁפְטִים וְשֹׁטְרִים** תתן לך פירוש לך בעצמך שהיא עבודתו יתברך תהיה ע"ד **שֹׁפְטִים** שהוא דברים שבין אדם לחבירו כמאמר מה דעלך סני לחברך וכו' מפני שהכל מאתו יתברך וזהו אשר ה' אלהיך נותן לך לשבטיך לכן **וְאָהַבְתָּ לְרֵעֲךָ כָּמוֹךָ**:

או יאמר **שֹׁפְטִים** שהוא המקום הבינה והתשובה כי המשפט לשפוט הוא ע"י הבינה **וְשֹׁטְרִים** הוא היראה פירוש להבין שהיראה היא ג"כ נבראת מאתו יתברך וחיים יש בה ובחרת בחיים, וזהו אשר ה' אלהיך נותן וכו' כידוע שמשם היא מוצא ההשתנות וההתפשטות לכל גבולי ישראל. ובכדי להבין המאמר ידוע שיש באדם ג"כ משוח מלחמת היצר, והיראה נקרא בית שהיא דרתא כמאמר חז"ל (שבת לא ע"ב) חבל על מאן דלית ליה דרתא וכו' והאהבה נקרא כרם שהוא עץ החיים אילנא דחיי ואיש הנקרא יחוד שניהם שנקראת יראת ה' הם שני מדות, וזהו למדה תורה דרך ארץ וכו'. ויספו השוטרים לדבר וכו' הירא מעבירות שבידו ישוב לביתו שהיא נקודה בהיכלי' שהוא מקום עלייתם בשרשם ודו"ק:

[י"ח]. פרשת כי תצא א'

(הקליפות כחיצונים, והקוב"ה כסתרו של עולם ורשות היחיד)

כִּי תֵצֵא לַמִּלְחָמָה עַל אֹיְבֶיךָ וּנְתָנוֹ... וְשָׁבִיתָ וכו'. פרש"י ז"ל לא דברה תורה אלא כנגד יצר הרע:

פתח הרב הנה ארז"ל (יומא פו ע"ב) אופני התשובה שנוי מעשה ושנוי השם ושנוי מקום וכמבואר בזוהר. הנה פירוש ענינו ע"ד הידיעה מאמר (משלי ו, כג) **כִּי נֵר מִצְוָה וְתוֹרָה אוֹר** הם רמ"ח פקודין נרות לאדלקא מאור תורה, והם אברי השכינה להתלבש בכל אברי נשמת האדם להאירו על ידם לנטלו ולנשאו ממלחמה לה' בעמלק מדור דור הוא השטן הוא היצר הרע מתגבר על האדם בכל יום והקב"ה עוזרו על ידם לחסות **בְּסֵתֶר** כנפיו **וּבְצֵל שַׁדַּ-י יִתְלוֹנָן** וטמיר בכל טמירין דעלמא ודינא לא שלטא ביה. כידוע (תענית ח ע"ב) שאין הברכה מצויה אלא בדבר הסמוי מן העין במקום דלא שלטא ביה **עַיִן לֹא רָאָתָה אֱלֹהִים זוּלָתְךָ יַעֲשֶׂה לִמְחַכֵּה לוֹ**, שכל עיקר השראת הקליפה ודינים הוא ההתגלות וכל היותר יותר, כענין לוחות הראשונות נתנו ברעש

ונשתברו (תנחומא כי תשא לא ע"א):

וזהו (בראשית מב, א) **לָמָּה תִּתְרָאוּ** (ישעי' סו, כד) **וְהָיוּ דֵרָאוֹן לְכָל בָּשָׂר**, ולכן נקראים חצונים לשון חיצונית ויצר הרע בהתגלות, והקב"ה נקרא **סִתְרוֹ** של עולם פנימית רה"י (הקדמת ת"ז יב ע"א), והתורה נקראת (מו"ק טז. עה"פ שה"ש ז, ב) חמוקי ירכיך מה ירך בסתר אף ד"ת, וזהו (קידושין ל ע"א) אם פגע בך וכו' משכהו לבית המדרש שהיא התורה לחסות בסתר. כי מבחר השמות הוא אדם ולא איש אם אמנם **יְהֹ-וָה אִישׁ מִלְחָמָה** כתיב (שמות טו, ג) זהו בשעת מלחמה שהוא לשבר הקליפות בקול ענות גבורה וזרוע נטויה והתגלות כמותם כי מניה וביה ליזל ולשדא ביה נרגא הס מלהזכיר עליהם שם ה' שם בסתר. כאשר אמרו רז"ל (ברכות נח ע"א) כי ברעם ורעש לא אתי מלכא כי אם בחשאי וקול דממה דקה תמן אתי מלכא ומלכותא דארעא כמלכותא דרקיע לכן הבין בלא ראות מעמד המלך ע"ש. והנה ידוע (מת"ז ס"ט קח ע"ב) שאפילו כל הקליפות שבעולם היותר חיצונים תלוים ועומדים במאמרו של מלך **וּנְהִירוּ דָּקִיק** מן הקודש להחיותם בסוד **וּמַלְכוּתוֹ בַּכֹּל מָשָׁלָה** (תהלים קג, יט), לכן כל עיקר רדיפתם להתדבק ולהאחד בקודש עבור חיותם אבל אחרי הבירור ניצוצי הקדושה ממנו **בִּלַּע הַמָּוֶת לָנֶצַח** (ישעיהו כה, ח): והנה אורייתא וקב"ה כולא חד (זח"ג עג ע"א) שהנה כן דרך התורה תיבותיה ואותיותיה מורים ומעוררים פנימיותה, כענין הטוב שכל הטוב שבעולם גנוז בגוה במלת אותיות אלו של טוב וכן השמחה במלת אותיות של שמחה. וכל הע' לשון יש להם חיות מלה"ק ולשון תורה לחוד בסוד **וּמַלְכוּתוֹ בַּכֹּל מָשָׁלָה**, כענין שכן קורין בלשון יוני לאחת הן (שבת לא ע"ב) זה מקום חיותו מן התורה וכן כל לשון. ולכן מתעוררים המדות כי מעשה אלהים המה ע"י הדבור בכל לשון, כענין השמחה המתעוררת מבשורה טובה וכן היגון מדבור הפכי וכן הכעס מדבור שכנגדו והתפארת והוד מספור שבחו בפניו וכן כל עניני המדות. אשר המדות בעצמם אין להם שום תמונה והשגה בעולם במלות אותיות שם המדה כמו חסד באותיות חסד וכן כולם כי אם ע"ד הנסתר. וסוד ה' להמשיך המדה בלשון תורה ואותיותיה וממנה לכל לשון. וזהו (בראשית א, י) **וַיַּרְא אֱלֹהִים כִּי טוֹב** כי הראיה הוא לשון המשכה כמאמר (ישעיהו ב, ב) **וְנָהֲרוּ אֵלָיו כָּל הַגּוֹיִם** שהוא לשון נהורא שהוא אור עין וזהו עין השכל עינא דליבא כמאמר (קהלת א, טז) **וְלִבִּי רָאָה הַרְבֵּה חָכְמָה**, וזהו הנאמר (מגילה ח ע"א) בזב ג' ראיות ב' ראיות שהיא המשכת זוב:

והנה מצא מין את מינו וניעור אם אדם גס הוא ומגושם אינם מתעוררים מדותיו כי אם בהשגת גשמיות ובשורשם כמו כסף וזהב ומגדנות לרוב ותענוגות בני אדם אף על פי שהדברים והחפצים הם עבים וגולם חומרי מתעוררים בו המדות שבלי תמונה בסוד **וּמַלְכוּתוֹ בַּכֹּל מָשָׁלָה**. אבל אינו משיגה כי אם ע"י כח החומר הנזכר וכפי ענינו, לכן כן דרך המדה שהיא חלשה ואינה קיימת כמאמר (אבות ה, טז) **בָּטֵל דָּבָר, בְּטֵלָה אַהֲבָה**, משא"כ אהבת ה' ...**כִּי עַזָּה כַמָּוֶת אַהֲבָה... מַיִם רַבִּים לֹא יוּכְלוּ לְכַבּוֹת ... אִם יִתֵּן אִישׁ אֶת כָּל הוֹן בֵּיתוֹ בָּאַהֲבָה בּוֹז יָבוּזוּ לוֹ**. לכן זהו (שם א, יז) **וְלֹא הַמִּדְרָשׁ הוּא הָעִקָּר, אֶלָּא הַמַּעֲשֶׂה** כי האותיות הם בסוד המעשה והתגין נקודות וטעמים מחשבה נר"נ (ת"ז יט לט ע"ב) וזהו (זח"א מז ע"א) באורייתא ברא קוב"ה עלמא, כי ששת ימים עשה ה' וביום השביעי שהם ז' (אותיות וט"ו) [תיבות וכ"ז] אותיות. וזה כל אדם לכך נברא להשיג המדות ולהשתמש עמהם ע"י אותיות התורה **וְנֵר מִצְוָה** כי בהשיג **מִצְוָה** אחת הבאה לידו יתעורר שמחתו כבהשיג חפצו הגשמי כענין שמח במצות הוא וכענין לא פסיק חוכא מפומיה כוליה יומא (ברכות ט ע"ב). כי העיקר להדבק במדותיו, והם על ידי השגת המצות כי בלתי גבול המצוה המדה אין סוף וגבול שהרי המדות אצולות מאתו יתברך שהוא אין סוף ודבר אין סוף אין לו השגה לכן הוצרך הצמצום, ואח"כ מאיר אור המדה דרך קו המדה וגבול בלי התפשטות בו יותר מדאי שלא יתבטל הכלי מהיכנו שהוא הצמצום הראשון כי אם במזג השוה לעשותה כלי אז אפשרית ההשגה במדה זו ע"י התגלות הצמצום כלי וגבול. ולכן

כל הצמצומים הם אינם רק בשביל התגלות כבודו והרחמנות על החסרון אח"כ מתגלה וכן דרך כל נס המתגלה מתוך הנסיון וזהו (עיין תנחומא מקץ ג) מתוך צרה המציא פדות. וכל עיקר צמצום המצוה בגשם מעשי הוא **נֵר** להשיג **אוֹר תּוֹרָה** המאיר בתוכו שהוא השמחה של מצוה וכן כל מדה ומדה כי בלתי הגבול אין להשיגו שהמדה אין סוף, והכל לפי מה שהוא אדם אם גשמי הוא הגבול וכלי התעוררות מדותיו הם חפצי גשמיים ואם צדיק צדקות אהב:

ולכן במקום שבעלי תשובה עומדין אין צדיקים גמורים יכולים לעמוד, כי מצות התשובה היא יותר עליונה ופנימית מכל המצות, אחרי שהבע"ת כבר השתמש במדותיו והשיגם בעניני הגשמים אם היו בדברי הרשות או איסור עכ"פ השיג מעט מן המדות שהתעורר בהשתמשם, ועתה מתעורר במדות היותר עליונים במצות התשובה שהוא לשוב מהשגת מדותיו שבתחילה. משא"כ כל המצות מעשיות הם גשמים והתעוררות המדות ע"י קטן מהכיל התעוררות מדת הבע"ת במצות התשובה:

והנה אחרי שובו באמת שהוא להגביר מדותיו שלא להשתמש בגשמיות ולא לשמוח ולהתעצב בהם כי שולחנו גדול משולחנם לכן אין הגשמים פועלים במדותיו כלום כי אם אהבת ה' ועשות חסד. הוא הנקרא שינוי מעשה ודאי ושינוי מקום שיצא מרה"ר לרה"י ושינוי השם שבודאי אין צירוף השמות שוים במדותיו דהשתא להקודמים כי עכשיו משתמש בלה"ק ומתפעל ע"י **כִּי נֵר מִצְוָה וְתוֹרָה אוֹר** ותחלה היה משתמש בשם א' הלשונות מע' לשון כנזכר. וזהו באותו פרק באותו מקום באותו אשה והוא ענין עולם שנה נפש כי השתנות המעשה נמשך מענין חילוף הזמנים ושורשם הוא:

וזהו **כִּי תֵצֵא** שהוא מרה"י לרה"ר שהוא התגלות המדות בודאי **לַמִּלְחָמָה עַל אֹיְבֶיךָ** שהקליפה רודפת אחרי הקדושה היכא דשלטא ביה עינא ואלמלא הקב"ה עוזרו זהו גלוי שכינה כנגדם ה' איש מלחמה. וזהו (אבות ג, ב) **הֱוֵי מִתְפַּלֵּל בִּשְׁלוֹמָהּ שֶׁל מַלְכוּת** שהיא שכינה (ת"ז כ"א ס ע"א) **שֶׁאִלְמָלֵא מוֹרָאָהּ, אִישׁ אֶת רֵעֵהוּ חַיִּים בְּלָעוֹ**. וזהו **וּנְתָנוֹ יְהֹ-וָה אֱלֹ-הֶיךָ בְּיָדֶךָ וְשָׁבִיתָ שִׁבְיוֹ** הם המדות שהשתמש עמהם תחלה **וְרָאִיתָ בַּשִּׁבְיָה** לשון המשכה **אֵשֶׁת יְפַת** הוא על שם המ"ן כי המדה שהשתמש עמה תחלה נעשה עכשיו מ"ן והתעוררות לשוב ממנה. וזהו **וְלָקַחְתָּ לְךָ לְאִשָּׁה** שעושה אותה כלי מדה וגבול וצמצום להתגלות מדותיו העליונים ממנה. ובוודאי אין האדם השלם צריך לכל זה אבל הכל לפי מה שהוא אדם כי אין דרך השגת מדותיו ע"י גבולים גשמים או יותר רוחנים שאינם מוגבלים כ"כ כי כאיש גבורתו לעמוד בקשרי המלחמה לעורר מדותיו לשמים:

וזהו לא דברה תורה אלא כנגד היצר הרע כי הדבור הוא הצמצום והתחלקות האותיות בתוך הקול בכדי להמשיך הקול והתגלותו אפילו בצמצום זה שהוא המשכת חיותו יתברך בתוך הדבור כידוע (מזח"ג רכ"ח ע"א) שהדבור והקול הוא יחוד קוב"ה, וזהו לא דברה תורה שאינו צריך הצמצום אלא כנגד יצה"ר שאם אין יכול לו בצמצום קל מצמצם יותר בגשמים כענין (ברכות ה ע"א) אי אזל מוטב ואם לאו יזכיר לו יום וכו' עד **בִּלַּע הַמָּוֶת לָנֶצַח**:

[י"ט]. פרשת כי תבא א'

(שורש מידות הנפש, הם עולמות ואורות עליונים מביאות דביקות, תענוג רוחני, ושמחה של מצווה)

אמר רבא כל המעביר על מדותיו מעבירין לו על כל פשעיו שנאמר (מיכה ז, יח) **נֹשֵׂא עָוֹן וְעֹבֵר עַל פֶּשַׁע** וכו' (ר"ה יז ע"א). הנה בפרשה. זו רבים מהמפרשים פותרים אותה **כִּי תָבוֹא אֶל הָאָרֶץ** העליונה שהוא העוה"ב וכו' **וְשַׂמְתָּ בַטֶּנֶא** דורשין נוטריקון **[טֶ"נֶא]** טעמים נקודות אותיות:

והענין הוא מאמר רבי יעקב (אבות ד, כא) **הַתְקֵן עַצְמְךָ בַּפְּרוֹזְדוֹר, כְּדֵי שֶׁתִּכָּנֵס לַטְּרַקְלִין** שאמר דרך משל על עוה"ז שהוא כפרוזדור לפני העוה"ב, אם אמנם **הַפְּרוֹזְדוֹר** הוא מקום מעבר קודם הכניסה ולא להתקין עצמו בתוכו עשוי, הנה המעבר דרך עליו הוא התיקון שבתוך כך מתקן עצמו. כי זה הוא ענין עולם הזה אשר

לכאורה נגדות לעוה"ב שהוא רוחני פשוט שאינו מושג למשיגי העוה"ז ואיך יתכן היות מעבר העוה"ז תיקון והכנה לכניסת עוה"ב. אבל באמת כתיב (תהלים פד, ו) **אַשְׁרֵי אָדָם עוֹז לוֹ בָךְ מְסִלּוֹת בִּלְבָבָם**, שהענין הוא **עוֹלָם חֶסֶד יִבָּנֶה** (שם פט, ג) ואין שום נברא בעולם בלתי ע"י המדות שבעת ימי הבנין כידוע, וזה כל האדם שלא להשתמש במדות לפעולות הגשם כי לא הקרה ה' לפניו אותה כי אם להזכיר בשם ה' ולהתדבק עמה בשורשה עד אין סוף, כי אחרי ידיעתו שמדות נפשו הם עולמות ואורות עליונים אשר לא ידע אנוש ערכה ונעלמה מעין כל חי **מָה רַב טוּבְ הצפון** בנשמת האדם ומדותיו **אֱלֹהִים זוּלָתְךָ יַעֲשֶׂה לִמְחַכֵּה לוֹ**, איך ישתמש עמהם להנאת גשמית וחיי שעה, כידוע ממשל מרגלית יקרה מאד שלא יתננה בדבר מועט או בפרוסת לחם אפילו אם ירעב מאד אחרי ידיעתו מגודל ערכה אם לא מי שהוא שוטה כל ימיו ולא ידע ערכה. וזהו **אַשְׁרֵי אָדָם עוֹז** לו בך כי המדות הם **ע"וז**, למטה ז' ולמעלה ע' כידוע שלמטה יחידות ולמעלה עשירות יותר בהתרחבות, שכל מדות נפשו הם רק ב"ך בה' יתברך, ואפילו כל המדות הגשמים החולפים ועוברים במחשבתו הם רק מסילות בלבבם כמו פרוזדור לטרקלין לעבור דרך עליהם להתקשר בשורשה בו יתברך:

והנה פירוש מעביר על מדותיו הוא שלא לעשות כפי התחייבות מדותיו אבל הוא מעביר ומשנה מדותיו, שהוא ענין הרהור תשובה שהוא עדיין התחלה וקבלה בלב לשוב אף על פי שעדיין לא נגמר במלואו וטובו, שהרי מדותיו הראשונים הם עדיין בתקפם וגבורתם שהרי הוא מעביר שלא לעשות כפי מדותיו אבל עדיין ישנם בו. וכבר כתבנו שהעיקר שירגיל האדם את מדותיו בלתי לה' לבדו ולשרש אחריהם, כענין (ע"ז מה ע"ב) העוקר עבודה זרה שצריך לשרש אחריה שלא ישאר בו שום **שֹׁרֶשׁ פֹּרֶה רֹאשׁ וְלַעֲנָה**, כי השורש הוא הכל וכל הענפים מסתעפים אחריה כענין (ב"ר נג, כ) זרוק חוטרא וכו' אעיקרא קאי. וכללו של דבר אי סייפא לא ספרא (ע"ז יז ע"ב) שאין האלהות מושג למשיגי הגוף וכל זמן שהמדה משגת בגוף גשמי איך תשיג עוה"ב האלהית פשוט ורוחני:

אבל האמת שתחלת ההרהור תשובה כלול מהכל ונעוץ סופה בתחלתה, שהרי בהרהור נעשה צדיק גמור כדברי חז"ל (קידושין מט ע"ב) ה"ז מקודשת. והענין כי ההרהור הוא נקודה שבלב והתחלה כענין הנקודה שהיא התחלה לכל האותיות ומנהיגם כידוע (ת"ז ת' ה, כ ע"ב), ולכן אינו קשה כי אם ההתחלה כמאמר (מכילתא יתרו יט, ה) כל התחלות קשות, אבל אחר ההתחלה הוא מוליך ומביא לסוף המעשה במחשבה תחלה שהוא התענוג מהשלמת הרצון. וענין התחלה הוא כמו הולדה שגם בהולד האדם יש בו כל שרשי כוחותיו שיבואו לו אח"כ, אבל אינם בהתגלות והתחלקות בפועל כי אם בכח נסתר כלולים בנקודה אחת כידוע, וצריכין למוד והרגל לחלק מדותיו ולהוציא הדבר מכח אל הפועל. כי אע"פ שכלול הכל בנקודה בלתי הלמוד וההרגל לא יגמור, כי הנקודה היא יכולה להשתנות לכל אות ולכל צד שתרצה עד אחר ההרגל בהמשך הזמן, אשר לחלק יצא כל שרשי הנקודות להתפשט כל מדה בפני עצמה הולך וגדול מקטנות אל הגדלות כל מדה הולך ובונה במה לעצמו עד כי גדל מאד לצרכי בנין שלם. כמאמר (בראשית ב, כב) **וַיִּבֶן יְהֹ-וָה אֱלֹהִים אֶת הַצֵּלָע** ונעשה קומה שלימה אשר עז פניו לא ישונה כמו הנקודה שיכולה להשתנות למה שתרצה:

כן ענין הרהור תשובה שהיא התחלה ונקודה שבלב הכלולה מכל מדות התשובה אבל אח"כ צריך להמשיך עצמו תמיד במדה זו עד כי ימשיך מדות גדולות מן הנקודה, ואחר שיתגדלו מדותיו כל צרכם להשתנות ממה שהיו על אופן הנהגת הנקודה הוא הנקרא אותיות, ומן האותיות יבא אל התענוג שהוא הטעמים שהיא השמחה של מצוה. ובודאי שגם בנקודה היה כלול השמחה בהעלם והוא לעשות נחת רוח ליוצרו שאמר ונעשה רצונו, אבל אינו מורגש כמו מן המדות הגדולות שהרגשת השמחה מהם הוא ענין השגתם וסדר השתמש עמם בעוה"ב ביתר שאת, זהו ענין התקן עצמך בפרוזדור בעה"ז כדי שתכנס לטרקלין עוה"ב **בְּשַׁנּוֹתוֹ אֶת טַעְמוֹ** ומדותיו מכל עיקר הרגשתם שלא בגשמיות כלל:

וזהו ענין ארז"ל (מגילה לא ע"ב) עזרא תיקן להם לישראל לקרות התוכחה הראשונה קודם עצרת והשניה קודם ראש השנה באמרו תכלה שנה וקללותיה כי עצרת גם כן ראש השנה לאילן. כידוע שבעולמות עליונים שלמעלה מן הזמן ענין השנה בהם לשון שינוי וכן חודש מלשון חידוש מעולם לעולם ומענין לענין, שהוא ענין אלפים שנה שקדמה התורה. וידוע מענין הקללות באמרם חז"ל (עירובין יח ע"א) תחלה נתקלל נחש כי הוא שורשה וכל הצ"ח קללות כולם הם הסתעפות להנמשך אחריו ומתפרד מאתו יתברך. וכן בתשובתו הרמתה אליו יתברך עד כי ישתנו מדותיו משרשם בלתי לה' לבדו בוודאי יחליפנו וימיר אותו רע בטוב, ויתהפכו כל הקללות לברכה לשון בריכה והמשכה. ויתהפך מנחש למטה שהוא המשכה, וזהו שתיקן לקרות התוכחה בצאת השנה שהוא גמר השינוי כי אז בודאי תכלה השנה וקללותיה, כי הקללות שבתורה הם תיקון הנחש וע"י קריאתם (בתורה בסוף השנה) [סוף שנה בתורה] הקדומה אלפים שנה שינו את מדתם להתהפך לברכה ועושה חסד לאלפים:

וזהו **וְהָיָה** שהוא לשון שמחה, **כִּי תָבוֹא אֶל הָאָרֶץ** העליונה שהיא שמחה של מצוה להשיג **וְלָקַחְתָּ מֵרֵאשִׁית** וכו' שהוא ענין התחלה והרהור תשובה שהיתה נקודה **וְשַׂמְתָּ בַטֶּנֶא** הוא פירוש טעמים נקודות אותיות שהוא להמשיך הנקודה עד שיגיעו למדות וממנה תשיג השמחה והתענוג והטעמים. אם אמנם הטעמים הם קודמים אפילו לנקודה וכל שכן לאותיות אבל ידוע סוף מעשה במחשבה תחלה:

וזהו שאמרו רז"ל כל המעביר על מדותיו מעבירין ממנו כל פשעיו, שכן בלשון מעביר ראשון ראשון ארז"ל (ר"ה יז ע"א) ועון עצמו אינו נמחק. מפני היותו עדיין מתחיל ומעביר על מדותיו שלא לעשות כמעשיהם אבל עדיין המדה עצמה לא נמחקה מאתו לשרש אחריה לכן מדה כנגד מדה מעבירין לו פשעיו והעון אינו נמחק עד שיגמור תשובתו הרמתה לעקור המדה מעיקרה מלהשתמש בה בגשמיות בלתי לה' לבדו, זהו הנקרא תשובה שלימה באותו פרק באותו מקום וכו', כי כל אופני חמימות חשק מדתו שהיה מגושם תחלה השיב לה' את כל עיקרה. ולא עוד אלא שהגדיל מדתו לה' ותוקף והחמימות חוזק אש האהבה אליו יתברך עד כי אהבתו יתברך מכבה עבירה אש אהבת היצה"ר, שאפילו אם יזדמן לו באותו פרק באותו מקום אינו חושק בה מפני אהבתו יתברך, זו היא תשובה מאהבה שזדונות נעשו כזכיות בודאי לא יחשוב ה' לו עון אשר חטא והעון עצמו נמחק מעיקרו:

סליק בעזרת האל שוכן מרומים:

פרשת כי תבא ב'

אמר (ר"י) רב נחמן תתי לי שקיימתי שלש סעודות בשבת (שבת קיח, ב):

פתח הרב והיה כי תבא וכו' **וְלָקַחְתָּ מֵרֵאשִׁית** וכו', על פי מאמר דוד המלך עליו השלום: **הַנֶּחֱמָדִים מִזָּהָב וּמִפַּז רָב** וכו' גם עבדך נזהר בהם בשמרם עקב רב. ומבואר בספרים ענין המשל מלך הדיוט שנותן ומוסר לשומר מבחר ומיטב וראשית גנזי אוצרותיו לשמור בכדי שישתמרו מן ההפסד והאבדה בכדי שיאיר האוצר לעולם כל אימת שירצו להשתמש עמו, מה שאין כן כשיפסד יאבד המאור שבו ולא יאיר וכל שכן כשיאבד מאתו. הנה אפילו במשל הדיוט יעידו ויגידו עינים הרואות את גודל החן שמצא השומר אצל המלך בתחלה קודם שמסר לו האוצר והמאור שבו שהרי השומר נהנה לאורו ילך אצל המלך בלא בר ומה לו עוד, ואמת משל הוא כשישמור השומר היטב ויזהר בשמירתו בוודאי השומר נעשה אוצר המלך לגנוז בידו כל שעשועיו.

והנה על דרך זה אמרו רבותינו זכרונם לברכה: **בְּרֵאשִׁית** בשביל התורה וישראל ובכורים שנקראים ראשית בשבילם נברא העולם, והענין ידוע מאמר הכל בחכמה עשית שהוא נקרא **רֵאשִׁית חָכְמָה יִרְאַת יְהֹ-וָה** היא אוצרו, ואמרבותינו זכרונם לברכה: אין לו להקב"ה בעולמו אלא אוצר של יראת שמים בלבד, כי המדות הם בתי גנזים לשמור האוצר בתוכם

שהוא החכמה. כי המדות הם מגבילים לחכמה בכל מדה ומדה שמשמרה על פי התורה, ובלתי המדות המשמרים להגנוז בתוכם אי אפשר להשתמש ולפעול פעולת החכמה כלל שהרי אינה מתגבלת כמאמר (איוב יא: ט') **אֲרֻכָּה מֵאֶרֶץ מִדָּהּ וּרְחָבָה** וכו', וכל דבר שאינו מוגבל ואין סוף אין לו בית יד להחזיק בו ולהשתמש בו, אבל המדות המה מגבלים אותה. אם אמנם המדות גם כן אינם מוגבלים שהרי על דרך משל נקודת הרחמנות שבלב אין לה גבול וסוף ויכולה היא להתפשט באמת על דה אין סוף, וכמו כן מדת החסד ושאר המדות גם כן מפני שהמדות הם גם כן אלהות עצמית כידוע. אבל יש להם מדה וגבול ותחום על ידי ערך המקבל אותה המדה מה שצריך רחמנות כשממלא אותו וכמו כן מדת החסד וכל המדות המה מוגבלים על ידי שלמטה מהם ומקבליהם, ועל דרך זה ראשית חכמה על כל פנים בוודאי מתפעלת ומאירה על ידי המדות כידוע ואי אפשר בשום אופן בלתם.

ולכן צריך האדם לשמור מדותיו בכדי שיוכל לפעול על ידי פעולות החכמה והחכמה תאיר בו (איוב כט, ט') **בְּהִלּה נֵרה, עֲלֵי ראשו** (קהלת ט, ח) **וְשֶׁמֶן עַל-ראשו אַל-יֶחְסָר** ולאורו ילך עד בית אלהים חיים ומלך עולם כמשל הנזכר לעיל. וכמו כן התורה נקראת ראשית שהיא החכמה שהיא גנוזה בתוך המדות וכן ישראל עלו במחשבה תחלה כידוע ונקראים ראשית, וזהו ענין הבכורים כמאמר (ישעיהו כח, ד') **כְּבִכּוּרָהּ** (בתאנה) **בְּטֶרֶם קַיִץ... בְּעוֹדָהּ בְּכַפּוֹ יִבְלָעֶנָּה** שהיא הדבר הנחמד מאד מפני היותו ראשית ואמרו רבותינו זכרונם לברכה כשנכנס אדם בכרמו ראה תאנה שבכרה כורך עליה גמי לסימן ולשמרה אל המלך, והוא ענין שאמרנו שישמור שמירה אל הראשית עבור המלך ויהנה לאורה גם כן, וזהו ענין קריאת ביכורים וכל הפרשה (דברים כו, ג) **הִגַּדְתִּי הַיּוֹם** וכו':

וזהו שאמרו רבותינו זכרונם לברכה בענין ביכורים בתר עניא אזלא עניותא עשירים שמביאים בקלתות של כסף וזהב מחזירים להם הכלים עניים שמביאין בסלי נצרים הכלים גם כן לכהן. שהוא כענין המדות גם כן על דרך זה עשירים שהם בעלי דעה כמאמר רבותינו זכרונם לברכה אין עני אלא מן הדעת כי הדעת היא המקשר המדות אל שרשם ואליו יתברך והמדות נקראים כסף וזהב כידוע, ולכן העשירים שמשמרים אוצר המלך והראשית שמסר לשומרו והוא משמרם בקלתות של כסף וזהב פירוש במדות כשרים ונאמנים כמו שהן בעצמם. נמצא נשארים הכלים לעצמן פי' מדותיו והוא ענין השארת הנפש לעולם ומה שהרויחה שלא לאכול נהמא דכסופא כי הם של הנפש, ואחר שנזהר בשמירת האוצר נעשה לעולם ועד אוצר המלך שהמלך גנוז אצלו ומחפש באוצרותיו כאות נפשו אחרי היותם גנוזים אצלו. מה שאין כן העני שאין בו דעת ואינו משמר הראשית חמודות המלך כי אם בסלים ונצרים אינו נשאר לו כלום, כי איזה צדיק מחויב להעלותם או שיתברר ויתלבן על ידי אופנים שונים ואינם נקראים על שמו כלל. וזהו(ישעיהו כ"ח: ד') **וְשֵׁם רְשָׁעִים יִרְקָב** תעלה בשמותם, אבל פעולתם בוודאי יתעלו ויתבררו ויתלבנו ויתצרפו כמ"ש (ישעיהו מ"ב: 'ח) **אֲנִי יְהֹ-וָה הוּא שְׁמִי וּכְבוֹדִי לְאַחֵר לֹא אֶתֵּן** וכמאמר **וְעַסּוֹתֶם רְשָׁעִים** כי נעשה מהם **אֵפֶר תַּחַת כַּפּוֹת רַגְלֵי** הצדיקים. (מלאכי ג': כ"א)

וזהו (דברים ג': כ"ג) **וָאֶתְחַנַּן אֶל יְהֹ-וָה** שהוא לשון חינון, והוא החן הראשון שמסר לו הקב"ה אוצרו הטוב לשמור וזהו אתה החלות להראות את עבדך וכו', ובזה החן שמצא קודם המדות בתחלה וקודם ששמרם במדות הואיל משה לבקש שיתנן עליו באותו חן שהוא למעלה מן המדות והיא ביטול המדות בשרשם. וזהו שאמר דוד המלך ע"ה הנחמדים מזהב ומפז רב כי הראשית שהוא התורה נחמדת מן המדות הנקרא זהב כנזכר לעיל שהרי המדות הם שומר לאוצר, וזהו (תהילים יט, יב) **גַּם עַבְדְּךָ נִזְהָר בָּהֶם בְּשָׁמְרָם עֵקֶב רָב**, וז"ש (ר"י) רב נחמן תיתי לי שקיימתי שלש סעודות כי הראשית הוא המקיים את הכל וכן על דרך זה בכל המצות השכל הפועל המצוה הוא המקיים ומחי' את המצוה וזהו שקיימתי וכו'.

ר' מנחם-מנדל מוויטבסק בדרך עלייתו לארץ ישראל

א

כשהיה ר' מנדלי מוויטבסק על הים סמוך לחופה של ארץ ישראל עמד עליו נחשול שבים לטבעו עם ספינתו. הגביה ר' מנדלי עיניו למרום ואמר: "רבונו של עולם אתה ראית את כל הכבוד שעשו לי בחוצה לארץ, רבי נחום מטשרנוביל בעצמו נטל מטאטא וטיאט לכבודי את חצרו ואני עמדתי וראיתי ולא עיכבתי בידו וקיבלתי עלי כל אותם היסורים בשביל כבודה של ארץ ישראל, ועכשיו שהגעתי סמוך לארץ ישראל אתה מרעיש עלי את הים לטבעני!" מיד נח הים מזעפו והגיע ר' מנדלי בשלום לארץ ישראל.[1]

ב

כשנסע להיפרד מהרב הקדוש רבי פנחס מקאריץ קודם שעלה לארץ הקודש, אמר הרב הקדוש רבי מקאריץ לבני ביתו: "כבר משתי שבועות קודם, שהיתחילו לנקות את חדרי הבית, והרב הקדוש רבי פנחס בעצמו טאטא את המדריגות לפניו. כשהגיע הרב הקדוש מוויטבסק לקאריץ אמר הרב הקדוש רבי פנחס מקאריץ: — הנה נוסע אלינו מלך ישראל...

לאחר ששהה אצלו כשמונה ימים נענה הרב הקדוש רבי מקאריץ ואמר לאנשי ביתו הייתי חפץ שיסע כבר כי אין ביכולתי לסבול עוד את רוב קדושתו.[2]

ג

בדרכו לארץ הקודש, נקלע לסכנה גדולה, והתפלל ואמר:

—רבונו של עולם זכור נא לי היסורים שסבלתי בחוץ לארץ ממה שכבונדי, וכשטאטא הרב הקדוש רבי מקאריץ המדריגות לפני, היסורים הנוראים שהיה לי מזה...[3]

ד

בבואו לארץ ישראל קבע את מקום מושבו בעיר העתיקה, צפת, ולאחר זמן עבר משם לעיר העתיקה, טבריא, ואמר הטעם משום שבצפת האויר זך ובכל שעה שומע בת קול משמיא, ואין בכוחו לסבול זאת, לכן עקר משם. אמר:

—כשבא לארץ ישראל מצא טבריא עיר שכולה צדיקים, וצפת עיר שכולה רשעים.[4]

ה

בבואו לארץ ישראל כשהיה פעם הרב הקדוש מקאברין אצל הרב הקדוש מרוזין היו שם משולחים אורחים מעיר העתיקה, ירושלים, ודיבר איתם הרב הקדוש אודות מה שלא קבע הרב הקדוש מוויטבסק את משכנו בירושלים, קרית מלך רב, וענו הם בתירוצים שונים משום האויר שלא היה טוב עבורו, או משום שנתירא מן הישמעאלים אל אודות החובות של רבי יהודה החסיד כשידוע תבעו זאת מכל יוצאי אשכנז, ולא הוטבו דבריהם בעיני הרב הקדוש מרוזין, ופנה אל הרב הקדוש מקאברין ושאלו:

—ומה אתה אומר?

וענה:

—שכנראה שהיה ירא מפני קדושת ירושלים!

ופנה הרב הקדוש להמשולחים ואמר להם:

—*איהר וואוינט ווי בהמות אין ירושלים*... [הנכם מתגוררים כבהמות בירושלים כלומר מבלי שום הרגשה...על שחשבו שבגלל דברים כאלו יוותר הרב הקדוש על ישיבת עיר הקדוש].[5]

ו

קודם שעלה לארץ ישראל נסע להפריד מצדיקי דורו והיה על שבת קודש בפולנה, ובצאת השבת בא אל הרב הקדוש בעל התולדות שעדיין הסיב אז בסעודה שלישית כדרכו הקודש שהיה מאריך מאוד, והרב הקדוש מוויטבסק נכנס לבית מדרשו והדליק את הלולקע שלו.

נענה הרב הקדוש מפולנה ואמר לו מעשה בעשיר שהיה לו אבן טובה ששויה מרובה וחביבה עליו כנפשו ונתחכך הרבה מאוד היכן

---

[1] ש"י עגנון, תכריך של סיפורים, (שוקן: תל אביב, תשל"ד), סימן א', ע' קמ"ט-ק"נ.

[2] ר' מרדכי מסלונים, מאמר מרדכי, כרך ב' (ישראל זאב סלונים: ירושלים, תשס"ז), סימן י', ע' נ"ט.

[3] ר' מרדכי מסלונים, מאמר מרדכי, כרך ב' (ישראל זאב סלונים: ירושלים, תשס"ז), סימן י"א, ע' ס'.

[4] ר' מרדכי מסלונים, מאמר מרדכי, כרך ב' (ישראל זאב סלונים: ירושלים, תשס"ז), סימן י"ג, ע' ס'.

[5] ר' מרדכי מסלונים, מאמר מרדכי, כרך ב' (ישראל זאב סלונים: ירושלים, תשס"ז), סימן י"ט, ע' ס"ב.

ר' מנחם-מנדל מוויטבסק בדרך עלייתו לארץ ישראל

להצניעה מפני הגנבים ועלה בדעתו להטמין מרגלית טובה זו

אצל האשפה שלא יעלה על דעת הגנבים שיש שם חפץ יקר, כן אתם שהנכם מופלגים בעניות ושפלים בעיניכם ופנינה יקרה זן מידת השפלות החבתם בתוך הנהגה של גדלות שנראה כגיאות אבל אותי לא תרמו.[6]

ז

וכמו ששמעתי ממרן הצדיק מרוזין זכר צדיק לברכה שסיפר לאדונינו מורינו הרב זכר צדיק לברכה שבימי הקדוש הצדיק רבי מנחם מענדל מוויטעפסק זכרונו לברכה כשהיה בירושלים אירע אשר איש פתי וחסר דעה עלה להר הזיתים ותקע בשופר ואין איש רואהו. והיה ההשרעה להמון ישראל כי זהו התקעת שופר המבשר הגאולה וכאשר הגיע הדבר לאוזני ההוא צדיק הנזכר לעיל פתח החלון והביט לאויר העולם [ורחרח באוויר פה ושם] ומיד אמר:[7]

— [לא, המשיח טרם בא], שאין שום התחדשות! כי ודאי שאם היה סימנא דגאולה דוודאי היה מרגיש ורואה באויר העולם...[8]

ח

...ויספר ר' ברוך מרדכי מבאברויסק כי פעם ישבו רבינו [ר' שינאור זלמן מליאדי] עם הרב הקדש ר' מנחם מנדל מטשערנוביל בסוכה, ואדונינו מורינו הרב האמצעי [ר' דב באר]

ועוד אברך בשם ברוך מרדכי (ר' ברוך מרדכי לא התבטא מעולם על עצמו "אני") שמעו כי הרב הקדש [ר' מנחם מנדל מטשערנוביל] שאל מרבינו [ר' שינאור זלמן מליאדי] במה היה ר' מענדלי הארעדאקער גדול?

ר' מענדלי ידע מחשבותיו של כל אדם— השיב רבינו [ר' שינאור זלמן מליאדי].

—ומה בכך?!

—גם ידע מחשבות האדם במשך כל ימי חייו.

—ומה בכך?! המשיך ר' מנחם מנדל מטשערנוביל להקשות.

—כשר' מענדלי עבר בבית— אמר רבינו [ר' שינאור זלמן מליאדי] — הרגיש כל מה שחשבו בבית הזה מעודו וכל מה שעתידים לחשוב בו עד עולם. וסיים הרבי כי זהו ההבדל בין מרכבה לאצילות ובין מרכבה לאדם קדמון שהוא עולם הכללי.

ויתפעל הר' מנחם מנדל מטשערנוביל המאד, אך לפתע יקרא: הרי סכמנו ששום אדם לא יאזין לשיחות[י]נו! בשמענו זאת—סיים ר' ברוך מרדכי מבאברויסק— קפצנו מגג הסוכה ולא זכינו לשמוע המשך דבוריהם הקדושים.[9]

ט

אצל הרב הגאון הקדוש המפורסם הר' מענדלי זכר צדיק לברכה מלובאוויטש היה המנהג בין החסידים שלו שלמדו בהקלויז שלו שבעת לימודם בלילה עמד לפני כל אחד ואחד מהלומדים נר אחד. ואחר שסיימו לימודם והיו מספרים ומדברים ביניהם איזו מעשיות מצדיקים היו מכבים את הנרות כולם. רק נר אחד או שתים השאירו להם והיו יושבים סביב הנר והיו מדברים. פעם אחת אירע שהיו יושבים במסיבה אחת בהקלויז אצל הנר היחידי ומדברים. נכנס אליהם הרב הקדוש הרב מענדלי זכרונו לברכה. שאל אותם:

—במה מדברים ביניהם?

השיבו לו:

—הרב מענדילי ווטיבסקר זכר צדיק לברכה!

אמר להם הרב:

—לכבודו של הרב הקדוש הזה תדליקו כל הנרות כמו שבעת הלימוד. ואני אספר לכם ממנו...[10]

---

[6] ר' מרדכי מסלונים, מאמר מרדכי, כרך ב' (ישראל זאב סלונים: ירושלים, תשס"ז), סימן ח', ע' נ"ט.

[7] מנחם זיגלבוים, סיפורים מחדרי הרבי, (א.מ: בני ברק, תשס"ט) , ע' 270.

[8] ר' אלימלך מגראדזיסק, דברי אלימלך, פרשת קרח, (א.מ: ווארשא, תר"נ) ע' קע"ז, ראה שם יהודה לייב לוין, חסידים מספרים, חלק ראשון, (מעין חכמה: ירושלים, א.ת.) פרק שביעי, סימן תר"א, ע' 196.

[9] יהושע מונדשיין, ספר מגדל עז, (מכון לויבאוויטש: כפר חב"ד, תש"מ), סימן י"ג, ע' ק"ס-קס"א.

[10] ספר סיפורי צדיקים החדש, אברהם יצחק סויבלמאן בן אשר ענזיל, (מו"ל מענדל זאלצמאן: וינה, תרפ"ב), סימן ל"ב, ע' ה'.